FOOD FOR FIFTY

FOOD FOR FIFTY

8th edition

Grace Shugart

Professor Emeritus of Hotel, Restaurant and Institution Management, and Dietetics
KANSAS STATE UNIVERSITY

Mary Molt

Administrative Dietitian, Housing and Foodservice
Instructor of Hotel, Restaurant and Institution Management, and Dietetics
KANSAS STATE UNIVERSITY

MACMILLAN PUBLISHING COMPANY
New York

COLLIER MACMILLAN PUBLISHERS
London

Macmillan Publishing Company
866 Third Avenue, New York, New York 10022

Collier Macmillan Canada, Inc.

Library of Congress Cataloging-in-Publication Data

Shugart, Grace Severance, 1910–
    Food for fifty/Grace Shugart, Mary Molt.—8th ed.
        p.   cm.
    Includes indexes.
    ISBN 0-02-410391-8
    1. Quantity cookery. 2. Menus. I. Molt, Mary. II. Title.
III. Title: Food for 50.
TX820.S45   1989
641.5'7—dc19   88-11084
                                                CIP

Printing: 4 5 6 7   Year: 0 1 2 3 4 5

Fifty Years of *Food for Fifty*

For over five decades *Food for Fifty* has served the needs of educators and practitioners in all segments of the foodservice industry. The first edition of *Food for Fifty* was written in 1937 under the leadership of the late Bessie Brooks West, who was then head of the Institutional Management Department at Kansas State University. Mrs. West was a recognized leader in foodservice administration, and her appreciation for fine food and service was well known by students and professional colleagues. Her goal in starting *Food for Fifty* was to introduce students to quantity food-production methods by providing a compilation of basic standardized recipes, with efficient procedures for their preparation. The editions that followed reinforced the primary focus of providing students and foodservice managers with a practical and reliable guide for quantity food production. In preparing the eighth edition, the authors have maintained the integrity of this tradition while addressing the needs of a modern foodservice industry.

Grace Shugart, M.S., Professor Emeritus of Hotel, Restaurant and Institution Management, and Dietetics at Kansas State University, has been a coauthor since the fourth edition, published in 1961. Mrs. Shugart graduated from Washington State University and earned a master's degree at Iowa State University. Her professional experience has included 24 years at Kansas State University, first as director of Residence Hall Foodservice and assistant professor of Institutional Management, then as professor and head of the Institutional Management Department upon the retirement of Bessie Brooks West. She has also served as food director of the cooperative dormitories and instructor in Institution Management at Iowa State University, and she has held positions in hospital dietetics as well. Mrs. Shugart has been active in The American Dietetic Association, having served as delegate-at-large, speaker of the House of Delegates, and president. She was a recipient of ADA's Medallion in 1978 and Copher Award in 1980, and she was named the Kansas Distinguished Dietitian in 1977. A member of the American School Food Service Association and Women in Communications, she also holds membership in the honor societies of Phi Kappa Phi, Omicron Nu, and Phi Upsilon Omicron. Mrs. Shugart was presented with the Distinguished Home Economics Alumnus Award in 1978 and with the Alumni Achievement Award in 1982 by Washington State University. She is also a coauthor of the text *Foodservice in Institutions*.

Mary Molt, M.S., R.D., is administrative dietitian in Housing and Foodservice and instructor in Hotel, Restaurant and Institution Management, and Dietetics (HRIMD) at Kansas State University. She holds a bachelor's degree from Kearney State College in Nebraska and a master's degree from Oklahoma State University. Mary Molt became a coauthor of *Food for Fifty* with the seventh edition. She has

15 years of professional practice experience at Kansas State University, with a joint appointment in academe and foodservice administration. Her current responsibilities include teaching supervised practice courses in the Department of HRIMD, directing a foodservice center serving more than 5000 meals per day, and operating a retail bakery for university students. Mary Molt is active in The American Dietetic Association, the Kansas Dietetic Association, and the National Association of College and University Food Service (NACUFS). In 1981 and 1986 she was recognized with the NACUFS President's Award for outstanding service to the association. Mary Molt holds membership in several honor societies: Delta Kappa Gamma, Kappa Omicron Phi, Omicron Nu, and Phi Kappa Phi.

Preface

The eighth edition of *Food for Fifty* was designed as a text for use by students in quantity food production and as a reference for persons in foodservice management. This revised edition includes new and updated tables, new contemporary recipes, standardized procedures, improved organization, and an expanded discussion of basic food information.

Food for Fifty compiles in one comprehensive text basic information, recipes, and guidelines needed for planning and preparing food in quantity. The four-part format organizes the material and allows users to locate information quickly. Part One, "General Information," is considered by many to be an indispensable reference. Purchasing, preparation, and serving guides, tables of weights and measures, and recipe adjustment instructions are included. An extensive variety of tested recipes, many variation suggestions, and basic food information for different categories of food make Part Two, "Recipes," valuable for anyone who prepares food in quantity. The recipes, written in an easy-to-use format with standardized procedures, allow quality products to be prepared consistently. Part Three, "Menu Development," includes guidelines and suggestions for planning meals. This section is a quick reference for selecting food items and also a resource for identifying factors that affect menu planning. Part Four, "Special Meals & Receptions," provides useful information for planning special foodservice events. Key points are highlighted so that specific information can be found easily.

The Appendix includes a glossary of menu and food-production terms that provides definitions of words used in quantity cooking. A chart suggesting uses for herbs and spices is also found in the Appendix. The index in *Food for Fifty* provides access to the extensive information in the book. Cross-referencing by name and category allows the user to find recipes quickly and easily.

Appreciation is extended to the many colleagues and friends who have, through the course of association with the authors, made this revision of *Food for Fifty* possible. Special acknowledgment is given to John Pence, Director of Residence Hall Foodservice at Kansas State University, and his management staff for their support and advice.

Grace Shugart
Mary Molt

Contents

Tables

Part four   SPECIAL MEALS & RECEPTIONS

FOOD FOR FIFTY

Part one

GENERAL INFORMATION

FOOD PRODUCTION INFORMATION

Information in this section is presented as a guide for ordering food, for adjusting recipes, and for the planning, preparation, and serving of food. Quantities to prepare are based on 50 average-size portions, as are most of the recipes, but adjustments may need to be made to fit individual situations. Rarely is 50 the exact number to be served, and the portion size will vary according to the type of foodservice and the needs of the individuals in the group. Tables are included that will assist with these recipe adjustments.

Most ingredients in the recipes are given in weights, but if volume measurements (teaspoons, tablespoons, cups, quarts, or gallons) are to be used, tables in this section will assist in converting from weights to measures. Metric measures were not used in the recipes, but charts for converting to metric are included.

Also given is basic information on cooking temperatures, food equivalents and substitutions, and equipment capacity. A guide for use of herbs and spices and a glossary of cooking and menu terms are found in the Appendix.

HOW TO USE TABLES AND GUIDES

Table 1.1 suggests amounts of food to purchase and prepare for 50 persons, based on the size portions listed in the table. If larger or smaller servings are needed or if the number of portions required is other than 50, an adjustment in the amount to prepare or purchase must be made.

When ordering fresh fruits and vegetables, the loss in preparation must be considered when determining the amount to buy. Table 1.2 gives approximate yields in the preparation of fresh fruits and vegetables, which will be helpful in ordering these products.

Tables 1.3 through 1.5 are tables of weights and measures intended as aids in converting recipe ingredients from weight to measure. Table 1.5 gives equivalent measures (teaspoons, tablespoons, and cups) for weights from 1 to 16 ounces for a few ingredients, such as flour, salt, and sugar, that appear repeatedly in recipes.

Tables 1.6 and 1.7 provide metric weight and measure equivalents.

Tables 1.8 through 1.20 include preparation and serving guides. Cooking temperatures are given in Tables 1.8 through 1.12, with Table 1.13 suggesting coatings for deep-fat fried foods. Recommended serving temperatures are shown in Figure 1.1. Dipper and ladle equivalents are given in Tables 1.14 and 1.15. Tables 1.16 and

1.17 will be helpful in determining batch sizes and scaling weights for selected pans. Figure 1.2 illustrates four commonly used mixer attachments. Table 1.18 lists common can sizes, and Tables 1.19 and 1.20 give food equivalents, substitutions, and proportions.

Information on adjusting recipes begins on p. 52. Tables 1.21 and 1.22 include information on rounding off weights and measures, and changing pounds and ounces to decimal parts of a pound. Tables 1.23 through 1.25 are direct-reading tables for adjusting yields of recipes. Table 1.24 is used when ingredient amounts in recipes are given in *weights* and portion yields are divisible by 25. In Table 1.23, ingredients are stated in *volume* measurement and portions are divisible by 25. Table 1.25 is especially useful when enlarging home-size recipes. Ingredients are in *volume* measurement for yields from 8 to 96 portions.

AMOUNTS OF FOOD TO SERVE 50

TABLE 1.1 AMOUNTS OF FOOD TO SERVE 50[a]

Food	Serving portion	Amount for 50 portions	Miscellaneous information
Beverages			
Cider	4 oz (½ cup)	2 gal	64 4-oz portions
Cocoa	6 oz (¾ cup)	2½ gal	
Unsweetened powder		8 oz	
Instant mix		2½ lb	
Coffee	6 oz (¾ cup)	2½ gal	
Regular or urn grind		1–1½ lb	
Freeze-dried		2–3 oz	
Instant		3 oz	
Lemonade	8 oz (1 cup)	3 gal	48 8-oz portions
Frozen concentrate		3 32-oz cans	dilute 1:4 parts water
Orange juice, see Juices			
Punch	4 oz (½ cup)	2–2½ gal	1 gal yields 32 4-oz portions
			2½ gal yields 50 4-oz portions plus 30 refills
Tea			
Hot	6 oz (¾ cup)	2½ gal	
Bulk		2 oz	Amount may vary with quality of tea
Iced	8 oz (1 cup)	3 gal	48 8-oz portions
1-oz bag		6 bags	6 1-oz bags make 3 gal
Instant		1–1½ oz	
Wine		See p.706	
Bread and crackers			
Biscuits, baking powder	1 biscuit	4½ doz	
Dough ready for baking		5 lb	
Mix		2½ lb	
Bread			
1½-lb loaf	1 slice	2½ loaves	24 slices per loaf
2-lb pullman	1 slice	1½ loaves	36 slices per loaf
Breads, quick, 5 × 9 × 2¾-inch loaves	1 slice	4 loaves	16 slices per loaf
Coffee cake, 12 × 18 × 2 inch	3 × 2¼-inch	2 pans	Cut 4 × 8
Batter, ready to bake		5–6 lb per pan	
Crackers			
Graham	2 crackers	1¾–2 lb	60–65 per lb
Saltines	4 crackers	1½ lb	150–160 per lb
Soda	2 crackers	1½–2 lb	65 per lb

(continued)

TABLE 1.1   *(Continued)*

Food	Serving portion	Amount for 50 portions	Miscellaneous information
Muffins	1 muffin	4½ doz	
Batter, ready to bake		5 lb	
Mix		3½ lb	
Pancakes	3½ oz	7 qt batter	2 4-inch cakes
Mix		6 lb	
Rolls			
Breakfast, 3-oz	1 roll	4½ doz	
Dinner, 1½-oz	1 roll	4½ doz	
Frozen dough		10 lb	
Mix		5 lb	
Toast			
French	2 slices	7 lb bread	
Buttered or cinnamon	2 slices	7 lb bread	
Waffles	3 oz	6 qt batter	1 waffle

Cereals			
Barley, for soup		14–16 oz	For 3 gal soup
Cream of wheat	⅔ cup	2 lb	2 gal cooked
Hominy grits	⅔ cup	2 lb	2 gal cooked
Prepared cereal, flakes, crisp	1 oz (½–¾ cup)	3 lb	
Rice	½ cup	3–4 lb	6–8 qt cooked
Rolled oats	⅔ cup	2 lb	2 gal cooked
See also Pasta			

Dairy products			
Butter or margarine			
For sandwiches		1 lb	To butter 100 slices
For table	1–2 pats	1–1½ lb	
For vegetables	½–1 tsp	4–8 oz	
Cheese, cheddar	1–1½ oz	3–5 lb	For sandwich or with cold cuts
Sandwich slices, cheddar or Swiss	1 oz	3¼ lb	
Cottage	2 oz (No. 20 dipper)	6½ lb	For salad or side dish
Cream	½ oz	2 lb	For salad or garnish
Dessert (cream, blue, Camembert)	1 oz	3 lb	
Cream			
Coffee		1–1½ qt	
Whipping	2 Tbsp	1½ pt	1½ qt whipped
Ice cream, bulk	No. 12 dipper	2 gal	Dish or sundae
	No. 16 dipper	1½ gal	With cake or cookie
	No. 20 dipper	1¼ gal	For à la mode

TABLE 1.1 *(Continued)*

Food	Serving portion	Amount for 50 portions	Miscellaneous information
Milk			
Fluid	8 oz (1 cup)	3 gal	
Nonfat dry	8 oz (1 cup)	3 lb	3.5 oz (1⅓ cups) dry milk per qt of water. Volume may vary with brand.
Nondairy creamer	1 tsp	3 oz	
Sherbet	No. 20 dipper	1¼ gal	
Whipped topping mix			
Dry	2 Tbsp	5 oz	
Frozen	2 Tbsp	18 oz (1½ qt)	
Liquid	2 Tbsp	1½ pt	1½ qt whipped
Desserts			
Cakes			
Angel food	1 oz	3–4 10-inch cakes	12–14 cuts per cake
Pound or loaf, 5 × 9-inch	3 oz	4 loaves	
Sheet, 12 × 18 × 2-inch	3 × 2¼-inch	2 pans	Cut 4 × 8
Batter, ready to bake		4–5 lb each	
Sheet, 18 × 26 × 2-inch	3 × 2½-inch	1 pan	Cut 6 × 10
Batter, ready to bake		8–10 lb	
Cake mixes			
Angel food		4 lb	
Chocolate, white, yellow		5 lb	
Pies, 8-inch	⅙ pie	8 pies	Cut 6 pieces per pie
Filling			
Chiffon	3 cups per pie	6 qt	
Cream or custard	3 cups per pie	6 qt	
Fruit	3 cups (1 lb 8 oz per pie)	6 qt (10–12 lb)	
Meringue	4 oz per pie	2 lb	
Pastry			
1 crust	5 oz per pie	2 lb 8 oz	
2 crust	9 oz per pie	4 lb 8 oz	
Pies, 9-inch	⅛ pie	7 pies	Cut 8 pieces per pie
Filling			
Chiffon	3¾ cups per pie	6–7 qt	
Cream or custard	3¾ cups per pie	6–7 qt	
Fruit	3¾–4 cups (1 lb 14 oz)	6–7 qt (10–12 lb)	
Meringue	5–6 oz per pie	2–2¼ lb	
Pastry			
1 crust	9 oz per pie	4 lb	
2 crust	16 oz per pie	7 lb	

(continued)

TABLE 1.1 *(Continued)*

Food	Serving portion	Amount for 50 portions	Miscellaneous information
Puddings	½ cup (4 oz)	6¼ qt	No. 10 dipper
Toppings, sauce	2–3 Tbsp	2–3 qt	
Eggs			
Eggs			
In shell	1 egg	4½ doz	
Fresh or frozen, whole	1 egg	5 lb (2½ qt)	
Fish and shellfish			
Fish			
Fillets and steaks, 4 per lb	3 oz	14–16 lb	1 lb AP = 0.70 lb cooked fish
Whole, dressed	3 oz	40 lb	1 lb AP = 0.27 lb cooked fish
Oysters, shucked	3–4 oz	1½–2 gal	1 lb AP = 0.38 lb cooked oysters
Scallops, frozen, to fry	3 oz	10–12 lb	
Shrimp			
Raw, in shell	2 oz	12½ lb	1 lb AP = 0.54 lb cooked shrimp
	3 oz	18–20 lb	
Raw, peeled and cleaned	3 oz	16 lb	1 lb peeled = 0.62 lb cooked shrimp
Cooked, peeled and cleaned	3 oz	10 lb	1 lb AP = 1.00 lb cooked shrimp
Fruits			
Canned			
For pies, see Desserts			
For salad or dessert	3–4 oz (½ cup)	2–2½ No. 10 cans	For fruits such as peach or pear halves and sliced pineapple, depends on count per can
Fresh			
Apples	1 apple	½ box	Size 113
8 8-inch pies	⅙ pie	14–16 lb AP	1 lb AP = 0.91 lb ready to cook or serve raw with peels; 0.78 lb pared, cooked
7 9-inch pies	⅛ pie	16 lb AP	
Salad or dessert	3–3½ oz	15 lb AP	
Apricots	2	9 lb AP	Medium size 12 per lb
Avocado	½	25 avocados	Medium size 2 per lb
Salad	3 slices	12 avocados	1 lb AP = 0.67 lb ready to serve raw

TABLE 1.1 *(Continued)*

Food	Serving portion	Amount for 50 portions	Miscellaneous information
Bananas	1	16 lb AP	Small, 5–6 inch 1 lb AP = 0.65 lb ready to serve raw
Salad	3 oz	10 lb AP	Medium, 7–8 inch, 3 per lb
Blueberries	4 oz	12–14 lb AP	1 lb AP = 0.96 lb ready to serve raw
Cherries, sweet	3 oz	10 lb AP	1 lb AP = 0.98 lb ready to serve with pits; 0.84 lb pitted
Cranberries, for sauce	¼ cup	4 lb AP	1 lb AP = 0.95 lb ready to cook
Fruit cup (mixed fruits)	3 oz (⅓ cup)	9 lb (6 qt)	
Grapefruit	½	25 fruit	64 to 80 size
Salad	5 sections	21 fruit	12 sections per fruit 1 lb AP = 0.52 lb ready to serve raw
Grapes, seedless	4 oz	12–15 lb AP	1 lb AP = 0.97 lb ready to serve raw
With seeds			1 lb AP = 0.89 lb raw seeded
Kiwi fruit	1 slice	6–8 fruit	For garnish
Lemons			
For tea or fish	⅙ lemon	8–10 lemons	Medium, size 165
For lemonade	8-oz glass	3 doz	Medium, size 165
Limes			
Garnish	1 wedge	12 limes	4 wedges per lime
Limeade	8-oz glass	4½ doz	
Mangoes, cubed or sliced	½ cup	12½ lb AP	1 lb AP = 0.69 lb ready to serve raw
Melon			
Cantaloupe	½ melon	25 melons	
Fruit cup		5 melons	1 lb AP = 0.52 lb ready to serve raw
Salad slices		6 melons	
Casaba, honeydew, or persian	⅛ melon	7 melons	1 lb AP = 0.46 lb ready to serve raw
Watermelon	12–16 oz	38–50 lb AP	1 lb AP = 0.57 lb fruit without rind
Nectarines	1 nectarine (5 oz)	15–16 lb AP	1 lb AP = 0.91 lb ready to serve raw
Oranges	1 orange	½ box	Size 113
Juice	4 oz (½ cup)	6¼ qt	16–18 doz size 113
Sections	5 sections	18 oranges	Size 150; 1 lb AP = 0.40 lb ready to serve, without membrane

(continued)

TABLE 1.1 *(Continued)*

Food	Serving portion	Amount for 50 portions	Miscellaneous information
Peaches	1 peach (4–5 oz)	12–15 lb AP	
Diced or sliced	½ cup	20 lb AP	1 lb AP = 0.76 lb ready to cook or serve raw
Pears	1 pear (5–6 oz)	17–19 lb AP	1lb AP = 0.92 lb ready to cook or serve raw, unpared; 0.78 lb pared
Salad	3 slices	15–17 lb AP	8–10 slices per pear
Pineapple, cubed	½ cup	24 lb AP (6 pineapples)	1 lb AP = 0.54 lb ready to serve raw
Plums, Italian or purple	2 plums	12½ lb AP	Medium size, 8 per lb 1 lb AP = 0.94 lb ready to cook or serve raw
Rhubarb, 8 8-inch pies	⅙ pie	12 lb AP	1 lb AP = 0.86 lb ready to cook
7 9-inch pies	⅛ pie		
Sauce	½ cup	14 lb AP	
Strawberries	4 oz	14 lb AP	1 lb AP = 0.88 lb ready to serve raw
Garnish	1 berry	1 qt AP	1 qt AP = about 1.32 lb ready to serve raw
Shortcake	¾ cup	8 qt AP	
Sundaes	½–¾ cup	6–8 qt AP	
Strawberries, frozen			
For pies, see Desserts			
For salad or dessert	4 oz (½ cup)	13–15 lb	
For topping	1½ oz	5 lb	
Juices			
Fruit or vegetable	4 oz (½ cup)	6¼ qt	
	6 oz (¾ cup)	9½ qt	
Canned	4 oz	4 46-oz cans	
	6 oz	7 46-oz cans	
Frozen	4 oz	4–5 12-oz cans	Dilute 1:3 parts water
		2 32-oz cans	Dilute 1:3 parts water
	6 oz	7 12-oz cans	Dilute 1:3 parts water
		3 32-oz cans	Dilute 1:3 parts water
MEAT **Beef**			
Brisket, corned, boneless	3 oz EP	25–30 lb AP	1 lb AP = 0.42 lb cooked lean meat
Brisket, fresh, boneless	3 oz EP	25–30 lb AP	1 lb AP = 0.46 lb cooked lean meat
Cubed, 1-inch, for stew	3 oz EP	12–15 lb AP	1 lb AP = 0.56 lb cooked lean meat

TABLE 1.1 *(Continued)*

Food	Serving portion	Amount for 50 portions	Miscellaneous information
Ground, no more than 30% fat	3 oz EP	13–15 lb AP	1 lb AP = 0.70 lb cooked meat
Liver	3½ oz EP	16 lb AP	1 lb AP = 0.70 cooked liver
Roast			
Chuck, pot roast, boneless	3 oz EP	18 lb AP	1 lb AP = 0.60 lb lean cooked meat
With bone	3 oz EP	20–22 lb AP	1 lb AP = 0.45 lb cooked lean meat
Rib, standing	6 oz EP	45–50 lb AP	Bone in, oven prepared
Ribeye	3 oz EP	12–15 lb AP	1 lb AP = 0.70 lb lean cooked meat
Round, boneless	3 oz EP	18 lb AP	1 lb AP = 0.61 lb cooked lean meat
Rump, boneless	3 oz EP	16–18 lb AP	1 lb AP = 0.62 lb cooked lean meat
Sirloin, boneless, trimmed	3 oz EP	16–18 lb AP	1 lb AP = 0.61 lb cooked lean meat
Short ribs, trimmed	3 oz EP	38–40 lb AP	1 lb AP = 0.25 lb cooked meat
Steaks			
Cubed, 4 per lb	3 oz EP	17 lb AP	
Flank, 4 per lb	3 oz EP	17 lb AP	1 lb AP = 0.67 lb cooked lean meat
Loin strip	8 oz AP	25 lb AP	Short cut, bone in
Round, boneless, 3 per lb	3½ oz EP	18–20 lb AP	1 lb AP = 0.59 lb cooked lean meat
Sirloin, boneless	3½ oz EP	14–16 lb AP	1 lb AP = 0.75 lb cooked lean meat
Tenderloin, trimmed	4 oz EP	14 lb AP	1 lb AP = 0.90 lb cooked lean meat
T-bone	8 oz AP	25 lb AP	
	12 oz AP	36–38 lb AP	

Lamb

Food	Serving portion	Amount for 50 portions	Miscellaneous information
Chops, rib, 4 per lb	2 each	25 lb AP	1 lb AP = 0.46 lb cooked lean meat
Roast, leg, boneless	3 oz EP	15 lb AP	1 lb AP = 0.61 lb cooked lean meat
With bone	3 oz EP	22 lb AP	1 lb AP = 0.45 lb cooked lean meat

(continued)

TABLE 1.1 *(Continued)*

Food	Serving portion	Amount for 50 portions	Miscellaneous information
Pork, fresh			
Chops, loin, with bone, 3 per lb	1 chop	17 lb AP	1 lb AP = 0.41 lb cooked lean meat
Cutlets, 3 or 4 per lb	3–3½ oz EP	12–15 lb AP	1 lb AP = 0.75 lb cooked meat
Roast, loin, boneless	3 oz EP	18–20 lb AP	1 lb AP = 0.54 lb cooked lean meat
With bone	3 oz EP	22–24 lb AP	1 lb AP = 0.41 lb cooked lean meat
Fresh ham, whole boneless	3 oz EP	18–20 lb AP	1 lb AP = 0.53 lb cooked lean meat
With bone	3 oz EP	20–22 lb AP	1 lb AP = 0.46 lb cooked lean meat
Shoulder, Boston butt, boneless	3 oz EP	18–20 lb AP	1 lb AP = 0.54 lb cooked lean meat
With bone	3 oz EP	19–21 lb AP	1 lb AP = 0.50 lb cooked lean meat
Shoulder, picnic, boneless	3 oz EP	20–22 lb AP	1 lb AP = 0.46 lb cooked lean meat
With bone	3 oz EP	25 lb AP	1 lb AP = 0.38 lb cooked lean meat
Sausage, bulk	2-oz pattie	12½–15 lb AP	1 lb AP = 0.47 lb cooked lean meat
Links, 12–16 per lb	2 links	7–8 lb AP	1 lb AP = 0.47 lb cooked lean meat
Spareribs	8–12 oz AP	25–40 lb AP	1 lb AP = 0.39 lb cooked meat
Pork, cured			
Bacon, sliced,			
Hotel pack	2 slices	4–5 lb	24 slices per lb
Sliced	2 slices	5–6 lb	17–20 slices per lb
Canadian	2 slices (2 oz)	10 lb	16 slices per lb
Ham, boneless	3 oz EP	15 lb AP	1 lb AP = 0.63 lb cooked lean meat
With bone	3 oz EP	18–20 lb AP	1 lb AP = 0.53 lb cooked lean meat
Fully cooked, ready to eat	3 oz EP	15 lb AP	
Pullman, canned	3 oz EP	12–15 lb AP	1 lb AP = 0.64 lb cooked lean meat
Shoulder, Boston butt, boneless	3 oz EP	16 lb AP	1 lb AP = 0.60 lb lean meat
Shoulder, picnic, boneless	3 oz EP	18 lb AP	1 lb AP = 0.53 lb cooked lean meat

TABLE 1.1 *(Continued)*

Food	Serving portion	Amount for 50 portions	Miscellaneous information
Variety and luncheon meats			
Braunschweiger	2 oz	7 lb	
Frankfurters			
8 per lb	2 franks	12½ lb	
10 per lb	2 franks	10 lb	
Knockwurst	3 oz	10 lb	
Sliced luncheon meat	1 oz	3¼ lb	16 slices per lb
Veal			
Cubed, 1-inch for stew	2 oz EP	12–15 lb AP	1 lb AP = 0.65 lb cooked lean meat
Cutlets, 3 or 4 per lb	3–3½ oz EP	12½–15 lb AP	1 lb AP = 0.80 lb cooked lean meat
Ground	3–4 oz EP	15–18 lb AP	1 lb AP = 0.73 lb cooked lean meat
Liver, calves	3–4 oz EP	15–18 lb AP	1 lb AP = 0.70 lb cooked liver
Roast, leg, boneless	3 oz EP	15–18 lb AP	1 lb AP = 0.61 lb cooked lean meat
Shoulder, boneless	3 oz EP	18 lb AP	1 lb AP = 0.59 lb cooked lean meat
Pasta			
Macaroni, noodles, and spaghetti	4 oz	4½–5 lb dry	12 lb cooked
In casseroles	2 oz	2–3 lb dry	6–7 lb cooked
Poultry			
Chicken, fryer parts			
½ breast (without back)	5 oz AP	15–16 lb AP	1 lb AP = 0.66 lb cooked chicken
1 drumstick and thigh	6 oz AP	19–20 lb AP	
1 drumstick	3 oz AP	10 lb AP	1 lb AP = 0.49 lb cooked chicken
1 thigh	3 oz AP	10–11 lb AP	1 lb AP = 0.50 lb cooked chicken
2 wings	5 oz AP	15 lb AP	1 lb AP = 0.34 lb cooked chicken
Whole	¼ fryer	13 fryers	2½–3 lb each
	½ fryer	25 fryers	1¾–2 lb each
Whole, for stewing	3 oz cooked chicken without bone	26–28 lb AP	1 lb AP = 0.36 lb cooked chicken, not using neck and giblets; 0.41 lb using neck meat and giblets.
Cooked, diced	2 oz	6 lb 4 oz	

(continued)

TABLE 1.1 *(Continued)*

Food	Serving portion	Amount for 50 portions	Miscellaneous information
Turkey, dressed, whole for roasting	3 oz EP (slices)	40–50 lb AP	1 lb AP = 0.53 lb cooked turkey with skin, without neck and giblets; without skin 0.47 lb
Boneless roll, raw	3–4 oz EP	16–18 lb AP	1 lb AP = 0.66 lb cooked turkey meat
Boneless roll, cooked	3–4 oz EP	12–15 lb AP	1 lb AP = 0.92 lb cooked turkey meat
Breasts, whole, raw	3 oz EP	19 lb AP	1 lb AP = 0.64 lb turkey meat with skin; 0.57 lb without skin
Leg quarters	3 oz EP	19 lb AP	1 lb AP = 0.53 lb cooked turkey; without skin 0.48 lb
Turkey ham, cooked	1½ oz	5 lb	
Turkey, cooked, cubed	1½–2 oz	5–6 lb EP (18–20 lb AP)	3¾–4½ qt
Canned, see Chicken			
Relishes			
Catsup	1 oz	½ No. 10 can	1 No. 10 can = about 12 cups
	1 oz	5 14-oz bottles	
Olives, green, whole	3	2 qt	88–90 per qt
Ripe, whole or pitted	3	1½ qt	120–150 per qt
Pickles, dill, whole	1 pickle	2½ qt	
Dill or sweet, sliced	1 oz	2¼ qt	
Pickle relish	1 oz	2 qt	1 gal = about 58 oz drained
Salads and salad dressings			
Salads			
Bulky vegetable	1 cup	3 gal	
Fish or meat	½ cup	6–7 qt	
Fruit	⅓ cup	4¼ qt	
Gelatin	½ cup	1 12 × 20 × 2-inch pan	24-oz pkg flavored gelatin, 1 gal liquid
Potato	½ cup	6–7 qt	
Dressings			
Mixed in salad			
French, thin	1 Tbsp	3–4 cups	
Mayonnaise	1–2 Tbsp	1 qt	

TABLE 1.1 *(Continued)*

Food	Serving portion	Amount for 50 portions	Miscellaneous information
Self-service			
Thousand Island or Roquefort	1–2 Tbsp	1½–2 qt	
French	1 Tbsp	1–1½ qt	
Sauces			
Gravy	3–4 Tbsp	3–4 qt	
Meat accompaniment	2 Tbsp	2 qt	
Pudding	2–3 Tbsp	2–3 qt	
Vegetable	2–3 Tbsp	2–3 qt	
Soups			
Soup			
First course	½–1 cup (4–8 oz)	2–3¼ gal	
Main course	1 cup (8 oz)	3¼ gal	
Soup			
Concentrated	1 cup (8 oz)	5 46-oz cans	
Soup base, paste		10 oz	For 2½ gal soup
Sugars, jellies, sweets, nuts			
Candies, small	2 each	1 lb	
Honey	2 Tbsp	5 lb (2 qt)	
Jam or jelly	1 Tbsp	2–3 lb	
Marshmallows	3	1–1½ lb	
Nuts, mixed	1½ Tbsp	1–½ lb	
Sugar, cubes	1–2 cubes	1½ lb	
Granulated	1½ tsp	12 oz	
Syrup	¼ cup	3 qt	
Toppings for dessert	2 Tbsp	1½–2 qt	
Vegetables			
Canned	2½ oz	2 No. 10 cans	Most vegetables yield 60–70 oz drained weight
Dried			
Dehydrated potatoes			
Diced or sliced	3–4 oz	2–2½ lb AP	
Instant for mashing	4 oz	2–2¼ lb AP	
Dried beans	4 oz	5–6 lb AP	
Split peas or lentils	4 oz	4 lb AP	

(continued)

TABLE 1.1 *(Continued)*

Food	Serving portion	Amount for 50 portions	Miscellaneous information
Fresh			
Alfalfa sprouts	2 Tbsp	1 lb	
Asparagus	3 oz	18–20 lb AP	1 lb AP = 0.53 lb ready to cook; 0.50 lb cooked
Beans, green or wax	3 oz	10–12 lb AP	1 lb AP = 0.88 lb ready to cook
Bean sprouts	2 Tbsp	12 oz	
Beets, topped	3 oz	12–14 lb AP	1 lb AP = 0.77 lb peeled; 0.73 lb cooked slices
Broccoli	3 oz	16–20 lb AP	1 lb AP = 0.81 lb ready to cook
Brussels sprouts	3 oz	12–14 lb AP	1 lb AP = 0.76 lb ready to cook
Cabbage			
Green	1 wedge or 3 oz shredded	12–14 lb AP	1 lb AP = 0.89 lb ready to cook or serve raw
Red, chopped or shredded	2 oz	10 lb AP	1 lb AP = 0.64 lb ready to cook or serve raw
Carrots, without tops	3 oz	14–16 lb AP	1 lb AP = 0.70 lb ready to cook or serve raw; 0.60 lb cooked
Strips for relish	3 strips, 4 × ½ inch	4–5 lb	
Cauliflower	3 oz	16–18 lb AP	1 lb AP = 0.62 lb ready to cook or serve raw; 0.61 lb cooked
Salad pieces	¼ cup	8 lb AP	1 medium head = about 6 cups (50–75) florets
Celery, sliced	3 oz	12 lb AP	1 lb AP = 0.83 lb ready to cook or serve raw; 0.74 lb cooked
Sticks for relishes	4 sticks, 4 × ½ inch	4–5 lb AP	
Celery cabbage	2 oz	9 lb AP	1 lb AP = 0.93 lb ready to serve raw
Corn, on cob	1 ear	5 doz (25 lb with husks)	1 lb AP = 0.33 lb edible portion cooked
Cucumbers	1½ oz	5–6 lb AP	1 lb AP = 0.84 lb pared ready to serve raw
Eggplant	3 oz	12–15 lb AP	1 lb AP = 0.81 lb ready to cook
Endive, escarole	½ cup	8–10 lb AP	1 lb AP = 0.78 lb ready to serve
Lettuce			
Head, wedges	⅙ head	8–10 heads	24 heads per crate
Broken, for salad	1 cup (2½ oz)	9½ lb AP	1lb AP = 0.76 lb ready to serve

TABLE 1.1 *(Continued)*

Food	Serving portion	Amount for 50 portions	Miscellaneous information
Garnish	1 leaf	4–5 lb AP	
Leaf, for garnish	1 leaf	3–4 lb AP	1 lb AP = 0.66 lb ready to serve
Bibb	2½ oz	9 lb	
Romaine, for salad	2½ oz	9 lb AP	1 lb AP = 0.64 lb ready to serve
Mushrooms, sliced	3 oz	12 lb AP	1 lb AP = 0.98 ready to serve raw or cook; 0.22 lb cooked
For sauce	1 oz	3–4 lb AP	
Onions			
Green, chopped for salad	¼ cup (with tops)	3½–4 lb AP	1 lb AP = 0.83 lb ready to serve raw with tops; 0.37 lb without tops
Mature	2 oz	7–8 lb AP	1 lb AP = 0.88 lb ready to serve raw or cook; 0.78 lb cooked
Whole, to bake	1 medium	12–15 lb AP	
Parsley, for garnish or seasoning		2 lb AP	1 lb AP = 0.92 lb ready to serve raw
Parsnips	3 oz	12–15 lb AP	1 lb AP = 0.83 lb ready to cook
Peppers, green, strips	3 strips	4–5 lb AP	1 lb AP = 0.80 lb ready to cook or serve raw; 0.73 lb cooked
Chopped for salads	½ oz	1–2 lb AP	
Potatoes, sweet, or yams to bake	1 potato (4½–5 oz)	18–20 lb AP	1 lb AP = 0.61 lb baked, without skins
Candied	4 oz	20–25 lb AP	1 lb AP = 0.80 lb peeled, ready to cook
Mashed	4 oz	18 lb AP	
Potatoes, white, baked	1 potato	17–25 lb AP	1 lb AP = 0.74 lb baked potato without skins
Mashed	4 oz (½ cup)	15 lb AP	1 lb AP = 0.81 lb ready to cook pared
Steamed	4 oz (1 potato)	16–17 lb AP	
French fried	4–5 oz	16–20 lb AP	1 lb AP = 0.81 lb ready to cook
Radishes, without tops, for relishes	2 oz	6 lb AP	1 lb AP = 0.94 lb ready to serve raw
Spinach	3 oz	12 lb AP	1 lb AP = 0.88 lb ready to cook or serve raw
For salad	1 oz	4–5 lb AP	
Squash, summer, yellow	3 oz	10 lb AP	1 lb AP = 0.95 lb ready to cook; 0.83 lb cooked

(continued)

TABLE 1.1 *(Continued)*

Food	Serving portion	Amount for 50 portions	Miscellaneous information
Zucchini	3 oz	10 lb AP	1 lb AP = 0.94 lb ready to cook; 0.86 lb cooked
Squash, winter, acorn	½ squash	20–25 lb AP	1 lb AP = 0.87 lb ready to cook in skin
Butternut	3 oz	12 lb AP	1 lb AP = 0.84 lb ready to cook pared
Hubbard, baked	2½-inch square	20–25 lb	
Mashed	3 oz	15 lb AP	1 lb AP = 0.64 lb ready to cook pared
Tomatoes	1 small	20 lb AP	
Sliced, salad	3 slices	15 lb AP	1 lb AP = 0.90 lb ready to cook or serve raw
Diced	½ cup	10 lb AP	
Cherry, salad	1 oz	4 lb AP	1 lb AP = 0.97 lb stemmed
Turnips	3 oz	12–15 lb AP	1 lb AP = 0.79 lb ready to cook or serve raw; 0.78 lb cooked
Watercress	1½ oz	4–5 lb AP	1 lb AP = 0.92 lb ready to serve raw
Yams, see Potatoes, sweet			
Frozen			
Asparagus spears	3 oz	10 lb	
Beans, cut green or lima	3 oz	10 lb	
Broccoli	3 oz	10 lb	
Brussels sprouts	3 oz	10 lb	
Cauliflower	3 oz	10 lb	
Corn, whole kernel	3 oz	10 lb	
Peas	3 oz	10 lb	
Potatoes			
French fried	4 oz	12–13 lb	
Hashed brown	4 oz	12–13 lb	
Spinach	3 oz	10 lb	

Miscellaneous

Food	Serving portion	Amount for 50 portions	Miscellaneous information
Ice			
For water glasses	3–4 oz	10–12 lb	
For punch bowl		10 lb	
Potato chips	1 oz	3 lb	

[a] Abbreviations used: AP, as purchased; EP, edible portion.

TABLE 1.2 APPROXIMATE YIELD IN THE PREPARATION OF FRESH FRUITS AND VEGETABLES (in lb)

Weight of ready to cook or ready to serve raw from 1 lb as purchased

Apples	0.78	Lettuce, head	0.76
Asparagus	0.53	Lettuce, leaf	0.66
Avocado	0.67	Lettuce, romaine	0.64
Bananas	0.65	Mangoes	0.69
Beans, green or wax	0.88	Mushrooms	0.98
Beans, lima	0.44	Nectarines	0.91
Beets	0.77	Okra	0.87
Blueberries	0.96	Onions, mature	0.88
Broccoli	0.81	Orange sections	0.40
Brussels sprouts	0.76	Parsnips	0.83
Cabbage, green	0.87	Peaches	0.76
Cabbage, red	0.64	Pears, served pared	0.78
Cantaloupe, served without rind	0.52	Peas, green	0.38
Carrots	0.70	Peppers, green	0.80
Cauliflower	0.62	Pineapple	0.54
Celery	0.83	Plums	0.94
Chard, Swiss	0.92	Potatoes, sweet	0.80
Cherries, pitted	0.87	Potatoes, white	0.81
Chicory	0.89	Radishes, without tops	0.94
Collards, leaves	0.57	Rhubarb, without leaves	0.86
Collards, leaves and stems	0.74	Rutabagas	0.85
Cranberries	0.95	Spinach, partly trimmed	0.88
Cucumbers, pared	0.84	Squash, acorn	0.87
Eggplant	0.81	Squash, butternut	0.84
Endive, escarole	0.78	Squash, Hubbard	0.64
Grapefruit sections	0.52	Squash, summer	0.95
Grapes, seedless	0.97	Squash, zucchini	0.94
Honeydew melon, served		Strawberries	0.88
without rind	0.46	Tomatoes	0.99
Kale	0.67	Turnips, without tops	0.79
		Watermelon	0.57

Adapted from *Food Buying Guide for School Food Service*, U.S. Department of Agriculture PA 1257, Washington, D.C., 1980.

How to use this table: To determine the amount of fruits or vegetables to yield the amount stated in a recipe as EP or as ready to cook in Table 2.19, Timetable for Boiling or Steaming Fresh Vegetables:

Divide the weight of ready to cook or EP desired by the figure given in this table. For example, the recipe for Mashed Potatoes calls for 12 lb EP potatoes. To change the 12 lb EP to AP, divide 12 lb by 0.81, the ready to cook weight from 1 lb AP.

12 lb EP divided by 0.81 lb = 14.8 or 15 lb to purchase

TABLES OF WEIGHTS AND MEASURES

TABLE 1.3 FOOD WEIGHTS AND APPROXIMATE EQUIVALENTS IN MEASURE

Food	Weight	Approximate measure
Alfalfa sprouts	1 lb	6 cups
Allspice, ground	1 oz	4½ Tbsp
Almonds, blanched, slivered, chopped	1 lb	3½ cups
Apples, canned, pie pack	1 lb	2 cups
Apples, fresh, AP[a]	1 lb	3–4 medium (113)
Apples, fresh, pared and sliced	1 lb	1 qt
Apples, pared and diced, 1½-inch cubes	1 lb	3½ cups
Applesauce	1 lb	2 cups
Apricots, canned halves, without juice	1 lb	2 cups or 12–20 halves
Apricots, canned, pie pack	1 lb	2 cups
Apricots, dried, AP	1 lb	3 cups
Apricots, dried, cooked, without juice	1 lb	4½–5 cups
Apricots, fresh	1 lb	5–8 apricots
Asparagus, canned, cuts	1 lb	2½ cups
Asparagus, canned tips, drained	1 lb	16–20 stalks
Asparagus, fresh	1 lb	16–20 stalks
Avocado	1 lb	2 medium
Bacon bits	1 lb	3⅓ cups
Bacon, cooked	1 lb	85–95 slices
Bacon, uncooked	1 lb	14–25 slices
Bacon, uncooked, diced	1 lb	2¼ cups
Baking powder	1 oz	2⅓ Tbsp
Baking powder	1 lb	2⅓ cups
Baking soda	1 oz	2⅓ Tbsp
Baking soda	1 lb	2⅓ cups
Bananas, AP	1 lb	3 medium
Bananas, diced	1 lb	2½–3 cups
Bananas, mashed	1 lb	2 cups
Barbecue sauce	1 lb	2 cups
Barley, pearl	1 lb	2 cups
Basil, sweet	1 oz	¾ cups
Bay leaves	1 oz	2 cups
Beans, baked	1 lb	2 cups
Beans, garbanzo, canned	1 lb	2½ cups
Beans, Great Northern, dried, AP	1 lb	2½ cups
Beans, green, cut, cooked	1 lb	3 cups
Beans, green, cut, frozen	1 lb	3 cups
Beans, kidney, dried, AP	1 lb	2½ cups
Beans, kidney, dried, 1 lb AP, after cooking	2 lb 6 oz	6–7 cups
Beans, lima, dried, AP	1 lb	2½ cups
Beans, lima, dried, AP, after cooking	2 lb 9 oz	6 cups
Beans, lima, fresh, canned, or frozen	1 lb	3 cups
Beans, navy, dried, AP	1 lb	2¼ cups
Beans, navy, dried, 1 lb AP, after cooking	2 lb 3 oz	5½–6 cups
Beans, pinto, dried, AP	1 lb	2½ cups

TABLE 1.3 *(Continued)*

Food	Weight	Approximate measure
Bean sprouts, canned, drained	1 lb	1 qt
Bean sprouts, fresh	1 lb	2 qt
Beef, cooked, diced	1 lb	3 cups
Beef, dried, solid pack	1 lb	3¾ cups
Beef, ground, raw	1 lb	2 cups
Beef base (paste)	1 lb	2½ cups
Beets, cooked, diced or sliced	1 lb	2½–3 cups
Beets, fresh, medium	1 lb	3–4 beets
Blackberries, fresh, frozen, IQF[b]	1 lb	3½ cups
Blackberries or boysenberries, pie pack	1 lb	2½ cups
Blackeyed peas, dried	1 lb	2¾ cups
Blueberries, canned	1 lb	2 cups
Blueberries, fresh, frozen, IQF	1 lb	3 cups
Bran, all bran	1 lb	2 qt
Bran flakes	1 lb	3 qt
Bread, dry, broken	1 lb	8–9 cups
Bread, fresh	1 lb	8 oz dry crumbs
Bread, loaf	1 lb	16–18 slices, ½ inch each
Bread, sandwich	2 lb	36–40 slices, thin
Bread, soft, broken	1 lb	2½ qt
Bread crumbs, dry, ground	1 lb	4 cups (1 qt)
Bread crumbs, soft	1 lb	2 qt
Brussels sprouts, AP	1 lb	1 qt
Butter	1 lb	2 cups
Buttermilk, dry	1 oz	¼ cup
Buttermilk, dry	1 lb	4 cups
Butterscotch chips	1 lb	2⅔ cups
Cabbage, raw, shredded	1 lb	1 qt lightly packed
Cabbage, AP, shredded, cooked	1 lb	1½ cups
Cake crumbs, soft	1 lb	6 cups
Cake mix	1 lb	4 cups
Cantaloupe	3 lb	1 melon, 6-inch diameter
Caraway seeds	1 oz	4 Tbsp
Carrots, diced, cooked	1 lb	3 cups
Carrots, diced, raw	1 lb	3–3¼ cups
Carrots, fresh	1 lb	4–5 medium
Carrots, ground, raw, EP[c]	1 lb	3 cups
Carrots, shredded	1 lb	4 cups
Carrots, sliced, frozen	1 lb	3½ cups
Catsup	1 lb	2 cups
Cauliflower, florets	1 lb	4 cups
Cauliflower, head	1 lb	1 medium
Cayenne pepper	1 oz	4 Tbsp
Celery, chopped	1 lb	3 cups
Celery, diced, EP	1 lb (1–2 bunches)	1 qt
Celery cabbage, shredded	1 lb	6 cups

(continued)

TABLE 1.3 *(Continued)*

Food	Weight	Approximate measure
Celery flakes, dried	1 oz	1⅓ cups
Celery salt	1 oz	2 Tbsp
Celery seed	1 oz	4 Tbsp
Cheese, cheddar or Swiss, shredded	1 lb	4 cups
Cheese, cottage	1 lb	2 cups
Cheese, cream	1 lb	2 cups
Cheese, loaf, slices	1 lb	16–20 slices
Cheese, mozzarella, shredded	1 lb	3½ cups
Cheese, Parmesan or Romano, grated	1 lb	3½ cups
Cherries, glacé, candied	1 lb	96 cherries or 2½ cups
Cherries, maraschino, drained	1 lb	50–60 cherries
Cherries, red, frozen	1 lb	2 cups
Cherries, red, pie pack, drained	1 lb	2½ cups
Cherries, Royal Anne, drained	1 lb	2½ cups
Chicken, cooked, cubed	1 lb	3 cups
Chicken, ready to cook	4–4½ lb	1 qt cooked, diced
Chicken base (paste)	1 lb	1¾ cups
Chili powder	1 oz	4 Tbsp
Chili sauce	1 lb	1⅓ cups
Chilis, green, diced	1 lb	2 cups
Chives, freeze-dried	1 oz	2⅞ cups
Chives, frozen	1 oz	⅓ cup
Chocolate, baking	1 lb	16 squares
Chocolate, grated	1 lb	3½ cups
Chocolate, melted	1 lb	2 cups (scant)
Chocolate chips	1 lb	2⅔ cups
Chocolate wafers	1 lb	4 cups crumbs
Cinnamon, ground	1 oz	4 Tbsp
Cinnamon, ground	1 lb	4 cups
Cinnamon sticks	1 oz	10 pieces
Citron, dried, chopped	1 lb	2½ cups
Cloves, ground	1 oz	4 Tbsp
Cloves, whole	1 oz	5 Tbsp
Cocoa	1 lb	4½ cups
Coconut, flaked or shredded	1 lb	4¾ cups
Coffee, ground coarse	1 lb	5–5½ cups
Coffee, instant	1 oz	½ cup
Corn, cream style, canned	1 lb	2 cups
Corn, whole kernel, canned, drained	1 lb	3 cups
Corn, whole kernel, frozen	1 lb	3 cups
Cornflake crumbs	1 lb	4½ cups
Cornflakes	1 lb	4 qt
Cornmeal, coarse	1 lb	3 cups
Cornmeal, 1 lb AP, dry, after cooking	6 lb	3 qt
Cornstarch	1 oz	3 Tbsp
Cornstarch	1 lb	3 cups
Corn syrup	1 lb	1½ cups
Crab in shell	1 lb	½ cup cooked meat
Crabmeat, flaked	1 lb	3½ cups
Cracked wheat	1 lb	3½ cups

TABLE 1.3 *(Continued)*

Food	Weight	Approximate measure
Cracker crumbs, medium fine	1 lb	5–6 cups
Crackers, 2⅝ × 2⅝-inch	1 lb	65 crackers
Crackers, graham	1 lb	60–65 crackers
Crackers, graham, crumbs	1 lb	4 cups
Crackers, saltines, 2 × 2-inch	1 lb	150–160 crackers
Cranberries, cooked	1 lb	1¾ cups
Cranberries, raw	1 lb	4 cups
Cranberry relish	1 lb	1¾ cups
Cranberry sauce, jellied	1 lb	2 cups
Cream of tartar	1 oz	3 Tbsp
Cream of Wheat or farina, quick, AP	1 lb	2⅔ cups
Cream of Wheat or farina, 1 lb AP, after cooking	8 lb	1 gal
Cream, sour	1 lb	2 cups
Cream, whipping	1 pt	1 qt whipped
Croutons	1 lb	2¼ qt
Cucumbers	1 lb	2–3 large
Cucumbers, diced, EP	1 lb	3 cups
Cucumbers, sliced	1 lb	50–60 slices
Cumin, ground	1 oz	4 Tbsp
Currants, dried	1 lb	3 cups
Curry powder	1 oz	4½ Tbsp
Dates, pitted	1 lb	2½ cups
Dill seed	1 oz	4½ Tbsp
Dill weed	1 oz	¾ cup
Eggplant	1 lb	8 slices, 4 × ½-inch
Eggplant	1 lb	1 qt diced
Eggs, dried, whites	1 lb	5 cups
Eggs, dried, whole	1 lb	5⅓ cups
Eggs, dried, yolks	1 lb	5⅔ cups
Eggs, hard-cooked, chopped	1 lb	2⅔ cups
Eggs, hard-cooked, chopped	1 doz	3½ cups
Eggs, shelled, fresh or frozen, whole	1 lb (approximately 1¾ oz per egg)	2 cups (8–10 eggs)
Eggs, shelled, fresh or frozen, whites	1 lb (approximately 1¼ oz per white)	2 cups (16–18 eggs)
Eggs, shelled, fresh or frozen, yolks	1 lb (approximately ½ oz per yolk)	2 cups (22–26 eggs)
Eggs, whole, in shell[d]	1 lb	8–10 large eggs
Fennel seed	1 oz	4 Tbsp
Figs, dry, cut fine	1 lb	2½ cups
Flour, all-purpose or bread	1 lb	4 cups
Flour, cake or pastry, unsifted	1 lb	3¾ cups
Flour, rye	1 lb	4 cups
Flour, whole wheat	1 lb	3¾–4 cups
Garlic, fresh	1 oz	6 large cloves
Garlic, fresh, minced	1 oz	3 Tbsp

(continued)

TABLE 1.3 *(Continued)*

Food	Weight	Approximate measure
Garlic powder	1 oz	3 Tbsp
Garlic salt	1 oz	2 Tbsp
Gelatin, granulated, flavored	1 lb	2¼ cups
Gelatin, granulated, unflavored	1 oz	3 Tbsp
Gelatin, granulated, unflavored	1 lb	3 cups
Ginger, candied, chopped	1 oz	2 Tbsp
Ginger, ground	1 oz	4 Tbsp
Ginger, ground	1 lb	4 cups
Graham cracker crumbs	1 lb	4 cups
Grapefruit, medium	1 lb	1 grapefruit, 10–12 sections, ⅔ cup juice
Grapefruit sections	1 lb	2 cups
Grapes, cut, seeded, EP	1 lb	2¾ cups
Grapes, seedless, fresh	1 lb	2½ cups
Grapes, on stem	1 lb	1 qt
Grits, hominy	1 lb	3 cups
Grits, hominy, 1 lb AP, after cooking	6½ lb	3¼ qt
Ham, cooked, diced	1 lb	3 cups
Ham, cooked, ground	1 lb	2 cups
Hominy, canned	1 lb	3 cups
Hominy grits, see Grits		
Honey	1 lb	1⅓ cups
Horseradish, prepared	1 oz	2 Tbsp
Ice cream	4½–6 lb	1 gal
Jam, jelly	1 lb	1⅓–1½ cups
Lard	1 lb	2 cups
Lemon juice	1 lb	2 cups (8–10 lemons)
Lemon peel, dried	1 oz	4 Tbsp
Lemon peel, fresh	1 oz	4 Tbsp
Lemon peel, fresh	1 lemon	2 Tbsp
Lemons, size 165	1 lb	4–5 lemons; yield, ¾ cup juice
Lettuce, average head	2 lb	1 head
Lettuce, chopped or shredded	1 lb	6–8 cups
Lettuce, leaf	1 lb	25–30 salad garnishes
Limes, fresh	1 lb	yield, ⅞ cup juice
Macaroni, 1-inch pieces, dry	1 lb	4 cups
Macaroni, 1 lb AP, after cooking	3 lb	2–2¼ qt
Macaroni, cooked	1 lb	3 cups
Mace	1 oz	4½ Tbsp
Margarine	1 lb	2 cups
Marjoram	1 oz	6 Tbsp
Marshmallows (1¼-inch)	1 lb	80–90
Marshmallows, miniature (10 miniature = 1 regular)	1 lb	8 cups
	1 oz	52
Mayonnaise	1 lb	2 cups (scant)
Meat, cooked, chopped	1 lb	2 cups
Milk, evaporated	1 lb	1¾ cups
Milk, fluid, whole	1 lb	2 cups
Milk, nonfat, dry	1 lb	6 cups

TABLE 1.3 *(Continued)*

Food	Weight	Approximate measure
Milk, nonfat, dry	1 oz	6 Tbsp
Milk, sweetened, condensed	1 lb	1½ cups
Mincemeat	1 lb	2 cups
Molasses	1 lb	1⅓ cups
Monosodium glutamate	1 oz	2 Tbsp
Mushrooms, canned	1 lb	2 cups
Mushrooms, fresh	1 lb	6¾ cups
Mustard, ground, dry	1 oz	5 Tbsp
Mustard, ground, dry	1 lb	5 cups
Mustard, prepared	1 oz	2 Tbsp
Mustard seed	1 oz	2½ Tbsp
Noodles, cooked	1 lb	2¾ cups
Noodles, 1 lb AP, after cooking	3 lb	2 qt
Nutmeats	1 lb	4 cups
Nutmeg, ground	1 oz	3½ Tbsp
Oats, rolled, quick, AP	1 lb	6 cups
Oats, rolled, 1 lb AP, after cooking	2½ lb	4 qt
Oil, vegetable	1 lb	2–2⅛ cups
Olives, AP	1 lb	⅔ cups chopped
Olives, green, small size, drained	1 lb	160 olives
Olives, green, stuffed	1 lb	2½ cups
Olives, ripe, sliced	1 lb	3⅓ cups
Olives, ripe, small size, drained	1 lb	160 olives
Onions, dehydrated	1 lb	8 lb raw (equivalent)
Onions, dehydrated, chopped	1 oz	5 Tbsp
Onions, dehydrated, chopped	1 lb	5–6 cups
Onions, fresh, chopped	1 lb	2–3 cups
Onions, green, sliced	1 lb	2 cups
Onions, mature, AP	1 lb	4–5 medium
Onion powder	1 oz	3 Tbsp
Onion salt	1 oz	2½ Tbsp
Onion soup mix	1 oz	2⅔ Tbsp
Onion soup mix	1 lb	2⅔ cups
Orange juice, frozen	6 oz	3 cups reconstituted
Orange juice, frozen	32 oz	4 qt reconstituted
Orange peel, dried	1 oz	4 Tbsp
Orange peel, fresh	1 medium orange	3 Tbsp grated peel
Oranges, medium (113)	1 lb	3–4 oranges, unpeeled; 5 oranges, peeled; 10–11 sections each; yield, 1 cup juice
Oranges	1 lb	2 cups bite-size pieces
Oregano, ground	1 oz	5 Tbsp
Oregano, leaf	1 oz	¾ cup
Oysters, shucked	1 lb	2 cups
Paprika, ground	1 oz	4 Tbsp
Parsley, coarsely chopped	1 oz	¾ cup
Parsley flakes, dry	1 oz	1⅓ cups
Parsnips, AP	1 lb	4 medium

(continued)

tinued)

	Weight	Approximate measure
...ned, sliced, drained	1 lb	2 cups
...fresh, AP	1 lb	4 medium
...es, sliced, frozen	1 lb	2 cups
...eanut butter	1 lb	2 cups
Peanuts, chopped, no skins	1 lb	3 cups
Peanuts, shelled	1 lb	3¼ cups
Pears, canned, drained, diced	1 lb	2½ cups
Pears, canned, large halves, drained	1 lb 14 oz	1 qt (9 halves)
Pears, fresh AP	1 lb	3–4 medium
Peas, cooked, drained	1 lb	2¼ cups
Peas, dried, 1 lb after cooking	2½ lb	5½ cups
Peas, in pod	1 lb	1 cup shelled
Peas, split, dried, AP	1 lb	2⅓ cups
Pecans, chopped	1 lb	4 cups
Pecans, shelled, pieces	1 lb	4 cups
Pepper, ground, black or white	1 oz	4 Tbsp
Pepper, ground, black or white	1 lb	4 cups
Peppercorns	1 oz	6 Tbsp
Peppers, green	1 lb	2–3
Peppers, green, chopped	1 lb	3 cups
Peppers, green, dried flakes	1 oz	¾ cup
Pickle relish	1 lb	2 cups
Pickles, chopped	1 lb	3 cups
Pickles, halves, 3-inch	1 lb	3 cups or 36 halves
Pimiento, chopped	1 lb	2 cups
Pineapple, canned, crushed	1 lb	2 cups
Pineapple, canned, slices, drained	1 lb	8–12 slices
Pineapple, canned, tidbits	1 lb	2 cups
Pineapple, fresh	2–4 lb	1 pineapple, 2–4 cups, cubed
Pineapple, frozen, chunks	1 lb	2 cups
Poppy seed	1 oz	3 Tbsp
Potato chips	1 lb	4–5 qt
Potato chips, crushed	1 lb	2 qt
Potatoes, dehydrated, diced	1 lb	5⅛ cups
Potatoes, dehydrated, flakes	1 lb	5 cups
Potatoes, dehydrated, granules	1 lb	2¼ cups
Potatoes, dehydrated, slices	1 lb	9⅔ cups
Potatoes, fresh, white, AP	1 lb	3 medium
Potatoes, fresh, white, cooked	1 lb	2½ cups
Potatoes, raw, white, cubed	1 lb	2¾ cups
Potatoes, sweet	1 lb	3 medium
Potatoes, sweet, cooked	1 lb	2 cups
Poultry seasoning, ground	1 oz	3 Tbsp
Prunes, dried, size 30/40, AP	1 lb	2½ cups
Prunes, dried, 1 lb AP, after cooking	2 lb	3–4 cups
Prunes, pitted, cooked	1 lb	3¼ cups
Pudding mix, dry, instant	1 lb	2½ cups
Pudding mix, dry, regular	1 lb	2⅔ cups
Pumpkin, cooked	1 lb	2 cups

TABLE 1.3 *(Continued)*

Food	Weight	Approximate measure
Radishes, AP	1 lb	45–50
Raisins, AP	1 lb	3 cups
Raisins, 1 lb AP, after cooking	1 lb 12 oz	1 qt
Raisins, chopped	1 lb	2⅔ cups
Raspberries, fresh AP, or frozen IQF	1 lb	3 cups
Raspberries, with syrup	1 lb	2 cups
Red-hots	1 lb	2¼ cups
Rhubarb, raw, 1-inch pieces	1 lb	4 cups
Rhubarb, 1 lb EP, after cooking		2½ cups
Rice, brown, AP	1 lb	2½ cups
Rice, converted, AP	1 lb	2½ cups
Rice, cooked	1 lb	2¼ cups
Rice, 1 lb AP, after cooking	4 lb	2 qt
Rice, precooked, AP	1 lb	4½ cups
Rice, puffed	1 oz	1⅔ cups
Rice, regular, AP	1 lb	2⅓ cups
Rice cereal, crisp	1 lb	4 qt
Rosemary leaves	1 oz	9 Tbsp
Rutabagas, raw, cubed, EP	1 lb	3⅓ cups
Sage, finely ground	1 oz	8 Tbsp (½ cup)
Sage, rubbed	1 oz	⅔ cup
Salad dressing, cooked	1 lb	2 cups
Salmon, canned	1 lb	2 cups
Salt	1 oz	1½ Tbsp
Salt	1 lb	1½ cups
Sauerkraut	1 lb	3 cups packed
Sausage, bulk, AP	1 lb	2 cups
Sausages, link, small	1 lb	16–17
Sesame seed	1 oz	3 Tbsp
Sherbet	6 lb	1 gal
Shortening, hydrogenated fat	1 lb	2¼ cups
Shrimp, cleaned, cooked, peeled	1 lb	3¼ cups
Soda, baking	1 oz	2⅓ Tbsp
Spaghetti, cooked	1 lb	2⅔ cups
Spaghetti, 1 lb AP, after cooking	3 lb	2 qt
Spinach, canned or frozen	1 lb	2 cups
Spinach, raw	1 lb	5 qt lightly packed
Spinach, raw, chopped	1 lb	3¼ qt
Spinach, 1 lb AP, after cooking	13 oz	2¾ cups
Squash, Hubbard, cooked	1 lb	2 cups
Starch, waxy maize	1 oz	3 Tbsp
Strawberries, fresh or frozen, IQF	1 lb	3 cups
Strawberries, sliced, frozen, with syrup	1 lb	2 cups
Suet, ground	1 lb	3¾ cups
Sugar, brown, lightly packed	1 lb	3 cups
Sugar, brown, solid pack	1 lb	2 cups
Sugar, cubes	1 lb	96 cubes
Sugar, granulated	1 lb	2¼ cups
Sugar, powdered, unsifted	1 lb	3¼ cups
Sugar, powdered, XXXX sifted	1 lb	3¾ cups

(continued)

TABLE 1.3   *(Continued)*

Food	Weight	Approximate measure
Tapioca, quick cooking	1 lb	3 cups
Tapioca, 1 lb AP, after cooking		7½ cups
Tarragon, leaf	1 oz	1 cup
Tea, bulk	1 lb	6 cups
Tea, instant	1 oz	½ cup
Thyme, ground	1 oz	6 Tbsp
Thyme, leaves	1 oz	½ cup
Tomatoes, canned	1 lb	2 cups
Tomatoes, fresh	1 lb	3–4 medium, 16 slices
Tomatoes, fresh, diced	1 lb	2¼ cups
Tortillas, corn, 8-inch	1 lb	16
Tortillas, flour, 8-inch	1 lb	12
Tortillas, flour, 10-inch	1 lb	9
Tuna, canned	1 lb	2 cups
Turkey, AP, dressed weight	14 lb	11–12 cups diced, cooked meat
Turmeric, ground	1 oz	4 Tbsp
Turnips, AP	1 lb	2–3
Vanilla and other extracts	1 oz	2 Tbsp
Vinegar	1 lb	2 cups
Walnuts, English, shelled	1 lb	4 cups
Water	1 lb	2 cups
Watercress, EP	1 oz	½ cup
Watermelon	1 lb	1-inch slice, 6-inch diameter
Whipped topping, liquid	1 lb	2 cups
Yeast, compressed	1 oz	1 pkg
Yeast, dry	¼ oz	1 envelope
Yeast, dry, regular or instant	1 oz	3 Tbsp + 1 tsp
Yeast, dry, regular or instant	1 lb	3⅓ cups
Zucchini, fresh, shredded	1 lb	3¼ cups

[a] AP denotes "as purchased," which refers to the status of the product before it is peeled, hulled, cored, or otherwise prepared for cooking.
[b] IQF denotes "individually quick frozen."
[c] EP denotes "edible portion," or the status of the product after it has been prepared for cooking or for serving raw.
[d] One case (30 doz) eggs weighs approximately 41–43 lb and yields approximately 35 lb liquid whole eggs.

TABLE 1.4   BASIC EQUIVALENTS IN MEASURES AND WEIGHTS

Equivalents	*Abbreviations*[a]	
1 Tbsp = 3 tsp, in liquids ½ fl oz	bu	bushel
⅛ cup = 2 Tbsp, in liquids 1 fl oz	c	cup
¼ cup = 4 Tbsp, in liquids 2 fl oz	fl oz	fluid ounce
⅓ cup = 5 Tbsp + 1 tsp	gal	gallon
½ cup = 8 Tbsp, in liquids 4 fl oz	g	gram
⅔ cup = 10 Tbsp + 2 tsp	kg	kilogram
¾ cup = 12 Tbsp, in liquids 6 fl oz	L	liter
1 cup = 16 Tbsp, in liquids 8 fl oz	lb	pound
1 pt = 2 cups, in liquids 16 fl oz	mL	milliliter
1 qt = 2 pt = 4 cups	oz	ounce
1 gal = 4 qt	pk	peck
1 lb = 16 oz	pt	pint
1 pk = 8 qt, approximately 12½ lb	qt	quart
1 bu = 4 pk, approximately 50 lb	Tbsp	tablespoon
1 ml = $\frac{1}{5}$ tsp	tsp	teaspoon
1 L = 1.06 qt		
1 g = 0.035 oz		
1 kg = 2.2 lb		

[a] Periods are usually not used in abbreviations for quantity recipes.

TABLE 1.5   WEIGHT (1–16 OZ) AND APPROXIMATE MEASURE EQUIVALENTS FOR COMMONLY USED FOODS

Food item	1 oz	2 oz	3 oz	4 oz
Baking powder	2⅓ Tbsp	¼ cup + 1 tsp	⅓ cup + 2 Tbsp	½ cup + 1 Tbsp
Baking soda	2⅓ Tbsp	¼ cup + 1 tsp	⅓ cup + 2 Tbsp	½ cup + 1 Tbsp
Bread crumbs, dry	¼ cup	½ cup	¾ cup	1 cup
Butter or margarine	2 Tbsp	¼ cup	⅓ cup + 2 tsp	½ cup
Celery, chopped	¼ cup	½ cup	¾ cup	1 cup
Cornstarch	3½ Tbsp	⅓ cup + 2 Tbsp	⅔ cup	¾ cup + 2 Tbsp
Eggs, whole, whites or yolks, fresh or frozen	2 Tbsp	¼ cup	⅓ cup + 2 tsp	½ cup
Flour, all-purpose, unsifted	¼ cup	½ cup	¾ cup	1 cup
Flour, cake, unsifted	¼ cup	½ cup	½ cup + 3 Tbsp	¾ cup + 3 Tbsp
Milk, nonfat dry	⅓ cup	¾ cup	1 cup + 2 Tbsp	1½ cups
Nutmeats	¼ cup	½ cup	¾ cup	1 cup
Onion, chopped	2 Tbsp	¼ cup	⅓ cup + 2 tsp	½ cup
Salt	1½ Tbsp	3 Tbsp	¼ cup + 1½ tsp	⅓ cup + 2 tsp
Shortening, hydrogenated fat	2 Tbsp + 1 tsp	¼ cup + 2 tsp	⅓ cup + 2 Tbsp	½ cup + 1 Tbsp
Sugar, brown, light pack	3 Tbsp	⅓ cup + 2 tsp	½ cup + 1 Tbsp	¾ cup
Sugar, granulated	2¼ Tbsp	¼ cup	¼ cup + 3 Tbsp	½ cup + 1 Tbsp
Sugar, powdered	3 Tbsp	⅓ cup + 2 tsp	½ cup + 1 tsp	¾ cup
Yeast, dry	3 Tbsp + 1 tsp	⅓ cup + 1 Tbsp	½ cup + 2 Tbsp	¾ cup + 1 Tbsp

5 oz	6 oz	7 oz	8 oz
¾ cup	¾ cup + 2 Tbsp	1 cup + 1 tsp	1 cup + 3 Tbsp
¾ cup	¾ cup + 2 Tbsp	1 cup + 1 tsp	1 cup + 3 Tbsp
1¼ cups	1½ cups	1¾ cups	2 cups
½ cup + 2 Tbsp	¾ cup	¾ cup + 2 Tbsp	1 cup
1¼ cups	1½ cups	1¾ cups	2 cups
1 cup + 2 Tbsp	1¼ cup + 1 Tbsp	1½ cup + 1 Tbsp	1¾ cups
½ cup + 2 Tbsp	¾ cup	¾ cup + 2 Tbsp	1 cup
1¼ cups	1½ cups	1¾ cups	2 cups
1 cup + 3 Tbsp	1¼ cups + 3 Tbsp	1½ cups + 2 Tbsp	1¾ cups + 2 Tbsp
1¾ cups + 2 Tbsp	2¼ cups	2½ cups + 2 Tbsp	3 cups
1¼ cups	1½ cups	1¾ cups	2 cups
½ cup + 2 Tbsp	¾ cup	¾ cup + 2 Tbsp	1 cup
⅓ cup + 2 Tbsp	½ cup + 1 Tbsp	⅔ cup	¾ cup
⅔ cup + 1 Tbsp	¾ cup + 2 Tbsp	1 cup	1 cup + 2 Tbsp
¾ cup + 3 Tbsp	1 cup + 2 Tbsp	1¼ cups + 1 Tbsp	1½ cups
½ cup + 3 Tbsp	¾ cup + 2 Tbsp	1 cup	1 cup + 2 Tbsp
¾ cup + 3 Tbsp	1 cup + 2 Tbsp	1¼ cups + 1 Tbsp	1½ cups
1 cup + 2 tsp	1¼ cups	1½ cups	1⅔ cups

(continued)

TABLE 1.5 *(Continued)*

Food item	9 oz	10 oz	11 oz	12 oz
Baking powder	1¼ cups + 1 Tbsp	1½ cups	1½ cups + 2 Tbsp	1¾ cups
Baking soda	1¼ cups + 1 Tbsp	1½ cups	1½ cups + 2 Tbsp	1¾ cups
Bread crumbs, dry	2¼ cups	2½ cups	2¾ cups	3 cups
Butter or margarine	1 cup + 2 Tbsp	1¼ cups	1⅓ cups + 1 Tbsp	1½ cups
Celery, chopped	2¼ cups	2½ cups	2¾ cups	3 cups
Cornstarch	2 cups	2 cups + 3 Tbsp	2⅓ cups + 2 Tbsp	2½ cups + 2 Tbsp
Eggs, whole, whites or yolks, fresh or frozen	1 cup + 2 Tbsp	1¼ cups	1⅓ cups + 1 Tbsp	1½ cups
Flour, all-purpose, unsifted	2¼ cups	2½ cups	2¾ cups	3 cups
Flour, cake, un-sifted	2 cups + 2 Tbsp	2¼ cups + 2 Tbsp	2½ cups + 1 Tbsp	2¾ cups
Milk, nonfat dry	3¼ cups + 2 Tbsp	3¾ cups	4 cups + 2 Tbsp	4½ cups
Nutmeats	2¼ cups	2½ cups	2¾ cups	3 cups
Onion, chopped	1 cup + 2 Tbsp	1¼ cups	1⅓ cups + 1 Tbsp	1½ cups
Salt	¾ cup + 2 Tbsp	¾ cup + 3 Tbsp	1 cup + 1 Tbsp	1 cup + 2 Tbsp
Shortening, hy-drogenated fat	1¼ cups	1⅓ cups + 1 Tbsp	1½ cups + 1 Tbsp	1⅔ cups
Sugar, brown, light pack	1⅔ cups	1¾ cups + 2 Tbsp	2 cups + 1 Tbsp	2¼ cups
Sugar, granu-lated	1¼ cups	1¼ cups + 3 Tbsp	1½ cups + 1 Tbsp	1½ cups + 3 Tbsp
Sugar, powdered	1⅔ cups	1¾ cups + 2 Tbsp	2 cups + 1 Tbsp	2¼ cups
Yeast, dry	1¾ cups + 2 Tbsp	2 cups + 1 Tbsp	2¼ cups + 1 Tbsp	2½ cups

13 oz	14 oz	15 oz	16 oz
1¾ cups + 2 Tbsp	2 cups + 1 Tbsp	2 cups + 3 Tbsp	2⅓ cups
1¾ cups + 2 Tbsp	2 cups + 1 Tbsp	2 cups + 3 Tbsp	2⅓ cups
3¼ cups	3½ cups	3¾ cups	4 cups
1½ cups + 2 Tbsp	1¾ cups	1¾ cups + 2 Tbsp	2 cups
3¼ cups	3½ cups	3¾ cups	4 cups
2¾ cups + 2 Tbsp	3 cups + 1 Tbsp	3¼ cups + 1½ tsp	3½ cups
1½ cups + 2 Tbsp	1¾ cups	1¾ cups + 2 Tbsp	2 cups
3¼ cups	3½ cups	3¾ cups	4 cups
3 cups + 1 Tbsp	3¼ cups + 1 Tbsp	3½ cups	3¾ cups
4¾ cups + 2 Tbsp	5¼ cups	5½ cups + 2 Tbsp	6 cups
3¼ cups	3½ cups	3¾ cups	4 cups
1½ cups + 2 Tbsp	1¾ cups	1¾ cups + 2 Tbsp	2 cups
1¼ cups	1¼ cups + 1 Tbsp	1⅓ cups + 1 Tbsp	1½ cups
1¾ cups + 1 Tbsp	2 cups	2 cups + 2 Tbsp	2¼ cups
2⅓ cups + 2 Tbsp	2½ cups + 2 Tbsp	2¾ cups + 1 Tbsp	3 cups
1¾ cups + 1 Tbsp	2 cups	2 cups + 2 Tbsp	2¼ cups
2⅓ cups + 2 Tbsp	2½ cups + 2 Tbsp	2¾ cups + 1 Tbsp	3 cups
2⅔ cups + 1 Tbsp	2¾ cups + 3 Tbsp	3 cups + 2 Tbsp	3⅓ cups

TABLE 1.6 U.S. MEASURES OF WEIGHT AND METRIC EQUIVALENTS[a]

U.S. weight	Metric	U.S. weight	Metric	U.S. weight	Metric
1 oz[b]	28 g[c]	1 lb	454 g	2 lb	908 g
1½ oz	43 g	1 lb 1 oz	482 g	2 lb 4 oz	1.02 kg
2 oz	57 g	1 lb 2 oz	510 g	2 lb 8 oz	1.14 kg
2½ oz	70 g	1 lb 3 oz	539 g	2 lb 12 oz	1.25 kg
3 oz	85 g	1 lb 4 oz	567 g	3 lb	1.36 kg
3½ oz	100 g	1 lb 5 oz	595 g	3 lb 4 oz	1.47 kg
4 oz (¼ lb)	114 g	1 lb 6 oz	624 g	3 lb 8 oz	1.59 kg
5 oz	142 g	1 lb 7 oz	652 g	3 lb 12 oz	1.70 kg
6 oz	170 g	1 lb 8 oz	680 g	4 lb	1.81 kg
7 oz	198 g	1 lb 9 oz	709 g	4 lb 4 oz	1.93 kg
8 oz (½ lb)	227 g	1 lb 10 oz	737 g	4 lb 8 oz	2.04 kg
9 oz	255 g	1 lb 11 oz	765 g	4 lb 12 oz	2.15 kg
10 oz	284 g	1 lb 12 oz	794 g	5 lb	2.27 kg
11 oz	312 g	1 lb 13 oz	822 g	6 lb	2.72 kg
12 oz (¾ lb)	340 g	1 lb 14 oz	851 g	7 lb	3.18 kg
13 oz	369 g	1 lb 15 oz	879 g	8 lb	3.63 kg
14 oz	397 g			9 lb	4.08 kg
15 oz	425 g			10 lb	4.54 kg

[a] Basic figures used to calculate metric weights are: 1 oz = 28.35 g; 1 lb = 453.59 g. Resulting figures were rounded to nearest gram and to 2 decimals for kilograms.
[b] Abbreviations used: oz, ounce; lb, pound; g, gram; kg, kilogram.
[c] To change grams to kilograms, move decimal 3 places to left; e.g., 28 g = 0.028 kg.

TABLE 1.7 U.S. MEASURES OF VOLUME AND METRIC EQUIVALENTS[a]

U.S. measure		Metric	U.S. measure		Metric
1 tsp[b]		5 mL	1 qt	¼ gal	0.95 L
1 Tbsp		15 mL	1½ qt		1.42 L
¼ cup (4 Tbsp)		60 mL	2 qt	½ gal	1.89 L
⅓ cup (5⅓ Tbsp)		80 mL	3 qt	¾ gal	2.84 L
½ cup (8 Tbsp)		120 mL	3½ qt		3.31 L
⅔ cup (10⅔ Tbsp)		160 mL	4 qt	1 gal	3.79 L
¾ cup (12 Tbsp)		180 mL	6 qt	1½ gal	5.68 L
1 cup (16 Tbsp) (¼ qt)		240 mL	8 qt	2 gal	7.57 L
2 cups (1 pt)		480 mL	10 qt	2½ gal	9.46 L
4 cups (1 qt)		950 mL	12 qt	3 gal	11.36 L

[a] Basic figures used to calculate metric volume are: 1 Tbsp = 14.8 mL rounded to 15 mL; 1 cup = 237 mL rounded to 240 mL; 1 qt = 0.95 L (4 × 237 mL divided by 1000).
[b] Abbreviations used: tsp, teaspoon; Tbsp, tablespoon; pt, pint; qt, quart; gal, gallon; mL, milliliter; L, liter.

PREPARATION AND SERVING GUIDES

TABLE 1.8   TEMPERATURES AND TIMES USED IN BAKING

Type of product	Approximate time required for baking[a] (minutes)	Oven temperature	
		°F	°C[b]
Bread			
Biscuits	10–15	425–450	220–230
Corn bread	30–40	350–400	175–205
Cream puffs	40–60	375	190
Muffins	20–25	400–425	205–220
Popovers	60	375	190
Quick loaf bread	60–75	350–375	175–190
Yeast bread	30–40	400	205
Yeast rolls			
Plain	15–25	400–425	205–220
Sweet	20–30	375	190
Cakes, with fat			
Cupcakes	15–25	350–375	175–190
Layer	20–35	350–375	175–190
Loaf	45–60	350	175
Sheet	35–40	350	175
Cakes, without fat			
Angel food and sponge	30–45	350–375	175–190
Cookies			
Bar	20–30	325–350	165–170
Drop	8–15	350–375	175–190
Rolled	8–10	375	190
Egg, meat, milk, cheese dishes			
Cheese soufflé (baked in pan of hot water)	30–60	350	175
Custard, plain, corn, other (baked in pan of hot water)	30–60	350	175
Macaroni and cheese	25–30	350	175
Meat loaf	60–90	325	165
Meat pie	25–30	400	205
Rice pudding (raw rice)	120–180	300	150
Scalloped potatoes	60	350	175

(*continued*)

TABLE 1.8 *(Continued)*

Type of product	Approximate time required for baking[a] (minutes)	Oven temperature	
		°F	°C[b]
Pastry			
1-crust pie (custard type)	30–40	400–425	205–220
Meringue on cooked filling in preheated shell	12–15	350–375	175–190
	or		
	4–4½	425	205
Shell only	10–12	450	230
2-crust pies and uncooked filling in prebaked shell	45–55	400–425	205–220
2-crust pies with cooked filling	30–45	400–425	205–220

[a] For convection ovens follow time and temperature recommendations of manufacturer or decrease time and temperature 10%.

[b] Metric temperatures were obtained by using the following formula: $\frac{5}{9}$ of °F after subtracting 32. Resulting figures were rounded to a functional temperature.

TABLE 1.9 SUGGESTED TIMES AND TEMPERATURES FOR BAKING IN A CONVECTION OVEN

Product	Oven temperature		Baking time[a]	Number of shelves
	°F	°C		
Meats				
Steamship round (50 lb, medium)	225	105	9 hr	1
Rolled beef roast (12–15 lb)	275	135	2½ hr	3
Standing rib choice (20 lb, trimmed, rare)	235	115	2¾ hr	2
Lasagna	250–270	130	90 min	3
Hog dogs, 10 per lb (18 × 26 pan)	325	165	10–15 min	5
Baked stuffed pork chops	375	190	20–30 min	5
Bacon (on racks in 18 × 26 pans)	400	205	5–7 min	5
Poultry				
Chicken breast and thigh	350	175	40 min	5
Chicken back and wing	350	175	35 min	5
Chicken (2½ lb quartered)	350	175	30 min	5
Turkey rolled (18 lb rolls)	310	155	3¾ hr	3
Chicken-turkey pot pies	325	165	30–35 min	5
Fish and seafood				
Fish sticks	335	170	16–18 min	5
Halibut steaks, codfish (frozen 5 oz)	350	175	20 min	5
Baked stuffed shrimp	400	205	6–7 min	5
Baked stuffed lobster (1½ lb)	400	205	10 min	3
Lobster tails (frozen)	425	220	9 min	5
Potatoes				
Idaho potatoes (120 count)	400	205	50 min	5
Oven roasted potatoes (sliced or diced)	325	165	10 min	5
Baked goods				
Frozen berry pies (22 oz)	350	175	34 min	5 (30 pies)
Frozen fruit pies (46 oz)	350	175	45–50 min	5 (20 pies)
Fresh apple pie (20 oz)	350–375	175–190	25–30 min	5 (30 pies)
Pumpkin pies	300	150	30–35 min	5
Fruit cobbler	300	150	30 min	5
Apple turnovers	350	175	15 min	5
Bread (24 1-lb loaves)	340	170	30 min	3
Corn bread (northern)	335	170	25 min	5
Corn bread (southern)	375	190	15–20 min	5
Hamburger rolls	300	150	15 min	5
Yeast rolls	325	165	25 min	5
Croissant	325	165	15–18 min	5
French bread	375	140	18–20 min	4

(*continued*)

TABLE 1.9 *(Continued)*

Product	Oven temperature		Baking time[a]	Number of shelves
	°F	°C		
Sheet cakes (5 lb mixed batter per pan)	300	150	20–25 min	4
Chocolate cake	335	170	20 min	5
Fruit cakes	275	135	70 min	3
Brownies	325	165	20 min	5
Danish	335	170	12 min	5
Cinnamon buns	335	170	20 min	5
Sugar cookies	300	150	15 min	5
Cream puffs	350	175	20–25 min	5
Chocolate chip cookies	350	175	10 min	5
Peanut butter cookies	325	165	10 min	5

Used by permission of the Blodgett Oven Company, Inc.

[a] Abbreviations used: hr, hour; min, minute.

Note: Actual times and temperatures may vary considerably from those shown. They are affected by weight of load, temperature of the product, recipe, type of pan, and calibration of thermostat.

TABLE 1.10 TERMS FOR OVEN TEMPERATURES

Term	Temperature	
	°F	°C[a]
Very slow	250–275	121–135
Slow	300–325	150–165
Moderate	350–375	175–190
Hot	400–425	205–220
Very hot (quick)	450–475	230–245
Extremely hot	500–525	260–275

[a] Metric temperatures were obtained by using the following formula: $\frac{5}{9}$ of °F after subtracting 32. Resulting figures were rounded to a functional temperature.

TABLE 1.11   METRIC TEMPERATURE EQUIVALENTS[a]

°F	°C	°F	°C	°F	°C	°F	°C
32	0	200	95	300	150	400	205
100	38	212	100	310	155	425	220
105	40	220	105	320	160	450	230
110	43	225	107	324	162	475	245
115	46	230	110	325	165	500	260
120	49	234	112	330	166	525	275
125	52	238	114	335	168	550	290
130	55	240	115	338	170	575	300
140	60	244	118	340	171	600	315
150	65	248	120	350	175		
160	70	250	121	360	180		
170	75	260	125	365	182		
175	80	266	130	370	185		
180	82	270	132	375	190		
185	85	275	135	380	195		
190	88	290	143	390	200		
195	90						

[a] Temperatures in this edition of *Food for Fifty* are given in Fahrenheit and Celsius (Centigrade). To convert from °F to °C, the following formula was used: $(°F - 32) \times \frac{5}{9} = °C$. Some temperatures were rounded to numbers that would be functional in ovens and other equipment.

TABLE 1.12 DEEP-FAT FRYING TEMPERATURES

Type of product	Preparation[a]	Temperature[b] °F	°C	Frying time[c] (minutes)
Bananas	Batter	375	190	1–3
Cauliflower, precooked	See p. 647	370	185	3–5
Cheese balls	See p. 319	360	180	2–3
Chicken, disjointed, 1½–2 lb fryers	Light coating or egg and crumb[b]	350	175	10–12
2–2½ lb fryers	Light coating or egg and crumb	350	175	12–15
Chicken, half 1½–2 lb fryers	Light coating or egg and crumb	350	175	12–15
Croquettes (all previously cooked foods)		360–375	180–190	2–5
Cutlets, ½ inch thick	Egg and crumb	325–350	165–175	5–8
Doughnuts	See p. 134	375	190	3–5
Eggplant	See p. 647	370	185	5–7
Fish fillets or sticks	Egg and crumb or batter	360–375	180–190	4–6
French toast	See p. 139	360	180	3–4
Fritters	See p. 140	375	190	2–5
Onion rings	Batter	350	175	3–4
Oysters	Egg and crumb	375	190	2–4
Potatoes, ½ inch	See p. 652			
Complete fry		365	182	6–8
Blanching		360	180	3–5
Browning		375	190	2–3
Frozen, fat blanched		375	190	2–3
Sandwiches	Batter	350–375	175–190	3–4
Scallops	Egg and crumb	360–375	180–190	3–4
Shrimp	Batter or egg and crumb	360–375	180–190	3–5
Zucchini	See p. 647	370	185	4–6

[a] See Table 1.13 for light coating, egg and crumb, and batter.
[b] If food is frozen, use lower temperatures listed and allow additional cooking time. At high altitudes, the lower boiling point of water in foods requires lowering of temperatures for deep-fat frying.
[c] The exact frying time will vary with the equipment used, size and temperature of the food pieces, and the amount of food placed in the fryer at one time. If the fryer is overloaded, foods may become grease-soaked.

Note: Use fat with a high smoking temperature. Filter fat regularly, at least once a day or more often if fryer is in constant use. The breakdown of fat may be caused by using the fat for too long a period, cooking product at too high a temperature, failure to filter the fat regularly, or salting the food over the fryer.

TABLE 1.13   COATINGS FOR DEEP-FAT FRIED FOODS

Ingredient	Light coating	Egg and crumb	Batter
Eggs		3[a]	6
Milk[b]	1 cup	1 cup	2 cups
Flour, all-purpose	1 lb	8 oz (optional)	12 oz
Salt[c]	2 tsp	1 tsp	2 tsp
Bread crumbs, fine		12 oz	
Baking powder			2 tsp
Shortening, melted, or cooking oil			3 Tbsp
Seasonings	As desired		

[a] For soft mixtures, such as egg cutlets, increase eggs to 6.
[b] Water may be substituted for milk except for batter.
[c] Seasoned Salt (p. 624) may be substituted.

Light Coating.   Dip prepared food in milk. Dredge with seasoned flour.
Egg and Crumb.   Dip prepared food in flour (may omit), then in mixture of beaten egg and milk. Drain. Roll in crumbs to cover (see Figure 2.33).
Batter.   Combine flour, salt, and baking powder. Add milk, beaten eggs, and shortening. Dip prepared foods in batter.

TABLE 1.14   DIPPER EQUIVALENTS

Dipper number[a]	Approximate measure	Approximate weight	Suggested use
6	10 Tbsp (⅔ cup)	6 oz	Entree salads
8	8 Tbsp (½ cup)	4–5 oz	Entrees
10	6 Tbsp (⅜ cup)	3–4 oz	Desserts, meat patties
12	5 Tbsp (⅓ cup)	2½–3 oz	Croquettes, vegetables, muffins, desserts, salads
16	4 Tbsp (¼ cup)	2–2¼ oz	Muffins, desserts, croquettes
20	3$\frac{1}{5}$ Tbsp	1¾–2 oz	Muffins, cupcakes, sauces, sandwich fillings
24	2⅔ Tbsp	1½–1¾ oz	Cream puffs
30	2$\frac{1}{5}$ Tbsp	1–1½ oz	Large drop cookies
40	1½ Tbsp	¾ oz	Drop cookies
60	1 Tbsp	½ oz	Small drop cookies, garnishes
100	Scant 2 tsp		Tea cookies

[a] Portions per quart.

Note: These measurements are based on level dippers. If a rounded dipper is used, the measure and weight are closer to those of the next larger dipper.

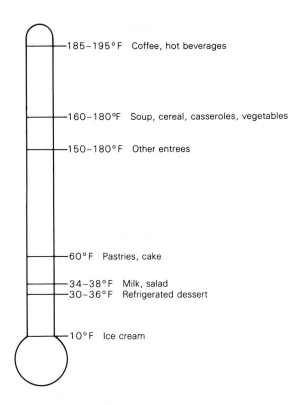

Figure 1.1 *Recommended serving temperatures.*

TABLE 1.15 LADLE EQUIVALENTS

Approximate measure	Approximate weight	Suggested use
⅛ cup	1 oz	Sauces, salad dressings
¼ cup	2 oz	Gravies, some sauces
½ cup	4 oz	Stews, creamed dishes
¾ cup	6 oz	Stews, creamed dishes, soup
1 cup	8 oz	Soup

Note: These measurements are based on level ladles. If a rounded ladle is used, the measure is closer to that of the next larger ladle.

TABLE 1.16 RECOMMENDED MIXER BOWL AND STEAM-JACKETED KETTLE SIZES FOR SELECTED PRODUCTS

	50 portions	*100 portions*	*200 portions*	*500 portions*
Breads, yeast	7 lb/12 qt MB[a]	14 lb/12 qt MB	28 lb/20 qt MB	70 lb/60 qt MB
Quick	10 lb/12qt MB	20 lb/20qt MB	40 lb/60 qt MB	100 lb/80 qt MB
Cakes, angel food	6 lb/12 qt MB	12 lb/30 qt MB	24 lb/60 qt MB	60 lb/2 batch sizes, 60 qt MB
Other	8 lb/12 qt MB	16 lb/20 qt MB	32 lb/30 qt MB	80 lb/80 qt MB
Cookies	5 lb/5 qt MB	10 lb/12 qt MB	20 lb/30 qt MB	50 lb/60 qt MB
Pastry	7 lb/12 qt MB	14 lb/20 qt MB	28 lb/30 qt MB	70 lb/80 qt MB
Pie fillings Fruit	12 lb/10 qt SJK 10 qt SP	24 lb/20 qt SJK 20 qt SP	48 lb/20 gal SJK	70 lb/20 gal SJK
Frozen/ chiffon	12 lb/20 qt MB	24 lb/60 qt MB	48 lb/80 qt MB	120 lb/2 batch sizes, 80 qt MB
Puddings/pie fillings	12 lb/10 qt SJK 10 qt SP	24 lb/20 qt SJK 10 qt SP	48 lb/20 gal SJK	120 lb/20 gal SJK
Scrambled eggs	10 lb/12 qt MB	20 lb/20 qt MB	40 lb/60 qt MB	100 lb/2 batch sizes, 60 qt MB
Cheese soufflé	14 lb/30 qt MB	28 lb/60 qt MB	56 lb/2 batch sizes, 60 qt MB	140 lb/3 batch sizes, 80 qt MB
Meat loaf	12 lb/20 qt MB	24 lb/30 qt MB	48 lb/60 qt MB	120 lb/2 batch sizes, 80 qt MB
Spaghetti sauce	19 lb/20 qt SJK 15 qt SP	38 lb/20 gal SJK 20 qt SP	76 lb/20 gal SJK	190 lb/40 gal SJK
Pasta (includes water)	45 lb/20 gal SJK 25 qt SP	90 lb/20 gal SJK	180 lb/40 gal SJK	450 lb/80 gal SJK
Salad dressing	8 lb/12 qt MB	16 lb/20 qt MB	32 lb/60 qt MB	80 lb/80 qt MB
Soups/stews	25 lb/20 qt SJK 15 qt SP	50 lb/20 gal SJK 25 qt SP	100 lb/20 gal SJK	250 lb/40 gal SJK
Mashed potatoes	15 lb/20 qt MB	30 lb/30 qt MB	60 lb/80 qt MB	150 lb/3 batch sizes, 80 qt MB
Whipped cream or topping	1½ qt/5 qt MB	3 qt/12 qt MB	6 qt/30 qt MB	15 qt/60 qt MB

[a] Abbreviations used: MB, mixer bowl; SJK, steam-jacketed kettle; SP, stock pot.

TABLE 1.17 PAN CAPACITIES

Pan size	Maximum capacity[a]	Portion	Suggested use
18 × 26 × 2-inch (cake pan)	8–10 lb	Cut 6 × 10 (3 × 2½ inches)	Cakes
18 × 26 × 1-inch (sheet pan)	4–6 lb	Cut 6 × 10 (3 × 2½ inches) Panned 8 × 12 Dropped 3 × 5	Sheet cakes, bar cookies Dinner rolls Cookies
13 × 18 × 1-inch (half sheet pan)	2–3 lb	Cut 5 × 6 (2½ × 3 inches)	Sheet cakes, bar cookies
12 × 18 × 2-inch	4–5 lb	Cut 5 × 6 (2½ × 3 inches)	Cakes
12 × 20 × 4-inch (full counter pan)	24–30 lb	Cut 48 portions cut 4 × 8 (3 × 2½ inches)	Meat loaf Lasagne Rice pilaf
12 × 20 × 2-inch (full counter pan)	12–15 lb	Cut 4 × 6 (3 × 3⅓ inches) Cut 4 × 8 (3 × 2½ inches)	Casseroles Baked desserts
12 × 10 × 4-inch (half counter pan)	12–15 lb		Casseroles Gravy
12 × 10 × 2-inch (half counter pan)	6–7 lb	Cut 4 × 3 (3 × 3 inches) Cut 4 × 4 (3 × 2½ inches)	Casseroles Baked desserts
9-inch round (cake)	1½ lb	Cut 1/16	Layer cakes, corn bread
8-inch round (cake)	1¼ lb	Cut 1/12–1/14	Layer cakes
9-inch round (pie)	1½ lb	Cut ⅛	Pies
8-inch round (pie)	1 lb	Cut ⅙	Pies
5 × 16 × 4 (loaf)	3–5 lb	Cut 1/24–1/32 Cut 1/24	Quick breads, yeast breads Cakes
5 × 8 × 4 (loaf)	1½–2½ lb	Cut 1/12–1/16 Cut 1/12	Quick breads, yeast breads Cakes

TABLE 1.17 *(Continued)*

Pan size	Maximum capacity[a]	Portion	Suggested use
5 × 9 × 2¾ (loaf)	1½–2 lb	Cut $\frac{1}{16}$	Quick breads, yeast breads, cakes
10-inch tube	2–2½ lb	Cut $\frac{1}{14}$	Chiffon cakes

[a] The type of product being scaled into the pans will dictate the weight per pan.

Notes:
1. See recipes for specific scaling instructions.
2. A formula for determining scaling weight of cakes is given on p. 176.

TABLE 1.18 COMMON CAN SIZES

Can size (industry term)	Approximate net weight or fluid measure	Approximate cups per can	Number of portions	Principal products
No. 10	6 lb–7 lb 5 oz	12–13	25	Institutional size for fruits, vegetables
No. 5 Squat	4 lb–4¼ lb	8	16–20	Institutional size for canned fish, sweet potatoes
No. 3 Cyl	46 fl oz or 51 oz	5¼	10–12	Fruit and vegetable juices, condensed soups
No. 2½	26–30 oz	3½	5–7	Fruits, some vegetables
No. 2	18 fl oz or 20 oz	2½	5	Juices, fruits, ready-to-serve soups
No. 303	1 lb	2	4	Fruits, vegetables, ready-to-serve soups
No. 300	14–16 oz	1¾	3–4	Some fruits and meat products
No. 1 (Picnic)	10½–12 oz	1¼	2–3	Condensed soups
8 oz	8 oz	1	2	Ready-to-serve soups, fruits, vegetables

Note: When substituting one can for another size, one No. 10 can is approximately equivalent to:
   7 No. 303 (1 lb) cans
   5 No. 2 (1 lb 4 oz) cans
   4 No. 2½ (1 lb 13 oz) cans
   2 No. 3 (46 to 50 oz) cans

Attachment		Uses
Flat beater	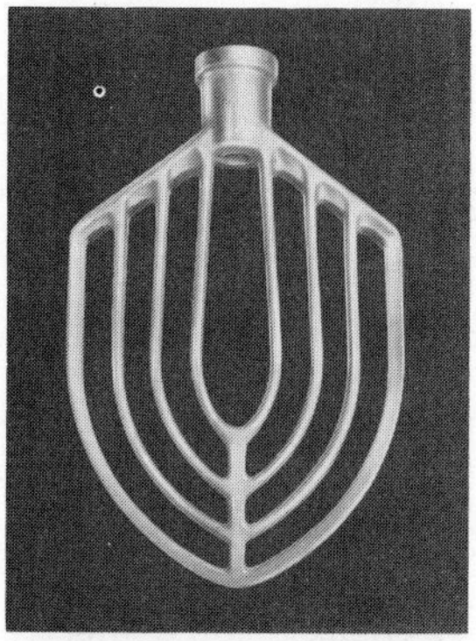	Creaming, mixing cake and cookie batters, mashing potatoes, general mixing
Wing whip (pictured) or wire whip	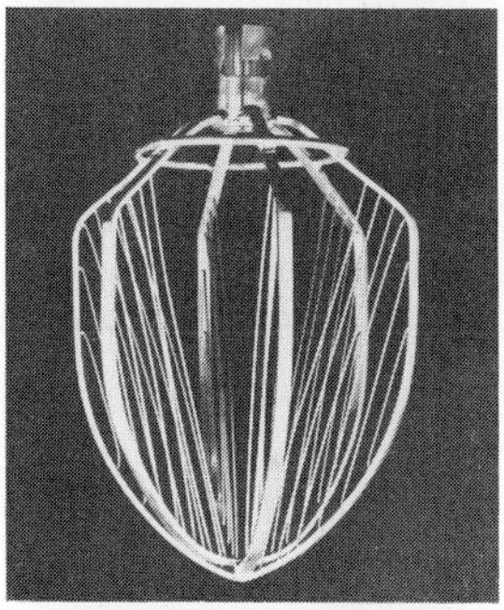	Whipping cream, eggs, sponges, meringues
Dough arm	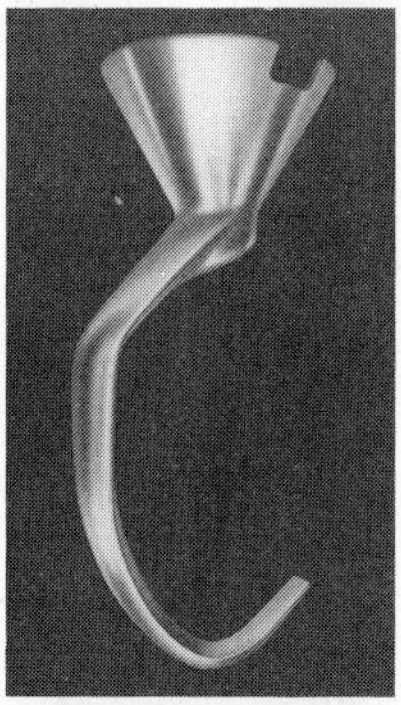	Kneading yeast dough
Pastry knife	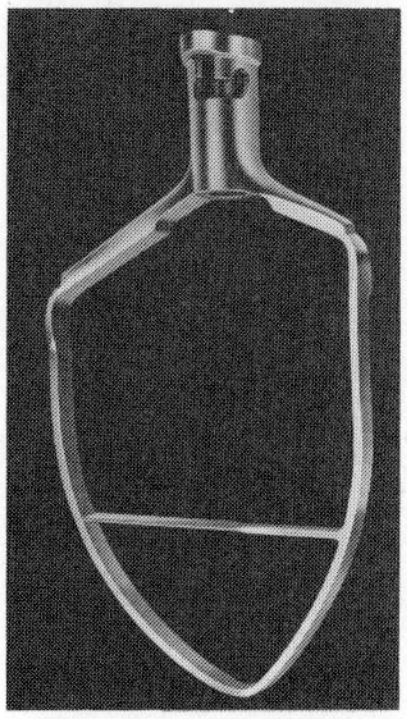	Cutting shortening into flour

Figure 1.2 *Commonly used mixer attachments. Photos courtesy of Hobart Corporation, Troy, Ohio.*

TABLE 1.19 INGREDIENT SUBSTITUTIONS (APPROXIMATE)

Recipe item	*Amount*	*Substitute ingredient*
Baking powder	1 tsp	¼ tsp baking soda + ½ tsp cream of tartar ¼ tsp baking soda + ½ cup buttermilk or sour milk (to replace ½ cup of the liquid)
Butter	1 lb	14 oz hydrogenated shortening + 1 tsp salt 14 oz lard + 1 tsp salt 14 oz (1⅜ cups) oil + 1 tsp salt
Buttermilk	1 cup	1 Tbsp lemon juice or vinegar + enough whole milk to make 1 cup (let stand 5 minutes before using) or 1 cup unflavored yogurt
Celery, fresh	8 oz	4 oz celery flakes, dry
Chocolate, unsweetened	1 oz (1 square)	3 Tbsp cocoa + 1 Tbsp (½ oz) fat
Cocoa	3 Tbsp	1 oz chocolate. Reduce fat in recipe by 1 Tbsp
Cornstarch (thickening)	1 Tbsp 1 oz 1 Tbsp 1 oz	2 Tbsp flour, all-purpose 2 oz flour, all-purpose 2 tsp waxy maize starch ¾ oz waxy maize starch
Cream		
Half and half	1 cup	¾ cup milk + 2–3 Tbsp fat
Whipping	1 cup	¾ cup milk + ⅓ cup fat
Flour, all-purpose	1 cup	1½ cups bread flour 1 cup + 2 Tbsp cake flour 1 cup rye or whole wheat flour 1 cup less 2 Tbsp cornmeal 1 cup rolled oats 1½ cups bread crumbs
Flour, all-purpose (thickening)	1 oz	1⅓ oz quick-cooking tapioca ½ cup cornmeal ⅔ oz cornstarch ½ oz waxy maize starch, arrowroot ¾ oz bread crumbs

TABLE 1.19 *(Continued)*

Recipe item	Amount	Substitute ingredient
Flour, cake	1 cup	1 cup less 2 Tbsp all-purpose flour
Garlic	1 medium clove	⅛ tsp garlic powder ½ tsp garlic, minced, dry ½ tsp garlic salt
Green peppers, chopped	8 oz EP	1 oz green pepper flakes, dry
Honey	1 cup	1¼ cup granulated sugar + ¼ cup liquid
Milk, fluid, whole	1 cup	1 oz (⅓ cup) nonfat dry milk + water to make 1 cup + 1 Tbsp fat (optional) ½ cup evaporated milk + ½ cup water
	1 qt	4 oz nonfat dry milk + water to make 1 qt + 1¼ oz fat (optional)
Milk, sour[a]	1 cup	1 Tbsp vinegar or lemon juice + sweet milk to make 1 cup
Onions, fresh, chopped	8 oz EP	1 oz dehydrated onions, chopped or minced[b]
Parsley, fresh, chopped	8 oz EP	3 oz parsley flakes, dry
Stock, chicken or beef	1 gal	3 oz concentrated soup base + 1 gal water (commercial products may vary in strength; follow manufacturer's directions)
Sugar, granulated	1 cup	1⅓ cups brown sugar 1½ cups powdered sugar 1¼–1½ cups corn syrup less ¼–½ cup liquid in recipe 1 cup honey less ¼–⅓ cup liquid in recipe 1⅓ cups molasses less ⅓ cup liquid in recipe
Tapioca, quick-cooking	1 Tbsp	1 Tbsp all-purpose flour (for thickening)
Yeast, active dry	¼ oz (1 pkg)	1 cake compressed
	1 oz	2 oz compressed

TABLE 1.19 *(Continued)*

Recipe item	Amount	Substitute ingredient
Yeast, instant		See manufacturer's directions for conversion from active dry or compressed

[a] To substitute buttermilk or sour milk for sweet milk, add ½ tsp baking soda and decrease baking powder by 2 tsp per cup of milk.

[b] Rehydrate onions unless they are to be used in a recipe in which there is a large volume of liquid. To rehydrate, cover onions with water, using the ratio of 1 oz dehydrated onions (½ cup) to ¾ cup water. Let stand 20–30 minutes.

TABLE 1.20   PROPORTIONS OF INGREDIENTS

Function	Ingredient	Relative proportion
Leavening agents	Baking powder Baking soda Yeast	1½–2 Tbsp to 1 lb flour 2 tsp to 1 qt sour milk or molasses ½–1 envelope dry (⅛–¼ oz) to 1 lb flour (varies with ingredients and time allowed)
Seasonings	Salt	1–2 tsp to 1 lb flour 1¼ tsp to 1 lb meat 2 tsp to 1 qt water (for cereal) 2½ tsp to 1 pt liquid (for rolls)
Thickening agents	Eggs	4–6 whole eggs to 1 qt milk 8–12 egg yolks to 1 qt milk 8–12 egg whites to 1 qt milk
	Flour	½ oz to 1 qt liquid—very thin sauce (cream soups, starchy vegetables) 1 oz to 1 qt liquid—thin sauce (cream soups, nonstarchy vegetables) 2 oz to 1 qt liquid—medium sauce (creamed foods, gravy) 3–4 oz to 1 qt liquid—thick sauce (soufflés) 4–5 oz to 1 qt liquid—very thick sauce (croquettes) 1 lb to 1 qt liquid—pour batter (popovers) 2 lb to 1 qt liquid—drop batter (cake muffins) 3 lb to 1 qt liquid—soft dough (biscuits, rolls) 4 lb to 1 qt liquid—stiff dough (pastry, cookies, noodles)
	Gelatin, granulated, unflavored	2 Tbsp to 1 qt liquid—plain gelatins (gelatin and fruit juices) 2 Tbsp to 1 qt liquid—whips (gelatin and fruit juices whipped) 3 Tbsp to 1 qt liquid—fruit gelatins (gelatin, fruit juices, and chopped fruit) 3 Tbsp to 1 qt liquid—vegetable gelatins (gelatin, liquid, and chopped vegetables) 3 Tbsp to 1 qt liquid—sponges (gelatin, fruit juice, and beaten egg whites) 4 Tbsp to 1 qt liquid—Bavarian cream (gelatin, fruit juice, fruit pulp, and whipped cream)

RECIPE ADJUSTMENT

Adjusting recipes to meet the needs of individual foodservices is often necessary. Recipes may need to be standardized for either weights or measures, or policies may require yields different from the recipes in this book. In either case, recipe adjustment is simplified by using the following procedures for converting from U.S. measurement to metric, converting from weight to measure, and increasing and decreasing recipe yields.

Converting from U.S. measurement to metric

Two approaches are possible for converting recipes from U.S. measurement to metric: soft conversion and hard conversion. In soft conversion, weights and measures are converted to their exact metric equivalents. An ounce would become 28.3 grams; a quart would be 0.95 liter. Hard conversion changes weights and measures to round metric sizes. For example, a one-ounce portion would convert to either 25 or 30 grams, but not to 28.3 grams; one quart would be changed to one liter. Tables 1.6, 1.7, and 1.11 show metric conversions.

The soft conversion method produces numbers that may become awkward to work with. Equipment may not be available to measure ingredients to the degree of accuracy that soft conversion requires. Hard conversion specifies numbers that are easier to use than the soft conversion procedure. This method may be satisfactory for recipes that are not sensitive to formula adjustments, such as soups and beverages, but may be unsatisfactory for products such as cakes, breads, and other baked products. Testing recipes to evaluate acceptability is recommended when using the hard conversion method.

Converting from weight to measure

Quantities of most dry ingredients in recipes in this book are given by weight in ounces and pounds. However, if accurate scales are not available or if scales do not have graduations for weighing small amounts, the weights of ingredients may need to be converted to measures. The following tables will be helpful:

Table 1.3 Food Weights and Approximate Equivalents in Measure (p. 20)

Table 1.4 Basic Equivalents in Measures and Weights (p. 29)

Table 1.5 Weight (1–16 oz) and Measure Equivalents for Commonly Used Foods (p. 30)

Table 1.21 A Guide for Rounding Off Weights and Measures (p. 57)

Table 1.22 Ounces and Decimal Equivalents of a Pound (p. 68)

The following example illustrates the procedure for converting ingredients in Baking Powder Biscuits (p. 116) from weight to measure:

- Change 5 pounds flour to measure by multiplying by 4 cups. Turn to Table 1.3 (p. 20).
- The resulting 20 cups would be equivalent to 5 quarts. Table 1.4 (p. 29). For ingredients other than flour, a gallon measure should be used.
- By referring to Table 1.5 (p. 30) the 5 ounces of baking powder and 1 pound 4 ounces of shortening may be converted quickly by finding the amount in the appropriate column or adding the columns together. The same information is included in the longer table (Table 1.3, p. 20), but for conversion of small amounts of commonly used foods, Table 1.5 is useful.

Increasing and decreasing recipe yields

Changing yields for recipes in this book may be required to meet the needs of individual situations. Recipes may need to be adjusted to produce batch sizes compatible with preparation equipment, such as mixers, ovens, and steam-jacketed kettles, or consistent with pan sizes available. See Tables 1.16 and 1.17 for recommended equipment sizes and pan capacities. Recipes may also need adjustment as portion sizes are increased or decreased or as purchase units for ingredients change.

Three methods commonly used to adjust recipe yields are the *factor method,* the *percentage method,* and *direct-reading measurement tables.*

FACTOR METHOD

In the factor method a conversion factor is determined and multiplied by each ingredient in the recipe. This process is explained in the following steps:

Step 1. Divide the desired yield by the known yield of the recipe being adjusted to obtain the conversion *factor.* For example, to increase a 50-portion recipe to 125 portions, divide 125 by 50 for a factor of 2.5.

Step 2. Wherever possible, convert ingredients to weight. If amounts of some ingredients are too small to be weighed, leave them in measure.

Step 3. Multiply the amount of each ingredient in the original recipe by the factor. To work with decimal parts of a pound instead of ounces for this multiplication, Table 1.22 will be helpful.

Step 4. Multiply the original total weight of ingredients by the factor. Multiply the pounds and ounces separately.

Step 5. Add together the new weights of all ingredients for the adjusted recipe. If the answers in Steps 4 and 5 are not the same, an error exists and the calculations should be checked. (A slight difference may exist because of rounding the figures.)

Step 6. Change weights of any ingredients that can be more easily measured than weighed to measure.

Step 7. Check all amounts and use Table 1.21 for rounding off unnecessary fractions to simplify weights or measures as far as accuracy permits.

The following example illustrates the procedure for adjusting Baking Powder Biscuits from 100 biscuits to 500, using the factor method of adjustment:

Step 1. Derive the factor:

$$\frac{500 \text{ (new)}}{100 \text{ (original)}} = 5 \text{ (factor)}$$

Ingredients	*Original recipe*	*Step 2: Convert to weight*	*Step 3: Multiply by factor*	*Steps 6 and 7: Change to measure and simplify*
Flour, all-purpose	5 lb	5 lb	25 lb	25 lb
Baking powder	5 oz	5 oz	25 oz	1 lb 9 oz
Salt	2 Tbsp	1⅓ oz	6½ oz	6½ oz
Shortening, hydrogenated	1 lb 4 oz	1 lb 4 oz	6 lb 4 oz	6 lb 4 oz
Milk	1¾ qt	3 lb 8 oz	17 lb 8 oz	2 gal + ¾ qt
Steps 4 and 5: Total weight		10 lb 2 oz	50 lb 11 oz	

PERCENTAGE METHOD

The percentage method of recipe adjustment often is desirable, especially for large-volume production where batch sizes may vary greatly. Once the ingredient percentage has been established, it remains constant for all future adjustments. Recipe increases and decreases are made by multiplying the percentage of each ingredient by the total weight desired. Checking ingredients for proper recipe balance is possible, because the percentage of each ingredient is available. Some computer recipe systems use the percentage method of recipe adjustment. This process is explained in the following steps:

Step 1. Convert all ingredients from measure or pounds and ounces to pounds and tenths of a pound (see Tables 1.3 and 1.22). Make desired equivalent ingredient substitutions such as frozen whole eggs for fresh eggs, nonfat dry milk and water for liquid milk. Use edible portion (EP) weights when a difference exists between EP and as purchased (AP) weights (see Table 1.1). Individual meat items and other meats in entree recipes that do not require the meat to be cooked prior to combining with other ingredients are calculated on AP weight. Examples are pork chops, meat loaf, and Salisbury steak.

Step 2. Total the weight of ingredients in the recipe, using EP weight where applicable.

Step 3. Calculate the percentage of each ingredient in relation to the total weight, using the following formula:

$$\frac{\text{individual ingredient weight}}{\text{total weight}} = \text{percentage of each ingredient}$$

The sum of the percentages must equal 100.

Step 4. Check the ratio of ingredients. Standards have been established for ingredient proportions of many items. The ingredients should be in proper balance before going further.

Step 5. Establish the weight needed to give the desired number of servings. The weight will be determined by portion size multiplied by the desired number of servings to be prepared. This weight may need to be adjusted because of pan sizes or equipment capacity (see Tables 1.16 and 1.17).

Step 6. Handling loss must be added to the weight needed, and it may vary from 1 to 10 percent, depending on the product. Similar items produce predictable losses, and with some experimentation these losses can be assigned accurately. The formula for incorporating handling loss is as follows:

$$\text{total weight needed} = \frac{\text{desired yield}}{100 \text{ percent} - \text{assigned handling loss percent}}$$

For example, cake has a handling loss of approximately 2 percent, and 72 lb of batter is needed to make nine 18 × 26 × 2-inch pans. To determine the total amount of batter to be made, divide 72 lb by 98 percent (100 percent − 2 percent handling loss). Using this formula, a recipe calculated for 73.47 lb of batter is needed.

Step 7. Multiply each ingredient percentage by the total weight to give the exact amount of each ingredient needed. The total weight of ingredients should equal the weight needed as calculated in Step 6. Once the percentages of a recipe have been established, any number of servings can be calculated, and the ratio of ingredients to the total will remain the same.

Step 8. Unless scales are calibrated to read in pounds and tenths of a pound, convert to pounds and ounces (Table 1.22) or to measure (Table 1.3). Use Table 1.21 for rounding off unnecessary fractions.

The following example illustrates the procedure for adjusting Baking Powder Biscuits (p. 116) from 100 biscuits to 500, using the percentage method of adjustment:

Ingredients	Original recipe	Step 1: Convert to decimal weights	Step 3: Calculate percentage	Step 7: Calculate weights	Step 8: Convert to pounds and ounces
Flour, all-purpose	5 lb	5.0 lb	49.276	25.52 lb	25 lb 8 oz
Baking powder	5 oz	0.313 lb	3.085	1.60 lb	1 lb 10 oz
Salt	2 Tbsp	0.0839 lb	0.827	0.43 lb	6¾ oz

(continued)

Ingredients	Original recipe	Step 1: Convert to decimal weights	Step 3: Calculate percentage	Step 7: Calculate weights	Step 8: Convert to pounds and ounces
Shortening, hydrogenated	1 lb 4 oz	1.25 lb	12.319	6.38 lb	6 lb 6 oz
Milk	1¾ qt	3.5 lb	34.493	17.86 lb	2¼ gal
Step 2: Total weight		10.1469 lb	100.00	51.79 lb	

Step 4.   Check ratio of ingredients to see if they are within acceptable guidelines.

Step 5.   Establish needed weight:

$$\frac{10.1469 \text{ (total weight of 100 biscuits)}}{100} = 0.1015 \text{ lb (weight per biscuit)}$$

500 (desired yield) × 0.1015 lb = 50.75 lb of dough needed before handling loss

Step 6.   Calculate handling loss. Estimated handling loss 2 percent:

$$\frac{50.75 \text{ lb (desired yield)}}{\substack{98 \text{ percent} \\ (100 \text{ percent} - 2 \text{ percent})}} = 51.79 \text{ lb total dough needed}$$

Enlarging home-size recipes

Before enlarging a small recipe, be sure the same quality can be achieved in large quantity and that the appropriate equipment and pans are available. Standardized quantity production procedures may need to replace small-scale techniques.

Enlarging a small-quantity recipe in steps is more likely to be successful than increasing size too quickly. Following are suggestions for expanding home-size recipes:

Step 1.   Prepare the product in the amount of the original recipe, following the quantities and procedures exactly and noting any procedures that are unclear or any problems with the preparation.

Step 2.   Evaluate the product and decide if it is acceptable for the foodservice. If adjustments are necessary, revise the recipe and make the product again. Prepare the small-size amount until the product is satisfactory.

Step 3.   Double the recipe or expand to an appropriate amount for the pan size that will be used, and prepare the product, making notations on the recipe of any changes you make. For example, additional cooking time may be needed for the larger amount. Use Table 1.25 for increasing recipe size. Evaluate the product and record the yield, portion size, and acceptability.

Step 4. Double the recipe again, or if the product is to be baked, calculate the quantities needed to prepare one baking pan of the size that will be used in the foodservice. Use Table 1.25 for increasing recipe size. If ingredients are to be weighed, home-size measures should be converted to pounds and ounces or to pounds and tenths of a pound before proceeding further. Prepare and evaluate the product as before.

Step 5. If the product is satisfactory, continue to enlarge by increments of 25 portions or by pans until approximately 100 portions are prepared. Recipes with larger yields should be evaluated for acceptability and adjustment made each time the yield is increased significantly.

TABLE 1.21 GUIDE FOR ROUNDING OFF WEIGHTS AND MEASURES

If the total amount of an ingredient is	*Round it to*
Weights	
Less than 2 oz	Measure unless weight is ¼-, ½-, or ¾-oz amounts
2–10 oz	Closest ¼ oz or convert to measure
More than 10 oz but less than 2 lb 8 oz	Closest ½ oz
2 lb 8 oz–5 lb	Closest full ounce
More than 5 lb	Closest ¼ lb
Measures	
Less than 1 Tbsp	Closest ⅛ tsp
More than 1 Tbsp but less than 3 Tbsp	Closest ¼ tsp
3 Tbsp–½ cup	Closest ½ tsp or convert to weight
More than ½ cup but less than ¾ cup	Closest full tsp or convert to weight
More than ¾ cup but less than 2 cups	Closest full Tbsp or convert to weight
2 cups–2 qt	Nearest ¼ cup
More than 2 qt but less than 4 qt	Nearest ½ cup
1–2 gal	Nearest full cup or ¼ qt
More than 2 gal but less than 10 gal[a]	Nearest full quart
More than 10 gal but less than 20 gal[a]	Closest ½ gal
Over 20 gal[a]	Closest full gallon

[a] For baked goods or products where accurate ratios are critical, always round to the nearest full cup or ¼ qt.

Note: This table is intended to aid in rounding fractions and complex measurements into amounts that are as simple as possible to weigh or measure while maintaining the accuracy needed for quality control.

TABLE 1.22   OUNCES AND DECIMAL EQUIVALENTS OF A POUND

Ounces	Decimal part of a pound	Ounces	Decimal part of a pound
¼	0.016	8¼	0.516
½	0.031	8½	0.531
¾	0.047	8¾	0.547
1	0.063	9	0.563
1¼	0.078	9¼	0.578
1½	0.094	9½	0.594
1¾	0.109	9¾	0.609
2	0.125	10	0.625
2¼	0.141	10¼	0.641
2½	0.156	10½	0.656
2¾	0.172	10¾	0.672
3	0.188	11	0.688
3¼	0.203	11¼	0.703
3½	0.219	11½	0.719
3¾	0.234	11¾	0.734
4	0.250	12	0.750
4¼	0.266	12¼	0.766
4½	0.281	12½	0.781
4¾	0.297	12¾	0.797
5	0.313	13	0.813
5¼	0.328	13¼	0.828
5½	0.344	13½	0.844
5¾	0.359	13¾	0.859
6	0.375	14	0.875
6¼	0.391	14¼	0.891
6½	0.406	14½	0.906
6¾	0.422	14¾	0.922
7	0.438	15	0.938
7¼	0.453	15¼	0.953
7½	0.469	15½	0.969
7¾	0.484	15¾	0.984
8	0.500	16	1.000

Note: This table is useful when increasing or decreasing recipes. The multiplication or division of pounds and ounces is simplified if the ounces are converted to decimal parts of a pound. For example, when multiplying 1 lb 9 oz by 3, first change the 9 oz to 0.563 lb, by using the table. Thus, the 1 lb 9 oz becomes 1.563 lb, which multiplied by 3 is 4.683 lb or 4 lb 11 oz.

DIRECT-READING MEASUREMENT TABLES

Recipe adjustment may be made by using tables that have been developed for different numbers of portions. Using these charts requires a minimum of calculation. Table 1.24 can be used when the desired yields are divisible by 25 and the ingredients are given in *weights*. Table 1.23 is used when recipe ingredients are given in *volume measurements* and the yields can be divided by 25. Table 1.25 has yields that can be divided by 8 and is useful in enlarging home-size recipes. Following are instructions for using direct-reading measurement tables.

Directions for using Tables 1.23 and 1.24. Tables 1.23 and 1.24, which follow, are used in the same manner but for different types of ingredients. Table 1.24 is used for converting weighed ingredients using recipe yields that are divisible by 25. Table 1.23 is used for converting volume measures of ingredients using recipe yields that are divisible by 25.

1. Locate the column that corresponds to the original yield of the recipe to be adjusted. For example, assume the original recipe yields 100 portions. Locate the "100" column across the top of the chart on Table 1.24.
2. Go down this column to the amount of the ingredient required (or to the closest number to that figure) in the recipe to be adjusted. If the recipe for 100 portions requires 21 lb of ground beef, for example, go down the column headed 100 to the figure "21."
3. Then go across the page, in line with that amount, to the column that is headed to correspond with the yield desired. For example, if only 75 portions are desired, begin with the 21 lb figure in the "100" column and slide across to the column headed "75" and read that figure. It indicates that 15 lb 12 oz of ground beef would be required to make 75 portions with this recipe.
4. Record this figure as the amount of the ingredient required for the new yield of the recipe. Repeat steps 1, 2, and 3 for each ingredient in the original recipe to obtain the adjusted ingredient weight needed for the new yield. Follow the same procedure using Table 1.23 in adjusting ingredient amounts indicated in volume measures. Yields can be either increased or decreased in this manner.
5. If two columns need to be combined to obtain the desired yield, follow steps 1 through 4 and add together the amounts given in the two columns to obtain the amount required for the adjusted yield. For example, to find the amount of ground beef for 225 portions of our hypothetical recipe, locate the figures in columns headed "200" and "25" and add them together. In this example it would be 42 lb + 5 lb 4 oz, so the required total for ground beef would be 47 lb 4 oz.
6. The figures given in these tables are given in exact weights including fractional ounces. After making yield adjustments for every ingredient, refer to Table 1.21 for rounding off fractional amounts that are not of sufficient proportion to change product quality.

Abbreviations used in the charts

oz	ounce	qt	quart
lb	pound	gal	gallon
tsp	teaspoon	(r)	slightly rounded
Tbsp	tablespoon	(s)	scant

Equivalents helpful in using the charts

3 tsp = 1 Tbsp	12 Tbsp = ¾ cup
4 Tbsp = ¼ cup	16 Tbsp = 1 cup
5 Tbsp + 1 tsp = ⅓ cup	4 cups = 1 qt
8 Tbsp = ½ cup	4 qt = 1 gal
10 Tbsp + 2 tsp = ⅔ cup	

* Amounts cannot be weighed accurately without introducing errors.

TABLE 1.23 DIRECT-READING TABLE FOR ADJUSTING RECIPES WITH INGREDIENT AMOUNTS GIVEN IN VOLUME MEASUREMENT AND DIVISIBLE BY 25[a]

25	*50*	*75*	*100*
¼ tsp	½ tsp	¾ tsp	1 tsp
¼ tsp (r)	½ tsp (r)	1 tsp (s)	1¼ tsp
¼ tsp + ⅛ tsp	¾ tsp	1 tsp + ⅛ tsp	1½ tsp
½ tsp (s)	¾ tsp (r)	1¼ tsp (r)	1¾ tsp
½ tsp	1 tsp	1½ tsp	2 tsp
½ tsp (r)	1 tsp + ⅛ tsp	1¾ tsp (s)	2¼ tsp
½ tsp + ⅛ tsp	1¼ tsp	2 tsp (s)	2½ tsp
¾ tsp (s)	1¼ tsp + ⅛ tsp	2 tsp (r)	2¾ tsp
¾ tsp	1½ tsp	2¼ tsp	1 Tbsp
1 tsp + ⅛ tsp	2¼ tsp	1 Tbsp + ¼ tsp + ⅛ tsp	1½ Tbsp
1½ tsp	1 Tbsp	1½ Tbsp	2 Tbsp
1¾ tsp + ⅛ tsp	1 Tbsp + ¾ tsp	1 Tbsp + 2½ tsp + ⅛ tsp	2½ Tbsp
2¼ tsp	1½ Tbsp	2 Tbsp + ¾ tsp	3 Tbsp
2¼ tsp + ⅛ tsp	1 Tbsp + 2¼ tsp	2 Tbsp + 1½ tsp + ⅛ tsp	3½ Tbsp
1 Tbsp	2 Tbsp	3 Tbsp	¼ cup
1 Tbsp + 1 tsp	2 Tbsp + 2 tsp	¼ cup	⅓ cup
2 Tbsp	¼ cup	¼ cup + 2 Tbsp	½ cup
2 Tbsp + 2 tsp	⅓ cup	½ cup	⅔ cup
3 Tbsp	6 Tbsp	½ cup + 1 Tbsp	¾ cup
¼ cup	½ cup	¾ cup	1 cup
¼ cup + 1 Tbsp	½ cup + 2 Tbsp	¾ cup + 3 Tbsp	1¼ cups
⅓ cup	⅔ cup	1 cup	1⅓ cups
⅓ cup + 2 tsp	¾ cup	1 cup + 2 Tbsp	1½ cups

200	300	400	500
2 tsp	1 Tbsp	1 Tbsp + 1 tsp	1 Tbsp + 2 tsp
2½ tsp	1 Tbsp + ¾ tsp	1 Tbsp + 2 tsp	2 Tbsp + ¼ tsp
1 Tbsp	1½ Tbsp	2 Tbsp	2½ Tbsp
1 Tbsp + ½ tsp	1 Tbsp + 2¼ tsp	2 Tbsp + 1 tsp	2 Tbsp + 2¾ tsp
1 Tbsp + 1 tsp	2 Tbsp	2 Tbsp + 2 tsp	3 Tbsp + 1 tsp
1½ Tbsp	2 Tbsp + ¾ tsp	3 Tbsp	3 Tbsp + 2¼ tsp
1 Tbsp + 2 tsp	2½ Tbsp	3 Tbsp + 1 tsp	4 Tbsp + ½ tsp
1 Tbsp + 2½ tsp	2 Tbsp + 2¼ tsp	3 Tbsp + 2 tsp	4 Tbsp + 1¾ tsp
2 Tbsp	3 Tbsp	¼ cup	5 Tbsp
3 Tbsp	¼ cup + 1½ tsp	⅓ cup + 2 tsp	¼ cup + 3½ Tbsp
¼ cup	¼ cup + 2 Tbsp	½ cup	½ cup + 2 Tbsp
¼ cup + 1 Tbsp	¼ cup + 3½ Tbsp	½ cup + 2 Tbsp	¾ cup + ½ Tbsp
⅓ cup + 2 tsp	½ cup + 1 Tbsp	¾ cup	¾ cup + 3 Tbsp
¼ cup + 3 Tbsp	½ cup + 2½ Tbsp	¾ cup + 2 Tbsp	1 cup + 1½ Tbsp
½ cup	¾ cup	1 cup	1¼ cups
⅔ cup	1 cup	1⅓ cups	1⅔ cups
1 cup	1½ cups	2 cups	2½ cups
1⅓ cups	2 cups	2⅔ cups	3⅓ cups
1½ cups	2¼ cups	3 cups	3¾ cups
2 cups	3 cups	1 qt	1¼ qt
2½ cups	3¾ cups	1¼ qt	1½ qt + ¼ cup
2⅔ cups	1 qt	1¼ qt + ⅓ cup	1½ qt + ⅔ cup
3 cups	1 qt + ½ cup	1½ qt	1¾ qt + ½ cup

(continued)

TABLE 1.23   *(Continued)*

25	50	75	100
6 Tbsp + 2 tsp	¾ cup + 4 tsp	1¼ cups	1⅔ cups
¼ cup + 3 Tbsp	¾ cup + 2 Tbsp	1¼ cups + 1 Tbsp	1¾ cups
½ cup	1 cup	1½ cups	2 cups
½ cup + 1 Tbsp	1 cup + 2 Tbsp	1½ cups + 3 Tbsp	2¼ cups
½ cup + 4 tsp	1 cup + 2 Tbsp + 2 tsp	1¾ cups	2⅓ cups
½ cup + 2 Tbsp	1¼ cups	1¾ cups + 2 Tbsp	2½ cups
⅔ cup	1⅓ cups	2 cups	2⅔ cups
½ cup + 3 Tbsp	1¼ cups + 2 Tbsp	2 cups + 1 Tbsp	2¾ cups
¾ cup	1½ cups	2¼ cups	3 cups
¾ cup + 1 Tbsp	1½ cups + 2 Tbsp	2¼ cups + 3 Tbsp	3¼ cups
¾ cup + 4 tsp	1⅔ cups	2½ cups	3⅓ cups
¾ cup + 2 Tbsp	1¾ cups	2½ cups + 2 Tbsp	3½ cups
¾ cup + 2 Tbsp + 2½ tsp	1¾ cups + 4 tsp	2¾ cups + ½ tsp	3⅔ cups
¾ cup + 3 Tbsp	1¾ cups + 2 Tbsp	2¾ cups + 1 Tbsp	3¾ cups
1 cup	2 cups	3 cups	1 qt
1¼ cups	2½ cups	3¾ cups	1¼ qt
1½ cups	3 cups	1 qt + ½ cup	1½ qt
1¾ cups	3½ cups	1¼ qt + ¼ cup	1¾ qt
2 cups	1 qt	1½ qt	2 qt

200	300	400	500
3⅓ cups	1¼ qt	1½ qt + ⅔ cup	2 qt + ⅓ cup
3½ cups	1¼ qt + ¼ cup	1¾ qt	2 qt + ¾ cup
1 qt	1½ qt	2 qt	2½ qt
1 qt + ½ cup	1½ qt + ¾ cup	2¼ qt	2¾ qt + ¼ cup
1 qt + ⅔ cup	1¾ qt	2¼ qt + ⅓ cup	2¾ qt + ⅔ cup
1¼ qt	1¾ qt + ½ cup	2½ qt	3 qt + 1½ cups
1¼ qt + ⅓ cup	2 qt	2½ qt + ⅔ cup	3 qt + 1⅓ cups
1¼ qt + ½ cup	2 qt + ¼ cup	2¾ qt	3¼ qt + ¾ cup
1½ qt	2¼ qt	3 qt	3¾ qt
1½ qt + ½ cup	2¼ qt + ¾ cup	3¼ qt	1 gal + ¼ cup
1½ qt + ⅔ cup	2½ qt	3¼ qt + ⅓ cup	1 gal + ⅔ cup
1¾ qt	2½ qt + ½ cup	3½ qt	1 gal + 1½ cups
1¾ qt + ⅓ cup	2¾ qt	3½ qt + ⅔ cup	1 gal + 1⅔ cups
1¾ qt + ½ cup	3 qt + ¼ cup	1 gal	1 gal + 3¾ cups
2 qt	3 qt	1 gal	1¼ gal
2½ qt	3¾ qt	1¼ gal	1½ gal + 1 cup
3 qt	1 gal + 2 cups	1½ gal	1¾ gal + 2 cups
3½ qt	1¼ gal + 1 cup	1¾ gal	2 gal + 3 cups
1 gal	1½ gal	2 gal	2½ gal

(continued)

TABLE 1.23 *(Continued)*

25	50	75	100
2¼ cups	1 qt + ½ cup	1½ qt + ¾ cup	2¼ qt
2½ cups	1¼ qt	1¾ qt + ½ cup	2½ qt
2¾ cups	1¼ qt + ½ cup	2 qt + ¼ cup	2¾ qt
3 cups	1½ qt	2¼ qt	3 qt
3¼ cups	1½ qt + ½ cup	2¼ qt + ¾ cup	3¼ qt
3½ cups	1¾ qt	2½ qt + ½ cup	3½ qt
3¾ cups	1¾ qt + ½ cup	2¾ qt + ¼ cup	3¾ qt
1 qt	2 qt	3 qt	1 gal
1¼ qt	2½ qt	3¾ qt	1¼ gal
1½ qt	3 qt	1 gal + 2 cup	1½ gal
1¾ qt	3½ qt	1¼ gal + 1 cup	1¾ gal
2 qt	1 gal	1½ gal	2 gal
2¼ qt	1 gal + 2 cups	1½ gal + 3 cups	2¼ gal
2½ qt	1¼ gal	1¾ gal + 2 cups	2½ gal
2¾ qt	1¼ gal + 2 cups	2 gal + 1 cup	2¾ gal
3 qt	1½ gal	2¼ gal	3 gal
3 qt + 1 cup	1½ gal + 2 cups	2¼ gal + 3 cups	3¼ gal
3½ qt	1¾ gal	2½ gal + 2 cups	3½ gal
3½ qt + 1 cup	1¾ gal + 2 cups	2¾ gal + 1 cup	3¾ gal

200	300	400	500
1 gal + 2 cups	1½ gal + 3 cups	2¼ gal	2¾ gal + 1 cup
1¼ gal	1¾ gal + 2 cups	2½ gal	3 gal + 2 cups
1¼ gal + 2 cups	2 gal + 1 cup	2¾ gal	3¼ gal + 3 cups
1½ gal	2¼ gal	3 gal	3¾ gal
1½ gal + 2 cups	2¼ gal + 3 cups	3¼ gal	4 gal + 1 cup
1¾ gal	2½ gal + 2 cups	3½ gal	4¼ gal + 2 cups
1¾ gal + 2 cups	2¾ gal + 1 cup	3¾ gal	4½ gal + 3 cups
2 gal	3 gal	4 gal	5 gal
2½ gal	3¾ gal	5 gal	6¼ gal
3 gal	4½ gal	6 gal	7½ gal
3½ gal	5¼ gal	7 gal	8¾ gal
4 gal	6 gal	8 gal	10 gal
4½ gal	6¾ gal	9 gal	11¼ gal
5 gal	7½ gal	10 gal	12½ gal
5½ gal	8¼ gal	11 gal	13¾ gal
6 gal	9 gal	12 gal	15 gal
6½ gal	9¾ gal	13 gal	16¼ gal
7 gal	10½ gal	14 gal	17½ gal
7½ gal	11¼ gal	15 gal	18¾ gal

(continued)

TABLE 1.23 *(Continued)*

25	50	75	100
1 gal	2 gal	3 gal	4 gal
1 gal + 1 cup	2 gal + 2 cups	3 gal + 3 cups	4¼ gal
1 gal + 2 cups	2¼ gal	3¼ gal + 2 cups	4½ gal
1 gal + 3 cups	2¼ gal + 2 cups	3½ gal + 1 cup	4¾ gal
1¼ gal	2½ gal	3¾ gal	5 gal
1¼ gal + 1 cup	2½ gal + 2 cups	3¾ gal + 3 cups	5¼ gal
1¼ gal + 2 cups	2¾ gal	4 gal + 2 cups	5½ gal
1¼ gal + 3 cups	2¾ gal + 2 cups	4¼ gal + 1 cup	5¾ gal
1½ gal	3 gal	4½ gal	6 gal
1½ gal + 1 cup	3 gal + 2 cups	4½ gal + 3 cups	6¼ gal
1½ gal + 2 cups	3¼ gal	4¾ gal + 2 cups	6½ gal
1½ gal + 3 cups	3¼ gal + 2 cups	5 gal + 1 cup	6¾ gal
1¾ gal	3½ gal	5¼ gal	7 gal

200	300	400	500
8 gal	12 gal	16 gal	20 gal
8½ gal	12¾ gal	17 gal	21¼ gal
9 gal	13½ gal	18 gal	22½ gal
9½ gal	14¼ gal	19 gal	23¾ gal
10 gal	15 gal	20 gal	25 gal
10½ gal	15¾ gal	21 gal	26¼ gal
11 gal	16½ gal	22 gal	27½ gal
11½ gal	17¼ gal	23 gal	28¾ gal
12 gal	18 gal	24 gal	30 gal
12½ gal	18¾ gal	25 gal	31¼ gal
13 gal	19½ gal	26 gal	32½ gal
13½ gal	20¼ gal	27 gal	33¾ gal
14 gal	21 gal	28 gal	35 gal

Used with permission from *Quantity Food Preparation: Standardizing Recipes and Controlling Ingredients.* Copyright 1983 by The American Dietetic Association, Chicago, Ill.

[a] To be used with Table 1.24, which is similarly constructed for weight measures.

TABLE 1.24 DIRECT-READING TABLE FOR ADJUSTING WEIGHT INGREDIENTS OF RECIPES DIVISIBLE BY 25[a]

25	50	75	100	200	300	400	500
*	*	*	¼ oz	½ oz	¾ oz	1 oz	1¼ oz
*	*	*	½ oz	1 oz	1½ oz	2 oz	2½ oz
*	*	*	¾ oz	1½ oz	2¼ oz	3 oz	3¾ oz
¼ oz	½ oz	¾ oz	1 oz	2 oz	3 oz	4 oz	5 oz
*	*	*	1¼ oz	2½ oz	3¾ oz	5 oz	6¼ oz
*	¾ oz	*	1½ oz	3 oz	4½ oz	6 oz	7½ oz
*	*	*	1¾ oz	3½ oz	5¼ oz	7 oz	8¾ oz
½ oz	1 oz	1½ oz	2 oz	4 oz	6 oz	8 oz	10 oz
*	*	1¾ oz	2¼ oz	4½ oz	6¾ oz	9 oz	11¼ oz
*	1¼ oz	2 oz	2½ oz	5 oz	7½ oz	10 oz	12½ oz
*	*	2 oz	2¾ oz	5½ oz	8¼ oz	11 oz	13¾ oz
¾ oz	1½ oz	2¼ oz	3 oz	6 oz	9 oz	12 oz	15 oz
*	*	2½ oz	3¼ oz	6½ oz	9¾ oz	13 oz	1 lb ¼ oz
*	1¾ oz	2¾ oz	3½ oz	7 oz	10½ oz	14 oz	1 lb 1½ oz
1 oz	2 oz	2¾ oz	3¾ oz	7½ oz	11¼ oz	15 oz	1 lb 2¾ oz
1 oz	2 oz	3 oz	4 oz	8 oz	12 oz	1 lb	1 lb 4 oz
1 oz	2¼ oz	3¼ oz	4¼ oz	8½ oz	12¾ oz	1 lb 1 oz	1 lb 5¼ oz
*	2½ oz	3½ oz	4½ oz	9 oz	13½ oz	1 lb 2 oz	1 lb 6½ oz
*	2½ oz	3½ oz	4¾ oz	9½ oz	14¼ oz	1 lb 3 oz	1 lb 7¾ oz
1¼ oz	2½ oz	3¾ oz	5 oz	10 oz	15 oz	1 lb 4 oz	1 lb 9 oz
*	2¾ oz	4¼ oz	5½ oz	11 oz	1 lb ½ oz	1 lb 6 oz	1 lb 11½ oz
1½ oz	3 oz	4½ oz	6 oz	12 oz	1 lb 2 oz	1 lb 8 oz	1 lb 14 oz
*	3¼ oz	4¾ oz	6½ oz	13 oz	1 lb 3½ oz	1 lb 10 oz	2 lb ½ oz
1¾ oz	3½ oz	5¼ oz	7 oz	14 oz	1 lb 5 oz	1 lb 12 oz	2 lb 3 oz
2 oz	3¾ oz	5¾ oz	7½ oz	15 oz	1 lb 6½ oz	1 lb 14 oz	2 lb 5½ oz
2 oz	4 oz	6 oz	8 oz	1 lb	1 lb 8 oz	2 lb	2 lb 8 oz
2¼ oz	4¼ oz	6½ oz	8½ oz	1 lb 1 oz	1 lb 9½ oz	2 lb 2 oz	2 lb 10½ oz
2¼ oz	4½ oz	6¾ oz	9 oz	1 lb 2 oz	1 lb 11 oz	2 lb 4 oz	2 lb 13 oz
2½ oz	4¾ oz	7¼ oz	9½ oz	1 lb 3 oz	1 lb 12½ oz	2 lb 6 oz	2 lb 15½ oz
2½ oz	5 oz	7½ oz	10 oz	1 lb 4 oz	1 lb 14 oz	2 lb 8 oz	3 lb 2 oz
2¾ oz	5½ oz	8¼ oz	11 oz	1 lb 6 oz	2 lb 1 oz	2 lb 12 oz	3 lb 7 oz
3 oz	6 oz	9 oz	12 oz	1 lb 8 oz	2 lb 4 oz	3 lb	3 lb 12 oz
3¼ oz	6½ oz	9¾ oz	13 oz	1 lb 10 oz	2 lb 7 oz	3 lb 4 oz	4 lb 1 oz
3½ oz	7 oz	10½ oz	14 oz	1 lb 12 oz	2 lb 10 oz	3 lb 8 oz	4 lb 6 oz
3¾ oz	7½ oz	11¼ oz	15 oz	1 lb 14 oz	2 lb 13 oz	3 lb 12 oz	4 lb 11 oz

25	50	75	100	200	300	400	500
4 oz	8 oz	12 oz	1 lb	2 lb	3 lb	4 lb	5 lb
4½ oz	9 oz	13½ oz	1 lb 2 oz	2 lb 4 oz	3 lb 6 oz	4 lb 8 oz	5 lb 10 oz
5 oz	10 oz	15 oz	1 lb 4 oz	2 lb 8 oz	3 lb 12 oz	5 lb	6 lb 4 oz
5½ oz	11 oz	1 lb ½ oz	1 lb 6 oz	2 lb 12 oz	4 lb 2 oz	5 lb 8 oz	6 lb 14 oz
6 oz	12 oz	1 lb 2 oz	1 lb 8 oz	3 lb	4 lb 8 oz	6 lb	7 lb 8 oz
6½ oz	13 oz	1 lb 3½ oz	1 lb 10 oz	3 lb 4 oz	4 lb 14 oz	6 lb 8 oz	8 lb 2 oz
7 oz	14 oz	1 lb 5 oz	1 lb 12 oz	3 lb 8 oz	5 lb 4 oz	7 lb	8 lb 12 oz
7½ oz	15 oz	1 lb 6½ oz	1 lb 14 oz	3 lb 12 oz	5 lb 10 oz	7 lb 8 oz	9 lb 6 oz
8 oz	1 lb	1 lb 8 oz	2 lb	4 lb	6 lb	8 lb	10 lb
8½ oz	1 lb 1 oz	1 lb 9½ oz	2 lb 2 oz	4 lb 4 oz	6 lb 6 oz	8 lb 8 oz	10 lb 10 oz
9 oz	1 lb 2 oz	1 lb 11 oz	2 lb 4 oz	4 lb 8 oz	6 lb 12 oz	9 lb	11 lb 4 oz
9½ oz	1 lb 3 oz	1 lb 12½ oz	2 lb 6 oz	4 lb 12 oz	7 lb 2 oz	9 lb 8 oz	11 lb 14 oz
10 oz	1 lb 4 oz	1 lb 14 oz	2 lb 8 oz	5 lb	7 lb 8 oz	10 lb	12 lb 8 oz
11 oz	1 lb 6 oz	2 lb 1 oz	2 lb 12 oz	5 lb 8 oz	8 lb 4 oz	11 lb	13 lb 12 oz
12 oz	1 lb 8 oz	2 lb 4 oz	3 lb	6 lb	9 lb	12 lb	15 lb
13 oz	1 lb 10 oz	2 lb 7 oz	3 lb 4 oz	6 lb 8 oz	9 lb 12 oz	13 lb	16 lb 4 oz
14 oz	1 lb 12 oz	2 lb 10 oz	3 lb 8 oz	7 lb	10 lb 8 oz	14 lb	17 lb 8 oz
15 oz	1 lb 14 oz	2 lb 13 oz	3 lb 12 oz	7 lb 8 oz	11 lb 4 oz	15 lb	18 lb 12 oz
1 lb	2 lb	3 lb	4 lb	8 lb	12 lb	16 lb	20 lb
1 lb 1 oz	2 lb 2 oz	3 lb 3 oz	4 lb 4 oz	8 lb 8 oz	12 lb 12 oz	17 lb	21 lb 4 oz
1 lb 2 oz	2 lb 4 oz	3 lb 6 oz	4 lb 8 oz	9 lb	13 lb 8 oz	18 lb	22 lb 8 oz
1 lb 3 oz	2 lb 6 oz	3 lb 9 oz	4 lb 12 oz	9 lb 8 oz	14 lb 4 oz	19 lb	23 lb 12 oz
1 lb 4 oz	2 lb 8 oz	3 lb 12 oz	5 lb	10 lb	15 lb	20 lb	25 lb
1 lb 5 oz	2 lb 10 oz	3 lb 15 oz	5 lb 4 oz	10 lb 8 oz	15 lb 12 oz	21 lb	26 lb 4 oz
1 lb 6 oz	2 lb 12 oz	4 lb 2 oz	5 lb 8 oz	11 lb	16 lb 8 oz	22 lb	27 lb 8 oz
1 lb 7 oz	2 lb 14 oz	4 lb 5 oz	5 lb 12 oz	11 lb 8 oz	17 lb 4 oz	23 lb	28 lb 12 oz
1 lb 8 oz	3 lb	4 lb 8 oz	6 lb	12 lb	18 lb	24 lb	30 lb
1 lb 10 oz	3 lb 4 oz	4 lb 14 oz	6 lb 8 oz	13 lb	19 lb 8 oz	26 lb	32 lb 8 oz
1 lb 12 oz	3 lb 8 oz	5 lb 4 oz	7 lb	14 lb	21 lb	28 lb	35 lb
1 lb 14 oz	3 lb 12 oz	5 lb 10 oz	7 lb 8 oz	15 lb	22 lb 8 oz	30 lb	37 lb 8 oz
2 lb	4 lb	6 lb	8 lb	16 lb	24 lb	32 lb	40 lb
2 lb 2 oz	4 lb 4 oz	6 lb 6 oz	8 lb 8 oz	17 lb	25 lb 8 oz	34 lb	42 lb 8 oz
2 lb 4 oz	4 lb 8 oz	6 lb 12 oz	9 lb	18 lb	27 lb	36 lb	45 lb
2 lb 6 oz	4 lb 12 oz	7 lb 2 oz	9 lb 8 oz	19 lb	28 lb 8 oz	38 lb	47 lb 8 oz

(continued)

TABLE 1.24 *(Continued)*

25	50	75	100	200	300	400	500
2 lb 8 oz	5 lb	7 lb 8 oz	10 lb	20 lb	30 lb	40 lb	50 lb
2 lb 12 oz	5 lb 8 oz	8 lb 4 oz	11 lb	22 lb	33 lb	44 lb	55 lb
3 lb	6 lb	9 lb	12 lb	24 lb	36 lb	48 lb	60 lb
3 lb 4 oz	6 lb 8 oz	9 lb 12 oz	13 lb	26 lb	39 lb	52 lb	65 lb
3 lb 8 oz	7 lb	10 lb 8 oz	14 lb	28 lb	42 lb	56 lb	70 lb
3 lb 12 oz	7 lb 8 oz	11 lb 4 oz	15 lb	30 lb	45 lb	60 lb	75 lb
4 lb	8 lb	12 lb	16 lb	32 lb	48 lb	64 lb	80 lb
4 lb 4 oz	8 lb 8 oz	12 lb 12 oz	17 lb	34 lb	51 lb	68 lb	85 lb
4 lb 8 oz	9 lb	13 lb 8 oz	18 lb	36 lb	54 lb	72 lb	90 lb
4 lb 12 oz	9 lb 8 oz	14 lb 2 oz	19 lb	38 lb	57 lb	76 lb	95 lb
5 lb	10 lb	15 lb	20 lb	40 lb	60 lb	80 lb	100 lb
5 lb 4 oz	10 lb 8 oz	15 lb 12 oz	21 lb	42 lb	63 lb	84 lb	105 lb
5 lb 8 oz	11 lb	16 lb 8 oz	22 lb	44 lb	66 lb	88 lb	110 lb
5 lb 12 oz	11 lb 8 oz	17 lb 4 oz	23 lb	46 lb	69 lb	92 lb	115 lb
6 lb	12 lb	18 lb	24 lb	48 lb	72 lb	96 lb	120 lb
6 lb 4 oz	12 lb 8 oz	18 lb 12 oz	25 lb	50 lb	75 lb	100 lb	125 lb
7 lb 8 oz	15 lb	22 lb 8 oz	30 lb	60 lb	90 lb	120 lb	150 lb
8 lb 12 oz	17 lb 8 oz	26 lb 4 oz	35 lb	70 lb	105 lb	140 lb	175 lb
10 lb	20 lb	30 lb	40 lb	80 lb	120 lb	160 lb	200 lb
11 lb 4 oz	22 lb 8 oz	33 lb 12 oz	45 lb	90 lb	135 lb	180 lb	225 lb
12 lb 8 oz	25 lb	37 lb 8 oz	50 lb	100 lb	150 lb	200 lb	250 lb

Used with permission from *Quantity Food Preparation: Standardizing Recipes and Controlling Ingredients.* Copyright 1983 by the American Dietetic Association, Chicago, Ill.

[a] To be used with Table 1.23, which is similarly constructed for volume measures.

Directions for using Table 1.25   Many quantity recipes can be expanded from home-size recipes. Table 1.25 is useful when enlarging small-quantity recipes. Instructions for using this table follow:

1. Locate column that corresponds to the yield of the recipe to be increased. For example, if the recipe yields 8 portions, use the figures in the first column under the heading 8.

2. Locate the ingredient amount for each ingredient to be adjusted. Example: the original recipe of 8 portions calls for 1 Tbsp sugar. Find 1 Tbsp in the column marked 8.

3. Locate the amount on the same line under the heading for the desired yield. Example: To increase the original recipe for 8 servings to 24, locate under the 24 column heading the number on the same line with the 1 Tbsp in the 8 column. In the case of 1 Tbsp sugar for 8 portions the enlarged amount is 3 Tbsp.

4. Repeat this procedure for each ingredient in the recipe. Refer to Table 1.21 for rounding off awkward fractions and complicated measurements.

Abbreviations in table	**Measuring spoon sizes**	**Equivalents**
tsp teaspoon	1 Tbsp	3 tsp = 1 Tbsp
Tbsp tablespoon	1 tsp	4 Tbsp = ¼ cup
qt quart	½ tsp	5 Tbsp + 1 tsp = ⅓ cup
gal gallon	¼ tsp	
(b) too small for accurate measure; use caution	for ¾ tsp combine ½ tsp + ¼ tsp	8 Tbsp = ½ cup
	for ⅛ tsp use half of the ¼ tsp	10 Tbsp + 2 tsp = ⅔ cup
(r) slightly rounded		12 Tbsp = ¾ cup
(s) scant		16 Tbsp = 1 cup
		4 cups = 1 qt
		4 qt = 1 gal

TABLE 1.25   DIRECT-READING TABLE FOR INCREASING HOME-SIZE RECIPES WITH INGREDIENT AMOUNTS GIVEN IN VOLUME MEASUREMENT AND DIVISIBLE BY 8

8	16	24	32
(b)	(b)	⅛ tsp	⅛ tsp (r)
(b)	⅛ tsp (r)	¼ tsp	¼ tsp (r)
¼ tsp (s)	¼ tsp (r)	½ tsp	¾ tsp (s)
¼ tsp	½ tsp	¾ tsp	1 tsp
¼ tsp (r)	¾ tsp (s)	1 tsp	1¼ tsp (r)
½ tsp (s)	¾ tsp (r)	1¼ tsp	1¾ tsp (s)
½ tsp	1 tsp	1½ tsp	2 tsp
½ tsp (r)	1¼ tsp (s)	1¾ tsp	2¼ tsp (r)
¾ tsp (s)	1¼ tsp (r)	2 tsp	2¾ tsp (r)
¾ tsp	1½ tsp	2¼ tsp	1 Tbsp
¾ tsp (r)	1¾ tsp (s)	2½ tsp	1 Tbsp + ¼ tsp (r)
1 tsp (s)	1¾ tsp (r)	2¾ tsp	1 Tbsp + ¾ tsp (s)
1 tsp	2 tsp	1 Tbsp	1 Tbsp + 1 tsp
1½ tsp	1 Tbsp	1½ Tbsp	2 Tbsp
2 tsp	1 Tbsp + 1 tsp	2 Tbsp	2 Tbsp + 2 tsp
2½ tsp	1 Tbsp + 2 tsp	2½ Tbsp	3 Tbsp + 1 tsp
1 Tbsp	2 Tbsp	3 Tbsp	¼ cup
1 Tbsp + ½ tsp	2 Tbsp + 1 tsp	3½ Tbsp	¼ cup + 2 tsp
1 Tbsp + 1 tsp	2 Tbsp + 2 tsp	¼ cup	⅓ cup
1 Tbsp + 2¼ tsp	3 Tbsp + 2¾ tsp	⅓ cup	¼ cup + 3 Tbsp
2 Tbsp + 2 tsp	⅓ cup	½ cup	⅔ cup
3 Tbsp + 1¾ tsp	⅓ cup + 5 tsp	⅔ cup	¾ cup + 2 Tbsp
¼ cup	½ cup	¾ cup	1 cup
⅓ cup	⅔ cup	1 cup	1⅓ cups
⅓ cup + 4 tsp	¾ cup + 4 tsp	1¼ cups	1⅔ cups
⅓ cup + 5¼ tsp	⅔ cup + 3½ Tbsp	1⅓ cups	1¾ cups + 1¼ tsp
½ cup	1 cup	1½ cups	2 cups
½ cup + 2¼ tsp	1 cup + 5¼ tsp	1⅔ cups	2 cups + 3½ Tbsp
½ cup + 4 tsp	1 cup + 3 Tbsp	1¾ cups	2⅓ cups
⅔ cup	1⅓ cups	2 cups	2⅔ cups
¾ cup	1½ cups	2¼ cups	3 cups
¾ cup + 1¼ tsp	1½ cups + 2¾ tsp	2⅓ cups	3 cups + 2 Tbsp
¾ cup + 4 tsp	1⅔ cups	2½ cups	3⅓ cups
⅔ cup + 3½ Tbsp	1¾ cups + 1¼ tsp	2⅔ cups	3½ + 1 Tbsp
⅔ cup + ¼ cup	1¾ cups + 4 tsp	2¾ cups	3⅔ cups

48	64	96
¼ tsp	¼ tsp (r)	½ tsp
½ tsp	¾ tsp (s)	1 tsp
1 tsp	1¼ tsp (r)	2 tsp
1½ tsp	2 tsp	1 Tbsp
2 tsp	2¾ tsp (s)	1 Tbsp + 1 tsp
2½ tsp	1 Tbsp + ¼ tsp	1 Tbsp + 2 tsp
1 Tbsp	1 Tbsp + 1 tsp	2 Tbsp
1 Tbsp + ½ tsp	1 Tbsp + 1¾ tsp	2 Tbsp + 1 tsp
1 Tbsp + 1 tsp	1 Tbsp + 2¼ tsp	2 Tbsp + 2 tsp
1 Tbsp + 1½ tsp	2 Tbsp	3 Tbsp
1 Tbsp + 2 tsp	2 Tbsp + ¾ tsp	3 Tbsp + 1 tsp
1 Tbsp + 2½ tsp	2 Tbsp + 1¼ tsp	3 Tbsp + 2 tsp
2 Tbsp	2 Tbsp + 2 tsp	¼ cup
3 Tbsp	¼ cup	⅓ cup + 2 tsp
¼ cup	⅓ cup	½ cup
¼ cup + 1 Tbsp	⅓ cup + 4 tsp	½ cup + 2 Tbsp
⅓ cup + 2 tsp	½ cup	¾ cup
¼ cup + 3 Tbsp	½ cup + 4 tsp	¾ cup + 2 Tbsp
½ cup	⅔ cup	1 cup
⅔ cup	¾ cup + 2 Tbsp	1⅓ cups
1 cup	1⅓ cups	2 cups
1⅓ cups	1¾ cups	2⅔ cups
1½ cups	2 cups	3 cup
2 cups	2⅔ cups	1 qt
2½ cups	3⅓ cups	1¼ qt
2⅔ cups	3½ cups + 2½ tsp	1¼ qt + ⅓ cup
3 cups	1 qt	1½ qt
3⅓ cups	4¼ cups + 3 Tbsp	1½ qt + ⅔ cup
3½ cups	1 qt + ⅔ cup	1¾ qt
1 qt	1¼ qt + ⅓ cup	2 qt
1 qt + ½ cup	1½ qt	2¼ qt
1 qt + ⅔ cup	1½ qt + ¼ cup	2¼ qt + ⅓ cup
1¼ qt	1½ qt + ⅔ cup	2½ qt
1¼ qt + ⅓ cup	1¾ qt + 2 Tbsp	2½ qt + ⅔ cup
1¼ qt + ½ cup	1¾ qt + ⅓ cup	2¾ qt

(continued)

TABLE 1.25 *(Continued)*

8	16	24	32
1 cup	2 cups	3 cups	1 qt
1 cup + 4 tsp	2 cups + 2½ Tbsp	3¼ cups	1 qt + ⅓ cup
1 cup + 5¼ tsp	2 cups + 3½ Tbsp	3⅓ cups	4¼ cups + 3 Tbsp
1 cup + 2 Tbsp + 2 tsp	2¼ cups + 4 tsp	3½ cups	1 qt + ⅔ cup
1 cup + 3½ Tbsp	2¼ cups + 3 Tbsp	3⅔ cups	4¾ cups + 2 Tbsp
1¼ cups	2½ cups	3¾ cups	1¼ qt
1⅓ cups	2⅔ cups	1 qt	1 ¼ qt + ⅓ cup
1⅔ cups	3⅓ cups	1¼ qt	1½ qt + ⅔ cup
2 cups	1 qt	1½ qt	2 qt
2⅓ cups	1 qt + ⅔ cup	1¾ qt	2¼ qt + ⅓ cup
2⅔ cups	1¼ qt + ⅓ cup	2 qt	2½ qt + ⅔ cup
3 cups	1½ qt	2¼ qt	3 qt
3⅓ cups	1½ qt + ⅔ cup	2½ qt	3¼ qt + ⅓ cup
3⅔ cups	1¾ qt + ⅓ cup	2¾ qt	3½ qt + ⅔ cup
1 qt	2 qt	3 qt	1 gal
1 qt + ⅓ cup	2 qt + ⅔ cup	3¼ qt	1 gal + 1⅓ cups
1 qt + ⅔ cup	2¼ qt + ⅓ cup	3½ qt	1 gal + 2⅔ cups
1¼ qt	2½ qt	3¾ qt	1¼ gal
1¼ qt + ⅓ cup	2½ qt + ⅔ cup	1 gal	1¼ gal + 1⅓ cups
1½ qt + ⅔ cup	3¼ qt + ⅓ cup	1¼ gal	1½ gal + 2⅔ cups
2 qt	1 gal	1½ gal	2 gal

48	64	96
1½ qt	2 qt	3 qt
1½ qt + ½ cup	2 qt + ⅔ cup	3¼ qt
1½ qt + ⅔ cup	2 qt + ¾ cup + 2 Tbsp	3¼ qt + ⅓ cup
1¾ qt	2¼ qt + ⅓ cup	3½ qt
1¾ qt + ⅓ cup	2¼ qt + ¾ cup	3 qt + 2⅔ cups
1¾ qt + ½ cup	2½ qt	3 qt + 3 cups
2 qt	2¾ qt + ⅓ cup	1 gal
2½ qt	3¼ qt + ⅓ cup	1¼ gal
3 qt	1 gal	1½ gal
3½ qt	1 gal + 2⅔ cups	1¾ gal
1 gal	1¼ gal + 1⅓ cups	2 gal
1 gal + 2 cups	1½ gal	2¼ gal
1¼ gal	1½ gal + 2⅔ cups	2½ gal
1¼ gal + 2 cups	1¾ gal + 1⅓ cups	2¾ gal
1½ gal	2 gal	3 gal
1½ gal + 2 cups	2 gal + 2⅔ cups	3¼ gal
1¾ gal	2¼ gal + 1⅓ cups	3½ gal
1¾ gal + 2 cups	2½ gal	3¾ gal
2 gal	2½ gal + 2⅔ cups	4 gal
2½ gal	3¼ gal + 1⅓ cups	5 gal
3 gal	4 gal	6 gal

Part two
RECIPES

RECIPE INFORMATION

YIELD

The recipes in this book produce servings for 50 people unless otherwise stated. Factors that may affect yield include portioning, ingredient weighing error, calculation mistake in increasing or decreasing quantities, abnormal handling loss, and variation in the edible portion (EP) and as purchased (AP) factors for food products such as fresh produce and meats.

A standard counter pan 12 × 20 inches has been indicated for many recipes. For baked desserts and some bread products, either a 12 × 18-inch or an 18 × 26-inch pan is specified, as they are standard bakeware sizes. Weight of product per pan may need to be changed if pans other than those specified in the recipe are used. Care should be taken to scale products so that portion weight will be accurate and recipe yield remains correct.

Many standard-sized baking or counter pans will yield from 24 to 32 servings per pan. The recipes in this case are generally calculated for 48 or 64 servings. Yield adjustments may be made by cutting the servings into sizes that will yield the desired number of portions. Some foodservices may wish to adjust yield based on the clientele to be served.

INGREDIENTS

In most cases, the type of ingredient used in testing the recipes has been specified; for example, granulated, brown, or powdered sugar, and all-purpose or cake flour. High-ratio or hydrogenated shortenings were used in cake and pastry recipes; margarine or butter in cookies, some quick breads, and most sauce recipes. Solid fats such as margarine, butter, and hydrogenated fats were used interchangeably in recipes that specify "shortening." Corn, soybean, or cottonseed oil was used in recipes that specify salad or vegetable oil. Sodium aluminum sulfate–type baking powder (double acting) and active dry yeast were used for leavening.

Fresh eggs, large size, weighing approximately 2 ounces unshelled (1¾ oz shelled) were used in the preparation of the recipes. Eggs are specified by both number and weight. In many foodservices, frozen eggs are used, in which case the eggs are weighed or measured. If the eggs are to be measured, the number and weight may easily be converted to volume by referring to Table 1.3.

Nonfat dry milk is indicated in some recipes, but in those specifying whole fluid milk, dry milk may be substituted. Table 1.19 gives a formula for conversion. In most cases, it is not necessary to rehydrate the dry milk. It is mixed with other dry ingredients, and water is added in place of the fluid milk. The amount of fat in the recipe may need to be increased slightly.

WEIGHTS AND MEASURES

Quantities of dry ingredients weighing more than 1 ounce are given by weight in ounces (oz) and pounds (lb). Weights are for foods as purchased (AP) unless otherwise stated. Liquid ingredients are indicated by measure, teaspoons (tsp), tablespoons (Tbsp), cups (cups), quarts (qt), and gallons (gal).

Accurate weighing and measuring of ingredients are essential for a satisfactory product. Weighing is more accurate than measuring and is recommended whenever possible. Reliable scales are necessary. A table-model scale of 15- to 20-pound capacity with ¼- to ½-ounce graduations or an electronic digital-readout scale with a 15- to 20-pound capacity is suitable for weighing ingredients for 50 portions.

Standard measuring equipment should be used to assure accuracy, and measurements should be level. Use the largest appropriate measure to reduce the possibility of error and to save time. For example, use a one-gallon measure once instead of a one-quart measure four times. Flour is the exception. Use a measure no larger than one quart for flour.

COOKING TIME AND TEMPERATURE

The cooking time given in each recipe is based on the size of pan and the amount of food in the pan. If a smaller or larger pan is used, an adjustment in cooking time may need to be made. The number of pans placed in the oven at one time also may affect the length of baking time; the larger the number of pans or the colder a product, the longer the cooking time. In convection ovens, the time and temperature should be reduced by approximately 10 percent.

ABBREVIATIONS USED IN RECIPES

AP	as purchased
EP	edible portion
°F	degrees Fahrenheit
fl oz	fluid ounce
gal	gallon
lb	pound
oz	ounce
psi	pounds per square inch
pt	pint
qt	quart
tsp	teaspoon
Tbsp	tablespoon

APPETIZERS & PARTY FOODS

"Appetizer" in this book is the term used to describe foods offered preceding a meal, as well as foods served informally for parties, receptions, and other functions where people serve themselves from a variety of offerings. In either case the appetizers should be attractive in appearance, pleasing in flavor, and tastefully displayed.

Selections for appetizers may be from one or more of the following categories:

Hors d'oeuvres are attractive hot and cold finger foods that may include crisp fresh fruits and vegetables, pickles, olives, cheese, fish, sausages, deviled eggs, or a combination of these.

Dips, hot or cold, are accompaniments to fruits, vegetables, crackers, or chips. They should be complementary to the foods being served with them.

Canapés are made by spreading a well-seasoned mixture of eggs, cheese, fish, or meat on a canapé base. Bases include toasted or untoasted bread slices cut into various shapes, crackers, chips, tiny biscuits, or puff pastry shells. Fruit and nut breads make good bases for many canapé mixtures.

Cocktails are made of pieces of fruit, fruit or vegetable juices, and carbonated or alcoholic beverages. They may be made also of seafood such as oysters, shrimp, crab, or lobster and served with a seasoned sauce.

Soup appetizers are light and generally served as a first course at the dining table. Hot or cold broth or cream soups may be served and should complement the remainder of the meal.

Table 2.1 is a general guide for quantities of appetizers needed to serve 50 people. Table 2.2 suggests foods appropriate for serving entree party trays to 50 people. The type of group being served, time of day, type of event and duration, and number of different items offered may necessitate increasing or decreasing the amount of food recommended.

TABLE 2.1 SUGGESTIONS FOR APPETIZERS

Food item	Guide to serving quantities for 50[a]
Beverages	
Punch	2–2½ gal, recipes pp. 100–107
Wine	See Tables 4.1 and 4.2, p. 705

(continued)

TABLE 2.1 *(Continued)*

Food item	Guide to serving quantities for 50[a]
Canapé spreads and fillings	
Chicken salad spread	Recipe p. 541, prepare ¼ recipe
Ham salad spread	Recipe p. 542, prepare ¼ recpie
Tuna salad spread	Recipe p. 543, prepare ¼ recipe
Miniature puffs	Recipe p. 289, prepare ½ recipe
Cocktails	
Broiled grapefruit	25 fruit
Fruit cup	10 lb
Melon balls or cubes	10 lb
Punch	2 gal, recipes pp. 100–107
Shrimp cocktail	Recipe for sauce p. 571
Dips	
Artichoke, hot	Recipe p. 88
Artichoke and crab, hot	Recipe p. 88
Basic, and variations	Recipe p. 86
Garden dressing (dip)	Recipe p. 522
Layered Mexican	Recipe p. 89
Nacho	Recipe p. 323
Salsa	Recipe p. 569
Summer fruit	Recipe p. 88
Vegetable	Recipe p. 87
Hors d'oeuvres	
Apple and cheese wedges	1½ lb cheese, 8 apples, cut in wedges
Carrot curls	3–4 lb
Celery sticks	3–4 lb
Cheese ball, party, with crackers	Recipe p. 91 125–150 crackers
Cheese balls, hot	Recipe p. 319, prepare ½ recipe, use No. 40 dipper
Cheese cubes	5 lb
Cheese olive balls	Recipe p. 92
Cherry tomatoes	2 lb
Chips	5 lb
Cocktail sausages	3–5 lb
Deviled eggs	Recipe p. 317, prepare ½ recipe
Fruit chunks	8 lb
Marinated mushrooms	Recipe p. 485
Meat balls in barbecue sauce	Recipe p. 363, prepare ⅓ recipe, use No. 70 dipper
Molded shrimp or crab	Recipe p. 90
Sausage balls	100, recipe p. 92
Vegetable relishes	See p. 472 for ideas

TABLE 2.1 *(Continued)*

Food item	Guide to serving quantities for 50[a]
Hors d'oeuvres *(continued)*	
Whole shrimp, with cocktail sauce	3–5 lb shrimp, recipe for sauce p. 571, prepare ½ recpie
Soups	
Bouillon	Recipe p. 591, prepare ½ recipe for 4 oz portion
French onion	Recipe p. 603, prepare ½ recipe for 4 oz portion
Gazpacho	Recipe p. 616
Vichyssoise	Recipe p. 617, prepare ½ recipe for 4 oz portion

[a] The quantity of appetizers needed for 50 portions will depend on the group being served, the type of function, and the number of different items offered. If food items are served in combination with other foods, adjust the amounts to yield the approximate total weight or total number recommended. Example: Carrot curls in combination with celery sticks require a total weight of 3–4 lb.

TABLE 2.2 ENTREE PARTY TRAYS

MEAT AND CHEESE TRAYS *(approximate amount to serve 50)*

Meat (shaved or thinly sliced)	Cheese (thinly sliced)	Bread (thinly sliced bread or buns)	Spreads/other
Choose 10 lb	*Choose 3 lb*	*Choose 125 small slices or 75 buns*	*Use suggested amount*
Cold cuts	American	Small buns	Margarine or butter, softened, 1 lb
Corned beef	Cheddar	Sliced bread	Mayonnaise or salad dressing, 1½ cups
Roast beef	Edam	Pumpernickel	Prepared mustard, 1 cup
Ham	Gouda	Rye	Horseradish, 1 cup
Pastrami	Monterey Jack	White	Leaf lettuce, 3 lb
Turkey	Muenster	Whole wheat	Alfalfa sprouts, 1 lb
	Provolone		Tomatoes, sliced, 7 lb
	Swiss		Onions, sliced, 2 lb

VEGETABLE TRAYS AND DIPS *(approximate amount to serve 50)*

Vegetables	Relishes	Dips
Choose 5 lb	*Choose 3 lb*	*Choose 1–1½ qt*
Broccoli florets	Black or green olives	Hot artichoke
Carrot sticks or slices	Dill spears	Blue cheese
Cauliflower florets	Green olives	Creamy herb
Celery sticks	Pickled beets	Creamy onion
Cherry tomatoes	Pickled eggs	Dill
Cucumber spears or circles	Pickled vegetables	Garden (prepare ½ recipe)
Green onions	Sweet pickles	Italian
Jicama		Picante
Kohlrabi		Seafood
Mushrooms		Summer fruit
Pea pods		
Radish roses		
Red, green, or yellow bell peppers		
Zucchini spears		

Notes:

1. Meat and cheese may be rolled, folded, or stacked and garnished with leaf lettuce, parsley, and colorful vegetables (Figures 2.1, 2.2, and 2.3). Vegetables look appealing when cut in creative shapes and garnished with crisp greens.
2. Arranging food neatly so the tray will remain attractive is important. Including larger quantities of more popular items will make food trays appear well supplied throughout the serving period. Color and flavor combinations should be considerations also for determining placement of food items.

Figure 2.1 *Vegetable deli tray. Courtesy of Dillon Food Stores.*

Figure 2.2 *Deli tray, with an arrangement of rolled cold meats. Courtesy of Dillon Food Stores.*

Figure 2.3 *Deli tray, with sliced meat and cheese. Courtesy of Dillon Food Stores.*

APPETIZER RECIPES

Basic dip

YIELD: 50 portions
PORTION: See Variations

Ingredient	Amount	Procedure
Cream cheese	8 oz	Mix cream cheese until softened, using flat beater.
Sour cream	1½ lb	Add sour cream. Mix until smooth. Add ingredients for variations from chart. Mix until evenly distributed. Chill.

Note:
Dip may be thinned by adding a small quantity of buttermilk or milk.

BASIC DIP VARIATIONS

Variation	Ingredients added to basic dip	Serve with
Avocado (guacamole)[a]	(Delete cream cheese; reduce sour cream to 8 oz) 1 lb 8 oz avocado pulp 1 Tbsp lemon juice 3 oz onion, finely chopped 2 Tbsp fresh cilantro, finely chopped ¼ tsp garlic powder 8 oz fresh tomatoes, diced	Tortilla chips Nacho chips
Blue cheese	8 oz blue cheese, crumbled 1½ tsp lemon juice 2 Tbsp onion, finely chopped ½ cup buttermilk or milk	Crackers Fresh vegetables Chips
Creamy herb	¼ cup fresh onion, finely chopped ¼ cup snipped fresh parsley ¼ cup chives, chopped 1 Tbsp Worcestershire sauce ¼ tsp garlic powder	Fresh vegetables
Creamy onion	2 oz dry onion soup mix ½ oz snipped fresh parsley or chives	Chips
Dill	1½ Tbsp chopped onion 1 Tbsp dill weed 1½ tsp Beau Monde seasoning	Fresh vegetables
Italian	1½ oz dry Italian salad dressing mix ½ oz snipped fresh parsley	Fresh vegetables
Picante	(Delete sour cream; increase cream cheese to 2 lb) 8 oz salsa[b] ¼ cup fresh cilantro, chopped 1 oz stuffed olives, chopped	Tortilla chips Nacho chips Fresh vegetables Spread for canapés
Seafood	8 oz cooked shrimp, clam, or crab, finely chopped 1 oz dry onion soup mix 2 oz chili sauce 1½ Tbsp horseradish	Crackers Toasted party bread

(continued)

BASIC DIP VARIATIONS *(Continued)*

Variation	Ingredients added to basic dip	Serve with
Summer fruit	(Delete cream cheese) 8 oz brown sugar or honey 1½ tsp vanilla	Fresh fruit

[a] Chunky avocado dip may be made by deleting sour cream and using 2 lb cubed fresh avocados.
[b] More salsa may be added for a thinner dip.

Hot artichoke dip

OVEN: 350°F	YIELD: 50 portions
BAKE: 20–25 minutes	PORTION: 1½ oz

Ingredient	Amount	Procedure
Artichoke hearts, canned	2 lb 10 oz	Drain and chop artichoke hearts.
Garlic clove, mashed Mayonnaise Worcestershire sauce Parmesan cheese, grated Pepper, white	3 cloves 2 cups 1½ tsp 3 cups ¼ tsp	Stir remaining ingredients into artichoke hearts.
		Pour into 2 one-quart ovenproof bowls or pans. Bake at 350°F for 20–25 minutes. Serve warm with chips or crackers.

Variation:
Hot crab and artichoke dip.   Add 1 lb chopped crabmeat before baking.

Layered Mexican dip

YIELD: 50 portions
          3 14-inch platters
PORTION: 4 oz

Ingredient	Amount	Procedure
Bean dip	4 lb (6 10½-oz cans)	Spread 1 lb 5 oz bean dip on each of 3 14-inch round platters.
Avocado pulp Lemon juice Salt Pepper, black	3 lb 6 Tbsp 1 tsp 1½ tsp	Blend avocado, lemon juice, salt and pepper. Spread 1 lb over bean dip layer.
Sour cream Mayonnaise Taco seasoning	1 lb 8 oz 1½ cups 3¾ oz	Blend sour cream, mayonnaise, and seasoning. Spread 12 oz over avocado layer.
Tomatoes, fresh, diced	3 lb	Sprinkle 1 lb tomatoes over sour cream–mayonnaise layer.
Green onions, sliced	9 oz	Sprinkle 3 oz onions over tomatoes.
Black olives, sliced	1 lb 4 oz	Sprinkle 6 oz olives over onions.
Cheddar cheese, shredded	12 oz	Sprinkle 4 oz cheese over olives.

Notes:
1. Serve with tortilla or nacho chips. Platter of dip will keep well in the refrigerator for up to two days.
2. Salsa may be substituted for diced tomatoes, taco seasoning, and mayonnaise. Use 7½ cups salsa (2½ cups on each tray).
3. Refried Beans (⅓ recipe, p. 633) may be substituted for purchased bean dip.

Shrimp ring

YIELD: 50 portions
2 one-quart molds
PORTION: 2 oz

Ingredient	Amount	Procedure
Gelatin, unflavored Water, cold	3 Tbsp 1 cup	Soften gelatin in cold water. Save for later step.
Tomato soup	1 lb 6 oz	Heat tomato soup to boiling.
Cream cheese	1 lb 2 oz	Add cheese to hot tomato soup. Stir until blended. Add gelatin. Set aside to cool.
Celery, finely chopped Onion, finely chopped Shrimp, small salad (frozen or canned and drained) Mayonnaise	6 oz 4 oz 8 oz 1 lb	Add to cooled cream cheese–tomato mixture.
Shrimp	12 oz	Line each of 2 one-quart molds with 6 oz shrimp. Carefully pour 1¼ qt cooled cheese mixture over shrimp. Chill until set.
		Unmold on 2 plates and garnish. Serve with canapé bases, crackers, or melba toast.

Note:
Canned shredded crabmeat may be substituted for shrimp.

Party cheese ball

YIELD: 50 portions
2 balls
PORTION: 1½ oz

Ingredient	Amount	Procedure
Cream cheese, softened	1 lb	Mix all ingredients until smooth, using flat beater.
Blue cheese, crumbled	1 lb 8 oz	
Sharp cheddar cheese, shredded	2 lb	Shape into two balls, 2 lb 4 oz each. Chill.
Onion, finely minced	3 oz	
Worcestershire sauce	1 tsp	

Notes:
1. Ball may be rolled in chopped pecans, snipped fresh parsley, or paprika.
2. Cheese mixture may be shaped into a long roll. After chilling, slice and serve on crackers or other canapé base.

Sausage balls

OVEN: 350°F	YIELD: 50 portions
BAKE: 20–25 minutes, both steps	PORTION: 2 balls

Ingredient	Amount	Procedure
Pork sausage, bulk	2 lb	Form sausage into 100 1-inch balls, using a No. 70 dipper. Place on baking sheet. Bake at 350°F for 15 minutes. Drain on paper towels.
Cheddar cheese, grated	1 lb	Combine cheese, margarine, flour, and seasonings in mixer bowl, using flat beater.
Margarine, softened	8 oz	
Flour, all-purpose	12 oz	
Salt	½ tsp	
Paprika	2 tsp	
		Wrap 2 Tbsp (No. 70 dipper) of dough around each sausage ball. Place on ungreased baking sheet. Bake at 350°F for 8–10 minutes. Serve hot.

Note:
Balls may be frozen after wrapping with dough. Bake while still frozen at 400°F for 12–15 minutes.
Variation:
Cheese olive puffs. Wrap dough around large stuffed green olives. Bake same as for Sausage Balls.

BEVERAGES

COFFEE

The type of coffee-making equipment used in a foodservice determines the method of preparation and the grind of coffee. The urn is used when large quantities of coffee are required, as on a rapidly moving cafeteria line or for a large catered function. Where the service is spread over a longer period, coffee may be prepared in small batches in a drip or vacuum coffee maker.

The equipment selected should make a clear, rich brew, hold the coffee at a consistent temperature, and provide the quantity needed at an appropriate speed with a minimum of labor. Regardless of the method used, certain precautions should be observed:

1. Select a blend of coffee that is well liked by the clientele. The grind should be suitable for the equipment to be used.

2. Use fresh coffee. Coffee deteriorates rapidly after it is ground. Large amounts should not be accumulated. Coffee should be protected from exposure to heat, moisture, and air. Coffee not needed for immediate use may be stored in the refrigerator or freezer.

3. Use a proportion of fresh cold water to coffee that makes a brew of the strength preferred by the clientele. A proportion of 2½ gallons of water per pound of coffee makes a commonly accepted brew. Use 3 gallons of water per pound of coffee when a milder flavor is preferred. See p. 95 for coffee recipes.

4. Measure coffee accurately. The number of servings per pound of coffee varies with the quality of the coffee bean, equipment used, and cup size. A pound of high-quality coffee properly made should yield about 50 6-ounce portions when properly brewed. Many foodservices purchase coffee in pre-measured packages.

5. Have the water cold, freshly drawn, accurately measured, and brought to a temperature of 195–200°. Water that is too hot will extract bitter solids. Water that is too cold will not extract enough flavor, and the coffee will be too cold for serving.

6. Hold coffee at a temperature of 185–190°F for not more than one hour, and do not allow it to boil.

7. Serve coffee very hot. The consumer often judges a foodservice by the quality of its coffee, and temperature is important to its acceptance.

8. Plan production so that coffee is always fresh.

9. Clean the urn or other equipment immediately after each use, following instructions that come with the equipment.

TEA

Tea is made by the process of infusion, in which boiling water is poured over tea leaves or tea bags. The mixture is allowed to stand until the desired concentration is reached. The tea bags are then removed, or the tea leaves are strained out. For large quantities, instant tea is convenient to use.

A stainless steel or earthenware container is preferable for brewing tea. Use freshly drawn cold water, heated just to the boiling point. For iced tea, make the brew stronger than for hot tea to compensate for the melting of the ice added at the time of service. Keep the tea at room temperature, because cloudiness develops in refrigerated tea.

PUNCH

Punch may be made easily from frozen or canned juices in various combinations. Lemonade (p. 101) or Foundation Fruit Punch (p. 101) makes a good base for many other fruit drinks by adding fresh, frozen, canned, or powdered juices of the desired flavor.

The amount of sugar needed varies with the sugar concentration of the juices and individual preference. A recipe for Simple Syrup for sweetening punch is given on p. 101. If time does not allow making the syrup, add the sugar directly to the punch. Stir until sugar is dissolved.

Most punch is served iced but may be served hot if desired. Ingredients for punch should be refrigerated, and the chilled ingredients may be combined several hours in advance of service. If ginger ale or other carbonated beverage is to be used, however, it should be chilled and added just before serving.

If punch is served from a bowl, it may be kept cold by adding ice cubes or ring molds of ice. Ring molds made with lemonade will accent the flavor of other juices without diluting the punch. To add color, arrange alternate slices of orange, lemon, and unstemmed strawberries or cherries in the molds. Sprigs of mint may be added as a garnish. Add water to fill the mold three-fourths full and freeze. Unmold the ring and place upside down in the punch bowl. To make decorative ice cubes, fill ice cube trays with pastel-colored water or fruit juice. Add a red cherry to each ice cube section before freezing for additional color.

The amount of punch or iced beverage to prepare depends on the size of the punch cup or glass, the number of guests to be served, and whether second servings will be offered. Service from a punch bowl requires slightly more punch than if it is to be poured from a pitcher for individual service. It is always desirable to have extra chilled, unopened cans of the main punch ingredients to facilitate serving a larger crowd than anticipated.

Most recipes in this book were developed for 2–2½ gallons of punch. Each gallon will yield 32 ½-cup portions. Punch cups vary in size from 3 to 6 ounces, so it is important that the size be considered in determining the correct amount of punch to prepare.

BEVERAGE RECIPES

Coffee

	YIELD:	50 portions
		2½ gal
	PORTION:	6 oz (¾ cup)

Ingredient	Amount	Procedure
Coffee	1 lb	Use proper blend and grind for the coffee maker used.
Water, cold	2½ gal	Use method recommended by the manufacturer of the coffee maker.

Note:
The amount of water will vary with the brand of coffee and the strength preferred.

Variations:
1. **Iced coffee.** Increase coffee to 2 lb. Pour over ice in glasses. Coffee may be cooled to room temperature but should not be refrigerated. Flavorings may be added for variety; i.e., vanilla.
2. **Instant coffee.** Use 3 oz instant coffee or 2 oz freeze-dried to 2½ gal boiling water. Dissolve the coffee in a small amount of boiling water and add to the remaining hot water. Keep hot just below the boiling point.

Steeped coffee

	YIELD:	50 portions
		2½ gal
	PORTION:	6 oz (¾ cup)

Ingredient	Amount	Procedure
Coffee, regular grind	1 lb	Tie coffee loosely in a cloth bag.
Water, cold	2½ gal	Immerse bag in water. Heat to boiling point. Boil 3 minutes or until of desired strength. Remove coffee bag. Cover container and hold over low heat to keep at serving temperature.

Note:
For an extra clear brew, beat 1 egg and 1 cup of water together and stir into dry coffee until dampened. Then proceed as above.

Hot tea

		YIELD: 50 portions
		2½ gal
		PORTION: 6 oz (¾ cup)

Ingredient	Amount	Procedure
Tea bags, 1-oz	2	Place tea bags in a stainless steel, enamel, or earthenware container.
Water, boiling	2½ gal	Pour water over tea bags. Steep for 3 minutes. Remove bags.

Notes:
1. If bulk tea is used, tie loosely in a bag.
2. The amount of tea to be used will vary with the quality.
3. Instant tea (¾–1 oz) may be used in place of the tea bags. The exact amount will vary according to the strength desired.

Spiced tea

		YIELD: 48 portions
		1½ gal
		PORTION: 4 oz (½ cup)

Ingredient	Amount	Procedure
Water, boiling	1½ gal	Mix all ingredients except tea.
Sugar, granulated	1 lb 8 oz	Simmer 20 minutes.
Lemon juice	¼ cup	Strain.
Lemon peel, grated	1 lemon	
Orange juice	1 cup	
Orange peel, grated	1 orange	
Cloves, whole	4 tsp	
Cinnamon sticks	8	
Tea bag, 1-oz	1	Add tea bag to hot liquid. Steep for 5 minutes. Remove tea bag. Serve hot.

Variation:
Russian tea.   Use only 1¼ gal water. Add 1 qt grape juice when adding other juice.

Iced tea

		YIELD: 48 portions
		3 gal
		PORTION: 8 oz (1 cup)

Ingredient	Amount	Procedure
Tea bags, 1-oz	6	Place tea bags in enamel, stainless steel, or earthenware container.
Water, boiling	1 gal	Pour boiling water over tea bags. Steep 4–6 minutes. Remove bags.
Water, cold	2 gal	Pour hot tea into cold water.
Ice, chipped or cubed	10–15 lb	Fill 12-oz glasses with ice. Pour tea over ice just before serving.

Notes:
1. Always pour the hot tea concentrate into the cold water. Do not refrigerate or ice the tea prior to service. Cloudiness develops in tea that has been refrigerated.
2. Instant tea (1 to 1½ oz) may be used in place of the tea bags.
3. Six to seven lemons, cut in eighths, may be served with the tea.

Cocoa

YIELD: 50 portions
2½ gal
PORTION: 6 oz (¾ cup)

Ingredient	Amount	Procedure
Sugar, granulated Cocoa Salt	1 lb 8 oz 8 oz ½ tsp	Mix sugar, cocoa, and salt.
Water	1 qt	Add water and mix until smooth. Boil approximately 3 minutes or to form a thin syrup.
Milk	2½ gal	Heat milk. Stir in syrup.
Vanilla	1 tsp	Just before serving, add vanilla and stir until well mixed.

Notes:
1. A marshmallow or 1 tsp whipped cream may be added to each cup if desired.
2. Cocoa syrup may be made in amounts larger than this recipe and stored in the refrigerator for three or four days. To serve, add 1 qt cocoa syrup to each 2 gal hot milk.

Variations:
1. **Hot chocolate.**   Substitute 10 oz unsweetened baking chocolate for cocoa. Add to syrup and stir until melted.
2. **Instant hot cocoa.**   Dissolve 2½ lb instant cocoa powder in 2 gal boiling water.

French chocolate

YIELD: 64 portions
3 gal
PORTION: 6 oz (¾ cup)

Ingredient	Amount	Procedure
Unsweetened chocolate Water, cold	1 lb 2 oz 3 cups	Combine chocolate and water. Cook over direct heat, stirring constantly, for 5 minutes or until chocolate is melted. Remove from heat. Beat with a wire whip until smooth.
Sugar, granulated Salt	2 lb 8 oz ½ tsp	Add sugar and salt to chocolate mixture. Return to heat. Cook over hot water 20–30 minutes or until thick. Chill.
Whipping cream	3½ cups	Whip cream. Fold into cold chocolate mixture.
Milk	2½ gal	Heat milk to scalding. To serve, place 1 Tbsp (rounded) chocolate mixture in each serving cup. Add hot milk to fill cup. Stir until well blended. Serve immediately.

Notes:
1. The milk must be kept very hot during the serving period.
2. The chocolate mixture may be stored for 24 hours in the refrigerator.
3. To make in quantity, prepare chocolate syrup and add hot milk. Whip cream to soft peaks and fold into hot chocolate. Keep hot.

Foundation fruit punch

YIELD: 80 portions
2½ gal
PORTION: 4 oz (½ cup)

Ingredient	Amount	Procedure
Sugar, granulated	2 lb 8 oz	Mix sugar and water.
Water	1 qt	Bring to boil. Cool.
Orange juice, frozen, undiluted	3 cups	Combine juices and water. Add sugar syrup and stir until mixed. Chill.
Lemon juice, frozen, undiluted	3 cups	
Water, cold	1½ gal	

Notes:
1. If time does not allow making and cooling syrup, the sugar may be added to the cold punch and stirred until dissolved. Increase cold water to 1¾ gal.
2. Ginger ale may be substituted for part or all of the water. Chill and add just before serving.

Variations:
1. **Golden punch.**   Reduce orange and lemon juice to one 12-oz can each. Add two 46-oz cans pineapple juice.
2. **Sparkling grape punch.**   Reduce orange and lemon juice to one 12-oz can each. Add two 12-oz cans frozen grape juice. Just before serving, add two 20-oz bottles of ginger ale.

Simple syrup

		YIELD:　2 qt
Ingredient	**Amount**	**Procedure**
Sugar, granulated	2 lb	Mix sugar and water.
Water	1 qt	Boil for 3 minutes.
		Chill before using in punch.

Notes:
1. For a thicker syrup, increase sugar to 2 lb 8 oz and add 1 Tbsp corn syrup.
2. May be stored in the refrigerator for use in beverages or where recipe specifies Simple Syrup.

Lemonade

		YIELD:　48 portions
		3 gal
		PORTION:　8 oz (1 cup)
Ingredient	**Amount**	**Procedure**
Lemon juice	1¼ qt (approximately 30 lemons)	Mix lemon juice and sugar.
Sugar, granulated	2 lb 8 oz	
Water, cold	2¼ gal	Add water. Stir until sugar is dissolved. Chill.

Notes:
1. Three 6-oz cans undiluted frozen lemon juice may be substituted for fresh lemon juice. Increase water to 2½ gal.
2. Three 32-oz cans frozen lemonade concentrate, diluted 1:4 parts water, will yield 60 1-cup portions.
3. Lemonade makes a good base for fruit punch.

Banana punch

<table>
<tr><td></td><td>YIELD:</td><td>64 portions</td></tr>
<tr><td></td><td></td><td>2 gal</td></tr>
<tr><td></td><td>PORTION:</td><td>4 oz (½ cup)</td></tr>
</table>

Ingredient	Amount	Procedure
Sugar, granulated	2 lb	Mix sugar and water.
Water, hot	1½ qt	Boil for 3 minutes. Cool.
Orange juice, frozen, undiluted	1½ cups or 1 12-oz can	Combine juices, fruits, and water. Add cooled sugar syrup. Chill.
Lemon juice, frozen, undiluted	¾ cup or 1 6-oz can	
Water, cold	1 qt	
Pineapple, crushed	3 qt or 1 No. 10 can	
Bananas, ripe, mashed	6 medium	
Ginger ale, chilled	1 qt	Add ginger ale just before serving.

Notes:
1. Mixture may be frozen before ginger ale is added and held for use later.
2. Two 46-oz cans of unsweetened pineapple juice and one 12-oz can lemonade may be substituted for the crushed pineapple and lemon juice.

Variation:
Banana slush punch.   Mix and freeze juices, syrup, and mashed bananas. To serve, fill glass about half full of partially frozen slush and add chilled ginger ale.

Sparkling apricot-pineapple punch

YIELD: 80 portions
2½ gal
PORTION: 4 oz (½ cup)

Ingredient	Amount	Procedure
Apricot nectar	3 qt or 2 46-oz cans	Combine juices and water. Chill.
Pineapple juice, unsweetened	3 qt or 2 46-oz cans	
Lemon or lime juice, frozen, undiluted	1½ cups	
Water, cold	2 qt	
Ginger ale, chilled	2 qt	Add ginger ale just before serving.

Cranberry punch

YIELD: 80 portions
2½ gal
PORTION: 4 oz (½ cup)

Ingredient	Amount	Procedure
Cranberry juice	3 qt	Mix juices and water. Chill.
Pineapple juice	3 qt or 2 46-oz cans	
Lemonade, frozen, undiluted	1 qt or 1 32-oz can	
Water, cold	1 qt	
Ginger ale, chilled	3 28-oz bottles	Add ginger ale just before serving.

Ginger ale fruit punch

		YIELD: 96 portions
		3 gal
		PORTION: 4 oz (½ cup)

Ingredient	Amount	Procedure
Sugar, granulated	3 lb	Mix sugar and water.
Water	1 qt	Bring to boil. Cool.
Lemon juice	1½ qt	Combine juices and water.
Orange juice	1½ qt	Add sugar syrup. Chill.
Pineapple juice	1 qt	
Water	1 gal	
Ginger ale, chilled	2 qt	Add ginger ale just before serving.

Note:
Lime, orange, lemon, or raspberry sherbet may be added to punch just before serving.

Blushing pineapple punch

		YIELD: 50 portions
		1¾ gal
		PORTION: 4 oz (½ cup)

Ingredient	Amount	Procedure
Sugar, granulated	6 oz	Cook sugar, water, and cinnamon candies
Cinnamon candies (red-hots)	6 oz	over low heat, stirring until candies are dissolved.
Water	1½ cups	
Pineapple juice	1 gal	Combine pineapple juice and cinnamon candy syrup.
Ginger ale	2 qt	Add ginger ale and ice just before serving.
Ice	8 oz	

Variation:
Red-hot tea. Use following ingredients in place of those in recipe: 12 oz cinnamon candies dissolved in 5½ qt hot water. Add 16 oz concentrated orange juice and lemon juice to taste. Serve hot.

Wassail bowl

YIELD: 80 portions
          2½ gal
PORTION: 4 oz (½ cup)

Ingredient	Amount	Procedure
Sugar, granulated	2 lb 8 oz	Mix sugar, water, and spices.
Water	2½ qt	Boil 10 minutes.
Cloves, whole	1½ tsp	Cover and let stand one hour in a warm place.
Cinnamon sticks	10	Strain.
Allspice berries	10	
Crystallized ginger, chopped	2 oz	
Orange juice, strained	2 qt	When ready to serve, add juices and cider.
Lemon juice, strained	1¼ qt	Heat quickly to boiling point.
Apple cider	5 qt	
Crabapples or small oranges	6–10	To serve, pour hot mixture over fruit, studded with cloves, in a punch bowl.
Cloves, whole		If using a glass bowl, temper by filling with warm water to prevent cracking when hot punch is poured in.

Tomato juice cocktail

YIELD: 72 portions
2¼ gal
PORTION: 4 oz (½ cup)

Ingredient	Amount	Procedure
Tomato juice	8½ qt or 6 46-oz cans	Mix all ingredients. Chill.
Lemon juice	¾ cup	
Worcestershire sauce	3 Tbsp	
Tabasco sauce	½ tsp	
Celery salt	3 Tbsp	

Hot spiced tomato juice

YIELD: 64 portions
2 gal
PORTION: 4 oz (½ cup)

Ingredient	Amount	Procedure
Tomato juice	4¼ qt or 3 46-oz cans	Add onions, celery, and seasonings to tomato juice.
Onions, chopped	8 oz	Simmer for about 15 minutes.
Celery stalks, cut in 1-inch pieces	6	Strain.
Bay leaves	3	
Cloves, whole	12	
Salt	1 tsp	
Dry mustard	1 Tbsp	
Consommé	1 gal	Add consommé to tomato mixture and reheat. Serve hot.

Note:
Two 50-oz cans condensed beef or chicken consommé, diluted with 2 qt water, may be used.

Spiced cider

YIELD: 80 portions
        2½ gal
PORTION: 4 oz (½ cup)

Ingredient	Amount	Procedure
Cinnamon sticks	10	Tie cinnamon, cloves, and allspice loosely in a cloth bag.
Cloves, whole	2½ Tbsp	
Allspice berries	2½ Tbsp	
Apple cider	2½ gal	Add spice bag, sugar, and other seasonings to cider.
Sugar, brown	12 oz	
Mace	½ tsp	Bring slowly to the boiling point.
Salt	1 tsp	Simmer for about 15 minutes.
		Remove spices.
		Serve hot or chilled.

Variation:
Cider punch.   Omit spices. Substitute 1 qt reconstituted frozen orange juice and 1 qt pineapple juice for an equal amount of cider. Garnish with thin slices of orange.

BREADS

QUICK BREADS

Basic ingredients in all quick breads are flour, liquid, a leavening agent, and flavorings. Fat and eggs are usually included also. The type and quantity of each of these ingredients and their interaction affect the characteristics of the finished product. They may be classified, according to the proportion of flour to liquid, as

Pour batter: pancakes, waffles, popovers, crepes
Drop batter: muffins, pan breads
Soft dough: biscuits

Quick breads are leavened by baking powder, baking soda, or steam, which act quickly, requiring them to be baked at once. If a double-acting baking powder is used, quick breads may be mixed, panned, refrigerated, and then baked as needed during the serving period. A variety of quick breads may be made from basic biscuit and muffin recipes by adding fruits, nuts, and other flavorings.

Quick bread mixes may be prepared by sifting together the dry ingredients, which generally include nonfat dry milk, and then cutting in the shortening. Such a mix may be made on days when the work load is light and stored for periods up to six weeks without refrigeration or longer if refrigerated. Many foodservices use some type of commercial mix. The decision to purchase a mix or to make their own depends on the amount of skilled labor available, food inventories, and the cost and quality of the mix.

Methods of mixing

Ingredients for most quick breads are combined by the muffin or biscuit method, although the cake method is used for some loaf breads. Most quick bread ingredients should be mixed only to blend, with as little handling as possible.

MUFFIN METHOD
The muffin method is used for muffins, pancakes, waffles, and popovers.

1. Mix the dry ingredients in a mixer bowl. If dry milk is used, add it to the other dry ingredients.
2. Combine beaten eggs, milk, and melted or liquid fat and add to the dry ingredients all at once.
3. Mix at low speed only enough to dampen the dry ingredients.

The mixture will be lumpy. Excess mixing causes gluten to develop and carbon dioxide to be lost, resulting in the formation of long "tunnels" in the baked product. Effects of overmixing are less evident in rich muffins and loaf breads that contain a higher proportion of fat and sugar, or when the batter is made with cake or pastry flour. The batter should be dipped into pans carefully to avoid additional mixing.

BISCUIT METHOD

The biscuit method is used mainly for baking powder biscuits.

1. Combine dry ingredients in a mixer bowl.
2. Cut fat into the flour with flat beater or pastry knife.
3. Add liquid and mix to form a soft dough.
4. Knead dough lightly 15–20 strokes to develop the gluten. This results in a biscuit that has good volume and a crumb that peels off in flakes. Over-kneading, however, produces a biscuit that is compact and less tender.

CONVENTIONAL AND DOUGH-BATTER METHODS

The conventional and dough-batter methods, described on p. 173, may be used successfully for coffee cakes, loaf breads, and rich muffins.

Quality standards for quick breads

Quality standards	Deviation: cause
Appearance:	
Golden brown	Pale: overmixing, oven too cool
Slightly rounded, pebbly top	Rough surface: undermixing, too much flour
Well-proportioned shape	
Tender crust	Peaked: wrong size pans, overmixing
	Undersized: incorrect proportions, inaccurate measurements, improper mixing
Texture:	
Even grain, no tunnels	Coarse, tunneled: incorrect proportions, inaccurate measurements, overmixing
	Dry: oven temperature too low, too much flour, overbaked
Tenderness:	
Moist crumb, breaks easily without crumbling	Tough, elastic: overmixed
Light and tender	
Flavor:	
Good flavor, characteristic of ingredients	Too flat: not enough salt
	Unpleasant: poor quality fat or flavorings

YEAST BREADS
Ingredients

An understanding of the functions of the main ingredients in yeast-raised doughs is essential to the production of good bread and rolls.

FLOUR

Flour used for baking must contain enough protein to make an elastic framework of gluten that will stretch and hold the gas bubbles formed as the dough ferments. Bread flour is made from hard wheat and contains more protein than other flour; it is used by bakers who make large quantities of bread. All-purpose flour is milled from a blend of hard and soft wheats and contains enough protein to provide the gluten essential to make good rolls and yeast breads for most foodservices. An all-purpose flour was used in testing the recipes in this book. Whole wheat, rye, and specialty flours add variety to breads, and they should be combined with white flour because they do not have enough gluten to effect proper bread structure.

YEAST

Compressed or dry yeast may be used in yeast doughs. Two types of dry yeast are available, active dry and instant active dry. Instant dry yeast differs from regular dry in that it contains more active yeast cells and does not require a separate step for rehydrating the yeast prior to use. When substituting active dry for compressed yeast, only 50 percent by weight is required. Water should be increased to make up the weight difference. Substitution of instant active dry yeast for compressed requires slightly less than 50 percent by weight and varies among brands. Manufacturers' equivalent charts should be followed when converting to instant active dry yeast from compressed or regular dry yeast.

Dry yeast does not require refrigeration and remains active a reasonable length of time in cool dry storage. Compressed yeast is perishable and must be held under refrigeration (30 to 34°F), and storage is limited to not more than two weeks. It may be frozen to extend its keeping time but must be used soon after defrosting.

Compressed yeast is softened in lukewarm water (95°F). Active dry yeast is softened in warm water (105–110°F) or may be mixed with the dry ingredients. In this method the yeast is blended with a portion of the flour, sugar, salt, and dry milk solids if used. The liquid ingredients may be heated to a very warm temperature (120°F). The yeast can withstand the higher temperature because of protection provided by flour particles. Instant dry yeast may be incorporated along with the dry ingredients or sprinkled on the dough after the dry and liquid ingredients are combined, then mixed as usual. Instant yeast is sensitive to temperatures below 65°F, and warmer than usual dough temperatures may provide a better growth environment for the yeast.

Yeast grows best between 80 and 85°F. Dough should be kept in this temperature range during fermentation and should be near 80°F when mixing is completed. A moderate increase in the amount of yeast speeds up fermentation, but too much gives the bread a yeasty flavor.

LIQUID

The amount of liquid necessary to produce an optimum dough varies with the flour and generally is related to the protein quantity in the flour. Flours with higher protein values absorb more water than low-protein flour.

The liquid used for yeast breads generally is milk or water, although potato water and fruit juice may be used also. Milk improves the browning and nutritive value of the bread and tends to delay its staling. Liquid used for bread should be lukewarm (95°F) for compressed yeast, warm (105–110°F) for active dry yeast, or very warm (120°F) if the dry yeast is mixed with the flour and other ingredients. If fresh fluid milk is used, it is scalded to stop enzyme action that may produce undesirable characteristics, then cooled to the appropriate temperature. Nonfat dry milk is used extensively in quantity baking and may be mixed with the dry ingredients or reconstituted and used in liquid form. The nutritive value of the bread may be increased by the addition of extra quantities of dry milk. Evaporated milk may be used also in bread making and generally is diluted with an equal amount of water.

OTHER INGREDIENTS

Although used in small quantities, other ingredients influence the quality of the finished product. Salt is added for flavor and also helps to control the rate of fermentation. Sugar, a ready source of food for the yeast, accelerates the action of the yeast. Although the addition of a small amount of sugar makes the dough rise faster, too much sugar inhibits yeast activity. Granulated sugar generally is used for bread making, but honey, corn syrup, brown sugar, and molasses are used also, especially in dark whole grain bread, sweet rolls, or coffee cake. Fat is added to improve flavor, tenderness, browning, and keeping quality. Fat in large amounts, or if added directly to the yeast, will slow its action. Eggs are added for flavor, richness, tenderness, and color.

BREAD BASES

Commercially available bread bases may include ingredients for dough conditioning, flavoring, and coloring, as well as flour, salt, eggs, and seeds or nuts. These bases generally require mixing with flour, yeast, and liquid. Mixing and proofing time and techniques may be different from standard procedures, so manufacturers' instructions should be followed.

Mixing the dough

Mixing and kneading are essential for uniformly incorporating ingredients and developing a good gluten network. Kneading is accomplished by continuing the mixing process beyond the point of combining. In a mixer, a dough arm is used. The mixing speed and length of time will be determined by the type of mixer and the amount of dough. Moisture content of the flour may vary making it necessary to add the last part of the flour gradually to determine if the full amount is needed. It may be necessary to use more or less flour than the recipe specifies. The dough should be soft but not sticky and is softer for rolls than for loaf bread. Soft dough makes a lighter and more tender product than a stiff dough. The dough is mixed only until it leaves the sides and bottom of the bowl. When adequately kneaded, a small piece of dough may be stretched, without tearing, to resemble a membrane. This test is often referred to as the membrane test. Overkneading dough results in a breakdown of gluten strands, resulting in a low-volume, dense bread.

Fermentation of dough

Fermentation begins when the dough is mixed and continues until the yeast is killed by the heat of the oven. After mixing is completed, the dough should be set in a warm place (80–85°F), free from drafts, to ferment. The length of the fermentation period depends on the type of product, amount of yeast, strength of the flour, amount of sugar, and temperature. Usually 1½ hours are required for the dough to double in bulk the first time.

After the dough has doubled, it is punched down to its original bulk by placing the hand in the center of the dough and folding edges to the center, then turning over the ball of dough. Punching forces out excess carbon dioxide and incorporates oxygen, which allows the yeast cells to grow more rapidly. The yeast cells are more uniformly distributed, producing an even-textured product with a fine grain. After the dough has been punched down, it must be handled lightly to avoid breaking the small air cells that have been formed. If the dough is made with bread flour, usually it is allowed to rise a second time before shaping, although if the dough has been made with all-purpose flour, the second rising may be omitted. Some commercial bread bases require no first fermentation period. Bread products are mixed, shaped, and allowed to proof, then baked.

The dough may be retarded at any point during the fermentation process by chilling the dough. The dough may also be allowed to rise first, scaled into rolls, and then refrigerated. The baking process may be halted at a time when the rising is complete and before browning occurs, as in brown-and-serve rolls.

Shaping and baking

After the dough has doubled in bulk and been punched down, it is divided into 3- to 4-lb balls and allowed to rest for 10–15 minutes, then shaped into loaves or rolls of the desired size. (See p. 141 for recipes and directions for shaping.)

Let the panned bread or rolls rise (proof) at 90–100°F and 80–95 percent relative humidity, until double in bulk. Dough that has not risen long enough makes a small, compact product with low volume and dense texture. Dough that has risen too long tends to have an open, crumbly texture and reduced volume. When proofed for the correct length of time, a slight indentation that slowly comes back will remain when the bread product is pressed lightly with a finger. Too short a proofing period will cause no indentation to remain, and too long a proofing will cause the product to collapse.

Crust texture may be determined partly by the treatment applied after rising and prior to baking. For a chewy or crisp crust, spray loaves or rolls with cold water before and during baking, as with French Bread (p. 141), or brush with an egg-white glaze (1 slightly beaten egg white with 1 teaspoon of water). For a shiny golden crust, brush loaves or rolls with egg or egg-yolk glaze (1 slightly beaten egg or egg yolk with 1 tablespoon of water or milk) prior to baking. For a soft or tender crust, brush with melted butter or margarine immediately after baking.

Bake bread at 375–400°F. For best volume and texture, preheat the oven before baking yeast breads. The final expansion of the dough called "oven spring" occurs in the first 10 to 15 minutes of baking in a hot oven. The bread is done when tapping the crust produces a hollow sound and the sides, bottom, and top are golden brown. Remove bread from the pans immediately and place on a wire rack to prevent steaming and softening of the crust. Cool the loaves uncovered. If insufficient time is available for the bread to rise fully, a lower oven temperature may be used for a brief period to permit the dough to rise. The best volume is obtained if fully risen dough is put into a hot oven. The heat of the oven causes a rapid expansion of the gas in the dough. Long baking thickens the crust.

Rolls made from plain bread dough should be baked quickly in a 400°F oven. Rich doughs are baked at lower temperatures (350–375°F) to prevent excessive browning of the crust. Roll doughs may be refrigerated and portions of the dough baked at intervals. Storage time should be limited to less than a week to prevent crust formation.

Two general rules should be followed when baking bread products: The smaller the product, the higher the baking temperature and the shorter the baking time; the larger the product, the lower the baking temperature and the longer the baking time.

Freezing yeast doughs and breads

Yeast doughs can be frozen up to six weeks either before or after shaping. Sugar and yeast usually are increased slightly in doughs to be retarded or frozen. If the dough is to be frozen before shaping, divide it into pieces, flatten on baking sheets for quick freezing and defrosting, cover, and place in the freezer. If rolls are to be shaped before freezing, place on greased baking sheets or in muffin pans, cover, and freeze. When completely frozen, the rolls may be removed from the pans and stored in freezer bags. Allow time for thawing and rising (about six hours for bread and two hours for rolls).

To freeze baked bread and rolls, allow to cool to room temperature, then wrap and freeze. Frozen baked products should be allowed to return to room temperature, then placed in a warm oven for about 3 minutes or in a microwave oven for the length of time recommended by the manufacturer.

Quality standards for yeast bread

Quality standards	Deviation: cause
Appearance:	
Symmetrical, uniform shape, rounded top	Excessive volume: too much yeast, too little salt
Golden brown top, bottom, sides	Poor volume: weak flour, not enough yeast, over- or underdeveloped gluten, over- or underproofing
Smooth tender crust	
Good volume	
	Pale: cool oven
	Dark: excessive sugar or milk, oven too hot or too long baking
	Cracked: overmixing, improper shaping
Texture:	
Fine, even grain, free from large air bubbles	Coarse: too long proofing period, too cool oven, not enough flour, underkneading, slack dough
Thin cell walls	Heavy: yeast partially killed, underkneaded, poor distribution of ingredients, too cool while proofing, too short proofing period, excessive dough in pan
Crumb:	
Moist, silky, elastic	Crumbly, dry: too stiff dough, too cool oven, underkneaded
Flavor:	
Fresh nutlike	Flat: too little salt
	Yeasty: too long rising period, too warm proofing
	Sour: too long rising period, poor-quality ingredients

QUICK BREAD RECIPES

Basic muffins (Cake method)

OVEN: 350°F
BAKE: 18–20 minutes

YIELD: 50 3-oz muffins
70 2¼-oz muffins

Ingredient	Amount	Procedure
Sugar, granulated Shortening	1 lb 3 oz 14 oz	Cream sugar and shortening until fluffy, about 10 minutes, using flat beater.
Eggs	5 (9 oz)	Add eggs slowly to creamed mixture. Mix until blended. Scrape sides of bowl.
Flour, all-purpose Baking powder Salt	3 lb 3 oz 3 oz 1 Tbsp	Combine dry ingredients.
Milk Vanilla	1½ qt 1 Tbsp	Add milk and vanilla alternately with dry ingredients to creamed mixture. Do not overmix.
		Portion into prepared muffin pans with No. 12 dipper for 3-oz muffins or No. 16 dipper for 2¼-oz muffins. Bake at 350°F for 18–20 minutes.

Variations:
1. **Chocolate chip muffins.**   Add 1 lb chocolate chips to batter.
2. **Coconut muffins.**   Add 1 lb flaked coconut to batter. For other variations, see Basic Muffins (Muffin method), p. 118.

Baking powder biscuits

OVEN: 425°F BAKE: 15 minutes		YIELD: 100 2½-inch biscuits or 130 2-inch biscuits

Ingredient	Amount	Procedure

Flour, all-purpose
Baking powder
Salt
	5 lb
	5 oz
	2 Tbsp
		Combine flour, baking powder, and salt in
		    mixer bowl.
		Mix on low speed until blended,
		    approximately 10 seconds, using flat beater.

Shortening,
    hydrogenated
	1 lb 4 oz	Add shortening to flour mixture.
		Mix on low speed for 1 minute.
		Stop and scrape sides and bottom of bowl.
		Mix 1 minute longer. The mixture will be
		    crumbly.

Milk	1¾ qt	Add milk. Mix on low speed to form a soft
		    dough, about 30 seconds. Do not overmix.
		    Dough should be as soft as can be handled.

1. Place one half of dough on lightly floured board or table. Knead lightly 15–20 times.
2. Roll to ¾-inch thickness. Biscuits will approximately double in height during baking. Cut with a 2½-inch (or 2-inch) cutter, or cut into 2-inch squares with a knife. When using round hand cutters, cut straight down and do not twist to produce the best shape. Space the cuts close together to minimize scraps. Use of a roller cutter or cutting the dough into squares eliminates or reduces scraps. The scraps can be rerolled, but the biscuits may not be as tender.
3. Place on baking sheets ½ inch apart for crusty biscuits, just touching for softer biscuits. Repeat, using remaining dough.
4. Bake at 425°F for 15 minutes, or until golden brown.
5. Biscuits may be held 2–3 hours in the refrigerator until time to bake.

Note:
7 oz nonfat dry milk and 1¾ qt water may be substituted for fluid milk. Combine dry milk with other dry ingredients. Increase shortening to 1 lb 6 oz.

Variations:
1. **Buttermilk biscuits.**   Substitute cultured buttermilk (or 7 oz dry buttermilk and 1¾ qt water) for milk. Add 1 Tbsp baking soda to dry ingredients.
2. **Butterscotch biscuits.**   Divide dough into 8 parts. Roll each part into a rectangle ¼ inch thick. Spread with melted margarine or butter and brown sugar. Roll the dough as for Jelly Roll. Cut off slices ¾ inch thick. Bake at 375°F for 15 minutes.
3. **Cheese biscuits.**   Reduce shortening to 1 lb and add 1 lb grated cheddar cheese.

4. **Cinnamon raisin biscuits.**   Substitute 2 lb 8 oz margarine for shortening. Combine 8 oz sugar and 2½ Tbsp cinnamon with dry ingredients. Add 1 lb 12 oz raisins to mixture after margarine has been mixed in. When baked, frost with Powdered Sugar Glaze (p. 213).
5. **Drop biscuits.**   Increase milk to 2 qt. Drop by spoon or No. 30 dipper onto greased baking sheets.
6. **Orange biscuits.**   Proceed as for Butterscotch Biscuits. Spread with orange marmalade.
7. **Raisin biscuits.**   Reduce shortening to 14 oz and use ½ cup less milk; add 4 whole eggs, 3 Tbsp grated orange rind, 8 oz sugar, and 8 oz chopped raisins.
8. **Scotch scones.**   Add 10 oz sugar and 7 oz currants to dry ingredients. Add 5 eggs, beaten, mixed with the milk. Cut dough in squares and then cut diagonally to form triangles. Brush lightly with milk before baking.
9. **Shortcake.**   Increase shortening to 1 lb 12 oz. Add 8 oz sugar.
10. **Whole wheat biscuits.**   Substitute 2 lb whole wheat flour for 2 lb all-purpose flour.

Banana whole wheat muffins

OVEN: 350°F
BAKE: 35–40 minutes

YIELD: 50 muffins

Ingredient	Amount	Procedure
Sugar, granulated Shortening	1 lb 9 oz 13 oz	Cream sugar and shortening on medium speed until fluffy, using flat beater.
Eggs	7 (12 oz)	Add eggs to creamed mixture and mix thoroughly. Scrape sides of bowl.
Bananas, mashed	2 lb 11 oz	Add bananas. Mix on medium speed for 10 minutes.
Flour, whole wheat Flour, all-purpose Baking soda Salt	10 oz 1 lb 8 oz 3½ tsp 1½ tsp	Combine dry ingredients. Add to banana mixture. Mix on low speed only until blended. Scrape sides of bowl as needed.
Vanilla	1 Tbsp	Add vanilla and mix to blend.
		Portion batter into prepared muffin pans with No. 16 dipper. Bake at 350°F for 35–40 minutes.

Variation:
Banana muffins.   Delete whole wheat flour. Increase all-purpose flour to 2 lb 2 oz.

Basic muffins (Muffin method)

OVEN: 400°F	YIELD: 50 muffins
BAKE: 25 minutes	PORTION: 2¼ oz

Ingredient	Amount	Procedure
Flour, all-purpose	2 lb 8 oz	Combine dry ingredients in mixer bowl.
Baking powder	2 oz	Blend on low speed for 10 seconds, using flat
Salt	1 Tbsp	beater.
Sugar, granulated	6 oz	
Eggs, beaten	4 (7 oz)	Combine eggs, milk, and melted shortening.
Milk	1½ qt	Add to dry ingredients. Mix on low speed
Shortening, melted, cooled to room temperature	8 oz	only long enough to blend, about 15 seconds.
		Batter will still be lumpy.
		Portion batter with No. 16 dipper into well-greased muffin pans, about ⅔ full. Batter should be dipped all at once with as little handling as possible, but may be refrigerated for 24 hours and baked as needed.
		Bake at 400°F for 20–25 minutes, or until golden brown.
		Remove muffins from pans as soon as baked.

Notes:
1. 6 oz nonfat dry milk and 1½ qt water may be substituted for fluid milk. Combine dry milk with other dry ingredients. Increase fat to 9 oz.
2. No. 24 dipper yields 6½ dozen muffins.

Variations:
1. **Apple muffins.**   Add 1 lb chopped peeled apples. Fold into batter.
2. **Apricot muffins.**   Add 1 lb cooked apricots, drained and chopped. Fold into batter.
3. **Blueberry muffins.**   Carefully fold 1 lb well-drained blueberries into the batter. Increase sugar to 10 oz.
4. **Cherry muffins.**   Add 1 lb well-drained, cooked cherries. Fold into batter.
5. **Cornmeal muffins.**   Substitute 1 lb white cornmeal for 1 lb flour.
6. **Cranberry muffins.**   Sprinkle 4 oz granulated sugar over 1 lb chopped raw cranberries. Fold into batter.
7. **Currant muffins.**   Add 8 oz chopped currants. Fold into batter.
8. **Date muffins.**   Add 1 lb chopped dates. Fold into batter.

9. **Jelly muffins.** Drop ¼–½ tsp jelly on top of each muffin just before placing in the oven.
10. **Nut muffins.** Add 10 oz chopped nuts. Fold into batter.
11. **Raisin nut muffins.** Add 6 oz chopped nuts and 6 oz chopped raisins. Fold into batter.
12. **Spiced muffins.** Add 1½ tsp cinnamon, 1 tsp ginger, and ½ tsp allspice to dry ingredients.
13. **Whole wheat muffins.** Substitute 12 oz whole wheat flour for 12 oz white flour. Add ¼ cup molasses with liquid ingredients.

Oatmeal muffins

OVEN: 400°F
BAKE: 15–20 minutes

YIELD: 50 muffins
PORTION: 2¼ oz

Ingredient	Amount	Procedure
Rolled oats	14 oz	Combine rolled oats and buttermilk in mixer
Buttermilk	1¼ qt	bowl. Let stand 1 hour.
Eggs, beaten	5 (9 oz)	Combine eggs, sugar, and shortening.
Sugar, brown	1 lb 4 oz	Add to rolled oat mixture. Mix 30 seconds.
Shortening, melted and cooled	1 lb	Scrape sides of bowl.
Flour, all-purpose	1 lb 4 oz	Combine dry ingredients.
Baking powder	5 tsp	Add to rolled oat mixture. Mix on low speed
Salt	2½ tsp	only until dry ingredients are moistened,
Baking soda	2½ tsp	about 15 seconds.
		Portion batter with No. 16 dipper into well-greased muffin pans (⅔ full). Bake at 400°F for 15–20 minutes.

Notes:
1. 4 oz dry buttermilk and 1¼ qt water may be substituted for liquid buttermilk.
2. Flavor may be varied by the addition of 1 tsp cinnamon to the dry ingredients.
3. No. 24 dipper yields 7 dozen muffins.

French breakfast puffs

OVEN: 350°F	YIELD: 50 puffs
BAKE: 20–25 minutes	PORTION: 2¼ oz

Ingredient	Amount	Procedure
Margarine or butter	1 lb 2 oz	Cream margarine and sugar on medium
Sugar, granulated	1 lb 10 oz	speed until light and fluffy, using flat beater.
Eggs	6 (10 oz)	Add eggs to creamed mixture. Blend on low speed, then beat on medium speed for 3–5 minutes.
Flour, all-purpose	2 lb 8 oz	Combine dry ingredients.
Baking powder	2½ Tbsp	
Salt	1 Tbsp	
Nutmeg, ground	1½ tsp	
Nonfat dry milk	3 oz	
Water	3⅓ cups	Add dry ingredients and water alternately, on low speed, to creamed mixture.
		Portion batter into greased muffin pans with No. 16 dipper. Bake at 350°F for 20–25 minutes.
Sugar, granulated	1 lb 10 oz	Mix sugar and cinnamon.
Cinnamon, ground	2 Tbsp	
Margarine or butter, melted	1 lb 4 oz	When muffins are baked, remove from pans. Roll in melted margarine or butter, then in sugar-cinnamon mixture.

Notes:
1. 3½ cups fluid milk may be used in place of the nonfat dry milk and water.
2. For small, tea-sized muffins, dip batter with No. 40 dipper into small (1½-inch) muffin pans.

Variations:
1. **Apple nut muffins.** Add 1 lb chopped apples and 8 oz chopped nuts.
2. **Plain cake muffins.** Delete nutmeg. Do not roll in sugar and cinnamon.

Bishop's bread

OVEN: 365°F	YIELD: 64 portions
BAKE: 35–45 minutes	2 pans 12 × 18 × 2-inch
	PORTION: 3 × 2¼-inch

Ingredient	Amount	Procedure
Shortening Sugar, brown	1 lb 3 lb 2 oz	Cream shortening and sugar on medium speed for 5 minutes, using flat beater.
Flour, all-purpose Salt Cinnamon, ground	2 lb 14 oz 2 tsp 1 Tbsp	Combine flour, salt, and cinnamon. Add to creamed mixture and mix until well blended. Remove 1 lb 12 oz of the mixture to sprinkle on top later.
Flour, all-purpose Baking powder Baking soda	1 lb 2 oz 5 tsp 1½ tsp	Combine flour, baking powder, and soda.
Eggs, beaten Buttermilk	5 (9 oz) 1½ qt	Combine eggs and buttermilk. Add alternately with dry ingredients to creamed mixture. Scrape sides of bowl. Mix on low speed about 30 seconds. (Batter will not be smooth.)
		Scale batter into 2 greased 12 × 18 × 2-inch baking pans, 5 lb per pan. Sprinkle 14 oz of the reserved topping over batter in each pan. Bake at 365°F for 35–45 minutes. Cut 4 × 8.

Notes:
1. May be baked in one 18 × 26 × 2-inch pan. Cut 6 × 10 for 60 portions 3 × 2½-inch.
2. 4 oz dry buttermilk and 1 qt water may be substituted for fluid buttermilk.

Blueberry coffee cake

OVEN: 350°F	YIELD: 64 portions
BAKE: 45 minutes	2 pans 12 × 18 × 2-inch
	PORTION: 3 × 2¼-inch

Ingredient	Amount	Procedure
Sugar, brown	12 oz	Combine sugars, flour, cinnamon, and margarine.
Sugar, granulated	4 oz	Mix on low speed to a coarse crumb consistency, about 5 minutes, using flat beater.
Flour, all-purpose	4 oz	Set aside for final step.
Cinnamon, ground	2 tsp	
Margarine or butter, soft	4 oz	
Shortening	14 oz	Cream shortening and sugar on medium speed for about 10 minutes.
Sugar, granulated	2 lb 10 oz	
Eggs	7 (12 oz)	Add eggs to creamed mixture and continue mixing, 3–5 minutes.
Flour, all-purpose	3 lb 6 oz	Combine flour, baking powder, and salt.
Baking powder	2 oz	
Salt	1 Tbsp	
Milk	3½ cups	Add dry ingredients and milk alternately to creamed mixture.
		Mix on low speed for 3 minutes.
		Scrape sides of bowl.
		Mix on medium speed 10 seconds.
Blueberries, frozen or canned (well-drained and rinsed)	2 lb	Carefully fold blueberries into batter. (Berries may be sprinkled on top of batter.)
		Scale into 2 greased 12 × 18 × 2-inch baking pans, 4 lb 12 oz per pan.
		Crumble topping mixture evenly over top of batter, 10 oz per pan.
		Bake at 350°F for 45 minutes.
		Cut 4 × 8.

Notes:
1. May be baked in one 18 × 26 × 2-inch pan. Cut 6 × 10 for 60 portions 3 × 2½-inch.
2. 3 oz nonfat dry milk and 3½ cups water may be substituted for fluid milk. Add dry milk to other dry ingredients. Increase shortening to 15 oz.
3. After cake is baked, thin Powdered Sugar Glaze (p. 213) may be drizzled in a fine stream over the top to form an irregular design.
4. Recipe can be used for blueberry muffins. Sprinkle blueberries on top.

Dutch apple coffee cake

OVEN: 365°F
BAKE: 50–60 minutes

YIELD: 64 portions
2 pans 12 × 20 × 2-inch
PORTION: 3 × 2½-inch

Ingredient	Amount	Procedure
Sugar, granulated	2 lb 8 oz	Cream sugar, shortening, and eggs on medium speed for 10 minutes, using flat beater.
Shortening	12 oz	
Eggs	8 (14 oz)	
Flour, all-purpose	2 lb 8 oz	Combine dry ingredients and mix until well blended.
Baking powder	2 oz	
Salt	2 tsp	
Milk	1 qt	Add milk and dry ingredients alternately to creamed mixture. Mix on low speed for 3 minutes. Scrape sides of bowl. Mix on medium speed for 10 seconds.
Apples, frozen or canned	2 lb 8 oz	Drain apples and chop. Combine with margarine, sugar, and cinnamon.
Margarine, melted	2 oz	
Sugar, granulated	1 lb 2 oz	
Cinnamon, ground	2 Tbsp	
		Scale batter into two 12 × 20 × 2-inch baking pans, 4 lb 6 oz per pan. Spread 1 lb 14 oz apple mixture over batter in each pan. Bake at 365°F for 50–60 minutes. Cut 4 × 8.

Note:
Cake batter may be mixed and panned the day before using. Refrigerate overnight, then add topping and bake.

Coffee cake

OVER: 350°F
BAKE: 25 minutes

YIELD: 64 portions
2 pans 12 × 18 × 2-inch
PORTION: 3 × 2¼-inch

Ingredient	Amount	Procedure
Margarine or butter	10 oz	Place margarine, sugar, flour, cinnamon, and salt in mixer bowl.
Sugar, granulated	1 lb 4 oz	
Flour, all-purpose	3 oz	Mix on low speed until crumbly, using flat beater. Set aside, to be used later as topping.
Cinnamon, ground	1 oz	
Salt	1½ tsp	
Flour, all-purpose	3 lb 6 oz	Combine dry ingredients in mixer bowl.
Baking powder	2 oz	
Sugar, granulated	2 lb	
Salt	1⅔ Tbsp	
Eggs, beaten	6 (10 oz)	Combine eggs and milk.
Milk	1¼ qt	Add to dry ingredients. Mix on low speed until dry ingredients are just moistened.
Shortening, melted and cooled	1 lb 10 oz	Add shortening and mix on low speed for one minute.
		Scale dough into 2 greased 12 × 18 × 2-inch baking pans, 4 lb 2 oz per pan. Sprinkle with reserved topping mixture, 1 lb per pan. Bake at 350°F for 25 minutes or until done. Cut 4 × 8.

Notes:
1. 5 oz nonfat dry milk and 1¼ qt water may be substituted for the fluid milk. Combine dry milk with other dry ingredients. Increase shortening to 1 lb 12 oz.
2. May be baked in one 18 × 26 × 2-inch pan. Cut 6 × 10 for 60 portions 3 × 2½ inches.
3. If used for breakfast, may be mixed and panned the day before. Refrigerate until morning, then bake. Allow 5–10 minutes extra time because batter will be cold.

Walnut coffee cake

OVEN: 350°F	YIELD: 4 cakes
BAKE: 45–50 minutes	PORTION: 16 slices per cake

Ingredient	Amount	Procedure
Sugar, granulated Margarine	3 lb 1 lb	Cream sugar and margarine on medium speed until light and fluffy, using flat beater.
Eggs Vanilla	16 (1 lb 12 oz) 1 Tbsp	Add eggs slowly to creamed mixture, beating well after each addition. Add vanilla.
Flour, all-purpose Baking powder Salt	3 lb 4 Tbsp 2 tsp	Mix flour, baking powder, and salt together.

Milk	1 qt	Add milk alternately with dry ingredients to
		    creamed mixture, beating well after each
		    addition.

Sugar, brown Margarine Flour, all-purpose Cinnamon, ground Walnuts, chopped	2 lb 4 oz 2 oz 1 Tbsp 1 lb	Combine brown sugar, margarine, flour, cinnamon, and walnuts for crumb mixture.

		Scale 1 lb 4 oz batter into each of 4 greased
		    10-inch tube pans.
		Sprinkle 6 oz crumb mixture over batter.
		Spread with 1 lb 4 oz batter.
		Top with 6 oz crumb mixture.
		Bake at 350°F for 45–50 minutes.
		Cool slightly. Remove from pans.
		Frost with Powdered Sugar Glaze (p. 213) if
		    desired.
		Slice 16 servings per cake.

Corn bread

OVEN: 350°F		YIELD: 64 portions
BAKE: 35 minutes		2 pans 12 × 18 × 2-inch
		PORTION: 3 × 2¼-inch

Ingredient	Amount	Procedure
Cornmeal, yellow	2 lb 3 oz	Combine dry ingredients in mixer bowl.
Flour, all-purpose	2 lb 5 oz	Blend on low speed, using flat beater.
Baking powder	3½ oz	
Salt	2½ Tbsp	
Sugar, granulated	10 oz	
Eggs, beaten	9 (1 lb)	Combine eggs, milk, and shortening.
Milk	1¾ qt	Add to dry ingredients. Mix on low speed
Shortening, melted and cooled	10 oz	only until dry ingredients are moistened.
		Scale batter into 2 greased 12 × 18 × 2-inch baking pans, 5 lb per pan. Bake at 350°F for 35 minutes. Cut 4 × 8.

Notes:
1. 7 oz nonfat dry milk and 1¾ qt water may be substituted for fluid milk. Mix dry milk with other dry ingredients. Increase shortening to 11 oz.
2. May be baked in one 18 × 26 × 2-inch pan. Cut 6 × 10 for 60 portions 3 × 3½ inches.
3. May be baked in corn stick or muffin pans. Reduce baking time to 15–20 minutes.

Spoon bread

OVER: 350°F	YIELD: 50 portions

OVEN: 350°F
BAKE: 45–60 minutes

YIELD: 50 portions
2 pans 12 × 20 × 2-inch
PORTION: 4 oz

Ingredient	Amount	Procedure
Milk	5¾ qt	Scald milk by heating to point just below boiling.
Cornmeal, yellow Salt	1 lb 12 oz 1 oz (1½ Tbsp)	Add cornmeal and salt to milk, stirring briskly with a wire whip. Cook 10 minutes, or until thick.
Eggs, beaten	25 (2 lb 12 oz)	Add eggs slowly to cornmeal mixture, while stirring.
Margarine or butter, melted Baking powder	6 oz 2 oz	Add margarine and baking powder to cornmeal mixture. Stir to blend.
		Pour into 2 greased 12 × 20 × 2-inch baking pans, 8 lb per pan. Place in pans of hot water. Bake at 350°F for 45–60 minutes or until set. Serve at once.

Note:
Serve with crisp bacon, Creamed Chicken (p. 442), or Creamed Ham (p. 390).

Boston brown bread

STEAM PRESSURE: 5 lb
STEAM: 1¼–1½ hours

YIELD: 64 portions
    8 round loaves, 3¼ × 4½ inches
PORTION: ½-inch slice

Ingredient	Amount	Procedure
Cornmeal, yellow	1 lb	Combine dry ingredients in mixer bowl.
Flour, whole wheat	12 oz	Blend on low speed for 10 seconds, using flat
Flour, all-purpose	12 oz	beater.
Salt	1 oz (1½ Tbsp)	
Baking soda	1½ Tbsp	
Buttermilk	1½ qt	Blend buttermilk and molasses.
Molasses	2¼ cups	Add all at once to dry ingredients.
		Mix on low speed only until ingredients are
		blended.
		Fill 8 greased 3¼ × 4½-inch cans ¾ full.
		Cover tightly with aluminum foil.
		Steam for 1¼–1½ hours.
		Cut 8 slices per loaf.

Notes:
1. 12 oz raisins may be added.
2. May be baked as loaves. Add 3 Tbsp melted fat. Scale into three 5 × 9-inch loaf pans, 2 lb 8 oz per pan. Bake at 375°F for one hour.

Banana nut bread

OVEN: 350°F	YIELD: 64 portions
BAKE: 50 minutes	4 loaves 5 × 9-inch
	PORTION: ½-inch slice

Ingredient	Amount	Procedure
Margarine	10 oz	Cream margarine and sugar on medium
Sugar, granulated	1 lb 10 oz	speed for 5 minutes, using flat beater.
Eggs	5 (9 oz)	Add eggs to creamed mixture. Beat 2 minutes.
Bananas, mashed	1 lb 10 oz	Add bananas. Beat 1 minute.
Flour, all-purpose	2 lb	Combine dry ingredients and nuts.
Baking powder	4 Tbsp	
Salt	2 tsp	
Baking soda	½ tsp	
Pecans or walnuts, chopped	8 oz	
Milk	¾ cup	Add dry ingredients and milk to creamed mixture. Mix on low speed for 1 minute.
		Scale batter into 4 greased loaf pans (5 × 9 × 2¾-inch), approximately 2 lb per pan. Bake at 350°F for 50 minutes. Cut 16 slices per loaf.

Cranberry nut bread

OVEN: 350°F	YIELD: 80 portions
BAKE: 50 minutes	5 loaves 5 × 9-inch
	PORTION: ½-inch slice

Ingredient	Amount	Procedure
Cranberries, raw	1 lb 4 oz	Wash and sort cranberries.
Orange peel	7 oz	Coarsely grind cranberries and orange peel.
Flour, all-purpose	2 lb 8 oz	Combine dry ingredients in mixer bowl.
Sugar, granulated	2 lb 4 oz	Blend on low speed for 10 seconds or until
Baking powder	1 oz	mixed, using flat beater.
Salt	2 tsp	
Baking soda	2 tsp	
Eggs, beaten	5 (9 oz)	Combine and add to dry ingredients.
Orange juice	1½ cups	Mix on low speed only until dry ingredients
Water	3¾ cups	are moistened.
Salad oil	½ cup	
Pecans or walnuts, chopped	1 lb	Add nuts and cranberry mixture to batter. Mix on low speed until blended. Batter may be lumpy.
		Scale batter into 5 greased loaf pans (5 × 9 × 2¾-inch), approximately 2 lb per pan. Bake at 350°F for about 50 minutes. Cut 16 slices per loaf.

Date nut bread

OVEN: 350°F	YIELD: 64 portions
BAKE: 50 minutes	4 loaves 5 × 9-inch
	PORTION: ½-inch slice

Ingredient	Amount	Procedure
Dates, chopped	1 lb 8 oz	Add water and soda to dates. Let stand 20 minutes.
Baking soda	1½ Tbsp	
Water, boiling	3¼ cups	
Shortening	3 oz	Cream shortening and sugar on medium speed for 5 minutes, using flat beater.
Sugar, granulated	1 lb 12 oz	
Eggs	4 (7 oz)	Add eggs and vanilla to creamed mixture. Mix on medium speed for 2 minutes.
Vanilla	1½ Tbsp	
Flour, all-purpose	2 lb	Combine flour, salt, and nuts. Add alternately with dates to creamed mixture.
Salt	1½ tsp	
Pecans or walnuts, chopped	8 oz	
		Scale batter into 4 greased loaf pans (5 × 9 × 2¾-inch), approximately 2 lb per pan. Bake at 350°F for about 50 minutes. Cut 16 slices per loaf.

Nut bread

OVEN: 350°F		YIELD: 80 portions
BAKE: 50 minutes		5 loaves 5 × 9-inch
		PORTION: ½-inch slice

Ingredient	Amount	Procedure
Flour, all-purpose	3 lb	Combine dry ingredients and nuts in mixer bowl.
Baking powder	1 oz	
Salt	1 Tbsp	Mix on low speed until blended, using flat beater.
Sugar, granulated	1 lb 8 oz	
Pecans or walnuts, chopped	1 lb	
Eggs, beaten	6 (10 oz)	Combine eggs, milk, and shortening.
Milk	1½ qt	Add to dry ingredients.
Shortening, melted and cooled	4 oz	Mix on low speed only until blended.
		Scale batter into 5 greased loaf pans (5 × 9 × 2¾-inch), approximately 1 lb 14 oz per pan.
		Bake at 350°F for about 50 minutes.
		Cut 16 slices per loaf.

Note:
5 oz nonfat dry milk and 1½ qt water may be substituted for fluid milk. Combine dry milk with other dry ingredients. Increase shortening to 6 oz.

Pumpkin bread

OVEN: 350°F	YIELD: 80 portions
BAKE: 50 minutes	5 loaves 5 × 9-inch
	PORTION: ½-inch slice

Ingredient	Amount	Procedure
Sugar, granulated	2 lb 12 oz	Combine sugar, oil, pumpkin, and eggs in mixer bowl.
Salad oil	2 cups	
Pumpkin, canned	2 lb 6 oz	Cream on medium speed for 10 minutes, using flat beater.
Eggs	9 (15 oz)	Scrape sides of bowl and beater.
Flour, all-purpose	2 lb 2 oz	Combine dry ingredients.
Baking soda	4 tsp	
Baking powder	2 tsp	
Salt	1 Tbsp	
Cinnamon, ground	1 Tbsp	
Nutmeg, ground	1 tsp	
Water	1¼ cups	Add dry ingredients and water alternately to creamed mixture.
		Mix 3 minutes on low speed. Scrape sides of bowl.
		Scale batter into 5 greased loaf pans (5 × 9 × 2¾-inch), approximately 1 lb 15 oz per pan. Bake at 350°F for 50 minutes or until done. Cool 30 minutes before removing from pans. Cut 16 slices per loaf.

Note:
8 oz raisins or chopped nuts may be added.

Cake doughnuts

DEEP-FAT FRYER: 375°F		YIELD: 8 dozen doughnuts
FRY: 3–4 minutes		

Ingredient	Amount	Procedure
Eggs	6 (10 oz)	Beat eggs until light.
Sugar, granulated Shortening, melted and cooled	1 lb 4 oz 3 oz	Add sugar and melted shortening to eggs. Mix on medium speed about 10 minutes.
Flour, all-purpose Baking powder Salt Nutmeg, ground Ginger, ground Orange peel, grated	3 lb 4 oz 3 oz 2½ tsp 2 tsp ¼ tsp 1 Tbsp	Combine dry ingredients.

Milk	1 qt	Add dry ingredients and milk alternately to
		   egg mixture.
		Mix to form a soft dough. Add more flour if
		   dough is too soft to handle. Chill.

		Roll dough to ⅜-inch thickness on floured board or table. Cut with floured 2½-inch doughnut cutter. Fry in deep fat for 3–4 minutes.
Sugar, granulated	8 oz	Sprinkle with sugar when partially cool.

Note:
4 oz nonfat dry milk and 1 qt water may be substituted for fluid milk. Increase shortening to 4 oz.

Variation:
Chocolate doughnuts. Substitute 2 oz cocoa for 2 oz flour.

Waffles

| | YIELD: | 6 qt batter |
| | | 50–60 waffles |

Ingredient	Amount	Procedure
Flour, all-purpose	3 lb	Combine dry ingredients in mixer bowl.
Baking powder	3 oz	Blend on low speed for 10 seconds, using flat
Salt	2 Tbsp	beater.
Sugar, granulated	4 oz	
Egg yolks	18 (11 oz)	Combine egg yolks, milk, and melted
Milk	2¼ qt	shortening.
Shortening, melted and cooled	1 lb	Add to dry ingredients. Mix on low speed just enough to moisten dry ingredients.
Egg whites	18 (1 lb 5 oz)	Beat egg whites until stiff but not dry. Fold into batter.
		Use No. 10 dipper to place batter on preheated waffle iron. Bake about 4 minutes.

Note:
9 oz nonfat dry milk and 2¼ qt water may be substituted for fluid milk. Mix dry milk with dry ingredients. Increase shortening to 1 lb 2 oz.

Variation:
Pecan waffles.   Add 6 oz chopped pecans.

Pancakes

| | | YIELD: 7 qt batter |
| | | 100 cakes 4-inch diameter |

Ingredient	Amount	Procedure
Flour, all-purpose	4 lb 8 oz	Place dry ingredients in mixer bowl.
Baking powder	4 oz	Mix on low speed until well blended, using
Salt	2 Tbsp	flat beater.
Sugar, granulated	12 oz	
Eggs	12 (1 lb 5 oz)	In another bowl, beat eggs until light.
Milk	3½ qt	Add milk and melted shortening to eggs.
Shortening, melted and cooled, or salad oil	12 oz	
		Add egg mixture to dry ingredients. Mix on low speed for 30 seconds. If batter is thicker than desired, thin with milk.
		Use No. 16 dipper to place batter on griddle, which has been preheated to 350°F. Cook until surface of cake is full of bubbles and golden brown. Turn pancakes and finish cooking.

Note:
14 oz nonfat dry milk and 3½ qt water may be substituted for the fluid milk. Add dry milk to other dry ingredients. Increase shortening to 1 lb.

Variations:
1. **Apple pancakes.**   Add 1 lb chopped cooked apples and 1 tsp cinnamon or nutmeg.
2. **Blueberry pancakes.**   Fold 1 lb individually quick frozen (IQF) blueberries or well-drained and rinsed canned blueberries carefully into batter after cakes are mixed. Handle carefully to avoid mashing berries. If a large batch is being prepared, add berries to a small portion of the batter at one time. Serve with Blueberry Syrup, p. 584.
3. **Buttermilk pancakes.**   Substitute buttermilk for milk. Add 1 Tbsp baking soda to dry ingredients. 14 oz dry buttermilk and 3½ qt water may be substituted for fluid buttermilk. Add dry buttermilk and soda to other dry ingredients. Increase shortening to 1 lb.
4. **Pecan pancakes.**   Add 1 lb chopped pecans.

Pancake mix

YIELD: 12 lb mix

Ingredient	Amount	Procedure
Flour, all-purpose	9 lb	Combine ingredients in mixer bowl.
Baking powder	8 oz	Blend well, using flat beater or whip.
Salt	¼ cup	Store in covered container.
Sugar, granulated	1 lb 8 oz	
Nonfat dry milk	1 lb 8 oz	

Variation:
Buttermilk pancake mix. Substitute 1 lb 8 oz dry buttermilk for nonfat dry milk and add 2 Tbsp baking soda.

TABLE FOR USING PANCAKE MIX

Ingredient	30 cakes	50 cakes	100 cakes	200 cakes
Pancake mix	2 lb	3 lb	6 lb	12 lb
Eggs, beaten	4 (7 oz)	6 (10 oz)	12 (1 lb 5 oz)	24 (2 lb 10 oz)
Water	1 qt	1½ qt	3 qt	1½ gal
Shortening, melted	4 oz	6 oz	12 oz	1 lb 8 oz

To use mix:
1. Weigh appropriate amount of mix as given in the table.
2. Add beaten eggs, water, and cooled melted fat.
3. Stir only until mix is dampened.
4. Place on hot griddle with No. 16 dipper.
5. Cook until cake is full of bubbles. Turn and finish cooking.

Crepes

YIELD: 50 portions
          5 qt batter
PORTION: 2 crepes

Ingredient	Amount	Procedure
Flour, all-purpose Salt	2 lb 8 oz 1 oz (1½ Tbsp)	Combine flour and salt in mixer bowl.
Eggs	24 (2 lb 10 oz)	Beat eggs until fluffy.
Milk Margarine or butter, melted	2¾ qt 6 oz	Add milk and margarine to eggs. Add to flour and mix until smooth. Batter will be thinner than pancake batter.
		Portion batter with No. 20 (1¾ oz) dipper onto lightly greased hot griddle. Brown lightly on both sides. Crepes will roll best if they are not overbrowned. Stack, layered with waxed paper, until ready to use.

Notes:
  1. Crepes may be folded or rolled around desired filling. (See recipe for Chicken Crepes, p. 440.)
  2. If used for dessert crepes, add 3 Tbsp sugar to dry ingredients. Fill with fruit filling.

French toast

YIELD: 50 slices

Ingredient	Amount	Procedure
Eggs	24 (2 lb 10 oz)	Beat eggs.
Milk Salt Sugar, granulated	1½ qt 1 Tbsp 4 oz	Add milk, salt, and sugar to eggs. Mix well.

Bread slices, day old	50	Dip bread into egg mixture. Do not let bread soak. Fry on a well-greased griddle or in deep fat at 360°F until golden brown. Serve sprinkled with powdered sugar.

Variations:

1. **Batter-fried French toast.** Use 1-inch thick bread slices. Cut into triangles or leave whole. Dip in mixture made from 18 eggs (2 lb), 1¼ qt milk, ⅓ cup vegetable oil, 2 lb 8 oz all-purpose flour, 1 oz (1½ Tbsp) salt, and 1 oz (2⅓ Tbsp) baking powder. Fry in deep fat at 350–375°F until golden brown. Dredge in powdered sugar. Serve with warm maple syrup.
2. **Cinnamon French toast.** Add 1 tsp cinnamon to egg mixture.

Dumplings

STEAM PRESSURE: 5 lb	YIELD: 50 portions
STEAM: 12–15 minutes	PORTION: 2 dumplings

Ingredient	Amount	Procedure
Flour, all-purpose Baking powder Salt	2 lb 8 oz 3 oz (6 Tbsp) 2 Tbsp	Combine dry ingredients in mixer bowl. Mix on low speed until blended, using flat beater.
Eggs, beaten Milk	6 (10 oz) 5½ cups	Combine eggs and milk. Add to dry ingredients. Mix on low speed only until blended.
		Portion batter with No. 24 dipper, onto trays. Do not cover trays. Steam for 12–15 minutes.

Notes:

1. 5 oz nonfat dry milk and 5½ cups water may be substituted for the fluid milk. Add dry milk to other dry ingredients.
2. Serve with meat stew or stewed chicken. Mixture may be dropped onto hot meat mixture in counter pans and steamed.

Variation:

Spaetzles (Egg dumplings). Use 1 lb 4 oz flour, 1 tsp baking powder, 1½ tsp salt, 6 eggs, and 3 cups milk. Mix as above. Drop small bits of dough or press through a colander into 3 gal simmering soup. Cook approximately 5 minutes. Soup must be very hot to cook dumplings.

Fritters

| DEEP-FAT FRYER: 375°F | YIELD: 50 portions |
| FRY: 4–6 minutes | PORTION: 2 fritters |

Ingredient	Amount	Procedure
Flour, all-purpose	4 lb	Combine dry ingredients in mixer bowl.
Salt	1 Tbsp	Mix on low speed for 10 seconds or until
Baking powder	4 oz	mixed, using flat beater.
Sugar, granulated	2 oz	
Eggs, beaten	12 (1 lb 5 oz)	Combine eggs, milk, and melted shortening.
Milk	2 qt	Add to dry ingredients. Mix only enough to
Shortening, melted	6 oz	moisten dry ingredients.
		Portion batter with No. 30 dipper into hot deep fat. Fry at 375°F for 4–6 minutes. Serve with syrup.

Note:
8 oz nonfat dry milk and 2 qt water may be substituted for fluid milk. Add dry milk to other dry ingredients.

Variations:
1. **Apple fritters.** Add 3 lb tart raw apple, peeled and finely chopped, and 1 tsp cinnamon (optional).
2. **Banana fritters.** Add 3 lb bananas, mashed.
3. **Corn fritters.** Add 2 qt whole kernel corn, drained.
4. **Fruit fritters.** Add 1 qt drained fruit: peach, pineapple, or other fruit.
5. **Green chili fritters.** Add 2 lb 8 oz chopped green chilies, drained. Serve with nacho sauce (Nachos, p. 323). Make ¼ recipe.

YEAST BREAD RECIPES

French bread

OVEN: 425°F	YIELD: 5 loaves 1 lb 12 oz
BAKE: 25–30 minutes	

Ingredient	Amount	Procedure
Yeast, active dry Water, warm (110°F) Sugar, granulated	1½ oz 2 cups 2 oz	Combine yeast, water, and sugar. Stir to dissolve yeast. Let stand 10 minutes.
Water, warm Shortening Salt	3 cups 3 oz 1¾ oz	Add to yeast mixture. Mix until blended, using dough arm.

Flour, all-purpose	5 lb	Add flour all at once. Mix on low speed to
		    blend.
		Mix on medium speed for 7–10 minutes, or
		    until sides of bowl are clean and dough
		    makes a rhythmic slapping sound against
		    side of bowl.

1. Let dough rise (proof) in a warm place for about 2 hours, or until double in bulk.
2. Punch down dough by pulling the dough up on all sides, folding over the center and pressing down, then turning over in the bowl.
3. Divide into 5 portions, 1 lb 12 oz each. On lightly floured surface, roll or pat dough to a 12 × 6-inch rectangle.
4. Starting with longer side, roll up tightly, pressing dough into roll with each turn. Pinch edges and ends to seal.
5. Place on greased baking sheet sprinkled with cornmeal.
6. Proof until double in bulk.
7. With sharp knife, make 2 or 3 diagonal slashes across top of loaf.
8. Spray or brush with cold water.
9. Bake at 425°F for 25–30 minutes until golden brown. Spray or brush loaf with cold water several times during baking for a crisp crust.

Notes:
   1. For a shiny, golden crust, brush loaves before baking with an egg glaze made from one slightly beaten egg and 1 Tbsp of water or milk.
   2. After baking, leave uncovered at room temperature to keep the crust crisp.

White bread

OVER: 400°F	YIELD: 16 1½-lb loaves
BAKE: 30–40 minutes	

Ingredient	Amount	Procedure
Yeast, active dry	5 oz	Soften yeast in warm water.
Water, warm (110°F)	3 cups	Let stand 10 minutes.
Sugar, granulated	10 oz	Combine sugar, salt, dry milk, water, and
Salt	5 oz	shortening.
Nonfat dry milk	14 oz	Add softened yeast.
Water, lukewarm	1 gal	Mix on medium speed until blended, using
Shortening, melted	12 oz	dough arm.
Flour, all-purpose	15 lb	Add flour. Mix on low speed about 10 minutes or until dough is smooth and elastic and small blisters appear on the surface.

1. Let dough rise in a warm place (80°F) approximately 2 hours, or until double in bulk.
2. Punch down dough by pulling the dough up on all sides, folding over the center and pressing down, then turning over in the bowl. Shape into 16 loaves, 1 lb 8 oz each (Figure 2.4). Place in greased 5 × 9 × 2¾-inch loaf pans.
3. Let rise approximately 1½ hours, or until double in bulk.
4. Bake at 400°F for 30–40 minutes or until loaves are golden brown and sound hollow when tapped (Figure 2.5).
5. Brush tops of loaves with melted margarine or butter.

Notes:
1. 1¼ gal fresh milk may be substituted for the water and dry milk. Scald milk, combine with sugar, salt, and shortening. Cool to lukewarm before adding to other ingredients.
2. The dough temperature should be about 80°F when mixed.
3. Mixing may be simplified by combining dry yeast with sugar, salt, dry milk, and 2 lb of the flour. Mix thoroughly. In mixer bowl, combine very warm water (120°F) and shortening. Blend on low speed. Add yeast-flour mixture while mixing on low speed. Add remaining flour gradually, mixing until a smooth, elastic dough is formed.
4. Shortening may be increased to 1 lb and sugar to 12 oz if a richer dough is desired.
5. A variety of shapes may be made from the dough (Figures 2.6 and 2.7).

Variations:

1. **Buffet submarine buns.**   Scale dough into 1-lb portions. Shape into 18-inch long loaves. (See Figure 2.4 for shaping instructions.) Use for Submarine Sandwiches (p. 545).
2. **Butter slices.**   Divide dough into thirds. Roll ⅓ inch thick. Cut with 3-inch biscuit cutter or shape into long rolls and cut into slices. Dip in melted margarine or butter. Stand pieces on edge in 5 × 9 × 2¾-inch loaf pans (8 pieces per pan). Let rise and bake.
3. **Cinnamon bread.**   After dough has been divided and scaled into loaves, roll each into a rectangular sheet. Brush with melted margarine or shortening; sprinkle generously with cinnamon and sugar. Roll as for Jelly Roll. Seal edge of dough and place in greased loaf pans sealed edge down. Sprinkle top with cinnamon and sugar.
4. **Raisin bread.**   Add 3 lb raisins to dough after mixing.
5. **Whole wheat bread.**   Substitute whole wheat flour for half of the all-purpose flour.

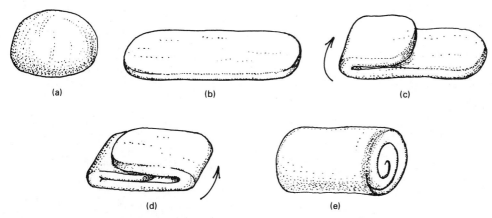

(a)   (b)   (c)

(d)   (e)

Figure 2.4 *Shaping bread loaves: (a) Divide into 1 lb 8 oz balls. (b) Flatten dough to force out air bubbles. (c) and (d) Fold into thirds. (e) Roll tightly and seal by pinching ends together. Smooth out or tuck sealed ends under loaf.*

Figure 2.5 *Well-shaped baked bread loaf, showing fine grain and evenly browned top and sides. Photo provided by Kansas Wheat Commission.*

Figure 2.6 *Basic bread or roll dough is shaped easily into a variety of products. Photo supplied by Fleischmann's Yeast, Inc.*

Figure 2.7 *Varying bread shapes and toppings. Photo supplied by Fleischmann's Yeast, Inc.*

Dilly bread

OVEN: 375°F	YIELD: 5 1½-lb loaves
BAKE: 30–35 minutes	

Ingredient	Amount	Procedure
Yeast, active dry	1¼ oz	Combine yeast, water, and sugar.
Water, warm (110°F)	½ cup	Stir to dissolve yeast.
Sugar, granulated	3 oz	Let stand for later step.
Cottage cheese, cream style	1 lb 12 oz	Combine cottage cheese and water in mixer bowl.
Water, warm	1¼ cups	
Vegetable oil	¼ cup	Add oil, onion, dill weed, and eggs to cottage cheese mixture. Mix to blend, using dough arm.
Dehydrated chopped onion	½ oz	
Dill weed	1 Tbsp	
Eggs, whole	3 (6 oz)	Add yeast mixture.
Flour, all-purpose	4 lb 2 oz	Combine dry ingredients. Add enough to cottage cheese mixture to make a smooth batter. Scrape sides of bowl occasionally. Add remaining flour gradually until dough pulls itself from sides of bowl. Dough will be sticky. Proof until double in bulk.
Salt	1 Tbsp	
Baking soda	½ tsp	
		Scale dough into 5 portions, 1 lb 8 oz each. Shape into loaves. Proof until double in size. Bake at 375°F for 30–35 minutes. Brush with melted margarine.

Whole wheat bread

OVEN: 365°F	YIELD: 5 1½-lb loaves
BAKE: 30–35 minutes	

Ingredient	Amount	Procedure
Yeast, active dry	1¼ oz	Combine yeast, water, and sugar.
Water, warm (110°F)	1¾ cups	Let stand 10 minutes.
Sugar, granulated	1 Tbsp	
Water, hot	1 qt	Combine water, milk, sugar, salt, and
Nonfat dry milk	5 oz	shortening in mixer bowl, using dough arm.
Sugar, granulated	5 oz	Mix until shortening is softened.
Salt	1½ oz	
Shortening	6 oz	
Flour, all-purpose	2 lb 12 oz	Add enough flour to mixture in mixer bowl to make a thin smooth batter. Add yeast mixture. Mix 15 minutes on medium speed.
Flour, whole wheat	1 lb	Add remaining all-purpose flour and whole wheat flour in small amounts to make a soft dough that pulls itself from side of bowl. Mix on low speed about 10 minutes or until dough is smooth and elastic and small blisters appear on the surface.

1. Let dough rise (proof) in warm place for about 2 hours or until double in bulk.
2. Punch down dough. Scale into 5 portions 1 lb 8 oz each.
3. Shape into loaves. Let rise until double in size.
4. Bake at 365°F for 30–35 minutes.
5. Remove bread from oven. Brush with melted margarine.

Note:
Recipe may be used for Whole Wheat Rolls. See p. 154 for procedure. Recipe makes approximately 100 1½-oz rolls. Bake at 375°F for 20–25 minutes.

Variations:
1. **Cornmeal bread.** Delete whole wheat flour. Increase all-purpose flour to 3 lb and add 1 lb cornmeal.
2. **Egg bread.** Delete whole wheat flour. Increase all-purpose flour to 3 lb 12 oz. Decrease water in second step to 1 qt. Add 5 eggs (8 oz), beaten.

3. **Jalapeño cheese bread.**   Delete whole wheat flour. Increase all-purpose flour to 4 lb. Increase yeast to 1½ oz. Reduce nonfat dry milk to 1 oz. Add 3 oz seeded jalapeño peppers, finely chopped, 8 oz green chilies, chopped, 10 oz shredded cheddar cheese, and 8 oz shredded processed cheese.
4. **White loaves.**   Delete whole wheat flour. Increase all-purpose flour to 4 lb.

English muffin bread

OVEN: 375°F
BAKE: 40–50 minutes

YIELD: 5 1½-lb loaves

Ingredient	Amount	Procedure
Water, hot Salad oil	2 cups 1½ cups	Combine water and oil in mixer bowl.
Flour, all-purpose Sugar, granulated Salt Eggs, beaten	2 lb 6 oz 2 oz 6 (10 oz)	Add flour, sugar, salt, and eggs to water-oil mixture.
Yeast, active dry Water, warm (110°F)	1¼ oz 1½ cups	Dissolve yeast in warm water. Add to flour mixture. Mix on medium speed for 2 minutes, using dough arm.
Flour, all-purpose	2 lb	Add enough remaining flour to make a stiff batter. Cover and let rise until light and double in bulk. Punch down dough.
Cornmeal	2 oz	Grease 5 loaf pans (5 × 9 × 2¾-inch). Sprinkle with cornmeal. Scale 1 lb 8 oz dough per pan. Shape and place in pans. Sprinkle with cornmeal. Cover. Let rise until double in bulk. Bake at 375°F for 40–50 minutes or until loaf sounds hollow when tapped lightly.

Oatmeal bread

| OVEN: | 375°F | YIELD: | 5 1½-lb loaves |
| BAKE: | 30–35 minutes | | |

Ingredient	Amount	Procedure
Yeast, active dry Water, warm (110°F) Sugar, granulated	1¼ oz 1 cup 2 tsp	Combine yeast, water, and sugar. Let stand 10 minutes.
Water, hot Rolled oats Molasses Shortening Salt	3 cups 6 oz 1 cup 6 oz 2 Tbsp	Combine in mixer bowl, using dough arm.
Flour, all-purpose	3 lb 8 oz	Add enough flour to rolled oats mixture to make a smooth, thin batter.
Eggs	4 (7 oz)	Add eggs and yeast mixture to batter. Mix 15 minutes on medium speed. Add remaining flour in small amounts, on low speed, to make a soft dough. Let rest 10 minutes. Knead on low speed for 10 minutes or until smooth and elastic, or until a small piece of dough can be stretched to resemble a thin membrane. Let rise until double in bulk.
Rolled oats	4 oz	Grease 5 loaf pans (5 × 9 × 2¾-inch). Coat each pan with ¼ cup rolled oats. Punch down dough. Scale 1 lb 8 oz dough for each pan and shape into a loaf. Place in prepared pans.
Egg whites Water	2 (2 oz) 1 Tbsp	Combine egg whites and water. Brush on loaves and sprinkle with rolled oats. Let rise until double in bulk. Bake at 375°F for 30–35 minutes.

Variation:
Molasses bran bread.   Delete rolled oats and eggs. Increase water to 1 qt. Add 10 oz whole wheat flour, 3 oz unprocessed bran, 1½ tsp ground ginger, and 4 oz nonfat dry milk.

Potato bread

OVEN: 375°F		YIELD: 5 1½-lb loaves
BAKE: 30–35 minutes		

Ingredient	Amount	Procedure
Instant potatoes Water, boiling	5 oz 2 cups	Pour boiling water over potatoes. Set aside for later step.
Yeast, active dry Water, warm (110°F) Sugar, granulated	1 oz 1 cup 1 tsp	Combine yeast, water, and sugar. Let stand 10 minutes.

Water, hot
Nonfat dry milk
Shortening
Sugar, granulated
Salt
	1½ cups
	4 oz
	8 oz
	8 oz
	2 Tbsp
		Combine water, milk, shortening, sugar, and
		  salt in mixer bowl, using dough arm to
		  mix and soften shortening.
		Add potato mixture and mix until well
		  blended.

Flour, all-purpose	3 lb 8 oz	Add enough flour to make a smooth batter. Add yeast mixture. Mix on medium speed for 15 minutes.
Eggs, beaten	5 (8 oz)	Add eggs and mix thoroughly. Add remaining flour in small amounts on low speed to make a soft dough. Proof until double in bulk.
		Punch down dough. Scale into 5 loaves, 1 lb 8 oz each. Place in greased baking pans (5 × 9 × 2¾-inch). Proof until double in size. Bake at 375°F for 30–35 minutes.

Note:
Dough may be shaped into rolls. Recipe makes approximately 100 1½-oz rolls. Bake at 375°F for 20–25 minutes.

Variation:
Portuguese sweet bread. Delete nonfat dry milk. Substitute 6 oz margarine for shortening. Increase sugar to 10 oz and eggs to 6 (10 oz).

Swedish rye bread

OVEN: 375°F	YIELD: 5 1½-lb loaves
BAKE: 40–50 minutes	

Ingredient	Amount	Procedure
Yeast, active dry Water, warm (110°F) Sugar, brown	2¼ oz 2 cups 1 oz	Combine yeast, water, and brown sugar. Let stand 10 minutes.
Water, hot Salt Sugar, brown Molasses Shortening	3 cups 1 Tbsp 6 oz 6 oz (½ cup) 3 oz	Combine in mixer bowl. Mix thoroughly until shortening is softened.
Flour, all-purpose Flour, rye	3 lb 8 oz 12 oz	Combine flours. Add enough to mixture in mixer bowl to make a thin smooth batter. Add yeast mixture. Mix on medium speed for 10 minutes, using dough arm. Reduce mixer speed. Add remaining flour in small amounts to make a soft dough that pulls itself from sides of bowl. Mix for about 10 minutes, until smooth and elastic, or until a small piece of dough can be stretched to resemble a thin membrane. Let rise until double in bulk.
		Punch down dough. Shape into 5 loaves, 1 lb 8 oz each. Place in 5 loaf pans (5 × 9 × 2¾-inch). Let rise until double in bulk. Bake at 375°F for 40–50 minutes or until bread sounds hollow when tapped lightly.

Variations:
1. **Caraway rye bread.**   Add 2 Tbsp caraway seeds to dough.
2. **Limpa rye bread.**   Decrease all-purpose flour to 2 lb and increase rye flour to 2 lb. Add 2 Tbsp fennel seed and 2 Tbsp grated orange peel.
3. **Rye rolls.**   Shape into 1½-oz rolls. Yield: 7 dozen.

Quick roll dough

OVEN: 400°F	YIELD: 10 dozen rolls
BAKE: 15–20 minutes	PORTION: 1½ oz

Ingredient	Amount	Procedure
Yeast, active dry	2 oz	Soften yeast in warm water in mixer bowl.
Water, warm (110°F)	2 qt	
Eggs, beaten	12 (1 lb 5 oz)	Add eggs and melted shortening to yeast
Shortening, melted	8 oz	mixture.
Flour, all-purpose	7 lb 4 oz (variable)	Combine dry ingredients. Add to yeast mixture.
Nonfat dry milk	7 oz	Mix with dough arm on low speed for
Sugar, granulated	8 oz	approximately 10 minutes or until dough is
Salt	2 oz (3 Tbsp)	smooth and elastic and leaves sides of bowl, 15–20 minutes.
		Divide dough into 10 equal portions, approximately 1½ lb each. Let rest 10 minutes.
		Work 1 portion at a time. This will be a rather soft dough.
		Shape into 1½-oz rolls and place on greased baking sheets.
		Let rise until double in bulk, about 45 minutes.
		Bake at 400°F for 15–20 minutes.
		Brush with melted margarine or butter if desired.

Note:
Mixing may be simplified by combining dry yeast with sugar, salt, dry milk, and 2 lb of the flour. Add very warm water (120°F) and melted fat to beaten eggs. Mix. Add remaining flour gradually, mixing until a smooth, elastic dough is formed.

Variations:
See variations for Basic Roll Dough, pp. 154–156.

Basic roll dough

OVEN: 400°F		YIELD: 8 dozen rolls
BAKE: 15–25 minutes		PORTION: 1½ oz

Ingredient	Amount	Procedure
Water, warm (110°F)	1 cup	Combine sugar and water. Add yeast.
Sugar, granulated	1 tsp	Let stand 10 minutes.
Yeast, active dry	1½ oz	
Water, hot	1¼ qt	Place hot water, dry milk, sugar, salt, and
Nonfat dry milk	5 oz	shortening in mixer bowl.
Sugar, granulated	4 oz	Mix thoroughly, using dough arm, until
Salt	2 oz	shortening is softened.
Shortening	8 oz	
Eggs, beaten	4 (7 oz)	Add eggs and softened yeast.
Flour, all-purpose	4 lb 12 oz (variable)	Add flour to make a moderately soft dough. Mix on low speed for about 10 minutes until smooth and satiny or until a small piece of dough can be stretched to resemble a thin membrane.

1. Turn into lightly greased bowl, turn over to grease top. Cover. Let rise in warm place (80°F) until double in bulk.
2. Punch down. Divide into thirds for ease in handling. Shape into 1½-oz rolls or into desired shapes. (See variations.)
3. Let rise until double in bulk.
4. Bake at 400°F for 15–25 minutes or until golden brown.

Notes:
1. 1¼ qt fluid milk may be used in place of nonfat dry milk and hot water. Scald milk, then add sugar, salt, and shortening, and cool to lukewarm.
2. Mixing may be simplified by combining dry yeast with sugar, salt, dry milk, and 2 lb of the flour. Mix thoroughly. In mixer bowl combine 1½ qt very warm water (120°F), shortening, and beaten eggs. Blend on low speed. Add remaining flour gradually, mixing until a smooth, elastic dough is formed.
3. 3–4 hours are required for mixing and rising. For a quicker rising dough, increase yeast to 2 oz.

Variations:
1. **Bowknots.**   Roll 1½-oz portions of dough into strips 9 inches long. Tie loosely into a single knot (see Figure 2.8).

2. **Braids.**   Roll dough ¼ inch thick and cut in strips 6 inches long and ½ inch wide. Cross 3 strips in the middle and braid from center to end. Press ends together and fold under (see Figure 2.9).
3. **Butterhorns.**   Proceed as for Crescents, but do not form crescent shape.
4. **Caramel crowns.**   Increase sugar in dough to 9 oz. Scale dough into balls 1½ oz each. Drop into mixture of 1 lb 4 oz sugar and 3 Tbsp cinnamon to coat balls. Arrange 18 balls in each of 5 greased tube pans, into which 2 oz pecans, halves or coarsely chopped, have been placed. The pan should be about one-third full. Let rise until double in bulk. Bake at 350°F for 30 minutes. Immediately loosen from pan with a spatula. Invert pans to remove. Cool. Serve irregular side up to resemble a crown. Garnish with maraschino cherries.
5. **Cloverleaf rolls.**   Pinch off 1-oz balls of dough. Fit into greased muffin pans, allowing 3 balls for each roll (see Figures 2.10 and 2.11).
6. **Crescents.**   Weigh dough into 12-oz portions. Roll each into a circle ⅛ inch thick and 8 inches in diameter. Cut into 12 triangles and brush top with melted margarine or butter. Beginning at base, roll each triangle, keeping point in middle of roll and bringing ends toward each other to form a crescent shape. Place on greased baking sheets 1½ inches apart (see Figure 2.12).
7. **Dinner or pan rolls.**   Shape dough into 1½-oz balls, place on well-greased baking sheets. Cover. Let rise until light. Brush with mixture made of egg yolk and milk—1 egg yolk to 1 Tbsp milk (see Figure 2.13).
8. **Fan tan or butterflake rolls.**   Weigh dough into 12-oz pieces. Roll out into very thin rectangular sheet. Brush with melted margarine or butter. Cut in strips about 1 inch wide. Pile 6 or 7 strips together. Cut 1½-inch pieces and place on end in greased muffin pans.
9. **Gooey buns.**   Grease sides of one 18 × 26 × 2-inch baking sheet. Combine in kettle or saucepan 8 oz margarine, 1 lb 8 oz brown sugar, and ¾ cup corn syrup. Cook until sugar is dissolved. Pour into prepared pan. Cool. If desired, sprinkle 1 lb pecans over mixture. Place 1½-oz portions of dough 8 × 12 on sugar mixture. Let rise. Bake at 375°F for 20–25 minutes. Remove from oven and turn upside down onto 18 × 26 × 1-inch baking sheet.

(continued)

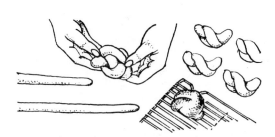

Figure 2.8 *Shaping Bowknot Rolls.*

Figure 2.9 *Braiding yeast dough. Photo supplied by Fleischmann's Yeast, Inc.*

10. **Half-and-half rolls.** Proceed as for Twin Rolls. Use 1 round plain dough and 1 round whole wheat dough for each roll.
11. **Hamburger buns.** Divide dough into 2 portions. Roll each piece of dough into a strip 1½ inches in diameter. Cut strips into pieces approximately 2½ oz each. Round the pieces into balls. Place balls in rows on greased baking sheets 1½–2 inches apart. Let stand 10–15 minutes, then flatten to desired thickness with finger, rolling pin, or another baking sheet.
12. **Hot cross buns.** Divide dough into thirds. Roll ½ inch thick. Cut rounds 3 inches in diameter. Brush tops with beaten egg. Score top of bun to make a cross before baking; or after baking, make a cross on top with frosting. (See p. 165 for variation.)
13. **Hot dog buns.** Divide dough into 2 portions. Roll each piece of dough into a strip 1½ inches in diameter. Cut strips of dough into pieces approximately 2½ oz each. Round pieces of dough; roll into pieces approximately 4½ inches long. Place in rows on greased baking sheets ½ inch apart.
14. **Parker house rolls.** Divide dough into thirds. Roll to ⅓ inch thickness. Cut rounds 2–2½ inches in diameter or form 1½-oz balls. Allow balls to stand for 10 minutes, then elongate with rolling pin. Crease middle of each roll with dull edge of knife. Brush with melted margarine or butter, fold over, and press together with palm of hand (see Figure 2.14).
15. **Popcorn rolls.** Shape dough into 1½-oz balls. Place on greased baking sheets. Snip top of each ball twice with scissors.
16. **Poppy seed rolls.** (a) Proceed as for Twists. Substitute poppy seeds for sugar and cinnamon. (b) Proceed as for Cinnamon Rolls. Substitute poppy seed for sugar, cinnamon, and raisins.
17. **Ribbon rolls.** Weigh dough into 12-oz pieces. Roll ¼ inch thick. Spread with melted margarine or butter. Place on top of this a layer of whole wheat dough rolled to the same thickness. Repeat, using the contrasting dough until 5 layers thick. Cut with a 1½-inch cutter. Place in greased muffin pans with cut surface down.

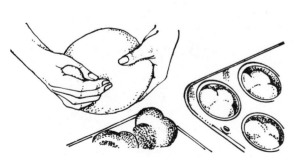

Figure 2.10 *Shaping Cloverleaf Rolls.*

Figure 2.11 *Panning Cloverleaf Rolls. Photo supplied by Fleischmann's Yeast, Inc.*

18. **Rosettes.** Follow directions for Bowknots. After tying, bring one end through center and the other over the side.
19. **Sesame rolls.** Proceed as for Twin Rolls. Brush tops with melted margarine or butter and sprinkle with sesame seeds.
20. **Twin rolls.** Weigh dough into 12-oz pieces. Roll ⅝ inch thick. Cut rounds 1 inch in diameter. Brush with melted margarine or butter. Place on end in well-greased muffin pans, allowing 2 rounds for each roll.
21. **Twists.** Weigh dough into 12-oz pieces. Roll ⅓ inch thick, spread with melted margarine or butter, sugar, and cinnamon. Cut into strips ⅓ × 8 inches, bring both ends together, and twist dough.
22. **Whole wheat rolls.** Substitute 2 lb 6 oz whole wheat flour for 2 lb 6 oz all-purpose flour. Proceed as for Basic Roll Dough.

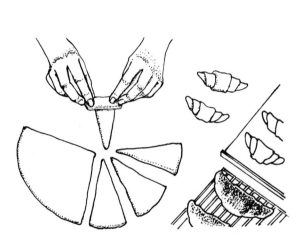

Figure 2.12 *Shaping Crescent Rolls.*

Figure 2.13 *Shaping Dinner or Pan Rolls.*

Figure 2.14 *Shaping Parker House Rolls.*

Refrigerator rolls

OVEN: 400°F	YIELD: 8 dozen rolls
BAKE: 15–20 minutes	

Ingredient	Amount	Procedure
Sugar, granulated	12 oz	Place sugar, shortening, salt, and potatoes in mixer bowl.
Shortening	12 oz	
Salt	2 oz	
Mashed potatoes, hot	1½ cups	
Milk	1¼ qt	Scald milk by heating to point just below boiling.
		Add to mixture in bowl. Mix to blend. Cool to lukewarm.
Yeast, active dry	1 oz	Soften yeast in warm water.
Water, warm (110°F)	1 cup	
Baking soda	1½ tsp	Add softened yeast, soda, and baking powder to milk mixture.
Baking powder	1 Tbsp	
Flour, all-purpose	4 lb	Add just enough flour to make a stiff batter. Let rise 15 minutes.
		Add remaining flour or enough to make a stiff dough.
		Mix until dough is smooth.
		Place in a greased container. Grease top.
		Cover and place in the refrigerator for 24 hours.
		Remove dough from refrigerator and shape into rolls, 1½ oz each.
		Let rise 1–1½ hours or until light.
		Bake at 400°F for 15–20 minutes.

Note:
5 oz nonfat dry milk and 1½ qt water may be substituted for fluid milk. Mix dry milk with soda, baking powder, and part of flour.

Variations:
See variations for Basic Roll Dough, pp. 154–156.

Butter buns

OVEN: 400°F	YIELD: 9–10 dozen buns
BAKE: 15–20 minutes	

Ingredient	Amount	Procedure
Sugar, granulated	1 lb	Place sugar, salt, and margarine in mixer bowl.
Salt	1 oz	
Margarine or butter	1 lb 8 oz	
Milk	3 cups	Scald milk by heating to a point just below boiling. Add to ingredients in mixer bowl and mix. Cool to lukewarm.
Yeast, active dry	2 oz	Soften yeast in warm water.
Water, warm (110°F)	1 cup	
Eggs	12 (1 lb 5 oz)	Beat eggs and yolks. Add eggs, lemon extract, and yeast to milk mixture. Mix until blended.
Egg yolks	16 (10 oz)	
Lemon extract (optional)	4 tsp	
Flour, all-purpose	4 lb 8 oz	Add flour and mix thoroughly, using dough arm. Let rise until double in bulk. Portion with No. 30 dipper into greased muffin pans. Let rise 1 hour. Bake at 400°F for 15–20 minutes.

Note:
3 oz nonfat dry milk and 3 cups water may be substituted for the fluid milk. Combine dry milk with the flour. Increase margarine to 1 lb 9 oz.

Raised muffins

OVEN: 350°F		YIELD: 8 dozen muffins
BAKE: 20 minutes		

Ingredient	Amount	Procedure
Sugar, granulated Salt Shortening	12 oz 2 oz 9 oz	Place sugar, salt, and shortening in mixer bowl.
Milk	1½ qt	Scald milk by heating to point just below boiling. Add to mixture in mixer bowl. Cool to lukewarm.
Yeast, active dry Water, warm (110°F)	1½ oz 1½ cups	Soften yeast in warm water.
Eggs, beaten	12 (1 lb 5 oz)	Add eggs and softened yeast to milk mixture.
Flour, all-purpose	2 lb	Add flour. Beat on medium speed for 10 minutes, using flat beater. Let rise in warm place for 1½ hours.
Flour, all-purpose	2 lb 12 oz (variable)	Add remaining flour. Beat until batter is smooth. Portion with No. 20 dipper into greased muffin pans. Let rise until double in bulk (about 1 hour). Bake at 350°F for 20 minutes.

Note:
6 oz nonfat dry milk and 1½ qt water may be substituted for the fluid milk. Combine dry milk with the first portion of flour.

Herbed tomato buns

OVEN: 375°F		YIELD: 60 buns
BAKE: 15–18 minutes		PORTION: 2 oz

Ingredient	Amount	Procedure
Sugar, brown, light	1 Tbsp	Combine sugar, yeast, and water in mixing bowl. Let stand 10 minutes.
Yeast, active dry	2 oz	
Water, warm (110°F)	1 cup	
Sugar, brown, light	1 oz	Combine in mixer bowl. Mix on low speed until shortening is softened, using dough arm.
Salt	1 oz	
Nonfat dry milk	3 oz	
Shortening	4 oz	
Water, hot	1¼ cups	
Flour, all-purpose	12 oz	Add flour. Mix to a smooth batter.
Tomatoes, canned, drained	1 lb 5 oz	Finely chop tomatoes. Add to mixture in mixer bowl.
Eggs, beaten	5 (8 oz)	Add eggs, seasonings, and yeast mixture. Mix on medium speed for 5 minutes.
Thyme, ground	2 tsp	
Basil leaves	1½ tsp	
Flour, all-purpose	3 lb 8 oz	Add flour gradually to make a soft dough that pulls itself away from sides of bowl, about 10 minutes, or until a small piece of dough can be stretched to resemble a thin membrane. Let rise until double in bulk.
		Punch dough down. Shape into buns, 2 oz each. Place 3 × 5 on greased 18 × 26 × 1-inch baking sheets. Press down to make a flat round bun; let rise (Figure 2.15). Bake at 375°F for 15–18 minutes.

Note:
To make loaves, scale dough into portions, 1 lb 8 oz each, shape into loaves, and place in greased loaf pans (5 × 9 × 2¾-inch). Bake at 375°F for 35–45 minutes or until golden brown and loaves sound hollow when tapped lightly.

Figure 2.15 *Bread or roll dough may be shaped into buns and topped with caraway seeds, coarse salt, or other topping. Used by permission of Red Star Yeast Products, Universal Foods Corporation.*

Figure 2.16 *Yeast breads are made festive by various shapes and frostings such as hot cross buns or frosted can-shaped loaves. Used by permission of Red Star Yeast Products, Universal Foods Corporation.*

Basic sweet roll dough

OVEN: 375°F	YIELD: 8 dozen rolls
BAKE: 20–25 minutes	PORTION: 2 oz

Ingredient	Amount	Procedure
Yeast, active dry	2 oz	Soften yeast in warm water.
Water, warm (110°F)	1½ cups	
Water, hot	3 cups	Combine hot water, dry milk, sugar,
Nonfat dry milk	3 oz	shortening, and salt in mixer bowl.
Sugar, granulated	1 lb	Mix until shortening is softened, using dough
Shortening	1 lb	arm. Cool to lukewarm.
Salt	2 oz	
Eggs, beaten	9 (1 lb)	Add eggs and yeast to mixture in bowl. Blend.
Flour, all-purpose	5–6 lb (variable)	Add flour gradually on low speed. Mix on medium speed to a smooth dough, 5–6 minutes. Do not overmix. Dough should be moderately soft.

1. The dough temperature just after mixing should be 78–82°F.
2. Place dough in lightly greased bowl. Grease top of dough, cover, and let rise in warm place until double in bulk, about 2 hours.
3. Punch down and let rise again, about 1 hour.
4. Punch down and divide into portions for rolls. Let rest 10 minutes.
5. Scale 2 oz per roll. Shape (see Variations) and let rise until rolls are almost double in bulk, about 45 minutes.
6. Bake at 375°F for 20–25 minutes.

Notes:
  1. Mixing may be simplified by combining dry yeast with sugar, salt, dry milk, and 2 lb of the flour. Mix thoroughly. Combine eggs, very warm water (120°F), and melted shortening. Add yeast-flour mixture on low speed. Add remaining flour gradually, mixing until a smooth, elastic dough is formed.
  2. 3 cups fluid milk may be used in place of nonfat dry milk and hot water. Scald milk, then add sugar, salt, and shortening, and cool to lukewarm.
  3. For a quicker rising dough, increase yeast to 3 oz.

Variations:
1. **Cherry nut rolls.** Add 1 tsp nutmeg, ½ tsp almond or lemon extract, 1 lb chopped glacé cherries, and 1 lb chopped pecans to dough. Shape into 1-oz balls. When baked, cover with glaze made of orange juice and powdered sugar.

2. **Cinnamon twists.** Combine 1 lb granulated sugar and 1 Tbsp cinnamon. Melt 4 oz margarine. Dip 2-oz portions of dough into melted margarine, then roll in sugar-cinnamon mixture. Elongate and twist dough portions into 3-inch-long rolls. Place side by side in two 13 × 18-inch baking pans. Bake at 375°F for 20–25 minutes.

3. **Coffee cake.** Scale 4 lb dough, roll out to size of 18 × 26 × 1-inch baking sheet. Cover top of dough with melted margarine or butter and topping (see p. 172). Fruit fillings may be used also.

4. **Crullers.** Roll dough ⅓ inch thick. Cut into strips ½ × 8 inches. Bring two ends together and twist dough. Let rise, then fry in deep fat. Frost with Powdered Sugar Glaze (p. 213) or dip in fine granulated sugar.

5. **Danish pastry.** Roll a 5-lb piece of dough into a rectangular shape about ¼ inch thick. Start at one edge and cover completely ⅔ of the dough with small pieces of hard butter, margarine, or special Danish pastry shortening. The latter is stable at bakeshop temperature and is easier to use than butter or margarine. Use 2–5 oz per lb of dough.

    Fold the unbuttered ⅓ portion of dough over an equal portion of buttered dough. Fold the remaining ⅓ buttered dough over the top to make 3 layers of dough separated by a layer of fat. Roll out dough ¼ inch thick. This completes the first roll. Repeat folding and rolling two or more times. Do not allow the fat to become soft while working with the dough. Let dough rest 45 minutes. Make into desired shapes.

6. **Hot cross buns.** Add to dough 8 oz chopped glacé cherries, 8 oz raisins, 2 Tbsp cinnamon, ¼ tsp cloves, and ¼ tsp nutmeg. Shape into round buns, 1 oz per bun. When baked, make a cross on top with Powdered Sugar Glaze. (Figure 2.16).

7. **Kolaches.** Add 2 Tbsp freshly grated lemon peel to dough. Shape dough into 1-oz balls. Place on lightly greased baking sheet. Let rise until light. Press down center to make cavity and fill with 1 tsp filling. Brush with melted margarine or butter and sprinkle with chopped nuts. Suggested fillings: chopped cooked prunes and dried apricots cooked with sugar and cinnamon; poppy seed mixed with sugar and milk; apricot or peach marmalade.

8. **Long johns.** Roll out dough to a thickness of ½ inch. Cut dough into rectangular pieces ½ × 4 inches. Let rise until double in bulk. Fry in deep fat.

9. **Swedish braids.** Add to dough 1 lb chopped candied fruit, 8 oz pecans, and ½ tsp cardamom seed. Weigh dough into 1¾ lb portions and braid. Place on greased 18 × 26 × 1-inch baking sheets, 4 per pan. When baked, brush with Powdered Sugar Glaze (p. 213) made with milk in place of water.

Cinnamon rolls

OVEN: 375°F		YIELD: 5 dozen rolls
BAKE: 20–25 minutes		PORTION: 3 oz

Ingredient	Amount	Procedure
Basic Roll Dough (p. 154) or Basic Sweet Roll Dough (p. 164)	10 lb (1 recipe)	Let dough rise until double in bulk. Divide dough into 8 portions, 1 lb 4 oz each. Roll each portion into rectangular sheet 9 × 14 × ⅓ inches.
Margarine or butter, melted	12 oz	Spread each sheet with melted margarine.
Sugar, granulated Cinnamon, ground	2 lb 3 Tbsp	Combine sugar and cinnamon. Sprinkle 6 oz over each sheet. Roll as for Jelly Roll (see Figure 2.17). Cut into 1-inch slices. Place cut side down on greased baking sheets, in muffin pans, or round pans (see Figure 2.18). Let rise until double in bulk, about 45 minutes. Bake at 375°F for 20–25 minutes. After removing from oven, spread tops with Powdered Sugar Glaze (p. 213) made with milk in place of water, Peanut Butter Glaze (p. 213), or Chocolate Glaze (p. 212).

Variations:
1. **Butterfly rolls.** Cut rolled dough into 2-inch slices. Press each roll across center parallel to the cut side, with the back of a large knife handle. Press or flatten out the folds of each end. Place on greased baking sheets 1½ inches apart.
2. **Butterscotch rolls.** Use brown sugar and omit cinnamon, if desired. Cream 8 oz margarine or butter, 1 lb 8 oz brown sugar, and 1 tsp salt. Gradually add 1 cup water, blending thoroughly. Spread 10 oz mixture over each of 4 greased 18 × 26 × 1-inch baking sheets or place 1 Tbsp mixture into each greased muffin pan cup. Place rolls cut side down in pans.
3. **Cinnamon raisin rolls.** Use brown sugar in place of granulated sugar and add 8 oz raisins to filling.
4. **Double cinnamon buns.** Proceed as for Butterfly Rolls. Roll sheet of dough from both sides to form a double roll.
5. **Glazed marmalade rolls.** Omit cinnamon. Dip cut slices in additional melted margarine or butter and granulated sugar. When baked, glaze with orange marmalade mixed with powdered

sugar until of a consistency to spread. Apricot marmalade, strawberry jam, or other preserves may be used for the glaze.

6. **Honey rolls.** Substitute honey filling for sugar and cinnamon. Whip 1 lb margarine or butter and 1 lb honey until light and fluffy.

7. **Jumbo cinnamon rolls.** Use 24 lb dough, 3 lb granulated sugar mixed with 5 Tbsp cinnamon, and 1 lb margarine or butter. Divide dough into four 6-lb portions. Roll each portion into approximately 26 × 26-inch square. Spread with 4 oz softened margarine and sprinkle with 1½ cups sugar-cinnamon mixture. Roll into a 26-inch-long roll. Cut into 12 slices 2-inches thick. Pan 2 × 4 in 12 × 18-inch baking pans. Proof until double in bulk. Bake at 350°F for 25 minutes or until done. Frost with Powdered Sugar Glaze (p. 213).

8. **Orange rolls.** Omit cinnamon. Spread with mixture of 1 lb 8 oz granulated sugar and 1 cup fresh grated orange peel. When baked, brush with a glaze made of powdered sugar and orange juice. If desired, use a filling made by creaming 1 lb margarine or butter, 2 Tbsp fresh grated orange peel, 2 lb granulated sugar, and ¾ cup undiluted frozen orange juice concentrate. Spread on dough.

9. **Pecan rolls.** Coarsely chop 1 lb 8 oz pecans. Sprinkle 8 oz over bottom of each of three 12 × 18 × 2-inch baking pans. Combine 2 lb margarine or butter, 2 Tbsp cinnamon, ⅓ cup corn syrup, ⅓ cup water, and 2 lb 8 oz brown sugar. Cook over medium heat until margarine melts. Pour over chopped nuts, 1 lb 12 oz per pan. Place rolls cut side down on mixture.

10. **Sugared snails.** Proceed as for Butterfly Rolls, rolling dough thinner before adding sugar filling. Cut rolled dough into slices ¾ inch thick. Dip cut surface of each roll in granulated sugar. Place on greased baking sheets ½ inch apart, with sugared side up. Allow to stand 10–15 minutes, then flatten before baking.

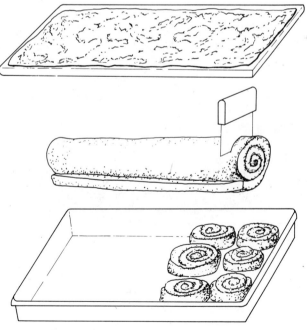

Figure 2.17 *Preparing Cinnamon Rolls.*

Figure 2.18 *Cinnamon Rolls baked in a round pan. Photo supplied by Fleischmann's Yeast, Inc.*

Fruit coffee rings

OVEN: 350°F	YIELD: 8 rings
BAKE: 30 minutes	

Ingredient	Amount	Procedure
Basic Roll Dough (p. 154) or Basic Sweet Roll Dough (p. 164)	10 lb (1 recipe)	Let dough rise until double in bulk. Divide dough into 1½-lb portions. Roll out each portion into a rectangular strip 9 × 14 × ⅓ inches.
Filling (see below)	2 qt	Spread each strip with 1 cup filling. Roll as for Cinnamon Rolls. Arrange in ring mold or 10-inch tube pan. Cut slashes in dough with scissors about 1 inch apart (Figure 2.19). Let rise until double in bulk. Bake at 350°F for 25–30 minutes. Brush with Powdered Sugar Glaze (p. 213).

Suggested Fillings:
Use 2 qt Apricot Filling (p. 218) or apricot preserves, Cranberry Filling (p. 214), Fig Filling (p. 216), Prune-Date Filling (p. 216), orange marmalade, or a mixture of 1 lb margarine or butter and 1 lb honey whipped together until light and fluffy. Dough may be shaped in a twist (see Figure 2.20).

Figure 2.19 *Yeast dough may be filled and shaped into a coffee ring. Used by permission of Red Star Yeast Products, Universal Foods Corporation.*

Figure 2.20 *Nuts, raisins, or other fruits may be added to bread or sweet roll dough and shaped in a twist. Photo supplied by Fleischmann's Yeast, Inc.*

Fillings or toppings for coffee cake and sweet rolls

1. **Almond filling.** Mix 1 lb almond paste, 1 lb granulated sugar, 12 oz margarine or butter, and 4 oz flour. Add 2 eggs and beat until smooth.

2. **Butter cinnamon topping.** Cream 8 oz margarine or butter, 1 lb granulated sugar, 3 Tbsp cinnamon, and ½ tsp salt. Add 4 beaten eggs and 3 oz flour and blend.

3. **Butter crunch topping.** Blend 1 lb granulated sugar, 1 lb margarine or butter, ½ tsp salt, 3 oz honey, and 2 lb flour together to form a crumbly mixture.

4. **Crumb topping.** Mix 8 oz margarine or butter, 12 oz granulated sugar, ½ tsp cinnamon, and 12 oz flour until crumbly. Add 4 oz chopped nuts if desired.

DESSERTS

Cakes, Frostings, and Fillings

CAKES

Cakes may be classified according to two major types: butter or shortened cakes and foam or sponge cakes. A properly balanced formula, correct temperature of ingredients, accurate measurements, controlled mixing of ingredients, proper relationship of batter to pan, and correct oven temperature and baking time are essential to good cake making. Cake flour yields better volume and texture than all-purpose flour and was used in testing recipes in this section, unless otherwise specified.

Butter or shortened cakes

Butter or shortened cakes contain butter, margarine, or other shortening and usually are leavened with baking powder or with baking soda and an acid. They may be mixed by one of the following methods:

CONVENTIONAL METHOD OF MIXING

1. Cream shortening and sugar on medium speed about 10 minutes, or until light and fluffy.
2. Add eggs and beat 3–5 minutes at high speed. Scrape sides of bowl and beater.
3. Combine flour, leavening, and other dry ingredients. Add alternately with the liquid to the creamed mixture.
4. Mix on low speed until thoroughly blended. Scrape sides of bowl occasionally for even mixing.

DOUGH-BATTER METHOD OF MIXING

1. Cream flour, baking powder, and shortening on low speed for 2 minutes. Scrape bowl. Mix 3 minutes.
2. Add sugar, salt, and half the milk. Mix 2 minutes. Scrape bowl. Mix 3 minutes.
3. Combine egg, flavoring, and remaining milk. Add half to flour mixture. Mix 30 seconds. Scrape bowl. Mix 1 minute.
4. Add remaining egg mixture. Mix 1 minute. Scrape bowl. Mix 2½ minutes.

This method requires less time and fewer utensils than the conventional method and yields a good product. See p. 188 for cake made by the dough-batter method.

MUFFIN METHOD OF MIXING
1. Mix dry ingredients, including dry milk if used, in a mixer bowl.
2. Combine liquids (beaten eggs, milk or water, and melted shortening or oil).
3. Add liquids all at once to dry ingredients. Mix at low speed only enough to combine ingredients.

This method is quick and most successful when the cake is used soon after baking.

DRY BLENDING AND WETTING METHOD OF MIXING
1. Blend dry ingredients in mixer bowl and mix on low speed for 1 minute, using flat beater.
2. Add 58.52 percent of the water to the dry ingredients. Mix slightly; flour is not all absorbed.
3. Add fat and mix on low speed for 1 minute, then on medium speed for 4 minutes.
4. Add 12.87 percent of water. Mix 1 minute on low speed, then 3 minutes on medium speed.
5. Add remainder of water (28.61 percent), eggs, and flavoring. Mix 3 minutes on low speed.

This method of mixing produces a cake with good volume and fine texture. Converting water from weight to liquid measurements may produce awkward numbers. A small adjustment of the three liquid additions may need to be made for easy measurement, but the total weight of water should be the same as the amount specified in the recipe. See p. 187 for White Cake made by the dry blending and wetting method of mixing.

Butter or other shortened cakes usually are baked as sheet cakes for ease of preparation and serving but may be baked in layers or as cupcakes. Layer cakes may be made by cutting 18 × 26-inch sheet cakes in half or layering two 13 × 18-inch sheet cakes. (See Figure 2.21 for layering and frosting a sheet cake.) Table 2.3 is a guide for scaling cake batter into various sizes of pans.

A variety of cakes may be made from a basic butter cake or white cake by using a variety of frostings and fillings. Suggested amounts are given in Table 2.4, p. 205.

Foam or sponge cakes

True sponge cakes are leavened chiefly by air incorporated in beaten eggs, although modified sponge cakes may have baking powder added. Foam cakes usually are baked in ungreased tube pans but may be baked in loaves. See Table 2.3 for batter weights.

Figure 2.21 *Layering and frosting a sheet cake: (a) Remove sheet cake from pan after loosening sides. Place top side down on inverted baking sheet. Spread frosting evenly over cake. (b) Carefully turn second cake onto frosted layer. (c) Remove parchment paper if used. (d) Frost top and sides of cake.*

Egg whites for angel food cakes should be at room temperature when beaten. Sugar is added gradually when whites are at the soft peak stage. Beating is continued until the whites are stiff but not dry. Flour and other ingredients are folded in carefully to minimize loss of air from the foam.

Cake mixes

Prepared cake mixes offer the foodservice a wide variety of products that can be produced with fewer and less skilled employees than cakes prepared "from scratch." However, care should be given to the selection of the mix, and the instructions for preparation should be followed carefully to assure high-quality products. The formulas in commercial mixes are balanced, and any deviation such as the substitution of milk for water or the addition of eggs can change the finished product. A dry cake mix may be prepared in the foodservice production area and stored for future use. The recipe for a Master Cake Mix is given on p. 183.

Scaling cake batters

Pans for butter cakes should be greased and/or dusted with flour or lined with parchment paper. Sides of the pan should be left ungreased. A coating mixture may be prepared and brushed on the pans (p. 179).

The correct amount of cake batter per pan is important in producing a cake with consistently high quality and volume. Approximate weights of batter for selected pan sizes are given in Table 2.3. The proper scaling weight for different batters, however, can be determined by actual baking tests and experimentation. Once it has been determined, scaling weights for all pan sizes using the same batter can be calculated mathematically. The formula follows:

Step 1. Experiment, using any pan, to determine the proper scaling weight.

Step 2. Determine the volume of the pan used, expressed as cubic inches.

$$\text{square pan volume} = \text{length} \times \text{width} \times \text{height}$$

$$\text{round pan volume} = 3.14 \times \text{radius squared} \times \text{height}$$

Step 3. Determine the cubic inches per ounce of batter (*factor*) by dividing the cubic inches (as found in Step 2) by the ounces of batter determined to be correct by experimentation in Step 1.

$$\text{factor} = \frac{\text{cubic inches in pan}}{\text{correct scaling weight per pan}}$$

Step 4. Find the proper scaling weight of the particular batter calculated for any pan by dividing the known factor into the pan volume.

$$\frac{\text{volume of cake pan to be used}}{\text{factor}} = \text{proper scaling weight of batter}$$

The following example illustrates the procedure for calculating proper scaling weight for a cake. The proper scaling weight of a 6 × 1½-inch round chocolate cake was determined to be 8 ounces. What would be the scaling weight for the same batter in a 10 × 1½-inch round pan?

Step 1. Through experimentation, it was determined that 8 oz in a 6 × 1½-inch pan was correct.

Step 2. Volume = $3.14 \times 3^2 \times 1.5 = 42$ cubic inches.

Step 3.

$$\frac{42 \text{ cubic inches}}{8 \text{ ounces}} = 5.25 \text{ cubic inches per ounce} = \text{factor}$$

Step 4. 10-inch pan volume = $3.14 \times 5^2 \times 1.5 = 118$ cubic inches.

$$\frac{118 \text{ cubic inches}}{5.25 \text{ (factor)}} = 22.5 \text{ ounces scaling weight}$$

TABLE 2.3 APPROXIMATE SCALING WEIGHTS AND YIELDS FOR CAKES

Pan size	Approximate weight per pan	Yield	Type of cake
12 × 18 × 2 inches	4–5 lb	30 portions (5 × 6)	Butter, sheet
13 × 18 × 1 inches (half size baking sheet)	2–2½ lb	48 portions (6 × 8)	Butter, layer
13 × 18 × 1 inches	1¼–1½ lb	12 portions	Jelly roll, sheet
18 × 26 × 2 inches	8–10 lb	60 portions (6 × 10)	Butter, sheet
9-inch round	20–32 oz	16 portions	Butter, layer
10-inch tube	28–40 oz	14 portions	Angel food, sponge
Cupcakes	1¾ oz each		Butter

Quality standards for cakes

Standards for butter cakes

Appearance:

Smooth surface, golden brown
Contour has slightly rounded top
High volume

Deviation: cause

Peaked or cracked: too much flour, oven too hot
Pale: too little sugar, wrong type pan, underbaked
Too dark: too much sugar, oven too hot, overbaked
Low volume: too much shortening, too much liquid, oven temperature too low, wrong size pan

(continued)

Texture:

Fine grained, small evenly distributed cell walls
Light but not crumbly

Large cells: too little liquid, insufficient mixing, too much shortening, too cool oven
Compact: overbeating
Crumbly: too much shortening or sugar, insufficient mixing
Tunnels: too much egg, too little sugar, overmixing, too hot oven

Crumb:

Soft, velvety, moist, light, tender

Dry: too little sugar, too much leavening, too long baking
Soggy: underbaking, too much shortening, undermixed
Tough: overmixing, overbaking, too much shortening

Flavor:

Delicate, sweet, well-blended

Flat: too little salt
Unpleasant, bitter: strong or rancid shortening, poor quality eggs or flavoring

Standards for angel, sponge, or chiffon cakes

Deviation: cause

Appearance:

Thin, golden brown crust, rounded top, slightly split in the middle

Thick, hard crust: too hot oven, too long baking
Sticky crust: too much sugar, insufficient baking
Large cracks: too stiff a mixture, overbeaten eggs, too hot an oven

Texture:

Fine texture, thin cell walls, light in weight in proportion to size

Heavy, low volume: loss of air in mixing, grease on equipment or bowl

Crumb:

Moist and tender

Dry: overbeaten egg whites, too much flour, too little sugar, overbaking, too cool an oven
Tough: too high a baking temperature, too much mixing
Coarse: underbeaten eggs, too little mixing, too hot an oven

Flavor:

Delicate

Unpleasant: poor quality eggs or flavorings

CAKE RECIPES

Coating for baking pans

		YIELD: 2 lb 12 oz
Ingredient	**Amount**	**Procedure**
Shortening	1 lb	Mix shortening until creamy.
Flour, all-purpose	12 oz	Add flour gradually, whipping until smooth. Start on low mixer speed, then move to medium.
Oil, cooking	2 cups	Add oil very slowly and whip until light and frothy. Store at room temperature in tightly closed containers. Apply to pans with pastry brush. Use to grease cake pans or cookie sheets.

Angel food cake

OVEN: 350°F	YIELD: 42 portions
BAKE: 50–55 minutes	3 10-inch cakes
	PORTION: 14 slices per cake

Ingredient	Amount	Procedure
Egg whites, fresh or frozen	2 lb 8 oz (5 cups)	Beat egg whites on high speed for 1 minute, using whip attachment.
Salt Cream of tartar	1 tsp 2 Tbsp	Add salt and cream of tartar. Continue beating until egg whites are just stiff enough to hold their shape.
Sugar, granulated	1 lb 8 oz	Add sugar slowly while beating on medium speed.
Vanilla Almond extract (optional)	1 Tbsp 1 tsp	Add flavorings. Continue beating on high speed for 2 minutes, or until mixture will stand in stiff peaks.
Sugar, granulated Flour, cake	12 oz 12 oz	Mix sugar and flour. Sift three times. Gradually add to egg whites on low speed. Continue folding 2 minutes after last addition. Scale into 3 ungreased tube cake pans, 1 lb 12 oz per pan. Bake at 350°F for 50–55 minutes or at 400°F for 35 minutes. Invert cakes to cool.

Note:
To add sugar-flour mixture by hand, remove bowl from machine and fold mixture into meringue, using wire whip or spatula, adding 1 cup at a time. Mix about 5 strokes after each addition.

Variations:
1. **Chocolate angel food cake.**   Substitute 1½ oz cocoa for 1½ oz flour.
2. **Frozen-filled angel food cake.**   Cut each cake crosswise into 3 slices. Spread 1 pt softened strawberry ice cream on first layer and cover with cake slice. Spread second slice with 1 pt softened pistachio ice cream. Top with remaining slice. Frost top and sides with sweetened whipped cream (1 cup cream, 2 Tbsp powdered sugar, and ½ tsp vanilla per cake). Cover with toasted coconut. Freeze. Remove from freezer 1 hour before serving. Other ice cream or sherbet may be used.
3. **Orange-filled angel food cake.**   Cut each cake crosswise into 3 slices. Spread Orange Filling (p. 217) between layers, and frost top and sides with Orange Frosting (p. 211).

Yellow angel food (Egg yolk sponge cake)

OVEN: 350°F
BAKE: 30–45 minutes

YIELD: 42 portions
      3 10-inch cakes
PORTION: 14 slices per cake

Ingredient	Amount	Procedure
Egg yolks	1 lb 8 oz (3 cups)	Beat egg yolks on medium speed, using whip attachment.
Water, boiling	2 cups	Add water to egg yolks. Beat on high speed until light, about 5 minutes.
Sugar, granulated	1 lb	Sift sugar. Add to egg mixture gradually, beating on high speed while adding.
Flour, cake Sugar, granulated	12 oz 12 oz	Combine flour and sugar. Add on low speed to egg mixture.
Flour, cake Baking powder Salt	10 oz 4½ tsp 1 tsp	Mix flour, baking powder, and salt.
Lemon juice Fresh lemon peel, grated	3 Tbsp 1 Tbsp	On low speed, gradually add flour alternately with lemon juice and peel to egg mixture.
Vanilla Lemon extract	1 Tbsp 1½ tsp	Add flavoring and continue mixing on low speed for 2 minutes.
		Scale into 3 ungreased tube cake pans, 1 lb 14 oz per pan. Bake at 350°F for 30–45 minutes. Immediately upon removal from oven, invert cakes to cool.

Orange chiffon cake

OVEN: 350°F
BAKE: 45–50 minutes

YIELD: 42 portions
3 10-inch cakes
PORTION: 14 slices per cake

Ingredient	Amount	Procedure
Flour, cake Baking powder Salt Sugar, granulated	1 lb 8 oz 1½ oz (3 Tbsp) 2 tsp 1 lb 3 oz	Combine dry ingredients in mixer bowl. Mix on low speed for about 10 seconds, or until blended, using flat beater.
Egg yolks, beaten Salad oil Water	1 lb (2 cups) 1½ cups 1½ cups	Combine egg yolks, salad oil, and water. Add to dry ingredients. Mix on medium speed until smooth.
Orange juice Orange peel, grated	1 cup 2 Tbsp	Add orange juice and peel gradually. Mix well after each addition, but avoid overmixing.
Egg whites Cream of tartar	1 lb 4 oz (2½ cups) 2 tsp	Whip egg whites until foamy. Add cream of tartar and continue beating until egg whites form soft peaks.
Sugar, granulated	1 lb 2 oz	Add sugar gradually and continue beating until very stiff. Fold gently into batter. Scale into 3 ungreased tube cake pans, 2 lb 12 oz per pan. Bake at 350°F for 45–50 minutes. Immediately on removal from oven, invert cakes to cool.
Orange Frosting (p. 211)	1½ qt	When cake has cooled, remove from pan and frost.

Variations:
1. **Cocoa chiffon cake.** Omit orange juice and peel. Add 5 oz cocoa to dry ingredients. Increase water to 2⅓ cups. Add 1 Tbsp vanilla.
2. **Walnut chiffon cake.** Omit orange juice and peel. Increase water to 2⅓ cups. Add 2 Tbsp vanilla and 12 oz finely chopped walnuts. Frost with Burnt Butter Frosting (p. 208).

Master cake mix

YIELD: 29 lb mix
7 cakes 12 × 18 × 2 inches

Ingredient	Amount	Procedure
Flour, cake	10 lb 8 oz	Mix flour, dry milk, baking powder, salt, and sugar on low speed for 1 minute.
Nonfat dry milk	1 lb 12 oz	
Baking powder, double-acting	8 oz	
Salt	2 oz	
Sugar, granulated	5 lb 4 oz	
Sugar, granulated	6 lb	Divide sugar into 2-lb portions.
Shortening, hydrogenated, emulsified	4 lb 14 oz	Cream shortening on medium speed for 3 minutes, using flat beater. Scrape sides of bowl and beater.
		Add 2 lb sugar. Cream on medium speed 1 minute. Repeat until all sugar is added. Scrape sides of bowl and beater.
		Add 4 qt blended dry ingredients. Mix on low speed 1 minute. Repeat once more. Lower bowl, add remaining dry ingredients. Blend on low speed 1 minute while slowly raising mixer bowl. Mix should resemble cornmeal in consistency. Store in tightly covered containers.

Note:
The recipe for using Master Cake Mix is on p. 186.

Plain cake

OVEN: 350°F
BAKE: 35–40 minutes

YIELD: 60 portions
  2 pans 12 × 18 × 2 inches
PORTION: 2½ × 3 inch

Ingredient	Amount	Procedure
Flour, cake Baking powder Shortening, hydrogenated	2 lb 5 oz 3¾ Tbsp 1 lb	Place flour, baking powder, and shortening in mixer bowl. Mix on low speed for 2 minutes, using flat beater. Scrape sides of bowl. Mix 3 minutes.
Sugar, granulated Salt Milk	2 lb 13 oz 2 tsp 2 cups	Combine sugar, salt, and milk. Add to flour mixture. Mix on low speed 2 minutes. Scrape sides of bowl. Mix 3 minutes.
Eggs Milk Vanilla	8 (14 oz) 2½ cups 2 Tbsp	Combine eggs, milk, and vanilla. Add half to flour mixture. Mix on low speed 30 seconds. Scrape sides of bowl. Mix 1 minute. Add remaining egg mixture. Mix 1 minute. Scrape sides of bowl. Mix 2½ minutes.
		Scale batter into 2 greased 12 × 18 × 2-inch baking pans 4 lb 10 oz per pan. Bake at 350°F for 35–40 minutes. Cut 5 × 6.

Notes:
  1. 4 oz nonfat dry milk and 4½ cups water may be substituted for fluid milk. Add dry milk to flour mixture. Divide water as stated in recipe.
  2. May be baked in one 18 × 26 × 2-inch pan. Cut 6 × 10 for 60 portions.
  3. For layer cakes, scale 1 lb 9 oz batter into each of six 9-inch layer cake pans.
  4. For cupcakes, portion with No. 30 dipper into muffin pans. Yield 8½ dozen.

Variations:
1. **Boston cream pie.** For two 12 × 18-inch pies, scale batter into 4 pans, 2 lb 5 oz each. When baked, spread Custard Filling (p. 215) on 2 cakes, 3 lb 3 oz each. Place other cakes on top. Cover with Chocolate Glaze (p. 212), 1 lb per cake. Cut 5 × 6.

For two 18 × 26-inch pies, scale 4 lb 10 oz into each of 2 pans. Use 6 lb 6 oz Custard Filling and 2 lb Chocolate Glaze. Cut 6 × 10.

For 9-inch layers, scale batter into 8 pans, 1 lb 2 oz per pan. Use ½ recipe Custard Filling. Spread 1½ cups on each of 4 layers. Use ½ recipe Chocolate Glaze, spreading ½ cup on each pie.

Powdered sugar sifted over top of pies may be substituted for Chocolate Glaze.

2. **Cottage pudding.**   Cut cake into squares and serve with No. 20 dipper of fruit, lemon, nutmeg, or other sauce.

3. **Dutch apple cake.**   After the cake batter is poured into baking pans, arrange 2 lb 8 oz peeled sliced apples in rows over each pan. Sprinkle over top of each pan 4 oz granulated sugar and 1 tsp cinnamon, mixed.

4. **Lazy daisy cake.**   Mix 1 lb 2 oz melted margarine or butter, 2 lb brown sugar, 2 lb coconut, and 1½ cups half and half, or enough to moisten to consistency for spreading. Spread over baked cake, 3 lb per pan, and brown under the broiler or in the oven.

5. **Marble cake.**   Divide batter into 2 portions after mixing. To 1 portion add 3 Tbsp cocoa, 1 Tbsp cinnamon, and 1 tsp nutmeg. Place batters alternately in cake pans; swirl with knife.

6. **Pineapple upside-down cake.**   Mix 1 No. 10 can drained crushed pineapple (or tidbits), 8 oz melted margarine or butter, 12 oz brown sugar, and 8 oz chopped nuts. Pour 4 lb 3 oz in each 12 × 18-inch baking pan. Pour cake batter over mixture. Apricots or peaches may be substituted for pineapple.

7. **Praline cake.**   Substitute chopped pecans for coconut in Lazy Daisy Cake.

Plain cake (Using master mix)

OVEN:	350°F
BAKE:	45 minutes

YIELD: 60 portions
2 pans 12 × 18 × 2 inches
PORTION: 2½ × 3 inches

Ingredient	Amount	Procedure
Master Cake Mix (p. 183)	5 lb 10 oz	Place mix in mixer bowl.
Eggs	9 (1 lb)	Add eggs, vanilla, and water.
Vanilla	4 tsp	Mix on low speed 2 minutes, using flat
Water	2 cups	beater. Scrape sides of bowl.
		Mix on medium speed 3 minutes. Scrape sides of bowl and beater.
Water	1⅓ cups	Add water gradually, mixing on low speed for 2 minutes.
		Scrape sides of bowl and mix on medium speed for 1 minute.
		Scale batter into 2 lightly greased 12 × 18 × 2-inch baking pans, 4 lb per pan. Bake at 350°F for 45 minutes. Cool and frost. Cut 5 × 6.

Note:
May be baked in one 18 × 26 × 2-inch pan. Cut 6 × 10 for 60 portions.

Variations:
1. **Chocolate cake.**   Blend 5 oz cocoa and 2 tsp baking soda with mix.
2. **Spice cake.**   Blend 2 Tbsp cinnamon, 1 Tbsp nutmeg, 2 Tbsp cloves, and 1½ tsp allspice with cake mix.
See p. 184 for additional variations.

White cake (Dry blending method)

OVEN: 350°F
BAKE: 25–30 minutes

YIELD: 60 portions
2 pans 12 × 18 × 2 inches
PORTION: 2½ × 3 inches

Ingredient	Amount	Procedure
Flour, cake	1 lb 13 oz	Combine dry ingredients in mixer bowl. Mix on low speed for 1 minute.
Sugar, granulated	2 lb 5 oz	
Nonfat dry milk	3 oz	
Salt	4 tsp	
Baking powder	1¾ oz	
Water	1¾ cups	Add water. Mix slightly.
Shortening	1 lb	Add shortening. Mix 1 minute on low speed. Mix 4 minutes on medium speed.
Water	½ cup	Add water. Mix 1 minute on low speed. Scrape bowl. Mix 3 minutes on medium speed. Scrape bowl and beater.
Egg whites	1 lb	Add eggs, water, and vanilla. Mix 3 minutes on low speed.
Eggs, whole	3 oz	
Water	1 cup	
Vanilla	2 Tbsp	
		Scale batter into two 12 × 18 × 2-inch pans, 4 lb per pan. Bake at 350°F for 25–30 minutes. Cool and frost.

Note:
May be baked in one 18 × 26 × 2-inch pan. Cut 6 × 10 for 60 portions.

Variations:
See p. 188.

White cake (Dough-batter method)

OVEN: 350°F
BAKE: 35–40 minutes

YIELD: 60 portions
2 pans 12 × 18 × 2 inches
PORTION: 2½ × 3 inches

Ingredient	Amount	Procedure
Flour, cake Baking powder Shortening, hydrogenated	2 lb 4 oz 1½ oz 1 lb 2 oz	Place flour, baking powder, and shortening in mixer bowl. Mix on low speed for 2 minutes, using flat beater. Scrape sides of bowl. Mix 3 minutes.
Sugar, granulated Salt Milk	2 lb 4 oz 1 Tbsp 2 cups	Combine sugar, salt, and milk. Add to flour mixture. Mix on low speed 2 minutes. Scrape sides of bowl. Mix 3 minutes.
Egg whites Milk Vanilla	12 (14 oz) 1⅓ cups 2 Tbsp	Combine egg whites, milk, and vanilla. Add half to mixture in bowl. Mix on low speed for 30 seconds. Scrape sides of bowl. Mix 1 minute. Add remaining egg-milk mixture. Mix on low speed for 1 minute. Scrape sides of bowl. Mix 2½ minutes.
		Scale batter into 2 greased 12 × 18 × 2-inch pans, 5 lb 7 oz per pan. Bake at 350°F for 35–40 minutes. Cool and frost. Cut 5 × 6.

Notes:
1. 3 oz nonfat dry milk and 3⅓ cups water may be substituted for fluid milk. Increase shortening to 1 lb 3 oz. Mix dry milk with flour.
2. May be baked in one 18 × 26 × 2-inch pan. Cut 6 × 10 for 60 portions.
3. For six 9-inch layer pans, scale 1 lb 6 oz per pan.

Variations:
1. **Chocolate chip cake.** Add 12 oz chocolate chips to batter.
2. **Coconut lime cake.** Scale into six 9-inch layer cake pans. When baked, cool, then spread Lime Filling (p. 217) between layers. Frost with Fluffy Frosting (p. 208) or Ice Cream Frosting (p. 207). Sprinkle with toasted flaked coconut.

3. **Cupcakes.**   Portion batter with No. 20 dipper into muffin pans or paper baking cups. Yield: 7 dozen.
4. **Lady Baltimore cake.**   Bake cake in layers. Prepare one recipe Ice Cream Frosting (p. 207). To 1½ qt frosting, add 1 tsp orange juice, 4 oz macaroon crumbs, 5 oz chopped almonds, and 6 oz chopped raisins. Spread on bottom layers; place second layers on top and spread with filling. Frost tops and sides with remaining frosting.
5. **Poppy seed cake.**   Add 6 oz poppy seeds that have been soaked in part of the milk. Frost with Chocolate Frosting (p. 209).
6. **Silver white cake.**   Scale batter into six 9-inch layer cake pans. When baked, cool and then spread Lemon Filling (p. 216) between layers. Frost with Ice Cream Frosting (p. 207).
7. **Starburst cake.**   Bake in two 12 × 18 × 2-inch pans. While cake is warm, perforate top with a meat fork every half inch. Prepare 2 qt flavored gelatin, and while still liquid slowly pour 1 qt over each cake. Cool and frost with Ice Cream Frosting (p. 207) or other white frosting.

Carrot cake

OVEN: 325°F
BAKE: 40–45 minutes

YIELD: 60 portions
        2 pans 12 × 18 × 2 inches
PORTION: 2½ × 3 inches

Ingredient	Amount	Procedure
Sugar, granulated	2 lb 6 oz	Combine sugar, oil, and eggs.
Cooking oil	2½ cups	Beat 2 minutes on medium speed, using flat
Eggs	1 lb (9)	beater.
Flour, all-purpose	1 lb 12 oz	Combine dry ingredients.
Salt	1 oz (1½ Tbsp)	Add to oil mixture and beat 1 minute.
Baking soda	⅔ oz (5 tsp)	
Cinnamon, ground	⅔ oz (3 Tbsp)	
Carrots, raw, grated	2 lb 8 oz	Add carrots and nuts. Mix until blended.
Nuts, chopped	1 lb	
		Scale batter into two 12 × 18 × 2-inch pans, 5 lb per pan.
		Bake at 325°F for 40–45 minutes.
		Frost with Cream Cheese Frosting (p. 210).
		Cut 5 × 6.

Note:
May be baked in one 18 × 26 × 2-inch pan cut 6 × 10 for 60 portions.

Applesauce cake

OVEN: 350°F	YIELD: 60 portions
BAKE: 40–45 minutes	2 pans 12 × 18 × 2 inches
	PORTION: 2½ × 3 inches

Ingredient	Amount	Procedure
Shortening, hydrogenated Sugar, granulated	1 lb 1 lb 14 oz	Cream shortening and sugar on medium speed for 10 minutes, using flat beater.
Eggs	8 (14 oz)	Add eggs to creamed mixture. Mix on medium speed for 5 minutes.
Flour, cake Baking powder Salt Baking soda Cinnamon, ground Cloves, ground Nutmeg, ground	1 lb 12 oz 2½ Tbsp 1¾ tsp ½ tsp 2½ tsp 1 tsp 1 tsp	Combine dry ingredients.
Water	2½ cups	Add dry ingredients alternately with water on low speed to creamed mixture, ending with dry.
Applesauce Raisins Nuts, chopped	2½ cups 1 lb 4 oz 10 oz	Add remaining ingredients. Mix on low speed only to blend.
		Scale batter into 2 greased 12 × 18 × 2-inch baking pans, 5 lb per pan. Bake at 350°F for 40–45 minutes. Cool and frost. See Note 3 for suggested frostings. Cut 5 × 6.

Notes:
1. May be baked in one 18 × 26 × 2-inch pan. Cut 6 × 10 for 60 portions.
2. This cake is too tender to bake in layers.
3. Suggested frostings: Ice Cream Frosting (p. 207), Fluffy Brown Sugar Frosting (p. 208), or Cream Cheese Frosting (p. 210).

Banana cake

OVEN: 350°F	YIELD: 48 portions
BAKE: 25–30 minutes	3 2-layer cakes (9-inch)
	PORTION: 16 slices per cake

Ingredient	Amount	Procedure
Shortening, hydrogenated	1 lb	Cream shortening, sugar, and vanilla on medium speed for 10 minutes, using flat beater.
Sugar, granulated	2 lb	
Vanilla	1 Tbsp	
Eggs	8 (14 oz)	Add eggs to creamed mixture and mix on medium speed for 3 minutes, then add bananas and mix for an additional 2 minutes.
Bananas, mashed	2 lb (4 cups)	
Flour, cake	2 lb	Combine dry ingredients.
Salt	1¼ tsp	
Baking powder	3⅓ Tbsp	
Baking soda	2 tsp	
Buttermilk	1 cup	Add dry ingredients alternately with buttermilk on low speed. Mix on medium speed 2–3 minutes.
		Scale batter into 6 greased 9-inch layer cake pans, 1 lb 6 oz per pan. Bake at 350°F for 25–30 minutes. Cool. Remove from pans and frost. See Note 3 for suggested frostings.

Notes:
1. May be baked in two 12 × 18 × 2-inch pans, scaled 4 lb 3 oz per pan. Cut 5 × 6 for 30 portions per pan.
2. For sheet cake, bake in one 18 × 26 × 2-inch pan. Cut 6 × 10 for 60 portions.
3. Suggested frostings: Creamy Frosting (p. 210) or Cream Cheese Frosting (p. 210).

Burnt sugar cake

OVER: 375°F
BAKE: 35–40 minutes

YIELD: 60 portions
        2 pans 12 × 18 × 2 inches
PORTION: 2½ × 3 inches

Ingredient	Amount	Procedure
Sugar, granulated Shortening, hydrogenated	2 lb 11 oz 1 lb	Cream shortening and sugar on medium speed for 10 minutes, using flat beater.
Egg yolks	8 (5 oz)	Add egg yolks to creamed mixture and mix on medium speed for 5 minutes.
Milk Water Burnt sugar syrup[a] Vanilla	2 cups 2 cups ⅔ cup 4 tsp	Combine liquids.
Flour, cake Baking powder Salt	2 lb 2 oz 2⅔ Tbsp 1¼ tsp	Combine dry ingredients. Add to creamed mixture alternately with liquids, on low speed. Scrape sides of bowl. Mix 2 minutes.
Egg whites	8 (9 oz)	Beat egg whites until they form soft peaks. Fold into batter on low speed.
		Scale batter into 2 greased 12 × 18 × 2-inch baking pans, 4 lb 8 oz per pan. Bake at 375°F for 35–40 minutes. Cool and frost. See Note 2 for suggested frostings. Cut 5 × 6.

Notes:
  1. May be baked in one 18 × 26 × 2-inch pan cut 6 × 10; or in eight 9-inch layers, scaled 1 lb 2 oz per pan.
  2. Suggested frostings: Burnt Butter Frosting (p. 208), Creamy Frosting (p. 210), Cream Cheese Frosting (p. 210), or Ice Cream Frosting (p. 207).

[a]**Burnt sugar syrup.** Place ⅓ cup granulated sugar in pan and melt slowly, stirring constantly. Cook until light brown (caramelized), being careful not to scorch. Add ⅓ cup boiling water. Cook slowly until a syrup is formed. For larger amounts, use 1 lb sugar and 2 cups boiling water.

Chocolate cake

OVEN: 350°F	YIELD: 60 portions	
BAKE: 25–30 minutes	2 pans 12 × 18 × 2 inches	
	PORTION: 2½ × 3 inches	

Ingredient	Amount	Procedure
Flour, cake	1 lb 8 oz	Combine dry ingredients in mixer bowl.
Cocoa	5 oz	Mix on low speed for 1 minute, using flat
Sugar, granulated	2 lb 5 oz	beater.
Nonfat dry milk	2½ oz	
Salt	1 Tbsp	
Baking powder	1 oz	
Baking soda	3½ tsp	
Water	1½ cups	Add to dry ingredients.
Shortening	1 lb	Mix on low speed for 1 minute.
		Mix on medium speed for 3 minutes.
		Scrape sides of bowl and beater.
Water	1½ cups	Add and mix on low speed for 1 minute.
		Mix on medium speed for 2 minutes.
Eggs	10 (1 lb 2 oz)	Blend in eggs. Mix on low speed for 2 minutes.
Water	1 cup	
Vanilla	¼ cup	
		Scale batter into two 12 × 18 × 2-inch baking pans, 4 lb 2 oz per pan.
		Bake at 350°F for 25–30 minutes.
		Cool and frost. See Note 2 for suggested frostings.
		Cut 5 × 6.

Notes:
 1. Cake may be baked in one 18 × 26 × 2-inch pan. Cut 6 × 10 for 60 servings.
 2. Suggested frostings: Chocolate Butter Cream Frosting (p. 209), Mocha Frosting (p. 212), or Ice Cream Frosting (p. 207).

Fudge cake

OVEN: 350°F	YIELD: 48 portions
BAKE: 25–30 minutes	3 2-layer cakes (9-inch)
	PORTION: 16 slices per cake

Ingredient	Amount	Procedure
Shortening, hydrogenated Sugar, granulated Vanilla	12 oz 2 lb 1 Tbsp	Cream shortening, sugar, and vanilla on medium speed for 10 minutes, using flat beater.
Eggs	6 (10 oz)	Add eggs and mix on medium speed for 5 minutes.
Cocoa Water, hot	5 oz 1½ cups	Mix cocoa and hot water.
Flour, cake Salt Baking soda	1 lb 12 oz 1 tsp 1½ Tbsp	Combine flour, salt, and soda.
Buttermilk	3 cups	Add dry ingredients alternately with buttermilk and cocoa to creamed mixture on low speed. Scrape sides of bowl. Continue mixing until smooth and ingredients are mixed.
		Scale batter into 6 greased 9-inch layer cake pans, 1 lb 4 oz per pan. Bake at 350°F for 25–30 minutes. Cool. Remove from pans and frost. See Note 2.

Notes:
  1. For 12 × 18-inch layer cake, scale into two 12 × 18 × 2-inch or two 13 × 18 × 1-inch pans, 3 lb 13 oz per pan. When baked and cooled, frost one cake, then remove cake from pan and place on top (see Figure 2.21). Frost top and sides.
  2. Suggested frostings: Chocolate Butter Cream Frosting (p. 209), Ice Cream Frosting (p. 207), or Mocha Frosting (p. 212).

Variations:
1. **Chocolate cupcakes.** Portion with No. 20 dipper into muffin pans or paper liners. Yield: 5 dozen.
2. **Chocolate sheet cake.** Bake in one 18 × 26 × 2-inch baking pan. Cut 6 × 10 for 60 portions.

German sweet chocolate cake

OVEN: 350°F
BAKE: 40–45 minutes

YIELD: 60 portions
       2 pans 12 × 18 × 2 inches
PORTION: 2½ × 3 inches

Ingredient	Amount	Procedure
German sweet chocolate Water, boiling Vanilla	10 oz 1¼ cups 2½ tsp	Melt chocolate in water. Cool. Add vanilla. Set aside.
Shortening, hydrogenated Sugar, granulated	1 lb 4 oz 2 lb 8 oz	Cream shortening and sugar on medium speed for 10 minutes, using flat beater.
Egg yolks	10 (6 oz)	Add egg yolks one at a time. Beat well after each addition. Add chocolate mixture and blend.
Flour, cake Salt Baking soda	1 lb 9 oz 1¼ tsp 2½ tsp	Combine flour, salt, and soda.

Buttermilk	2½ cups	Add dry ingredients alternately with
		   buttermilk to creamed mixture.
		Mix on low speed until smooth. Scrape sides
		   of bowl.

Egg whites	10 (11 oz)	Beat egg whites until stiff peaks form. Fold into batter on low speed. Do not overmix. Scale batter into 2 greased 12 × 18 × 2-inch baking pans, 4 lb 7 oz per pan. Bake at 350°F for 40–45 minutes.
Coconut Pecan Frosting (p. 209)	2 qt	When cool, frost with Coconut Pecan Frosting. Cut 5 × 6.

Notes:
1. May be baked in one 18 × 26 × 2-inch pan. Cut 6 × 10 for 60 portions.
2. For four 2-layer cakes, scale into eight 9-inch layer cake pans, 1 lb 1 oz per pan. Cut 16 slices per cake for 64 portions.

Pineapple cashew cake

OVEN: 350°F
BAKE: 25–30 minutes

YIELD: 40 portions
         3 2-layer cakes (9-inch)
PORTION: 16 slices per cake

Ingredient	Amount	Procedure
Margarine or butter Sugar, granulated Vanilla	1 lb 2 oz 1 lb 14 oz 1 Tbsp	Cream margarine, sugar, and vanilla on medium speed for 10 minutes, using flat beater.
Egg yolks	10 (6 oz)	Add egg yolks in 3 portions, while creaming. Mix 2 minutes.
Flour, cake Baking powder Salt	1 lb 14 oz 1½ oz 1½ tsp	Combine flour, baking powder, and salt.
Milk	2¼ cups	Add dry ingredients alternately with milk on low speed to creamed mixture.
Crushed pineapple, drained	1 lb	Add pineapple to batter. Mix on low speed only to blend.
Egg whites	10 (11 oz)	Beat egg whites on high speed until stiff but not dry. Fold into batter on low speed. Scale batter into 6 greased 9-inch layer cake pans, 1 lb 5 oz per pan. Bake at 350°F for 25–30 minutes.
Pineapple Butter Frosting (p. 211) Cashew nuts, toasted, coarsely chopped	2 qt 8 oz	When cool, remove cake from pans. Cover with frosting and sprinkle with toasted cashews.

Note:
May be baked in one 18 × 26 × 2-inch pan, cut 6 × 10 for 60 portions; or in two 12 × 18 × 2-inch pans, scaled 4 lb per pan, and cut 5 × 6 for 30 portions per pan.

Fruit cake

OVEN:	300°F	YIELD:	64 portions

OVEN: 300°F
BAKE: 2½ hours

YIELD: 64 portions
4 loaves 5 × 9 inches
PORTION: ½-inch slice

Ingredient	Amount	Procedure
Shortening, hydrogenated	8 oz	Cream shortening and sugar on medium
Sugar, granulated	1 lb	speed for 10 minutes, using flat beater.
Eggs	4 (7 oz)	Add eggs to creamed mixture. Mix 5 minutes.
Jelly	8 oz	Add ingredients in order listed.
Cinnamon, ground	2 tsp	Mix on low speed only until fruit is coated
Cloves, ground	2 tsp	with flour mixture.
Raisins	2 lb	
Currants	1 lb	
Dates, chopped	1 lb	
Nuts	8 oz	
Flour, cake	1 lb 4 oz	
Baking soda	2 tsp	Dissolve soda in cold coffee.
Coffee, brewed, cold	1½ cups	Add to other ingredients and mix until blended.
		Scale batter into 4 loaf pans (5 × 9 × 2¾ inches) lined with 2 layers of heavy waxed paper, 2 lb 3 oz per pan. Bake at 300°F for 2½ hours. Cut 16 slices per cake.

Notes:

1. May be steamed for 4 hours.
2. Store in a container with a tight cover. Most fruit cakes mellow in flavor if kept about 2 weeks before using.

Gingerbread

OVEN:	350°F	YIELD:	60 portions
BAKE:	40 minutes		2 pans 12 × 18 × 2 inches
		PORTION:	2½ × 3 inches

Ingredient	Amount	Procedure
Shortening, hydrogenated	14 oz	Cream shortening and sugar on medium
Sugar, granulated	14 oz	speed for 10 minutes, using flat beater.
Molasses or sorghum	3½ cups	Add molasses and mix on low speed until blended.
Flour, cake	2 lb 4 oz	Combine dry ingredients.
Baking soda	2 Tbsp	
Salt	1½ tsp	
Cinnamon, ground	1 Tbsp	
Cloves, ground	1 Tbsp	
Ginger, ground	1 Tbsp	
Water, hot	3¾ cups	Add dry ingredients alternately with water to creamed mixture.
Eggs, beaten	7 (12 oz)	Add eggs and mix on low speed 2 minutes. Scale batter into 2 greased 12 × 18 × 2-inch baking pans, 4 lb 3 oz per pan. Bake at 350°F for 40 minutes. Sprinkle with powdered sugar and serve warm or serve with Lemon Sauce (p. 583). Cut 5 × 6.

Note:
May be baked in one 18 × 26 × 2-inch pan. Cut 6 × 10 for 60 portions.

Variations:
1. **Almond meringue gingerbread.** Cover baked Gingerbread with Meringue (p. 255). Sprinkle with slivered or chopped almonds and brown in 375°F oven.
2. **Ginger muffins.** Measure into greased muffin pans with No. 20 dipper. Yield: 7 dozen.
3. **Praline gingerbread.** Combine 1 lb melted margarine or butter, 2 lb brown sugar, 2 lb chopped pecans, and 1½–2 cups cream. Spread 2 lb 12 oz mixture over each pan. Brown under broiler, or return to oven and heat until topping is slightly browned.

Pound cake

OVEN: 325°F
BAKE: 1 hour 15 minutes

YIELD: 48 portions
2 cakes (10-inch tube pans)
PORTION: 24 slices per cake

Ingredient	Amount	Procedure
Flour, cake Sugar, granulated Salt Baking powder	1 lb 10 oz 2 lb 1 Tbsp ½ tsp	Combine dry ingredients in mixer bowl. Blend on low speed for 1 minute, using flat beater.
Eggs	10 (1 lb 2 oz)	Add eggs to dry ingredients. Mix until ingredients are mixed evenly and lumps disappear. Batter will be stiff.
Shortening Milk	1 lb 2 oz ¼ cup	Add shortening and milk to mixture in bowl. Cream on medium speed until very light, about 10 minutes.
Milk Almond extract Vanilla	1½ cups 1½ tsp 1½ tsp	Add milk and extracts slowly. Mix on low speed for 2–3 minutes or just until blended.
		Scale batter into 2 greased 10-inch tube pans, 3 lb 6 oz per pan. Bake at 325°F for 1 hour 15 minutes to 1 hour 25 minutes, or until cake tests done. Drop bottom of cake pans onto counter from a distance of 2–3 inches as cakes are removed from oven to produce a compact texture. Cool. Remove from pans. Cut into 24 slices.

Note:
May be baked in four loaf pans (5 × 9 × 2¾ inches), 1 lb 10 oz batter per pan. Cut in 12 slices.

Pumpkin cake

OVEN:	350°F	YIELD:	48 portions
BAKE:	60–70 minutes		3 cakes (10-inch tube pans)
		PORTION:	16 slices per cake

Ingredient	Amount	Procedure
Eggs	12 (1 lb 4 oz)	Beat eggs on medium speed until blended.
Sugar, granulated	2 lb 10 oz	Add sugar to eggs gradually, beating on high speed until thick and ivory colored.
Vegetable oil	1 qt	Add oil very slowly on low speed.
Flour, all-purpose Baking powder Baking soda Salt Cinnamon, ground	2 lb 10 oz 2 Tbsp 2 Tbsp 1 Tbsp 3 Tbsp	Combine dry ingredients in a separate bowl.
Pumpkin, canned	3 lb	On low speed, add pumpkin alternately with dry ingredients, beginning and ending with dry ingredients.
		Scale batter into 3 ungreased 10-inch tube pans, 3 lb 12 oz per pan. Bake at 350°F for 60–70 minutes Cool in pans.

Chocolate roll

OVEN: 325°F	YIELD:	48 portions
BAKE: 20 minutes		4 pans 12 × 18 × 2 inches
	PORTION:	1-inch slice

Ingredient	Amount	Procedure
Egg yolks	24 (14 oz)	Beat egg yolks on high speed, using flat beater.
Sugar, granulated	2 lb 4 oz	Add sugar and continue beating until mixture is lemon colored, thick, and fluffy.
Unsweetened chocolate, melted Vanilla	12 oz 2 Tbsp	Add chocolate and vanilla. Blend on low speed.
Flour, cake Baking powder Salt	9 oz 1 Tbsp 1½ tsp	Combine flour, baking powder, and salt. Add to creamed mixture on low speed.
Egg whites	24 (1 lb 11 oz)	Beat egg whites on high speed until they form rounded peaks. Fold into cake mixture on low speed. Scale batter into 4 greased 12 × 18 × 2-inch pans lined with heavy waxed paper, 1 lb 7 oz per pan. Bake at 325°F for 20 minutes.
		When baked, remove from pans and quickly remove waxed paper. Trim edges if hard. Roll (Figure 2.22) and let stand a few minutes. Unroll and spread with one of the fillings suggested below. Roll up securely. Cover with a thin layer of Chocolate Frosting (p. 209).

Note:
Suggested fillings: Custard Filling (p. 215), Fluffy Frosting (p. 208), or whipped cream, plain or flavored with peppermint.

Variation:
Ice cream roll.   Spread with a thick layer of softened vanilla ice cream. Roll up securely and wrap in waxed paper. Place in freezer for several hours before serving.

Figure 2.22 *Rolling and filling a jelly roll: (a) Turn baked cake onto a cloth sprinkled with powdered sugar. Remove waxed or parchment paper. (b) While still warm, roll tightly. (c) When cooled but not cold, unroll and spread with filling. (d) Roll firmly. (e) Sprinkle finished jelly roll with powdered sugar.*

Jelly roll

OVEN: 375°F
BAKE: 12 minutes

YIELD: 48 portions
4 pans 12 × 18 × 2 inches
PORTION: 1-inch slice

Ingredient	Amount	Procedure
Eggs	27 (3 lb)	Beat eggs on high speed for 1–2 minutes, using flat beater.
Sugar, granulated Vanilla	3 lb 1 Tbsp	Add sugar and vanilla to eggs. Beat 10–15 minutes.
Flour, cake Cream of tartar Baking powder Salt	1 lb 8 oz 2 Tbsp 2 Tbsp 2 tsp	Mix dry ingredients. Fold on low speed into egg-sugar mixture.
		Scale batter into four 12 × 18 × 2-inch baking pans lined with heavy waxed paper, 1 lb 14 oz per pan. Bake at 375°F for 12 minutes.
		When baked, turn onto a cloth or heavy paper covered with powdered sugar (Figure 2.22). Quickly remove waxed paper and trim edges if hard. Immediately roll cakes tightly.
Jelly or Custard Filling (p. 215)	1 qt	When cooled but not cold, unroll, spread with Jelly or Custard Filling, 1 cup per roll. Roll firmly and wrap with waxed paper.
Sugar, powdered	1 lb	Sprinkle top of each roll with 4 oz powdered sugar. Slice each roll into 12 portions.

Note:
May be baked in two 18 × 26 × 1-inch pans, scaled 3 lb 12 oz per pan.

Variation:
Apricot roll. Cover cakes with Apricot Filling (p. 218) and roll. Cover outside with sweetened whipped cream or whipped topping and toasted coconut.

Pumpkin cake roll

OVEN: 375°F
BAKE: 15 minutes

YIELD: 50 portions
              2 rolls
PORTION: cut 25 per roll

Ingredient	Amount	Procedure
Eggs	18 (2 lb)	Whip eggs on high speed until thick and lemon colored, using flat beater.
Sugar, granulated	2 lb 13 oz	Add sugar gradually while mixing on medium speed.
Pumpkin, canned Lemon juice	2 lb 3 oz 2 Tbsp	Add pumpkin and lemon juice to egg mixture, mixing until blended.
Flour, all-purpose Baking powder Salt Cinnamon, ground Ginger, ground Nutmeg, ground	1 lb 2 oz 1 oz 1 Tbsp 1 oz 4 tsp 1 Tbsp	Combine dry ingredients in a bowl. Fold into pumpkin mixture.
		Scale batter into two 18 × 26 × 1-inch silicone paper-lined baking pans, 4 lb per pan. Bake at 375°F for 15 minutes or until cake tests done.
Sugar, powdered	6 oz	Sift powdered sugar generously onto a large white towel. Loosen edges of cake and turn onto towel. Remove silicone paper. Roll cake and towel up jelly roll fashion. Cool completely.
Cream cheese, softened Margarine	2 lb 10 oz	Beat cream cheese and margarine until creamy, using flat beater.
Sugar, powdered Vanilla	1 lb 6 oz 1 Tbsp	Add sugar and vanilla to cream cheese mixture. Beat until smooth and creamy.

		Unroll cooled cake. Spread cream cheese filling over unrolled cakes, 2 lb per cake. Reroll cake.
Nuts, chopped	2 cups	Garnish with 1 cup nuts sprinkled over each roll. Chill. Cut each roll into 25 portions.

Note:
If needed, sift additional powdered sugar over top of rolled cake.

FROSTINGS AND FILLINGS

The presentation of cakes may be varied by the use of different fillings and frostings. The amount to use will depend on the kind of cake to be frosted and the individual preference of the patrons. Table 2.4 may serve as a guide. Figure 2.23 suggests cutting configurations for cakes.

TABLE 2.4 APPROXIMATE SCALING WEIGHTS FOR FROSTINGS AND FILLINGS

Pan size	*Approximate weight per pan*
13 × 18 × 2-inch	3 cups (1 lb 8 oz)
18 × 26 × 2-inch	1½ qt (3 lb)
9-inch layer	2 cups (1 lb) ¾ cup in the middle 1¼ cups top and sides
10-inch tube	1½ cups (12 oz)

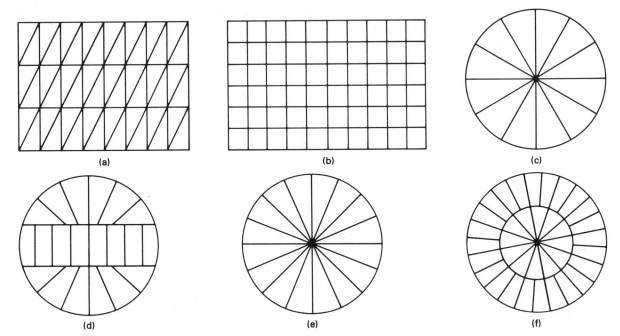

Figure 2.23 *Suggested cutting configurations for cakes: (a) 18 × 26-inch baking sheet, 48 portions; (b) 18 × 26-inch baking sheet, 60 portions; (c) 8 to 12-inch round, 12 portions; (d) 10 to 12-inch round, 20 portions; (e) 8 to 12-inch round, 16 portions; (f) 10 to 12-inch round, 36 portions.*

FROSTING RECIPES

Boiled frosting

YIELD: 2 qt

Ingredient	Amount	Procedure
Sugar, granulated Water, hot	2 lb 1¼ cups	Combine sugar and water. Stir until sugar is dissolved. Boil without stirring to soft ball stage (238°F).
Egg whites	4 (4 oz)	Beat egg whites on high speed until stiff but not dry, using wire whip attachment. Gradually pour syrup over egg whites while

		beating. Continue beating until frosting is of consistency to spread.
Vanilla	1 Tbsp	Add vanilla. Spread on cake at once.

Variations:
See variations of Ice Cream Frosting below.

Ice cream frosting

	YIELD: 2½ qt	
Ingredient	**Amount**	**Procedure**
Sugar, granulated Water, hot	1 lb 8 oz 1 cup	Combine sugar and water. Boil without stirring to soft ball stage (238°F).
Egg whites	9 (10 oz)	Beat egg whites until frothy, using wire whip attachment.
Sugar, powdered, sifted	3 oz	Add powdered sugar to egg whites and beat on high speed to consistency of meringue. Add hot syrup slowly and continue beating until mixture is thick and creamy.
Sugar, powdered, sifted Vanilla	8 oz 1 Tbsp	Add powdered sugar and vanilla. Beat until smooth. Add more sugar if necessary to make frosting hold its shape when spread.

Note:
This frosting may be kept several days in a covered container in the refrigerator.

Variations:
1. **Bittersweet frosting.** Melt 8 oz unsweetened chocolate over hot water. Gradually stir in 1½ oz margarine or butter. When slightly cool, pour over white frosting to form a design.
2. **Candied fruit frosting.** Add 8 oz chopped candied fruit.
3. **Chocolate frosting.** Add 8 oz melted chocolate.
4. **Coconut frosting.** Frost cake. Sprinkle with 4 oz dry shredded coconut.
5. **Maple nut frosting.** Delete vanilla. Flavor with 1½ tsp maple flavoring. Add 6 oz chopped nuts.
6. **Maraschino cherry frosting.** Delete vanilla. Add ½ tsp almond extract and 8 oz chopped maraschino cherries.
7. **Peppermint frosting.** Add 8 oz finely crushed peppermint candy.

Fluffy frosting

		YIELD: 2 qt
Ingredient	**Amount**	**Procedure**
Sugar, granulated Water Corn syrup, white Salt	1 lb 4 oz ¾ cup 2½ Tbsp ⅛ tsp	Boil sugar, water, syrup, and salt until mixture reaches the soft ball stage (238°F).

Egg whites	5 (6 oz)	Beat egg whites on high speed until stiff but
		    not dry, using wire whip attachment.
		Gradually add half of the hot syrup, beating
		    constantly.
		Cook remaining half of syrup until it forms a
		    hard ball (250°F).
		Gradually add to first mixture. Beat on high
		    speed until it holds its shape.

Vanilla	1½ tsp	Add vanilla.

Variation:
Fluffy brown sugar frosting.   Substitute brown sugar for granulated sugar.

Burnt butter frosting

		YIELD: 1¼ qt
Ingredient	**Amount**	**Procedure**
Butter or margarine	9 oz	Heat butter in sauce pan until golden brown.
Sugar, powdered	1 lb 8 oz	Add sugar to butter and blend.

Vanilla
Water, hot
	1 Tbsp
	½ cup
		Add vanilla and water. Beat until of
		    spreading consistency. Add more water if
		    necessary.

Note:
This amount will frost 8 dozen 1½-inch cookies. If used for cake, increase by one-fourth.

Chocolate butter cream frosting

YIELD:　2 qt

Ingredient	Amount	Procedure
Margarine or butter	1 lb 8 oz	Cream margarine on medium speed until fluffy.
Evaporated milk	½ cup	Add milk and blend.
Sugar, powdered, sifted	1 lb 8 oz	Add sugar gradually. Mix on medium speed until smooth.
Unsweetened chocolate, melted	6 oz	Add chocolate and vanilla. Beat on high speed until light and fluffy.
Vanilla	1 tsp	

Note:
Milk may be substituted for evaporated milk.

Coconut pecan frosting

YIELD:　2 qt

Ingredient	Amount	Procedure
Evaporated milk	2 cups	Combine milk, egg yolks, sugar, and margarine.
Egg yolks, beaten	6 (4 oz)	
Sugar, granulated	1 lb	Cook in steam-jacketed kettle or over hot water until thickened.
Margarine or butter	8 oz	
Pecans, finely chopped	12 oz	Add pecans, coconut, and vanilla.
Coconut, flaked	12 oz	Cool, then beat well until thick enough to spread.
Vanilla	2 tsp	

Cream cheese frosting

YIELD: 1¾ qt

Ingredient	Amount	Procedure
Cream cheese, softened	12 oz	Blend cream cheese, margarine, and milk on medium speed until smooth.
Margarine or butter, softened	2 oz	
Milk	¼ cup	
Sugar, powdered, sifted	2 lb 12 oz	Add sugar gradually to cheese-margarine mixture.
Vanilla	1 Tbsp	Add vanilla and beat until smooth and of spreading consistency.

Variation:
Orange cheese frosting. Substitute 1 Tbsp orange juice and 1 Tbsp grated orange peel for vanilla.

Creamy frosting

YIELD: 1½ qt

Ingredient	Amount	Procedure
Margarine or butter	12 oz	Cream margarine on medium speed for 1 minute or until soft.
Evaporated milk	½ cup	Add milk, salt, and vanilla. Mix until blended.
Salt	1 tsp	
Vanilla	1 Tbsp	
Sugar, powdered, sifted	2 lb	Add sugar gradually. Whip on medium speed until mixture is smooth and creamy.

Note:
Milk or cream may be substituted for evaporated milk.

Variations:
1. **Cocoa frosting.** Increase liquid to 1¼ cups. Add 6 oz cocoa sifted with the sugar.
2. **Lemon butter frosting.** Substitute ¼ cup lemon juice for an equal amount of milk, and 1½ Tbsp fresh grated lemon peel for the vanilla.
3. **Orange butter frosting.** Substitute ½ cup orange juice for an equal amount of milk, and 1 Tbsp fresh grated orange peel for the vanilla.

Orange frosting

		YIELD: 1½ qt
Ingredient	**Amount**	**Procedure**
Margarine or butter	8 oz	Cream margarine until fluffy.
Sugar, powdered, sifted	2 lb 8 oz	Add sugar gradually on medium speed. Mix until creamy.
Vanilla Salt Orange juice Lemon juice Orange peel, grated	2 Tbsp ½ tsp ¼ cup ¼ cup 1 tsp	Add remaining ingredients. Blend until smooth.

Pineapple butter frosting

		YIELD: 2½ qt
Ingredient	**Amount**	**Procedure**
Margarine or butter Sugar, powdered Salt	1 lb 8 oz 3 lb ½ tsp	Mix margarine, sugar, and salt on medium speed until creamy.
Egg yolks	3 (2 oz)	Add egg yolks. Whip on high speed until light and fluffy.
Crushed pineapple, drained	1 lb	Add pineapple to creamed mixture. Blend on low speed. Refrigerate until ready to use.

Note:
Frosting for Pineapple Cashew Cake (p. 196).

Mocha frosting

	YIELD: 2 qt	
Ingredient	**Amount**	**Procedure**
Hot coffee, strong	1½ cups	Add coffee to margarine and cocoa.
Margarine or butter, softened	3 oz	Mix on medium speed until blended.
Cocoa	4 oz	
Sugar, powdered, sifted	3 lb	Add sugar, salt, and vanilla. Mix until smooth.
Salt	½ tsp	Add more sugar if necessary to make
Vanilla	½ tsp	frosting hold its shape when spread.

Note:
Instant coffee, 2 Tbsp dissolved in 1½ cups hot water, may be used in place of brewed coffee.

Chocolate glaze

	YIELD: 1 qt	
Ingredient	**Amount**	**Procedure**
Unsweetened chocolate	4 oz	Melt chocolate and margarine over low heat.
Margarine or butter	3 oz	
Sugar, powdered, sifted	1 lb 5 oz	Add sugar, vanilla, and water gradually.
Vanilla	1 Tbsp	Beat until smooth. If needed, add boiling
Water, boiling	½ cup	water, a few drops at a time, to make
		spreading consistency.

Peanut butter glaze

	YIELD: 3½ cups	
Ingredient	**Amount**	**Procedure**
Margarine, melted	3 oz	Cream margarine and peanut butter.
Peanut butter	8 oz	
Sugar, powdered	1 lb 10 oz	Add sugar and milk alternately to make a
Milk	1 cup	spreading consistency.
		Spread over rolls.

Powdered sugar glaze

	YIELD: 1 qt	
Ingredient	**Amount**	**Procedure**
Sugar, powdered, sifted	2 lb	Gradually add water to sugar.
Water, boiling	¾ cup	Add vanilla. Beat until smooth.
Vanilla	2 tsp	Thin, if necessary, to spread.

Note:
Use for frosting baked rolls or products requiring a thin frosting.

FILLING RECIPES

Chocolate cream filling

YIELD: 3 qt

Ingredient	Amount	Procedure
Chocolate chips	2 lb 4 oz (3 12-oz pkg)	Combine chocolate chips, orange juice, and sugar.
Orange juice or water	1 cup	Melt over hot water. Cool.
Sugar, granulated	8 oz	
Cream, whipping	1½ qt	Whip cream until stiff. Fold into chocolate mixture.

Note:
Use as filling for Orange Cream Puffs (p. 289).

Variation:
Chocolate mousse. Whip 10 egg whites to a soft peak and fold into chocolate-whipped cream mixture. Chill. May be frozen.

Cranberry filling

YIELD: 2 qt

Ingredient	Amount	Procedure
Cranberry relish	1 lb 8 oz	Make relish according to recipe on p. 517.
Crushed pineapple	1 No. 2 can	Add pineapple, sugar, and flour to relish. Cook until thick.
Sugar, granulated	8 oz	
Flour, all-purpose	¼ cup	
Margarine or butter	1 oz	Add margarine. Stir until blended.

Note:
Use for Fruit Coffee Ring (p. 169).

Custard filling

	YIELD: 3 qt	
Ingredient	**Amount**	**Procedure**
Cornstarch	6 oz	Combine dry ingredients.
Sugar, granulated	1 lb	
Salt	½ tsp	
Milk, cold	2 cups	Add cold milk to dry ingredients and stir until smooth.
Milk, hot	2½ qt	Add cold mixture to hot milk, stirring constantly with wire whip. Cook over hot water until thick.
Eggs, beaten	10 (1 lb)	Add, while stirring, a small amount of hot mixture to the beaten eggs. Add to remainder of hot mixture, stirring constantly. Cook 7 minutes.
Vanilla	2 tsp	Remove from heat. Add vanilla. Cool.

Notes:
1. Use as a filling for cakes, Cream Puffs (p. 289), Chocolate Roll (p. 201), and Eclairs (p. 289).
2. To fill three 9-inch layer cakes, use ⅓ recipe.

Date filling

	YIELD: 1½ qt	
Ingredient	**Amount**	**Procedure**
Dates, pitted, chopped	2 lb	Combine dates, water, and sugar.
Water	2¼ cups	Cook until mixture is thick. Cool.
Sugar, granulated	12 oz	

Notes:
1. Use as cake or cookie filling.
2. To add flavor, 6 oz jelly or ¼ cup orange juice may be used in place of ¼ cup of the water.

Fig filling

YIELD: 2 qt

Ingredient	Amount	Procedure
Figs, dried, chopped Water	2 lb 2 cups	Soak figs in water, then cook together.
Sugar, granulated Flour, all-purpose Salt Lemon juice	1 lb 4 oz ½ tsp 1 cup	Add sugar, flour, salt, and lemon juice to figs. Cook to a paste.
Margarine or butter	1 lb	Blend margarine into hot mixture.

Variations:
1. **Apricot filling.**   Substitute 2 lb dried apricots, cooked and chopped, for the figs. Reduce lemon juice to ½ cup.
2. **Prune date filling.**   Substitute 1 lb cooked, pitted, and chopped prunes and 1 lb chopped dates for the figs.

Lemon filling

YIELD: 1 qt

Ingredient	Amount	Procedure
Sugar, granulated Water	1 lb 3 cups	Heat sugar and water to boiling point.
Cornstarch Water, cold	2½ oz ¾ cup	Blend cornstarch and cold water. Gradually add to boiling sugar and water while stirring with a wire whip. Cook until thickened and clear, stirring constantly.
Egg yolks, beaten	4 (3 oz)	Blend egg yolks into hot mixture with wire whip. Cook 5–8 minutes while stirring.

Salt	¾ tsp	Add remaining ingredients. Stir to blend.
Lemon juice	½ cup	Cool.
Fresh lemon peel, grated	2 tsp	
Margarine or butter	1 oz (2 Tbsp)	

Variations:
1. **Lime filling.**   Substitute fresh lime for the lemon. Add a few drops of green food coloring.
2. **Orange filling.**   Substitute orange juice for the water and fresh orange peel for the lemon peel. Reduce lemon juice to 3 Tbsp.

Marmalade nut filling

YIELD: 2 lb 8 oz filling

Ingredient	Amount	Procedure
Margarine	2 oz	Melt margarine.
Walnuts, pieces	1 lb	Add nuts. Cook and stir until nuts are toasted.
Sugar, brown	6 oz	Add sugar and cinnamon. Cook until heated
Cinnamon, ground	1 tsp	through.
Orange marmalade	1 lb	Add marmalade. Mix well.

Prune filling

	YIELD: 1 qt	
Ingredient	**Amount**	**Procedure**
Prunes, pitted, cooked and chopped	2 cups	Add cream, margarine, and eggs to prunes. Heat over hot water.
Sour cream	1 cup	
Margarine or butter	2 oz	
Eggs, beaten	4 (7 oz)	
Sugar, granulated	1 lb	Mix dry ingredients. Add to prune mixture. Cook and stir over hot water until thick. Cool.
Salt	½ tsp	
Flour, all-purpose	1 oz (¼ cup)	

Note:
8 oz chopped nuts may be added.

Variation:
Apricot filling.   Substitute dried apricots for prunes.

Cookies

Cookies are made in a variety of shapes, sizes, and textures. They may be crisp, soft, or chewy, depending on the proportion of ingredients, the method of mixing, and baking time and temperature.

Proportion of ingredients

Crisp cookies generally have a low proportion of liquid and a high sugar and fat content. Soft cookies have a high proportion of liquid and are low in fat and sugar. Chewy cookies have high sugar and liquid content but are low in fat and have a high proportion of eggs. A high sugar or liquid content may increase spread of the cookie during baking.

Methods of mixing

Most cookies are prepared by one of the following methods:

1. **Creaming method.** Cream shortening, sugar, and flavorings at low speed until blended. The amount of creaming can affect the texture of the cookies. A short creaming time is used for a chewy cookie; and for a cookie with cakelike texture, the shortening and sugar are creamed until light and fluffy. The amount of creaming may also affect the spread of the cookie while it is baking. After the creaming is completed, blend in the eggs and liquid, then the flour and leavening. Mix the dough only until ingredients are combined.
2. **One-stage method.** Place all ingredients in the mixer and mix at low speed until blended.
3. **Sponge method.** Beat eggs (whites, yolks, or whole) until light. Add the remaining ingredients and blend, being careful not to overmix or deflate the eggs.

Shaping

Drop cookies are made from a soft dough, which is portioned onto prepared baking sheets with a dipper (Figure 2.24). A No. 40 dipper, which was used for most of the recipes in this book, makes a medium size cookie weighing about ¾ oz. Larger cookies may be made by using a No. 20 or No. 30 dipper, and Nos. 60 and 70 make small cookies. If using the recipe for larger or smaller cookies, the yield may need to be adjusted by using the procedure on p. 53.

Bar cookies are made from a soft dough or batter that is spread evenly on prepared baking pans. Most recipes in this section suggest using two 13 × 18 × 1-inch pans (half baking sheet) or one 18 × 26 × 1-inch pan (baking sheet). The

Figure 2.24 *Portioning cookie dough. Spacing on baking sheet will depend on type of cookie dough, size of dipper used, and spread of the dough while baking.*

13 × 18-inch pan will yield 30 2½ × 3-inch bars by cutting 5 × 6. An 18 × 26-inch pan may be cut 6 × 10 to yield 60 bars 3 × 2½ inches or 8 × 12 for 96 cookies.

Rolled cookies are made from a stiff dough that has been chilled thoroughly. The dough is rolled out to ⅛ inch thickness on a lightly floured board and cut with a cookie cutter.

Refrigerator cookies are made by shaping dough into rolls of uniform size (1–2 inches in diameter) and chilling, then cutting into slices. Use of a slicing machine ensures uniform thickness. The dough may be made into rolls, wrapped in waxed or parchment paper, refrigerated or frozen, and baked as needed.

Molded or pressed cookies are made by shaping into small balls, then flattened by pressing with a mold or other flat utensil dipped in sugar. Cookies may be shaped also with a cookie press or, if using a soft dough, with a pastry bag.

Baking

Pans are prepared by lightly greasing or lining with silicone or parchment paper. A heavily greased pan increases the spread of the cookie. Some high-fat cookies can be baked on ungreased pans. Most cookies are baked at a relatively high temperature. Too low a temperature increases spreading and may produce dry, pale cookies. Too high a temperature decreases spreading and may burn the edges or bottoms.

Cookies should be watched carefully to prevent overbaking or burning. To test for doneness, press center of the cookie lightly with a finger. If almost no imprint remains and the cookie is browned, it is done. Fudge-type bars will be done when the top has a dull crust, and cakelike bars when a pick inserted in the center comes out clean. Soft cookies should be removed from the oven when they are still soft to the touch.

In most cases, to prevent sticking, the cookies should be removed from pans while they are still warm. If silicone or parchment paper is used, the cookies may be left on the pan to cool. Very soft cookies, however, should not be removed until they are cool enough and firm enough to handle. Cookies should be completely cooled before storing.

Storing

Proper storage is important to maintain the quality and freshness of cookies. Crisp cookies may become soft if they absorb moisture, so they should be stored loosely covered away from moisture. Soft cookies should be stored tightly covered because they will become dry if allowed to lose moisture. All cookies are best if served soon after baking.

Quality standards for cookies

Drop cookies	**Deviation: cause**
Appearance:	
Uniform mound shape	Misshapen: improper dropping of dough, oven too hot or too cool, improper mixing
	Excessive spreading: dough too warm, incorrect oven temperature, not peaked when dropped
Color:	
Delicately browned, uniform	Dark: too hot oven temperature
	Pale: too low oven temperature
Texture:	
Crisp or chewy, true to type	Soft, tough, crumbly, dry: incorrect proportion of ingredients, inaccurate measuring, poor mixing or baking techniques

(continued)

Flavor:
Sweet, characteristic of ingredients

Unpleasant flavor: poor quality fat or other ingredients

Rolled cookies

Appearance:
Retains shape of cutter
Color:
Lightly browned surface
Texture:
Crisp thin cookie or soft thick cookie (depending on variety)

Tough: excessive rerolling
Dry: rolling in too much flour or rerolling

Bar cookies

Appearance:
Uniform, well-cut shape

Crumbles when cut: cutting while too warm

Texture:
Rich, moist eating quality

Dry, crumbly: overbaking, improper proportion of ingredients

Tenderness:
Thin delicate crust
Flavor:
Appealing flavor

Hard crusty top: overmixing

Unpleasant: poor quality ingredients

Molded cookies

Appearance:
Uniform, well-shaped
Color:
Delicately browned
Texture:
Crisp and tender
Flavor:
Pleasing, well blended

Misshapen: poor molding

Too brown: overbaking

Crumbly: insufficient shaping

Unpleasant: poor quality ingredients

Refrigerator cookies

Appearance:
Uniform thin slices

Irregular shape: improper molding of dough roll, dough not chilled before slicing, improper slicing technique

Color:

Lightly browned surface

Too brown: overbaked

Texture:

Crisp and crunchy

Soft: cut too thick

Flavor:

Rich and flavorful

Unpleasant: poor quality ingredients

Pressed cookies

Appearance:

Well-shaped and well-defined pattern

Misshapen: improper use of cookie press, dough too cold or too warm, placing dough on hot baking sheet, oven temperature too low

Color:

Delicately browned edges

Overbrowned: overbaking

Texture:

Very tender and crisp

Crumbly, dry: incorrect proportions of ingredients

Flavor:

Rich and buttery

Unpleasant: poor quality ingredients overbaked

COOKIE RECIPES
Drop cookies

Butterscotch drop cookies

OVEN: 375°F	YIELD: 8 dozen cookies
BAKE: 10–15 minutes	PORTION: ¾ oz per cookie

Ingredient	Amount	Procedure
Margarine or butter Sugar, brown	8 oz 1 lb	Cream margarine and brown sugar on medium speed for 5 minutes, using flat beater.
Eggs Vanilla	4 (7 oz) 2 tsp	Add eggs and vanilla to creamed mixture. Mix on medium speed until well blended.
Flour, all-purpose Baking powder Baking soda Salt	1 lb 4 oz 1 tsp 2 tsp 1 tsp	Combine dry ingredients.
Sour cream	1 lb	Add dry ingredients alternately with sour cream to dough. Mix on low speed until blended.
Walnuts, chopped	8 oz	Add nuts. Mix until blended. Chill dough until firm.
		Portion with No. 40 dipper 3 × 5 onto lightly greased or silicone-paper-lined 18 × 26-inch baking sheets. Bake at 375°F for 10–15 minutes. Cover with Burnt Butter Frosting (p. 208) while cookies are still warm.

Variations:
1. **Butterscotch squares.** Spread batter in 12 × 18 × 2-inch baking pan. Bake at 325°F for 25 minutes.
2. **Chocolate drop cookies.** Add 4 oz unsweetened chocolate, melted, to creamed mixture.

Butterscotch pecan cookies

OVEN: 375°F	YIELD: 10 dozen cookies
BAKE: 10–12 minutes	PORTION: ¾ oz per cookie

Ingredient	Amount	Procedure
Margarine or butter Sugar, brown	1 lb 2 lb	Cream margarine and sugar on medium speed for 5 minutes, using flat beater.
Eggs Vanilla	4 (7 oz) 1 Tbsp	Add eggs and vanilla to creamed mixture. Mix on low speed until blended.
Flour, all-purpose Pecans, chopped	1 lb 8 oz 1 lb	Add flour and pecans. Mix on low speed until blended.
		Portion with No. 40 dipper 3 × 5 onto lightly greased or silicone-paper-lined 18 × 26-inch baking sheets. Bake at 375°F for 10–12 minutes.

Coconut macaroons

OVEN: 325°F	YIELD: 9 dozen cookies
BAKE: 15 minutes	PORTION: ½ oz per cookie

Ingredient	Amount	Procedure
Egg whites Salt	8 (9 oz) ⅛ tsp	Beat egg whites and salt on high speed until frothy, using whip attachment.
Sugar, granulated Sugar, powdered	12 oz 12 oz	Combine sugars and add gradually to egg whites.
Vanilla	2 tsp	Add vanilla. Continue beating on high speed until stiff.
Coconut, shredded	1 lb 6 oz	Carefully fold in coconut on low speed. Portion with No. 60 dipper 4 × 6 onto lightly greased or silicone-paper-lined 18 × 26-inch baking sheets. Bake at 325°F for 15 minutes.

Chocolate chip cookies

OVEN: 375°F	YIELD: 10 dozen cookies
BAKE: 8–10 minutes	PORTION: ¾ oz per cookie

Ingredient	Amount	Procedure
Margarine or butter	12 oz	Cream margarine and sugars on medium
Sugar, granulated	8 oz	speed for 5 minutes, using flat beater.
Sugar, brown	8 oz	
Eggs	4 (7 oz)	Add eggs and vanilla to creamed mixture
Vanilla	2 tsp	and beat until light and fluffy.
Flour, all-purpose	1 lb 4 oz	Combine dry ingredients. Add on low speed
Salt	1 tsp	to creamed mixture.
Baking soda	2 tsp	
Nuts, coarsely chopped	1 lb	Add nuts and chocolate chips. Mix until
Chocolate chips	1 lb 8 oz	blended.
		Portion with No. 40 dipper 3 × 5 onto lightly greased or silicone-paper-lined 18 × 26-inch baking sheets.
		Bake at 375°F for 8–10 minutes.

Note:
For jumbo cookies, use No. 20 dipper. Bake at 365°F for 12–15 minutes.

Jumbo chunk chocolate cookies

| OVEN: | 350°F | | YIELD: | 5 dozen cookies |
| BAKE: | 10–12 minutes | | PORTION: | 3½ oz |

Ingredient	Amount	Procedure
Sugar, brown	1 lb 8 oz	Cream sugars and shortening on medium speed for 5 minutes, using flat beater.
Sugar, granulated	1 lb	
Shortening	2 lb	
Eggs, beaten	9 (1 lb)	Add eggs and vanilla to creamed mixture.
Vanilla	1½ Tbsp	
Flour, all-purpose	2 lb 8 oz	Combine dry ingredients and add to creamed mixture. Mix thoroughly.
Baking soda	4 tsp	
Salt	4 tsp	
Semisweet chocolate chunks	4 lb 12 oz	Add chocolate and nuts.
Nuts, chopped	1 lb	
		Portion with No. 20 dipper 3 × 5 onto lightly greased or silicone-paper-lined 18 × 26-inch baking sheets. Flatten slightly. Bake at 350°F for 10–12 minutes.

Note:
These cookies are best when served the same day they are baked.

Drop molasses cookies

OVEN: 350°F
BAKE: 8–10 minutes

YIELD: 8 dozen cookies
PORTION: ¾ oz per cookie

Ingredient	Amount	Procedure
Flour, all-purpose	2 lb	Stir together flour, soda, and spices. Set aside.
Baking soda	2⅔ Tbsp	
Cinnamon, ground	¼ cup	
Cloves, ground	1 tsp	
Nutmeg, ground	1 tsp	
Ginger, ground	2 tsp	
Salt	2 tsp	
Shortening, melted and cooled	1 lb 8 oz	Combine shortening and sugar in mixer bowl. Beat on medium speed for 5 minutes, using flat beater.
Sugar, granulated	2 lb	
Eggs	4 (7 oz)	Add eggs, one at a time, beating well after each addition.
Molasses	1 cup	Add molasses gradually to egg mixture. Add dry ingredients gradually on low speed and mix well.
		Portion with No. 40 dipper 3 × 5 onto lightly greased or silicone-paper-lined 18 × 26-inch baking sheets. Bake at 350°F for 8–10 minutes.

Note:
Cookies will be soft in center.

Oatmeal cookies

OVEN: 375°F	YIELD: 8 dozen cookies
BAKE: 8–11 minutes	PORTION: ¾ oz per cookie

Ingredient	Amount	Procedure
Margarine Sugar, brown Sugar, granulated	1 lb 4 oz 12 oz 8 oz	Cream margarine and sugars on medium speed for 5 minutes, using flat beater.
Eggs Vanilla	2 (4 oz) 2 tsp	Add eggs and vanilla to creamed mixture. Continue to cream until well mixed.
Flour, all-purpose Salt Baking soda	12 oz 1 tsp 1 tsp	Combine dry ingredients. Add to creamed mixture.
Rolled oats, uncooked	12 oz	Add oats. Mix on low speed until blended.
Raisins, softened	12 oz	Add raisins. Mix only to blend. Portion with No. 40 dipper 3 × 5 onto lightly greased or silicone-paper-lined 18 × 26-inch baking sheets. Bake at 375°F for 8–9 minutes for a chewy cookie, 10–11 minutes for a crisp cookie.

Note:
For variety, add 8 oz chopped nuts, chocolate chips, or coconut.

Peanut butter cookies

OVEN: 375°F		YIELD: 9 dozen cookies
BAKE: 8 minutes		PORTION: ¾ oz per cookie

Ingredient	Amount	Procedure
Margarine or butter	1 lb	Cream margarine and sugars on medium speed for 5 minutes, using flat beater.
Sugar, granulated	1 lb	
Sugar, brown	10 oz	
Eggs	4 (7 oz)	Add eggs and vanilla. Continue beating until blended.
Vanilla	2 tsp	
Peanut butter	1 lb 2 oz	Add peanut butter to creamed mixture. Blend on low speed.
Flour, all-purpose	1 lb	Combine dry ingredients. Add to creamed mixture. Mix on low speed until well blended.
Baking soda	2 tsp	
Salt	1 tsp	
		Portion dough with No. 40 dipper 3 × 5 onto lightly greased or silicone-paper-lined 18 × 26-inch baking sheets. Flatten with tines of a fork. Bake at 375°F for 8 minutes.

Variations:
1. **Chocolate chip peanut butter cookies.** Add 1 lb chocolate chips.
2. **Chunky peanut butter cookies.** Use chunky peanut butter or add 12 oz chopped peanuts.

Peanut cookies

OVEN: 350°F	YIELD: 9 dozen cookies	
BAKE: 12–15 minutes	PORTION: ¾ oz per cookie	

Ingredient	Amount	Procedure
Margarine or butter	12 oz	Cream margarine and sugars on medium speed for 5 minutes, using flat beater.
Sugar, granulated	8 oz	
Sugar, brown	1 lb	
Eggs	4 (7 oz)	Add eggs and vanilla. Mix for 5 minutes.
Vanilla	2 tsp	
Flour, all-purpose	12 oz	Combine dry ingredients. Add to creamed mixture.
Baking soda	1 tsp	
Salt	1 tsp	
Rolled oats, quick, uncooked	10 oz	Add rolled oats and peanuts. Mix until blended.
Peanuts, salted	1 lb	
		Portion dough with No. 40 dipper 3 × 5 onto lightly greased or silicone-paper-lined 18 × 26-inch baking sheets.
		Bake at 350°F for 12–15 minutes.

Snickerdoodles

OVER: 375°F	YIELD: 8 dozen cookies
BAKE: 8–10 minutes	PORTION: ¾ oz per cookie

Ingredient	Amount	Procedure
Margarine or butter	1 lb	Cream margarine and sugar on medium
Sugar, granulated	1 lb 8 oz	speed for 5 minutes, using flat beater.
Eggs	4 (7 oz)	Add eggs to creamed mixture. Mix thoroughly.
Flour, all-purpose	1 lb 6 oz	Mix dry ingredients. Add to creamed mixture.
Cream of tartar	4 tsp	Mix on low speed until well blended.
Baking soda	2 tsp	
Salt	½ tsp	
Sugar, granulated	8 oz	Combine sugar and cinnamon.
Cinnamon	5 Tbsp	Portion dough with No. 40 dipper.
		Roll in sugar-cinnamon mixture.
		Place 3 × 5 onto lightly greased or silicone-paper-lined 18 × 26-inch baking sheets.
		Bake at 375°F for 8–10 minutes or until lightly browned but still soft. These cookies puff up at first, then flatten out with crinkled tops.

Drop sugar cookies

OVEN: 375°F	YIELD: 8 dozen cookies	
BAKE: 8–10 minutes	PORTION: ¾ oz per cookie	

Ingredient	Amount	Procedure
Shortening	1 lb	Cream fats and sugar, starting on low speed, progressing to medium, then high speed for 5 minutes. Use flat beater.
Margarine or butter	1 lb 2 oz	
Sugar, granulated	2 lb	
Eggs	3 (5 oz)	Add eggs and vanilla to creamed mixture and mix thoroughly.
Vanilla	4 tsp	
Flour, all-purpose	1 lb 14 oz	Combine dry ingredients. Add gradually to creamed mixture. Blend well.
Cream of tartar	2 tsp	
Baking soda	2½ tsp	
Salt	½ tsp	
		Portion with No. 40 dipper 3 × 5 onto lightly greased or silicone-paper-lined 18 × 26-inch baking sheets. Bake at 375°F for 8–10 minutes.

Notes:
1. Cookies will be soft in center.
2. For jumbo cookies, use No. 20 dipper.

Whole wheat sugar cookies

OVEN: 375°F
BAKE: 8–10 minutes

YIELD: 8 dozen cookies
PORTION: ¾ oz per cookie

Ingredient	Amount	Procedure
Margarine or butter	1 lb	Cream margarine and sugar for 5 minutes or until light and fluffy, using flat beater.
Sugar, granulated	2 lb	
Eggs	4 (7 oz)	Add eggs, vanilla, and milk. Mix well.
Vanilla	4 tsp	
Milk	½ cup	
Flour, whole wheat	1 lb 8 oz	Combine dry ingredients.
Baking powder	4 tsp	Add gradually to creamed mixture.
Baking soda	2 tsp	Blend well.
Salt	2 tsp	
Nutmeg, ground	2 tsp	
Orange peel, grated	4 Tbsp	
Sugar, granulated	4 oz	Portion with No. 40 dipper 3 × 5 onto lightly greased or silicone-paper-lined 18 × 26-inch baking sheets.
Cinnamon, ground	2 tsp	Flatten slightly and sprinkle with sugar and cinnamon mixture. Bake at 375°F for 8–10 minutes.

Note:
Cookies will be soft in center.

Bar cookies

Brownies

OVEN: 325°F	YIELD: 60 portions
BAKE: 20 minutes	2 pans 12 × 18 × 1 inches
	PORTION: 2½ × 3 inches

Ingredient	Amount	Procedure
Eggs	15 (1 lb 10 oz)	Beat eggs on high speed for 5 minutes, using flat beater.
Sugar, granulated Shortening, melted Margarine, melted Vanilla	2 lb 4 oz 10 oz 8 oz 2 Tbsp	Add sugar, fats, and vanilla to eggs. Mix on medium speed for 5 minutes.
Flour, cake Cocoa Baking powder Salt	14 oz 10 oz 2 tsp ½ tsp	Combine dry ingredients. Add to creamed mixture. Mix on low speed about 5 minutes.
Nuts, chopped	12 oz	Add nuts to batter. Mix to blend.
		Scale batter into 2 lightly greased 12 × 18 × 1-inch baking pans, 3 lb 8 oz per pan. Bake at 325°F for 20 minutes. Do not overbake. Should be soft to touch when done. While warm, sprinkle with powdered sugar, or cool and cover with a thin layer of mocha or chocolate frosting if desired.

Notes:
1. 1 lb unsweetened chocolate may be substituted for the cocoa. Melt and add to the fat-sugar-egg mixture.
2. 2 lb chopped dates may be added.
3. May be baked in one 18 × 26 × 1-inch baking sheet.

Butterscotch squares

OVEN: 325°F   YIELD: 60 portions
BAKE: 25 minutes   2 pans 12 × 18 × 1 inches
                                        PORTION: 2½ × 3 inches

Ingredient	Amount	Procedure
Margarine or butter Sugar, brown	1 lb 2 lb 8 oz	Cream margarine and sugar on medium speed for 5 minutes, using flat beater.
Eggs Vanilla	10 (1 lb) 1 Tbsp	Add eggs, one at a time, and vanilla. Mix on low speed until blended.
Flour, all-purpose Baking powder Salt	1 lb 8 oz 2 Tbsp 1 tsp	Combine dry ingredients. Add to creamed mixture. Mix on low speed until blended.
Nuts, chopped (optional)	12 oz	Add nuts to batter. Mix to blend.
		Spread batter evenly in 2 lightly greased 12 × 18 × 1-inch baking pans, 3 lb 6 oz per pan. Bake at 325°F for 25 minutes. Cut 5 × 6.

Note:
May be baked in one 18 × 26 × 1-inch baking sheet. Cut 6 × 10.

Variation:
Butterscotch chocolate chip brownies.   Add 1 lb chocolate chips.

Coconut pecan bars

OVEN: 350°F
BAKE: 15–20 minutes, first layer
       20–25 minutes, second layer

YIELD: 96 portions
       2 pans 12 × 18 × 1 inches
PORTION: 2 × 2¼ inches

Ingredient	Amount	Procedure
Margarine or butter	1 lb 8 oz	Blend margarine, brown sugar, and flour on low speed until mixture resembles coarse meal, using flat beater.
Sugar, brown	12 oz	
Flour, all-purpose	1 lb 4 oz	
		Press even layer of mixture into two 12 × 18 × 1-inch baking pans, 1 lb 12 oz per pan.
		Bake at 350°F until light brown, 15–20 minutes.
Eggs, beaten	8 (14 oz)	Combine remaining ingredients to form topping.
Flour, all-purpose	4 oz	
Baking powder	1 Tbsp	
Salt	2 tsp	
Sugar, brown	2 lb 8 oz	
Vanilla	1 Tbsp	
Coconut, shredded or flaked	8 oz	
Pecans, chopped	12 oz	
		Spread topping over baked crust, 3 lb per pan.
		Bake 20–25 minutes.
		Frost with Orange Frosting (p. 211) if desired.
		Cut 6 × 8.

Note:
May be baked in one 18 × 26 × 1-inch baking sheet.

Variation:
Dreamland bars. Reduce coconut to 4 oz. Increase pecans to 1 lb. Add 12 oz chopped maraschino cherries and 1 lb chopped dates. Combine 2 oz margarine or butter and 8 oz powdered sugar. Spread over top. Bake.

Date bars

OVEN: 350°F	YIELD: 60 portions
BAKE: 25–30 minutes	2 pans 12 × 18 × 1 inches
	PORTION: 2½ × 3 inches

Ingredient	Amount	Procedure
Egg yolks	12 (7 oz)	Beat egg yolks on high speed until lemon colored, using flat beater.
Sugar, granulated	2 lb	Add sugar to yolks gradually and continue beating after each addition.
Flour, all-purpose Salt Baking powder	1 lb ½ tsp 1½ Tbsp	Combine flour, salt, and baking powder.
Dates, chopped Nuts, chopped	3 lb 1 lb	Add dates and nuts to flour mixture. Combine with egg-sugar mixture.
Egg whites	12 (14 oz)	Beat egg whites on high speed until they form soft peaks, using wire whip attachment. Fold into batter.
		Spread batter evenly into 2 lightly greased 12 × 18 × 1-inch baking pans, 4 lb 3 oz per pan. Bake at 350°F for 25–30 minutes.
Sugar, powdered	6 oz	Sift powdered sugar over top of warm baked bars. Cut 5 × 6.

Note:
May be baked in one 18 × 26 × 1-inch baking sheet. Cut 6 × 10.

Oatmeal date bars

OVEN: 325°F
BAKE: 45 minutes

YIELD: 96 portions
          2 pans 12 × 18 × 1 inches
PORTION: 2 × 2¼ inches

Ingredient	Amount	Procedure
Margarine or butter	1 lb 10 oz	Cream margarine and sugar on medium speed for 5 minutes, using flat beater.
Sugar, brown	2 lb 12 oz	
Flour, all-purpose	2 lb	Combine dry ingredients.
Rolled oats, quick, uncooked	1 lb 8 oz	Add to creamed mixture. Mix on low speed until crumbly.
Baking soda	2⅔ Tbsp	Spread 2 lb 10 oz prepared mixture into each of two 12 × 18 × 1-inch baking pans. Flatten to an even layer.
Date Filling (p. 215)	3 qt	Spread date filling over oatmeal mixture, 1½ qt per pan. Cover with remainder of dough, 1 lb 4 oz per pan. Bake at 325°F for 45 minutes. Cut 6 × 8 into bars.

Notes:
1. May be baked in one 18 × 26 × 1-inch baking sheet. Cut 8 × 12.
2. Crushed pineapple or cooked dried apricots may be used in place of dates in the filling.

Marshmallow krispie squares

YIELD: 60 portion
2 pans 12 × 18 × 1 inches
PORTION: 2½ × 3 inches

Ingredient	Amount	Procedure
Margarine or butter	1 lb	Melt margarine. Add marshmallows and vanilla.
Marshmallows	4 lb	
Vanilla	1 Tbsp	Stir until completely melted. Cook over low heat 3 minutes longer, stirring constantly. Remove from heat.
Rice Krispies	2 lb 8 oz	Stir Rice Krispies into marshmallow mixture until well coated. Using buttered spatula, press mixture evenly into 2 lightly greased 12 × 18 × 1-inch baking pans, 3 lb per pan. Cut while warm, 5 × 6.

Note:
May be made in one 18 × 26 × 1-inch baking sheet. Cut 5 × 6.

Variations:
1. **Chocolate marshmallow squares.**   Cover squares with a thin, rich chocolate frosting.
2. **Peanut butter squares.**   Add 1 lb 2 oz peanut butter to marshmallow mixture. Proceed as above. Frost with Chocolate Glaze (p. 212).

Pressed and molded cookies

Butter tea cookies

OVEN: 375°F		YIELD: 10 dozen cookies
BAKE: 10–12 minutes		

Ingredient	Amount	Procedure
Butter Sugar, granulated	1 lb 9 oz	Cream butter and sugar on medium speed for 5 minutes, using flat beater.
Egg yolks Vanilla	6 (4 oz) 1 tsp	Add egg yolks and vanilla to creamed mixture. Mix on medium speed until blended.
Flour, all-purpose	1 lb 4 oz	Add flour and mix on low speed. Chill dough.
		Shape with cookie press onto ungreased baking sheets. Bake at 375°F for 10–12 minutes.

Variation:
Thimble cookies.   Roll dough into 1-inch balls. Dip in egg white and roll in finely chopped pecans. Bake 3 minutes at 325°F, then make indentation in center of cookies and fill with jelly. Bake 10–12 minutes longer.

Chocolate tea cookies

OVEN: 350°F   YIELD: 10 dozen cookies
BAKE: 6–10 minutes

Ingredient	Amount	Procedure
Margarine or butter Sugar, granulated	1 lb 12 oz	Cream margarine and sugar on medium speed for 5 minutes, using flat beater.
Eggs Vanilla	2 (4 oz) 1 Tbsp	Add eggs and vanilla to creamed mixture. Blend on medium speed for 5 minutes.
Flour, all-purpose Salt Baking powder Cocoa	1 lb 2 oz ¼ tsp 1 tsp 1 oz (¼ cup)	Combine dry ingredients. Add to creamed mixture and mix on low speed until blended. Chill dough.
		Shape dough with cookie press onto ungreased baking sheets. Bake at 350°F for 6–10 minutes.

Sandies

OVEN: 325°F		YIELD: 8 dozen cookies
BAKE: 20 minutes		

Ingredient	Amount	Procedure
Margarine or butter Sugar, granulated Vanilla	12 oz 3 oz 1 tsp	Cream margarine, sugar, and vanilla on medium speed for 5 minutes, using flat beater.
Flour, all-purpose Salt	1 lb 2 oz 1 tsp	Add flour and salt to creamed mixture. Mix on low speed until blended.
Water Pecans, finely chopped	1 Tbsp 8 oz	Add water and pecans and blend. Chill dough.
		Shape dough into small balls ¾ inch in diameter. If mixture crumbles so it will not stick together, add a small amount of melted margarine. Place on lightly greased or silicone-paper-lined baking sheets. Bake at 325°F until lightly browned, about 20 minutes.
Sugar, powdered, sifted	8 oz (approximate)	Roll in powdered sugar while still hot.

Variation:
Frosty date balls.   Add 1 lb finely chopped pitted dates.

Refrigerator and rolled cookies

Butterscotch refrigerator cookies

OVEN: 375°F   YIELD: 8 dozen cookies
BAKE: 8–10 minutes

Ingredient	Amount	Procedure
Margarine or butter	8 oz	Cream fats and sugars on medium speed for 5 minutes, using flat beater.
Shortening	8 oz	
Sugar, granulated	12 oz	
Sugar, brown	1 lb	
Eggs	4 (7 oz)	Add eggs and vanilla to creamed mixture. Mix on medium speed for 5 minutes.
Vanilla	2 tsp	
Flour, all-purpose	2 lb	Combine dry ingredients.
Cream of tartar	2 tsp	
Baking soda	2 tsp	
Dates, finely chopped	8 oz	Add dry ingredients, dates, and nuts to dough. Mix on low speed until well blended.
Nuts, chopped	8 oz	
		Place dough on waxed paper. Form into three 2-lb rolls, 2 inches in diameter. Wrap. Chill several hours.
		Slice cookies ⅛ inch thick. Place on ungreased baking sheets.
		Bake at 375°F for 8–10 minutes.

Crisp ginger cookies

OVEN: 375°F
BAKE: 8–10 minutes

YIELD: 8 dozen cookies

Ingredient	Amount	Procedure
Molasses Sugar, granulated	1 cup 8 oz	Combine molasses and sugar. Boil 1 minute. Cool.
Shortening	8 oz	Place shortening and molasses in mixer bowl. Blend on medium speed, using flat beater.
Eggs	2 (4 oz)	Add eggs and mix thoroughly.
Flour, all-purpose Salt Baking soda Ginger, ground	1 lb 12 oz (or more) ½ tsp 1 tsp 2 tsp	Combine dry ingredients. Add to molasses-egg mixture. Mix on low speed until well blended.
		Form dough into a roll 2 inches in diameter. Chill thoroughly. Cut into ⅛-inch slices. Place on lightly greased baking sheets. Bake at 375°F for 8–10 minutes.

Note:
Dough may be rolled and cut with cookie cutter.

Oatmeal crispies

| OVEN: 350°F | | YIELD: 8 dozen cookies |
| BAKE: 12–15 minutes | | |

Ingredient	Amount	Procedure
Flour, all-purpose	12 oz	Combine flour, salt, and soda in mixer bowl.
Salt	2 tsp	
Baking soda	2 tsp	
Shortening	1 lb	Add shortening, sugars, eggs, and vanilla to flour mixture.
Sugar, granulated	1 lb	
Sugar, brown	1 lb	Mix on low speed about 5 minutes, using flat beater.
Eggs	4 (7 oz)	
Vanilla	2 tsp	
Rolled oats, quick, uncooked	1 lb	Add rolled oats and nuts. Mix on low speed to blend.
Nuts, chopped	8 oz	Shape dough into three 2-lb rolls, 2 inches in diameter. Wrap in waxed paper and chill overnight.
		Cut dough into slices ¼ inch thick.
		Place 2 inches apart on ungreased baking sheets.
		Bake at 350°F for 12–15 minutes.

Note:
For smaller cookies form into four 1½-inch rolls and slice ⅛ inch thick. Yield: approximately 25 dozen.

Variation:
Oatmeal coconut crispies. Add 1 cup flaked coconut.

Rolled sugar cookies

OVEN: 375°F	YIELD: 10 dozen cookies	
BAKE: 7 minutes	PORTION: 2-inch cookie	

Ingredient	Amount	Procedure
Margarine or butter	1 lb	Cream margarine and sugar on medium
Sugar, granulated	1 lb	speed for 5 minutes, using flat beater.
Eggs	4 (7 oz)	Add eggs and vanilla to creamed mixture.
Vanilla	1 Tbsp	Blend on medium speed for 2 minutes.
Flour, all-purpose	1 lb 8 oz	Combine dry ingredients.
Salt	2 tsp	Add to creamed mixture. Mix on low speed
Baking powder	2 tsp	until blended.
Flour, all-purpose	4 oz	Mix flour and sugar.
Sugar, granulated	2 oz	Roll dough ⅛ inch thick on a surface that has been lightly dusted with flour-sugar mixture.
		Cut into desired shapes. Place on ungreased baking sheets.
		Bake at 375°F for 7 minutes or until lightly browned.

Variations:
1. **Christmas wreath cookies.** Cut rolled dough with doughnut cutter. Brush with beaten egg and sprinkle with chopped nuts. Decorate with candied cherry rings and pieces of citron arranged to represent holly.
2. **Coconut cookies.** Cut rolled dough with round cookie cutter. Brush with melted margarine or butter and sprinkle with shredded coconut, plain or tinted with food coloring.
3. **Filled cookies.** Cut dough with round cutter. Cover half with Fig or Date Filling (pp. 216, 215). Brush edges with milk and cover with remaining cookies. Press edges together with tines of a fork.
4. **Pinwheel cookies.** Divide dough into 2 portions. Add 2 oz melted unsweetened chocolate to one portion. Roll each portion into the same size sheet, ⅛ inch thick. Place chocolate dough over the white dough and press together. Roll as for jelly roll. Chill thoroughly. Cut into thin slices.

Pies

A good pie should have a tender, flaky crust that will just hold its shape. The type of crust produced is partially determined by the method of combining the fat and flour. A flaky crust results when fat and flour are mixed until small lumps are formed throughout the mixture. A mealy crust results when fat and flour are mixed thoroughly.

Tenderness depends largely on the kind of flour and the amount of fat and water used. The tenderness of pastry increases with the proportion of fat; excess fat, however, may cause the crust to be too tender to remove from the pan. Excess water gives a less tender product. Overmixing after the water has been added or using too much flour when rolling toughens pastry also.

A pie crust mix, made by cutting the fat into the flour and salt mixture, may be stored in the refrigerator for four to six weeks and used as needed by adding water to make fresh pie crusts. If freezer storage is adequate, crusts may be made and frozen unbaked until needed, and fruit pies can be made ahead and frozen unbaked also. The quality of the filling for frozen fruit pies is best when waxy maize starch is used.

Quality standards for pastry

Quality standard	Deviation: possible cause
Appearance:	
Golden brown color, blistery surface uniform, attractive edges, fits pan well	Dark: overbaking
	Pale: underbaking, overhandling
	Smooth surface: overhandling, too much flour when rolling
	Shrunken: stretched crust when easing into pan
Tenderness:	
Cuts easily	Tough: too much water, overhandling
	Too tender: undermixing, not enough liquid, too much shortening
Texture:	
Flaky or mealy texture	Compact: underbaked, too much liquid
	Dry: shortening cut in too finely, not enough liquid
Flavor:	
Pleasant bland flavor	Burned: overbaked
	Rancid: poor quality shortening

PIE RECIPES

Pastry

		YIELD: 50 lb dough
Ingredient	**Amount**	**Procedure**
Flour, all-purpose Shortening, hydrogenated	25 lb 18 lb	Mix flour and shortening on low speed, using flat beater. Mix until fat particles are the size of small peas for a flaky crust. For a mealy crust, mixture should resemble cornmeal.
Water, cold Salt	3¾ qt 12 oz	Add water and salt to flour-fat mixture. Mix on low speed only until dough will hold together.

Notes:
1. For seven 9-inch one-crust pies, use 4 lb; for seven 9-inch two-crust pies, use 7 lb. See pp. 250 and 252 for directions for preparation.
2. For eight 8-inch one-crust pies, use 2 lb 8 oz; for eight 8-inch two-crust pies, use 4 lb 8 oz. See pp. 250 and 252 for directions for preparation.

Pastry for one-crust pies

YIELD: 56 portions
4 lb dough
7 9-inch pies
PORTION: cut 8 per pie

Ingredient	Amount	Procedure
Flour, all-purpose Shortening, hydrogenated	2 lb 1 lb 6 oz	Mix flour and shortening on low speed for 1 minute, using pastry knife or flat beater. Scrape sides of bowl and continue mixing until shortening is evenly distributed, 1 to 2 minutes.
Water, cold Salt	1–1¼ cups 1 oz (1½ Tbsp)	Dissolve salt in smaller amount of water (use reserved amount of water if needed). Add to flour mixture. Mix on low speed only until a dough is formed, about 40 seconds. Portion into 9-oz balls for 9-inch pies. See note for 8-inch pies.

Note:
For eight 8-inch pies, use 1 lb 3 oz flour, 13 oz shortening, 1 cup water, and 2½ tsp salt. Scale 5 oz for each crust. To serve, cut pies in six portions.

To make a one-crust pie:
1. Roll dough into a circle 2 inches larger than pie pan.
2. Fit pastry loosely into pan so that there are no air spaces between the crust and pan (Figure 2.25).
3. Trim, allowing ½ inch extra to build up edge.
4. For custard-type pie, crimp edge, add filling, and bake according to the recipe.
5. For cream or chiffon pies, crimp edge and prick crust with fork. Bake according to directions below.
6. Bake in a hot oven (425°F) for 10 minutes or until light brown. Cool. A second pan may be placed over the crust for the first part of baking, then removed and the crust allowed to brown. The second pan helps to keep the crust in shape.
7. Fill baked crust with desired filling.

Figure 2.25 *Preparing pastry for a baked pie shell. Holes are made in shells to keep them flat during baking.*

Pastry for two-crust pies

YIELD: 56 portions
7 lb dough
7 9-inch pies
PORTION: cut 8 per pie

Ingredient	Amount	Procedure
Flour, all-purpose Shortening, hydrogenated	3 lb 6 oz 2 lb 7 oz	Mix flour and shortening on low speed for one minute, using pastry knife or flat beater. Scrape sides of bowl and continue mixing until shortening is evenly distributed, 1–2 minutes.
Water, cold Salt	1¾–2 cups 1¾ oz (2½ Tbsp)	Dissolve salt in smaller amount of water (use reserved amount if water is needed). Add to flour mixture. Mix on low speed only until a dough is formed, about 40 seconds. Portion into 9-oz balls for bottom crust and 7-oz for top crust. See note for 8-inch pies.

Note:
For eight 8-inch pies, use 2 lb flour, 1 lb 8 oz shortening, 1½–1¾ cups water, and 1 oz (1½ Tbsp) salt. Scale 5 oz for bottom crust and 4 oz for top crust. To serve, cut into six portions.

To make a two-crust pie:
1. Roll each ball of dough into a circle. Place pastry for bottom crust in pie pans, easing into pans without stretching the dough.
2. Trim off overhanging dough. If desired, leave ½ inch extra pastry around the edge and fold over to make a pocket of pastry to prevent fruit juices from running out.
3. Add desired filling.
4. Moisten edge of bottom crust with water (Figure 2.26).
5. Cover with top crust, in which slits or vents have been cut near the center to allow steam to escape.
6. Trim top pastry to extend ½ inch beyond edge of pan.
7. Fold edge of top pastry under edge of lower pastry, seal by pressing the two crusts together and fluting with fingertips.
8. If desired, brush top crusts with milk and sprinkle with sugar.
9. Bake as directed in the recipe.

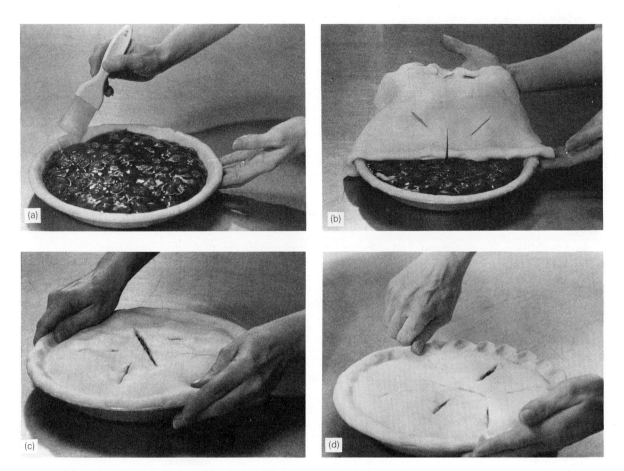

Figure 2.26 *Preparing pastry for a two-crust pie. (a) Moistening edge of crust. (b) Placing top crust on filled pie. (c) Pressing top crust to seal tightly. (d) Fluting edge of pie.*

Graham cracker crust

OVEN: 375°F	YIELD: 56 portions
BAKE: 5 minutes	7 9-inch pies
	PORTION: cut 8 per pie

Ingredient	Amount	Procedure
Graham cracker crumbs	2 lb	Mix all ingredients.
Sugar, granulated	15 oz	Pat 9 oz crumb mixture evenly into each pie
Margarine or butter, melted	15 oz	pan. For 8-inch crusts, see Note 1. Bake at 375°F for about 5 minutes.

Notes:
1. For eight 8-inch shells, use 1 lb 5 oz crumbs, 10 oz sugar, and 10 oz melted margarine or butter. Portion 5 oz per shell.
2. Vanilla wafer crumbs or chocolate cookie crumbs may be substituted for graham cracker crumbs.
3. Crusts may be refrigerated several hours instead of baking.

Variation:
Chocolate crumb crust. Add 6 oz cocoa to graham cracker crumbs and sugar. Mix, then add melted margarine or butter.

Meringue for pies

OVEN: 375°F
BAKE: 10–12 minutes

YIELD: meringue for 7 9-inch pies

Ingredient	Amount	Procedure
Egg whites, at room temperature Salt Cream of tartar	16 (2 cups/1 lb) ½ tsp ½ tsp	Add salt and cream of tartar to egg whites. Whip past frothy stage, on high speed, approximately 1½ minutes, using wire whip attachment.
Sugar, granulated	1 lb	Add sugar gradually while beating. Beat until sugar has dissolved. The meringue should be stiff enough to hold peaks but not dry.
		Spread meringue on filled pies while filling is hot, 5–6 oz per pie. The meringue should touch all edges of the crust. Brown in oven at 375°F for 10–12 minutes or until golden brown.

Notes:
1. For 8-inch pies, use 4 oz per pie.
2. For proper volume, egg whites must have no yolk mixed in them, and the beater and bowl must be free of any trace of fat. Even a small trace of fat will prevent the whites from foaming properly.
3. Egg whites should be at room temperature before beating. The meringue will be higher and lighter.

Meringue shells

OVEN: 275°F	YIELD: 50 shells
BAKE: 1 hour	PORTION: 3 oz

Ingredient	Amount	Procedure
Egg whites	28 (3 cups/1 lb 8 oz)	Add salt and cream of tartar to egg whites. Beat on high speed until frothy, using wire whip attachment.
Salt	1 tsp	
Cream of tartar	1 tsp	
Sugar, granulated	3 lb	Add sugar ½ cup at a time, beating on high speed between each addition until sugar is dissolved and mixture will hold its shape, 20–30 minutes.
		Place mixture on greased and floured baking sheets with No. 10 dipper and shape into nests with spoon; or place on pans with pastry tube. Bake at 275°F for about 1 hour. Watch carefully the last 15–20 minutes to avoid overcooking. Meringues should be white, not brown. If overcooked, they are too brittle. Serve ice cream or fruit in the center.

Variations:
1. **Angel pie.**   Place meringue in well-greased and floured pie pans, about 1¼ qt per pan. Use spoon to build up sides. After baking fill each shell with 3 cups Cream Pie filling (p. 264), Lemon Pie filling (p. 267), or Chocolate Pie filling (p. 265). Then top with a thin layer of whipped cream.
2. **Meringue sticks.**   Force mixture through pastry tube to form sticks. Sprinkle with chopped nuts. Bake.

Pies made with canned fruit

OVEN: 400°F	YIELD: 56 portions
BAKE: 30 minutes	7 9-inch pies
	PORTION: cut 8 per pie

Ingredient	Amount	Procedure
Pastry for Two-Crust Pies (p. 252)	7 lb	Make pastry. Divide into 9-oz balls for bottom crust and 7-oz balls for top crusts. Roll and place bottom crusts in seven 9-inch pie pans. For 8-inch pies, see Note 1.
Fruit, pie pack	2 No. 10 cans	Drain fruit. Measure liquid and add water to make 2 qt. Bring 1½ qt of the liquid to boiling point.
Cornstarch	8 oz	Mix remaining liquid with cornstarch and add gradually, while stirring with a wire whip, to hot liquid. Cook until thick and clear.
Sugar, granulated Salt	3 lb 8 oz 2 tsp	While still hot, add sugar and salt. Mix thoroughly and bring to boiling point. Add drained fruit and mix carefully to avoid breaking or mashing fruit. Cool slightly.
		Scale 1 lb 12 oz–2 lb (3½–4 cups) filling into each unbaked pie shell. Moisten edge of bottom crust with water. Cover with top crust. Seal edge, trim, and flute edges (p. 253). Bake at 400°F for 30 minutes or until crust is browned.

Notes:
1. For eight 8-inch pies, make 4 lb 8 oz dough for crusts and portion into 5 oz for bottom crust and 4 oz for top crust. For filling, use 1½ No. 10 cans fruit, 3 lb sugar (variable), 6 oz cornstarch, and 1½ tsp salt. Drain liquid from fruit and add water to make 1½ qt liquid. Scale 1 lb–1 lb 8 oz (approximately 3 cups) filling per pie.
2. Suggested fillings: apple, apricot, blackberry, cherry, gooseberry, or peach.
3. Other thickening agents may be used, such as waxy maize (6 oz total for 9-inch or 4½ oz total for 8-inch pies) or tapioca (9 oz total for 9-inch or 7½ oz total for 8-inch pies).

TABLE 2.5   GUIDE FOR USING FROZEN FRUIT IN PIES OR COBBLERS (SEVEN 9-INCH PIES)

| Fruit 10 lb | Sugar[a] | Thickening | | Seasonings |
		Cornstarch[a]	Waxy maize[a]	
Apples	1 lb 8 oz	3 oz	2½ oz	Salt, 1 tsp; nutmeg, 1 tsp; cinnamon, 1 Tbsp; butter, 2 oz
Apricots	2 lb	5½ oz	4 oz	Cinnamon, 2 tsp
Berries	2½–3½ lb	6½ oz	5 oz	Lemon juice, 2 Tbsp; salt, 1 tsp
Blueberries	3 lb	8 oz	6 oz	Salt, 1 tsp; butter, 2 oz; lemon juice, 1½ cup; cinnamon, 1 tsp
Blue plums	2–2½ lb	5½ oz	4 oz	Salt, 1 tsp; butter, 2 oz
Cherries	1 lb 12 oz	7 oz	5 oz	Salt, 1 tsp
Gooseberries	6 lb	14 oz	10 oz	Salt, ½ tsp
Peaches	1 lb 6 oz	5½ oz	4 oz	Butter, 1 oz; salt, 1 tsp; almond extract, ¼ tsp; cinnamon, 1 tsp; nutmeg, 1 tsp
Pineapple	2 lb	5½ oz	4 oz	Salt, 1 tsp
Rhubarb	5 lb	7 oz	5 oz	Salt, 1 tsp
Strawberries	2 lb	12 oz	8½ oz	Lemon juice, ¾ cup; red color, ¾ tsp

[a] The amount of sugar and cornstarch or waxy maize added to the fruit will vary according to the pack of the fruit and individual preferences of flavor and consistency. Frozen fruits packed without the addition of sugar are known as "dry pack." When sugar is added during the freezing process, the ratio is usually 3, 4, or 5 parts by weight of fruit to 1 part by weight of sugar. Use less thickening for cobblers. Some fruits are available individually quick frozen (IQF) without added sugar.

Pies made with frozen fruit

OVEN: 400°F
BAKE: 30–40 minutes

YIELD: 56 portions
        7 9-inch pies
PORTION: cut 8 per pie

Ingredient	Amount	Procedure
Pastry for Two-Crust Pies (p. 252)	7 lb	Make pastry. Divide into 9-oz balls for bottom crust, 7-oz balls for top crust. Roll and place bottom crusts in seven 9-inch pie pans. For 8-inch pies, see note.
Fruit, frozen	10 lb	Thaw fruit. Measure juice. If necessary, add water to bring total liquid to 1½–2 qt according to consistency desired.
Sugar, granulated Cornstarch or waxy maize[a]	See Table 2.5 See Table 2.5	Combine sugar and starch. Add to hot liquid, stirring with wire whip.
Seasonings	See Table 2.5	Add seasonings to thickened liquid and pour over fruit. Mix carefully to avoid breaking or mashing fruit.
		Scale 1 lb 12 oz–2 lb (3½–4 cups) filling into each unbaked pie shell. Moisten edge of bottom crust with water. Cover with top crust in which slits have been made for steam to escape. Seal edge, trim and flute edges (see p. 253). Bake at 400°F for 30–40 minutes or until fruit is done and crust is golden brown.

[a] Allow 2–3 oz cornstarch or 2–2½ oz waxy maize per qt of liquid. Use of waxy maize or other waxy starch products results in a translucent soft gel through which the fruit shows clearly. The color is brighter and the gel is less opaque and less rigid, making it ideal for thickening fruit fillings. It is important to use a waxy starch if the pies are to be frozen.

Note:
For eight 8-inch pies, use 4 lb 8 oz pastry, portioned 5 oz for bottom crust and 4 oz for top crust. Portion 1 lb–1 lb 8 oz (approximately 3 cups) filling per pie.

Fresh apple pie

OVEN: 400°F		YIELD: 56 portions
BAKE: 45 minutes		7 9-inch pies
		PORTION: cut 8 per pie

Ingredient	Amount	Procedure
Pastry for Two-Crust Pies (p. 252)	7 lb	Make pastry. Divide into 9-oz balls for bottom crust, 7-oz for top crust. Roll and place bottom crusts in seven 9-inch pie pans. For 8-inch pies, see Note 1.
Apples, tart, fresh	12 lb (EP) 15 lb (AP)	Peel, core, and slice apples.
Sugar, granulated Flour, all-purpose Cinnamon	3 lb 4 oz 1 Tbsp	Combine sugar, flour, and cinnamon. Add to apples and mix carefully.
Margarine or butter	8 oz	Portion 2 lb 4 oz filling into each unbaked crust. Add 1 oz margarine or butter to each pie. Moisten edge of bottom crust. Cover with perforated top crust. Seal edge, trim excess dough, and flute edges (see p. 253). Bake at 400°F for 45 minutes or until apples are tender.

Notes:
1. For eight 8-inch pies, use 4 lb 8 oz dough for crust and portion 5 oz for bottom crust and 4 oz for top crust. Portion filling, 2 lb per pie.
2. Suggested apples are Jonathan, Granny Smith, and Winesap.

Variation:
Apple crumb pie.   Omit top crust. Sprinkle apples with **Streusel topping:** Mix 1 lb flour, 1 lb 10 oz sugar, 2 oz nonfat dry milk, and 1 tsp salt. Cut in 10 oz margarine or butter and add 6 oz chopped pecans. Use 1 cup per pie. Bake until apples are tender and topping is brown.

Sour cream apple nut pie

OVEN: 450°F, 350°F
BAKE: 10 minutes, 55 minutes

YIELD: 56 portions
              7 9-inch pies
PORTION: cut 8 per pie

Ingredient	Amount	Procedure
Pastry for One-Crust Pies (p. 250)	4 lb	Make pastry. Line seven 9-inch pie pans, 9 oz per pan. For 8-inch pies, see note.
Sour cream Sugar, granulated Flour, all-purpose Eggs Vanilla Salt	3 lb 8 oz 6 oz 4 (6 oz) 2 Tbsp 1 tsp	Combine and mix until thoroughly blended.
Apples, sliced, frozen	8 lb 8 oz	Combine apples and sour cream mixture, being careful not to break apples.
		Scale 1 lb 12 oz filling into each unbaked crust. Bake at 450°F for 10 minutes. Reduce temperature to 350°F and continue baking until filling is slightly puffed and golden brown, about 40 minutes.

TOPPING

Ingredient	Amount	Procedure
Flour, all-purpose Sugar, brown Sugar, granulated Cinnamon	5 oz 4 oz 5 oz 2 Tbsp	Combine flour, sugars, and cinnamon.
Margarine or butter	5 oz	Add margarine to dry ingredients. Mix until crumbly.
Walnuts, coarsely chopped	8 oz	Add nuts. Mix in. Scale 3½ oz topping over each pie and bake for 15 minutes.

Note:
For eight 8-inch pies, use 2 lb 8 oz dough portioned 5 oz per pie. For filling, scale apple mixture 1 lb 8 oz per pie and topping 3 oz per pie.

Raisin pie

OVER: 400°F		YIELD: 56 portions
BAKE: 30 minutes		7 9-inch pies
		PORTION: cut 8 per pie

Ingredient	Amount	Procedure
Pastry for Two-Crust Pies (p. 252)	7 lb	Make pastry. Divide into 9-oz balls for bottom crust, 7-oz for top crust. Roll and place bottom crusts in seven 9-inch pie pans. For 8-inch pies, see note.
Raisins	4 lb	Simmer raisins in water until plump.
Water, hot	4½ qt	Cool slightly.
Sugar, granulated	2 lb 4 oz	Combine sugar, cornstarch, and salt.
Cornstarch	6 oz	Add to raisins and cook until thickened.
Salt	2 tsp	Remove from heat.
Lemon juice	6 Tbsp	Add lemon juice and margarine to raisin mixture. Cool slightly.
Margarine or butter	3 oz	
		Portion 2 lb 4 oz (3½–4 cups) filling into each unbaked crust. Moisten edge of bottom crust. Cover with perforated top crust. Seal edge, trim excess dough, and flute edges (see p. 253). Bake at 400°F for 30 minutes or until crust is golden brown.

Note:
For eight 8-inch pies, use 4 lb 8 oz dough, portioned 5 oz for bottom crust and 4 oz for top crust. For filling, portion 1 lb 14 oz (3–3½ cups) filling per pie.

Variation:
Dried apricot pie. Use 5 lb dried apricots. Cover with hot water; let stand 1 hour. Cook slowly without stirring until tender. Combine 4 lb granulated sugar and 2½ oz cornstarch. Mix with ½ cup cold water. Add to fruit a few minutes before it is done. Continue cooking until juice is clear. Proceed as for Raisin Pie.

Rhubarb pie

OVEN: 400°F	YIELD: 56 portions
BAKE: 35 minutes	7 9-inch pies
	PORTION: cut 8 per pie

Ingredient	Amount	Procedure
Rhubarb, fresh or frozen	10 lb (EP)	If fresh rhubarb is used, wash and trim. Do not peel. Cut in 1-inch pieces.
Sugar, granulated Tapioca, quick-cooking Salt Orange peel, grated	5 lb 8 oz 6 oz 2 tsp 3 Tbsp	Combine and stir into rhubarb. Let stand 30 minutes.
Pastry for Two-Crust Pies (p. 252)	7 lb	Make pastry. Divide into 9-oz balls for bottom crust, 7-oz for top crust. Roll and place bottom crusts in seven 9-inch pie pans, 9 oz per pan. For 8-inch pies, see Note 1.
Margarine or butter, melted	5 oz	Portion 2 lb 4 oz filling into each unbaked crust. Distribute margarine over filling in each pie. Moisten edges with cold water. Cover with top crust or pastry strips. Press edges together. Bake at 400°F for 35 minutes or until crust is golden brown and fruit is tender.

Notes:
  1. For eight 8-inch pies, use 4 lb 8 oz dough portioned 5 oz for bottom crust and 4 oz for top crust. Scale 1 lb 14 oz filling per pie.
  2. 8 oz cornstarch or 5 oz waxy maize starch may be substituted for the tapioca.

Rhubarb custard pie

OVEN: 375°F
BAKE: 45–50 minutes

YIELD: 56 portions
       7 9-inch pies
PORTION: cut 8 per pie

Ingredient	Amount	Procedure
Pastry for One-Crust Pies (p. 250)	4 lb	Make pastry. Line seven 9-inch pie pans, 9 oz per pan. Flute edges. For 8-inch pies, see Note 1.
Rhubarb, fresh or frozen	8 lb (EP)	If fresh rhubarb is used, wash and trim. Do not peel. Cut into ¼-inch pieces.
Eggs, beaten	12 (1 lb 5 oz)	Add eggs to rhubarb.
Sugar, granulated Flour, all-purpose Salt Lemon peel, grated	4 lb 8 oz 9 oz 1 tsp 1 tsp	Mix dry ingredients. Add to rhubarb mixture. Scale 2 lb (4½ cups) filling into each unbaked crust. Bake at 375°F for 45–50 minutes or until custard is set.

Notes:
1. For eight 8-inch pies, use 2 lb 8 oz dough, portioned 5 oz per pie. Use 1 lb 12 oz filling per pie.
2. May be topped with Meringue (p. 255).
3. Unbaked pie may be covered with a top crust or a latticed top made of ⅛-inch pastry strips.

Cream pie

OVEN: 425°F for pastry
       375°F for meringue
BAKE: 10 minutes, 12 minutes

YIELD: 56 portions
       7 9-inch pies
PORTION: cut 8 per pie

Ingredient	Amount	Procedure
Pastry for One-Crust Pies (p. 250)	4 lb	Make pastry. Line seven 9-inch pie pans, 9 oz per pan. For 8-inch pies, see note. Flute edges and prick crust with fork (p. 251). Bake at 425°F for 10 minutes or until light brown. Cool.

Milk	3¾ qt	Heat milk to boiling point in a steam-jacketed or other large kettle.
Sugar, granulated Cornstarch Salt Milk, cold	2 lb 12 oz 13 oz 2½ tsp 1¼ qt	Mix sugar, cornstarch, and salt. Add cold milk and stir until smooth. Add to hot milk gradually, stirring briskly with a wire whip. Cook until smooth and thick, approximately 10 minutes.
Egg yolks, beaten	20 (13 oz)	Add, while stirring, a small amount of hot mixture to the egg yolks. Add to remaining hot mixture, stirring constantly. Stir slowly and cook 5–10 minutes. Remove from heat.
Margarine or butter Vanilla	5 oz 2½ Tbsp	Stir in margarine and vanilla. Pour 2 lb (4 cups) filling into each baked pie shell.
Egg whites Salt Sugar, granulated Cream of tartar	20 (1 lb 6 oz) ½ tsp 1 lb 4 oz ½ tsp	Prepare Meringue (p. 255). Cover each filled pie with 5 oz meringue. Bake at 375°F for 10–12 minutes or until meringue is golden brown.

Note:
For eight 8-inch pies, use 2 lb 8 oz dough, portioned 5 oz per pie. Use 1 lb 12 oz (3½ cups) filling per pie.

Variations:
1. **Banana cream pie.**   Slice 1 large banana into each pie shell before adding cream filling.
2. **Chocolate cream pie.**   Add 6 oz cocoa or 8 oz unsweetened chocolate. Increase sugar to 3 lb. If using cocoa, mix with cornstarch and sugar. If using chocolate, melt and add to hot milk.
3. **Coconut cream pie.**   Add 10 oz toasted coconut to filling and sprinkle 2 oz coconut over meringue.
4. **Date cream pie.**   Add 3 lb chopped, pitted dates to cooked filling.
5. **Fruit glazed pie.**   Use frozen blueberries, strawberries, or cherries. Thaw 6 lb frozen fruit and drain. Measure 1 qt fruit syrup, adding water if needed to make that amount. Add slowly to a mixture of 6 oz sugar, 4 oz cornstarch, and ¾ cup lemon juice. Cook until thick and clear. Cool slightly. Add drained fruit. Spread over cream pies.
6. **Nut cream pie.**   Add ½ cup chopped pecans or other nuts.
7. **Pineapple cream pie.**   Add 3½ cups crushed pineapple, drained, to cooked filling.

Butterscotch cream pie

OVER: 425°F for pastry
         375°F for meringue
BAKE: 10 minutes, 12 minutes

YIELD: 56 portions
        7 9-inch pies
PORTION: cut 8 per pie

Ingredient	Amount	Procedure
Pastry for One-Crust Pies (p. 250)	4 lb	Make pastry. Line seven 9-inch pie pans, 9 oz per pan. For 8-inch pies, see Note 1. Flute edges and prick crust with fork (p. 251). Bake at 425°F for 10 minutes or until light brown.
Margarine or butter	1 lb	Melt margarine. Stir in sugar.
Sugar, brown	2 lb 8 oz	Cook over low heat to 220°F, stirring occasionally.
Milk	3 qt	Add milk slowly to margarine-sugar mixture while stirring with wire whip. Stir until all sugar is dissolved. Heat mixture to boiling.
Cornstarch	6 oz	Combine cornstarch, flour, and salt.
Flour, all-purpose	6 oz	
Salt	1 Tbsp	
Milk, warm	1 qt	Combine milk and eggs. Add to cornstarch and flour mixture and mix.
Eggs, whole	5 (9 oz)	Add to the hot mixture while stirring. Cook until thick.
Egg yolks	10 (6 oz)	Remove from heat.
Margarine or butter	4 oz	Add margarine and vanilla. Cool partially.
Vanilla	2 Tbsp	Fill baked pie shells, 1 lb 12 oz (3½ cups) per pie.
Egg whites	16 (1 lb 2 oz)	Prepare Meringue (p. 255).
Salt	½ tsp	Cover each filled pie with 5 oz meringue.
Sugar, granulated	1 lb	Bake at 375°F for 10–12 minutes, or until meringue is golden brown.
Cream of tartar	½ tsp	

Notes:
1. For eight 8-inch pies, use 2 lb 8 oz dough portioned 5 oz per pie. Use 1 lb 8 oz (3 cups) filling per pie.
2. Recipe may be used for pudding. Omit flour, increase cornstarch to 8 oz.

Lemon pie

OVEN: 425°F pastry		YIELD: 56 portions
375°F meringue		7 9-inch pies
BAKE: 10 minutes, 12 minutes		PORTION: cut 8 per pie

Ingredient	Amount	Procedure
Pastry for One-Crust Pies (p. 250)	4 lb	Make pastry. Line seven 9-inch pie pans, 9 oz per pan. For 8-inch pies, see note. Flute edges and prick with fork. Bake at 425°F for 10 minutes or until light brown.
Water Salt Lemon rinds, grated	2¼ qt 2 tsp 3	Heat water, salt, and lemon peel to boiling point.
Sugar, granulated Cornstarch Water, cold	3 lb 8 oz 12 oz 3 cups	Mix sugar and cornstarch. Add cold water and stir until mixed. Add slowly to boiling water, stirring constantly with wire whip. Cook until thickened and clear. Remove from heat.
Egg yolks, beaten	16 (1½ cups)	Add, while stirring, a small amount of hot mixture to egg yolks. Add to remaining hot mixture, stirring constantly. Return to heat and cook about 5 minutes. Remove from heat.
Margarine or butter Lemon juice	3 oz 1½ cups	Add margarine and lemon juice. Blend. Scale into baked pie shells, 1 lb 10 oz (3½ cups) per pie.
Egg whites Salt Sugar, granulated Cream of tartar	16 (1 lb 2 oz) ½ tsp 1 lb ½ tsp	Prepare Meringue (p. 255). Cover each pie with 5 oz meringue. Bake at 375°F for 10–12 minutes, or until meringue is golden brown.

Note:
For eight 8-inch pies, use 2 lb 8 oz dough portioned 5 oz per pie. Use 3 cups filling per pie.

Custard pie

OVEN: 450°F, 350°F	YIELD: 56 portions
BAKE: 35 minutes	7 9-inch pies
	PORTION: 8 per pie

Ingredient	Amount	Procedure
Pastry for One-Crust Pies (p. 250)	4 lb	Make pastry. Line seven 9-inch pie pans, 9 oz per pan. For 8-inch pies, see note. Flute edges.
Eggs, large	30 (3 lb 4 oz)	Beat eggs slightly.
Sugar, granulated	1 lb 14 oz	Add sugar, salt, and vanilla. Mix.
Salt	1¼ tsp	
Vanilla	2½ Tbsp	
Milk, scalded	1¼ gal	Add hot milk, slowly at first, then more rapidly. Pour into unbaked pie shells, 1 qt per pie.
Nutmeg, ground	2 tsp	Sprinkle nutmeg over top of pies. Bake at 450°F for 15 minutes. Reduce heat to 350°F and bake for 20 minutes, or until a knife inserted halfway between the edge and center comes out clean.

Note:
For eight 8-inch pies, use 2 lb 8 oz dough portioned 5 oz per pie. For filling, use 24 (2 lb 8 oz) eggs, 1 lb 8 oz sugar, 1 tsp salt, 2 Tbsp vanilla, and 1 gal milk, portioned 3 cups per pie.

Variation:
Coconut custard pie. Add 1 lb flaked coconut. Omit nutmeg.

Pumpkin pie

OVEN:	450°F, 350°F	YIELD:	56 portions
BAKE:	15 minutes, 30 minutes		7 9-inch pies
		PORTION:	cut 8 per pie

Ingredient	Amount	Procedure
Pastry for One-Crust Pies (p. 250)	4 lb	Make pastry. Line seven 9-inch pie pans, 9 oz per pan. For 8-inch pies, see Note 1. Flute edges.
Eggs, beaten Pumpkin	14 (1 lb 8 oz) 2½ qt (3 No. 2½ cans	Combine eggs and pumpkin in mixer bowl.
Sugar, granulated Sugar, brown Ginger, ground Cinnamon, ground Salt	1 lb 12 oz 10 oz 1½ tsp 1½ Tbsp 1 Tbsp	Combine sugars and seasonings. Add to pumpkin mixture.
Milk, hot	2¾ qt	Add milk to pumpkin mixture. Mix. Pour into unbaked pie shells, 1 qt per pie. Bake at 450°F for 15 minutes. Reduce heat to 350°F and bake for 30 minutes, or until a knife inserted halfway between the edge and center comes out clean.

Notes:
1. For eight 8-inch pies, use 2 lb 8 oz pastry portioned 5 oz per pie. Use 3½ cups filling per pie.
2. Undiluted evaporated milk may be substituted for fresh milk.
3. One pound chopped pecans may be sprinkled over tops of pies after 15 minutes of baking. Continue baking.

Variation:
Praline pumpkin pie. Mix 12 oz finely chopped pecans, 14 oz brown sugar, and 8 oz margarine or butter. Pat 4 oz of mixture into each unbaked pie shell before pouring in filling.

Pecan pie

OVEN: 350°F	YIELD: 56 portions
BAKE: 40 minutes	7 9-inch pies
	PORTION: cut 8 per pie

Ingredient	Amount	Procedure
Pastry for One-Crust Pies (p. 250)	4 lb	Make pastry. Line seven 9-inch pie pans, 9 oz per pan. For 8-inch pies, see note. Flute edges.
Sugar, granulated Margarine or butter Salt	5 lb 5 oz 1 Tbsp	Cream sugar, margarine, and salt on medium speed until fluffy, using flat beater.
Eggs, beaten	30 (3 lb 4 oz)	Add eggs to creamed mixture and mix well.
Corn syrup, white Vanilla	1¼ qt 3 Tbsp	Add corn syrup and vanilla. Blend thoroughly.
Pecan halves or pieces	2 lb	Place 4½ oz pecans in each unbaked pie shell. Pour 1 lb 8 oz (3 cups) egg-sugar mixture over pecans. Bake at 350°F for 40 minutes, or until filling is set.

Note:
For eight 8-inch pies, use 2 lb 8 oz pastry portioned 5 oz per pie. Use 2½ cups filling and 4 oz pecans per pie.

Pecan cream cheese pie

OVEN: 375°F, 350°F
BAKE: 10 minutes, 40–45 minutes

YIELD: 56 portions
        7 9-inch pies
PORTION: 8 per pie

Ingredient	Amount	Procedure
Pastry for One-Crust Pies (p. 250)	2 lb 8 oz	Make pastry. Line seven 9-inch pie pans, 5 oz per pan. For 8-inch pies, see note. Flute edges and prick crust with fork (p. 251). Bake at 375°F for 10 minutes or until set. Cool.
Cream cheese, softened Sugar, granulated	3 lb 12 oz 1 lb	Combine cream cheese and sugar in mixer bowl. Beat on medium until smooth, using flat beater.
Eggs Salt Vanilla	7 (12 oz) 1 tsp 2 Tbsp	Add eggs, salt, and vanilla to creamed mixture. Beat until smooth. Spread 12 oz filling into each pie shell.
Pecan pieces	2 lb 3 oz	Sprinkle 5 oz pecans over cream cheese layer.
Eggs Sugar, brown Corn syrup Vanilla	11 (1 lb 4 oz) 8 oz 2 lb 8 oz 1 Tbsp	Combine eggs, sugar, corn syrup, and vanilla in mixer bowl. Mix until blended. Scale 10 oz (approximately 1 cup) over pecans. Bake at 350°F for 40–45 minutes. Cool. Refrigerate overnight.

Note:
For eight 8-inch pies, use 2 lb 8 oz pastry portioned 5 oz per pie. For the filling, portion 11 oz cream cheese filling, 8 oz (1 cup) syrup mixture, and 4 oz pecans per pie.

Chocolate chiffon pie

OVEN: 425°F pastry
BAKE: 10 minutes

YIELD: 56 portions
       7 9-inch pies
PORTION: cut 8 per pie

Ingredient	Amount	Procedure
Pastry for One-Crust Pies (p. 250)	4 lb	Make pastry. Line seven 9-inch pie pans, 9 oz per pan. For 8-inch pies, see Note 1. Flute edges and prick crust with a fork (p. 251). Bake at 425°F for 10 minutes or until light brown.
Gelatin, unflavored Water, cold	1½ oz 1½ cups	Sprinkle gelatin over water. Let stand 10 minutes.
Unsweetened chocolate Water, boiling	8 oz 3 cups	Melt chocolate. Add hot water slowly. Stir until mixed. Add gelatin and stir until dissolved.
Egg yolks, beaten Sugar, granulated Salt	24 (1 lb) 1 lb 8 oz 1½ tsp	Combine egg yolks, sugar, and salt. Cook until mixture begins to thicken.
Vanilla	2 Tbsp	Add vanilla and chocolate to egg mixture. Chill until mixture begins to congeal.
Egg whites Sugar, granulated	24 (1 lb 12 oz) 1 lb 8 oz	Beat egg whites until frothy. Gradually add sugar and beat at high speed until meringue can be formed into soft peaks. Fold into chocolate mixture. Scale into baked pie shells, 1 lb (4 cups) per pie. Refrigerate.
Cream, whipping Sugar, granulated	1 qt ¼ cup	Just before serving, whip cream. Add sugar. Spread 1 cup whipped cream over each pie.

Notes:
1. For eight 8-inch pies, use 2 lb 8 oz pastry portioned 5 oz per pie. For filling, use 12 oz (3 cups) per pie.
2. Graham Cracker Crust (p. 254) may be used in place of pastry.

Variations:
1. **Chocolate peppermint chiffon pie.** Cover pie with whipped cream to which 1 lb crushed peppermint candy sticks has been added.
2. **Chocolate refrigerator dessert.** Use ⅔ recipe Chocolate Chiffon Pie. Spread 12 oz vanilla wafer crumbs over bottom of 12 × 20 × 2-inch pan. Pour in chocolate chiffon mixture and cover with 1 lb 12 oz crumbs.
3. **Frozen chocolate chiffon pie.** Fold in 3 cups cream, whipped. Pile into pastry or graham cracker crust. Spread over tops of pies 1½ cups cream, whipped and sweetened with 3 Tbsp sugar. Freeze. Serve frozen.

Ice cream pie

OVEN: 500°F	YIELD: 56 portions
BAKE: 2–3 minutes	7 9-inch pies
	PORTION: cut 8 per pie

Ingredient	Amount	Procedure
Graham Cracker Crusts (p. 254)	1 recipe	Prepare seven 9-inch crusts. For 8-inch pies, see Note 1.
Vanilla ice cream	2 gal	Soften ice cream. Dip into prepared crusts, using 4½ cups per pie. Freeze several hours.
Egg whites	24 (2 lb 10 oz)	Add salt to egg whites. Beat until frothy, using whip attachment.
Salt	¾ tsp	
Sugar, granulated	1 lb 8 oz	Add sugar gradually, beating at high speed until sugar has dissolved.
Vanilla	1½ tsp	Add vanilla. Cover pies with meringue, 9 oz per pie. Brown quickly (2–3 minutes) in oven at 500°F. Return to freezer if not served immediately.
Chocolate Sauce (p. 581)	1½ qt	Serve with chocolate sauce or fresh strawberries.

Notes:
1. For eight 8-inch pies, portion 1 qt ice cream per pie. Cover with 8 oz meringue.
2. Pastry crust, baked, may be used in place of graham cracker crust.
3. Other flavors of ice cream may be used.

Variation:
Raspberry Alaska pie. Thicken three 40-oz packages frozen red raspberries with 2 oz cornstarch. Make thin layers of thickened berries and ice cream in graham cracker crusts, using about half of the berries. Proceed as for Ice Cream Pie. Spoon remaining berries over individual servings of pie.

Lemon chiffon pie

OVEN: 425°F pastry
BAKE: 10 minutes

YIELD: 48 portions
       7 9-inch pies
PORTION: cut 8 per pie

Ingredient	Amount	Procedure
Pastry for One-Crust Pies (p. 250)	4 lb	Make pastry. Line seven 9-inch pie pans, 9 oz per pan. For 8-inch pies, see Note 1. Flute edges and prick crust with fork (p. 251). Bake at 425°F for 10 minutes or until light brown.
Gelatin, unflavored Water, cold	1½ oz 1¾ cups	Sprinkle gelatin over water. Let stand 10 minutes.
Egg yolks, beaten Sugar, granulated Salt Lemon juice	21 (13 oz) 1 lb 8 oz 2 tsp 2½ cups	Add sugar, salt, and lemon juice to egg yolks. Cook in steam-jacketed kettle or over hot water until consistency of custard. Remove from heat. Add softened gelatin. Stir until dissolved.
Lemon peel, grated	2 Tbsp	Add lemon peel. Chill until mixture begins to congeal.
Egg whites Sugar, granulated	21 (1 lb 8 oz) 1 lb 2 oz	Beat egg whites until frothy. Gradually add sugar and beat until meringue will form soft peaks. Fold into lemon mixture. Scale into baked pie shells, 1 lb (4 cups) per pie. Refrigerate.
Cream, whipping Sugar, granulated	1 qt ½ cup	Just before serving, whip cream. Spread 1 cup cream over each pie.

Notes:
1. For eight 8-inch pies, use 2 lb 8 oz pastry portioned 5 oz per pie. For the filling, use 12 oz (3 cups) per pie.
2. Graham Cracker Crust (p. 254) may be used in place of pastry.

Variations:
1. **Frozen lemon pie.** Increase sugar in custard to 2 lb. Delete sugar from meringue. Beat egg whites, fold into 2 qt cream, whipped. Fold into chilled lemon mixture. Pour into Graham Cracker Crusts (p. 254). Freeze. Serve frozen.

2. **Lemon refrigerator dessert.** Crush 3 lb 8 oz vanilla wafers. Spread half of crumbs in bottom of 12 × 20 × 2-inch pan. Pour chiffon pie mixture over crumbs and cover with remaining crumbs.
3. **Orange chiffon pie.** Substitute 2 cups orange juice for 2 cups lemon juice. Substitute grated orange peel for lemon peel.

Strawberry chiffon pie

OVEN: 425°F pastry
BAKE: 10 minutes

YIELD: 56 portions
        7 9-inch pies
PORTION: cut 8 per pie

Ingredient	Amount	Procedure
Pastry for One-Crust Pies (p. 250)	4 lb	Make pastry. Line seven 9-inch pie pans, 9 oz per pan. For 8-inch pies, see note. Flute edges and prick crust with fork (p. 251). Bake at 425°F for 10 minutes or until light brown.
Strawberries, sliced frozen	3 lb 12 oz	Drain strawberries. Reserve juice.
Strawberry gelatin Water, boiling	1 lb 4 oz 1¼ qt	Dissolve gelatin in boiling water.
Strawberry juice drained from berries Lemon juice	2 lb (1 qt) ⅔ cup	Add enough water to reserved juice to make 1 qt. Combine lemon and strawberry juices. Add to gelatin mixture. Chill until partially set. Stir occasionally.
Whipped topping	3 cups	Whip topping stiff but not dry. Whip gelatin mixture until soft peaks form. Fold in whipped topping.
Egg whites Salt Sugar, granulated	10 (12 oz) 1 tsp 12 oz	Add salt to egg whites. Beat until soft peaks form. Gradually add sugar. Beat until stiff peaks form. Fold in gelatin mixture. Fold strawberries into mixture. Portion 1 lb 4 oz filling into each baked pie shell. Chill until firm.

Note:
For eight 8-inch pies, use 2 lb 8 oz pastry portioned 5 oz per pie. For the filling, use 1 lb per pie.

Frozen mocha almond pie

YIELD: 56 portions
           7 9-inch pies
PORTION: cut 8 per pie

Ingredient	Amount	Procedure
Graham Cracker Crusts (p. 254)	1 recipe	Prepare seven 9-inch crusts. For 8-inch pies, see note.
Gelatin, unflavored Water, cold	1½ oz 1 cup	Sprinkle gelatin over water. Let stand 10 minutes.
Egg yolks, beaten Sugar, granulated Salt Coffee, hot	18 (11 oz) 1 lb 8 oz 1 Tbsp 2 qt	Add sugar, salt, and coffee to egg yolks. Cook in steam-jacketed kettle or over hot water until coats spoon. Remove from heat. Add softened gelatin. Stir until dissolved. Chill until mixture is consistency of unbeaten egg whites.
Egg whites Cream of tartar Sugar, granulated	18 (1 lb 5 oz) 1½ tsp 1 lb 8 oz	Add cream of tartar to egg whites. Beat until frothy. Add sugar gradually and beat on high speed until consistency of meringue. Fold into gelatin mixture.
Cream, whipping Sugar, granulated	1 qt ¼ cup	Whip cream. Add sugar to one-third of the whipped cream. Save for topping.
Almonds, toasted Vanilla	1 lb 2 Tbsp	Add almonds and vanilla to remaining whipped cream. Fold into gelatin mixture. Pour into prepared crusts. Spread remaining whipped cream over pies and freeze. Remove from freezer 15–20 minutes before serving.

Note:
For eight 8-inch pies, use 2 lb 8 oz pastry, portioned 5 oz per pie. Portion filling 3 cups per pie.

Puddings and Other Desserts

Recipes in this section include custards and other puddings made with milk and eggs, fruit desserts, cake-type puddings, gelatin desserts, and refrigerator desserts. All are used extensively in foodservices.

Basic custard consists of milk, sugar, eggs, and flavoring and may be of two types. Soft or stirred custard is cooked slowly over low heat, while stirring, until it is slightly thickened. It remains pourable when cooked. Baked custard, which is not stirred, is baked until it sets and becomes firm. It is used as a dessert by itself, as a pie filling, or as a basis for many baked puddings. Custards should be cooked to an internal temperature of not more than 185°F because the egg-liquid mixture coagulates at this temperature. If heated beyond this point, the custard tends to curdle and become watery. Cooking baked custards in a water bath, in which the custard cups or baking pan are placed in a pan of hot water, helps to prevent curdling.

Cream puddings contain starch thickeners as well as eggs, resulting in a thicker and more stable product. The thickener may be cornstarch, flour, tapioca, or a cereal product. These desserts require sweetening, usually sugar. Too much sugar interferes with the thickening of the eggs and the starch; therefore, it is important to use a properly balanced formula. To make a cream pudding, the milk is added slowly to the combined dry ingredients while stirring with a wire whip. The mixture is stirred occasionally and cooked until thickned in a steam-jacketed or other kettle over low heat to prevent scorching. The method of adding the eggs is important to a smooth pudding also. To avoid curdling when the eggs are added, a small amount of the hot mixture is first added to the beaten eggs, then this mixture is stirred into the rest of the pudding. Cream puddings should be smooth and creamy. A product that is too thick, too thin, or lumpy is unappealing. A basic vanilla pudding may be varied by the addition of different flavorings. Pudding mixes and canned puddings are available, but as with other convenience foods, the quality and cost of the product should be evaluated critically and its acceptability tested before a decision is made to purchase rather than prepare puddings on the premises.

Fruit offers a wide range of dessert possibilities and may be served fresh, poached, baked, as a sauce, or combined with other ingredients to make a baked dessert such as strawberry shortcake, fruit cobbler, or fruit crisp.

In the preparation of gelatin desserts, a firm but delicate product is desired. The use of too much gelatin will produce a tough, rubbery product; too little will prevent the dessert from setting. Fruit blended with gelatin usually is known as jellied fruit or molded fruit. Proportions for gelatin and fruit are given on p. 496. If the mixture is whipped and beaten egg whites are added, it becomes a whip or chiffon pudding. Whipped cream may be folded into the whipped mixture for a Bavarian cream. If milk and eggs are combined with gelatin in a custard-type pudding it is called a Spanish cream. Gelatin mixtures may also form the basis for refrigerator desserts, in which the filling is placed between layers of cake, cookie, or cracker crumbs.

PUDDING AND OTHER DESSERT RECIPES

Butterscotch pudding

YIELD: 50 portions
           6 qt
PORTION: ½ cup

Ingredient	Amount	Procedure
Margarine or butter Sugar, brown	10 oz 3 lb 12 oz	Cook margarine and sugar in steam-jacketed kettle until sugar starts to dissolve.
Water, warm	5½ cups	Add water slowly, while stirring. Turn off heat.
Milk	1½ qt	Add milk to warm mixture.
Cornstarch Flour, all-purpose Salt Milk	7 oz 3 oz ½ tsp 3 cups	Combine dry ingredients in mixer bowl. Add milk to make a smooth paste. Slowly add to warm sugar-milk mixture, stirring constantly. Cook until mixture thickens. Turn off heat.
Eggs	9 (1 lb)	Beat eggs on medium speed for 3 minutes. Add some of the hot mixture to the beaten eggs while still beating. Gradually add egg mixture to hot mixture. Turn on heat. Cook to 185°F. (Eggs must be cooked thoroughly or mixture will thin upon standing.)
Vanilla	2 Tbsp	Stir in vanilla. Cover with plastic wrap or waxed paper while cooling to prevent formation of film. Serve with No. 10 dipper.

Chocolate Pudding

YIELD:	50 portions
	6 qt
PORTION:	½ cup

Ingredient	Amount	Procedure
Sugar, granulated	2 lb 6 oz	Combine dry ingredients.
Flour, all-purpose	6 oz	
Cornstarch	3 oz	
Salt	1 tsp	
Cocoa	8 oz	
Milk	1 gal	Pour milk into steam-jacketed kettle or stock pot.
		Gradually add dry ingredients while stirring briskly with a wire whip.
		Heat to boiling point, then cook until thickened, about 20 minutes. Stir occasionally.
		Remove from heat.
Margarine or butter	8 oz	Add margarine and vanilla. Blend.
Vanilla	2 Tbsp	Cover with plastic wrap or waxed paper while cooling to prevent formation of film.
		Serve with No. 10 dipper.

Variations:
1. **Chocolate banana pudding.**   Slice 12 bananas into cooled pudding.
2. **Chocolate pudding with chips.**   Stir 8 oz peanut butter, butterscotch, or chocolate chips into cooled pudding.

Tapioca cream pudding

YIELD: 50 portions
6 qt
PORTION: ½ cup

Ingredient	Amount	Procedure
Milk	1 gal	Heat milk to boiling point in a steam-jacketed kettle or stock pot.
Tapioca, quick-cooking	9 oz	Add tapioca gradually while stirring with a wire whip. Cook until clear, stirring frequently.
Egg yolks, beaten Sugar, granulated Salt	10 (6 oz) 1 lb 2 tsp	Mix egg yolks, sugar, and salt. Add slowly to hot mixture while stirring. Cook about 10 minutes. Remove from heat.
Egg whites Sugar, granulated	10 (12 oz) 4 oz	Beat egg whites until frothy. Add sugar and beat on high speed to form a meringue.
Vanilla	2 Tbsp	Fold egg whites and vanilla into tapioca mixture. Serve with No. 10 dipper.

Variation:
Fruit tapioca cream.   Add 1 qt chopped canned peaches or crushed pineapple, drained. Add ½ tsp almond extract for peach tapioca.

Vanilla cream pudding

YIELD: 50 portions
         6 qt
PORTION: ½ cup

Ingredient	Amount	Procedure
Milk Sugar, granulated	3 qt 1 lb	Heat milk and sugar in steam-jacketed kettle.

Sugar, granulated
Cornstarch
Salt
Milk, cold
	1 lb 4 oz
	6 oz
	1½ tsp
	2¼ qt
		Combine dry ingredients with cold milk in
		   mixer bowl. Whip until smooth.
		Add to hot milk mixture slowly, stirring
		   constantly with a wire whip.
		Cook mixture until it is thickened and there
		   is no starch taste, approximately 10
		   minutes.

Egg yolks, beaten	20 (12 oz)	Add, while stirring, a small amount of hot
		   mixture to the beaten eggs.
		Add to remainder of hot mixture in kettle,
		   stirring constantly.
		Stir slowly and cook about 2 minutes.
		   Remove from heat.

Margarine or butter Vanilla	4 oz 2 Tbsp	Stir in margarine and vanilla. Cover with waxed paper while cooling to prevent formation of film. Serve with No. 10 dipper.

Variations:
1. **Banana cream pudding.**   Use ¾ recipe. Add 12 bananas, sliced, to cooled pudding.
2. **Chocolate cream pudding.**   Add 6 oz sugar and 8 oz cocoa.
3. **Coconut cream pudding.**   Add 8 oz shredded coconut just before serving.
4. **Pineapple cream pudding.**   Add 1 qt crushed pineapple, well drained.

Baked date pudding

OVEN: 350°F	YIELD: 54 portions
BAKE: 45 minutes	1 pan 12 × 20 × 2 inches
	PORTION: 3 oz

Ingredient	Amount	Procedure
Dates	2 lb 4 oz	Pour hot water over dates in mixer bowl.
Water, hot	2½ cups	Cover and let dates steam for 15 minutes.
		Mix on low speed and then on medium speed until dates are broken into small pieces.
Sugar, granulated	1 lb	Combine dry ingredients in bowl and stir until well blended.
Flour, all-purpose	1 lb	
Baking powder	1½ oz	Add to date mixture. Mix on low speed only until blended.
Nonfat dry milk	2 oz	
Salt	1½ tsp	Scale into well-greased 12 × 20 × 2-inch baking pan.
Walnuts, coarsely chopped	12 oz	
Sugar, brown	1 lb 4 oz	Mix sugar, margarine, and water. Heat to boiling point.
Margarine or butter	2 oz	
Water, boiling	1½ qt	Pour hot sauce over batter in pan. Do not stir.
		Bake at 350°F for 45 minutes. Cool.
		Cut 6 × 9 for 54 portions or 6 × 8 for 48 portions.
		Serve with whipped cream or whipped topping.

Lemon cake pudding

OVEN: 350°F	YIELD: 60 portions
BAKE: 1 hour	2 pans 12 × 20 × 2 inches
	PORTION: 2½ × 3 inches

Ingredient	Amount	Procedure
Egg yolks	35 (1 lb 6 oz)	Beat egg yolks, lemon juice, and margarine together until lemon colored.
Lemon juice	5 cups	
Margarine, softened	3 oz	
Sugar, granulated	6 lb	Combine sugar, flour, and salt.
Flour, all-purpose	1 lb 3 oz	
Salt	1 oz (1½ Tbsp)	
Milk	3 qt	Add dry ingredients and milk alternately to egg mixture on low speed, ending with dry ingredients.
Egg whites	27 (2 lb)	Beat egg whites on high speed, until stiff, using wire whip attachment. Blend into egg mixture on low speed.
		Pour pudding into two 12 × 20 × 2-inch counter pans, 9 lb 8 oz per pan. Set filled pans in two other counter pans that have been filled half full with boiling water. Bake at 350°F for 1 hour. Cut 5 × 6.

Fudge pudding

OVEN:	350°F	YIELD:	64 portions
BAKE:	50–60 minutes		2 pans 12 × 18 × 2 inches
		PORTION:	3 oz

Ingredient	Amount	Procedure
Margarine or butter	14 oz	Cream margarine, sugar, and vanilla on medium speed for 10–15 minutes, using flat beater.
Sugar, granulated	2 lb	
Vanilla	¼ cup	
Unsweetened chocolate, melted	6 oz	Add chocolate to creamed mixture. Cool.
Flour, all-purpose	2 lb 2 oz	Combine dry ingredients.
Baking powder	2 oz	
Salt	1 Tbsp	
Nonfat dry milk	8 oz	
Water	1 qt	Add water to creamed mixture alternately with dry ingredients.
Nuts, chopped	14 oz	Add nuts and mix only until blended. Scale into two 12 × 18 × 2-inch baking pans, 4 lb 8 oz per pan.

TOPPING

Ingredient	Amount	Procedure
Sugar, granulated	2 lb 5 oz	Combine sugars, cocoa, salt, and cornstarch.
Sugar, brown	2 lb 5 oz	
Cocoa	5 oz	
Salt	1 Tbsp	
Cornstarch	2 oz	
Water, boiling	3 qt	Add water to sugar mixture. Mix thoroughly. Pour over batter in pans, 2¾ qt per pan. Bake at 350°F for 50–60 minutes. Pudding is done when cake layer springs back when touched lightly. Serve with whipped cream.

Note:
Pudding separates into two layers when baked, a cakelike topping with chocolate sauce on the bottom. Serve with sauce on top.

Cheese cake

OVEN: 350°F	YIELD: 48 portions
BAKE: 45 minutes	6 8-inch cakes
	PORTION: cut 8 per cake

Ingredient	Amount	Procedure
Graham cracker crumbs	1 lb 8 oz	Combine crumbs, sugar, and melted margarine.
Sugar, granulated	12 oz	
Margarine or butter, melted	12 oz	Place 1 cup crumb mixture into each of six 8-inch pie pans or six 6 × 6-inch square cake pans.
		Press crumbs to sides and bottom of pans.
Cream cheese	4 lb 8 oz	Let cheese stand until it reaches room temperature.
		Cream until smooth, using flat beater.
Eggs	11 (1 lb 3 oz)	Add eggs slowly to cream cheese while beating.
Sugar, granulated	1 lb 2 oz	Add sugar and vanilla to cheese mixture.
Vanilla	2 Tbsp	Beat on high speed for about 5 minutes.
		Place about 3 cups filling in each shell.
		Bake at 350°F for 30–35 minutes. Do not overbake.
Sour cream	1¼ qt	Mix sour cream, sugar, and vanilla.
Sugar, granulated	4 oz	Spread 1 cup topping on each cake.
Vanilla	1½ tsp	
Graham cracker crumbs	4 oz	Sprinkle with a few graham cracker crumbs.
		Bake 10 minutes.

Variation:
Cheese cake with fruit glaze. Cover baked cheese cake with the following glaze: Thaw and drain 6 lb frozen strawberries, raspberries, or cherries. Measure 1 qt fruit syrup, adding water if needed to make that amount. Add slowly to mixture of 4 oz cornstarch, 6 oz granulated sugar, and ¾ cup lemon juice. Cook until thick and clear. Cool slightly. Add drained fruit. Spread over cheese cakes. Canned fruit pie fillings may be used for the glaze.

Baked custard

OVEN: 325°F	YIELD: 50 custards
BAKE: 40 minutes	PORTION: 4 oz

Ingredient	Amount	Procedure
Eggs	20 (2 lb 3 oz)	Beat eggs slightly, using wire whip attachment.
Sugar, granulated	1 lb 4 oz	
Salt	½ tsp	Add sugar, salt, cold milk, and vanilla.
Milk, cold	1 qt	Mix on low speed only until blended.
Vanilla	2 Tbsp	
Milk	1 gal	Scald milk by bringing to point just below boiling.
		Add to egg mixture and blend.
Nutmeg	2 tsp	Pour mixture into custard cups that have been arranged in baking pans.
		Sprinkle nutmeg over tops.
		Pour hot water around cups.
		Bake at 325°F for 40–45 minutes or until a knife inserted in custard comes out clean.

Note:
Custard may be baked in a 12 × 20 × 2-inch pan set in a pan of hot water. Cut 5 × 8 for 40 portions.

Variations:
1. **Bread pudding.** Pour liquid mixture over 1 lb dry bread cubes and let stand until bread is softened. Add 1 lb raisins if desired. Bake. Day-old sweet rolls may be substituted for bread.
2. **Caramel custard.** Add 1 cup Burnt Sugar Syrup (p. 192) slowly to scalded milk and stir carefully until melted.
3. **Rice custard.** Use ½ Baked Custard recipe, adding 1 lb rice (AP) cooked, 1 lb raisins, and 3 oz melted margarine or butter.

Floating island

YIELD:	50 portions	
	6 qt	
PORTION:	½ cup (4 oz)	

Ingredient	Amount	Procedure
Milk	4½ qt	Heat milk to boiling point.
Sugar, granulated Cornstarch Salt	1 lb 4 oz ½ tsp	Combine sugar, cornstarch, and salt. Add gradually to hot milk, stirring briskly with wire whip. Cook over hot water or in steam-jacketed kettle until slightly thickened.
Egg yolks, beaten Vanilla	24 (15 oz) 2 Tbsp	Gradually stir egg yolks and vanilla into hot mixture. Continue cooking until thickened, about 5 minutes.
Egg whites Sugar, granulated	24 (1 lb 12 oz) 12 oz	Beat egg whites on high speed past the frothy stage, approximately 1½ minutes, using wire whip attachment. Add sugar gradually, while beating. Beat until sugar has dissolved and mixture resembles meringue. Drop by spoonfuls onto hot water and bake at 375°F until set.
		Cool custard slightly and pour into sherbet dishes; or dip, using a No. 10 dipper. Lift meringues from water with a fork and place on top of portioned custards. Add dash of nutmeg. Chill before serving.

Christmas pudding

STEAM PRESSURE: 5–6 lb	YIELD: 48 portions
STEAM: 40–45 minutes	PORTION: 3 oz

Ingredient	Amount	Procedure
Carrots, raw, peeled	1 lb 4 oz (EP)	Peel and grate carrots and potatoes.
Potatoes, raw, peeled	1 lb 11 oz (EP)	
Sugar, granulated	2 lb	Cream sugar and margarine on medium
Margarine or butter	1 lb	speed, using flat beater.
Raisins	1 lb 4 oz	Add raisins, dates, and nuts to creamed
Dates, chopped	1 lb 4 oz	mixture.
Nuts, chopped	12 oz	Add carrots and potatoes.
		Mix on low speed until blended.
Flour, all-purpose	1 lb	Combine dry ingredients.
Baking soda	4 tsp	Add to fruit mixture. Mix on low speed until
Cinnamon	1 Tbsp	blended.
Cloves	1 Tbsp	
Nutmeg	1 Tbsp	
Salt	¼ tsp	
		Portion mixture with No. 16 dipper into greased muffin pans.
		Cover each filled pan with an inverted empty muffin pan.
		Steam for 40–45 minutes.
		Serve warm with Vanilla Sauce (p. 583), Hard Sauce (p. 586), or Nutmeg Sauce (p. 583).
		Garnish with holly leaf and whole cranberries for Christmas.

Variation:
Flaming pudding. Dip sugar cube in lemon extract. Place on hot pudding and light just before serving.

Cream puffs

OVEN: 425°F, 325°F		YIELD: 50 portions
BAKE: 45 minutes		PORTION: 1 puff

Ingredient	Amount	Procedure
Margarine or butter	1 lb	Melt margarine in boiling water.
Water, boiling	1 qt	
Flour, all-purpose	1 lb 3 oz	Add flour and salt all at once to boiling mixture. Beat vigorously.
Salt	1 tsp	Remove from heat as soon as mixture leaves sides of pan.
		Transfer to mixer bowl. Cool slightly.
Eggs	16 (1 lb 12 oz)	Add eggs one at a time, beating on high speed after each addition.
		Drop batter with No. 24 dipper onto greased baking sheets.
		Bake at 425°F for 15 minutes.
		Reduce heat to 325°F and bake 30 minutes longer.
		When ready to use, make a cut in top of each puff with a sharp knife.
		Fill with Custard Filling (p. 215), using a No. 16 dipper.
		Top with Chocolate Sauce (p. 581) if desired.

Variations:

1. **Butterscotch cream puffs.** Fill cream puffs with Butterscotch Pudding (p. 278). Top with Butterscotch Sauce (p. 580) if desired.
2. **Éclairs.** Shape cream puff mixture with pastry tube into 4½-inch strips. Bake. Split lengthwise. Proceed as in directions for Cream Puffs.
3. **Ice cream puffs.** Fill puffs with vanilla ice cream and serve with Chocolate Sauce (p. 581).
4. **Orange cream puffs with chocolate filling.** Add ½ cup grated orange peel and 10 oz chopped almonds to cream puff mixture. Bake. Fill with Chocolate Cream Filling (p. 214) or Chocolate Pudding (p. 279).
5. **Puff shells.** Make bite-size shells with pastry tube or No. 100 dipper. Bake. Fill with chicken, fish, or ham salad. Yield: approximately 200 puffs.

English toffee dessert

YIELD: 60 portions
2 pans 12 × 20 × 2 inches
PORTION: 2½ × 3 inches

Ingredient	Amount	Procedure
Vanilla wafers, finely crushed	2 lb 3 oz	Mix crumbs, nuts, and margarine. Cover bottoms of two 12 × 20 × 2-inch baking pans with crumb mixture, 1 lb 8 oz per pan. Reserve rest of crumbs for the top.
Nuts, finely chopped	1 lb 8 oz	
Margarine or butter, melted	1 lb	
Margarine or butter, soft	1 lb 12 oz	Cream margarine in mixer, using flat beater. Add sugar, milk, chocolate, egg yolks, and vanilla. Beat on medium speed until smooth and fluffy, about 15 minutes.
Sugar, powdered	4 lb 5 oz	
Nonfat dry milk	12 oz	
Unsweetened chocolate, melted	12 oz	
Egg yolks	23 (14 oz)	
Vanilla	¼ cup	
Egg whites	23 (1 lb 10 oz)	Beat egg whites until stiff but not dry. Fold into chocolate mixture on low speed. Pour over crumbs in pans, 4 lb 14 oz per pan. Sprinkle remaining crumbs over top, 12 oz per pan. Refrigerate for 3–4 hours. Cut 5 × 6. Garnish with whipped cream if desired.

Note:
Graham cracker crumbs may be used in place of vanilla wafers.

Pineapple Bavarian cream

YIELD: 60 portions
2 pans 12 × 20 × 2 inches
PORTION: 2½ × 3 inches

Ingredient	Amount	Procedure
Gelatin, unflavored Water, cold	3 oz 1 qt	Sprinkle gelatin over water. Let stand 10 minutes.
Crushed pineapple Sugar, granulated	1 No. 10 can 1 lb 12 oz	Heat pineapple and sugar to boiling point.
Lemon juice	¼ cup	Add gelatin to pineapple mixture. Stir until dissolved. Add lemon juice. Chill until mixture begins to congeal.
Whipping cream	1 qt	Whip cream and fold into pineapple mixture. Pour into 50 individual molds or two 12 × 20 × 2-inch pans. Cut 5 × 6.

Note:
May be used for pie filling.

Variations:
1. **Apricot Bavarian cream.** Substitute 3 lb dried apricots, cooked, or 6 lb canned apricot, sieved, for the crushed pineapple. Fold 6 beaten egg whites into the whipped cream.
2. **Strawberry Bavarian cream.** Substitute 6 lb fresh or frozen sliced strawberries for pineapple.

Russian cream

YIELD: 50 portions
        5 qt
PORTION: 4 oz

Ingredient	Amount	Procedure
Gelatin, unflavored Water, cold	1½ oz 1¼ qt	Sprinkle gelatin over cold water. Let stand 10 minutes.
Half-and-half Sugar, granulated	1½ qt 2 lb	Combine half-and-half and sugar. Heat until warm in steam-jacketed kettle or over hot water. Stir in softened gelatin. Heat until gelatin and sugar are dissolved but do not boil. Cool.
Sour cream Vanilla	2 lb 8 oz 2½ Tbsp	When mixture begins to thicken, fold in sour cream and vanilla, which have been beaten until smooth. Chill.
Raspberries, frozen	5 lb	Dip pudding with No. 12 dipper. Serve with No. 30 dipper of partially defrosted raspberries.

Apple brown betty

OVEN: 350°F
BAKE: 1 hour

YIELD: 64 portions
2 pans 12 × 20 × 2 inches
PORTION: 3 × 2½ inches

Ingredient	Amount	Procedure
Apples, fresh	12 lb (AP) 10 lb (EP)	Pare, core, and slice apples.
Cake or bread crumbs	2 lb	Arrange apples and crumbs in layers in 2 greased 12 × 20 × 2-inch baking pans: 2 lb 8 oz apples 8 oz crumbs 2 lb 8 oz apples 8 oz crumbs
Sugar, brown Cinnamon, ground Nutmeg, ground Water or fruit juice Lemon juice	1 lb 8 oz 1 tsp ½ tsp 2 qt (or less) 2 Tbsp	Mix sugar, spices, water, and juice. Pour 1½ qt over each pan.
Margarine or butter, melted	8 oz	Pour melted margarine over top. Bake at 350°F for 1 hour or until apples are tender. Cut 4 × 8.

Notes:
1. Serve warm with Lemon Sauce (p. 583) or cold with whipped cream.
2. 10 lb of canned or frozen apples may be used.
3. The amount of water will vary according to the dryness of the crumbs.
4. Graham cracker crumbs may be substituted for cake crumbs; 8 oz nuts may be added.
5. Peaches, apricots, or rhubarb may be substituted for the apples.

Apple crisp

OVEN:	350°F	YIELD:	64 portions
BAKE:	45–50 minutes		2 pans 12 × 20 × 2 inches
		PORTION:	3 × 2½ inches

Ingredient	Amount	Procedure
Apples, sliced	15 lb (EP)	Mix sugar and lemon juice with apples.
Sugar, granulated	12 oz	Arrange in 2 greased 12 × 20 × 2-inch
Lemon juice	⅓ cup	baking pans, 8 lb per pan.
Margarine or butter, soft	1 lb 4 oz	Combine remaining ingredients and mix
Flour, all-purpose	12 oz	until crumbly.
Rolled oats, quick-cooking, uncooked	12 oz	Spread evenly over apples, 2 lb 4 oz per pan. Bake at 350°F for 45–50 minutes.
Sugar, brown	2 lb	Serve with whipped cream, ice cream, or cheese.
		Cut 4 × 8.

Notes:
1. Fresh, frozen, or canned apples may be used.
2. 1 tsp cinnamon or nutmeg may be added to the topping.

Variations:
1. **Cheese apple crisp.**   Add 8 oz grated cheese to topping mixture.
2. **Cherry crisp.**   Substitute frozen pie cherries for apples. Increase granulated sugar to 1 lb. Add ½ tsp almond extract.
3. **Fresh fruit crisp.**   Combine 3 lb granulated sugar, 12 oz flour, 1 Tbsp nutmeg, and 1 Tbsp cinnamon. Add to 15 lb fresh fruit, pared and sliced. Top with mixture of 2 lb 6 oz margarine or butter, 2 lb 8 oz brown sugar, and 2 lb 6 oz flour. Cream margarine, add brown sugar and flour, and mix until of dough consistency. Spread over fruit. Bake. Serve warm with cream.
4. **Peach crisp.**   Substitute sliced peaches for apples.

Baked apples

| OVEN: 375°F | YIELD: 50 portions |
| BAKE: 45 minutes | PORTION: 1 apple |

Ingredient	Amount	Procedure
Apples	50	Wash and core apples. Peel down about one-fourth of the way from the top. Place in baking pans, peeled-side up.
Sugar, granulated Water, hot Salt Cinnamon, ground	3 lb 3 cups 1 tsp 1 Tbsp	Mix sugar, water, salt, and cinnamon. Pour over apples. Bake at 375°F until tender, about 45 minutes, basting occasionally while cooking to glaze. Test for doneness with a pointed knife inserted in the apple.

Notes:
1. Use apples of uniform size, suitable for baking, such as Rome Beauty or Jonathan.
2. Amount of sugar will vary with tartness of apples.
3. ½ cup red cinnamon candies may be substituted for cinnamon.
4. Apple centers may be filled with chopped dates, raisins, nuts, or mincemeat.
5. 3 oz margarine or butter may be added to the syrup for flavor.

Apple dumplings

OVEN: 350°F	YIELD: 50 dumplings
BAKE: 25–30 minutes	PORTION: 1 dumpling

Ingredient	Amount	Procedure
Pastry (p. 252)	7 lb	Make pastry. Scale into 10-oz balls. Chill for 10 minutes or more.
Flour, all-purpose Sugar, granulated Salt Cinnamon, ground	10 oz 6 lb 1 Tbsp 1 Tbsp	Make sauce. Combine flour, sugar, salt, and cinnamon.
Water, hot	1½ gal	Add dry ingredients to water while stirring with a wire whip. Cook until thickened.
Margarine or butter	1 lb	Add margarine and stir until margarine is melted. Remove from heat.
Vanilla	2 Tbsp	Add vanilla.
Apples, medium size	50	Wash, core, and peel apples.
Margarine or butter	1 lb 8 oz	Roll pastry to ⅛-inch thickness. Position apple on dough and cut a circle approximately 7 inches in diameter around it. Insert 1 Tbsp margarine into center of each apple. Push toward center of apple.
Sugar, granulated Cinnamon, ground Nutmeg, ground	1 lb 5 oz 1½ Tbsp 2 tsp	Combine sugar, cinnamon, and nutmeg. Use mixture to fill centers of apples. Enclose the apple in the cut dough, pinching to seal the edges. Turn the apple over so that the bottom is the top and make three slashes in the top of the apple. Place in lightly greased baking pans. Bake for 15 minutes at 350°F.

> Baste dumplings with one-half of the sauce and bake 10–15 minutes longer or until golden brown.
>
> Serve dumplings with additional warm sauce as desired.

Notes:

1. Apples may be wrapped with dough and frozen for later use. To serve, make sauce and bake as directed but allow 15–20 minutes longer baking time.
2. Sliced apples, frozen or fresh, may be used in place of whole apples. Cut pastry into 6-inch squares. Place No. 10 dipper of fruit in the center and sprinkle with sugar-cinnamon mixture. Fold corners of pastry to the center and on top of fruit and seal edges together. Bake as directed for Apple Dumplings.

Applesauce

YIELD: 50 portions
PORTION: ½ cup (4 oz)

Ingredient	Amount	Procedure
Apples, tart	15 lb (AP)	Wash, peel and core apples. Cut into quarters.
Water	1 qt	Add water to apples. Cook slowly until soft.
Sugar, granulated	3 lb	Add sugar and stir until dissolved. Serve with No. 12 dipper.

Notes:

1. Thin slices of lemon, lemon juice, or 1 tsp cinnamon may be added.
2. Peaches or pears may be substituted for apples.
3. Apples may be cooked unpeeled.
4. Amount of sugar will vary with tartness of apples.

Variation:

Apple compote.   Combine sugar and water and heat to boiling point. Add apples and cook until transparent.

Fruit cobbler

OVEN: 425°F		YIELD: 64 portions
BAKE: 30 minutes		2 pans 12 × 20 × 2 inches
		PORTION: 3 × 2½ inches

Ingredient	Amount	Procedure
Fruit, frozen	10 lb	Drain fruit. Reserve juice.
Juice drained from fruit, plus water to make total amount needed	2 qt	Heat juice and water to boiling point.
Sugar, granulated	1–2 lb (see Table 2.5, p. 258)	Mix sugar, cornstarch, salt, and seasonings, if any.
Cornstarch	6 oz	
Seasonings	See Table 2.5, p. 258	
Water, cold	2 cups	Add cold water to dry ingredients and stir until smooth. Add to hot juice while stirring briskly with a wire whip. Cook until thickened.
		Add cooked, drained fruit to thickened juice. Mix carefully to prevent breaking or mashing fruit. Cool. Pour into two 12 × 20 × 2-inch baking pans, 9 lb 6 oz per pan.
Pastry (p. 249) or Biscuit Topping for Fruit Cobbler (p. 299)	3 lb	Roll pastry or topping to fit pans. Place on top of fruit. Seal edges to sides of pan. Perforate top. Bake at 425°F for 30 minutes or until top is browned. Cut 4 × 8.

Notes:
1. Use cherries, berries, peaches, apricots, apples, plums, or other fruits.
2. The amount of sugar will vary with the tartness of the fruit.
3. For canned fruit, see p. 259.

Variations:
1. **Fruit slices.**   Use 2 lb 12 oz pastry. Line an 18 × 26 × 2-inch baking pan with 1 lb 8 oz of the pastry. Add fruit filling prepared as for cobbler. Moisten edges of dough and cover with crust made of remaining pastry. Trim and seal edges and perforate top. Bake at 400°F for 1–1¼ hours.
2. **Peach cobbler with hard sauce.**   Use 10 lb frozen sliced peaches, thawed, and mixed with 1 lb sugar, 1 tsp nutmeg, 4 oz flour, and 6 oz margarine or butter, melted. Top with pastry crust and bake. Serve warm with Hard Sauce (p. 586) or ice cream.

Biscuit topping for fruit cobbler

YIELD: topping for two 12 × 20-inch pans

Ingredient	Amount	Procedure
Flour, all-purpose	1 lb 6 oz	Blend dry ingredients in mixer bowl.
Baking powder	1 oz	
Salt	1 tsp	
Sugar, granulated	3 oz	
Nonfat dry milk	2 tsp	
Shortening	8 oz	Cut shortening into dry ingredients on low speed until it appears as coarse as cornmeal.
Eggs	2 (4 oz)	Beat eggs. Add water and blend.
Water	1¼ cups	Add to flour-shortening mixture. Blend on low speed until a soft dough is formed.
		Scale 1 lb 8 oz dough per pan. Roll to fit 12 × 20-inch pan. Roll onto rolling pin. Place over filling in pan, allowing dough to extend up edge of pan, about 1 inch all around (to allow for shrinkage). Cut several slits in dough.
Milk	¼ cup	Brush top of each pan with 2 Tbsp milk and 2 Tbsp sugar.
Sugar, granulated	2 oz	

Old-fashioned strawberry shortcake

OVEN: 375°F
BAKE: 15 minutes

YIELD: 50 individual shortcakes
PORTION: 1 shortcake
¾ cup (6 oz) strawberries

Ingredient	Amount	Procedure
Strawberries, fresh Sugar, granulated	9 qt 2 lb (variable)	Wash, drain, and stem strawberries. Slice and sweeten. Adjust sugar according to sweetness of berries.
Flour, all-purpose Baking powder Salt Sugar	4 lb 5 oz 2 Tbsp 1 lb 5 oz	Mix dry ingredients in mixer bowl.
Butter or margarine	2 lb	Cut butter into dry ingredients, using pastry blender or flat beater. Mixture should have coarse, mealy consistency.
Milk	1½ qt	Stir milk quickly into flour mixture. Mix just enough to moisten.
		Portion dough with No. 20 dipper onto ungreased baking sheets. Place about 2 inches apart to allow for spreading. Bake at 375°F for 12–15 minutes or until golden brown.
Cream, half-and-half, or whipping cream	1½ qt (3 qt if whipped)	To serve, dip ¾ cup (6 oz) strawberries over shortcake. Serve with cream or top with whipped cream.

Note:
For frozen strawberries, use 12 lb. Portion ½ cup over shortcake.

EGGS & CHEESE

Eggs, cheese, and milk are basic ingredients in many quantity recipes, and their cookery requires carefully controlled temperatures and cooking times.

EGGS
Market forms

FRESH EGGS

Federal quality standards classify fresh shell eggs as AA, A, and B. Grades AA and A are best for poaching, frying, and cooking in the shell because the yolks are firm, round, and high, and the thick white stands high around the yolk.

Eggs are graded also according to size, and the most readily available are extra large, large, and medium. Fresh eggs deteriorate rapidly at room temperature and should be refrigerated and stored away from foods with strong odors.

PROCESSED EGGS

Although fresh shell eggs are used extensively for table service, processed eggs are convenient to use in quantity food preparation and eliminate the time-consuming task of breaking eggs. Whole eggs, whites, yolks, and various blends are available in liquid, frozen, and dried forms. Thawed frozen eggs and reconstituted dried eggs are highly perishable, and careful handling by the user is essential to prevent contamination.

Frozen eggs Eggs may be purchased frozen whole or in the form of whites or yolks. High-quality eggs generally are used for frozen eggs, and they are suitable for omelets, scrambled eggs, and French toast, as well as in baking. Frozen eggs are pasteurized and can be purchased in containers of various sizes. If 30-lb cans are used, they require at least two days to defrost in the refrigerator. To speed thawing, the container may be placed in cold running water without submerging it. Thawed eggs should be used immediately or refrigerated promptly in an air-tight container and used within 24 hours.

Dried eggs Dried eggs are used less frequently than frozen and fresh eggs and are used primarily for baking. They should be stored in a cool, dry place where the temperature is not more than 50°F, preferably in the refrigerator. After opening a package, any unused portion should be refrigerated in a container with a close-fitting lid.

Only the amount needed at one time should be reconstituted. The dried eggs may be blended with water, but more often dried eggs are combined with other dry ingredients in the recipe, and the amount of water needed to reconstitute is added. Reconstituted eggs should be used immediately or refrigerated promptly in an airtight container and used within an hour.

A guide for substituting processed eggs for shell eggs is included in Table 1.3.

Egg cookery

An important rule in egg cooking is to use low temperatures and short cooking times. Poached, soft- or hard-cooked, and scrambled eggs should be prepared as close to service as possible by batch cooking or cooking to order. If eggs must be held on a hot counter, they should be undercooked slightly to compensate for the additional heating that will occur. Directions for cooking eggs are given on p. 306.

Hard-cooked eggs will peel easier if the raw eggs have been held in the refrigerator for 24 hours before cooking. A greenish color sometimes appears on the yolks of hard-cooked eggs when the eggs have been overcooked or allowed to cool slowly in the cooking water. Cooking the eggs for the minimum length of time required to make them solid and cooling them in cold running water or ice water help to prevent this color formation.

CHEESE AND MILK
Cheese cookery

Cheese used in cooking should be appropriate in flavor and texture to the item being prepared and should blend well with other ingredients. Aged natural cheese or processed cheese blends more readily than green or unripened cheese. Processed cheese is a blend of fresh and aged natural cheeses that have been melted, pasteurized, and mixed with an emulsifier. It has no rind or waste, is easy to slice, and melts readily. But, during processing, it loses some of the characteristic flavor of natural cheese. For this reason, a natural cheese with a more pronounced flavor may be preferred for cheese sauce and as an addition to other cooked foods where a distinctive cheese flavor is desired.

Cheese to be combined with other ingredients usually is ground, shredded, or diced to expedite melting and blending. Cheese melts at 325°F, and baked dishes containing cheese should be cooked at a temperature no higher than 350°F. Excessive temperature and prolonged cooking cause cheese to toughen and become stringy and the fat to separate. When making cheese sauce, the cheese should be added after the white sauce is completely cooked and the mixture heated only enough to melt the cheese. When cheese is used as a topping, a thin layer of buttered bread crumbs will protect it from the heat and from becoming stringy.

Cheddar cheese is one of the leading types used in quantity food preparation. It is available in many forms and ranges in flavor from mild to very sharp. Other kinds of cheese are used for appetizers, sandwiches, and salads or with crackers and fruit for dessert. Table 2.6 lists some of the most common cheeses used in foodservices.

TABLE 2.6   GUIDE TO NATURAL CHEESES

Type	*Characteristics*	*Mode of serving*
American	Mild flavor; semisoft to soft; smooth, plastic body	In sandwiches, on crackers
Bel Paese	Mild to moderately robust flavor; soft; smooth waxy body	On crackers, with fruit, in sandwiches, as such (dessert)
Blue (bleu)	Tangy, piquant flavor; semisoft, pasty sometimes crumbly texture; white interior marbled or streaked with blue veins of mold; resembles Roquefort	In dips, salad dressings, and cooked foods; as such (dessert)
Brick	Mild to moderately sharp flavor; semisoft to medium firm, elastic texture; creamy white-to-yellow interior; brownish exterior; slices well without crumbling	In salads and sandwiches; as such (dessert)
Brie	Mild to pungent flavor; soft, smooth texture; creamy yellow interior; edible thin brown and white crust	As such (dessert)
Camembert	Distinctive mild to tangy flavor; smooth texture, almost fluid when fully ripened; creamy yellow interior; edible thin white or gray-white crust	As such (dessert)
Cheddar	Mild to very sharp flavor; hard, smooth, firm body; can be crumbly; light cream to orange	As such; in sandwiches, cooked foods
Colby	Mild to mellow flavor, similar to cheddar; softer body and more open texture than cheddar; light cream to orange	As such; in sandwiches, cooked foods
Cottage	Mild, slightly acid flavor; soft open texture with tender curds of varying size; white to creamy white	As such; in salads, dips, cooked foods
Cream	Delicate, slightly acid flavor; soft, smooth texture; white	As such; in salads, in sandwiches, in dips, on crackers
Edam	Mellow, nutlike, sometimes salty flavor; rather firm, rubbery texture; creamy yellow or medium yellow-orange interior; surface coated with red wax; usually shaped like a flattened ball	As such; on crackers, with fresh fruit
Feta	Salty; soft, flaky, similar to very dry, high-acid cottage cheese; white	As such; in cooked foods

(continued)

TABLE 2.6 *(Continued)*

Type	Characteristics	Mode of serving
Gouda	Mellow, nutlike flavor, similar to Edam; smooth texture, often containing small holes; creamy yellow or medium yellow-orange interior; usually has a red wax coating; usually shaped like a flattened ball	As such; on crackers, with fresh fruit, in cooked dishes
Gruyère	Nutlike, salty flavor, similar to Swiss but sharper; firm, smooth texture with small holes or eyes; light yellow	As such (dessert); fondue
Monterey Jack	Very mild flavor; semisoft (whole milk), hard (lowfat or skim milk); smooth texture with small openings throughout; creamy white	As such; in sandwiches; grating cheese if made from lowfat or skim milk
Mozzarella	Delicate, mild flavor; semisoft, plastic texture; creamy white	Generally used in cooking, on pizza, or as such
Muenster	Mild to mellow flavor; semisoft; smooth, waxy body, numerous small mechanical openings; yellow, tan, or white surface, creamy white interior	As such; in sandwiches
Neufchâtel	Soft, smooth, creamy	As such; in sandwiches, dips, salads
Parmesan	Sharp, distinctive flavor, very hard, granular texture; yellowish white	Grated cheese on salads, soups, and pasta dishes
Port du Salut	Mellow to robust flavor similar to Gouda; semisoft, smooth elastic texture; creamy white or yellow	As such (dessert); with fresh fruit; on crackers
Provolone	Bland, acid flavor to sharp and piquant, usually smoked; hard, stringy texture; cuts without crumbling, plastic	As such (dessert) after it has ripened for 6 to 9 months; grating cheese
Ricotta	Bland but semisweet; soft, moist, and grainy or dry	As such; in cooked foods; as seasoning when grated
Romano	Sharp, peppery, piquant flavor; semisoft pasty, sometimes crumbly texture; white interior streaked with blue-green veins of mold	In salad dressings, on crackers, as such (dessert)
Swiss, Emmentaler	Mild, sweet, nutlike flavor; hard, smooth with large gas holes or eyes; pale yellow	As such; in sandwiches, with salads; fondue

Based on information from the National Dairy Council, Rosemont, IL.

Milk cookery

Milk should be heated or cooked at a low temperature. At high temperatures the protein in milk coagulates into a film on top and a coating on the sides of the kettle. This coating tends to scorch when milk is heated over direct heat. To prevent formation of this coating, milk should be heated over water, in a steamer, or in a steam-jacketed kettle. Whipping the milk to form a foam or tightly covering the pan and heating the milk below boiling temperature helps to prevent formation of a top film.

Curdling may be caused by holding the milk at high temperature or by the addition of foods containing acids and tannins. For example, the tannins in potatoes often cause curdling of the milk used in scalloped potatoes. Milk in combination with ham or certain vegetables, such as asparagus, green beans, carrots, peas, or tomatoes, may curdle. Curdling may be lessened by limiting the salt used, adding the milk in the form of a white sauce, keeping the temperature below boiling, and shortening the cooking time. Danger of curdling in tomato soup may be lessened by adding the tomato to the milk, by having both the milk and tomato hot when they are combined, or by thickening the milk or tomato juice before they are combined.

Dry milk is substituted extensively for fluid milk in quantity cooking because dry milk is comparatively low in cost and easy to handle and store. It is available as whole milk, nonfat milk, and buttermilk. Nonfat dry milk is pure fresh milk from which only the fat and water have been removed. It has better keeping qualities than dry whole milk, although both should be kept dry and cool. There are various types of nonfat dry milk of equal nutritional food value. Instant nonfat milk is the type that is readily reconstituted in liquid form. Whatever the type, it may be used in dry form or reconstituted as fluid milk. Once it has been reconstituted, it should be refrigerated immediately.

When dry milk is used in recipes that contain a large proportion of dry ingredients, such as bread, biscuits, and cakes, the only change in method would be to mix the unsifted dry milk with the other dry ingredients and use water in place of fluid milk. For best results, dry milk should be weighed, not measured. Package directions for reconstituting dry milk solids should be followed. A general guide is to use 3.5 ounces, by weight, of instant or regular spray process nonfat dry milk plus 3¾ cups water to make 1 quart liquid milk, or 1 pound plus 3¾ quarts water to make 1 gallon. The same proportion is used for dry buttermilk. For some foods, additional fat (1.2 ounces per quart of liquid) should be added. Additional amounts of nonfat dry milk may be added to some foods to supplement their nutritional value, although excessive amounts that affect palatability should not be used.

EGG RECIPES

Procedure for cooking eggs

Method	Equipment	Procedure
Hard- or soft-cooked (in shell)	Kettle	1. Place room temperature eggs in wire baskets. Lower into kettle of boiling water. Simmer (do not boil), timing as follows: *Soft-cooked* *Hard-cooked* 3–5 minutes 10–15 minutes 2. Immerse hard-cooked eggs in cold water or serve immediately. Serve soft-cooked eggs immediately after cooking.
	Steamer	1. Place room temperature eggs in perforated counter pans: 3 doz per 12 × 20 × 2-inch pan. 2. Place in a preheated steamer and time as follows: *Pressure* *Soft-cooked* *Hard-cooked* 5 lb 5–7 minutes 8–10 minutes 15 lb 4–6 minutes 7–9 minutes 3. Immerse in cold water or serve immediately.
Hard-cooked (out of shell)	Steamer	1. Crack room temperature eggs into a 12 × 20 × 2-inch solid, greased counter pan. Eggs should be thick enough in pans so whites come up to level of yolks (4 doz per pan). 2. Place in preheated steamer and time as follows: *Pressure* *Hard-cooked* 5 lb 6–8 minutes 15 lb 5–7 minutes 3. Remove from steamer and drain off any accumulated condensate. Chop and cool.
Poached	Fry pan or kettle	1. Break eggs into individual dishes. Carefully slide eggs into simmering water in fry pan or other shallow pan (Figure 2.27). The addition of salt (1 Tbsp) or vinegar (2 tsp) to the water increases the speed of coagulation and helps maintain shape. 2. Keep water at simmering (not boiling) temperature. Cook 5–7 minutes. 3. Remove eggs with slotted spoon.
	Steamer	1. Break eggs into water in 12 × 20 × 2-inch counter pans. 2. Place eggs into preheated steamer and time as follows: *Pressure* *Soft-poached* 5 lb 3–5 minutes 15 lb 2–4 minutes 3. To serve, lift out of water into a warmed pan.

| Fried | Skillet or griddle | 1. Break eggs into individual dishes. Slide carefully into hot fat in skillets or on griddle. |
| | | 2. Cook over low heat until of desired hardness, 5–7 minutes. |

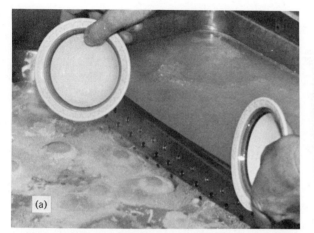

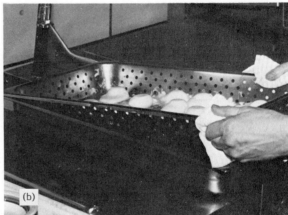

Figure 2.27 *Poaching eggs. (a) Place perforated pan (a tilting fry pan in this illustration) in simmering water. Carefully slide eggs individually into the water. (b) Remove cooked eggs by lifting the pan from the water and placing it into a solid counter pan to drain. (c) Eggs may be poached in a steamer. For timing, see Procedure for Cooking Eggs.*

Scrambled eggs

YIELD: 50 portions
PORTION: 3 oz

Ingredient	Amount	Procedure
Eggs	75 (8 lb 3 oz)	Break eggs into mixer bowl. If using frozen eggs, defrost. Beat slightly on medium speed, using wire whip attachment.
Milk Salt	1½ qt 2 Tbsp	Add milk and salt to eggs. Beat until blended.
Margarine or butter	8 oz	Melt margarine in fry pan, griddle, or steam-jacketed kettle. Pour in egg mixture (see Note 1). Cook over low heat, stirring occasionally, until of desired consistency. Eggs should be glossy. Serve with No. 10 dipper.

Notes:
1. The type of equipment used will determine batch size. Eggs should be cooked in small batches and held for a minimum amount of time before serving.
2. **Steamer method.**   Melt 4 oz margarine or butter in each of two steamer or counter pans. Pour egg mixture into pans. Steam for 6–8 minutes at 5 lb pressure until desired degree of hardness is reached.
3. **Oven method.**   Melt 4 oz margarine or butter in each of two counter or baking pans. Pour egg mixture into pans. Bake approximately 20 minutes at 350°F, stirring once after 10 minutes of baking.
4. Bacon fat may be used in place of margarine or butter.

Variations:
1. **Scrambled eggs and cheese.**   Add 1 lb grated cheddar cheese.
2. **Scrambled eggs and chipped beef.**   Add 1 lb chopped chipped beef. Reduce salt to 1 Tbsp or less.
3. **Scrambled eggs and ham.**   Add 1 lb 4 oz chopped cooked ham. Reduce salt to 1 Tbsp or less.

Creamed eggs

YIELD: 50 portions
PORTION: 5 oz

Ingredient	Amount	Procedure
Margarine or butter Flour, all-purpose Salt Pepper, white	1 lb 8 oz 1 oz (1½ Tbsp) ¼ tsp	Melt margarine. Add flour, salt, and pepper. Stir until smooth. Cook for 5 minutes.
Milk	1 gal	Add milk gradually, stirring constantly with wire whip. Cook until thickened.
Eggs, hard-cooked (p. 306)	75	Peel eggs. Slice or quarter. When ready to serve, pour hot sauce over eggs. Mix carefully. Reheat to serving temperature.

Variations:
1. **Curried eggs.** Substitute chicken broth for 2 qt of the milk. Add 2 Tbsp curry powder. May be served with steamed rice or chow mein noodles.
2. **Eggs à la king.** Substitute Chicken Stock for 2 qt of the milk. Add 1 lb mushrooms that have been sautéed, 12 oz chopped green peppers, and 8 oz chopped pimiento.
3. **Goldenrod eggs.** Mash or rice egg yolks. Add sliced whites to sauce. Serve on toast. Sprinkle mashed yolks over the top.
4. **Scotch woodcock.** Add 1 lb sharp cheddar cheese to sauce. Cut eggs in half lengthwise and place in pans. Pour sauce over eggs. Cover with buttered crumbs. Bake until heated through and crumbs are brown.

Baked omelet

OVEN: 325°F	YIELD: 48 portions
BAKE: 45 minutes	2 pans 12 × 20 × 2 inches
	PORTION: 3 oz

Ingredient	Amount	Procedure
Margarine or butter	12 oz	Melt margarine. Add flour and seasonings.
Flour, all-purpose	8 oz	Stir until smooth.
Salt	2 Tbsp	Cook 5 minutes.
Pepper, white	½ tsp	
Milk	3 qt	Add milk gradually, stirring constantly with a wire whip. Cook until thick.
Egg yolks, beaten	24 (15 oz)	Add egg yolks and mix well with wire whip.
Egg whites	24 (1 lb 12 oz)	Beat egg whites until they form rounded peaks. Fold into egg yolk mixture. Pour mixture into 2 greased 12 × 20 × 2-inch baking pans, 5 lb per pan. Set pans in counter pans with 3 cups of hot water in each. Bake at 325°F for 45 minutes or until set. Cut 4 × 6.

Variations:
1. **Bacon omelet.**   Fry 1 lb 8 oz diced bacon; substitute bacon fat for margarine in white sauce. Add diced bacon to egg mixture.
2. **Cheese omelet.**   Add 12 oz grated cheese before placing pans in oven.
3. **Ham omelet.**   Add 3 lb finely diced cooked ham. Reduce salt to 1 Tbsp or less.
4. **Jelly omelet.**   Spread 1 lb tart jelly over cooked omelet.
5. **Mushroom and cheese omelet.**   Add 8 oz grated cheese and 6 oz sliced mushrooms.
6. **Spanish omelet.**   Add 8 oz chopped green chilies to egg mixture. Serve with Spanish Sauce (p. 570).

Chinese omelet

OVEN: 325°F
BAKE: 45 minutes

YIELD: 48 portions
       2 pans 12 × 20 × 2 inches
PORTION: 4 oz

Ingredient	Amount	Procedure
Rice, long-grain Water Salt Cooking oil	2 lb (AP) 2½ qt 4 tsp 4 tsp	Cook rice according to directions on p. 422.
Margarine or butter Flour, all-purpose Salt	4 oz 2 oz 1 tsp	Melt margarine. Add flour and salt. Stir until smooth. Cook 5 minutes.
Milk	1 qt	Add milk gradually, stirring constantly with wire whip. Cook until thickened.
Cheddar cheese, sharp, shredded	1 lb	Add cheese to white sauce. Stir until cheese is melted.
Egg yolks Mustard, dry Salt Paprika	24 (15 oz) 1 tsp 2 Tbsp 1 tsp	Beat egg yolks until light and fluffy. Add seasonings. Add to cheese sauce. Stir until smooth. Add rice and mix to blend.
Egg whites	24 (1 lb 12 oz)	Beat egg whites until they form soft peaks. Fold into rice mixture.
		Pour into 2 greased 12 × 20 × 2-inch pans, 7 lb per pan. Bake at 325°F for 45 minutes or until set. Cut 4 × 6. Serve with Cheese Sauce (p. 561) or Tomato Sauce (p. 571).

Potato omelet

OVEN: 325°F	YIELD: 56 portions
BAKE: 1 hour	2 pans 12 × 20 × 2 inches
	PORTION: 6 oz

Ingredient	Amount	Procedure
Bacon slices	50	Arrange bacon, slightly overlapping, in baking pans. Cook in oven at 400°F until crisp. Remove from pans. Place on paper towels to absorb grease.
Potatoes, cooked, diced	9 lb (EP)	Brown potatoes slightly in bacon fat. Remove to 2 greased 12 × 20 × 2-inch baking pans, 4 lb 8 oz per pan.
Eggs, beaten Salt Pepper, white Cayenne Milk, hot	36 (3 lb 15 oz) 2 oz 1 tsp few grains 3 qt	Combine eggs, milk, and seasonings. Pour over potatoes.
		Bake at 325°F for 1 hour. Serve as soon as removed from oven. Cut 4 × 7. Place a slice of crisp bacon on top of each serving.

Variation:
Potato-ham omelet.   Omit bacon. Add 4 lb diced cooked ham to potatoes. Reduce salt to 1 Tbsp.

Egg and sausage bake

OVEN: 325°F
BAKE: 1 hour

YIELD: 48 portions
        2 pans 12 × 20 × 2 inches
PORTION: 6 oz

Ingredient	Amount	Procedure
Bread, sliced	2 lb 8 oz	Remove crusts from bread. Cut in cubes. Cover bottoms of 2 greased 12 × 20 × 2-inch baking pans with bread cubes. Pans should be well covered.
Sausage, bulk	9 lb	Brown sausage. Drain well.
Cheddar cheese, shredded	2 lb 8 oz	Spread cheese and sausage over bread cubes.
Eggs, beaten Milk Mustard, dry	42 (4 lb 8 oz) 3 qt 1½ Tbsp	Combine eggs, milk, and mustard. Pour over mixture in pans, 2½ qt per pan. May be mixed, covered, and refrigerated overnight.
		Bake uncovered at 325°F for 1 hour or until set. If browning too fast, cover with foil. Cut 4 × 6.

Note:
Chopped ham or bacon may be substituted for sausage.

Variations:
1. **Sausage-potato bake.** Substitute frozen hashed brown potatoes, thawed, for bread cubes.
2. **Egg-potato bake.** Delete sausage. Substitute frozen hashed brown potatoes for bread cubes.

Quiche

OVEN: 375°F	YIELD: 48 portions
BAKE: 25–30 minutes	12 8-inch quiches
	PORTION: ¼ quiche

Ingredient	Amount	Procedure
Flour, all-purpose	1 lb 13 oz	Make pastry according to directions on p. 249.
Salt	1 Tbsp	Line twelve 8-inch pie pans with pastry, 5 oz
Shortening	1 lb 4 oz	per pan.
Water, cold	1¼ cups	Partially bake shells at 375°F for about 10 minutes.
Eggs	30 (3 lb 4 oz)	Beat eggs. Add cream, milk, and seasonings.
Cream or half-and-half	2 qt	
Milk	2 qt	
Salt	1½ tsp	
Pepper, white	½ tsp	
Swiss cheese, grated	3 lb	Sprinkle partially baked shells with Swiss
Bacon, chopped, cooked, and drained, or ham, finely diced	1 lb	cheese, 4 oz per pie, and bacon or ham, 2 oz per pie. Pour egg mixture into shells, 15 oz (approximately 2 cups) per pie.
Parmesan cheese, grated	8 oz	Sprinkle with Parmesan cheese, 2 Tbsp per pie. Bake until custard is set and lightly browned.

Variations:
1. **Mushroom quiche.** Delete bacon or ham and Parmesan cheese. Sprinkle 3 lb sliced fresh mushrooms and 8 oz finely chopped onions sautéed in 4 oz margarine over bottoms of shells, approximately 4 oz per pie.
2. **Sausage quiche.** Substitute 1 lb cooked, drained sausage (1 lb 12 oz AP) for bacon or ham.
3. **Seafood quiche.** In place of bacon, use 3 lb flaked crab meat, shrimp pieces, or other seafood, 1 lb sliced fresh mushrooms, and 12 oz finely chopped onions sautéed in 4 oz margarine, approximately 5 oz per pie. Delete Parmesan cheese.
4. **Swiss spinach quiche.** Delete bacon or ham and Parmesan cheese. Increase Swiss cheese to 6 lb. Add 3 lb 8 oz chopped spinach, well drained. Add 1 tsp nutmeg.

Egg cutlets

| DEEP-FAT FRYER: 375°F | YIELD: 50 cutlets |
| FRY: 3 minutes | PORTION: 3 oz |

Ingredient	Amount	Procedure
Margarine or butter	12 oz	Melt margarine. Add flour and salt. Stir until
Flour, all-purpose	10 oz	smooth.
Salt	2 oz	Cook for 5 minutes.
Milk	2 qt	Add milk gradually, stirring constantly with wire whip.
		Cook until very thick.
Eggs, hard-cooked (p. 306)	48	Peel eggs. Chop or grind coarsely.
		Add white sauce to eggs. Mix.
		Portion with No. 12 dipper onto greased sheet pans. Chill.
		Shape into cutlets. Chill.
Eggs, beaten	6 (10 oz)	Combine eggs and milk.
Milk	1 cup	Dip cutlets in egg mixture and roll in crumbs.
Bread crumbs	12 oz	Chill 2 hours.
		Fry in deep fat for 3 minutes.

Note:
Cutlets may be baked. Place on greased baking sheets and bake at 350°F for 1 hour.

Variation:
Chicken cutlets. Substitute finely chopped cooked chicken for hard-cooked eggs. Substitute 1 qt Chicken Stock (p. 590) for 1 qt of the milk.

Egg foo yung

YIELD: 50 portions
PORTION: 4 oz with 1½ oz sauce

Ingredient	Amount	Procedure
Mushrooms, canned	1 lb	Drain and coarsely chop mushrooms and bean sprouts. Reserve liquid for use in final step.
Bean sprouts	1 No. 10 can	
Onions, shredded	1 lb 8 oz	Combine onions and green peppers with mushrooms and bean sprouts.
Green peppers, shredded	8 oz	
Cooking oil	1 cup	Fry vegetable mixture in hot oil for 2 minutes.
Eggs, beaten	40 (4 lb 6 oz)	Combine eggs and ham.
Ham, cooked, shredded	1 lb	Add to vegetables and mix.
		Portion with No. 10 dipper onto preheated grill or frying pan. Brown on one side, fold in half. Serve with the following sauce.
Cornstarch	2 oz	Combine cornstarch and soy sauce into a smooth paste.
Soy sauce	1½ cups	
Reserved vegetable juice or chicken stock	2 qt	Add to vegetable juice, stirring with a wire whip. Cook until thickened.

Note:
Roast pork, chicken, or bacon may be used in place of ham; green onions in place of shredded onions; and bamboo shoots and shredded water chestnuts in place of bean sprouts.

Deviled eggs

YIELD: 50 portions
PORTION: 2 halves

Ingredient	Amount	Procedure
Eggs, hard-cooked (p. 306)	50	Peel eggs. Cut in half lengthwise. Remove yolks to mixer bowl. Arrange whites in rows on a tray.
Milk	½ cup	Mash yolks, using flat beater. Add milk and mix until blended.

Mayonnaise or salad
  dressing
Salt
Dry mustard
Sugar, granulated
Vinegar, cider
	1½ cups
	
	1 Tbsp
	2 tsp
	1 tsp
	½ cup
		Add remaining ingredients to yolks and mix
		  until smooth.

		Refill whites with mashed yolks,
		  approximately 1½ Tbsp for each half egg
		  white.
		Sprinkle with paprika (optional).

Notes:
1. Pastry bag may be used to fill egg whites. Yolk mixture should be smooth and creamy. Use plain or rose tip.
2. 6 oz finely chopped pimientos may be added to yolk mixture.

Variation:
Hot stuffed eggs. To mashed egg yolks, add 3 oz melted margarine or butter, 2 tsp salt, ⅛ tsp cayenne, 1 Tbsp prepared mustard, and 1 lb ham, minced. Arrange stuffed eggs in two 12 × 20 × 2-inch baking pans. Cover with 1 gal White Sauce (p. 560), 2 qt per pan. Bake at 325°F for 30 minutes. Sprinkle with chopped parsley. Ham may be added to the White Sauce instead of to egg yolks.

Pickled eggs

YIELD: 50 portions
PORTION: 1 egg

Ingredient	Amount	Procedure
Eggs	50	Hard-cook eggs (p. 306). Peel.
Beet juice	3½ cups	Combine beet juice, vinegar, sugar, and salt in mixing bowl.
Vinegar, cider	3½ cups	
Sugar, granulated	12 oz	Stir until sugar is dissolved.
Salt	¼ tsp	Pour over eggs.
		Cover tightly and refrigerate overnight.

Variations:
1. **Dilled eggs.**   Use the following ingredients in place of those in recipe: 50 hard-cooked eggs, 1¾ qt vinegar, 1¼ qt water, 1 Tbsp dill weed, 1 tsp white pepper, 1 oz (1½ Tbsp) salt, ¼ tsp dry mustard, 1 Tbsp onion juice, and 3 cloves garlic.
2. **Smoked eggs.**   Combine ½ cup soy sauce, 1 Tbsp salad oil, 2 tsp liquid smoke, 5 tsp granulated sugar, and 1¼ cups water. Pour over eggs. Marinate for 2–3 hours. Stir eggs gently every half hour to keep them moistened with marinade.

CHEESE RECIPES

Cheese balls

DEEP-FAT FRYER: 360°F		YIELD: 50 portions
FRY: 2–3 minutes		150 balls
		PORTION: 3 balls

Ingredient	Amount	Procedure
Cheddar cheese, grated	9 lb	Mix cheese, flour, salt, and cayenne.
Flour, all-purpose	8 oz	
Salt	2 Tbsp	
Cayenne	few grains	
Egg whites	48 (3 lb 8 oz)	Beat egg whites until stiff. Fold into cheese mixture.
		Shape into balls 1–1¼ inches in diameter or dip with No. 30 dipper onto trays or baking sheets.
		Chill.
Eggs, beaten	6 (10 oz)	Combine eggs and milk.
Milk	2 cups	Dip cheese balls in egg mixture, then roll in crumbs.
Bread crumbs	1 lb 8 oz	Chill for several hours.
		Fry in deep fat for 2–3 minutes.

Notes:
1. Serve cheese balls in center of hot buttered pineapple rings, three per ring.
2. For serving as first-course accompaniment, use half the recipe and shape into balls ½–¾ inch in diameter. Yield: 150 balls.
3. For two cheese balls per portion, use No. 24 dipper. Yield: 40 portions.

Cheese fondue

OVEN: 350°F		YIELD: 50 portions
BAKE: 50–60 minutes		2 pans 12 × 20 × 2 inches
		PORTION: 6 oz

Ingredient	Amount	Procedure
Milk, scalded	4½ qt	Add margarine and seasonings to milk.
Margarine or butter, melted	4 oz	
Dry mustard	1½ tsp	
Salt	1 Tbsp	
Cayenne	few grains	
Bread cubes, soft	3 lb 8 oz	Pour milk mixture over bread, 2¼ qt per pan. Cool slightly.
Cheddar cheese, shredded	4 lb 8 oz	Add cheese and egg yolks to bread mixture. Mix until blended.
Eggs yolks, beaten	24 (1 lb)	
Egg whites	24 (1 lb 12 oz)	Beat egg whites until stiff. Fold into cheese mixture.
		Pour mixture into 2 greased 12 × 20 × 2-inch pans, 10 lb per pan. Set pans in counter pans with 3 cups of hot water. Bake at 350°F for 50–60 minutes.

Note:
Serve with Cheese Sauce (p. 561), Clam Sauce (p. 406), or Shrimp Sauce (p. 406).

Cheese soufflé

OVEN: 300°F	YIELD: 48 portions
BAKE: 1 hour	2 pans 12 × 20 × 2 inches
	PORTION: 4 oz

Ingredient	Amount	Procedure
Margarine or butter	1 lb 4 oz	Melt margarine. Add flour and salt. Stir until
Flour, all-purpose	10 oz	smooth.
Salt	1 tsp	Cook 5 minutes.
Milk	3 qt	Add milk gradually, stirring constantly with wire whip. Cook until thick.
Egg yolks, beaten	38 (1 lb 8 oz)	Add egg yolks to white sauce, stirring constantly. Cook for 2 minutes.
Cheddar cheese, shredded	1 lb 8 oz	Add cheese to sauce and stir until cheese is melted. Remove from heat.
Egg whites	38 (2 lb 12 oz)	Add cream of tartar to egg whites. Beat until
Cream of tartar	2 tsp	stiff, but not dry.
		Fold into cheese mixture.
		Scale mixture into two 12 × 20 × 2-inch baking pans, greased only on the bottoms, 6 lb 12 oz per pan.
		Bake at 300°F for 55–60 minutes or until set.
		Cut 4 × 6.

Note:
Serve with Cheese Sauce (p. 561), Mushroom Sauce (p. 564), or Shrimp Sauce (p. 406).

Variation:
Mushroom soufflé. Add 1 lb chopped mushrooms and 5 oz chopped green peppers to uncooked mixture. Serve with Béchamel Sauce (p. 563).

Cheese and broccoli strata

OVEN: 325°F		YIELD: 56 portions
BAKE: 1–1½ hours		2 pans 12 × 20 × 2 inches
		PORTION: 8 oz

Ingredient	Amount	Procedure
Bread slices, dry	2 lb	Cut bread into 1½-inch cubes. Set aside.
Broccoli cuts, frozen	5 lb	Cook broccoli until tender.

Cheddar cheese, shredded	2 lb	Layer as follows in each pan:
		   8 oz bread cubes
		   2 lb 8 oz broccoli
		   1 lb cheese
		   8 oz bread cubes

Eggs, beaten Milk Salt Prepared mustard Tabasco sauce Paprika	9 doz (12 lb) 1 gal 2 oz 3 oz (6 Tbsp) 1½ tsp ½ tsp	Combine eggs, milk, and seasonings. Pour 1¼ gal into each pan. Smooth down evenly. Sprinkle with paprika, ¼ tsp per pan.

		Set each pan in another counter pan
		   containing 3 cups hot water.
		Bake uncovered at 325°F until custard sets,
		   1–1½ hours.
		Cut 4 × 7.

Notes:
1. Baking time may be reduced if milk mixture is warmed to 140°F before baking.
2. May be served with 1 oz Cheese Sauce (p. 561).

Nachos

YIELD: 50 portions
PORTION: 3½ oz sauce
            1 oz chips

Ingredient	Amount	Procedure
Shortening	1 oz	Sauté onions in shortening until tender.
Onions, chopped	3 oz	
Green chili peppers, chopped	6 oz	Add chilies and tomatoes to onions. Simmer for 15 minutes.
Tomatoes, diced, canned	1 lb 8 oz	
Chicken Stock (p. 590)	2 qt	Add stock and seasonings. Bring to a boil. Reduce heat to medium.
Cumin, ground	1 Tbsp	
Garlic powder	2 tsp	
Processed cheese, shredded	6 oz 10 oz	Add cheese to hot mixture. Stir until melted.
Cornstarch	3 oz	Combine cornstarch and water to make a smooth paste. Add slowly to cheese mixture, stirring constantly. Cook and stir until mixture thickens. Turn heat to low.
Water	½ cup	
Nacho chips	4 lb	Place 12 nacho chips on dinner plate. Pour 4 oz ladle of sauce over chips. Garnish with sliced jalapeño peppers.

Note:
The sauce may be thinned with chicken broth.

Welsh rarebit

YIELD: 50 portions
6½ qt
PORTION: ½ cup (4 oz)

Ingredient	Amount	Procedure
Margarine or butter	10 oz	Melt margarine. Add flour and salt. Stir until smooth.
Flour, all-purpose	8 oz	
Salt	1 oz (1½ Tbsp)	Cook 5 minutes.
Milk	1 gal	Add milk gradually, stirring constantly with wire whip.
		Cook until thickened.
Cheddar cheese, shredded or ground	5 lb	Add cheese and seasonings to sauce.
		Cook over hot water until cheese is melted.
Dry mustard	2 Tbsp	Serve on toast or toasted buns.
Worcestershire sauce	2 Tbsp	
Pepper, white	½ tsp	

Variation:
Welsh rarebit with bacon. Serve rarebit over toast, with 2 slices cooked bacon and 2 slices fresh tomato.

FISH

PURCHASING AND STORAGE
Market forms of fin fish

Fish may be purchased fresh or frozen, and some are available canned. Following are the most common market forms:

Aberdeen cuts. Rhombus-shaped cuts from a block of frozen fish are known as Aberdeen cuts; sides may be squared off or cut with a tapered edge. These usually are breaded or battered. Also called diamond cuts, French cuts.

Bits or nuggets. Small pieces of fish breaded or coated with batter, weighing less than 1 ounce each, are called bits or nuggets. Shape may be round, square, or irregular. Some are cut from regular blocks of fish; others are cut from frozen blocks of minced fish. Also called bites, cubes, nuggets, petites, tidbits. Generally sold by count per pound, for example, 25–35 per pound.

Boneless fillet. The pinbones are removed from the fillet. Boneless fillets do not have to be completely boneless; the U.S. federal grade standards allow for an occasional small bone in Grade A fillets.

Butterfly fillet. Fish is cut along both sides, with the two pieces remaining joined by a piece of skin and flesh.

Drawn fish. Drawn fish have had the entrails, gills, and scales removed.

Fillet. A slice of fish flesh of irregular size and shape which is removed from the carcass by a cut made parallel to the backbone is called a fillet. Its weight is usually 2 to 12 ounces.

Fingers. Fingers are irregularly shaped pieces of fish, similar to a long, thin fillet breaded or battered, raw or precooked. Weight per piece varies; they are usually available in portions of 1 to 3 ounces or in bulk.

Fish sticks. Sticks are rectangles of fish cut from a frozen block, usually 2 by 3 inches, weighing 1 to 2 ounces each, breaded or battered.

Headed and gutted. Head, tails, fins, and viscera have been removed before sale.

Portion. Usually square or rectangular, portions are cut from a block of frozen fish. Weights vary from 1½ ounces to about 6 ounces. They may be plain or breaded, raw or precooked.

Steaks. Slices of dressed fish, smaller than chunks, ready for cooking, are called steaks. Salmon, halibut, swordfish, and other large fish are commonly processed and sold as steaks.

Whole or round fish. Fish are sold just as they came from the water. They must be dressed before cooking.

The cost per edible pound in terms of both convenience and waste should be considered when deciding which form of fish to buy. Whole or round fish yield about 50 percent edible flesh after they have been eviscerated and scaled and the head, tail, and fins have been removed; dressed fish yield 70 percent, steaks 90 percent, and fillets and portions 100 percent. The U.S. government standard on breaded portions is 25 percent breading and 75 percent fish when raw; 35 percent breading and 65 percent fish when oven finished. Battered portions are typically 50 percent batter and 50 percent fish.

Market forms of shellfish

Shellfish may be purchased fresh, frozen, and canned.

Clams. Clams are available alive in the shell; shucked, fresh or frozen; and canned, whole or chopped. Frozen clam strips are available for deep-fat frying.

Crabs. Crabs may be purchased alive, but most are marketed cooked and frozen in the shell, as crab legs or claws, or as frozen or canned crabmeat.

Lobsters. Northern lobsters are marketed alive in the shell and as cooked meat, fresh or frozen. A 1-pound lobster will yield about 4 ounces of cooked meat. Rock lobsters are marketed only as lobster tails, usually individually quick frozen (IQF).

Oysters. Oysters are marketed alive in the shell; shucked, fresh or frozen; and canned. Shucked oysters are in far greater demand in foodservices than those in the shell. Eastern oysters are larger and more readily available than Pacific oysters. Both are graded according to the number per gallon. The following table gives the sizes of oysters that are available:

Eastern oysters		Pacific oysters	
Size	*Count per gallon*	*Size*	*Count per gallon*
Counts or extra large	160	Large	fewer than 65
Extra selects or large	161–200	Medium	65–95
Selects or medium (preferred for frying)	201–300	Small	96–114
		Extra small	more than 144
Standards or small	301–400		
Very small	more than 500		

Based on information from the National Fisheries Institute, Washington D.C.

Scallops. Scallops are always sold shucked and are available fresh, by the gallon or pound; and frozen, as individually quick frozen (IQF), in 3- to 5-pound units, or frozen in block form in 5-pound units. Frozen breaded scallops for deep-fat frying are typically sold in 2½- to 3-pound units. They may be breaded whole or cut from a frozen block in uniform pieces before breading. Large sea scallops are graded in sizes from 10 to 70 count per pound; bay scallops are smaller, graded in sizes from 70 to 120 per pound.

Shrimp. Most shrimp are marketed frozen, although they are available canned and fresh. Shrimp are available in several forms, including "green"—that is, raw shrimp in the shell; peeled and deveined (P&D)—raw shrimp with shell and sand vein removed; peeled, deveined, and cooked (P&DC)—peeled shrimp, deveined and cooked; and broken—imperfect raw P&D shrimp. The name *prawn* is usually given to large shrimp, those designated jumbo or larger.

Count and description names for raw shrimp are as follows*:

Number per pound	Description
Fewer than 10	Extra colossal
10–15	Colossal
16–20	Extra jumbo
21–25	Jumbo
26–35	Extra large to large
36–50	Medium large to medium
51–70	Small to extra small
More than 70	Tiny

* Based on information from National Fisheries Institute, Washington D.C.

Two pounds of raw shrimp in the shells will yield about 1 pound of cooked, shelled, and deveined meat; about 1½ pounds of cooked shrimp in the shells are needed to yield 1 pound of shelled meat.

Storage

Seafood is perishable and should be handled with great care during storage, thawing, preparation, cooking, and serving. Fresh fish should be delivered packed in crushed ice and stored in the refrigerator at 32°F, live shellfish at 35°F but not in direct contact with ice or water. Frozen seafood should be delivered hard frozen and stored in the freezer at 0°F to −20°F until it is removed for cooking. Neither fresh nor thawed fish or shellfish should be held longer than one day before cooking.

Frozen fish does not need to be thawed prior to cooking if is not to be breaded. Some tempering may be necessary, however, to separate fish portions or cut into appropriate size pieces. Breaded fish portions should *not* be thawed before cooking.

COOKING METHODS
Fish

Fish by nature is tender and free of tough fibers that need to be softened by cooking, and it should be cooked only until the fish flakes easily when tested with a fork. Fish may be cooked in many ways, but the best method is determined by size, fat content, and flavor. Baking and broiling are suitable for fat fish. If lean fish is baked or broiled, fat is added to prevent dryness, and it often is baked in a sauce. Fish cooked in moist heat requires very little cooking time and usually is served with a sauce. Frying is suitable for all types, but those with firm flesh that will not break apart easily are best for deep-fat frying. Table 2.7 suggests cooking methods for specific types of fish. Table 2.8 lists cooking times and temperatures.

BAKING

Fish fillets Brush frozen fish in melted fat or dip in fat, then in flour. Place in greased shallow pan or pan lined with silicone paper or aluminum foil; do not cover. Season with spices. A thin slice of lemon may be placed on each piece. See p. 624 for herb seasoning. Bake frozen fish at 350–400°F for 20–25 minutes per inch of thickness. If fish is thawed or fresh, reduce cooking time to 10–12 minutes per inch of thickness.

Whole fish for buffet display Rinse and dry fish, then salt inside and out. Bake at 325°F until fish flakes easily, about 2 hours for a 12-pound fish and approximately 3 hours for a 20–24-pound fish. When done, gently remove skin, then garnish, being careful to arrange garnish so that fish can be cut and served easily.

BROILING

Fish fillets or steaks should be as dry as possible and at least 1 inch thick. Brush both sides with melted fat or basting sauce, then season. See p. 624 for herb seasoning. Place frozen fish on greased broiler rack or pan. If the skin is on, place skin side down. Broil 2–4 inches from preheated heating unit. Broiling time will range from 5 to 20 minutes. Thicker fillets may need to be turned once halfway through cooking time.

TABLE 2.7   FIN FISH BUYING AND COOKING GUIDE

Species	Characteristics	Fat or lean	Usual market forms	Cooking methods
Bass, sea	Flaky, white; rich flavor	Fat	Fillets, steaks; whole, pan-dressed	Fry, boil, bake
Bluefish	Dark, turning light when cooked; mild, soft	Fat	Fillets	Bake, poach

TABLE 2.7 *(Continued)*

Species	Characteristics	Fat or lean	Usual market forms	Cooking methods
Catfish	Firm flesh, abundant flavor	Lean	Whole, dressed; fillets	Fry
Cod	Mild flavor; soft white meat, flakes easily	Lean	Fillets, steaks; breaded portions	Bake, fry, broil
Dolphin (mahimahi)	Firm, white meat; delicate flavor	Lean	Fillets	Broil, sauté, bake
Flounder	Delicate flavor, white	Lean	Whole, pan-dressed; fillets; breaded	Fry, bake, broil
Grouper	Flaky white, firm; rich flavor	Lean	Whole, steaks, fillets	Fry, bake, poach
Haddock	White meat, mild flavor	Lean	Whole, steaks, fillets, breaded portions	Bake, fry, broil, poach
Halibut	Tender, white; mild flavor	Lean	Drawn, dressed, steaks	Broil, bake, fry, poach
Mackerel	Firm, slightly dark flesh; rich flavor	Fat	Whole, drawn; fillets	Broil, bake, poach, fry
Monkfish	Firm, white flesh; mild lobster-like flavor	Lean	Fillets, tails	Broil, sauté
Orange roughy	Snow-white flesh; delicate flavor, sweet taste	Lean	Fillets	Sauté, broil
Perch, ocean	Firm, white, flaky; mild flavor	Lean	Whole, pan-dressed; fillets; breaded fillets and portions	Pan fry, bake, deep-fat dry
Pike, walleye	Snowy white meat, sweet flavor	Lean	Whole, fillets, round	Pan fry
Pollack	Firm texture, white meat; mild	Lean	Fillets, breaded and pre-cooked sticks and portions	Fry, broil, bake
Pompano	Firm white flesh	Fat	Whole, fillets	Sauté, broil
Redfish	Light firm flesh, sweet flavor	Lean	Whole, fillets	Pan fry, blackened
Red snapper	Firm, white flesh; mild flavor	Lean	Dressed, fillets, portions	Bake, fry, broil
Salmon	Pink to red flesh, rich flavor	Fat	Dressed, steaks, fillets	Bake, poach, broil, pan fry
Shad	Oily, rich flavor; many bones	Fat	Whole, drawn, fillets	Bake, poach, broil, fry
Sole	Firm, white flesh; delicate flavor	Lean	Whole, fillets	Bake, fry, broil, poach
Swordfish	Firm flesh, mild flavor	Fat	Steaks, chunks	Broil, bake, poach
Trout, lake	Firm texture, rich flavor	Fat	Whole, drawn, fillets	Bake, poach, pan fry
Trout, rainbow	Delicate flesh, excellent flavor	Lean	Whole, dressed; boned and breaded fillets	Pan fry, oven fry, broil, bake
Tuna (ahi)	Light flesh, good flavor	Fat	Steaks, drawn, chunks	Bake, broil, sauté
Turbot	Very tender, white; mild flavor	Lean	Fillets	Fry, bake, broil
Whitefish	Rich flavor; tender, white flesh	Fat	Whole, drawn, dressed; fillets	Bake, broil, poach
Whiting	Firm texture, abundant flavor	Lean	Drawn; breaded portions and fillets	Deep-fat fry, broil, sauté

TABLE 2.8 SUGGESTED METHODS OF COOKING FIN FISH AND SHELLFISH[a]

		Baking[b]		Broiling	
Type	Approximate weight or thickness	Temperature (°F)	Time (minutes)	Distance from heat (inches)	Time (minutes)
Fin fish					
Dressed	3–4 lb	350–400	40–60		
Pan-dressed	½–1 lb	350–400	25–30	2–4	5–15
Steaks	½–1¼ inch	350–400	25–35	2–4	5–15
Fillets		350–400	25–35	2–4	5–15
Portions	1–6 oz	350–400	30–40		
Sticks	¾–1¼ oz	400	15–20		
Shellfish					
Clams, live, shucked		450	12–15	4	5–8
Crabs, live, soft-shell				4	8–10
Lobsters, live	¾–1 lb	400	15–20	4	12–15
Spiny lobster tails, frozen	¼–½ lb	450	20–30	4	8–12
Oysters, live, shucked		450	12–15	4	5–8
Scallops, shucked		350	25–30	3	6–8
Shrimp Headless, raw					
Headless, raw, peeled		350	15–20	3	5–8

Adapted from *How to Eye and Buy Seafood*, National Marine Fisheries Service, U.S. Department of Commerce, Chicago, Ill., 1976; and *Seafood, Foodservice Training Manual*, National Fisheries Institute, Washington, D.C.

[a] See p. 332 for microwave cooking methods.
[b] A basic guide is to bake or pan fry for 20–25 minutes (350–400°F) per inch of thickness for frozen fish; 10–15 minutes per inch of thickness for thawed or fresh fish.

FRYING

Pan frying and sautéing To pan fry, season fillets, steaks, or small whole fish with salt and pepper. Dip in milk and roll in flour or cornmeal or a combination of both. To sauté, lightly dust thawed, dry fish with seasoned flour. Cook in a small amount of fat at 360–375°F. Turn halfway through cooking time to brown each side.

Boiling, poaching, or steaming		Deep-fat frying		Pan frying[b]	
Method	Time (minutes)	Temperature (°F)	Time (minutes)	Temperature	Time (minutes)
Poach	10/lb				
Poach	10	360–375	4–5	Moderate	15–20
Poach	10	360–375	4–5	Moderate	15–25
Poach	10	360–375	4–5	Moderate	8–10
		360–375	4–5	Moderate	8–10
		360–375	3–5		
Steam	5–10	350	2–3	Moderate	4–5
Boil	10–15	375	2–4	Moderate	8–10
Boil	15–20	350	2–4	Moderate	8–10
Boil	10–15	350	3–5	Moderate	8–10
Steam	5–10	350	2–3	Moderate	4–5
Boil	3–4	350	2–3	Moderate	4–6
Boil	3–5				
Boil	3–5	350	2–3	Moderate	8–10

Deep-fat frying   Dip frozen fish fillets, steaks, or small whole fish in milk or egg mixture and seasoned crumbs; or purchase breaded or battered product. Fry 4–5 minutes at 360–375°F (thicker whole fish will require more time). Fish usually float when done.

Oven frying   Dip frozen fillets or steaks in seasoned milk; drain, then coat with fine bread crumbs. Place in greased shallow pan or pan lined with silicone paper or aluminum foil; do not cover. Drizzle melted fat over fish. Bake at 400°F.

MICROWAVE

Primary cooking guidelines The source for the following microwave cooking directions is the *Seafood Foodservice Training Manual,* published by the National Fisheries Institute, Washington, D.C.

1. Maximum moisture retention and even cooking can be achieved by generously brushing the fish and seafood item with butter or margarine and tightly covering or wrapping the item before cooking.
2. If the item is to be browned under a broiler after microwave cooking, it should be cooked to only 75–80 percent doneness in the microwave. Fish will not yet be flaky, and shellfish will be slightly translucent.
3. Microwave individual portions on medium-high setting to retain juices and flavor.
4. Let fish or seafood stand 2–3 minutes prior to serving.
5. Test for doneness: Fish is flaky when lifted gently with a fork near the center. It should be opaque in color; bones should be easily removed from meat. Shellfish will be slightly translucent in center. Let stand for a short period to finish cooking.

OVEN STEAMING

Place frozen fish on greased aluminum foil. Season, flavor with lemon juice, spices, and thinly sliced vegetables. Wrap securely. Place in shallow baking pan. Bake at 400°F for 20–25 minutes per inch of thickness.

POACHING

Prepare poaching liquid: acidulated water, court bouillon, fish stock, milk, or milk and water. Place fish fillets or thick steaks in a flat shallow baking pan. Barely cover fish with boiling liquid, then cover with parchment paper or a lid. Cook in a 350°F oven or in a steamer until fish loses its transparent appearance or until fish flakes easily when tested with a fork, usually 5–10 minutes. Remove fish from liquid and serve with a sauce or garnish.

Acidulated water Use 1 Tbsp salt and 3 Tbsp lemon juice or vinegar for each quart of water.

Court bouillon Add to 1 gal water ¾ cup each of chopped carrots, chopped onion, and chopped celery; 3 Tbsp salt; ½ cup vinegar; 2 or 3 bay leaves; 6 peppercorns; 9 cloves; and 3 Tbsp margarine or butter. Boil gently for 20–30 minutes. Strain to remove spices and vegetables.

Shellfish

Crabs. Simmer hard-shelled crabs for 10–15 minutes in salted water. Cool rapidly in ice water. Break the shells apart and remove meat to be used in cooked dishes and salads. One 2-pound crab yields about 12 ounces of cooked body and leg meat. Soft-shelled crabs usually are parboiled, dipped in egg and crumbs (p. 41), pan fried, or cooked in deep fat.

Lobsters.   To prepare frozen lobster tails, follow instructions on the package. Lobster meat, frozen or canned, may be used for salads and in cooked dishes. Live lobsters may be broiled or boiled.

Oysters.   Oysters are not ordinarily washed before using. If washing seems necessary, care should be taken to remove the oysters from the water quickly, so that they do not become soaked or waterlogged. Any bits of shell should be removed. Cook oysters just enough to heat through to keep oysters juicy and plump. Overcooking makes them shrunken and dry. To fry, dip oysters in egg and crumbs (p. 41) before frying.

Scallops.   To prepare fresh scallops, wash and remove any shell particles. Drain. Dip in egg and crumbs (p. 41). Fry in deep fat at 350°F for 2–3 minutes.

Shrimp.   Raw, or green, shrimp should be washed carefully. Cover with water and bring to a boil. Let simmer for 3–5 minutes in water to which has been added 1½ tsp salt to each quart, 2 bay leaves, and mixed spices. Drain. Remove shell and dark vein from the center back of each shrimp. To fry, dip peeled and cleaned raw or cooked shrimp in batter, or egg and crumb (p. 41). Fry in deep fat at 360–375°F for 2–3 minutes. Breaded frozen shrimp may be cooked from their hard-frozen state.

FISH RECIPES

Baked fish fillets

OVEN: 375°F
BAKE: 25–35 minutes

YIELD: 50 portions
PORTION: 5 oz

Ingredient	Amount	Procedure
Frozen fish fillets, 5 oz	50	Dip fish in margarine.
Margarine or butter, melted	1 lb	
Bread crumbs	1 lb 12 oz	Combine bread crumbs, flour, and seasonings.
Flour, all-purpose	10 oz	
Salt	1 Tbsp	
Paprika	1½ Tbsp	
Seasoned salt	1 Tbsp	
Marjoram	1 tsp	
Grated lemon peel	1 tsp	
		Dredge fish with crumb mixture and place on greased baking pans.
		Bake at 375°F for 25–35 minutes or until fish flakes easily.

Note:
Fish portions or steaks may be substituted for fish fillets.

Lemon baked fish

OVEN: 375°F	YIELD: 50 portions	
BAKE: 25–35 minutes	PORTION: 5 oz	

Ingredient	Amount	Procedure
Shortening, melted	1 lb	Mix shortening, salt, pepper, and lemon juice.
Salt	1 Tbsp	
Pepper, white	1 tsp	
Lemon juice	½ cup	
Frozen fish fillets, 5 oz	50	Dip each fish portion into seasoned fat.
Flour, all-purpose	14 oz	Dredge fish with flour.
		Place close together in single layer in greased baking pans.
Margarine or butter, melted	2 oz	Mix margarine and milk and pour over fish.
		Bake at 375°F for 25–35 minutes or until fish
Milk	¾ cup	flakes easily.

Breaded fish fillets

| DEEP-FAT FRYER: 375°F | | YIELD: 50 portions |
| FRY: 4–5 minutes | | PORTION: 5 oz |

Ingredient	Amount	Procedure
Frozen fish fillets,[a] 5 oz Flour, all-purpose Salt Pepper, white	50 8 oz 1 Tbsp 1 tsp	Dredge fish in mixture of flour, salt, and pepper.
Eggs, beaten Milk	6 (11 oz) 2 cups	Combine eggs and milk.

Bread crumbs	1 lb 4 oz	Dip fish in egg mixture, then in crumbs.
		Fry in deep fat for 4–5 minutes or until fish
		  is golden brown.
		Serve at once or place in uncovered counter
		  pans in 250°F oven until served.

[a] Suggested fish: flounder, sole, haddock, perch, grouper.

Filet of sole amandine

OVEN: 375°F		YIELD: 50 portions
BAKE: 15–20 minutes		PORTION: 5 oz

Ingredient	Amount	Procedure
Fillet of sole, 3 per lb	17 lb	Dredge fish in combined flour, salt, and
Flour, all-purpose	8 oz	pepper.
Salt	1 Tbsp	Place in greased counter pans in single layers.
Pepper, white	1 tsp	
Margarine or butter	1 lb 8 oz	Sauté onion and garlic in margarine.
Onion, finely chopped	4 oz	
Garlic, minced	1 clove	
Water	2 cups	Combine water, lemon juice, and seasonings.
Lemon juice	1½ cups	Add onions and garlic.
Salt	1 Tbsp	Heat, but do not boil.
Pepper, white	1 tsp	Just before baking, pour sauce over fish, 1 cup per pan.
Almonds, slivered	8 oz	Sprinkle almonds over fish. Bake at 375°F for 15–20 minutes.

Note:

Other white fish, such as halibut, haddock, cod, or flounder, may be used. Baking time on thicker fillets or steaks will be 25–35 minutes.

Deviled crab

OVER: 400°F	YIELD: 50 portions
BAKE: 15 minutes	PORTION: 3 oz

OVEN: 400°F

Ingredient	Amount	Procedure
Crabmeat	6 lb	Separate crabmeat into flakes.
Eggs, beaten	5 (9 oz)	Combine eggs, lemon juice, and seasonings.
Lemon juice	¼ cup	Add to crabmeat. Mix lightly.
Salt	1 oz (1½ Tbsp)	
Pepper	2 tsp	
Cayenne	few grains	
Worcestershire sauce	1 Tbsp	
Onion juice (optional)	2 Tbsp	
Margarine or butter	12 oz	Melt margarine in steam-jacketed or other kettle.
Flour, all-purpose	8 oz	Add flour and stir until smooth. Cook 5 minutes.
Milk	2 qt	Add milk gradually to flour mixture, stirring constantly with wire whip. Cook until thick.
Prepared mustard	1½ tsp	Add mustard to sauce. Combine with crab mixture. Mix lightly. Fill individual casseroles or shells.
Bread crumbs	8 oz	Combine crumbs and margarine.
Margarine or butter, melted	4 oz	Sprinkle over crab. Bake at 400°F for 15 minutes.

Scalloped oysters

OVEN: 400°F
BAKE: 30 minutes

YIELD: 50 portions
        2 pans 12 × 20 × 2 inches
PORTION: 5 oz

Ingredient	Amount	Procedure
Oysters	6 qt	Drain oysters, saving liquor.
Cracker crumbs	3 qt	Mix crumbs, margarine, and seasonings.
Margarine or butter, melted	1 lb	Spread a third of the crumbs over bottoms of 2 greased 12 × 20 × 2-inch baking pans.
Salt	1 oz (1½ Tbsp)	Cover with half of the oysters; repeat with
Paprika	½ tsp	crumbs and oysters.
Pepper, white	½ tsp	
Milk or cream	1 qt	Mix milk or cream and oyster liquor. Pour over top of oysters.
Oyster liquor (or milk)	3 cups	Cover with remaining crumbs.
		Bake at 400°F for 30 minutes.

Note:
2 cups finely chopped, partially cooked celery may be added.

Creole shrimp with rice

YIELD: 50 portions
PORTION: 4 oz creole shrimp
4 oz rice

Ingredient	Amount	Procedure
Shortening	8 oz	Cook onion, celery, and garlic in shortening until almost tender but not brown.
Onion, finely chopped	10 oz	
Celery, finely chopped	12 oz	
Garlic, minced	1 tsp	
Flour, all-purpose	6 oz	Add flour and seasonings. Stir until smooth. Cook 5 minutes.
Salt	1 oz (1½ Tbsp)	
Cayenne	¾ tsp	
Tomato juice	2 cups	Add tomato juice, tomatoes, and sugar. Cook 10 minutes.
Tomatoes, canned	2½ qt	
Sugar, granulated	1 Tbsp	
Shrimp, cooked, peeled, and deveined	6 lb EP	Add shrimp and green pepper to sauce. Heat to serving temperature.
Green pepper, chopped	8 oz	
Rice, long-grain	3 lb 8 oz	Cook rice according to directions on p. 422. Serve shrimp with 4-oz ladle over No. 10 dipper of rice.
Water, boiling	4¼ qt	
Salt	2 Tbsp	
Cooking oil	2 Tbsp	

Note:
If raw shrimp are used, purchase 12–14 lb. Cook as directed on p. 333.

Salmon loaf

OVEN: 325°F	YIELD: 50 portions
BAKE: 1¼ hours	5 loaves 5 × 9 inches
	PORTION: 4½ oz

Ingredient	Amount	Procedure
Milk, scalded	3¾ cups	Mix milk and bread cubes.
Bread cubes, soft	1 lb 4 oz	
Eggs, beaten	18 (2 lb)	Add eggs to milk and bread mixture.
Salmon, flakes	10 lb	Add salmon and other ingredients.
Salt	1 oz (1½ Tbsp)	Mix lightly.
Paprika	1 tsp	Scale salmon mixture into 5 greased 5 × 9-
Pepper, white	1 tsp	inch loaf pans, 2 lb 14 oz per pan.
Onions, chopped	3 oz	Bake at 325°F for 1–1½ hours.
Lemon juice	½ cup	

Note:
For a lighter-textured product, beat egg whites separately and fold into salmon mixture.

Variation:
Tuna loaf.   Substitute drained tuna for salmon.

Scalloped salmon

OVEN: 375°F
BAKE: 25 minutes

YIELD: 50 portions
2 pans 12 × 20 × 2 inches
PORTION: 6 oz

Ingredient	Amount	Procedure
Margarine or butter	1 lb	Melt margarine in steam-jacketed or other kettle.
Flour, all-purpose	12 oz	
Salt	1 oz (1½ Tbsp)	Add flour and stir until smooth.
Pepper, white	½ tsp	Cook 5 minutes.
Milk	1 gal	Add milk gradually, stirring constantly with wire whip. Continue cooking until thickened.
Parsley, chopped	¼ cup	Add parsley, onion, and celery salt to sauce.
Onion, chopped	4 oz	
Celery salt	1 tsp	
Salmon, canned	10 lb	Drain salmon. Remove skin and bones. Flake.
Bread crumbs	8 oz	Arrange salmon, sauce, and crumbs in layers in 2 greased 12 × 20 × 2-inch baking pans, 10 lb per pan.
Bread crumbs	4 oz	Combine buttered crumbs and sprinkle over the top.
Margarine or butter, melted	4 oz	Bake at 375°F for 25 minutes.

Note:
Diced hard-cooked eggs and frozen peas are good additions.

Variation:
Scalloped tuna.   Substitute tuna for salmon.

Tuna and noodles

OVEN: 350°F	YIELD: 48 portions
BAKE: 45 minutes	2 pans 12 × 20 × 2 inches
	PORTION: 8 oz

Ingredient	Amount	Procedure
Noodles	3 lb AP (9 lb cooked)	Cook noodles according to directions on p. 402. Drain.
Water, boiling	3 gal	
Salt	2 oz (3 Tbsp)	
Oil (optional)	2 Tbsp	
Tuna	5 lb 8 oz	Flake tuna and add to noodles.
Margarine or butter	8 oz	Melt margarine in steam-jacketed or other kettle. Add onions and celery. Sauté until tender.
Onions, chopped	1 lb 8 oz	
Celery, chopped	1 lb 8 oz	
Flour, all-purpose	6 oz	Add flour and pepper to onion mixture. Stir until blended. Cook 5–10 minutes.
Pepper, black	½ tsp	
Chicken base	3 oz	Stir in chicken base. Add water gradually, stirring constantly with wire whip. Cook until thickened. Add tuna and noodles to sauce. Stir gently until well blended.
Water	1 gal	
Processed cheese, shredded	8 oz	Scale into 2 greased 12 × 20 × 2-inch baking pans, 13 lb per pan. Sprinkle cheese over the noodles, 4 oz per pan. Sprinkle lightly with paprika. Bake at 350°F until mixture is heated through and cheese is melted, 30–45 minutes.
Paprika	½ tsp	

Note:
Two 46-oz cans cream of mushroom or cream of celery soup and 1 qt milk may be substituted for the sauce made from margarine, flour, chicken base, and water.

Variations:
1. **Tuna macaroni casserole.** Substitute macaroni for noodles.
2. **Tuna and rice.** Substitute 1 lb 8 oz rice for the noodles. Cook rice according to directions on p. 422.

Creamed tuna

YIELD: 50 portions
7½ qt
PORTION: 4 oz

Ingredient	Amount	Procedure
Eggs, hard-cooked (p. 306)	9	Peel eggs and chop coarsely.
Margarine or butter Flour, all-purpose Salt	12 oz 6 oz 1 Tbsp	Melt margarine in steam-jacketed or other kettle. Add flour and salt. Stir until smooth. Cook 5 minutes.
Milk	1 gal	Add milk gradually, stirring constantly with a wire whip. Cook until thickened.
Green pepper, chopped Pimiento, chopped Worcestershire sauce (optional) Cayenne	6 oz 6 oz 6 Tbsp ¼ tsp	Add green pepper, pimiento, and seasonings to sauce.
Tuna, flaked	5 lb	Add tuna and eggs to sauce. Reheat to serving temperature. Serve with 4-oz ladle on toast, biscuits, or corn bread.

Note:
Other cooked fish may be substituted for tuna.

Variations:
1. **Creamed salmon.**   Substitute salmon for tuna.
2. **Creamed tuna and celery.**   Delete hard-cooked eggs and green pepper. Add 1 lb diced cooked celery, 3 oz chopped onion sautéed in margarine, and 3 oz chopped pimiento.
3. **Creamed tuna and peas.**   Delete hard-cooked eggs and green pepper. Add 3 lb frozen peas, cooked until just tender and drained.
4. **Tuna rarebit.**   Delete hard-cooked eggs. Add 1 lb 8 oz shredded cheddar cheese.

MEAT

PURCHASING AND STORAGE

The quality of cooked meat depends on the quality purchased, the storage and handling of meat after delivery, and cooking methods. All meats marketed in interstate commerce in the United States must meet federal inspection standards for wholesomeness. This requirement includes all processed meat products and fresh and frozen meats. Meat slaughtered, processed, and sold within a given state must be inspected by programs "at least equal to" federal inspection standards.

Federal grading is on a voluntary basis. Federal and packer brand grades of meat are based on three factors—conformation, finish, and quality of the flesh. The federal grades are prime, choice, select, and standard.

Beef and lamb, when federally graded, also must be given a yield grade that measures the amount of lean meat that can be cut from a carcass. The yield grade of a beef carcass is determined by considering four characteristics: (1) the amount of external fat, (2) the amount of kidney, pelvic, and heart fat, (3) the area of rib-eye muscle, and (4) the warm carcass weight. Lamb yield grade is based on (1) the amount of external fat, (2) the amount of kidney and pelvic fat, and (3) the conformation grade of the leg.

Meat for foodservice use is available in wholesale cuts, fabricated roasts, and preportioned items. The form in which meat is purchased depends on the policies and size of the institution, the type of service it offers, and its storage and meat-cutting facilities. Portion-ready cuts require less storage space, eliminate skilled labor for cutting, and do away with waste. Costs are easily controlled, since the weight and price of each portion are predetermined and only the amount needed is ordered.

Fresh meat may be stored unwrapped or loosely covered with waxed paper at a temperature of 35–40°F, with a relative humidity of 80–90 percent. It should be used as soon after purchase as possible.

Frozen meat requires a uniform holding temperature of 0°F or below. It should be well wrapped to exclude air and to prevent drying. If the meat is to be frozen on the premises, the temperature should be even lower, with some air movement. If possible, meat should be frozen in a blast freezer set at −20 to −40°F with forced air convection.

Frozen meat should not be unwrapped before defrosting in the refrigerator at 30–35°F and should be cooked soon after defrosting. Once thawed, it should not be refrozen unless in an emergency, and then there will be some sacrifice in juiciness. Cooked meat may be frozen provided it is frozen soon after cooking and cooling.

Cured and cured and smoked meats such as ham and bacon, sausages, and dried beef require refrigerator storage. The type of ham used most often in food-services is the fully cooked ham, which has been cooked sufficiently that it may be served without further cooking or may be heated just enough to serve hot; fully cooked hams require storage at refrigerator temperature before and after heating. Most canned hams, which are also fully cooked, require refrigeration. Cook-before-eating hams are partially cooked in processing and must be kept under refrigeration. Commercially processed hams indicate on the label which they are or to what degree they have been cooked. Although ham, bacon, and other cured meats can be frozen, it should be only for short periods, since undesirable flavor changes occur because of the salt and spices in them.

COOKING METHODS

Meat is cooked by either dry or moist heat. The method used will depend on the grade and location of the cut. Meat cuts containing relatively small amounts of connective tissue are cooked by dry heat (roasting, broiling, or frying). Moist heat (braising or cooking in liquid) is used for less tender cuts that have larger amounts of connective tissue. Veal, lamb, and pork, all tender meats, often are cooked with moist heat to develop their flavor and to provide variety in menu items. Veal, because of its delicate flavor and low fat content, combines well with sauces and other foods.

Dry-heat cooking does not improve tenderness, and under some conditions it reduces it. Cooking with moist heat tends to soften some connective tissue and to make meat tender. A low temperature, regardless of the method, is desirable. The degree of doneness affects percentage losses, with a smaller loss in rare meat than in medium or well-done meat, provided other factors are the same.

Roasting

The term "roasting," which is a dry-heat method, refers to cooking meat in an oven, in an open pan, with no moisture added. The term also refers to large meat cuts cooked over or under coals and is often used interchangeably with baking. Meat cuts must be tender to be roasted. In beef, these are the lesser-used muscles, or those attached to the backbone. Most veal, pork, and lamb cuts may be cooked by this method.

Meats may be completely or partially defrosted or frozen at the time the cooking process is begun. Research has shown that meat roasted from the frozen state will yield as much meat as roasts partially or completely thawed before cooking. However, when time is a factor, defrosting meat before cooking usually is the accepted method. The additional cooking time required for frozen roasts is from one-third to one-half again the amount of time recommended for cooking a similar cut from the chilled state. Oven temperature does not change. Steps in roasting are as follows:

1. Place the meat, fat side up, on a rack in an open roasting pan. As the fat on top melts and runs down over the meat, it bastes the roast. Basting adds flavor and keeps the surface of the roast from drying out.

2. Insert a meat thermometer in the roast so that the bulb rests in the center of the cut but does not rest on bone or fat (Figure 2.28). If the meat is frozen, the thermometer is inserted toward the end of the cooking period after the meat has thawed.

3. Season the roast with salt, pepper, and other spices. See p. 624 for Seasoned Salt recipe. Salt penetrates less than an inch during cooking, so it may make little difference whether the roast is seasoned at the beginning, middle, or end of cooking.

4. Do not add water and do not cover. If water is added to the pan, the cooking will be by moist heat.

5. Roast at a constant low oven temperature, 250–350°F, depending on the kind of meat and size of the roast. If cooking in a convection oven, the temperature should be reduced by 50°F to minimize drying of the surface of the roast by moving air. Searing the roast initially at a high temperature does not hold in meat juices and may increase cooking losses. A constant low temperature reduces shrinkage and produces a more evenly done roast that is easier to carve and more attractive to serve.

6. Roast to the desired degree of doneness. The length of the cooking period depends on several factors: oven temperature, size and shape of the roast, style of cut (boned or bone in), oven load, quality of meat, and degree of doneness desired. Approximate cooking times and temperatures are given in Tables 2.9, 2.10, and 2.11. Although approximate total cooking time can be used as a general guide, the interior temperature of the meat as measured by a meat thermometer is a more reliable indicator of doneness. Roasts will continue cooking for a period of time after removal from the oven, and the internal temperature of the roast may rise as much as 5°F. The roast should be allowed to set in a warm place for 15–20 minutes before it is sliced. The roast becomes more firm, retains more of its juices, and is easier to slice. Refrigerating the roast for an extended period of time prior to slicing and service, however, results in loss of flavor. To ensure the highest quality, roasts should be served as soon as possible after cooking and slicing. Table 1.1 provides information on serving yields.

Broiling

Broiling is a dry-heat method of cooking using direct or radiant heat. It is used for small individualized tender cuts such as steaks, chops, and patties. Low-temperature cooking methods apply to proper broiling. Broiled meats should not be seared,

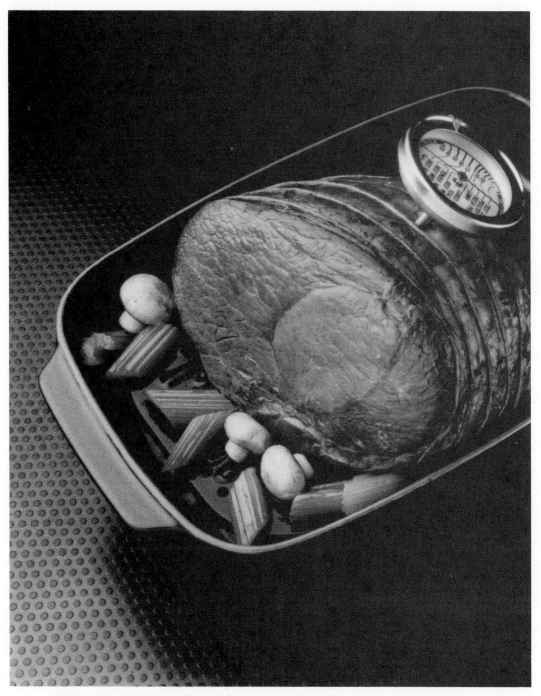

Figure 2.28 *Proper placement of meat thermometer in roast. Photo courtesy of the National Live Stock and Meat Board.*

for searing increases broiling losses. If marking on a hot broiler rack is desired, the remainder of the broiler time after marking should be at a moderate temperature.

Broiling is most successful for cuts 1–2 inches thick. Veal should not be broiled unless it is fairly mature and well marbled with fat, and then only loin chops or steaks. Broiling is an acceptable cooking method for pork chops, but because pork should be cooked to an internal temperature of 170°F, the temperature should be moderate so the chop does not become charred by the time it is cooked well done.

Frozen cuts may be successfully broiled, especially those 1½ inch thick or less. They should be broiled at a greater distance from the heat or at a lower temperature than unfrozen cuts to provide more uniform doneness. Although cooking times will vary, a general guideline is that frozen steaks will take nearly twice as long as unfrozen steaks.

Meat may be broiled in an oven broiler or other type of heat-from-above gas or electric broiler, or on an open hearth, which is heated from below. In pan broiling or griddle broiling, the heat is transferred from the pan or grill to the meat being cooked.

Following is the standard procedure for broiling:

1. Preheat the broiler. A preheated broiler rack will provide desired markings on the meat.
2. Place the meat on the broiler rack. A distance of 3–5 inches is recommended. If frozen meat is used, increase distance from the heat source.
3. Broil the meat until the side closest to the heat source is attractively browned and the cut is cooked almost halfway through.
4. Turn meat only once during cooking.
5. Broil second side to desired doneness. Season. See Table 2.12 for approximate time.

PAN BROILING AND GRIDDLE BROILING

1. Place meat on a preheated ungreased griddle or heavy frying pan.
2. Cook slowly, turning as necessary. Since the meat is in contact with the hot metal of the pan or griddle, turning more than once may be necessary for even cooking. If the steak is thick, reduce the temperature after browning. Griddle boiling requires more attention than true broiling, but it is more rapid than cooking in some types of broilers.
3. Cook the meat at a moderate temperature. Care should be taken not to puncture the meat while cooking. Use a long-handled tongs or spatula for turning.
4. Do not add additional fat or water. Pour off or scrape away any excess fat as it accumulates.
5. Cook meat to the desired degree of doneness. See Table 2.13 for approximate cooking times.

TABLE 2.9 TIMETABLE FOR ROASTING BEEF

Cut	Approximate weight of single roast (pounds)	Number of roasts in oven	Approximate total weight of roasts (pounds)	Oven temperature (°F)
Rib, roast ready, No. 109	20 to 25			250
Rib, roast ready, No. 109	20 to 25			300
Rib, roast ready, No. 109		2	56	300
Ribeye roll, No. 112 or 112A	4 to 6			350
Full tenderloin, No. 189 or 190	4 to 6			425
Strip loin, boneless, No. 180	10 to 12			325
Top sirloin butt, No. 184	8			300
Top (inside) round, No. 168	10			300
Top (inside) round, No. 168	15			300
Round, rump and shank off, boneless, tied, special, No. 165B	50			250

From National Live Stock and Meat Board, *Meat in the Foodservice Industry* (Chicago, reviewed 1987, copyright 1977), p. 62.

Frying

Frying is cooking in fat and may be accomplished by pan frying or griddle frying in a small amount of fat or by deep-fat frying, which uses a large amount of fat.

Meat for frying generally is cut thinner than that for broiling and may be breaded or tenderized by scoring, cubing, or grinding. Cuts lacking fat, such as veal cutlets and liver or other variety meats, usually are fried.

Interior temperature of roast when removed from oven (°F)	Minutes per pound based on one roast	Minutes per pound based on total weight of roasts in oven	Approximate total cooking time (hours)
130 (rare)	13 to 15		4½ to 5
140 (medium)	15 to 17		5 to 6
150 (well)	17 to 19		6 to 6½
130 (rare)	10 to 12		4 to 4½
140 (medium)	12 to 14		4½ to 5
150 (well)	14 to 16		5 to 5½
130 (rare)		5 to 6	5 to 5½
140 (medium)		6	6
150 (well)		7 to 8	6 to 7
140 (rare)	18 to 20		1⅓ to 1⅔
160 (medium)	20 to 22		1½ to 2
170 (well)	22 to 24		1⅔ to 2¼
140 (rare)			¾ to 1
140 (rare)	10		1½ to 2
140 (rare)	25		3½
140 (rare)	18 to 19		3 to 3¼
150 (medium)	22 to 23		3½ to 4
140 (rare)	15		3½ to 4
150 (medium)	17		4 to 4½
140 (medium)	12		10
155 (well)	14		11 to 12

PAN FRYING OR GRIDDLE FRYING

Procedures for pan frying or griddle frying are similar to pan or griddle broiling, but the meat may be dredged with seasoned flour, and a small amount of fat is used for cooking. Confusion often surrounds whether or not to cover the pan. Covering is not recommended for griddle frying, because in doing so the method of cooking changes from dry-heat to moist-heat cooking.

Pan frying and sautéing are terms sometimes used interchangeably. Generally

TABLE 2.10 TIMETABLE FOR ROASTING LAMB AND VEAL

Cut	Approximate weight (pounds)	Oven Temperature (°F)	Interior temperature of roast when removed from oven (°F)	Minutes per pound based on one roast	Approximate total cooking time (hours)
Lamb					
Leg, shank off, No. 233C	5 to 9	325	140 (rare)	20 to 25	2 to 3
			160 (medium)	25 to 30	2½ to 3¾
			170–180 (well)	30 to 35	3 to 4½
Leg, shank off, boneless, No. 233D	4 to 7	325	140 (rare)	25 to 30	2 to 3
			160 (medium)	30 to 35	2¼ to 3½
			170–180 (well)	35 to 40	2½ to 4
Shoulder, boneless and tied, No. 208	3½ to 5	325	140 (rare)	30 to 35	2 to 2½
			160 (medium)	35 to 40	2¼ to 3
			170–180 (well)	40 to 45	2½ to 3½
Rib rack, No. 204	1½ to 2	375	140 (rare)	30 to 35	¾ to 1
			160 (medium)	35 to 40	1 to 1¼
			170–180 (well)	40 to 45	1 to 1½
Rib rack, No. 204	2 to 3	375	140 (rare)	25 to 30	1 to 1¼
			160 (medium)	30 to 35	1¼ to 1½
			170–180 (well)	35 to 40	1½ to 1¾
Veal					
Leg, shank off, oven-prepared, boneless, No. 336	3½ to 7	325	170	25 to 30	2 to 3
Loin, two ribs, trimmed, No. 332 or 332A	4 to 6	325	170	30 to 35	2½ to 3
Square cut chuck, No. 309A	4 to 6	325	170	40 to 45	3 to 3½

From National Live Stock and Meat Board, *Meat in the Foodservice Industry* (Chicago, reviewed 1987, copyright 1977), p. 63.

sautéing refers to cooking small thin pieces of meat in a pan with a small amount of fat, usually at a high temperature and for a short period of time.

Following is the standard procedure for pan frying or griddle frying:

1. Dredge the meat with seasoned flour, crumbs, cornmeal, or similar coatings.
2. Brown the meat on both sides in a small amount of fat. Allow the fat to remain on the griddle or in the pan as the meat cooks.

TABLE 2.11 TIMETABLE FOR ROASTING FRESH AND CURED PORK

Cut	Approximate weight (pounds)	Oven temperature (°F)	Interior temperature of roast when removed from oven (°F)	Minutes per pound based on one roast[a]	Approximate total cooking time[a] (hours)
Fresh pork					
Loin, boned and tied, No. 413A	8 to 10	325	170	30 to 35	4½ to 5½
Loin, center-cut, No. 412	3 to 5	325	170	30 to 35	1¾ to 2½
Shoulder picnic, No. 405	5 to 8	325	170	30 to 35	3 to 4
Boston butt, boned and tied, No. 405A	4 to 6	325	170	40 to 45	3 to 4
Ham, skinned, short shank, No. 402A	12 to 16	325	170	22 to 26	5 to 6
Ham, boned and tied, No. 402B	10 to 14	325	170	24 to 28	4½ to 5½
Spareribs, No. 416	2 to 3	325	Cooked well-done		1½ to 2½
Cured pork					
Ham,[b] No. 503	10 to 14	325	160	18 to 20	3 to 4
Loin, bladeless, No. 546	3 to 5	325	160	25 to 30	1½ to 2½
Shoulder butt, boneless, No. 530	2 to 4	325	170	35 to 40	1 to 2
Shoulder picnic, No. 526	5 to 8	325	170	30 to 35	3 to 4
Canadian-style bacon, No. 550	2 to 4	325	160	35 to 40	1 to 1¾

From National Live Stock and Meat Board, *Meat in the Foodservice Industry* (Chicago, reviewed 1987, copyright 1977), pp. 62–63.

[a] Cooking times are for cook-before-eating products.
[b] Heat "fully cooked" hams to 140°F, allowing 15 to 18 minutes per pound for whole ham, 18 to 24 minutes per pound for half ham.

TABLE 2.12   TIMETABLE FOR BROILING MEAT

Cut	Approximate thickness (inches)	Approximate total cooking time (minutes)		
		Rare	Medium	Well done
Rib, club, top loin, T-bone, porterhouse, tenderloin, or individual servings of beef sirloin steak	1 1½ 2	15 25 35	20 35 50	
Beef sirloin steak	1 1½	20 to 25 30 to 35	30 to 35 40 to 45	
Ground beef patties	1 (4 oz)	15	20	
Pork chops (rib or loin)	¾ to 1			20 to 25
Pork shoulder steaks	½ to ¾			20 to 22
Smoked pork chops (rib or loin)	½ to ¾			15 to 20
Lamb shoulder, rib, loin and sirloin chops or leg chops (steaks)	1 1½ 2		12 to 16 17 to 20 20 to 25	
Ground lamb patties	1 (4 oz)		18 to 20	
Smoked ham slice (cook-before-eating)[a]	½ 1			10 to 12 16 to 20
Bacon				4 to 5

From National Live Stock and Meat Board, *Meat in the Foodservice Industry* (Chicago, reviewed 1987, copyright 1977), p. 66.

[a] Allow 8 to 10 minutes for broiling ½-inch-thick fully cooked ham slice and 14 to 16 minutes for 1-inch-thick fully cooked ham slice.

3. Do not cover meat. Cook at moderate temperature until done, turning occasionally.

4. Drain meat and serve at once.

DEEP-FAT FRYING

1. Coat or bread meat. (See p. 41 for methods of preparing food for deep-fat frying.) Portioned, prebreaded items may be cooked from a frozen state in the deep-fat fryer.

2. Heat the fat to approximately 350°F.

TABLE 2.13 TIMETABLE FOR GRIDDLE BROILING MEAT

Cut	Approximate thickness (inches)	Approximate total cooking time (minutes)		
		Rare	Medium	Well done
Beef steaks	¾	4	8	12
	1	6	10	15
	1½	10 to 12	15 to 18	20
Ground beef patties	¾	4 to 5	8 to 10	12
	1 (4 oz)	6 to 8	10 to 12	15
Lamb chops	1		10	15
	1½		15	20 to 25
Ground lamb patties	¾		10	12 to 15
	1 (4 oz)		10 to 15	15 to 20
Smoked ham slice	½			6 to 10
Bacon				2 to 3

From National Live Stock and Meat Board, *Meat in the Foodservice Industry* (Chicago, reviewed 1987, copyright 1977), p. 68.

3. Place pieces of meat in the wire basket and carefully lower into the fryer. Do not fill the basket while holding over the fat, because crumbs could fall into the fat.

4. Do not overload the basket or the fryer. An overload drastically reduces the temperature of the fat, thereby increasing fat absorption and inhibiting browning. This is especially true when the product is frozen. A ratio of about 5 to 1 by weight of fat to product is the maximum effective load.

5. Continue cooking until the outside of the product is browned and crisp and the meat reaches the desired doneness. Cooking time depends on the size of the piece, whether it is frozen or chilled, and whether the meat has been precooked.

6. Remove meat from fat and let drain. Do not shake the basket over the fat if the product is coated; shaking will cause particles and crumbs to fall into the fat. The product should not be salted over the fat, either, because salt shortens the life of the fat.

Braising

Braising is a moist-cookery method adapted to the less tender cuts of meat, particularly the much-used muscles and low grades of beef. Certain cuts of veal and thin cuts of pork such as chops and steaks are better if braised, although they are tender. The terms "pot roasting" and "fricasseeing" also are applied to this method of cooking. Steps in braising are as follows:

1. Season meat and dredge with flour. Flour increases browning but may be omitted.
2. Brown meat in a small amount of fat. The meat can be browned in its own fat or added fat. Browning develops the aroma, flavor, and color of the meat. Large cuts can be browned in a heavy pot on top of the range, in a pan in the oven, or in a steam-jacketed kettle. Smaller individual pieces can be browned in a tilting fry pan, on the grill, in the oven, or in the deep-fat fryer.
3. Add a small amount of water or other liquid. Use additional liquid as needed during the cooking. Braising or pot roasting in a steam-jacketed kettle will require more water than pot roasting in the oven. Other liquid, such as meat stock, tomato juice, or sour cream, may be used.
4. Cover with a tight-fitting lid or aluminum foil. Long, slow cooking in moisture will produce meat that is well done without being dried out.
5. Cook at low temperature until tender. Simmer in a steam-jacketed kettle or heavy pot on top of the range or in the oven at 300–325°F. See Table 2.14 for approximate cooking times.

Cooking in liquid

This method of moist cookery involves cooking meat covered with water or other liquid and is sometimes referred to as simmering, boiling, or stewing. This method

TABLE 2.14   TIMETABLE FOR BRAISING MEAT

Cut	Average weight or thickness	Approximate total cooking time (hours)
Pot roast	4 to 6 lb	3 to 4
Swiss steak	1 to 2½ inches	2 to 3
Short ribs	pieces 2 × 2 × 2 inches	1½ to 2
Lamb shanks	½ lb each	1 to 1½
Lamb riblets	¾ × 2½ × 3 inches	1½ to 2½
Pork chops or steaks	¾ to 1 inch	¾ to 1
Spareribs	2 to 3 lb	1½
Veal cutlets	½ × 3 × 5½ inches	¾ to 1
Veal steaks or chops	½ to ¾ inch	¾ to 1

From National Live Stock and Meat Board, *Meat in the Foodservice Industry* (Chicago, reviewed 1987, copyright 1977), p. 73.

is suitable for the least tender cuts, such as shank, neck, and brisket, and for variety meats such as heart and tongue.

Following is the procedure for cooking large cuts in liquid:

1. Cover meat with liquid. Water or meat stock are used and may be hot or cold when added to the meat. If desired, the meat may be browned first, but some cuts such as corned beef, cured and smoked meats, and variety meats generally are not browned.

2. Season with salt and pepper. Herbs, spices, and vegetables, used wisely, add to the variety and flavor of stewed meats. Suggested seasonings are carrots, celery, onions, bay leaves, thyme, marjoram, and parsley.

3. Cover and cook below boiling point until tender. Cooking may be in a steam-jacketed kettle, tilting fry pan, or a tightly covered heavy utensil on top of the range. See Table 2.15 for approximate cooking times.

TABLE 2.15 TIMETABLE FOR COOKING MEAT IN LIQUID (LARGE CUTS AND STEWS)

| | | Approximate cooking time | |
Cut	Average size or average weight	Minutes per pound	Total hours
Fresh beef	4 to 8 lb	40 to 50	3 to 4
Corned beef	6 to 8 lb	40 to 50	4 to 6
Beef shank crosscuts	¾ to 1 lb		2½ to 3½
Lamb or veal for stew	1- to 2-inch cubes		1½ to 2½
Beef for stew	1- to 2-inch cubes		2 to 3

From National Live Stock and Meat Board, *Meat in the Foodservice Industry* (Chicago, reviewed 1987, copyright 1977), p. 73.

	YIELD: 50 portions
F	PORTION: 3 oz

Ingredient	Amount	Procedure
Beef, boneless, inside round	18 lb	Season meat with salt and pepper. Place in roasting pan and brown at 450°F for about 30 minutes.
Salt	1 oz (1½ Tbsp)	
Pepper, black	½ tsp	
Water	2 qt	When meat is browned, add water. Reduce heat to 300°F. Cover and cook slowly until tender (3–5 hours). Add water as necessary. When meat is done, remove from pan. Let stand ½ hour before slicing.
Flour, all-purpose	6 oz	Mix flour and cold water, stirring with wire whip until smooth.
Water, cold	1½ cups	Add to drippings in pan.
Salt	1 oz (1½ Tbsp)	Remove excess fat if necessary and add water to make 1 gal gravy.
Pepper, black	½ tsp	Add salt and pepper.
Water	As necessary	

Notes:
1. Beef chuck may be used. Increase to 20 lb (AP).
2. Meat may be cooked in a steam-jacketed kettle. Brown in a small amount of fat. Add water, salt, and pepper. Cover kettle and cook until tender. Add water as necessary.

Variations:
1. **Savory pot roast or brisket.** Place meat in baking pan. Sprinkle with 5 oz dry onion soup mix. Cover tightly with aluminum foil. Bake at 300°F for 5–6 hours. Remove foil and bake ½ hour longer. Use juice for gravy. If brisket is used, increase to 25 lb. Cooked Barbecue Sauce (p. 568) may be added for the last half hour of cooking.
2. **Smoked beef brisket.** Use 25 lb well-trimmed beef brisket. Combine ⅔ cup liquid smoke, 2 Tbsp salt, 2 Tbsp onion salt, ¼ cup celery salt, ¼ cup garlic salt, ½ cup Worcestershire sauce, and ¼ cup black pepper. Spread on brisket. Cover with aluminum foil. Seal. Refrigerate overnight. Bake at 275°F for 4 hours covered. Uncover and spread with Cooked Barbecue Sauce (p. 568). Bake 1 hour longer. To serve, slice in thin slices across the grain of the meat.
3. **Yankee pot roast.** Add 1½ qt tomato puree and one bay leaf to the water used in cooking the pot roast.

Sauerbraten

OVEN: 350°F	YIELD: 50 portions	
BAKE: 2–2½ hours	PORTION: 4 oz	

Ingredient	Amount	Procedure
Red cooking wine	3 cups	Heat to boiling point. Do not boil.
Red wine vinegar	2½ cups	Cool to room temperature.
Water	2½ cups	
Bay leaves	5	
Juniper berries, whole	14	
Peppercorns, black	18	
Beef, boneless, inside round	20 lb	Rub beef with salt and pepper.
Salt	4 oz	
Pepper, black	2 Tbsp	
Onions, sliced	4 lb EP	Place meat and onions in deep pans. Pour marinade over beef. Turn beef to moisten all sides with marinade. Cover tightly. Refrigerate 2 or 3 days, turning the meat twice a day if meat is not covered with marinade. Strain marinade and reserve liquid to pour over beef. Place meat in roasting pan. Pour strained marinade over meat. Cover tightly. Roast at 350°F until internal temperature reaches 130°F. Remove meat from liquid. Reserve liquid for gingersnap sauce. Slice beef. Place in two 2-inch counter pans.

GINGERSNAP SAUCE

Ingredient	Amount	Procedure
Liquid from roast	3½ qt	Measure liquid from roast. Add water if needed. Add gingersnaps. Bring to boil, stirring constantly until mixture thickens. Ladle gingersnap sauce over beef. Additional sauce may be served with meat.
Gingersnaps, crushed	1 lb	

Salisbury steak

OVEN: 325°F	YIELD: 50 portions
BAKE: 25 minutes	PORTION: 5 oz

Ingredient	Amount	Procedure
Ground beef	12 lb 8 oz	Combine all ingredients and mix on low speed until blended. Do not overmix.
Bread crumbs	1 lb 8 oz	
Eggs	14 (1 lb 8 oz)	
Onions, chopped	8 oz	
Salt	2½ oz	
Pepper, black	½ tsp	
Milk	4½ cups	
		Portion meat with No. 8 dipper onto lightly greased baking sheets.
		Flatten slightly.
		Bake at 325°F for 25 minutes.
		Pour off grease.

Notes:
1. Steaks may be browned on a grill.
2. 1 oz (½ cup) dehydrated onions, rehydrated in ¾ cup water, may be substituted for fresh onions (p. 50).

Variation:

Bacon-wrapped beef. To 15 lb ground beef, add 4 oz chopped green pepper, 8 oz chopped onion, 2½ cups catsup, 2 Tbsp salt, and 1 Tbsp black pepper. Shape as for Salisbury Steak and wrap one slice bacon around each portion. Place on baking sheet. Bake at 350°F for 30–45 minutes.

Swiss steak

OVEN: 350°F		YIELD: 50 portions
BAKE: 2–2½ hours		PORTION: 5 oz

Ingredient	Amount	Procedure
Beef round, sliced, ¾ inch thick	17 lb	Cut meat into portions, 3 per lb.
Flour, all-purpose	1 lb	Mix flour, salt, and pepper. Pound into meat
Salt	3 oz	with mallet or cleaver.
Pepper, black	2 tsp	
Shortening, hot	1 lb 8 oz	Brown meat in shortening. Place, slightly overlapping, in two 12 × 20 × 2-inch counter pans.
Fat (meat drippings), hot	6 oz	Make gravy according to directions on p. 566.
Flour, all-purpose	6 oz	Add 1½ qt gravy to each pan of meat.
Salt	2 tsp	Cover tightly with aluminum foil.
Pepper, black	¾ tsp	Bake at 350°F for 2–2½ hours.
Water or beef stock	3 qt	

Note:
Portioned steaks, cut 3 per pound, may be substituted for beef round. Reduce cooking time to 1½ hours.

Variations:
1. **Chicken-fried steak.** Dip portioned steaks or beef cutlets into mixture of 6 eggs and 3 cups milk, then into crumb mixture (1 lb 4 oz bread crumbs, 12 oz flour, 3 oz salt, and 2 Tbsp pepper). Brown steaks in hot shortening. Arrange slightly overlapping in lined counter pans. Cover with aluminum foil. Bake at 325°F for 30–45 minutes or until tender.
2. **Country-fried steak.** Use beef round cut ⅜ inch thick. Proceed as for Swiss Steak except for adding gravy. Place steaks on racks in roaster or counter pans. Cover bottom of pan with water, 2 cups per pan. Cover with aluminum foil and bake. Make Cream Gravy (p. 566) to serve with the steaks.
3. **Spanish steak.** Substitute Spanish Sauce (p. 570) for gravy.
4. **Steak smothered with onions.** Proceed as for Swiss Steak. Add 3 lb sliced onions slightly browned.
5. **Baked steak teriyaki.** Combine 2 cups pineapple juice, drained from canned sliced pineapple, 1 qt water, 1½ cups soy sauce, ½ tsp garlic powder, ¼ tsp ginger, and ¼ cup honey. Bring to a boil. Thicken with 1½ cups cold water and ½ cup cornstarch, mixed. Pour 2 lb 8 oz mixture over each pan of browned steaks. Cover tightly. Bake at 325°F for 1–1½ hours or until tender. Garnish with green pepper rings and pineapple slices.
6. **Swiss steak with tomatoes.** Substitute 1 No. 10 can tomatoes for the gravy. Add 8 oz chopped onions.

Pepper steak

YIELD: 50 portions
PORTION: 6 oz meat
                 4 oz rice

Ingredient	Amount	Procedure
Beef round or sirloin, cut into thin strips	13 lb	Cook meat in shortening until lightly browned, about 10 minutes.
Shortening	8 oz	
Beef Stock (p. 589)	2 qt	Add stock, tomatoes, onions, and seasonings to meat.
Tomatoes, canned, diced	1 No. 10 can	
Onions, chopped	1 lb	Simmer until tender, 1–1½ hours, stirring occasionally.
Garlic	3 cloves, cut in half	
Salt	2 Tbsp	
Green peppers, thinly sliced in rings	12	Add green pepper and cook until tender but firm.
Cornstarch	3 oz	Combine cornstarch, water, and soy sauce into a smooth paste.
Water, cold	2½ cups	
Soy sauce	⅔ cup	Add to meat-vegetable mixture. Cook 5 minutes.
Rice, converted	3 lb 8 oz	Cook according to directions on p. 422.
Water, boiling	4¼ qt	Serve 6 oz meat mixture over 4 oz rice.
Salt	2 Tbsp	
Cooking oil	2 Tbsp	

Meat loaf

OVEN: 325°F	YIELD: 50 portions
BAKE: 1½ hours	5 loaves 5 × 9 inches
	PORTION: 4 oz

Ingredient	Amount	Procedure
Ground beef	10 lb	Mix all ingredients on low speed until blended, using flat beater. Do not overmix.
Ground pork	2 lb	
Bread crumbs, soft	12 oz	
Milk	1 qt	
Eggs	12 (1 lb 5 oz)	
Onion, finely chopped	4 oz	
Salt	2 Tbsp	
Pepper, black	1 tsp	
Cayenne	few grains	
		Press meat mixture into five 5 × 9-inch pans, 3 lb 4 oz per pan.
		Bake at 325°F for 1½ hours.
		Meat loaf may also be made in a 12 × 20 × 4-inch counter pan. Press mixture into pan. Divide into 2 loaves (Figure 2.29). Increase baking time to 2 hours.

Notes:

1. Ground pork may be omitted. Increase ground beef to 12 lb.
2. Topping of 8 oz brown sugar, 2 Tbsp dry mustard, 1¼ cups catsup, and 1 Tbsp nutmeg may be spread over loaves for the last half hour of cooking.
3. ½ oz (¼ cup) dehydrated onions, rehydrated in ½ cup water, may be substituted for fresh onions (p. 50).

Variations:

1. **Barbecued meatballs.** Measure with No. 8 dipper and shape into balls. Cover with 1 gal Barbecue Sauce (p. 568).
2. **Meatballs.** Measure with No. 8 dipper and shape into balls. Proceed as for Swedish Meatballs (p. 366) or Spaghetti with Meatballs (p. 420).
3. **Meat loaf sandwiches.** For *hot* sandwiches, serve one slice meat loaf on top of one slice of bread. Ladle 2 oz gravy over sandwich. If whipped potatoes are served, use 4 oz gravy. For *cold* sandwiches, serve a thin slice of meat loaf and lettuce leaf between two slices of bread.
4. **Vegetable meat loaf.** Add 2 cups catsup, 8 oz each raw carrots, onions, and celery, and 4 oz green peppers. Grind vegetables. Pour a small amount of tomato juice over loaves before baking.

Figure 2.29 *Shaping meat loaf. (a) Press mixture into counter pan, then smooth top. (b) Form into two loaves.*

Chuck wagon steak

OVEN: 400°F	YIELD: 50 portions
BAKE: 10–15 minutes	PORTION: 6 oz

Ingredient	Amount	Procedure
Ground beef patties, 3 per lb	50	Mix eggs and milk. Dip meat in egg mixture. Drain.
Eggs, beaten	6 (10 oz)	
Milk	1¾ cups	
Bread crumbs, dry	1 lb 3 oz	Combine bread crumbs, flour, and seasonings. Dredge steaks in crumb mixture and place 3 × 4 onto lightly greased 18 × 26-inch baking sheets. Brown steaks in 400°F oven for 10–15 minutes.
Flour, all-purpose	12 oz	
Salt	1½ tsp	
Pepper, black	½ tsp	

Variation:
Chuck wagon steak on a bun. Serve on steak bun, with lettuce and thick slices of tomato and onion.

Spanish meatballs

| OVEN: 325°F | YIELD: 50 portions |
| BAKE: 1½ hours | PORTION: 2 3-oz meatballs |

Ingredient	Amount	Procedure
Rice, converted	1 lb 2 oz	Cook rice (p. 422) until slightly underdone.
Water	1¼ qt	Drain off excess liquid.
Salt	1 tsp	
Ground beef	12 lb	Place ground beef in mixer bowl.
Eggs	12 (1 lb 5 oz)	Add cooked rice and other ingredients.
Potatoes, cooked and mashed	1 lb	Mix until blended, using flat beater. Do not overmix.
Onion, grated	4 oz	
Green peppers, chopped	4 oz	
Salt	2 oz (3 Tbsp)	
Pepper, black	1½ Tbsp	
		Form meatballs, using a No. 12 dipper. Place in a single layer on two 12 × 20 × 2-inch baking pans. Bake at 325°F for 1½ hours. Drain off fat.
Chili sauce	3 qt	Mix chili sauce and water.
Water	2 qt	Pour over meatballs. Cover tightly and bake an additional 30 minutes. Add more liquid if necessary.

Notes:
  1. Spanish Sauce (p. 570) or tomato puree may be substituted for chili sauce.
  2. ½ oz (¼ cup) dehydrated onions, rehydrated in ½ cup water, may be substituted for fresh onions (p. 50).

Swedish meatballs

OVEN:	300°F		YIELD:	50 portions
BAKE:	1 hour		PORTION:	2 2½-oz meatballs

Ingredient	Amount	Procedure
Bread	2 lb 8 oz	Soak bread in milk for 1 hour.
Milk	1½ qt	
Ground beef	5 lb	Combine meat, potato, onion, and seasonings
Ground pork	3 lb	in mixer bowl.
Potato, raw, grated	1 lb 4 oz	Add bread. Mix to blend, using flat beater.
Onion, minced	12 oz	Do not overmix.
Salt	2 oz	
Pepper, black	2 tsp	
		Form meatballs, using a No. 16 dipper. Place in a single layer on baking pans.
		Brown in hot oven (400°F).
		Transfer to two 12 × 20 × 2-inch counter pans.
Meat drippings	6 oz	Add flour and seasonings to meat
Flour, all-purpose	6 oz	drippings and blend.
Salt	2 tsp	Add milk gradually, stirring constantly with
Pepper, black	¾ tsp	a wire whip.
Milk	3 qt	Cook until smooth and thickened.
		Pour over meatballs.
		Bake at 300°F for 1 hour.

Notes:
1. Veal may be substituted for part of beef.
2. 1½ oz (¾ cup) dehydrated onions, rehydrated in 1 cup water, may be substituted for fresh onions (p. 50).

Beef stew

YIELD: 50 portions
PORTION: 7 oz

Ingredient	Amount	Procedure
Beef, 1-inch cubes	15 lb AP (10 lb EP)	Brown beef in kettle or oven.
Water Salt Pepper, black Worcestershire sauce	2 qt 2 oz (3 Tbsp) 2 tsp ¾ cup	Add water and seasonings to meat. Cover and simmer 2 hours. Add more water as necessary.
Potatoes, cubed Carrots, sliced or cubed Onion, cubed Celery, diced	4 lb 3 lb 1 lb 12 oz	Cook vegetables in steamer or in small amount of water in kettle or oven.
Flour, all-purpose Water	12 oz 1 qt	Mix flour and water until smooth. Add to meat and cook until thickened. Add vegetables.

Note:
One 40-oz package of frozen green peas may be added.

Variations:
1. **Beef pot pie.**   Add one 40-oz package of frozen peas. Place cooked stew in two 12 × 20 × 2-inch counter pans, 13 lb per pan. Make Pastry for One-Crust Pies (p. 250). Roll out 2 lb per pan and place on stew. Bake at 425°F for 20–25 minutes.
2. **Beef stew with biscuits.**   Place hot stew in two 12 × 20 × 2-inch counter pans. Prepare ½ recipe of Baking Powder Biscuits (p. 116). Cut into 48 2½-inch biscuits. Place on hot stew, 24 per pan. Bake at 425°F for 15–20 minutes.
3. **Beef stew with dumplings.**   Drop Dumplings (p. 139) on meat mixture and steam 15–18 minutes.
4. **Beef stew with tomatoes.**   Delete carrots and celery. Add 4 lb diced canned tomatoes and 1 lb 8 oz green pepper strips the last 5 minutes of cooking.

Beef stroganoff

YIELD: 50 portions
          2 gal
PORTION: 6 oz Stroganoff
           4 oz noodles

Ingredient	Amount	Procedure
Beef round, cut in ¼-inch strips	12 lb	Brown meat in shortening. Add onion and seasonings.
Shortening	8 oz	
Onion, chopped	1 lb 4 oz	
Salt	1 Tbsp	
Pepper, black	1 tsp	
Beef Stock (p. 589)	2½ qt	Add stock to meat and simmer 35–40 minutes or until meat is tender.
Flour, all-purpose	8 oz	Mix flour, water, and Worcestershire sauce and stir until smooth.
Water, cold	2 cups	Add to meat while stirring and cook until thickened.
Worcestershire sauce	¾ cup	
Mushrooms, fresh, sliced	2 lb 8 oz	Sauté mushrooms in margarine.
Margarine, melted	4 oz	
Sour cream	1 qt	Add sour cream to meat mixture, stirring constantly. Add mushrooms. Heat to serving temperature.
Noodles	4 lb 8 oz	Cook noodles according to directions on p. 402.
Water	4½ gal	Serve 6 oz Stroganoff over 4 oz noodles.
Salt	2 oz	
Oil (optional)	3 Tbsp	

Note:
May be served over rice. Cook 3 lb 8 oz rice in 4¼ qt water, 2 Tbsp salt, and 2 Tbsp oil. See p. 422.

Variation:
Ground beef stroganoff.   Substitute ground beef for beef round. Add 1 lb 8 oz chopped celery, ¼ cup paprika, ¼ cup Worcestershire sauce, and 2 tsp dry mustard.

Spanish rice

OVEN: 350°F
BAKE: 1 hour

YIELD: 50 portions
2 pans 12 × 20 × 2 inches
PORTION: 8 oz

Ingredient	Amount	Procedure
Rice, converted, uncooked	2 lb 8 oz	Cook rice according to directions on p. 422.
Water, boiling	3 qt	
Salt	1 oz (1½ Tbsp)	
Vegetable oil	1½ Tbsp	
Ground beef	7 lb	Cook beef until meat loses pink color.
Onions, chopped	1 lb 8 oz	Add onion, peppers, and celery to meat.
Green pepper, chopped	8 oz	Cook about 10 minutes.
Celery, chopped	8 oz	
Tomatoes, canned, diced	1 No. 10 can	Add remaining ingredients to meat mixture.
Chili sauce	3 cups	Combine with cooked rice.
Tomato paste	3 cups	
Salt	2 oz (3 Tbsp)	
Pepper, black	¼ tsp	
Cayenne	few grains	
Sugar, granulated	2 Tbsp	
Water	2 cups	
		Scale into two 12 × 20 × 2-inch pans, 15 lb per pan.
		Bake at 350°F for 1 hour.

Notes:
1. 3 lb bacon, diced and cooked, may be substituted for the ground beef.
2. Spanish Rice may be used as a filling for Stuffed Peppers (p. 373).
3. 3 oz (1½ cups) dehydrated onions, rehydrated in 2 cups water, may be substituted for fresh onions (p. 50).

Chop suey

YIELD: 50 portions
PORTION: 5 oz chop suey
             4 oz rice

Ingredient	Amount	Procedure
Beef, julienne strips	5 lb	Brown meat in steam-jacketed or other kettle.
Pork, julienne strips	2 lb	
Water	2 qt	Add water and salt to meat.
Salt	2 tsp	Simmer until tender.
Cornstarch	8 oz	Make a smooth paste of cornstarch and water.
Water, cold	1¼ cups	Pour slowly into meat and broth, stirring constantly while pouring. Cook until thickened.
Soy sauce	1 cup	Add soy sauce and Worcestershire sauce. Stir to blend.
Worcestershire sauce	1 cup	
Green peppers, sliced	4 oz	Steam vegetables until tender crisp.
Onions, sliced	1 lb	
Celery, diagonally sliced	2 lb	
Bean sprouts, canned, undrained	3 lb	Add bean sprouts and vegetables to meat mixture just before serving.
Rice, converted	3 lb 8 oz	Cook rice according to directions on p. 422.
Water	4¼ qt	Serve 5 oz chop suey over 4 oz rice.
Salt	2 Tbsp	
Vegetable oil	2 Tbsp	

Notes:
  1. 8 oz water chestnuts may be added.
  2. May be served over 2 oz chow mein noodles (6 lb) instead of rice.

Variation:
Chicken chow mein.   Substitute cubed, cooked chicken or turkey for beef and pork; and chicken stock for water. Delete green peppers and add 1 lb sliced mushrooms. Serve over rice or chow mein noodles.

Cheeseburger pie

OVEN: 400°F	YIELD: 48 portions
BAKE: 30–35 minutes	2 pans 12 × 20 × 2 inches
	PORTION: 8 oz (6 oz meat)

Ingredient	Amount	Procedure
Ground beef	12 lb AP (8 lb EP)	Brown beef in steam-jacketed or other kettle. Drain off fat.
Onions, chopped Green peppers, chopped	1 lb 4 oz 1 lb 4 oz	Add onions and green peppers to meat. Cook until vegetables are tender.
Garlic powder Salt Chili powder Cumin, ground Cayenne Sugar, brown Tomatoes, diced, canned	1 tsp 1 oz (1½ Tbsp) 3 oz 1 tsp ¼ tsp 1 oz 7 lb 12 oz	Add seasonings and tomatoes. Simmer 30 minutes or until thick. Scale meat mixture into two 12 × 20 × 2-inch pans, 9 lb per pan.

CHEESE BISCUIT TOPPING

Ingredient	Amount	Procedure
Flour, all-purpose Baking powder Salt Dry mustard Nonfat dry milk	2 lb 14 oz 2¾ oz (6 Tbsp) 2 Tbsp 1 tsp 7 oz	Combine dry ingredients in mixer bowl on low speed for 1 minute, using flat beater.
Shortening Processed cheese, shredded	12 oz 10 oz	Cut shortening and cheese into flour on low speed for 1–1½ minutes.
Water	1½ qt	Add water to make a thick batter. Mix only until flour is moistened.
		With No. 20 dipper, place topping 4 × 6 over meat mixture just before baking. Bake at 400°F for 30–35 minutes. Cut 4 × 6.

Note:
2½ oz (1¼ cups) dehydrated onions, rehydrated in 2 cups water, may be substituted for fresh onions (p. 50).

Beef biscuit roll

OVEN: 450°F		YIELD: 50 portions
BAKE: 15 minutes		PORTION: 5 oz

Ingredient	Amount	Procedure
Flour, all-purpose	3 lb	Mix ingredients as for Baking Powder
Baking powder	3 oz	Biscuits (p. 116).
Salt	1 Tbsp	Divide dough into 4 portions. Roll each
Shortening	12 oz	portion ¼ inch thick.
Milk	1 qt	
Cooked beef, chopped	8 lb	Combine meat, onion, and gravy.
Onion, finely chopped	1 lb	Season as needed. Mix well.
Salt	1 Tbsp	
Pepper, black	1 tsp	
Gravy, cold	1 qt	
		Spread 2 lb meat mixture over each portion of rolled biscuit dough.
		Roll as for jelly roll.
		Slice each roll into pieces 1 inch thick. Place 4 × 5 onto lightly greased 18 × 26-inch baking sheets.
		Bake at 450°F for 15 minutes or until lightly browned.
Brown Gravy (p. 566) or Mushroom Sauce (p. 564)	3 qt	Serve with gravy or mushroom sauce.

Note:
2 oz (1 cup) dehydrated onions, rehydrated in 1½ cups water, may be substituted for fresh onions (p. 50).

Variations:
1. **Chicken or turkey biscuit roll.** Substitute cooked poultry for meat. Serve with Mushroom Sauce (p. 564).
2. **Ham biscuit roll.** Use ground cooked ham. Delete salt in filling mixture. Serve with Mushroom Sauce (p. 564) or Cheese Sauce (p. 561).
3. **Tuna or salmon biscuit roll.** Substitute tuna or salmon for meat and combine with Thick White Sauce (p. 560). Serve with Cheese Sauce (p. 561).

Stuffed peppers

OVEN: 350°F	YIELD: 50 portions
BAKE: 45–60 minutes	PORTION: 5 oz

Ingredient	Amount	Procedure
Green peppers, large	25	Wash peppers and remove stem end. Cut peppers in half lengthwise. Remove seeds and tough white portion. Reserve trimmings for filling. Place in baking pans and steam or parboil for 3–5 minutes.
Rice, converted Water, boiling Salt Cooking oil	1 lb 1¼ qt 2 tsp 2 tsp	Cook rice according to directions on p. 422.
Ground beef	9 lb	Cook meat until it loses pink color. Drain off excess fat.
Onions, chopped Celery, chopped Green pepper trimmings, chopped	8 oz 12 oz 4 oz	Add onions, celery, and green pepper to meat. Sauté for 5 minutes.
Bread crumbs Eggs, beaten Tomato sauce Salt	12 oz 18 (2 lb) 3 cups 2 Tbsp	Add to meat mixture. Add cooked rice. Mix only until blended. Place No. 8 dipper of meat mixture in each pepper half.
Tomato soup Tomato sauce	2 50-oz cans 2 qt	Combine soup and sauce. Ladle 2 oz over each pepper. Bake at 350°F for 45–60 minutes. Ladle extra sauce over peppers during baking.

Note:
1 oz (½ cup) dehydrated onions, rehydrated in ¾ cup water, may be substituted for fresh onions (p. 50).

Baked hash

OVEN: 350°F	YIELD: 48 portions
BAKE: 1 hour	2 pans 12 × 20 × 2 inches
	PORTION: 7 oz

Ingredient	Amount	Procedure
Cooked beef	10 lb	Chop meat and vegetables coarsely.
Cooked potatoes	8 lb	
Onions	1 lb	
Salt	¼ cup	Add seasonings and gravy to meat mixture.
Pepper, black	1 tsp	Mix to blend.
Gravy (p. 566)	2 qt	
		Scale into two greased 12 × 20 × 2-inch baking pans, 11 lb 8 oz per pan.
		Bake at 350°F for 1 hour.
		Cut 4 × 6.

Note:
Raw potatoes, ground or chopped, or hashed brown potatoes may be used in place of cooked potatoes. Increase baking time to 1¼–1½ hours.

Variations:
1. **Corned beef hash.**   Substitute cooked corned beef for the cooked beef and delete salt.
2. **Saucy beef hash.**   Substitute 2 qt condensed cream of celery soup for meat stock. Add 2 Tbsp Worcestershire sauce. Delete salt.

Chili con carne

YIELD: 3 gal
PORTION: 1 cup (8 oz)

Ingredient	Amount	Procedure
Ground beef	10 lb	Cook beef, onions, and garlic in steam-jacketed kettle until meat loses pink color.
Onions, chopped	8 oz	
Garlic, minced	1 clove	
Tomatoes, canned, diced	3 qt	Mix tomato and seasonings.
Tomato puree	1 qt	Add to beef. Cook until blended.
Water	2 qt	
Chili powder	3 oz	
Cumin seed, ground	1½ Tbsp	
Salt	2 oz (3 Tbsp)	
Pepper, black	½ tsp	
Sugar, granulated	3 oz	
Beans, pinto, kidney, or red, canned	9 lb 8 oz	Add beans to meat mixture. Cover and simmer for 1 hour. Add water if chili becomes too thick.

Notes:
1. If dried beans are used, substitute 3 lb for canned beans. Wash and prepare according to directions on p. 622.
2. If desired, thicken chili by mixing 5 oz flour and 2 cups cold water. Add to chili mixture and heat until flour is cooked.
3. 1 oz (½ cup) dehydrated onions, rehydrated in ¾ cup water, may be substituted for fresh onions (p. 50).

Variations:
1. **Chili and cheese.**   Sprinkle grated cheddar or Monterey Jack cheese over chili, 1 Tbsp per bowl.
2. **Chili spaghetti.**   Use only 7 lb ground beef. Cook 1 lb 8 oz spaghetti according to directions on p. 402. Add to chili mixture just before serving. Macaroni or other pasta shapes may be used also.
3. **Chili buffet.**   Serve chili with accompaniments: chopped onions, tomatoes, and green peppers; sliced black olives; shredded cheese; and sliced jalapeño peppers.

Creamed beef

YIELD: 6¼ qt
PORTION: 6 oz (¾ cup)

Ingredient	Amount	Procedure
Ground beef	13 lb AP	Brown beef and onion.
Onions, chopped	3 oz	Drain off fat.
Margarine	8 oz	Melt margarine. Stir in flour and cook for 4–5 minutes.
Flour, all-purpose	8 oz	
Beef Stock (p. 589)	2 qt	Add stock and milk to fat-flour mixture while stirring.
Milk	2 qt	
Salt	2 oz (3 Tbsp)	Cook until thickened.
Pepper, black	1½ tsp	Add seasonings and meat. If beef soup base has been used for stock, salt may need to be reduced.
		Serve 6 oz meat over toast, biscuits, or baked potato.

Variation:
Sausage gravy on biscuits.   In place of ingredients in recipe, substitute the following: 10 lb AP (6 lb EP) sausage, browned and well drained, 6 oz margarine, 8 oz flour, 3 qt milk, and salt and pepper to taste. Serve over hot Baking Powder Biscuits.

Creamed chipped beef

YIELD: 6¼ qt
PORTION: 4 oz (½ cup)

Ingredient	Amount	Procedure
Chipped beef Margarine or butter	2 lb 8 oz 8 oz	Chop beef coarsely. Sauté in margarine until edges curl.
Margarine or butter Flour, all-purpose Pepper, white	1 lb 4 oz 10 oz 1 tsp	Melt margarine. Stir in flour and pepper. Cook 4–5 minutes.
Milk	5 qt	Add milk, stirring constantly. Cook until thickened. Add chipped beef. Serve 4 oz beef over toast, biscuit, or baked potato.

Variations:
1. **Chipped beef and eggs.** Add 2 dozen hard-cooked eggs, sliced or coarsely chopped. Reduce white sauce to 1 gal.
2. **Chipped beef and noodles.** Add 2 lb ground cheddar cheese to white sauce. Combine with 2 lb (AP) noodles, cooked. Top with buttered crumbs. Bake at 350°F for 30 minutes.
3. **Creamed chipped beef and peas.** Reduce beef to 2 lb and add 1 40-oz package frozen peas, cooked until peas are tender, before serving.

Pizza

OVEN:	400°F		YIELD:	48 portions
BAKE:	15–20 minutes			3 pans 18 × 26 × 1 inches
			PORTION:	7 oz

Ingredient	Amount	Procedure
Flour, all-purpose	5 lb	Place flour, salt, sugar, and dry milk in mixer
Salt	1½ oz	bowl. Mix on low speed, using dough hook.
Sugar, granulated	4 oz	
Nonfat dry milk	2 oz	
Yeast, active dry	1½ oz	Soften yeast in warm water.
Water, warm (110°F)	1½ qt	
Shortening	4 oz	Add softened yeast and shortening to dry
		ingredients.
		Mix on low speed to form dough.
		Continue kneading until smooth and elastic.
		Cover and let rise until double in bulk, about
		2 hours.
		Punch down dough according to directions
		on p. 112 and let rest 45 minutes.
		Divide into 3 portions, 2 lb 8 oz each.
		Roll out very thin, stretching to fit three 18
		× 26 × 1-inch baking sheets, allowing ¼
		inch to extend up sides of pans.
Tomato paste	1½ qt	Mix tomato and seasonings.
Tomato puree	1½ qt	Spread over dough, 1 qt per pan.
Salt	4 tsp	
Basil or oregano	1 Tbsp	
Cumin, ground	¾ tsp	
Thyme	½ tsp	
Pepper, black	1 tsp	
Garlic, crushed	1 clove	
Sausage	3 lb 12 oz	Cook meat and drain fat.
Ground beef	3 lb 12 oz	Add onions and cook until tender.
Onion, chopped	5 oz	Sprinkle evenly over tomato sauce,
		approximately 1 lb 8 oz per pan.

Mozzarella cheese, shredded	3 lb 12 oz	Top with 1 lb 4 oz cheese per pan. Bake at 400°F for 15–20 minutes. Cut each pan 2 × 4 and then each of the 8 pieces diagonally, yielding 16 portions per pan (see Figure 2.30).

Notes:

1. Active dry yeast may be mixed with dry ingredients. See p. 110 for procedure.
2. Processed cheese may be substituted for mozzarella. Sweet basil (1 tsp) may be sprinkled over top of each pan.

Variations:

1. **Beef pizza.** Delete sausage. Increase ground beef to 7 lb.
2. **Cheese pizza.** Delete meat. Top each pan with 2 lb 8 oz shredded mozzarella cheese, 2 lb shredded processed cheese, and 1 lb Parmesan cheese, combined.
3. **Pepperoni pizza.** Substitute sliced pepperoni for ground beef.

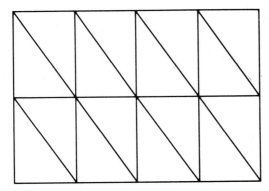

Figure 2.30 *Cutting pizza baked in 18 × 26 × 1-inch baking sheet. Cut lengthwise into 2 sections, then cut crosswise into 8 pieces. Cut each of the 8 pieces diagonally, yielding 16 portions.*

Taco salad casserole

YIELD: 48 portions
           3 pans 12 × 20 × 2 inches
PORTION: 8 oz

Ingredient	Amount	Procedure
Corn chips	2 lb 8 oz	Spread corn chips in bottoms of three 12 × 20 × 2-inch counter pans, 14 oz per pan.
Ground beef	8 lb	Brown meat in steam-jacketed kettle. Drain off fat.
Onions, minced Garlic, minced	8 oz 3 cloves	Add onions and garlic to meat. Cook until tender.
Flour, all-purpose Tomato juice	3 oz 1¼ qt	Combine flour and tomato juice and add to meat mixture.
Vinegar, cider Catsup Chili sauce Sugar, granulated Salt Pepper, black Chili powder Cayenne Tabasco sauce Worcestershire sauce Red beans, canned	2 Tbsp 1½ cups 1 cup 2 Tbsp 2 Tbsp ½ tsp 2 tsp ¼ tsp ¾ tsp 1 tsp 3 lb 12 oz	Add to meat mixture. Blend. Heat until very hot. Scale 4 lb 5 oz meat sauce over each pan of chips. Keep warm and serve soon after vegetables are layered on top. (See Note 2 for an alternate assembly method.)
Lettuce, chopped Green peppers, chopped Onions, finely chopped Tomatoes, fresh, diced	4 lb 12 oz 12 oz 2 lb 10 oz	Combine vegetables. Mix gently. Sprinkle over hot meat mixture, 2 lb 8 oz per pan.
Processed cheese, shredded	2 lb 10 oz	Sprinkle 14 oz cheese over each pan. Cut 4 × 4. Serve immediately.

Notes:

1. Chips will become soggy if held for very long. Spread meat on chips only as needed.
2. Casserole may be assembled on each plate individually. Place ¾ oz taco chips on plate. Ladle 4 oz hot meat mixture over chips and top with 2½ oz salad mixture and ¾ oz shredded cheese.
3. Serve with Salsa Sauce (p. 569) or commercial salsa.
4. 1 oz (½ cup) dehydrated onion, rehydrated in ¾ cup water (p. 50), may be substituted for the fresh onions that are added to the ground beef.

Beef liver with Spanish sauce

OVEN: 350°F
BAKE: 1 hour

YIELD: 50 portions
PORTION: 4 oz

Ingredient	Amount	Procedure
Beef liver, sliced, cut 5 per lb	10 lb	Dredge liver in seasoned flour.
Flour, all-purpose	8 oz	
Salt	2 oz (3 Tbsp)	
Pepper, black	2 tsp	
Shortening	1 lb 8 oz	Brown liver in hot shortening. Place in two 12 × 20 × 2-inch baking pans.
Spanish Sauce (p. 570)	1 recipe	Pour sauce over liver, 5 cups per pan. Cover with aluminum foil. Bake at 350°F until tender, about 1 hour.

Note:
Liver may be soaked in milk before cooking.

Variations:
1. **Baked liver and onions.** Brown liver as above. Sauté 5 lb sliced onions in 8 oz shortening. Arrange liver in 2 counter pans. Spread onions over liver. Cover pans with aluminum foil. Bake 30–40 minutes.
2. **Braised liver.** Brown liver as above. Cover with sauce made of 10 oz shortening, 5 oz flour, 3 qt beef stock, 2 oz salt, and 2 tsp pepper.
3. **Grilled liver and onions.** Have liver cut ⅜ inch thick. Preheat grill to 350°F. Oil grill slightly. Cook liver quickly, browning on one side, then turning and browning on the other side. Serve immediately with steamed or grilled sliced onions.
4. **Liver and bacon.** Dredge liver with seasoned flour and fry in bacon fat. Top each serving with one slice of crisp bacon.

Veal

Breaded veal cutlets

OVEN: 325°F		YIELD: 50 portions
BAKE: 1 hour		PORTION: 4 oz

Ingredient	Amount	Procedure
Veal cutlets, 4 oz	12 lb 8 oz	Dredge cutlets in seasoned flour.
Flour, all-purpose	8 oz	
Salt	1 oz (1½ Tbsp)	
Pepper, black	¼ tsp	
Eggs, beaten	7 (12 oz)	Combine eggs and milk.
Milk	1½ cups	Dip cutlets in egg mixture, then roll in crumbs.
Bread crumbs, fine	1 lb	
Shortening	2 lb	Brown meat in hot fat.
		Place, slightly overlapping, in two 12 × 20 × 2-inch counter pans.
		Add 2 cups water to each pan. Cover with aluminum foil.
		Bake at 325°F for 45–60 minutes.

Note:
Veal round, sliced ¼-inch thick and cut into 5-oz portions, may be used.

Variations:
1. **Veal cacciatore.** Dredge cutlets in flour. Brown in fat and place in baking pans. Pour over sauce made of 1 lb chopped peppers, 1 lb chopped onions, and ⅛ tsp minced garlic, simmered in margarine or butter for 10 minutes; 1 lb 8 oz sautéed sliced mushrooms; 1½ qt canned tomatoes; ¼ cup vinegar; 2 qt Chicken Stock (p. 590); 1 oz salt; and 1 tsp pepper. Bake 45 minutes.
2. **Veal New Orleans.** To 2 qt medium White Sauce (p. 560), add 8 oz chopped onions, 12 oz sliced mushrooms, 2 Tbsp Worcestershire sauce, ¼ tsp salt, ¼ tsp pepper, ¼ tsp paprika, and 3½ cups tomato soup. Arrange browned breaded cutlets in two 12 × 20 × 2-inch counter pans. Pour 1¾ qt sauce over each pan. Cover with aluminum foil and bake at 325°F for 1 hour.
3. **Veal Parmesan.** Add 8 oz grated Parmesan cheese to bread crumbs. After cutlets are browned and arranged in baking pans, pour 2 qt Tomato Sauce (p. 571) over them. Top with 1 lb 8 oz grated mozzarella cheese. Bake 1 hour.
4. **Veal piccata.** Flour cutlets and brown in hot shortening. Arrange in two 12 × 20 × 2-inch counter pans. Sauté 1 lb sliced mushrooms and 2 cloves garlic, minced, in 2 Tbsp margarine. Add 2½ cups Beef Stock (p. 589) and 2 Tbsp lemon juice. Bring to a boil. Pour 2 cups over each pan. Sprinkle ¼ cup Parmesan cheese over each pan. Cover with aluminum foil. Bake at 325°F for 1 hour.
5. **Veal scallopini.** Dredge cutlets in seasoned flour and sauté in hot shortening. Arrange in baking pans. Sauté 3 lb fresh mushrooms, sliced, and 1 lb chopped onion in 8 oz margarine or butter. Add 2 qt Chicken Stock (p. 590), 1½ cups lemon juice or vinegar, and 1 tsp each of parsley, rosemary, and oregano or marjoram. Pour over cutlets. Bake 1 hour.

Veal birds

OVEN: 300°F		YIELD: 50 portions
BAKE: 2 hours		PORTION: 4 oz

Ingredient	Amount	Procedure
Margarine or butter	8 oz	Sauté onion and celery in margarine.
Onions, finely chopped	8 oz	
Celery, finely chopped	8 oz	
Beef base	1½ oz	Combine beef base, seasonings, and water.
Salt	1 tsp (see Note 3)	Add to sautéed vegetables.
Pepper, black	1½ tsp	
Sage, ground	1 Tbsp	
Water	2 qt	
Bread, dry, cubed	2 lb	Add bread gradually to vegetable mixture, tossing lightly until thoroughly mixed.
Veal cutlets, 4 oz	50	Place No. 16 dipper of bread mixture on each piece of meat. Roll and fasten with a pick.
Flour, all-purpose	8 oz	Combine flour and salt.
Salt	2 oz	Roll each bird in flour and brown in hot shortening.
Shortening	2 lb 8 oz	Place in two 12 × 20 × 2-inch counter pans.
Water	1 qt	Add 2 cups water to each pan. Cover with aluminum foil.
		Bake at 300°F for 2 hours.

Notes:
1. Veal round, ¼-inch thick, cut into 4-oz pieces, may be substituted for the cutlets.
2. 1 oz (½ cup) dehydrated onion, rehydrated in ¾ cup water, may be substituted for fresh onion (p. 50).
3. If beef base is highly salted, reduce or delete salt in recipe.

Variations:
1. **Beef birds.** Make with beef cubed or flank steaks.
2. **Pork birds.** Make with pork cutlets.
3. **Veal birds with sausage stuffing.** Reduce bread to 2 lb 8 oz. Reduce salt to 1 tsp and sage to 1 Tbsp. Add 2 lb 8 oz sausage, cooked and drained.

Pork

Breaded pork chops

OVEN: 400°F, 325°F
BAKE: 10 minutes, 1 hour

YIELD: 50 chops
PORTION: 5 oz

Ingredient	Amount	Procedure
Pork chops, cut 3 per lb	17 lb	Dredge chops in seasoned flour.
Flour, all-purpose	12 oz	
Salt	3 oz	
Pepper, black	2 Tbsp	
Eggs, beaten	6 (10 oz)	Combine eggs and milk.
Milk	3½ cups	Dip chops in egg mixture, then roll in crumbs.
Bread crumbs	1 lb 4 oz	Place in single layer on greased sheet pans.
Shortening, melted	8 oz	Pour melted shortening over top of chops. Bake at 400°F until browned, about 10 minutes.
Water	1 qt	Remove chops from oven and arrange in partially overlapping rows in two 12 × 20 × 2-inch counter pans. Add 2 cups water to each pan. Cover pans. Bake at 325°F until tender, approximately 1 hour.

Variations:
1. **Baked pork chops.**   Dredge chops in 1 lb flour, ¼ cup vegetable oil, 2 oz salt, and 1 tsp black pepper, mixed. Place on well-greased sheet pans. Bake at 350°F until thoroughly cooked and browned, approximately 1¼ hours.
2. **Baked pork chops and apples.**   Brown chops as for Breaded Pork Chops. Place in two greased 12 × 20 × 2-inch baking pans. Pour over 1 qt apple juice, 2 cups per pan. Bake at 350°F for 1 hour. Serve with Buttered Apples (p. 518).
3. **Pork chops and dressing.**   Serve chops with No. 16 dipper of Bread Dressing (p. 458) and ladle of gravy dipped over.
4. **Stuffed pork chops.**   Use 6-oz pork chops and cut a pocket in each chop. Fill with Bread Dressing (use ¼ recipe, p. 458) or Apple Stuffing (p. 458, ½ recipe). Brown chops and place in baking pans. Pour 2 cups water or chicken broth in each pan. Cover and bake at 350°F for 1½ hours.

Deviled pork chops

OVEN: 350°F	YIELD: 50 chops	
BAKE: 1½ hours	PORTION: 5 oz	

Ingredient	Amount	Procedure
Chili sauce	1½ qt	Combine into a sauce.
Water	3 cups	
Dry mustard	1 tsp	
Worcestershire sauce	3 Tbsp	
Lemon juice	3 Tbsp	
Onion, grated	2 tsp	
Pork chops, cut 3 per lb	17 lb	Dip each chop in sauce. Place in single layer on greased baking sheets. Bake at 350°F for 1½ hours.

Note:
Chops may be placed on edge, close together, with fat side up in a 12 × 20 × 2-inch counter pan. Bake 2–2½ hours.

Variations:
1. **Barbecued pork chops.**   Place chops on greased baking sheets. Brush with melted fat. Sprinkle with salt. Brown chops in 450°F oven for 12–15 minutes. Transfer to counter pans. Pour Barbecue Sauce (p. 568) over chops. Bake at 325°F for 1½ hours or until chops are tender.
2. **Honey glazed pork chops.**   Marinate pork chops for 4 hours in a mixture of 2 cups soy sauce, 6 oz honey, 1 cup applesauce, 1 oz salt, and 4 oz sugar. Place in single layer on greased baking sheets. Bake at 350°F for 1 hour. Turn and brush with marinade as needed.
3. **Pork chops supreme.**   Arrange chops in single layer in baking pans. Sprinkle with salt. Combine 1 lb brown sugar, 3 cups catsup, and 1 cup lemon juice. Place about 2 Tbsp, No. 30 dipper, on each chop. Cut 4 medium-size onions into thin slices. Place 1 slice on top of each chop. Cover and bake at 350°F for 45 minutes. Uncover and bake 30 minutes longer.

Barbecued spareribs

| OVEN: 350°F | YIELD: 50 portions |
| BAKE: 2½ hours | PORTION: 8 oz |

Ingredient	Amount	Procedure
Pork spareribs or loin back ribs	25 lb	Separate ribs into 8-oz portions. Place in roasting pans. Brown uncovered in oven at 350°F until browned lightly, about 30 minutes. Pour off fat.
Barbecue Sauce (p. 568)	3 qt	Pour sauce over ribs. Cover with aluminum foil. Bake at 350°F until meat is tender, about 1½ hours. Uncover and bake an additional 20–30 minutes.

Note:
For larger portions, use 40 lb spareribs and 1 gal Barbecue Sauce.

Variations:
1. **Baked spareribs with dressing.** Brown ribs as above. Pour off fat. Spread with mixture of 2 oz salt, 2 tsp pepper, 1½ tsp ground sage, 1 lb chopped apples, 2 tsp caraway seeds, 1 tsp ground cloves, and 12 oz brown sugar. Bake 1½ hours until tender. Baste to keep moist. Serve with Bread Dressing (p. 458).
2. **Baked spareribs with sauerkraut.** Sprinkle ribs with 2 oz seasoned salt. Brown lightly. Pour off fat. Remove ribs from pan. Add 2 No. 10 cans sauerkraut to baking pan and place ribs on top. Bake for 1 hour.
3. **Barbecued short ribs.** Substitute beef short ribs for spareribs.
4. **Sweet-sour spareribs.** Brown spareribs for 30 minutes in 400°F oven, or simmer in water for 1 hour. Drain and cover with Sweet-Sour Sauce (p. 573). Bake at 350°F until meat is done. Serve with Steamed Rice or Fried Rice with Almonds (p. 424).

Sweet-sour pork

YIELD: 50 portions
PORTION: 5 oz pork
4 oz rice

Ingredient	Amount	Procedure
Pork strips, julienne	10 lb AP (7 lb EP)	Brown pork in steam-jacketed kettle.
Water	2 qt	Add water to pork and simmer until meat is tender.
Vinegar	1¼ qt	Combine and add to pork.
Soy sauce	1½ cups	Simmer until sugar is dissolved and
Catsup	1½ cups	pineapple is hot, 10–15 minutes.
Sugar, granulated	2 lb	
Pineapple juice	1 qt	
Pineapple chunks	1 lb	
Cornstarch	8 oz	Combine to make a smooth paste.
Water	2 cups	Pour slowly into pork mixture, stirring
Ginger, ground	1½ tsp	constantly.
Garlic powder	½ tsp	Cook until thickened and clear.
Carrots, fresh, sliced	1 lb 12 oz	Steam carrots until tender crisp. Add to mixture.
Snow peas	1 lb	Stir in just before serving.
Rice, converted	3 lb 8 oz	Cook rice according to directions on p. 422.
Water, boiling	4¼ qt	Serve 5 oz pork over 4 oz rice.
Salt	2 Tbsp	
Oil (optional)	2 Tbsp	

Variations:
1. **Sweet-sour beef.** Substitute beef strips for pork.
2. **Sweet-sour chicken.** Substitute cooked chicken or turkey for the pork. Do not brown.

Glazed baked ham

OVEN: 325°F	YIELD: 50 portions
BAKE: 2–2½ hours	PORTION: 3 oz

Ingredient	Amount	Procedure
Ham, boneless, fully cooked	15 lb	Place ham fat side up on a rack in roasting pan. Do not cover. Bake at 325°F for 2–2½ hours.
Cloves, whole	3 Tbsp	Remove ham from oven about 30 minutes before it is done. Drain off drippings. Score ham ¼ inch deep in diamond pattern. Stud with whole cloves. Cover with glaze.

HAM GLAZE

Ingredient	Amount	Procedure
Sugar, brown	8 oz	Combine ingredients for glaze.
Cornstarch	2 Tbsp	Spoon over ham. Repeat if heavier glaze is desired.
Corn syrup	¼ cup	Return ham to oven and bake until internal temperature reaches 140°F (see timetable, p. 353).
Pineapple juice	2 Tbsp	

Note:
If using a whole cured ham, not precooked, increase cooking time to 4–4½ hours; or simmer 3–4 hours in a kettle, then trim, glaze, and complete cooking in the oven.

Glaze variations:
1. **Apricot glaze.** 1 cup apricot jam and ¼ cup fruit juice or enough to cover ham.
2. **Brown sugar glaze.** 6 oz brown sugar, 1½ tsp dry mustard (or 3 Tbsp prepared mustard), and ¼ cup vinegar.
3. **Cranberry glaze.** 1¼ cups strained cranberry sauce, or enough to cover.
4. **Honey glaze.** 1 cup honey, ½ cup brown sugar, and ¼ cup fruit juice. Baste with fruit juice or ginger ale.
5. **Orange glaze.** 1 cup orange marmalade and ¼ cup orange juice.

Ham loaf

OVEN:	350°F	YIELD:	50 portions
BAKE:	1–1½ hours		5 pans 5 × 9 inches
		PORTION:	4 oz

Ingredient	Amount	Procedure
Ground cured ham	7 lb	Combine all ingredients in mixer bowl. Mix on low speed, using flat beater, only until ingredients are blended. *Do not overmix.*
Ground fresh lean pork	7 lb	
Onion, finely chopped	4 oz	
Milk	1 qt	
Eggs, beaten	14 (1 lb 8 oz)	
Pepper, black	1 tsp	
Bread crumbs	1 lb	
		Press meat mixture into five 5 × 9-inch loaf pans, 3 lb 8 oz per pan.
		Bake at 350°F for 1–1½ hours.
		If desired, cover tops of loaves with glaze (see Variation 2) during last 30 minutes of cooking.
		Cut 10 slices per pan.

Notes:
1. Meat may be baked in 12 × 20 × 4-inch baking or counter pan. Press mixture into pan and divide into 2 loaves. Increase baking time to 1½–2 hours.
2. 4 lb ground beef may be substituted for 4 lb fresh pork.
3. ½ oz (¼ cup) dehydrated onion, rehydrated in ½ cup water, may be substituted for fresh onion (p. 50).

Variations:
1. **Glazed ham balls.**   Measure with No. 8 dipper and shape into balls. Place on baking sheets. Brush with glaze (Variation 2) and bake 1 hour.
2. **Glazed ham loaf.**   Cover tops of loaves with a mixture of 1 lb 8 oz brown sugar, 1 cup vinegar, and 1½ Tbsp dry mustard.
3. **Ham patties with cranberries.**   Measure with No. 8 dipper and shape into patties. Spread pan with Cranberry Sauce (p. 519). Place ham patties on sauce and bake 1 hour.
4. **Ham patties with pineapple.**   Measure with No. 8 dipper and shape into patties. Top each with slice of pineapple and a clove. Pour pineapple juice over patties and bake 1 hour.

Creamed ham

	YIELD:	50 portions
		6¼ qt
	PORTION:	4 oz (½ cup)

Ingredient	Amount	Procedure
Margarine or butter Flour, all-purpose	1 lb 6 oz	Melt margarine. Add flour and stir until smooth. Cook 5 minutes.
Milk	1 gal	Add milk gradually, stirring constantly with wire whip. Cook until thickened.
Ham, cooked Salt Pepper, white	6 lb To taste ½ tsp	Cut ham in cubes or grind coarsely. Add to sauce and heat slowly for about 20 minutes. Add salt, if needed, and pepper. Serve 4 oz ham over biscuits, toast, spoon bread, corn bread, or cheese soufflé.

Note:
1 lb chopped celery or sliced mushrooms or 1 dozen chopped hard-cooked eggs may be added. Reduce ham to 5 lb.

Variation:
Plantation shortcake. Substitute 3 lb cooked turkey for 3 lb cooked ham. Substitute Chicken Stock for half of milk in sauce. Add 1 lb grated cheddar cheese. Serve over hot corn bread.

Oven-fried bacon

OVEN: 400°F
BAKE: 6–10 minutes

YIELD: 50 portions
PORTION: 2 slices

Ingredient	Amount	Procedure
Bacon, 17–20 slices per lb	100 slices (5–6 lb)	Arrange bacon slices on sheet pans. Bake at 400°F, without turning, until crisp, about 6–10 minutes. Pour off accumulating fat as necessary. Drain on paper towels or place in perforated pans for serving.

Note:
Bacon may be purchased, separated and placed on parchment paper, ready to be placed on baking sheets and baked.

Scrapple

		YIELD: 50 portions
		5 loaf pans 5 × 9 inches
		PORTION: 2 slices

Ingredient	Amount	Procedure
Sausage, bulk	8 lb	Fry sausage until slightly brown. Do not overcook. Drain off fat.
Water Salt	1½ gal 1 oz (1½ Tbsp)	Add salt to water. Bring to a boil.
Cornmeal Water, cold	3 lb 2 qt	Mix cornmeal with cold water. Pour gradually into boiling water, stirring constantly. Cook until very thick, 10–15 minutes.
		Add cooked sausage to cornmeal mixture. Scale into 5 greased 5 × 9-inch loaf pans, 4 lb 5 oz per pan. Cover with waxed paper to prevent formation of crust. Chill for 24 hours.
		Cut into ½-inch slices. Cook on greased grill preheated to 350°F. Grill until browned and crisp on both sides. Serve with warm syrup.

Note:
8 lb fresh pork, simmered until done and chopped finely, may be used in place of the sausage. Increase salt to 2 oz and add 1 Tbsp ground sage.

Variation:
Fried cornmeal mush.   Delete sausage. Increase cornmeal to 4 lb, salt to 2 oz, boiling water to 2 gal, and cold water to 2½ qt. Proceed as for Scrapple.

Cheese-stuffed frankfurters

| OVEN: 350°F | | YIELD: 50 portions |
| BAKE: 30 minutes | | PORTION: 2 frankfurters |

Ingredient	Amount	Procedure
Frankfurters, 10 per lb	10 lb	Split frankfurters lengthwise, but do not cut completely through.
Cheddar cheese Pickle relish	3 lb 1 qt	Cut cheese into strips about 3½ inches long. Place a strip of cheese and ½ Tbsp relish in each frankfurter.
Bacon, 24–26 slices per lb	100 slices (4–5 lb)	Wrap a slice of bacon around each frankfurter. Secure with a pick. Place on greased baking sheets. Bake at 350°F for 30 minutes.

Note:

8 lb 4 oz wieners, 12 per lb, may be substituted for the frankfurters. With the wieners, 1 slice of bacon may be wrapped around 2 wieners.

Variations:

1. **Barbecued frankfurters.** Place frankfurters in counter pans. Cover with Barbecue Sauce (p. 568). Bake at 400°F for about 30 minutes. Add more sauce if necessary.
2. **Chili dog.** Serve 2 oz Chili Con Carne (p. 375) over a frankfurter or wiener in a hot dog bun. Chili may be made with or without beans.
3. **Frankfurters and sauerkraut.** Steam frankfurters or cook in boiling water. Serve with sauerkraut (2 No. 10 cans), which has been heated.
4. **Nacho dog.** Serve 2 oz Nacho Sauce (p. 323) over a frankfurter or wiener in a hot dog bun. Sprinkle over the top one or more of the following: chopped green chilies or jalapeño peppers, chopped tomatoes, chopped black olives, or chopped onion.

Sausage rolls

OVEN: 400°F	YIELD: 50 rolls
BAKE: 20 minutes	PORTION: 1 roll, 2 oz gravy

Ingredient	Amount	Procedure
Sausages, link	12 lb 8 oz	Partially cook sausages. Save fat for gravy.
Flour, all-purpose Baking powder Salt Shortening Milk	3 lb 3 oz 3½ tsp 12 oz 1 qt	Make into biscuit dough, according to directions on p. 116.
		Divide biscuit dough into 2 portions. Roll each portion to ½-inch thickness and cut into 3 × 4-inch rectangles. Place 2 sausages in the center of each piece of dough and fold over. Place seam side down on greased baking sheets. Bake at 400°F for 20 minutes.
Sausage fat Flour, all-purpose Salt Pepper, black Water or chicken stock	6 oz 6 oz 2 tsp ½ tsp 3 qt	Add flour to fat and blend. Add salt and pepper. Cook for 5 minutes. Add water or stock gradually, stirring constantly. Cook until smooth and thickened. Serve 2-oz ladle of gravy over each sausage roll.

Variations:
1. **Italian sausage sandwich.**   Grill fifty 5-to-6-inch-long Italian sausages. Serve one sausage in a long bun with 1 oz Sandwich Tomato Sauce (p. 411) ladled on top. May be sprinkled with 1 oz shredded mozarella cheese.
2. **Pigs in blankets.**   Substitute 50 wieners for link sausages. Place each wiener diagonally on dough portion and roll up. Delete gravy. May serve with Cheese Sauce (p. 561).
3. **Pigs in blankets with cheese.**   Wrap 1 oz cheese around each wiener. Proceed as above.

PASTA, RICE & CEREALS

The cooking of pasta, rice, and cereals is similar. Water is added, heat is applied, and cooking is continued until gelatinization of the starch granules is completed.

PASTA

Pasta is a generic name for a basic dough mixture of durum or other high-protein hard wheat flour and water. With the exception of noodles, which contain eggs, the various pasta products are made from the same basic dough. Flavor variations may include whole wheat, herb, carrot, tomato, and spinach. Pasta comes in many different forms, and it is estimated that there are 150 different varieties. A few of the more popular types appear in Figures 2.31 and 2.32. Pasta may be purchased fresh, frozen, or dry.

Dry pasta will approximately double in *volume* after cooking, except egg noodles which remain about the same. The *weight* of dry noodles and most dry pasta will approximately triple when cooked. See p. 402 for the weight increase of selected pastas. Fresh and frozen pasta weight and volume do not expand or increase after cooking as much as dry products. Thickness varies among pasta shapes, and the volume increase is directly related to this variation. Certain shapes such as ziti, lasagna, and rigatoni have more fluctuation in their volume increase than do spaghetti and macaroni.

A general rule for cooking pasta is to allow 1 gallon of water, 1 ounce (1½ tablespoons) salt, and 1½ teaspoons cooking oil for every pound of pasta. Directions for cooking are given on p. 402. Pasta should be cooked until it is tender but firm (*al dente,* "to the tooth"). Overcooking produces a soft, pasty product that breaks easily when combined with sauces or other ingredients.

RICE

Rice is used in foodservices as a side dish, as an accompaniment to many stir-fried and Oriental foods, and as an ingredient in casseroles and other entrees. Four major types of rice are available:

1. **Regular milled white rice** is available as short-grain or medium-grain, with small, round kernels that become sticky when cooked; or long-grain, which has long, slender grains that stay separate and fluffy when properly cooked. In milling rice, the outer bran coating is removed; this process removes some vitamins and minerals but produces a white, light-textured

Figure 2.31 *Frequently used pasta shapes (see description of pasta shapes in Figure 2.32). Photo courtesy of the National Pasta Association.*

product. Enriched rice has had a coating of vitamins to compensate for some of the nutrients lost in milling.

2. **Parboiled or converted rice** is a specially processed long-grain rice that has been partially cooked under steam pressure, redried, and then milled or polished. Converted rice is the most widely used in foodservices. The grains stay firm, separate, and light, and the product holds well in the steam table without becoming sticky or mushy. The flavor and texture are not exactly like those of regular long-grain rice, so it is not always preferred by all foodservice customers.

3. **Instant rice** has been precooked and dried so that it can be prepared quickly. It does not hold well after cooking, and the grains quickly lose their shape and become mushy.

4. **Brown rice** has the bran layer left on, giving it a light brown color, slightly coarse crunchy texture, and nutty flavor. Brown rice is available as short-, medium-, or long-grain.

Rice is cooked until all of the water is absorbed, so the key to properly cooked rice is the proportion of rice to water and the correct cooking time. Converted (parboiled long-grain) white rice requires slightly more water and a longer cooking time than does regular long-grain or medium-grain rice. The cooking time for brown rice is almost double that of white rice. Rice may be cooked in a kettle, steamer, or oven. See pp. 422–423 for cooking directions.

CEREALS

Cereals may be whole, cracked, flaked or rolled, or granular. The amount of water used for cooking determines the volume of the finished product. Cereal swells to the extent of water used until the limit of the grain is reached. As a rule, granular cereals absorb more water than whole or flaked. The fineness of grind of the cereal and the amount of bran or cellulose are factors that determine the length of time a cereal needs to be cooked. Cereals cooked in quantity usually are prepared in a steam-jacketed kettle or steamer but may be cooked in a heavy kettle on top of the range. Directions for cooking breakfast cereals are given on p. 426.

Name	Shape	Description
Alphabets		Miniature pasta in letter shapes. Used in soups.
Bow ties	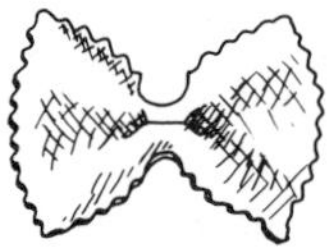	Bow-shaped noodles. Used with entree sauces and also salads.
Capellini		Delicate long thin threads. Used with light sauces.
Conchiglie		Shell-shaped. Used with sauces; larger shells stuffed, smaller shells used in salads.
Elbow macaroni		Short tubes that are slightly curved. Used in salads and casseroles.
Fettuccine	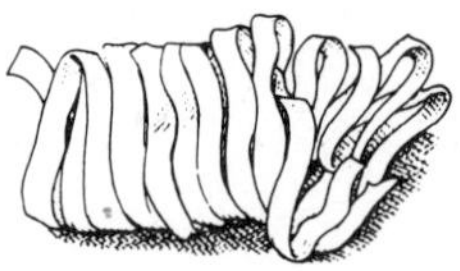	Pasta shaped like ribbons, slightly thick. Used with cream or meat sauces.
Fusilli		Long strands of spiraled spaghetti, cork + screw-shaped. Used with thick cream sauces.

Figure 2.32 *Shapes and descriptions of selected pasta.*

Name	Shape	Description
Lasagne	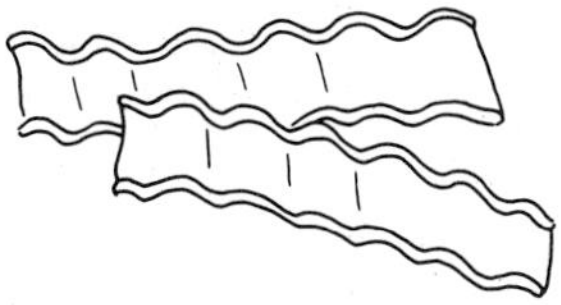	Wide, long, flat noodles with wavy edges. Baked layered with cheese and sauces.
Linguine	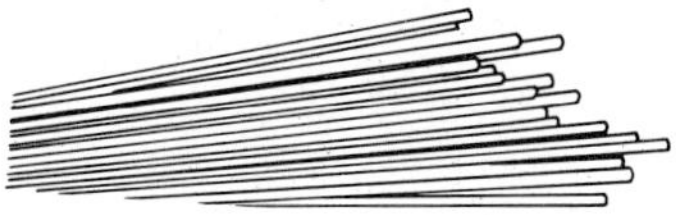	Thin narrow rods, slightly flattened. Used with sauces, especially cream sauces.
Macaroni	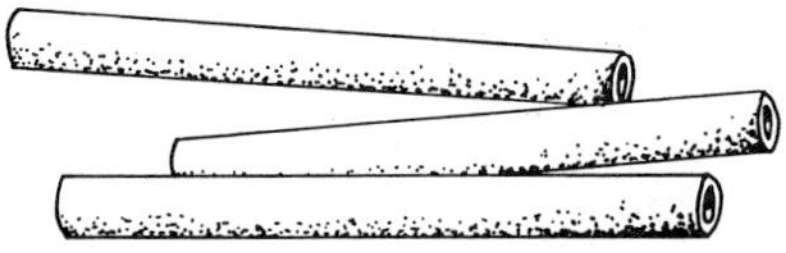	Long hollow round tubes, straight cut end. Baked in casseroles or with sauces.
Manicotti		Giant pasta tubes. Stuffed with cheese or meat fillings.
Mostaccioli	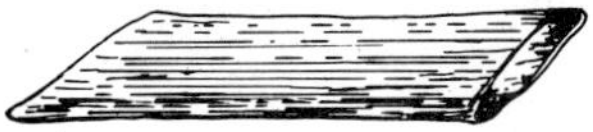	Grooved medium-sized hollow tubes, ends cut diagonally. Used in baked casseroles or with sauces.
Noodles	 X-Wide Noodles  Wide Noodles  Medium Noodles	Narrow flat pasta; typically contains egg. Used in a variety of casseroles, with sauces, and as a side dish.

Figure 2.32 *(Continued)*

Name	Shape	Description
Pastina (tiny dough) Ditalini		Used in soups and salads. Very short hollow tube.
Orzo		Shaped like rice.
Stelline		Star-shaped.
Acini		Small round shape.
Rigatoni		Large ribbed hollow tubes. Used in baked casseroles or with sauces.
Rotini	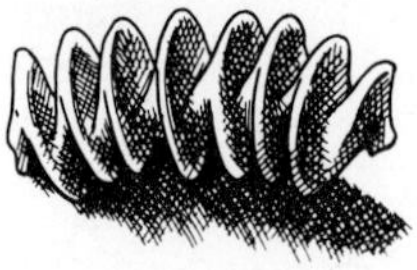	Spiraled pasta. Used in baked casseroles or salads.
Spaghetti	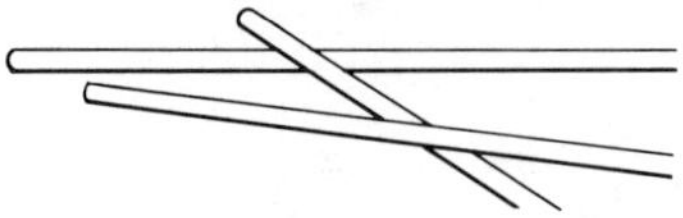	Long round rods. Used with all sauces, especially tomato.

Figure 2.32   *(Continued)*

Name	Shape	Description
Spaghettini	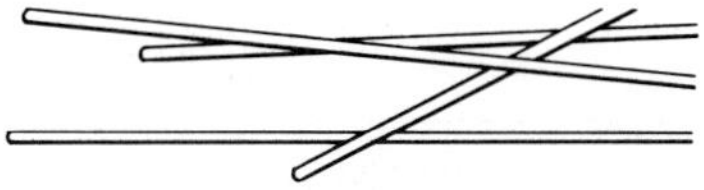	Thin round rods. Used like spaghetti, typically with light sauces.
Vermicelli	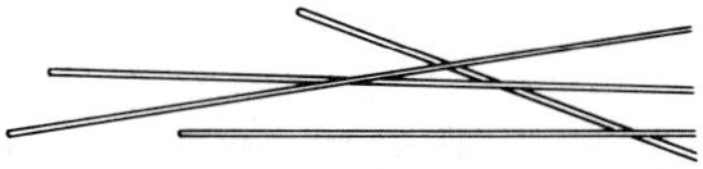	Extra thin spaghetti-like rods. Used with light delicate sauces.
Ziti		Short hollow round tubes with straight cut ends; resembles large macaroni. Used in baked casseroles or with sauces.

Figure 2.32   *(Continued)*

PASTA RECIPES

Cooking pasta

YIELD: 50 portions
PORTION: 4 oz

Ingredient	Amount	Procedure
Pasta	5 lb	Bring water to a rapid boil. Add salt and oil.
Water	5 gal	Add pasta gradually while stirring.
Salt	5 oz	Return to boiling. Cook uncovered at a fast
Vegetable oil (optional)	3 Tbsp	boil until tender, 5–10 minutes. Stir
		occasionally to prevent sticking.
		Test for doneness. The pasta should still be
		firm to the bite.
		Drain.

Notes:

1. Weight of cooked pasta will vary, depending on length of time cooked.
2. Addition of oil is optional. It helps prevent foaming and sticking.
3. Pasta is done when it is tender but firm (*al dente*).
4. If pasta is to be used as an ingredient in a recipe requiring further cooking, undercook slightly.
5. If product is not to be served immediately, drain and cover with cold water. Stir to aid in cooling. When pasta is cold, drain off water and toss lightly with a little salad oil. This will keep pasta from sticking or drying out. Cover tightly and store in the refrigerator. To reheat, put pasta in a colander and immerse in rapidly boiling water just long enough to heat through. *Do not continue to cook.* Or, reheat in a microwave oven.
6. Pasta can be covered tightly and refrigerated or frozen. Reheat to serving temperature.
7. Approximate reheating times for one 8-oz portion are 15 seconds in boiling water or 3 minutes in a microwave (650 watts); for four 8-oz portions, 15 seconds in boiling water or 10 minutes in a microwave (650 watts).
8. Approximate yield for selected dry pastas after cooking are as follows:

Type of pasta	Yield from 1 lb dry pasta
Acini	3 lb 4 oz
Bow ties	2 lb
Elbow macaroni	3 lb
Noodles	3 lb
Rigatoni	2 lb 8 oz
Rotini	2 lb 4 oz
Shells (small)	2 lb 8 oz
Spaghetti	3 lb

Macaroni and cheese

OVEN: 350°F	YIELD: 48 portions	
BAKE: 35 minutes	2 pans 12 × 20 × 2 inches	
	PORTION: 8 oz	

Ingredient	Amount	Procedure
Macaroni	3 lb 8 oz	Cook macaroni according to directions on p. 402.
Water, boiling	3½ gal	
Salt	2 Tbsp	Drain.
Margarine or butter	12 oz	Melt margarine. Stir in flour and seasonings.
Flour, all-purpose	8 oz	Cook 5–10 minutes.
Salt	2 Tbsp	
Dry mustard	1 Tbsp	
Worcestershire sauce	¼ cup	
Milk	1 gal	Add milk gradually, stirring constantly with wire whip.
		Cook until thickened.
Cheddar cheese, sharp, shredded	4 lb	Add cheese to sauce. Stir until cheese melts.
		Pour over macaroni and mix carefully.
		Scale into 2 greased 12 × 20 × 2-inch baking pans, 12 lb per pan.
Bread crumbs	1 lb	Mix crumbs and melted margarine.
Margarine or butter, melted	6 oz	Sprinkle over macaroni and cheese, 8 oz per pan.
		Bake at 350°F for about 35 minutes.

Note:
For variety, use rotini, shells, or other shapes of pasta.

Variation:
Macaroni, cheese, and ham. Add 3 lb chopped ham, 1 lb 8 oz per pan. Reduce salt to 1 Tbsp.

ni

YIELD: 50 portions
PORTION: 4 oz

Ingredient	Amount	Procedure
Margarine Garlic, minced	1 lb 10 oz 6 cloves	Melt margarine in steam-jacketed or other kettle. Add garlic and cook until golden.
Cream cheese, softened	3 lb 4 oz	Mix cream cheese on medium speed until fluffy, using flat paddle.
Parsley, fresh, minced Basil, leaf Pepper, black Salt	½ cup 2 Tbsp 1 tsp 2 tsp	Blend into cream cheese.
Water, boiling	1 qt	Add water gradually to cream cheese mixture. Mix until smooth. Add margarine and garlic. Mix until smooth.
Fettuccini Water, boiling Salt Vegetable oil	1 lb 12 oz (AP) 2 gal 1½ oz 2 Tbsp	Cook fettuccini according to directions on p. 402. Drain.
		Place 2 lb 12 oz cooked fettuccini in each of two 12 × 10 × 4-inch pans. Stir 3 lb 6 oz cream cheese sauce into each pan of pasta. Cover. Keep hot. Sprinkle with Parmesan cheese and snipped fresh parsley just before serving.

Note:
Other fresh herbs may be substituted for parsley.

Noodles romanoff

OVEN:	350°F	YIELD:	50 portions
BAKE:	45 minutes		2 pans 12 × 20 × 2 inches
		PORTION:	5 oz

Ingredient	Amount	Procedure
Noodles	3 lb	Cook noodles according to directions on p. 402.
Water, boiling	3 gal	Drain.
Salt	3 oz	
Vegetable oil (optional)	1 Tbsp	
Margarine or butter	10 oz	Sauté onions in margarine until tender.
Onions, chopped	6 oz	
Flour, all-purpose	4 oz	Add flour and seasonings to onions, stirring constantly.
Salt	1 oz (1½ Tbsp)	Cook 5–10 minutes.
Garlic powder	¼ tsp	
Milk	1¼ qt	Add milk gradually to flour mixture, stirring constantly.
		Cook until thickened.
Parmesan cheese, grated	4 oz	Add cheese, sour cream, and paprika to sauce.
Cottage cheese	2 lb 8 oz	Combine noodles and sauce.
Sour cream	2½ cups	
Paprika	1 Tbsp	
Cheddar cheese, shredded	8 oz	Scale pasta mixture into two 12 × 10 × 2-inch counter pans, 8 lb per pan.
		Sprinkle with cheese, 4 oz per pan.
		Bake at 350°F for 45 minutes or until heated through.

Note:
Linguini or other pasta may be substituted for the noodles.

Pasta with clam sauce

YIELD: 50 portions
PORTION: 6 oz sauce
4 oz pasta

Ingredient	Amount	Procedure
Margarine or butter	1 lb 8 oz	Melt margarine in a large kettle.
Flour, all-purpose	1 lb	Stir in flour and cook for 5–10 minutes.
Milk, hot	6½ qt	Add milk and seasonings to flour-margarine
Salt	2 oz	mixture, while stirring.
Nutmeg	½ tsp	Heat to boiling.
Cream	1½ qt	Reduce heat. Add cream slowly and continue to cook until thickened.
Minced clams	2 lb	Stir clams into sauce.
Pasta	5 lb	Cook pasta according to directions on p. 402.
Water, boiling	5 gal	Serve 6 oz sauce over 4 oz pasta.
Salt	5 oz	
Vegetable oil (optional)	3 Tbsp	

Notes:
1. Clam sauce is excellent served on whole wheat pasta.
2. 2 oz chopped green onion tops, 2 oz chopped chives, or 6 oz sliced mushrooms may be added for variety and color.

Variations:
1. **Pasta with cheese sauce.**   Delete salt, nutmeg, and clams. Reduce margarine to 1 lb, flour to 12 oz, milk to 5 qt, and cream to 1 qt. Stir in 4 oz chicken base. Add 2 oz Parmesan cheese, 8 oz provolone cheese, and 4 oz shredded Swiss cheese, and stir until melted. Thin with hot milk if sauce becomes too thick.
2. **Pasta with shrimp sauce.**   Substitute 4 lb cooked salad shrimp for the clams.

Pasta primavera

YIELD: 50 portions
PORTION: 5 oz sauce
               4 oz pasta

Ingredient	Amount	Procedure
Carrots, fresh	1 lb	Cut carrots into thin julienne strips 1½ inches long. Steam until tender-crisp. Drain. Save for later step.
Broccoli cuts	1 lb	Steam broccoli until tender-crisp. Drain. Save for later step.
Margarine, melted Onion, chopped Garlic, minced	12 oz 4 oz 4 cloves	Add onion and garlic to melted margarine. Cook until onions are tender.
Flour, all-purpose	12 oz	Add flour. Stir with wire whip until flour is mixed in. Cook for 5–10 minutes, stirring often.
Water Milk Chicken base	2¾ qt 2½ qt 4 oz	Add water, milk, and chicken base gradually, stirring with wire whip. Cook and stir often until no starchy flavor remains.
Parsley, snipped Basil leaves, dried Ham, diced, ½-inch cubes Frozen peas Mushrooms, sliced	2½ cups ½ cups 1 lb 8 oz 10 oz 8 oz	Add to sauce. Add carrots and broccoli cuts. Keep hot. Thin as needed with warm milk or chicken stock.
Pasta Water, boiling Salt Vegetable oil	5 lb 5 gal 5 oz 3 Tbsp	Cook pasta according to directions on p. 402. Drain. Serve 5 oz sauce over 4 oz pasta, accompanied by Parmesan cheese.

Note:
½ oz (¼ cup) dehydrated onion, rehydrated in ½ cup water, may be substituted for fresh onion (p. 50).

pasta

YIELD: 50 portions
PORTION: 4 oz

Ingredient	Amount	Procedure
Broccoli cuts	1 lb 12 oz	Steam broccoli until tender-crisp. Drain. Save for later step.
Margarine, melted	8 oz	Combine melted margarine and flour in steam-jacketed or other kettle.
Flour, all-purpose	8 oz	Stir and cook until smooth (5–10 minutes).
Milk	3¼ qt	Add milk gradually. Cook over low heat, stirring constantly, until thick. Do not boil. Turn off heat.
Swiss cheese, shredded	3 lb 4 oz	Add cheese and stir until melted.
Nutmeg, ground	¼ tsp	Stir in nutmeg.
Mushrooms, sliced, canned, drained	1 lb	Stir in mushrooms and broccoli.
Pasta	5 lb	Cook pasta according to directions on p. 402.
Water, boiling	5 gal	Drain.
Salt	5 oz	Serve 4 oz sauce over 4 oz pasta.
Vegetable oil	3 Tbsp	Thin sauce as necessary with hot milk.

Variation:
Ham and Swiss broccoli pasta. Omit nutmeg. Reduce cheese to 2 lb 8 oz, broccoli to 1 lb, and mushrooms to 8 oz. Add 2 lb diced ham and 8 oz diced green pepper.

Lasagne

OVEN: 350°F		YIELD: 48 portions
BAKE: 40–45 minutes		2 pans 12 × 20 × 2 inches
		PORTION: 6 oz

Ingredient	Amount	Procedure
Ground beef	5 lb	Cook beef, onion, and garlic until meat has
Onions, finely chopped	12 oz	lost pink color.
Garlic, minced	2 cloves	Drain off fat.
Tomato sauce	3 qt	Add tomato and seasonings to meat.
Tomato paste	1 qt	Continue cooking for about 30 minutes,
Pepper, black	1 tsp	stirring occasionally.
Basil, crumbled	1 tsp	
Oregano, crumbled	1 Tbsp	
Noodles, lasagne	2 lb 8 oz	Cook noodles according to directions on p. 402.
Water, boiling	2 gal	Store in cold water to keep noodles from
Salt	2 oz	sticking.
Vegetable oil	2 Tbsp	Drain when ready to use.
Mozzarella cheese, shredded	2 lb 8 oz	Combine cheeses.
		Arrange in two greased 12 × 20 × 2-inch
Parmesan cheese, grated	6 oz	counter pans in layers in the following
Ricotta cheese or cottage cheese, dry or drained	2 lb 8 oz	order:
		Meat sauce, 1 qt
		Noodles, overlapping, 1 lb 12 oz
		Cheeses, 1 lb 4 oz
		Repeat sauce, noodles, and cheeses.
		Spoon remainder of meat sauce on top.
		Bake at 350°F for 40–45 minutes.
		Cut 4 × 6.

Note:
1½ oz (¾ cup) dehydrated onions, rehydrated in 1 cup water, may be substituted for fresh onions (p. 50).

Pasta with vegetable sauce

	YIELD:	50 portions
		2½ gal sauce
	PORTION:	6 oz sauce
		4 oz pasta

Ingredient	Amount	Procedure
Onions, chopped	2 lb	Sauté onion in oil until tender, using a steam-jacketed or other large kettle.
Olive oil	1 cup	
Oregano, leaf	¼ cup	Add spices to onion. Mix well.
Basil, dried	½ oz (½ cup)	
Pepper, black	1 Tbsp	
Garlic powder	1 Tbsp	
Salt	1 oz (1½ Tbsp)	
Bay leaves	2	
Tomato juice	5 46-oz cans	Add tomato to spices and onion. Heat to boiling.
Tomato paste	1 lb 12 oz	Reduce heat and simmer uncovered for 15–20 minutes.
		Remove bay leaves.
Zucchini, sliced	2 lb 8 oz	Add zucchini and mushrooms just before serving. Cook only until zucchini is tender.
Mushrooms, sliced	1 lb 8 oz	
Pasta	5 lb	Cook pasta according to directions on p. 402.
Water, boiling	5 gal	Serve 6 oz sauce over 4 oz pasta.
Salt	5 oz	
Vegetable oil (optional)	3 Tbsp	

Notes:
1. 2 cups finely chopped fresh basil may be substituted for dry basil.
2. 4 oz (2 cups) dehydrated onions, rehydrated in 3 cups water, may be substituted for fresh onions (p. 50).

Variations:
1. **Italian sausage pasta.** Delete olive oil, salt, and zucchini. Brown 5 lb bulk Italian sausage in steam-jacketed kettle. Drain. Add onions to sausage and continue to cook until onions are tender. Add spices, tomato juice, and tomato paste. Simmer for 15–20 minutes. Add meat sauce to 6 lb 8 oz cooked pasta (approximately 3 lb AP) and mix gently. Be careful not to overcook pasta. Scale 12 lb

per 12 × 20 × 2-inch pan. Sprinkle 1 lb shredded mozzarella cheese over each pan and place in low oven until cheese is melted. Suggested pasta combination: 1 lb (AP) rotini, 1 lb (AP) bow ties, 1 lb (AP) rigatoni.
2. **Italian tomato sauce.**   Delete zucchini and mushrooms. Use for any pasta or in lasagne.
3. **Pizza sauce.**   Reduce olive oil to 4 oz. Delete zucchini and mushrooms. Increase tomato paste to 5 lb 8 oz and decrease tomato juice to 5¼ qt. Add 1 tsp fennel seed, 2 Tbsp sugar, 1 tsp paprika, and ¼ tsp cayenne. Spread 1 qt sauce on top of 18 × 26-inch pizza dough before adding toppings.
4. **Sandwich tomato sauce.**   Delete salt, zucchini, and mushrooms. Add 1 Tbsp sugar. Reduce shortening to 1 Tbsp, onions to ½ cup, oregano to 1 tsp, basil to 1 Tbsp, pepper to ½ tsp, garlic powder to ½ tsp, bay leaf to 1, tomato juice to 1¼ qt, and tomato paste to 1½ cups. Yield: 50 1-oz servings.

Beef, pork, and noodle casserole

OVEN: 325°F
BAKE: 30 minutes

YIELD: 50 portions
      2 pans 12 × 20 × 2 inches
PORTION: 6 oz

Ingredient	Amount	Procedure
Ground beef	4 lb	Brown meat and onion.
Ground pork	4 lb	Drain off fat.
Onion, finely chopped	1 lb	
Tomato soup	1½ qt	Mix soup, water, and seasonings. Add to meat.
Water	1½ qt	
Salt	1 Tbsp	
Pepper, black	1 tsp	
Noodles	1 lb 12 oz	Cook noodles according to directions on p. 402. Drain.
Water, boiling	1¼ gal	
Salt	2 Tbsp	
Vegetable oil (optional)	1 Tbsp	
Cheddar cheese, grated or ground	2 lb	Combine noodles, meat mixture, and cheese. Scale into two 12 × 20 × 2-inch pans, 8 lb 4 oz per pan.
Bread crumbs	1 lb 2 oz	Combine crumbs and margarine.
Margarine or butter, melted	5 oz	Sprinkle over meat and noodle mixture, 10 oz per pan. Bake at 325°F for 30 minutes.

Note:
2 oz (1 cup) dehydrated onions, rehydrated in 1½ cups water, may be substituted for fresh onions (p. 50).

Spinach lasagne (Deep dish)

OVEN: 350°F	YIELD: 64 portions	
BAKE: 1½–2 hours		2 pans 12 × 20 × 4 inches
	PORTION: 10 oz	

Ingredient	Amount	Procedure
Onions, chopped	1 lb 8 oz	Sauté vegetables in hot oil.
Green pepper, chopped	12 oz	
Garlic, minced	2 oz	
Vegetable oil	½ cup	
Tomatoes, diced, canned	8 lb	Stir tomato and seasonings into sautéed vegetables. Simmer uncovered for about 20 minutes.
Tomato juice	3 qt	
Tomato paste	2 lb 8 oz	
Parsley, chopped	3 oz	Remove bay leaf. Use sauce in layering steps.
Oregano, leaf	1 Tbsp	
Basil, leaf	1 Tbsp	
Bay leaves	2	
Spinach, chopped	3 lb	Cook spinach. Drain.
Cottage cheese	5 lb	Mix. Add to spinach.
Parmesan cheese	1 lb	
Eggs, beaten	5 (8 oz)	
Salt	1 Tbsp	
Pepper, black	2 tsp	
Lasagne noodles, dry	5 lb	See directions below for layering.
Mozzarella cheese, shredded	3 lb 12 oz	

Layer ingredients in each of two 12 × 20 × 4-inch pans as follows:

1. Tomato sauce, 3 lb 4 oz
2. Dry noodles, 13 oz
3. Spinach-cheese mixture, 2 lb 5 oz
4. Mozzarella cheese, 11 oz
5. Repeat layers 1 through 4
6. Dry noodles, 13 oz
7. Tomato sauce, 3 lb 4 oz
8. Mozzarella cheese, 8 oz

Bake at 350°F covered with aluminum foil for 1 hour. Remove foil and bake an additional 30–60 minutes or until hot and bubbly. If browning too fast, cover again with foil. Let set for 15–20 minutes before cutting. Cut 4 × 8.

Notes:
1. Frozen lasagne noodle sheets may be used. Reduce diced tomatoes to 5 lb 8 oz, tomato juice to 2¼ qt, and tomato paste to 2 lb. Replace dry noodles with 6 lb frozen lasagne sheets, using 3 lb per pan.
2. 3¾ oz (1¾ cups) dehydrated onions, rehydrated in 3 cups water, may be substituted for fresh onions (p. 50).

Beef on noodles

YIELD: 50 portions
PORTION: 6 oz meat and sauce
4 oz noodles

Ingredient	Amount	Procedure
Beef, cubed	15 lb AP (10 lb EP)	Brown beef in steam-jacketed or other kettle.
Onions, chopped Celery, chopped	2 lb 8 oz 1 lb 8 oz	Add onions and celery to meat. Sauté until vegetables are tender.
Water Pepper, black Worcestershire sauce	2 qt 1 Tbsp ½ cup	Add water and seasonings to meat-vegetable mixture. Simmer until beef is tender.
Flour, all-purpose Water Beef base	12 oz 1½ qt 5 oz	Make a smooth paste of flour, water, and beef base. Add to meat mixture to make a gravy. Cook until thickened.
Noodles Water, boiling Salt Vegetable oil	4 lb AP (12 lb cooked) 4 gal 4 oz 2 Tbsp	Cook noodles according to directions on p. 402. Drain. Serve 6 oz beef and sauce over 4 oz cooked noodles.

Note:
5 oz (2½ cups) dehydrated onions, rehydrated in 3¾ cups water, may be substituted for fresh onions.

Hungarian goulash

YIELD: 50 portions
PORTION: 6 oz goulash
        4 oz noodles

Ingredient	Amount	Procedure
Beef, cubed	10 lb	Brown beef and vegetables in shortening in
Onion, chopped	1 lb 8 oz	steam-jacketed kettle or tilting fry pan.
Garlic, finely chopped	1 clove	
Shortening	8 oz	
Sugar, brown	5 oz	Combine sugar, seasonings, and liquid
Mustard, dry	1 Tbsp	ingredients.
Paprika	1 oz (¼ cup)	Add to browned meat.
Cayenne	⅛ tsp	Cover container and simmer 2½–3 hours or
Salt	2½ oz	until meat is tender.
Worcestershire sauce	1½ cups	
Vinegar	2 Tbsp	
Catsup	1 qt	
Water	3 qt	
Flour, all-purpose	1 lb 4 oz	Mix flour and water until smooth.
Water, cold	1 qt	Add gradually to hot mixture and cook until thickened.
Noodles	4 lb 8 oz	Cook noodles according to directions on p. 402.
Water, boiling	4½ gal	Serve 6 oz goulash over 4 oz noodles.
Salt	2 oz	
Oil (optional)	¼ cup	

Notes:
1. Beef may be browned in a roasting pan in 450°F oven.
2. 3 lb 8 oz dry rice, cooked, may be substituted for the noodles. See p. 422 for directions for cooking.
3. 3 oz (1½ cups) dehydrated onions, rehydrated in 2¼ cups water, may be substituted for fresh onions.

Pasta, beef, and tomato casserole

YIELD: 50 portions
PORTION: 8 oz

Ingredient	Amount	Procedure
Ground beef	10 lb AP (7 lb EP)	Cook meat in kettle. Stir often to prevent lumps from forming. Drain off fat.
Onions, chopped	6 oz	Add onions and celery to meat.
Celery, chopped	3 oz	Cook until tender.
Tomatoes, canned, diced	1½ gal	Add tomatoes and seasonings to meat mixture.
Tomato puree	2 cups	Simmer 45–60 minutes.
Chili sauce	3 cups	
Salt	2 oz (3 Tbsp)	
Pepper, black	1½ tsp	
Sugar, granulated	2 Tbsp	
Macaroni, elbow	2 lb 8 oz	Cook macaroni according to directions on p. 402.
Water, boiling	2½ gal	Fold into tomato-meat mixture.
Salt	2 oz	Simmer until hot.
Vegetable oil (optional)	2 Tbsp	

Notes:
1. Other pasta shapes may be substituted for macaroni.
2. ¾ oz (⅓ cup) dehydrated onions, rehydrated in ¾ cup water, may be substituted for fresh onions.

Chicken tetrazzini

OVEN: 350°F
BAKE: 30–40 minutes

YIELD: 50 portions
           2 pans 12 × 20 × 2 inches
PORTION: 8 oz

Ingredient	Amount	Procedure
Cooked chicken	6 lb	Dice chicken.
Pimiento, chopped	4 oz	Add pimiento and parsley.
Parsley, chopped	2 Tbsp	
Spaghetti	3 lb AP (9 lb cooked)	Cook spaghetti according to directions on p. 402. Drain.
Water, boiling	3 gal	
Salt	1 oz (1½ Tbsp)	
Vegetable oil (optional)	2 Tbsp	
Margarine	6 oz	Sauté vegetables in margarine.
Onions, finely chopped	1 lb	
Green peppers, chopped	4 oz	
Mushrooms, sliced	1 lb 8 oz	
Flour, all-purpose	9 oz	Blend flour and seasonings into sautéed vegetables.
Salt	1 tsp	Stir in chicken base. Cook 5 minutes.
Pepper, black	1 tsp	
Chicken base	3 oz	
Water	1 gal	Add water, stirring constantly. Cook until thickened. Combine cooked spaghetti, chicken, and sauce. Scale into 2 greased 12 × 20 × 2-inch baking pans, 10 lb per pan.
Processed cheese, shredded	1 lb	Sprinkle 8 oz cheese over top of each pan. Bake at 350°F for 30–40 minutes or until heated through and cheese is bubbly.

Notes:
   1. 18–20 lb chickens AP will yield approximately 6 lb cooked meat.
   2. 2 oz (1 cup) dehydrated onions, rehydrated in 1½ cups water, may be substituted for fresh onions (p. 50).

Variations:
1. **Tuna tetrazzini.**   Substitute tuna for chicken.
2. **Turkey tetrazzini.**   Substitute turkey for chicken.

Spaghetti with chicken sauce

YIELD: 50 portions
PORTION: 6 oz sauce
4 oz spaghetti

Ingredient	Amount	Procedure
Margarine or butter	7 oz	Sauté vegetables in margarine until tender crisp.
Celery, chopped	1 lb 8 oz	
Onions, chopped	1 lb 8 oz	
Green peppers, chopped	2 oz	
Flour, all-purpose	10 oz	Stir in flour. Cook over low heat for 10 minutes.
Chicken Stock (p. 590)	4¾ qt	Add stock to vegetable mixture, stirring constantly. Cook until thickened.
Salt	2 tsp	Season with salt and pepper.
Pepper, white	1 tsp	
Chicken, cooked, cubed	7 lb	Fold in chicken and pimiento.
Pimiento, chopped	2 oz	
Spaghetti	5 lb	Cook spaghetti according to directions on p. 402.
Water, boiling	5 gal	Serve 6 oz sauce over 4 oz spaghetti.
Salt	5 oz	
Vegetable oil (optional)	3 Tbsp	

Notes:
1. Sauce may be combined with spaghetti and served as a casserole.
2. 3 oz (1½ cups) dehydrated onions, rehydrated in 2¼ cups water, may be substituted for fresh onions (p. 50).

spaghetti

YIELD: 50 portions
2 pans 12 × 20 × 2 inches
PORTION: 8 oz

Ingredient	Amount	Procedure
Ground beef	7 lb AP (4 lb 10 oz EP)	Cook beef in steam-jacketed or other kettle until meat loses its red color. Drain off fat.
Onion, chopped	8 oz	Add onion and green pepper to meat.
Green pepper, chopped	5 oz	Cook until vegetables are tender.
Water	2 qt	Add water and tomatoes.
Tomatoes, canned, diced	2 qt	
Tomato puree	2 qt	
Tomato paste	1 qt	
Salt	1 Tbsp	Add seasonings to meat mixture. Stir to blend.
Sugar, granulated	2 tsp	
Cayenne	½ tsp	
Garlic, fresh, minced	1 clove	
Worcestershire sauce	2 Tbsp	
Bay leaves	2 leaves	
Thyme, ground	½ tsp	
Oregano leaves	1 tsp	
Spaghetti	2 lb AP (6 lb cooked)	Cook spaghetti according to directions on p. 402.
Water, boiling	3 gal	
Salt	3 oz	
Vegetable oil (optional)	2 Tbsp	
Cheddar cheese, shredded	1 lb 4 oz	Combine sauce and cooked spaghetti. Pour into two 12 × 20 × 2-inch baking pans, 13 lb 12 oz per pan. Sprinkle cheese over top. Bake at 325°F for 30 minutes.

Note:

1 oz (½ cup) dehydrated onions, rehydrated in ¾ cup water, may be substituted for fresh onions (p. 50).

Spaghetti with meat sauce

YIELD: 50 portions
PORTION: 6 oz sauce
4 oz spaghetti

Ingredient	Amount	Procedure
Ground beef	8 lb	Brown beef. Drain off fat.
Tomato puree (or tomatoes)	5 qt	Add remaining sauce ingredients to cooked beef.
Water	1 qt	Cook slowly, stirring frequently, until thickened, approximately ½ hour.
Catsup	1¾ qt	Remove bay leaves before serving.
Onions, chopped	1 lb	
Bay leaves	2	
Thyme	½ tsp	
Garlic, minced	1 clove	
Oregano	1 Tbsp	
Basil	1 tsp	
Sugar, granulated	1 oz (2 Tbsp)	
Worcestershire sauce	¼ cup	
Cayenne	2 tsp	
Salt	1 oz (1½ Tbsp)	
Spaghetti	5 lb	Cook spaghetti according to directions on p. 402.
Water, boiling	5 gal	Serve 6 oz sauce over 4 oz spaghetti.
Salt	5 oz	
Vegetable oil (optional)	3 Tbsp	

Notes:
1. Grated Parmesan cheese may be sprinkled over top of each serving.
2. 2 oz (1 cup) dehydrated onions, rehydrated in 1½ cups water, may be substituted for fresh onions (p. 50).

Spaghetti with meatballs

OVEN: 400°F, 350°F
BAKE: 15, 30 minutes

YIELD: 50 portions
PORTION: 3 2-oz or 2 3-oz meatballs
4 oz spaghetti

Ingredient	Amount	Procedure
MEATBALLS		
Ground beef	15 lb	Mix meat, bread crumbs, eggs, milk, and seasonings on low speed. Do not overmix.
Bread crumbs, dry	8 oz	
Eggs	16 (1 lb 10 oz)	
Milk	3¾ cups	
Salt	3 oz	
Pepper, black	4 tsp	
Basil leaves, dry	4 Tbsp	
Garlic, minced	6 cloves	
Parsley, fresh, chopped (optional)	3 cups	
		Portion meat with No. 20 dipper onto baking sheets for 150 2-oz balls; use No. 12 dipper for 100 3-oz balls.
		Brown in 400°F oven for 15–20 minutes.
		Remove to 12 × 20 × 4-inch counter pan or roasting pan.
SAUCE		
Italian Tomato Sauce	2 gal (1 recipe)	Make sauce according to directions on p. 411.
		Pour over browned meatballs.
		Cover and cook in 350°F oven for about 30 minutes.
PASTA		
Spaghetti	5 lb	Cook spaghetti according to directions on p. 402.
Water, boiling	5 gal	
Salt	5 oz	Serve 2 or 3 meatballs and 5 oz sauce over 4 oz spaghetti.
Vegetable oil (optional)	3 Tbsp	

Note:
If desired, mix the cooked spaghetti with the tomato sauce. Place in 2 counter pans, arrange meatballs over top, and bake at 375°F for 20–30 minutes.

Vegetarian spaghetti

YIELD: 50 portions
          1 pan 12 × 20 × 4 inches
PORTION: 8 oz

Ingredient	Amount	Procedure
Margarine or butter, melted	1 lb	Combine margarine and flour in steam-jacketed kettle.
Flour, all-purpose	12 oz	Cook and stir until smooth. Cook 5–10 minutes, stirring frequently.
Milk	1 gal	Add milk gradually. Cook over low heat until thick, stirring constantly. Turn off heat.
Salt	1 Tbsp	Add salt and cheese to sauce. Stir until cheese melts.
Cheese, American	1 lb 6 oz	
Carrots, sliced	1 lb 12 oz	Steam vegetables until tender. Drain. Combine with cheese sauce.
Green peppers, chopped	8 oz	
Celery, chopped	1 lb	
Broccoli, cut	1 lb	
Mushrooms, pieces and stems, canned	3 lb	Add mushrooms to sauce.
Spaghetti	2 lb 12 oz	Cook spaghetti according to directions on p. 402. Drain. Combine cooked spaghetti gently with cheese sauce.
Water, boiling	2¾ gal	
Salt	3 oz	
Vegetable oil (optional)	1 Tbsp	

Variations:
1. **Garden pasta.**   Substitute 3 lb rotini for spaghetti. Omit green peppers and salt. Reduce mushrooms to 2 lb. Increase milk to 1¼ gal and cheese to 2 lb. Add 4 oz chicken base. Add 1 lb 8 oz cauliflower florets, steamed only until tender-crisp.
2. **Spaghetti with vegetarian sauce.**   Serve 4-oz ladle of sauce over 4 oz cooked spaghetti. Increase spaghetti to 5 lb AP for 50 servings.

RICE RECIPES

Steamed or baked rice

YIELD: 50 portions
PORTION: 4 oz

Ingredient	Amount	Procedure
Rice, converted	3 lb 8 oz	**Steamer**
Salt	2 Tbsp	Weigh rice into a 12 × 20 × 2-inch counter pan.
Margarine or vegetable oil (optional)	2 Tbsp	Add salt and margarine.
Water, hot	4¼ qt	Pour hot water over rice. Stir.
		Steam uncovered for 30–40 minutes.
		Fluff with fork.
		Oven
		Weigh rice into a 12 × 20 × 2-inch counter pan.
		Add salt and margarine.
		Pour hot water over rice. Stir.
		Cover pans tightly with aluminum foil.
		Bake at 350°F for one hour.
		Remove from oven and let stand covered for 5 minutes.
		Fluff with fork.

Notes:
1. If regular white rice is used in place of converted rice, the cooking time may need to be reduced.
2. For brown rice, increase cooking time to 50–60 minutes for steamed rice, 1½ hours for baked rice.
3. For buttered rice, add 5 oz butter or margarine. Add to dry rice in counter pan. Add salt and hot water.
4. 1 lb uncooked rice yields 2 qt cooked rice.

Boiled rice

YIELD: 50 portions
PORTION: 4 oz

Ingredient	Amount	Procedure
Water	4¼ qt	Bring water to a boil in steam-jacketed kettle or other large kettle.
Salt	2 Tbsp	
Rice, converted	3 lb 8 oz	Add salt, rice, and margarine. Stir. Cover tightly.
Margarine or vegetable oil (optional)	2 Tbsp	Cook on low heat until rice is tender and all water is absorbed, about 15–20 minutes.
		Remove from heat and let stand covered 5–10 minutes.
		Fluff with fork.

Notes:
  1. If using regular white rice in place of converted rice, the cooking time may need to be reduced.
  2. For brown rice, increase cooking time to 40–45 minutes.
  3. 1 lb uncooked rice yields 2 qt cooked rice.

Fried rice

YIELD: 50 portions
PORTION: 4 oz

Ingredient	Amount	Procedure
Rice, converted	2 lb 8 oz	Cook rice according to directions on p. 422.
Water	3 qt	Do not overcook. Let cool.
Salt	2 tsp	
Frozen peas	1 lb 8 oz	Cook peas and drain. Set aside.
Eggs	6 (11 oz)	Break eggs into bowl and stir until yolks and whites are mixed. Add salt.
Salt	2 tsp	
Vegetable oil	2 Tbsp	Cook in oil, stirring to break into small pieces. Set aside.
Onions, chopped	1 lb	Sauté onions and carrots in oil until tender.
Carrots, shredded	8 oz	Add rice and cook until heated.
Vegetable oil	¾ cup	
Soy sauce	1 cup	Add soy sauce to rice mixture, stirring to mix evenly.
		Stir in cooked peas and eggs. Serve immediately.

Note:
2 oz (1 cup) dehydrated onions, rehydrated in 1½ cups water, may be substituted for fresh onions.

Variations:
1. **Fried rice with almonds.**   Cook 3 lb rice according to directions on p. 422. Sauté 4 oz chopped onions and 4 oz chopped green peppers in 1 cup vegetable oil. Add cooked rice, 1 Tbsp pepper, 1 tsp garlic salt, ½ cup soy sauce, and 2 lb slivered almonds. Add salt if needed. Bake until thoroughly heated.
2. **Fried rice with ham.**   Delete peas. Reduce chopped onions to 4 oz. Increase carrots to 12 oz. Add 4 oz sliced green onions, 12 oz sliced celery, and 1 lb chopped ham.
3. **Green rice.**   To 2 lb rice, cooked, add 4 lb finely chopped raw or frozen spinach, 2 Tbsp onion juice, and 1¼ qt medium White Sauce (p. 560). Place in one 12 × 20 × 2-inch counter pan. Bake at 325°F for 30–40 minutes.
4. **Jalapeño rice.**   Cook 2 lb 8 oz rice (p. 422). Combine in mixer bowl the cooked rice, 4 oz chopped jalapeño peppers, 1 cup chopped chives, 7 oz chopped green chili peppers, 3 lb 6 oz sour cream, 1 tsp salt, and 3 lb shredded American cheese. Scale 5 lb 12 oz into each of three 12 × 10 × 2-inch half counter pans. Sprinkle 4 oz shredded processed cheese over each pan. Bake uncovered at 250°F for 1–1½ hours. Cut 4 × 4.

5. **Pork fried rice.** Delete peas. Add 4 lb cubed, cooked pork. Fry 1 lb bacon. Use bacon fat for sautéing vegetables and rice. Crumble bacon and add.
6. **Shrimp fried rice.** Add 1 lb 8 oz cooked shrimp.

Rice pilaf

OVEN: 350°F	YIELD: 50 portions
BAKE: 45 minutes	1 pan 12 × 20 × 4 inches
	PORTION: 4 oz

Ingredient	Amount	Procedure
Onions, finely chopped	1 lb 8 oz	Sauté onion in margarine until it begins to
Margarine, melted	8 oz	soften. Do not brown.
Rice, converted	3 lb	Add uncooked rice to onions and stir over heat until completely coated with the margarine.
Salt	1 tsp	Place rice in a 12 × 20 × 4-inch counter pan.
Pepper, white	¼ tsp	Add seasonings and stock.
Bay leaf	1	Stir to combine.
Chicken Stock (p. 590)	1 gal	Cover tightly with aluminum foil. Bake at 350°F for 45 minutes; or steam uncovered for 30 minutes. Stir before serving.

Notes:
1. Suggested additions for variety: chopped green pepper, pimiento, tomato, or nuts; sliced mushrooms or water chestnuts; ground or diced ham.
2. 3 oz (1½ cups) dehydrated onions, rehydrated in 2¼ cups water, may be substituted for fresh onions (p. 50).

Variations:
1. **Curried rice.** Add 3 Tbsp curry powder.
2. **Mexican rice.** Sauté 14 oz chopped onion, 10 oz chopped green pepper, and 3 oz chopped celery in ⅓ cup vegetable oil. Add raw rice and stir 2–3 minutes until grains are coated with oil. Stir in 3 Tbsp salt, 2 oz chili powder, and 1 tsp garlic powder. Place in a 12 × 20 × 4-inch counter pan. Pour a mixture of 2½ qt tomato juice and 1¾ qt Beef Stock (p. 589) over rice. Steam 25–35 minutes. Stir before serving.
3. **Mushroom rice pilaf.** Reduce rice to 1 lb 12 oz and Chicken Stock to 2½ qt. Delete bay leaf and add 1½ tsp thyme. Add 2 lb mushroom pieces and stems and 1 lb 8 oz chopped celery.

CEREAL RECIPES

Breakfast cereals

| | | YIELD: 2 gal |
| | | PORTION: ⅔ cup |

Ingredient	Amount	Procedure
Water Salt	2–2¼ gal 2 oz (3 Tbsp)	Measure water into steam-jacketed kettle or heavy stock pot. Add salt and bring to a rolling boil.
Cereal, granular or flaked	2 lb	Stir dry cereal gradually into boiling water, using wire whip. Stir until some thickening is apparent. Reduce heat and cook until cereal reaches desired consistency and raw starch taste has disappeared. Cereal should be thick and creamy but not sticky.

Notes:
1. Granular cereals may be mixed with cold water to separate particles and prevent formation of lumps.
2. Do not stir excessively; overstirring or overcooking produces a sticky, gummy product.
3. 1 lb raisins may be added to cereal the last 2 minutes of cooking.

Variation:
Rice and raisins.   Cook 8 oz raw rice (2 lb cooked) according to directions on p. 422. Heat 1 gal milk. Add cooked rice, 8 oz softened raisins, 12 oz granulated sugar, and 2 Tbsp cinnamon.

Granola

OVEN: 300°F		YIELD: 50 portions	
BAKE: 1 hour		PORTION: 2¾ oz	

Ingredient	Amount	Procedure
Sugar, brown	6 oz	Place in mixer bowl. Mix on medium speed to combine.
Almonds, slivered	14 oz	
Sesame seeds	4 oz	
Sunflower seeds, shelled	8 oz	
Bulgar	1 oz	
Coconut, shredded	2 lb 12 oz	
Salt	1 Tbsp	
Vanilla	2 tsp	
Almond extract	2 tsp	
Water	1 cup	
Salad oil	1 cup	
Rolled oats, quick	2 lb 11 oz	Mix rolled oats into other ingredients carefully so flakes are not broken. Spread mixture on sheet pans ½ inch deep. Bake at 300°F for 1 hour or until golden brown and crispy. Stir every 15 minutes while baking. Cool and store in airtight container until served.

Note:
Use for snacks, ice cream topping, or breakfast cereal.

Barley casserole

OVEN: 350°F	YIELD: 50 portions
BAKE: 1½ hours	1 pan 12 × 20 × 2 inches
	PORTION: 4 oz

Ingredient	Amount	Procedure
Margarine	6 oz	Sauté barley and vegetables in margarine.
Pearl barley	2 lb 6 oz	
Onions, chopped	1 lb 4 oz	
Mushroom pieces and stems, canned	1 lb 11 oz	
Chicken Stock (p. 590)	3½ qt	Add stock to barley mixture. Pour into a 12 × 20 × 2-inch counter pan. Bake at 350°F for 1½ hours. Serve with No. 10 dipper.

Note:
2½ oz (1¼ cups) dehydrated onions, rehydrated in 2 cups water, may be substituted for fresh onions (p. 50).

POULTRY

PURCHASING AND STORAGE

Poultry is used extensively in all types of foodservices. It is available ready to cook, either fresh or frozen, whole or cut up, and in a variety of other forms. Common forms include the following:

Whole birds, fresh and frozen

Broiler: 2½–4 lb, about 7 weeks of age.

Roaster: 4–8 lb, about 10 weeks of age.

Capon: 9½ lb approximately, 16 weeks old, desexed male chicken.

Stewing hen (or fowl): 4½–6 lb, 15-month-old broiler or egg industry hen.

Rock Cornish: 1½ lb or less, 4–5-week-old chicken (a hybrid developed from a Cornish chicken).

Turkeys: 4–24 lb or heavier.

Ducks: 3–7 lb, 7 weeks of age.

Geese: 6–12 lb, 7–10 weeks of age.

Ready to cook, frozen or fresh pieces

Halves, quarters, breasts, split breasts, thighs, drumsticks, whole legs, wings, drumettes.

Other forms

Cooked or raw turkey breasts, roasts, rolls.

Canned chicken or turkey.

Frozen raw or precooked diced chicken or turkey cubes.

Frozen breaded chicken pieces, fillets, and patties.

Nontraditional products, such as turkey pastrami, turkey hot dogs, and other poultry cold cuts.

Costs and quality can be controlled by selecting the poultry form that best suits the product being prepared. Keeping current on new poultry products and packaging is important to foodservice managers.

All poultry is highly perishable, and caution regarding cleanliness should be exercised in preparing, cooking, cooling, storing, and serving poultry products. Fresh-chilled poultry should be kept at a temperature of 28–32°F and used within one to two days. Frozen poultry should be kept hard-frozen at 0°F until it is removed from storage for thawing and cooking.

Poultry should be defrosted in a refrigerator. Place wrapped birds on trays to catch any drippings and arrange on refrigerator shelves so that air can circulate around them. Never thaw poultry in a manner that will cause cooked foods to become contaminated by the dripping from the raw birds. Allow one to two days for chickens and turkey roasts, two to four days for large birds, and one day or less for cut up chicken or small poultry pieces.

If faster thawing is necessary, partially defrost in the original wrapper in the refrigerator and then place in cold running water until thawed. Once thawed, poultry may be kept safely no longer than 24 hours at 32°F before cooking. It should never be refrozen.

COOKING METHODS

Most frozen poultry, except breaded and precooked products, is thawed prior to cooking. If frozen poultry is cooked, it will take approximately 1½ times as long as thawed poultry.

Poultry should be cooked at moderate heat (325–350°F) for optimum tenderness and juiciness, and the cookery method chosen should be appropriate for the age of the bird. Dry-heat methods (broiling, frying, or roasting) are used for young, tender birds. Moist-heat methods (stewing, steaming, and braising or fricasseeing) are suitable for the older, more mature birds. Recommended cooking methods for various classes of poultry are given in Table 2.16.

Poultry is easily flavored by imaginative use of herbs and spices. Possible spice choices for poultry include celery salt, curry, dill weed, fennel seed, garlic, marjoram, ground mustard, oregano, paprika, parsley, poultry seasoning, rosemary, saffron, savory, sesame seeds, sweet basil, tarragon, and thyme. A salt-free recipe for seasoning is on p. 624.

Broiling

Young tender chickens, 2½ lb or under, or 3–5 lb ready-to-cook turkeys may be broiled or cooked on the grill. The procedure for broiling poultry follows:

- Split each bird in half lengthwise or into quarters, depending on size. Fold wing tip back onto cut side.
- Brush with melted fat. Season with salt and pepper.
- Place, skin side down, on broiler. Place poultry 7 inches below source of heat; chicken and turkey should broil slowly. Turn and brush with fat while broiling in order to brown and cook evenly. The cooking time required varies from 50 to 60 minutes for chicken and 1 to 2¼ hours for turkey.

Poultry browns very quickly and may become too dark before it is cooked through. The chicken or turkey may be placed in an oven on sheet pans or racks to complete cooking after it has been browned on the grill or under the broiler.

TABLE 2.16 COOKING METHODS FOR POULTRY

Kind of poultry	Class	Average ready-to-cook weight (pounds)	Cookery method	Per person allowance, ready-to-cook weight (ounces)
Chicken	Broiler-fryer	2–4	Fry, broil, grill, roast	¼–½ bird
	Roaster	3–5	Roast	12–16
	Hen or fowl	4–5	Stew or fricassee	8–12
Turkey	Whole	8–24	Roast	12–16
	Roast, boned and tied	12	Roast	4–5
	Roast, cooked	8–10	Slice and heat in broth; or heat in an uncovered pan	2½–3
	Roll, ready to cook	3–6	Roast	4–5
Duck		3–7	Roast	12–16
Goose		6–12	Roast	12–16

Note: For cooked yields for chicken and turkey, see p. 435.

Deep-fat frying

Broiler-fryers may be cooked by submerging pieces in hot fat—that is, deep-fat frying. Pressure frying, or deep-fat frying in a covered fryer that allows steam to build up and cook the product under pressure, is also a common way to cook poultry.

Poultry products are usually breaded before deep-fat frying or are purchased with a batter or breaded coating. The recipe for coating chicken is on p. 41. Figure 2.33 shows the technique for breading. Guidelines for deep-fat frying of raw broiler-fryer pieces are as follows:

- Fry at proper temperature, 350–375°F for regular deep-fat frying, 345–350°F for pressure frying.

- Baskets should not be overloaded.

- Use a good quality fat with a high smoke point.

- 15–20 percent fresh fat should be added after each daily use. Old fat should be discarded.

- Cook until chicken reaches an internal temperature of 185°F.

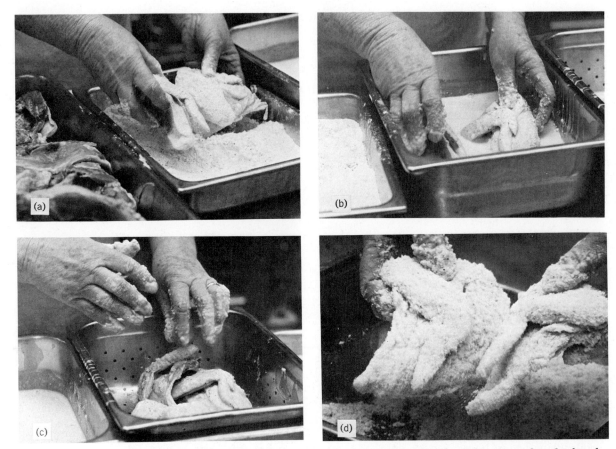

Figure 2.33 *Breading chicken. Arrange work station in the following order: food to be breaded, flour, egg-milk mixture, pan for draining, bread or cracker crumbs, and baking sheet on which to place the breaded product. See Table 1.13 for amounts of breading ingredients. (a) Dredge chicken with seasoned flour. (b) Dip in egg-milk mixture. (c) Drain. Picture shows a perforated pan set inside a solid counter pan. (d) Roll in crumbs. Place on baking sheet. If chicken is to be baked, line pan with parchment paper.*

The time will vary because of size differences. Approximate frying times for raw chicken pieces are 15–20 minutes for regular deep-fat frying and 14–18 minutes for pressure frying.

Quality deep-fat fried chicken will be plump and juicy with minimum fat absorption, attractive golden color, and crisp surface.

Pan frying

Pan-fried chicken pieces are usually coated with flour or breading before cooking. See recipe on p. 41 and description of breading technique above. Chicken may be purchased breaded and ready to pan fry. Follow these guidelines for pan frying raw chicken pieces:

- Heat ½ inch of fat to 350°F. Arrange breaded chicken in hot fat skin side down. Brown on all sides.
- Reduce temperature to 325°F and cook slowly until tender, usually 40–60 minutes, or until internal temperature reaches 180°F. Cooking time depends on size of pieces. Turn as necessary to assure even browning and doneness.

Sautéing thin slices of poultry in a small amount of fat is popular for many poultry dishes. Large pieces may require pan sautéing for browning, then finishing by another method, such as braising or baking.

Oven frying

Oven frying is a satisfactory method for producing fried chicken without large quantities of fat. When properly cooked, the finished product is tender, moist, and crispy. The following guidelines are for oven frying chicken:

- Dredge chicken in seasoned flour, then roll in melted fat.
- Place on sheet pans and bake approximately 1 hour at 350–375°F or until internal temperature reaches 185°F.

This method of cooking chicken should result in a nicely browned product with no turning. See recipe on p. 438.

Braising

Braising—cooking meat slowly in a closely covered pan with a small amount of moisture—is often required for mature, less tender poultry. Guidelines for braising whole and cut-up poultry follow:

Braising whole poultry
- Preheat oven to 450°F for young poultry, 325°F for more mature birds.
- Season and brush ready-to-cook poultry with fat.
- Place poultry in a heavy pan and cover tightly.
- Poultry is done when internal temperature reaches 185°F, 1–2 hours. Uncovering the poultry for the last 30 minutes of cooking will brown it.

Braising cut-up poultry
- Roll serving-size pieces of chicken in seasoned flour, then brown in fat in a heavy fry pan. Drain off fat. Place chicken in a baking pan.
- Add a small amount of hot water to chicken. Cover tightly and cook in a 325°F oven. Add more water as necessary to prevent sticking.
- Remove cover during the final 30 minutes of cooking to brown. Total cooking time will be 1½–2½ hours, depending on size of the pieces and maturity of the bird.

Stewing or simmering and poaching

Stewing or simmering and poaching all refer to cooking in a liquid. Stewing or simmering requires that the temperature be kept just below the boiling point, bubbling very gently. Poaching temperature is slightly lower and less liquid is used. This moist-heat method of stewing and simmering is used for larger, older, and tougher birds that require longer cooking times to soften. Poaching is used to gently cook tender poultry and develop a delicate subtle flavor. Guidelines are as follows:

Stewing or simmering
- Barely cover poultry with seasoned boiling water.
- Simmer until tender, approximately 2½ hours.
- For cooking in a steamer, place whole or parts of birds in a solid steamer pan. Cook until tender.

Poaching
- Place tender poultry product in a pan.
- Pour cold liquid, usually stock, in the pan to cover poultry part way up. Cover the pan.
- Heat gently on the range top or in the oven at 325°F until internal temperature reaches 185°F.
- Drain poultry well after cooking. Liquid may be used for making a sauce.

When stewed or simmered chicken meat is to be used in salads or creamed dishes, the following may be added to the cooking water for additional flavor: 1 carrot, 1 medium onion, 1 celery stock, and 2 whole peppercorns for each bird.

Cooked poultry must be cooled immediately if prepared for use at a later time. Remove from broth and place on sheet pans. When poultry is cool enough to handle, remove meat from bones, place in shallow pans and store in the refrigerator at 38°F or below. Broth should be cooled rapidly by stirring frequently during cooling.

Roasting

For large-quantity cookery, it usually is recommended that poultry be roasted unstuffed and that dressing be baked separately. If turkey is to be stuffed, mix the stuffing just before it is needed. Do not prepare dressing or stuff the bird in advance. Follow this order of procedure in roasting poultry:

1. Prepare bird. Remove pin feathers if necessary. Rinse bird well inside and out.
2. Season inside and outside of bird.
3. Brush with soft fat or oil.
4. Place bird on a rack in a shallow baking pan, breast up. If not for show, bake breast down.

5. Baste with fat and hot water (4 oz fat to 1 qt hot water) if desired. Drippings also may be used for basting.

6. Roast at 325–350°F to an internal temperature of 185°F. Insert thermometer in center of inside thigh muscle. Allow approximately 15–18 minutes per lb for a 20-lb unstuffed turkey. Allow approximately 30 minutes per lb for a 5-lb chicken. (See Table 2.17 for roasting guide.) If thermometer is not available, test doneness by moving drumstick. It moves easily at the thigh joint when done.

7. To roast turkey halves or quarters, place skin side up in an open pan. Roast at 325°F for 2–3 hours.

8. To roast a boneless turkey roast or roll, place on rack in an open pan. Roast at 325°F until a meat thermometer inserted in the center registers 170–175°F, or follow cooking directions on the package.

The yield of cooked meat from poultry is influenced by the size of the bird, the amount of bone, the method of preparation and service, and the size of portions desired. Whole ready-to-cook turkey will yield approximately 47 percent edible cooked meat without skin, neck meat, or giblets; turkey roast or roll will yield about 66 percent. Ready-to-cook chickens (large fryers) will yield approximately 35–40 percent usable cooked meat for combination dishes.

TABLE 2.17 ROASTING GUIDE FOR POULTRY (DEFROSTED)

Kind of Poultry	Ready-to-cook weight (pounds)	Approximate total roasting time at 325°F (hours)	Internal temperature of poultry when done[a] (°F)
Chicken, whole, roasters	2½–4	1–1½	185
Ducks	3–7	1–2	180
Geese	6–8	2½–3½	180
	8–12	3½–4½	180
Turkeys, whole	6–8	3–3½	180–185
	8–12	3½–4½	180–185
	12–16	4½–5½	180–185
	16–20	5½–6½	180–185
	20–24	6½–7	180–185
Turkeys, halves Quarters and pieces	3–8	2–3	
	8–12	3–4	
Turkey, boneless roasts	3–10	3–4	170–175

[a] Thermometer inserted in thigh of whole turkeys, in center of turkey roasts.

POULTRY RECIPES

Pan-fried chicken

YIELD: 50 portions
PORTION: 8–12 oz AP

Ingredient	Amount	Procedure
Chicken fryers, 2–3 lb	13	Cut chickens into pieces of desired serving size.
Flour, all-purpose	1 lb	Mix flour and seasonings.
Salt	2 Tbsp	Roll chicken pieces in the seasoned flour.
Paprika or poultry seasoning	1 Tbsp	
Pepper, black	1 tsp	
Shortening	1 lb	Brown chicken in hot shortening, ½ inch deep in pan. Reduce heat and cook slowly until tender, 45–60 minutes. Turn for even browning.

Notes:
1. Chicken portions (quarters, thighs, or breasts) may be used.
2. Chicken may be browned in a skillet, then placed in counter pans or baking pans, skin side up, and finished in the oven at 325°F for 20–30 minutes.

Variations:
1. **Chicken Cantonese.** Flour chicken and brown as above. Place in 12 × 20 × 2-inch counter pans. Cover with aluminum foil. Bake at 350°F for approximately 1 hour. Before serving, cover with sauce made of 3 qt pineapple juice, 3 qt orange juice, 12 oz flour, 3 lb pineapple cubes, 12 oranges peeled and diced, 1 lb 4 oz almonds slivered and browned, 2 tsp nutmeg, and 2 tsp salt. Combine juice and flour; cook until thickened. Add seasonings, fruit, and almonds. Pour over chicken. Bake uncovered about 10 minutes. Serve with cooked rice.
2. **Chicken cacciatore.** Brown chicken as above. Arrange in two 12 × 20 × 4-inch counter pans. Sauté 1 lb 8 oz coarsely diced onions and 2 cloves garlic, minced, in 5 oz margarine. Add 1 lb 8 oz green peppers cut into strips, 2 lb sliced mushrooms, 1 No. 10 can diced tomatoes with juice, ½ tsp oregano, ½ tsp thyme, and 1 qt Chicken Stock. Thicken with 4 oz flour mixed with 2 cups cold water. Pour over chicken, 3½ qt per pan. Cover with aluminum foil. Bake at 325°F for 1 hour.
3. **Deep-fat fried chicken.** Use 1¾ to 2-lb broiler-fryers, cut in serving pieces, or chicken quarters. Dredge in seasoned flour as above; or dredge in flour, dip in egg and milk mixture (3 eggs to 1 cup

milk), and roll in crumbs (12 oz); or dip in batter (p. 41). Fry in deep fat at 325°F for 12–15 minutes or until golden brown and cooked through. For larger fryers, brown in deep fat, drain, then place in baking pans and finish in the oven at 325°F for 20–30 minutes.

Fricassee of chicken

| OVEN: 325°F | YIELD: 50 portions |
| BAKE: 1½–2 hours | PORTION: 3 oz cooked meat |

Ingredient	Amount	Procedure
Chicken[a]	35 lb AP	Mix flour and seasonings.
Flour, all-purpose	12 oz	Dip chicken in seasoned flour.
Salt	2 Tbsp	
Pepper, white	1 tsp	
Shortening	1 lb	Brown chicken in hot shortening. Remove to roasting pan or steam-jacketed kettle and cover with boiling water. Cook slowly, adding more water if necessary, until chicken is tender, 1½–2 hours.
Margarine	10 oz	When tender, remove chicken from stock.
Flour, all-purpose	6 oz	Make gravy, using liquid in which chicken
Chicken broth	3½ qt	was cooked (see p. 566). Serve over chicken.

[a] Thirteen 2½- to 3-lb fryers.

Variations:
1. **White fricassee of chicken.** Do not brown chicken. Simmer until tender. Remove from liquid. Boil liquid until concentrated. Add milk or cream to make 1½ gal; thicken to make a Medium White Sauce (p. 560). Beat constantly with wire whip while pouring sauce gradually over 10 beaten egg yolks. Season to taste. Add chicken.
2. **Chicken with black olives.** Brown floured chicken. Place in baking pans. Cover with chicken gravy. Bake 1–1½ hours. Prior to serving, sprinkle with sliced ripe olives and sautéed fresh mushrooms.

Oven-fried chicken

OVEN: 350°F	YIELD: 50 portions
BAKE: 1 hour	PORTION: 1 chicken quarter
	or 2 pieces

Ingredient	Amount	Procedure
Chicken quarters	50	Mix flour and seasonings.
or chicken breasts and	100	Dredge chicken with seasoned flour.
thighs		Place in single layer on greased or silicone-
Flour, all-purpose	1 lb	paper-lined baking sheets.
Nonfat dry milk	8 oz	
Salt	2 Tbsp	
Paprika	1 Tbsp	
Pepper, black	1 tsp	
Margarine, melted	1 lb	Brush chicken with melted margarine.
		Bake at 350°F for 1 hour or until chicken is
		browned and tender.

Note:
Chicken may be breaded. See Table 1.13 for coating and Figure 2.33 for procedures.

Variations:
1. **Barbecued chicken.** Brown chicken at 425°F for 20–30 minutes. Reduce heat to 325°F. Pour 1½ gal Cooked Barbecue Sauce (p. 568) over chicken. Bake 40–45 minutes.
2. **Chicken Parmesan.** Combine 1 lb flour, 1 oz salt, ½ tsp pepper, and ¾ cup Parmesan cheese. Dredge chicken pieces in flour mixture, then dip in mixture of 12 (1 lb 5 oz) eggs and 1 qt milk, then back into flour mixture. Arrange chicken on greased or silicone-paper-lined baking sheets. Dribble lemon butter (8 oz melted butter or margarine and ¼ cup lemon or lime juice) over chicken. Bake at 325°F for 1 hour. Use drippings from baking sheets for gravy.
3. **Chicken teriyaki.** Marinate chicken overnight in a marinade of 3 cups soy sauce, 10 oz brown sugar, 1½ Tbsp garlic powder, and 1½ Tbsp ground ginger. Arrange chicken pieces in single layer on greased or silicone-paper-lined baking sheets. Bake at 350°F for 30 minutes. Remove from oven. Brush chicken with remaining marinade and bake until tender, about 30 minutes. 1 cup orange juice or pineapple juice may be added to the marinade.
4. **Herb baked chicken.** Combine 1 lb 8 oz dry bread crumbs, 8 oz flour, 1½ oz salt, 1 Tbsp paprika, 1½ tsp onion salt, 1 tsp garlic salt, 1 Tbsp rosemary, and ¾ cup salad oil. Dredge chicken in crumb mixture. Place on silicone-paper-lined 18 × 26 × 1-inch baking sheets. Bake at 350°F for 1 hour.
5. **Italian baked chicken.** Melt 3 lb butter. Dip chicken in melted butter, then roll in coating mixture of 3 lb dry bread crumbs, 1 cup chopped parsley, 2 Tbsp paprika, 1 Tbsp salt, 3 Tbsp garlic salt, 2 Tbsp oregano leaves, 1½ tsp basil leaves, 1 tsp black pepper, and 12 oz grated Parmesan cheese. Place in shallow baking pans with skin side up. Bake at 350°F for 1 hour.

Chicken tahitian

OVEN: 425°F, 325°F	YIELD: 52 portions
BAKE: 65–70 minutes	PORTION: 3 oz cooked meat

Ingredient	Amount	Procedure
Chicken, cut into quarters[a]	35 lb AP	Melt shortening in baking pans.
Shortening	12 oz	Arrange chicken in pans in single layer.
		Brown in 425°F oven for 30 minutes.
Frozen orange juice, undiluted	2 12-oz cans	Combine juice, margarine, ginger, and soy sauce.
Margarine, melted	1 lb	
Ginger, ground	2 Tbsp	
Soy sauce	2 Tbsp	
		Brush chicken with orange mixture.
		Bake at 325°F for 30–40 minutes, basting as needed until chicken is glazed.
		Serve with Steamed Rice (p. 422) and garnish with slivered almonds and avocado wedges.

[a] Thirteen 2½- to 3-lb fryers.

Chicken crepes

OVEN: 325°F		YIELD: 50 portions
BAKE: 10 minutes		PORTION: 2 crepes

Ingredient	Amount	Procedure
Margarine Flour, all-purpose Salt	1 lb 8 oz 12 oz 1 oz (1½ Tbsp)	Melt margarine in steam-jacketed or other large kettle. Add flour and salt. Blend and cook for 5 minutes.
Chicken Stock (p. 590) or milk	1½ gal	Gradually add stock, stirring constantly with wire whip.
Cooked chicken, diced Mushrooms, chopped Worcestershire sauce Curry powder Salt	10 lb 2 8-oz cans 2 Tbsp 2 Tbsp To taste	Combine chicken, mushrooms, and seasonings. Add enough sauce to hold chicken together (1–2 qt). Reserve remaining sauce to pour over crepes.
Crepes (p. 138)	1 recipe	Make batter. Fry on lightly greased griddle, using No. 20 dipper (1¾ oz) batter. Brown lightly on one side. Turn and cook to set batter. Place Crepes on trays, with waxed paper between layers. Hold for next step.
		Portion No. 20 dipper of chicken mixture onto each crepe; roll and place on baking sheets. Heat in 325°F oven for 10 minutes. Serve with remaining sauce, ladled on top.

Note:
1 lb sautéed mushrooms may be added to sauce that is ladled over crepes.

Variations:
1. **Fruit cheese crepes.** Fill Crepes (recipe on p. 138) with 1½ Tbsp of the following mixture: 2 lb cream cheese, whipped and combined with 2 cups sour cream. Serve with frozen strawberries or raspberries, thickened slightly, or with prepared fruit pie filling, heated.
2. **Spinach crepes.** Omit chicken and sauce. Fill crepes with cooked Spinach Soufflé (p. 663). Serve with Cheese Sauce (p. 561) or Swiss Cheese and Mushroom Sauce (p. 561).

Chicken turnovers

OVEN: 400°F	YIELD: 50 portions
BAKE: 25–30 minutes	PORTION: 4 oz

Ingredient	Amount	Procedure
Cooked chicken	6 lb	Dice or coarsely chop chicken.
Margarine Flour, all-purpose Salt	6 oz 4 oz 1 oz (1½ Tbsp)	Melt margarine. Stir in flour and salt. Cook 5 minutes.
Chicken Stock (p. 590)	1 qt	Add stock to margarine-flour mixture, stirring constantly with wire whip. Cook until thickened. When thick, fold in chicken.
Pastry (p. 249)	5 lb	Roll out Pastry. Cut into 50 rounds with 6-inch cutter. Place No. 20 dipper chicken mixture on each pastry round just below center. Fold rounds over and seal by pressing edges together with a fork. Bake at 400°F for 25–30 minutes. Serve with Chicken Gravy or Mushroom Sauce (1 gal).

Note:
18–20 lb of chickens AP will yield approximately 6 lb cooked meat.

Variations:
1. **Beef turnovers.** Substitute coarsely chopped cooked beef for chicken and Beef Stock for Chicken Stock. Serve with beef gravy.
2. **Ham turnovers.** Substitute ground ham for chicken. Delete salt. Serve with Mushroom Sauce (p. 564).

Creamed chicken

YIELD: 50 portions
PORTION: 6 oz (¾ cup)

Ingredient	Amount	Procedure
Cooked chicken	6 lb	Dice chicken.
Margarine or butter Onions, minced	1 lb 12 oz 4 oz	Melt margarine in steam-jacketed or other large kettle. Add onions and sauté until tender.
Flour, all-purpose Salt Pepper, white	1 lb 4 oz 1 oz (1½ Tbsp) 1 tsp	Add flour and seasonings to onions. Stir and cook for 5 minutes.
Chicken Stock (p. 590) Milk	3 qt 2¼ qt	Add stock and milk, stirring constantly with wire whip. Cook until thickened.
		Fold chicken gently into sauce. Check for seasonings. Heat to serving temperature. Serve over biscuits, toast, or rice.

Notes:
1. 18–20 lb of chickens AP will yield approximately 6 lb cooked meat.
2. ½ oz (¼ cup) dehydrated onions, rehydrated in ½ cup water, may be substituted for fresh onions (p. 50).

Variations:
1. **Chicken à la king.** Add 4 oz chopped green pepper, 4 oz shredded pimiento, and 1 lb sautéed sliced mushrooms.
2. **Tuna à la king.** Substitute tuna for chicken. Stir carefully to avoid breaking up of tuna pieces.
3. **Turkey à la king.** Substitute turkey for chicken.

Hot chicken salad

OVEN: 350°F		YIELD: 56 portions
BAKE: 25–30 minutes		2 pans 12 × 20 × 2 inches
		or 50 individual casseroles
		PORTION: 5 oz

Ingredient	Amount	Procedure
Cooked chicken	6 lb	Dice chicken.
Celery, diced	4 lb	Combine and add to chicken. Mix lightly.
Onion, chopped	3 oz	
Almonds, browned and chopped coarsely	1 lb	
Lemon juice	½ cup	
Lemon peel, grated	3 Tbsp	
Pepper, white	1 tsp	
Salt	1 Tbsp	
Mayonnaise	1½ qt	
		Scale mixture into two 12 × 20 × 2-inch counter pans, 7 lb per pan. If using individual casseroles, portion with No. 8 dipper.
Cheddar cheese, shredded	3 lb	Sprinkle cheese over top of salad mixture.
Potato chips, crushed	12 oz	Distribute potato chips uniformly over cheese. Bake at 350°F for 25–30 minutes, or until bubbly. Cut 4 × 7 or serve with No. 8 dipper.

Notes:
1. 18–20 lb of chickens AP will yield approximately 6 lb cooked meat.
2. Swiss cheese may be substituted for cheddar cheese.
3. 2 lb of the cheese may be added to the chicken mixture and 1 lb sprinkled on top.

Variation:
Hot turkey salad. Substitute turkey for chicken. A 16- to 18-lb turkey AP will yield approximately 6 lb cooked meat.

Scalloped chicken

OVEN: 350°F
BAKE: 30–40 minutes

YIELD: 48 portions
       2 pans 12 × 20 × 2 inches
PORTION: 8 oz

Ingredient	Amount	Procedure
Cooked chicken	6 lb	Cut chicken into ½-inch pieces. Save for layering step.
Margarine Flour, all-purpose Chicken base	1 lb 8 oz 3 oz	Melt margarine in steam-jacketed or other kettle. Stir in flour and chicken base. Cook 5 minutes.
Water	1 gal	Add water to roux, while stirring with wire whip. Cook until thickened.
Eggs, beaten	12 (1 lb 5 oz)	When sauce is thick, add small amount of hot mixture to eggs, then stir into remainder of sauce. Save for layering step.
Dry bread, cubed Salt Pepper, black Sage, ground, or poultry seasoning	2 lb 6 oz 1 tsp 2 tsp 1½ tsp	Add seasonings to bread. Mix to distribute seasonings.
Margarine Celery, chopped Onion, chopped Chicken base	10 oz 8 oz 8 oz 2 oz	Sauté celery and onion in melted margarine. Stir in chicken base. Add to bread.
Water	2½ qt	Add water to bread. Toss lightly. Do not overmix.
		Place dressing, sauce, and chicken in 2 greased 12 × 20 × 2-inch counter pans, layered in each pan as follows: 4 lb 8 oz dressing 1¼ qt sauce

Cracker crumbs, coarse	6 oz
Margarine, melted	3 oz

Notes:
1. Scalloped Turkey or Chicken may be mad
   and scaling it in the following manner in e
   into pans and spread evenly. Arrange 3 lb
   dressing over turkey, spreading evenly. Ba
   (p. 566).
2. 1 oz (½ cup) dehydrated onions, rehydrated in ¼ cup water, may be u
   onions (p. 50).

Variation:
Scalloped turkey.   Substitute turkey for chicken.

Chicken loaf

OVEN: 325°F
BAKE: 1½ hours

Ingredient

Rice, c
Wat
Sa

Batter crust for individual chicken pot pies

OVEN: 400°F
BAKE: 20–25 minutes

YIELD: 6 qt
PORTION: ½ cup per individual pie

Ingredient	Amount	Procedure
Flour, all-purpose	2 lb 4 oz	Combine dry ingredients.
Baking powder	1½ oz	
Salt	1 Tbsp	
Sugar, granulated	2 oz	
Milk	2 qt	Combine milk, egg yolks, and margarine.
Egg yolks, beaten	18 (11 oz)	Add to dry ingredients. Stir only enough to
Margarine, melted	4 oz	mix.
Egg whites	18 (1 lb 5 oz)	Beat egg whites until stiff. Fold into batter.
		Pour ½ cup batter over contents of each individual casserole. Pour around edges and then in center to form a thin covering over chicken mixture.

Note:
Batter may be refrigerated until needed. Thin mixture with cold milk if too thick.

YIELD: 50 portions
             5 loaves 5 × 9 inches
PORTION: 5 oz

	Amount	Procedure
...nverted ...er, boiling ...lt Vegetable oil (optional)	12 oz 1 qt 1½ tsp 2 tsp	Cook rice according to directions on p. 422.
Cooked chicken	6 lb	Dice chicken.
Pimiento, chopped Onion, grated	4 oz 2 oz	Combine chicken, cooked rice, pimiento, and onion. Mix lightly.
Eggs, beaten Salt Pepper, white Chicken Stock (p. 590) Milk Bread crumbs, soft	12 (1 lb 5 oz) 1 Tbsp ¾ tsp 1½ qt 3 cups 12 oz	Add remaining ingredients. Mix only until blended.
		Divide mixture into 5 greased loaf pans, 3 lb 2 oz per pan. Bake at 325°F for 1½ hours. Cut each loaf in 10 slices. Serve with Chicken Gravy (p. 566) or Mushroom Sauce (p. 560).

Notes:
1. 18–20 lb of chickens AP will yield approximately 6 lb cooked meat.
2. May be baked in 12 × 20 × 4-inch counter pan.
3. Turkey or tuna may be used in place of chicken.
4. ¼ oz (2 Tbsp) dehydrated onions, rehydrated in ¼ cup water, may be substituted for fresh onions (p. 50).

Szechwan chicken with cashews

YIELD: 50 portions
PORTION: 6 oz chicken
4 oz rice

Ingredient	Amount	Procedure
Salad oil	1 qt	Add ginger root and garlic to oil in stock pot.
Ginger root, fresh, sliced	½ oz	Heat, then remove ginger root and garlic and
Garlic	3 cloves	discard.
Chicken, raw, cut in cubes	6 lb	Add chicken to hot oil. Stir fry until chicken turns white, 3–5 minutes.
Green onions	1 lb 10 oz	Cut onions into 1-inch lengths.
Green peppers	4 lb	Cut peppers into 1-inch squares. Add to chicken mixture.
Mushrooms, pieces and stems, canned	4 lb	Add and stir fry 1–2 minutes.
Water chestnuts, sliced	1 lb	
Mushroom liquid plus water	1¾ qt	Combine and mix until smooth. Stir into chicken mixture. Cook and stir until thickened, 1–2 minutes.
Chicken base	1 oz	
Soy sauce	¼ cup	
Cornstarch	5 oz	
Cayenne	1 Tbsp	
Cashew nuts	1 lb	Stir in nuts and pimiento.
Pimiento, chopped	2 oz	
Rice, converted	3 lb 8 oz	Cook rice according to directions on p. 422.
Water, boiling	4¼ qt	Serve 6 oz chicken over 4 oz rice.
Salt	2 Tbsp	
Margarine	2 Tbsp	

Brunswick stew

YIELD: 50 portions
         3 gal
PORTION: 8 oz (1 cup)

Ingredient	Amount	Procedure
Cubed fresh pork	2 lb	Brown pork. Drain off fat.
Cooked chicken	7 lb 8 oz	Cube chicken.
Celery, diced Carrots, diced Potatoes, diced Onions, finely chopped	1 lb 8 oz 2 lb 4 oz 2 lb 10 oz	Cook vegetables until partially done.
Margarine Flour, all-purpose	8 oz 8 oz	Melt margarine in steam-jacketed or other large kettle. Add flour and stir until smooth.
Chicken Stock (p. 590) Salt Pepper, white	1 gal 1 Tbsp 1½ tsp	Add stock gradually, stirring constantly with wire whip. Add chicken, pork, and vegetables. Simmer until vegetables are tender. Do not overcook.
Green peas, frozen	1 lb	Add peas. Cook an additional 5 minutes. Stew should be fairly thick. Serve in soup bowls or deep plates.

Note:
If large fryers are used, cook 15 lb AP. Remove meat from bones and cube. Save broth for sauce.

Chicken pot pie

OVEN: 400°F	YIELD:	50 portions
BAKE: 20–25 minutes		2 pans 12 × 20 × 2 inches
	PORTION:	8 oz

Ingredient	Amount	Procedure
Margarine	12 oz	Sauté onions in margarine in steam-jacketed
Onions, chopped	14 oz	or other large kettle.
Flour, all-purpose	1 lb 6 oz	Add flour and pepper to onions. Stir until
Pepper, black	½ tsp	blended.
		Cook 30 minutes.
Chicken Stock (p. 590)	1¼ gal	Add stock, stirring constantly with wire whip.
		Cook until thickened, stirring often.
		Check for seasoning. Add salt if necessary.
Cooked chicken	6 lb	Cut chicken into ½- to ¾-inch pieces. Add to
		sauce.
Celery, sliced	1 lb 8 oz	Cook celery and carrots until partially done.
Carrots, sliced	2 lb	Drain. Fold into sauce.
Green peas, frozen	2 lb	Add peas uncooked to chicken mixture. Mix
		carefully.
		Scale chicken into two 12 × 20 × 2-inch
		counter pans, 12 lb per pan.
Pastry (p. 249)	3 lb	Roll out 1 lb 8 oz Pastry to fit each pan. Place
		on chicken mixture and seal edges to pan.
		Bake at 400°F for 20–25 minutes or until
		crust is done.

Notes:
1. 18–20 lb of chickens AP will yield approximately 6 lb cooked meat.
2. Chicken mixture may be topped with Baking Powder Biscuits (p. 116).
3. 1¾ oz (¾ cup) dehydrated onions, rehydrated in 1¼ cups water, may be substituted for fresh onions (p. 50).

Variations:
1. **Individual chicken pie with batter crust.**   Scale 8 oz hot chicken pie mixture into each of 50 casseroles. Pour ½ cup Batter Crust (p. 445) over each. Bake as above.
2. **Turkey pie.**   Substitute turkey for chicken.

Chicken soufflé

OVER: 325°F   YIELD: 48 portions
BAKE: 1 hour   2 pans 12 × 20 × 2 inches
                                       PORTION: 6 oz

Ingredient	Amount	Procedure
Cooked chicken	6 lb	Dice chicken.
Margarine	1 lb	Melt margarine. Add flour and seasonings. Stir until smooth.
Flour, all-purpose	4 oz	
Salt	1 oz (1½ Tbsp)	
Pepper, white	1 tsp	
Chicken Stock (p. 590)	2½ cups	Add stock and milk gradually, stirring constantly with wire whip.
Milk	3¾ qt	
Egg yolks, beaten	24 (15 oz)	Add egg yolks and crumbs to sauce and mix well.
Bread crumbs	1 lb	Add chicken and mix lightly.
Egg whites	24 (1 lb 12 oz)	Beat egg whites until they form a rounded peak. Fold into chicken mixture.
		Scale mixture into 2 greased 12 × 20 × 2-inch baking pans, 9 lb per pan. Bake at 325°F for 1 hour or until soufflé is set. Cut 4 × 6. Serve immediately. Serve with Béchamel Sauce (p. 563) or Mushroom Sauce (p. 564).

Note:
18–20 lb of chickens AP will yield approximately 6 lb cooked meat.

Variations:
1. **Ham soufflé.** Substitute coarsely ground cooked ham for chicken. Delete salt.
2. **Tuna soufflé.** Substitute tuna for chicken.
3. **Turkey soufflé.** Substitute turkey for chicken.

Chicken croquettes

| DEEP-FAT FRYER: 375°F | YIELD: 50 portions |
| FRY: 3–4 minutes | PORTION: 2 2½-oz croquettes |

Ingredient	Amount	Procedure
Cooked chicken	6 lb	Chop chicken finely.
Rice, converted Chicken Stock (p. 590)	1 lb 8 oz 3 qt	Cook rice in stock according to directions on p. 422.
Salt Celery salt Lemon juice Grated onion	1 oz (1½ Tbsp) 1 tsp 1 Tbsp 2 Tbsp	Add seasonings to rice. Mix lightly.
Flour, all-purpose Chicken Stock, cold	6 oz 2 cups	Make a smooth paste of flour and cold stock.
Chicken Stock	2 cups	Bring stock to boiling point. Add flour paste gradually, stirring with wire whip. Stir and cook until thick.
		Combine sauce, chicken, and rice. Mix well. Measure with No. 16 dipper onto greased baking sheets. Chill.
Eggs, beaten Milk Bread crumbs	6 (11 oz) 2 cups 1 lb 8 oz	Shape chicken mixture into croquettes. Mix eggs and milk. Dip croquettes into mixture, then roll in crumbs. Chill for 2 hours. Fry in deep fat for 3–4 minutes.

Notes:
1. 18–20 lb of chickens AP will yield approximately 6 lb cooked meat.
2. Croquettes may be baked at 350°F for about 30 minutes.

Variations:
1. **Ham croquettes.** Substitute ground cooked ham for chicken. Delete salt.
2. **Meat croquettes.** Substitute cooked chopped meat for chicken and Beef Stock for Chicken Stock. Add 2 oz finely chopped onion.

Chicken and noodles

OVEN: 350°F
BAKE: 30 minutes

YIELD: 50 portions
2 pans 12 × 20 × 2 inches
PORTION: 8 oz

Ingredient	Amount	Procedure
Cooked chicken	7 lb 8 oz	Cut chicken into ½-inch pieces.
Noodles Water, boiling Salt Vegetable oil	3 lb 3 gal 3 oz 1 Tbsp	Cook noodles according to directions on p. 402. Drain.
Margarine Onions, chopped	12 oz 2 oz	Melt margarine in a steam-jacketed or other large kettle. Add onions and sauté until tender.
Flour, all-purpose Salt	7 oz 1 Tbsp	Add flour and salt to onions. Stir until blended. Cook 5 minutes.

Chicken Stock (p. 590) or
    milk
	3½ qt	Add stock or milk gradually, stirring
		    constantly with wire whip.
		Cook until thickened.

		Combine chicken, cooked noodles, and sauce. Scale into two 12 × 20 × 2-inch counter pans, 11 lb 12 oz per pan. Bake at 350°F for 30 minutes.

Notes:
1. 20–22 lb of chickens AP will yield approximately 7 lb 8 oz cooked meat.
2. ¼ oz (2 Tbsp) dehydrated onion, rehydrated in ¼ cup water, may be substituted for fresh onions (p. 50).

Variations:
1. **Chicken and noodles with mushrooms.** Add 2 lb sliced mushrooms, sautéed with the onions.
2. **Pork and noodle casserole.** Substitute 10 lb pork, diced and cooked, for chicken.
3. **Turkey and noodle casserole.** Substitute cooked turkey for chicken (cook 18- to 20-lb turkey).

Chicken and rice casserole

OVEN: 350°F	YIELD: 50 portions
BAKE: 1 hour	2 pans 12 × 20 × 2 inches
	PORTION: 8 oz

Ingredient	Amount	Procedure
Cooked chicken	6 lb	Dice chicken.
Rice, converted	2 lb 8 oz	Cook rice according to directions on p. 422.
Water, boiling	2 qt	
Salt	2 Tbsp	
Margarine, melted	6 oz	Sauté onion, celery, and mushrooms in
Onion, chopped	3 oz	margarine.
Celery, chopped	8 oz	
Mushrooms, sliced	1 lb	
Flour, all-purpose	8 oz	Add flour to vegetables and stir to blend.
Milk	1½ qt	Add milk and stock, stirring constantly with
Chicken Stock (p. 590)	2 qt	wire whip.
Pepper, white	¼ tsp	Cook until thickened.
		Add pepper. Add salt if needed.
Almonds, slivered	6 oz	Add almonds, pimiento, and chicken to
Pimiento, chopped	3 oz	sauce. Combine carefully.
		Scale into two lightly greased 12 × 20 × 2-inch baking pans, 10 lb 8 oz per pan.
Bread crumbs	9 oz	Combine bread crumbs, margarine, and
Margarine, melted	3 oz	cheese.
Cheddar cheese, shredded	6 oz	Sprinkle over mixture in pans, 9 oz per pan.
		Bake at 350°F for 1 hour or until heated through.

Notes:
1. 18–20 lb of chickens AP will yield approximately 6 lb cooked meat.
2. Sliced water chestnuts may be substituted for almonds.
3. Chopped parsley may be sprinkled over the baked product just before serving.
4. ¼ oz (2 Tbsp) dehydrated onions, rehydrated in ¼ cup water, may be substituted for fresh onions (p. 50).

Turkey divan

OVEN: 350°F	YIELD: 50 portions
BAKE: 15 minutes	PORTION: 3 oz broccoli
	2 oz turkey

Ingredient	Amount	Procedure
Broccoli spears, fresh or frozen	10 lb EP	Cook broccoli according to directions on p. 636. Arrange in 3-oz portions in two 12 × 20 × 2-inch counter pans.
Margarine, melted	8 oz	Pour margarine over broccoli.
Salt Pepper, black Parmesan cheese, grated	1 oz (1½ Tbsp) ½ tsp 9 oz	Sprinkle broccoli with salt, pepper, and cheese.
Cooked turkey roll or breast	7 lb	Slice turkey in 2-oz portions. Arrange turkey slices over broccoli. Serving will be easier if edges of turkey slices are tucked under the broccoli portions.
Margarine Flour, all-purpose Salt	12 oz 6 oz 1 oz (1½ Tbsp)	Melt margarine. Add flour and salt. Stir until blended. Cook 5 minutes.
Milk	3 qt	Add milk, stirring constantly with wire whip. Cook until thickened.
Egg yolks, slightly beaten	1 cup	Add egg yolks to sauce. Stir until blended. Pour sauce over turkey and broccoli. Bake at 350°F for 15 minutes or until bubbly and golden brown.

Note:
Turkey or Chicken Stock may be substituted for part of milk in sauce; salt may then need to be reduced.

Turkey and dumplings

YIELD: 48 portions
 2 pans 12 × 20 × 2 inches
PORTION: 8 oz

Ingredient	Amount	Procedure
Margarine	14 oz	Melt margarine in steam-jacketed or other
Onions, chopped	1 lb	kettle. Sauté onions until tender.
Flour, all-purpose	1 lb 8 oz	Stir flour and pepper into onions. Cook for 5–
Pepper, black	1½ tsp	10 minutes, stirring often.
Water	1½ gal	Add water and chicken base to mixture in
Chicken base	6 oz	kettle. Cook until thickened, stirring often.
Turkey roll, cooked	6 lb 10 oz	Cut turkey into ½-inch cubes. Add to sauce.
Celery, chopped	1 lb 10 oz	Steam celery and carrots until tender-crisp.
Carrots, sliced	2 lb 4 oz	Fold into turkey mixture. Scale into two 12 × 20 × 2-inch pans, 13 lb per pan.

STEAMED DUMPLINGS

Ingredient	Amount	Procedure
Flour, all-purpose	2 lb 4 oz	Combine flour, baking powder, and salt in
Baking powder	3 oz	mixer bowl. Mix until blended.
Salt	2 Tbsp	
Eggs, beaten	5 (9 oz)	Combine eggs, milk, and seasonings.
Milk	1½ qt	Add to dry ingredients and mix only until
Parsley, fresh, chopped	1 oz	blended.
Poultry seasoning	2 tsp	Portion 4 × 6 with No. 24 dipper onto turkey and gravy. Steam for 20 minutes.

Notes:
1. Steam as soon as dumplings are portioned onto gravy. Product holds well after cooking.
2. 2 oz (1 cup) dehydrated onions, rehydrated in 1½ cups water, may be substituted for fresh onions (p. 50).

Singapore curry

YIELD: 50 portions
PORTION: 8 oz curry
           6 oz rice

Ingredient	Amount	Procedure
Cooked chicken	15 lb	Cut chicken into ¾-inch pieces.
Margarine Flour, all-purpose	1 lb 1 lb 4 oz	Melt margarine in steam-jacketed or other large kettle. Add flour and stir until smooth. Cook 5 minutes.
Chicken Stock (p. 590) Salt Pepper, white Curry powder	5 qt 1 tsp ½ tsp 2 oz	Add stock gradually, stirring constantly with wire whip. Cook until thickened. Add salt, pepper, and curry powder. Add chicken and stir gently to prevent breaking of chicken pieces. Taste and add more seasonings as the chicken takes up the curry flavor. It should be quite yellow and have a distinct curry flavor.
Rice, converted Salt Water, boiling	5 lb 3 oz 6¼ qt	Cook rice according to directions on p. 422. This amount of rice will allow very generous servings.
French fried onion rings Tomatoes, fresh, sliced Bananas, cut in thick slices or chunks Pineapple chunks, drained Coconut, shredded or flaked Salted peanuts Chutney	50 servings 10 lb 10 lb 1 No. 10 can 1 lb 8 oz 1 lb 2 1-lb jars	Serve curried chicken over rice, with accompaniments. See directions for serving in Note 2.

Notes:

    1. Shrimp, veal, lamb, or a combination of chicken and pork may be used, allowing 6 oz cooked meat per person.

2. For a Singapore Curry dinner, arrange foods on a buffet table in the following order: rice, curried chicken or other meat, and accompaniments in the order listed in the recipe. Each guest serves rice in the center of the plate, dips a generous serving of curried meat over the rice, and then adds accompaniments as desired.

Corn bread dressing

OVEN: 375°F
BAKE: 20–30 minutes

YIELD: 50 portions
1 pan 12 × 20 × 2 inches
PORTION: 4 oz

Ingredient	Amount	Procedure
Corn Bread (p. 126)	3 lb 10 oz	Prepare Corn Bread. Crumble.
Bread, cubed or torn	1 lb 12 oz	Crumble bread. Add to Corn Bread.
Margarine Onions, chopped Celery, chopped	4 oz 1 lb 1 lb 8 oz	Melt margarine in steam-jacketed or other kettle. Add onions and celery. Sauté until vegetables are tender. Add bread.
Chicken base Water, hot Salt[a] Poultry seasoning Pepper, black	2 oz 3 qt 1 tsp 1 Tbsp 1 tsp	Combine chicken base, water, and seasonings. Pour over bread mixture. Stir to moisten.
		Scale mixture (12 lb) into lightly greased 12 × 20 × 2-inch pan. Bake at 375°F for 20–30 minutes or until hot. Serve with No. 12 dipper.

[a] If chicken base is highly salted, reduce or delete salt in recipe.

Bread dressing (or stuffing)

OVEN: 325°F
BAKE: 1 hour 15 minutes

YIELD: 50 portions
             1 pan 12 × 20 × 2 inches
PORTION: 4½ oz

Ingredient	Amount	Procedure
Onion, chopped	1 lb	Sauté onion and celery in margarine until lightly browned.
Celery, chopped (optional)	1 lb	
Margarine	1 lb	
Water[a]	1 gal	Add water, chicken base, and seasonings to sautéed vegetables. Heat until hot.
Chicken base	3 oz	
Salt[b]	1 Tbsp	
Pepper, black	1 Tbsp	
Poultry seasoning[c]	1 Tbsp	
Thyme	1 Tbsp	
Dry bread, cubed	3 lb 12 oz	Add bread gradually to vegetable mixture, tossing lightly until thoroughly mixed. Avoid overmixing, which causes dressing to be soggy and compact.
		Scale dressing (15 lb) into lightly greased 12 × 20 × 2-inch pan. Bake at 325°F for 1 hour 15 minutes. Serve with No. 10 dipper.

[a] The amount of liquid will depend on the dryness of the bread.
[b] If chicken base is highly salted, reduce or delete salt in recipe.
[c] Sage may be used for part or all of the poultry seasoning.

Variations:
1. **Apple stuffing.**   Add 1 lb finely chopped apples. Reduce bread cubes to 3 lb 4 oz.
2. **Chestnut stuffing.**   Add 1 lb 4 oz cooked chestnuts, chopped. Reduce bread to 3 lb 8 oz. Substitute 2 qt milk for 2 qt water.
3. **Mushroom stuffing.**   Reduce celery and onions to 8 oz each. Sauté 2 lb fresh mushrooms with the vegetables.
4. **Nut stuffing.**   Add 2 cups chopped almonds or pecans that have been browned lightly in 4 oz melted margarine. Substitute 1 qt milk for 1 qt water.
5. **Oyster stuffing.**   Add 1 lb 8 oz oysters.
6. **Raisin stuffing.**   Add 1 lb seedless raisins.
7. **Sausage stuffing.**   Reduce bread cubes to 3 lb 4 oz. Add 2 lb sausage, cooked and drained, and 1 lb tart apples, peeled and chopped.

SALADS & SALAD DRESSINGS

SALADS

Salads are popular menu items, versatile enough to be served in a variety of ways. Appetizer salads are served as a first course and play an important role in stimulating the appetite and creating a sense of anticipation for the remainder of the meal. The visual appearance as well as taste and flavor combinations must be considered.

Accompaniment salads are considered side dishes to the entree. These salads should be selected carefully so that the flavor and food group characteristics will be in harmony. Many accompaniment salads have traditional significance: turkey and cranberries, pork and applesauce, sandwiches and pasta or potato salad, and fish and cole slaw.

Entree salads have become an upscale approach to dining, particularly at the noon meal and among the health-conscious patron. Other than bread or crackers and a beverage, the salad is generally the only menu item, making the ingredient selections especially important. Entree salads should be substantial in the amount of food provided, and they may include at least one ingredient that is a source of protein. The salad should be fresh in appearance and attractive in design.

A salad course is occasionally offered after the entree. The objective is to "cleanse the palate" in preparation for dessert. The salad served as a separate course should be light and refreshing. Fruit salads or lightly dressed delicate greens are appropriate choices.

With the exception of separate course salads, which are always served, the presentation of salads may be either individually placed and served or self-service from a buffet line or salad bar. The choice of method will depend on the clientele expectations and objectives of the foodservice.

Placed salads

Placed salads may be served to the patron either after they have been seated, on the table as for some banquets and catered functions, or a la carte from a cafeteria counter. Regardless of the serving method, the principles of placed salad construction are the same:

- Select plates or bowls that are appropriately sized and will add to the attractiveness of the salad.

- Place salad green underliners on the dish. The curly edge should be at the back and top of the salad and should not extend over the edge of the plate. Tossed green salads usually have no underliner.
- To gain height, place chopped lettuce on the underliner and under salad ingredients.
- Place the main salad ingredients neatly on the plate. They should be prepared and arranged attractively with careful consideration given to color and balance.
- Garnish appropriately to give accent in color and flavor.
- Keep chilled and sprinkle with salad dressing just before serving or pass dressings for individual service.

Salad bars

Salad bars have expanded the selection of items available and are very popular in many types of foodservices. For a salad bar to be successful, enough variety must be offered so that patrons will enjoy creating their own salad. See Table 2.18 for components of a basic salad bar and Figure 2.34 for a suggested salad bar arrangement.

Basic rules for salad bars are as follows:

- The salad bar should be equipped with a sneeze guard, and standards of good sanitation should be maintained. A clean plate should be used each time a patron visits the salad bar.
- A salad bar should look well supplied throughout the serving period. This purpose can be accomplished by selecting appropriate size containers and resupplying them when one-half to two-thirds empty. Avoid arranging too few food items on plates that will look empty after only a few servings are taken.
- Spills, drips, and misplaced food items should be cleaned up regularly. Arranging food containers so spills are reduced is important, and items that could become unsightly should be placed where they will be easy to reach without spilling onto other food. Correct serving utensils will help eliminate untidiness.
- The selections should be varied and creative enough to appeal to many different people. The variety of items offered should be changed periodically when serving repeat customers.

Salad ingredients and their preparation

Many salad ingredients may be purchased that have some or all of the preliminary preparation completed. Torn salad greens, prepared grapefruit sections, and diced

TABLE 2.18   BASIC SALAD BAR COMPONENTS

Item	Number of choices[a]	Ideas for choices
Greens	1 bowl	Combine 2–3 different greens. See below for types of greens.
Fresh vegetables	2–3 containers	Alfalfa sprouts, broccoli, cabbage (red or green), carrots, cauliflower, celery, cucumber, green onions, mushrooms, peppers (red, green, yellow), radishes, snow peas, tomatoes, zucchini
Toppings	1–2 containers	Bacon bits, garbanzo beans, croutons, pickles, olives, peanuts, raisins, sesame seeds, sunflower seeds
Gelatin	1–2 molds	Fruit or vegetable gelatin salads
Fruit, pasta, and vegetable salads	2–3 containers	Rice salads, potato salad, pasta salad, ambrosia, applesauce, other fruit or marinated vegetable salads
Protein	1–2 containers	Chopped hard-cooked eggs, egg salad, meat salad, cottage cheese, shredded cheese
Crackers and bread	1 basket	Variety crackers, warm breads
Dressings	3–4 containers	Blue cheese, buttermilk, French, Italian, oil and vinegar, Thousand Island

[a] More choices are appropriate if the salad bar or buffet serving area can accommodate the variety.

or chopped vegetables are examples. In many foodservices, however, salad ingredients are prepared on the premises. Information about the most commonly used salad ingredients and their preparation is provided in the following sections.

SALAD GREENS

Major types   Many kinds of greens may be used for salads. The most common ones are described below and shown in Figure 2.35.

Iceberg lettuce (Head lettuce).   The most popular lettuce used in green salads. Firm round heads ranging in color from bright to light green. Mild in flavor; combines well with other greens.

Bibb lettuce.   Small cup-shaped lettuce with a deep rich green color that

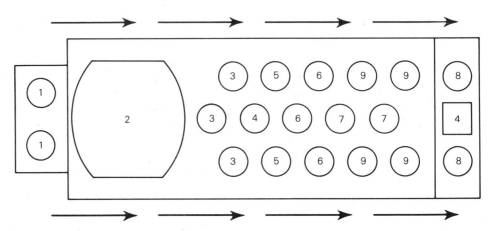

Figure 2.34 *Suggested salad bar arrangement: (1) plates and bowls; (2) greens; (3) fresh vegetables; (4) toppings; (5) gelatins; (6) fruit, pasta, and vegetable salads; (7) protein salads; (8) crackers and breads; (9) dressings.*

blends into whitish green near the core. Flavor is buttery and sweet, texture delicate and tender.

    Boston lettuce.   Soft pliable leaf and delicate sweet flavor. Not as tender or sweet as Bibb lettuce. Deep green outside blending to light yellow near the core.

    Leaf lettuce.   Most varieties have soft fragile leaves with curly edges. Color varies by variety but may be all green or various shades of red. May be mixed with other greens in a combination salad or used as an underliner or garnish.

    Romaine or cos.   Long, loaf-shaped head and long, narrow leaves. Tender, sweet, and tasty. Coarse dark green outer leaves and golden-yellow inner ones. Used in combination salads.

    Belgian or French endive.   An upright, thin, elongated stock resembling a spear. Off-white or pale green color. Served typically as a small, separate course salad after a meal.

    Curly endive.   A bunchy head with narrow, ragged-edge leaves. Mild center leaves, slightly bitter outer leaves. Used sparingly in combination salads. Primarily used for underliners and garnishing.

    Escarole.   A variety of endive with broad leaves that do not curl at the tips. Texture is coarse and slightly tough, flavor somewhat bitter. May be mixed sparingly with other greens.

    Spinach.   Curly dark green flat leaves. Very young tender leaves are often served fresh, more mature leaves cooked.

    Kale.   A hardy dark green, curly leaf. Often used as a garnish for salad bars, or may be cooked.

Figure 2.35 *Salad greens. Photo courtesy of the United Fresh Fruit and Vegetable Association.*

Celery cabbage (Chinese cabbage). Long oval-shaped head with broad white ribs. Mild cabbage flavor, tender and crisp.

Preparation Greens should be clean, crisp, chilled, and well drained. It may be necessary to separate leaves for thorough washing. Wash in a spray of water or in a large container of water. Shake off excess water, drain thoroughly, and refrigerate. Draining in a colander or on a rack placed on a baking sheet will keep the greens from standing in water while chilling. Cover with a clean damp cloth or plastic to prevent dehydration.

When preparing head lettuce for garnish, remove stem end or core (Figure 2.36). Hold inverted head under cold, running water to loosen tightly wrapped leaves. Do not soak. Turn heads open-side down to drain. Separate the leaves and stack 6 or 7 leaves to a nest. Invert and pack in a covered container or plastic bag. Refrigerate 2 hours or more to complete crisping.

Leaf lettuce is convenient to use for salad liners. Wash lettuce thoroughly (Figure 2.37). Cut stem end and place in perforated pan to drain. Chill 2 to 3 hours for crisping.

Spinach should be carefully examined, removing veins and tough stems. Discard all dry, yellow, wilted, or decayed leaves. Wash first in tepid water, then in cold, as many times as necessary to remove sand.

VEGETABLES

Whether vegetables are used raw or cooked, strive to preserve their shape, color, flavor, and crispness. Marinating in a well-seasoned French dressing adds flavor.

Figure 2.36 *Coring head lettuce. (a) Hit stem end of lettuce sharply on flat surface. (b) Remove loosened core.*

Figure 2.37 *Preparing leaf lettuce. (a) Wash lettuce under cold running water. (b) Remove stem end by cutting with a sharp knife. (c) Place leaf end up in a perforated pan to drain. Chill 2 to 3 hours to crisp.*

Asparagus.   Break or cut off tough part of stems. Thoroughly wash remaining portions. Cook and marinate in French Dressing (Light).

Beans, dry.   Cook, keeping beans whole (p. 626).

Beans, green.   Leave whole or cut lengthwise. Wash, cook, and marinate.

Beets.   Wash, cook, peel, remove any blemishes. Cut into desired shape and marinate.

Cabbage.   Remove outer leaves. Wash heads, cut into 4–6 pieces. Remove center stalk. Shred remaining portions as desired with a long sharp knife or shredder. Crisp in ice water 15–30 minutes.

Carrots.   Pare and remove blemishes. Cut into wedges, rounds, or strips.

Grind, shred, or cook; then cut into desired shapes and marinate. For carrot curls, see Relishes, p. 472.

Cauliflower. Remove all leaves and cut away dark spots. Separate into florets, leaving 1-inch stem. Soak in salt water (1 oz salt or ⅓ cup vinegar per gal). Cauliflower may be cooked and marinated, or it may be marinated and served raw (Figures 2.38 and 2.39).

Celery. Separate outer stalks from the heart. (Outer stalks may be used for soup.) Wash, trim, and remove bruised and blemished parts and strings. If necessary to sanitize, add 1 Tbsp household bleach to each gallon of water. Submerge celery for 30 seconds. Rinse well. Air dry. Use within 8 hours. To dice, cut lengthwise. Several stalks may be cut at one time. Place on a board and cut crosswise with a French knife. For celery curls, see p. 472.

Celery cabbage. Remove outer leaves and wash. Shred as lettuce or cut into 1- to 2-inch slices.

Chives. Remove roots and any objectionable portions. Wash. Drain. Cut leaves crosswise with a sharp knife or scissors.

Figure 2.38 *Cruciferous vegetables. Shown are brussels sprouts, kohlrabi, red cabbage, turnips, broccoli, cauliflower, and nappa. Photo courtesy of the United Fresh Fruit and Vegetable Association.*

Figure 2.39 *Less commonly used produce adds variety to the menu. Photo courtesy of the United Fresh Fruit and Vegetable Association.*

Cucumbers.   Wash and peel, or score lengthwise with a fork. Crisp and let stand in salted ice water 15 minutes. Cut into slices or wedges.

Green peppers.   Wash. Remove seeds and stems. Cut into rings or strips, or dice or chop.

Onions.   Pour water over onions to cover. Under water, remove wilted leaves, outer layer of the bulb, firm root end, and all bruised or decayed parts. Cut as desired (Figure 2.40).

Potatoes.   Peel. Remove eyes and bruised parts. Cut into ½-inch cubes and cook; or wash, cook with skins on, peel, and dice. Marinate 2 hours before using.

Tomatoes.   Wash and peel. If skins are difficult to remove, place in a wire basket and dip in boiling water until skins begin to loosen. Dip in cold water and remove skins. Chill.

Turnips.   Remove tops, wash, pare by hand. Shred or cut into fine strips.

FRESH FRUITS

Apples.   Wash, pare, core, remove bruises and spots. If the skins are tender and the desired color, do not pare.

To dice, cut into rings and dice with sectional cutter. Drop diced pieces into salad dressing, lemon, pineapple, or other acid fruit juice to prevent discoloration. If diced apple is placed in fruit juice, drain before using in a salad.

To section, cut into uniform pieces, with the widest part of the section not more than ½ inch thick. Remove core from each section. If the peeling has not been removed, score it in several places to facilitate cutting when it is served. Prevent discoloration by the same method as for diced apples, only do not use salad dressing.

Apricots.   Cut into halves or sections and remove seed. Remove skins if desired.

Avocados.   If hard, ripen at room temperature. Peel shortly before serving, cut into halves or quarters, and remove seed. Slice, dice, or cut into balls. Dip into French dressing or lemon juice to prevent discoloration.

Bananas.   Remove skins and bruised or discolored parts. Cut into strips, sections, wedges, or slices. Dip each piece into pineapple juice, other acid fruit juice, or salad dressing to prevent discoloration.

Cantaloupes and other melons.   Pare, dice, and cut into balls, or cut into uniform wedges or strips (Figure 2.41).

Cherries and grapes.   Wash, drain, halve, and remove seeds. To frost, brush with slightly beaten egg white. Sprinkle with sugar. Let dry before using.

Grapefruit.   For sections, select large grapefruit, wash and dry. Cut off a thick layer of skin from the top and bottom. Place grapefruit on cutting board, start at the top, and cut toward the board (Figure 2.42). Always cut with a downward stroke and deeply enough to remove all the white membrane. Turn grapefruit while cutting. When paring is completed and pulp is exposed, remove sections by cutting along the membrane of one section to the center of the fruit.

Figure 2.40 *Types of onions used in food production. Photo courtesy of the United Fresh Fruit and Vegetable Association.*

Figure 2.41 *Melons are available in many varieties. (clockwise from top left): watermelon, casaba, Persian, Crenshaw, cantaloupe, honeydew, and Santa Claus. Photo courtesy of the United Fresh Fruit and Vegetable Association.*

Turn the knife and force the blade along the membrane of the next section to the exterior of the fruit. Repeat for each section.

Kiwi.   Peel and slice crosswise.

Oranges.   Peel, section as grapefruit, or slice or dice (Figure 2.42).

Peaches.   Remove skins only a short time before using. Peel or submerge in boiling water for a few seconds and remove skins. Chill. Cut into halves, wedges, or slices. Drop into acid fruit juice to prevent discoloration.

Pears.   Peel and remove core and seeds a short time before serving. Cut into halves, wedges, or slices. Dipping in lemon juice or other acid fruit juice will prevent oxidation and discoloration.

Pineapples.   Remove crown by holding pineapple in one hand and crown in the other, then twisting in opposite directions (Figure 2.43). Trim top of pineapple and cut off base. Using a sharp knife, remove peel by using a downward cutting motion. Remove eyes by making narrow wedge-shaped grooves into the pineapple. Cut diagonally around the fruit, following the pattern of the eyes. Cut away as little of the fruit as possible. Cut pineapple vertically into eighths, then cut hard center core from each spear. To make pineapple chunks, cut each spear into pieces of the desired size.

Pomegranates.   Cut open and remove seeds. Discard peeling and white membrane.

CANNED FRUIT

Select whole pieces uniform in size and shape and with a firm appearance. Drain. If cubes or sections are desired, cut into pieces uniform in size and shape with well-defined edges. Pieces should not be too small.

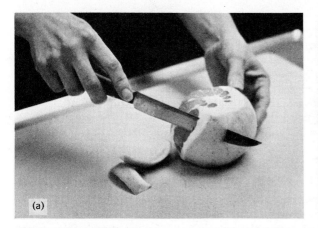 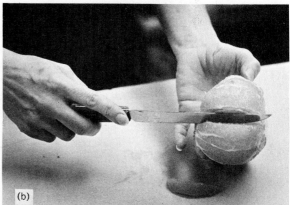

Figure 2.42 *Peeling and sectioning grapefruit: (a) Cut layer of peel from top and bottom of grapefruit. Using a sharp knife, remove peel. Cut with a downward stroke and deeply enough to remove all the white membrane. (b) Section grapefruit by cutting along membrane of one section to the center of the fruit. Turn the knife and force the blade along the membrane of the next section.*

Figure 2.43 *Preparing fresh pineapple: (a) Remove crown by holding pineapple in one hand and crown in the other, then twisting in opposite directions. (b) Trim top of pineapple and cut off base. Using a sharp knife, remove peel by using a downward cutting motion. (c) Remove eyes by making narrow wedge-shaped grooves into the pineapple. Cut diagonally around the fruit, following the pattern of the eyes. Cut away as little of the fruit as possible. (d) Cut pineapple vertically into eighths, then cut the hard center core from each spear. To make pineapple chunks, cut each spear into pieces of the desired size.*

RELISHES

Carrot curls.   Cut long, paper-thin slices. Roll each strip around finger, fasten with toothpick, and chill in ice water for several hours.

Carrot sticks.   Cut carrots into thin strips. Chill in ice water for several hours.

Celery curls or fans.   Cut celery into 2½-inch lengths. Make lengthwise cuts ⅛ inch apart about 1 inch in length on one or both ends of celery strips. Place in ice water about 2 hours before serving.

Celery rings. Cut celery into 2-inch lengths and then into pieces ⅛ inch thick. Place in ice water for several hours. Each strip of celery will form a ring.

Green pepper rings. Remove stem and seeds. Cut into thin slices.

Green pepper sticks. Cut pepper lengthwise into narrow strips.

Radish accordions. Cut long radishes not quite through into 10–12 narrow slices. Place in ice water. Slices will fan out accordion-style.

Radish roses. Cut off root end of radish with sharp knife. Leave an inch or two of the green stem. Cut 4 or 5 petal-shaped slices around the radish from cut tip to center. Place radishes in ice water, and petals will open.

OTHER FOODS

Almonds, blanched. To blanch almonds, cover with boiling water and let stand until skins will slip. Drain. Cover with cold water and rub off skins. Place skinned almonds between dry clean towels to remove water.

Almonds, toasted. Spread blanched almonds in a shallow pan in a thin layer. Heat at 250°F, stirring occasionally until nuts are light brown in color.

Cheese. Grate, shred, or cut in tiny cubes; or soften and put through a pastry tube.

Chicken or turkey. Cook, remove skin, gristle, and bone. Cut into ⅓-inch cubes. Marinate if desired. Mix with dressing and other ingredients just before serving.

Eggs. Hard-cook (p. 306). Use whole, halved, sliced, or sectioned. Slice or mince whites. Force yolks through ricer.

Fish. Cook, remove skin and bones. Flake. Marinate if desired. Mix with dressing just before serving. See p. 332 for preparation of crab, lobster, and shrimp.

Meat. Cut cooked meat into ⅓-inch cubes. Marinate with French or Italian dressing. Mix just before serving.

Nuts. Heat in hot oven to freshen if desired. Use whole, shredded, or chopped.

SALAD DRESSINGS

A salad dressing's function is to "dress" or accent the salad; it should not mask the flavor of the other ingredients. Care should be taken to choose an appropriate dressing to match the salad.

The basic ingredients of a salad dressing are oil and either vinegar or other acid food such as lemon juice. Added to the basic ingredients are emulsifiers or binding agents. Temporary emulsifiers may be herbs, spices, sugar, and salt. More permanent emulsifiers include egg yolk, as in mayonnaise, or a starch paste and egg mixture, as in a cooked dressing.

Salad dressings should be stored in glass, plastic, or stainless steel containers with tight-fitting lids at 40–50°F.

SALAD RECIPES
Vegetable and pasta salads

Basic mixed green salad

		YIELD: 50 portions
		10 lb
		PORTION: 3 oz

Ingredient	Amount	Procedure
Head lettuce (iceberg)	7 lb	Cut or tear lettuce and other greens into bite-sized pieces. (Use sharp steel-bladed knife if greens are cut.)
Leaf lettuce, Bibb or romaine	3 lb	
French dressing, oil and vinegar, or Italian dressing	1¼ qt	Just before serving, toss lightly with dressing, or portion greens into individual salad bowls, 3 oz per bowl, and serve with choice of dressings.

Notes:
   1. Any combination of salad greens may be used. For contrast, mix dark greens with light, crisp with tender, and smooth leaves with curly. With pale iceberg lettuce, use dark green spinach, romaine, curly endive, or red-tipped leaf lettuce.
   2. If serving on a salad bar, place greens in a large bowl and offer choice of dressing and garnishes (see p. 475).

Variations:
1. **Hawaiian tossed salad.**   To 7 lb mixed greens, add sections from 8 grapefruit, 8 oranges, 4 avocados, and 1 fresh pineapple, cubed. Serve with Honey French Dressing, p. 526.
2. **Salad greens with grapefruit.**   Place 3 oz greens in each bowl. Garnish each with 3 sections of pink grapefruit. Serve with Poppy Seed Dressing (p. 529) or French Dressing (Light) (p. 525).
3. **Spinach salad.**   Use 4 lb lettuce and 6 lb fresh spinach, 2 bunches green onions, sliced, and 12 eggs hard-cooked and sliced. To serve, toss lightly with French Dressing (Light) (p. 525) or Dijon Mustard Vinaigrette Dressing (p. 528) and portion into bowls. Sprinkle with bacon (1 lb) that has been diced, cooked until crisp, and drained.
4. **Spinach mushroom salad.**   Use 10 lb fresh spinach (may be part lettuce), 4 lb fresh mushrooms, sliced, and 2 bunches green onions, sliced. Toss lightly with French Dressing (Light) (p. 525) just before serving. Sprinkle with cooked crumbled bacon if desired.

Tossed vegetable salad

	YIELD:	50 portions
		10 lb
	PORTION:	3 oz

Ingredient	Amount	Procedure
Salad greens[a]	7 lb	Wash greens thoroughly and drain. Tear into bite-sized pieces.
Salad ingredients[b]	3 lb	Add salad ingredients to greens. Toss lightly. Portion into individual salad bowls or plates, 3 oz per portion.
Garnish[c]	As needed	Garnish salads if desired.
Salad dressing[d]	1¼ qt	Serve with choice of dressings. If preferred, French, Italian, or oil and vinegar dressing may be added to the salad just before serving.

[a] **Salad greens.**   Select one or more: iceberg, leaf, Bibb, Boston, or romaine lettuce, endive, spinach, escarole, celery cabbage, watercress. See Figure 2.35 for kinds of lettuce.

[b] **Salad ingredients.**   Select one or more: diagonally sliced asparagus, sliced Jerusalem artichokes, artichoke hearts, sliced avocado, bean sprouts, garbanzo beans, broccoli florets or sliced broccoli stems, chopped or shredded red cabbage, shredded or thinly sliced carrots, sliced cauliflower florets, sliced or diced celery, sliced or diced cucumbers, sliced green onions or scallions, diced green peppers, sliced fresh mushrooms, cooked green peas, sliced radishes, halved cherry tomatoes, fresh tomato wedges, sliced water chestnuts, sliced zucchini.

[c] **Garnishes.**   Alfalfa sprouts, crumbled crisp-cooked bacon, crumbled blue cheese, shredded cheddar cheese, cheese strips or cubes, seasoned croutons, sliced or quartered hard-cooked eggs, sliced olives, onion rings (fresh or French fried), parsley sprig, green pepper rings or strips, sunflower seeds, cherry tomatoes, tomato wedges, toasted wheat germ.

[d] **Salad dressings.**   French, Italian, Oil and Vinegar, Roquefort, Thousand Island, Buttermilk, Horseradish Cream, Green Peppercorn Cream, Sour Cream Basil.

Brown bean salad

YIELD: 50 portions
6 qt
PORTION: ½ cup (4 oz)

Ingredient	Amount	Procedure
Eggs, hard-cooked (p. 306)	12	Peel and dice eggs.
Brown or kidney beans	1½ No. 10 cans	Rinse beans with cold water. Drain.
Celery, diced	12 oz	Combine with beans. Add eggs.
Green pepper, chopped	3 oz	
Onion, minced	3 oz	
Pickle relish	10 oz	
Salad dressing or mayonnaise	3 cups	Combine and add to bean mixture. Mix lightly.
Salt	2 Tbsp	
Vinegar, cider	¾ cup	

Notes:
1. 4 lb dried beans, cooked according to directions on p. 622, may be substituted for canned beans.
2. Great Northern or pinto beans may be substituted for half of the kidney beans.

Garbanzo bean salad

YIELD: 50 portions
4½ qt
PORTION: ⅓ cup (3 oz)

Ingredient	Amount	Procedure
Garbanzo beans, canned	2 lb 8 oz	Rinse beans with cold water. Drain.
Red beans, canned	1 lb 8 oz	
Pinto beans, canned	2 lb	
Celery, sliced	1 lb	Combine with beans.
Cucumbers, peeled and sliced	12 oz	
Green onions, sliced	5 oz	
Radishes, sliced	8 oz	
Black olives, sliced	4 oz	
French Dressing (Light), p. 525	1 cup	Pour dressing over bean mixture. Toss lightly. Marinate for 2 hours.

Notes:
1. Cooked Great Northern beans may be substituted for garbanzo beans.
2. Vegetable Marinade (p. 579) may be substituted for French Dressing (Light).

Variation:
Garbanzo pasta salad. Delete pinto beans. Cook 8 oz shell macaroni to the *al dente* stage. Combine with other ingredients.

Triple bean salad

YIELD: 50 portions
        6 qt
PORTION: ½ cup (4 oz)

Ingredient	Amount	Procedure
Green beans, French style or cut	3 lb 8 oz (1 No. 10 can)	Drain green and wax beans thoroughly.
Wax beans, cut	2 lb 8 oz	
Kidney beans, canned	3 lb	Rinse kidney beans. Drain.
Onion, thinly sliced	1 lb 8 oz	Add onion, green pepper, and seasonings to beans.
Green pepper, diced	6 oz	Cover. Marinate overnight in the refrigerator.
Vinegar	3 cups	
Sugar, granulated	1 lb 8 oz	
Soy sauce	¼ cup	
Celery salt	¼ cup	
Salt	2 tsp	
Pepper, black	2 tsp	
Salad oil	1 cup	Just before serving, drain vegetables well. Add oil and toss lightly. Serve with No. 12 dipper.

Variations:
1. **Cauliflower bean salad.**   Delete kidney beans and add 3 lb cauliflower florets, slightly cooked.
2. **Oriental bean salad.**   Delete kidney beans. Add 1 lb 8 oz cooked red beans, drained and rinsed, and 1 lb 8 oz bean sprouts.

Carrot raisin salad

YIELD: 50 portions
4¼ qt
PORTION: ⅓ cup (2½ oz)

Ingredient	Amount	Procedure
Raisins	8 oz	Soften raisins in steamer or simmer in a small amount of water for about 3 minutes.
Carrots, raw	7 lb AP	Peel carrots. Shred or grind coarsely. Combine with raisins.
Mayonnaise	2 cups	Mix mayonnaise, salad dressing, and salt.
Salad dressing	2 cups	Add to carrot raisin mixture. Mix lightly.
Salt	1 Tbsp	Serve with No. 12 dipper.

Variations:
1. **Carrot celery salad.** Omit raisins. Use 5 lb ground carrots. Add 2 lb chopped celery and 2 oz sugar.
2. **Carrot-apple-celery salad.** Substitute 3 lb diced apples for 2 lb carrots.
3. **Carrot-celery-cucumber salad.** Use 4 lb 8 oz shredded carrots, 1 lb 8 oz chopped celery, and 1 lb 8 oz chopped cucumber.
4. **Carrot coconut salad.** Substitute 1 lb toasted coconut for raisins.

Marinated carrots

YIELD: 50 portions
PORTION: ⅓ cup (3 oz)

Ingredient	Amount	Procedure
Carrots, fresh, cut in ¼-inch slices	5 lb	Cook carrots until tender-crisp. Drain.
Tomato soup	2 cups	Combine and heat to boiling point.
Sugar, granulated	1 lb	Pour over warm carrots.
Salad oil	½ cup	Marinate for at least 4 hours.
Vinegar	1½ cups	
Salt	2 tsp	
Pepper, black	1 tsp	
Prepared mustard	1 Tbsp	
Worcestershire sauce	1 Tbsp	
Onions, chopped	12 oz	
Green pepper, chopped	3 oz	

Notes:
1. Frozen crinkle-sliced carrots, cooked until tender-crisp, may be substituted for fresh carrots.
2. Marinated carrots will keep in the refrigerator for a week.

Carrifruit salad

YIELD: 50 portions
4½ qt
PORTION: ⅓ cup (3 oz)

Ingredient	Amount	Procedure
Carrots, shredded	4 lb 8 oz	Combine ingredients. Mix lightly.
Pineapple tidbits, drained	2 lb 12 oz	
Flaked coconut	8 oz	
Miniature marshmallows	9 oz	
Mayonnaise	2¼ cups	Mix mayonnaise and cream.
Half-and-half	¾ cup	Add to salad ingredients. Mix carefully. Serve with No. 12 dipper.

Notes:
1. 8 oz raisins may be added.
2. Best when served the same day it is prepared.

Sliced cucumber and onion in sour cream

YIELD: 50 portions
4¼ qt
PORTION: ⅓ cup (2½ oz)

Ingredient	Amount	Procedure
Cucumbers	5 lb	Cut cucumbers and onions in thin slices.
Onions	8 oz	
Sour cream	3 cups	Blend rest of ingredients to form a thin cream dressing.
Mayonnaise	3 cups	
Salt	1½ tsp	Pour over cucumbers and onions. Mix lightly.
Sugar, granulated	3 Tbsp	
Vinegar	¾ cup	

Note:
This cream dressing may be used as a dressing for lettuce.

Variation:
German cucumbers. Reduce onions to 4 oz. Delete cream dressing. Pour mixture of 1 cup vinegar, ½ cup water, 1 Tbsp salt, and 8 oz sugar over cucumbers and onions. Marinate at least 1 hour.

Cole slaw

		YIELD: 50 portions
		4½ qt
		PORTION: ⅓ cup (2½ oz)

Ingredient	Amount	Procedure
Cabbage	7 lb EP (9 lb AP)	Shred or chop cabbage.
Vinegar	3 cups	Combine vinegar, sugar, and seasonings.
Sugar, granulated	1 lb 8 oz	Add to cabbage. Mix lightly.
Salt	1 oz (1½ Tbsp)	
Celery seed	1 Tbsp	

Note:
Red cabbage may be substituted for part or all of green cabbage.

Variations:
1. **Cauliflower broccoli salad.** Substitute 3 lb 8 oz EP each of cauliflower and broccoli for the cabbage. Add 3 oz chopped onion. Serve soon after preparing.
2. **Green pepper slaw.** Add 4 oz chopped green pepper, 2 oz chopped onion, and 4 Tbsp celery seed.
3. **Oriental cole slaw.** Substitute ⅓ recipe Sesame Seed Dressing (p. 525) for dressing given in recipe.

Creamy cole slaw

YIELD: 50 portions
4¼ qt
PORTION: ⅓ cup (2½ oz)

Ingredient	Amount	Procedure
Cabbage	7 lb EP (9 lb AP)	Shred or chop cabbage.
Mayonnaise or salad dressing	2 cups	Combine and add to cabbage. Mix lightly. Serve with No. 12 dipper.
Cream, half-and-half	2 cups	
Vinegar	½ cup	
Sugar, granulated	4 oz	
Salt	1 oz (1½ Tbsp)	
Pepper, white	½ tsp	

Note:
Whipped topping may be used in place of cream. Reduce sugar to 2 oz.

Variations:
1. **Cabbage apple salad.** See p. 501.
2. **Cabbage carrot slaw.** Reduce cabbage to 5 lb. Add 1 lb shredded or chopped carrots, 8 oz chopped green pepper, and 4 oz chopped onion.
3. **Cabbage-pineapple-marshmallow salad.** To 4 lb shredded or chopped cabbage, add 2 lb pineapple tidbits, drained, 1 lb miniature marshmallows, and a dressing made of 2 cups mayonnaise or salad dressing and 2 cups cream, whipped.
4. **Creamy cauliflower-broccoli salad.** Substitute 3 lb 8 oz EP each of cauliflower and broccoli for the cabbage. Add 3 oz chopped green onion.

Marinated garden salad

YIELD: 50 portions
        8 lb
PORTION: ⅓ cup (2½ oz)

Ingredient	Amount	Procedure
Carrots, sliced	1 lb EP	Steam carrots just until tender-crisp. Drain.
Cauliflower, fresh	2 lb EP	Cut cauliflower into florets.
Broccoli spears	2 lb EP	Cut broccoli into florets and slice stems.
Mushrooms, fresh	1 lb	Clean mushrooms. Cut large mushrooms in half. Combine all vegetables.
French Dressing (Light) p. 525	1½ qt	Combine dressing and seasonings. Pour over vegetables.
Dill weed	¼ oz	Marinate at least 2 hours.
Basil leaves	1 Tbsp	
Oregano leaves	1 tsp	

Marinated mushrooms

YIELD: 50 portions
PORTION: 3 oz

Ingredient	Amount	Procedure
Mushrooms, fresh, small	6 lb	Clean mushrooms and trim ends. Leave whole.
Water Lemon juice	1 qt ½ cup	Combine water and lemon juice. Bring to a boil. Add mushrooms and cook 1–3 minutes. Drain.
Vegetable Marinade (p. 579)	1½ qt	Pour marinade over mushrooms. Refrigerate for 2–3 hours. Drain off most of the marinade before serving.

Note:
Before serving, mushrooms may be tossed with fresh minced parsley or other fresh herb.

Variations:
1. **Marinated asparagus.**   Cook fresh or frozen asparagus spears until tender-crisp. Marinate.
2. **Marinated green beans.**   Cover whole green beans with marinade. If fresh green beans are used, cook until tender-crisp.
3. **Vegetable collage.**   Pour 3 cups Italian Salad Dressing (p. 525) or Vegetable Marinade (p. 579) over the following: 2 lb broccoli florets, 2 lb cauliflower florets, 12 oz sliced celery, 1 lb 8 oz cherry tomatoes cut in half, 2 lb sliced zucchini, 1 lb sliced green onions, 6 oz sliced carrots, and 1 lb 8 oz sliced black olives. Marinate in refrigerator for 4 hours, but if salad is to be held longer than that, add broccoli shortly before serving. Add 1 lb cooked crumbled bacon and toss.

Oriental salad

YIELD: 50 portions
PORTION: 3 oz

Ingredient	Amount	Procedure
Bean sprouts, canned	2 lb 8 oz	Drain bean sprouts.
Celery, sliced	10 oz	Combine vegetables with bean sprouts. Toss lightly.
Cucumbers, peeled and sliced	10 oz	
Green peppers, chopped	3 oz	
Tomatoes, fresh, diced	5 lb	
Chives, chopped	2 oz	
Tomato Dressing (p. 525)	1½ cups	Combine dressing, soy sauce, and salt.
Soy sauce	¼ cup	Pour over vegetables and toss lightly.
Salt	½ tsp	

Note:
2 lb fresh bean sprouts may be substituted for canned bean sprouts.

Spinach cheese salad

YIELD: 50 portions
PORTION: 3 oz

Ingredient	Amount	Procedure
Spinach, chopped, frozen	3 lb	Thaw spinach. Squeeze out excess moisture and drain.
Eggs, hard-cooked (p. 306)	10	Peel and chop eggs coarsely.
Onion, chopped Celery, chopped Cheddar cheese, shredded	6 oz 8 oz 1 lb	Add onions, celery, cheese, and eggs to spinach. Mix lightly.
Mayonnaise or salad dressing Salt Tabasco sauce Vinegar Horseradish	1¼ qt 2 tsp 2 tsp 2 Tbsp ⅔ cup	Combine mayonnaise and seasonings. Pour over spinach mixture. Mix lightly. Refrigerate for 2 hours. Serve with No. 12 dipper.

Basic pasta salad

YIELD: 50 portions
PORTION: 4 oz

Ingredient	Amount	Procedure
Pasta	3 lb 8 oz (AP)	Cook pasta according to directions on p. 402.
Water, boiling	3½ gal	Do not overcook. Pasta should be *al dente*.
Salt	3 oz	There should be approximately 9 lb cooked
Vegetable oil	2 Tbsp	pasta. Information on cooked weights of pasta is given on p. 402.
Dressing	1½–1¾ qt	Add dressing and toss gently to mix.
Vegetables and/or other ingredients	1 lb 8 oz–2 lb	Fold in other ingredients. Chill.

Suggested ingredients   (Figures 2.44 and 2.45):
Pasta: Rotini, rigatoni, shell macaroni, elbow macaroni.
Dressing: Vinaigrette and variations (p. 528), Lemon Basil (p. 528), Pepper Cream (p. 523), Green Peppercorn (p. 523), Thousand Island (p. 523), Italian (p. 525), Sour Cream Basil (p. 523).
Vegetables (cooked until tender-crisp):   Asparagus cuts, broccoli florets, carrot coins, Italian green beans, snow peas.
Vegetables (raw):   Broccoli, cauliflower, chives, cucumbers, green peppers, parsley, radishes, tomatoes, water chestnuts.
Other: Chicken, cooked beef strips, crabmeat, ham, shrimp, turkey, olives, pickles.

Figure 2.44 *Layering pasta and other ingredients makes an attractive presentation. Courtesy of the National Pasta Association.*

Figure 2.45 *Different pasta shapes may be combined with other ingredients in salads. Photo courtesy of Hershey Kitchens and reprinted with permission of Hershey Foods Corporation.*

Macaroni salad

YIELD: 50 portions
                6 qt
PORTION: ½ cup (4 oz)

Ingredient	Amount	Procedure
Elbow macaroni	2 lb	Cook macaroni according to directions on p. 402.
Water, boiling	2 gal	
Salt	2 oz (3 Tbsp)	Rinse in cold water. Drain well after rinsing.
Vegetable oil (optional)	1 Tbsp	
Eggs, hard-cooked (p. 306)	14	Peel and coarsely chop eggs.
Cheddar cheese, diced or shredded	1 lb 8 oz	Add eggs and remaining ingredients to macaroni. Mix lightly.
Pickle relish	1 lb	Chill
Celery, finely chopped	1 lb 8 oz	Serve with No. 12 dipper.
Onion, finely chopped	1 oz	
Pimiento, chopped	3 oz	
Salt	1 Tbsp	
Pepper, white	¾ tsp	
Mayonnaise	3 cups	

Note:
Other types of pasta may be substituted for elbow macaroni (see p. 488).

Variations:
1. **Ham and pasta salad.**   Delete eggs and reduce cheese to 1 lb. Add 2 lb cooked ham, diced.
2. **Chicken and pasta salad.**   Delete cheese, pickle relish, and eggs. Cook 2 lb 8 oz fettuccini or other type of pasta according to directions on p. 402. Add 3 lb cooked chicken, diced.

Italian pasta salad

YIELD: 50 portions
PORTION: 4 oz

Ingredient	Amount	Procedure
Rotini or other pasta	2 lb 8 oz	Cook pasta according to directions on p. 402.
Water, boiling	2½ gal	Rinse in cold water. Drain.
Salt	2 Tbsp	
Vegetable oil	1 Tbsp	
Thousand Island Dressing (p. 523)	1¾ qt	Combine dressing and seasonings. Pour over pasta. Mix gently.
Basil leaves	1 Tbsp	Chill.
Salt	1 Tbsp	
Garbanzo beans, canned	8 oz	Drain and rinse beans. Add to pasta mixture.
Tomatoes, fresh, cut in wedges	1 lb 8 oz	Add vegetables and olives to pasta mixture. Toss gently. Refrigerate until served.
Cucumbers, peeled and sliced	1 lb	
Cauliflower, fresh, sliced	8 oz	
Black olives, large, pitted	4 oz	

Note:
An oil-base dressing may be substituted for Thousand Island Dressing.

Potato salad

	YIELD:	50 portions
		7 qt
	PORTION:	4 oz

Ingredient	Amount	Procedure
Potatoes, pared	10 lb EP (12 lb AP)	Cook potatoes until tender. Dice while warm.
Salad oil	½ cup	Make a marinade of oil, vinegar, lemon juice,
Vinegar, cider	½ cup	and seasonings.
Lemon juice	1 Tbsp	Add to warm potatoes and mix gently.
Prepared mustard	2 Tbsp	Marinate until cold.
Sugar, granulated	3 oz	
Salt	1 Tbsp	
Tabasco sauce	Few drops	
Eggs, hard-cooked (p. 306), diced	12	Add eggs, celery, onion, and pepper to marinated potatoes.
Celery, diced	1 lb	Mix lightly.
Onion, finely chopped	8 oz	
Pepper, black	½ tsp	
Mayonnaise	2 cups	Add mayonnaise. Mix carefully to blend. Chill at least 1 hour before serving. Serve with No. 10 dipper.

Notes:
1. 2 cups French Dressing (Light), p. 525, may be substituted for the marinade given in the recipe.
2. Sour cream or yogurt may be substituted for half of the mayonnaise.
3. Potatoes may be cooked with skins on, then peeled. Use 12 lb AP.
4. 4 oz pickle relish, chopped pimiento, or chopped green pepper may be added.

Variation:
Sour cream potato salad.   Reduce eggs to 8 and mayonnaise to 1 cup. Add 2 cups sour cream, 1 tsp celery seed, and 12 oz peeled, sliced cucumbers.

Hot potato salad

YIELD: 50 portions
PORTION: ⅔ cup (6 oz)

Ingredient	Amount	Procedure
Potatoes	12 lb EP (15 lb AP)	Wash potatoes and trim as necessary. Steam until just tender, about 30 minutes. Peel and slice.
Bacon	1 lb	Dice bacon. Cook until crisp. Drain. Reserve fat.
Onion, chopped	8 oz	Sauté onion in bacon fat.
Flour, all-purpose	4 oz	Add flour to onions and stir until well mixed. Cook 5 minutes.
Sugar, granulated	1 lb	Mix sugar, spices, vinegar, and water. Boil 1 minute.
Salt	2½ oz	Add to fat-flour mixture gradually while stirring.
Pepper, black	2 tsp	Cook until slightly thickened.
Celery seed	1 Tbsp	
Vinegar, cider	3 cups	
Water	1 qt	
		Add hot dressing to warm potatoes and bacon. Mix lightly. Serve hot.

Notes:
1. 12 hard-cooked eggs, sliced or diced, may be added.
2. Mayonnaise or a combination of mayonnaise and salad dressing may be used in place of the hot vinegar dressing. Add to potato mixture and heat to serving temperature.

Gelatin salads

Perfection salad

YIELD: 40 or 48 portions
1 pan 12 × 20 × 2 inches
PORTION: 2¼ × 2½ or 2 × 2½ inches

Ingredient	Amount	Procedure
Gelatin, unflavored	3 oz	Sprinkle gelatin over cold water.
Water, cold	2 cups	Let stand 10 minutes.
Water, boiling	3 qt	Add boiling water to gelatin.
		Stir until gelatin is dissolved.
Vinegar, cider	1 cup	Add to gelatin mixture. Stir until sugar is
Lemon juice	1 cup	dissolved.
Salt	1 oz (1½ Tbsp)	Chill.
Sugar, granulated	1 lb	
Cabbage, chopped	1 lb 8 oz	When liquid begins to congeal, add vegetables.
Celery, chopped	10 oz	Pour into a 12 × 20 × 2-inch counter pan.
Pimiento, chopped	4 oz	Place in the refrigerator to congeal.
Green pepper, chopped	4 oz	Cut 5 × 8 for 40 portions.
Paprika	1 Tbsp	Cut 6 × 8 for 48 portions.

Fruit gelatin salad

YIELD: 40 or 48 portions
               1 pan 12 × 20 × 2 inches
PORTION: 2¼ × 2½ or 2 × 2½ inches

Ingredient	Amount	Procedure
Gelatin, flavored	1 lb 8 oz	Pour boiling water over gelatin.
Water, boiling	2 qt	Stir until dissolved.
Fruit juice or water, cold	2 qt	Add to hot liquid. Chill.
Fruit, drained	4 lb	Place fruit in counter pan. When gelatin begins to congeal, pour over fruit. Place in refrigerator to congeal. Cut 5 × 8 for 40 portions. Cut 6 × 8 for 48 portions.

Notes:

1. For quick preparation, dissolve 1 lb 8 oz flavored gelatin in 1½ qt boiling water. Measure 2½ qt chipped or finely crushed ice, then add enough cold water or fruit juice to cover ice. Add to gelatin and stir constantly until ice is melted. Gelatin will begin to congeal at once. Speed of congealing depends on proportion of ice to water and size of ice particles.
2. One or more canned, frozen, or fresh fruits, cut into desired shapes and sizes, may be used. Fresh or frozen pineapple must be cooked before adding to gelatin salad.
3. Fruit juice may be used for part or all of the liquid. Not more than 50 percent of heavy syrup, however, should be substituted for water.
4. If unflavored granulated gelatin is used, sprinkle 2½ oz over 2 cups cold water and let stand for 10 minutes. Add 3½ qt boiling fruit juice and 1 lb sugar.

Variations:

1. **Apple cinnamon swirl.** Heat 1¼ qt water to boiling. Add 1 lb lemon gelatin and 10 oz cinnamon candies (red-hots). Stir until dissolved. Stir in 3 lb (1½ qt) applesauce, ¼ cup lemon juice, and 1 Tbsp salt. Pour into a 12 × 20 × 2-inch pan and chill until partially set. Fold in 8 oz coarsely chopped walnuts. Beat 10 oz cream cheese, ½ cup milk, and ¼ cup mayonnaise until smooth. Spoon mixture (2 cups) on top of gelatin. Swirl through gelatin with rubber spatula to marble.
2. **Applesauce gelatin salad.** Heat 6 lb 10 oz (1 No. 10 can) applesauce, 8 oz granulated sugar, 1 Tbsp ground cinnamon, and 2 tsp ground nutmeg, stirring frequently. Add 1 lb 8 oz strawberry gelatin and stir until dissolved. Add 2 qt cold water and ⅓ cup lemon juice.
3. **Arabian peach salad.** Drain 1 No. 10 can sliced peaches, saving juice. Combine peach juice, 1½ cups white vinegar, 1 lb 12 oz granulated sugar, 1 oz stick cinnamon, and 2 tsp whole cloves. Simmer 10 minutes. Strain, and add enough hot water to make 1 gal liquid. Add to 1 lb 8 oz orange gelatin and stir until dissolved. When slightly thickened, add peaches. Apricot halves may be substituted for peaches.
4. **Autumn salad.** Dissolve 1 lb 8 oz orange gelatin in 2 qt boiling water. Add 2 qt cold liquid, 2 lb 8 oz sliced fresh peaches, and 3 lb 8 oz fresh pears.
5. **Blueberry gelatin salad.** Make in two layers. First layer: Drain 1 No. 10 can blueberries. Add water to juice if necessary to make 1 qt and heat to boiling. Add 12 oz raspberry gelatin and stir

until dissolved. Pour into 12 × 20 × 2-inch pan and chill. Second layer: Drain 1 No. 10 can crushed pineapple. Add water if necessary to make 1 qt liquid. Heat to boiling and add 12 oz lemon gelatin. Stir until dissolved. Stir in the crushed pineapple and 1 qt sour cream. Cool. Pour over first layer and chill.

6. **Boysenberry mold.** Thaw 2 lb 12 oz frozen boysenberries in a colander. Reserve juice. Heat juice plus water if needed to make 2 qt. Add 1 lb 8 oz raspberry gelatin and stir until dissolved. Stir in 1½ cups cold water. Chill until gelatin is the consistency of egg whites. Whip 1¼ qt whipped topping until soft peaks form. Fold in the thickened gelatin mixture and boysenberries. Pour into molds and refrigerate until firm.

7. **Cranberry apple salad.** Dissolve 1 lb 8 oz cherry or raspberry gelatin in 2 qt boiling water. Add 3 lb fresh or frozen cranberry relish, 1 lb chopped apples, and 1 lb crushed pineapple. One No. 10 can whole cranberry sauce and 4 oranges, ground, may be used in place of the relish. Delete pineapple.

8. **Cranberry mold.** Drain 3½ cups crushed pineapple (2½ cups drained). Heat juice, plus enough water to make 3¼ cups, to boiling. Add 1 lb raspberry gelatin and stir until dissolved. Stir in 1½ qt cranberry relish. Chill until consistency of unbeaten egg whites. Fold in 3 cups mandarin oranges, drained and chopped, and 3¼ cups whipped topping whipped until stiff (6½ cups whipped). Spread in oiled gelatin molds.

9. **Cucumber soufflé salad.** Dissolve 1 lb 8 oz lime or lemon gelatin in 1½ qt boiling water. Add 2 qt ice and cold water. Chill until partially set. Whip until fluffy. Add 3 cups mayonnaise and ⅓ cup lemon juice. Fold in 5 lb cucumbers, chopped.

10. **Frosted cherry salad.** Dissolve 1 lb 8 oz cherry gelatin in 2 qt boiling water. Add 2 qt cold fruit juice, 2 lb drained, pitted red cherries, and 2 lb crushed pineapple. When congealed, frost with whipped cream cheese and chopped toasted almonds.

11. **Frosted lime mold.** Dissolve 1 lb 8 oz lime gelatin in 2 qt boiling water. Add 2 qt cold fruit juice and, when mixture begins to congeal, add 4 lb crushed pineapple, drained, 2 lb 8 oz cottage cheese, 8 oz diced celery, 4 oz chopped pimiento, and 4 oz chopped nuts. When congealed, frost with mixture of 4 lb cream cheese blended with ½ cup mayonnaise.

12. **Jellied Waldorf salad.** Dissolve 1 lb 8 oz raspberry or cherry gelatin in 2 qt boiling water. Add 1 cup red cinnamon candies (red-hots) and stir until dissolved. Add 2 qt cold water or fruit juice. When mixture begins to congeal, add 2 lb diced apple, 12 oz finely diced celery, and 8 oz chopped pecans or walnuts.

13. **Lemon cream mold.** Dissolve 1 lb 8 oz lemon gelatin in 1 qt boiling water. Stir in 1 qt cold water, ¾ cup vinegar, and ¼ tsp salt. Cool to room temperature. Add to 3 lb 12 oz sour cream and mix until smooth. Garnish with very thin slices of lemon and cucumber.

14. **Molded pineapple cheese salad.** Dissolve 1 lb 8 oz lemon gelatin in 2 qt boiling water. Add 2 qt cold fruit juice, 1 lb grated cheddar cheese, 3 lb drained crushed pineapple, 3 oz chopped green pepper or pimiento, and 4 oz finely chopped celery.

15. **Ribbon gelatin salad.** Dissolve 1 lb 8 oz raspberry gelatin in 1 gal boiling water. Divide into three equal parts. Pour one-third into one 12 × 20 × 2-inch pan and chill. Add 1 lb cream cheese to another third and whip to blend; pour on the first part when it is congealed. Return it to the refrigerator until it, too, is congealed, then top with remaining portion.

16. **Sunshine salad.** Dissolve 1 lb 8 oz lemon gelatin in 2 qt boiling water. Add 2 qt cold fruit juice, 3 lb drained crushed pineapple, and 8 oz grated raw carrot.

17. **Swedish green-top salad.** Dissolve 12 oz lime gelatin in 2 qt boiling water. Pour into a 12 × 10 × 2-inch pan. Dissolve 12 oz orange gelatin in 2 qt boiling water. While still hot, add 1 lb 8 oz marshmallows and stir until melted. When cool, add 12 oz cream cheese, 1½ cups mayonnaise, and ½ tsp salt, blended together. Fold in 1 pt cream, whipped. Pour over congealed lime gelatin and return to the refrigerator to chill. To serve, invert so that green portion is on top.

18. **Under-the-sea salad.** Dissolve 1 lb 8 oz lime gelatin in 1 gal boiling water. Divide into two parts. Pour one part into a 12 × 20 × 2-inch pan and chill. When it begins to congeal, add 12 oz drained crushed pineapple or sliced pears. To the remaining gelatin mixture, add 1 lb cream cheese and whip until smooth. Pour over first portion.

Tomato aspic

YIELD: 40 or 48 portions
1 pan 12 × 20 × 2 inches
PORTION: 2¼ × 2½ or 2 × 2½ inches

Ingredient	Amount	Procedure
Gelatin, unflavored	4 oz	Sprinkle gelatin over cold water.
Water, cold	1 qt	Let stand 10 minutes.
Tomato juice	1 gal	Combine tomato juice and seasonings.
Onions, small, sliced	2	Boil 5 minutes. Strain.
Bay leaf	1	Add gelatin. Stir until dissolved.
Celery stalks	4	
Cloves, whole	8	
Dry mustard	2 tsp	
Sugar, granulated	14 oz	
Salt	1 Tbsp	
Vinegar or lemon juice	2 cups	Add vinegar or lemon juice.
		Pour into a 12 × 20 × 2-inch counter pan.
		Place in refrigerator to congeal.
		Cut 5 × 8 for 40 portions.
		Cut 6 × 8 for 48 portions.

Fruit salads

Ambrosia fruit salad

YIELD:　50 portions
PORTION:　2½ oz

Ingredient	Amount	Procedure
Mandarin oranges, canned, drained	3 lb	Combine fruits, marshmallows, and coconut.
Pineapple tidbits, canned, drained	3 lb 8 oz	
Miniature marshmallows	12 oz	
Shredded coconut	6 oz	
Sour cream	12 oz	Add sour cream to fruit. Toss lightly to combine. Serve with No. 12 dipper.

Note:
Salad does not hold well and is best when served soon after mixing.

Acini de pepe fruit salad

YIELD: 50 portions
PORTION: 4 oz

Ingredient	Amount	Procedure
Acini de pepe (small macaroni)	2 lb 6 oz (AP)	Cook according to directions on p. 402. Drain and cool slightly. There should be 7 lb 8 oz cooked product. Save for later step.
Water, boiling	2 gal	
Salt	1 oz (1½ Tbsp)	
Sugar, granulated	7 oz	Combine sugar, flour, and salt in steam-jacketed kettle.
Flour, all-purpose	2 Tbsp	
Salt	1 tsp	
Pineapple juice drained from pineapple	1½ cups	Pour juice slowly into mixture while stirring with wire whip. Cook over moderate heat, stirring until slightly thickened.
Eggs, beaten	2 (3 oz)	Stir a small amount of the hot mixture into eggs, then stir eggs into the hot mixture. Cook and stir until thickened.
Lemon juice	1 Tbsp	Add lemon juice. Cool to room temperature. Combine with cooked pasta. Mix lightly. Chill.
Mandarin oranges, drained	1 lb	Add fruit to pasta mixture. Mix lightly but thoroughly.
Crushed pineapple, drained	1 lb 12 oz	
Pineapple tidbits, drained	1 lb 12 oz	
Whipped topping	1¼ cups	Whip topping to stiff peaks. There should be 2½ cups whipped. Fold into salad. Chill until served. Serve with No. 8 dipper.

Waldorf salad

YIELD: 50 portions
6 qt
PORTION: ⅓ cup (3 oz)

Ingredient	Amount	Procedure
Cream, whipping (optional)	½ cup	Whip cream. Combine with mayonnaise.
Mayonnaise or salad dressing	2 cups	
Apples, tart (peeled or unpeeled)	8 lb EP	Dice apples into fruit juice to prevent apples from turning dark. Drain and stir into salad dressing.
Celery, chopped	2 lb EP	Add celery, seasonings, and nuts to apples.
Salt	1 oz (1½ Tbsp)	Mix lightly until all ingredients are coated with dressing.
Sugar, granulated (optional)	6 oz	Serve with No. 12 dipper.
Walnuts, coarsely chopped	8 oz	

Notes:
1. Add walnuts only to salad that will be used immediately, as nuts will cause the salad to become gray.
2. Fruit Salad Dressing (p. 530) may be substituted for mayonnaise.

Variations:
1. **Apple cabbage salad.**   Use 6 lb diced apples and 4 lb crisp shredded cabbage. Omit celery. Sour cream or plain yogurt may be substituted for half the mayonnaise.
2. **Apple carrot salad.**   Use 6 lb diced apples, 3 lb shredded carrots, and only 1 lb chopped celery.
3. **Apple celery salad.**   Delete walnuts. Add 8 oz marshmallows.
4. **Apple date salad.**   Substitute 2 lb cut dates for celery.
5. **Apple fruit salad.**   Substitute 4 lb fresh fruit in season for half the apples.

Spiced apple salad

| | | YIELD: 50 portions |
| | | PORTION: 1 apple |

Ingredient	Amount	Procedure
Sugar, granulated	6 lb	Combine sugar, water, and flavorings.
Water	2 qt	Boil for about 5 minutes to form a thin syrup.
Vinegar, cider	1 cup	Set aside for next step.
Red coloring	½ tsp	
Whole cloves	1 oz	
Cinnamon sticks	1 oz	
Apples, fresh	50	Core and peel apples. Leave apples whole unless they are large; then cut in half crosswise.
		Place apples in a flat pan.
		Pour syrup over apples. Cook on top of range or in oven until tender. Turn while cooking.
		Cool.
Celery, chopped	8 oz	Combine celery and nuts.
Nuts, chopped	4 oz	Add mayonnaise and salt.
Mayonnaise	¾ cup	Fill centers of cooked apples with this mixture.
Salt	½ tsp	

Notes:
1. Select apples that will hold their shape when cooked, such as Jonathan, Rome Beauty, or Winesap. Approximately 12 lb will be needed.
2. 8 oz softened cream cheese may be substituted for mayonnaise.

Grapefruit orange salad

YIELD: 50 portions
PORTION: 2 orange, 3 grapefruit sections

Ingredient	Amount	Procedure
Grapefruit, medium	16	Peel and section fruit according to directions on p. 468.
Oranges, large	17	For each salad, arrange 3 grapefruit sections and 2 orange sections alternately on lettuce or other salad greens.
		Serve with Celery Seed Fruit Dressing (p. 529) or Honey French Dressing (p. 526).

Variations:
1. **Citrus pomegranate salad.**   Arrange grapefruit and orange sections on curly endive. Sprinkle pomegranate seeds over fruit. Serve with Celery Seed Dressing (p. 529).
2. **Fresh fruit salad bowl.**   Place chopped lettuce or other salad greens in individual salad bowls, 2 oz per bowl. Arrange wedges of cantaloupe, honeydew melon, and avocado, and sections of orange or grapefruit on the lettuce. Garnish with green grapes, Bing cherries, or fresh strawberries. Fresh pineapple, peaches, or apricots are good also in this salad. Serve with Celery Seed Fruit Dressing (p. 529) or Honey French Dressing (p. 526).
3. **Grapefruit apple salad.**   Substitute wedges of unpeeled red apples for oranges.
4. **Grapefruit-orange-avocado salad.**   Place avocado wedges between grapefruit and orange sections. Garnish with fresh strawberries.
5. **Grapefruit-orange-pear salad.**   Alternate slices of fresh pear with grapefruit and orange sections.

Frozen fruit salad

YIELD: 48 portions
1 pan 12 × 20 × 2 inches
PORTION: 4 oz

Ingredient	Amount	Procedure
Gelatin, unflavored	1 oz	Sprinkle gelatin over cold water.
Water, cold	½ cup	Let stand 10 minutes.
Orange juice	1¾ cups	Combine juices and heat to boiling point.
Pineapple juice	1¾ cups	Add gelatin and stir to dissolve.
		Cool until slightly congealed.
Cream, whipping	2 cups	Whip cream. Combine with mayonnaise.
Mayonnaise	1 cup	Fold into the slightly congealed gelatin
		mixture.
Pineapple chunks, drained	1 lb 12 oz	Fold fruit into gelatin mixture.
Orange sections, cut in halves	1 lb 8 oz	Pour into a 12 × 20 × 2-inch counter pan or into molds.
Peaches, sliced, drained	1 lb 8 oz	Freeze.
Bananas, diced	2 lb	Cut 6 × 8.
Pecans, chopped	12 oz	
Maraschino cherries	8 oz	
Miniature marshmallows	8 oz	

Notes:
1. Whipped topping may be used in place of whipped cream.
2. Other combinations of fruit (a total of 8 lb) may be used.

Entree salads

Chef's salad bowl

		YIELD: 50 portions PORTION: 7 oz
Ingredient	**Amount**	**Procedure**

Head lettuce or mixed
  greens
	12 lb	Cut or tear lettuce into bite-sized pieces.
		Portion into individual salad bowls, 4 oz per
		  bowl.

Cooked turkey
Cooked ham
Cheddar cheese or Swiss
  cheese
	6 lb
	3 lb
	3 lb
		Cut meat and cheese into thin strips.
		Arrange on top of lettuce, 2 oz turkey, 1 oz
		  ham, and 1 oz cheese per bowl.

Green pepper rings
Tomatoes, cut into wedges
Eggs, hard-cooked,
  quartered (p. 306)
	50 (8 lb AP)
	6 lb AP
	25
		Garnish with 1 green pepper ring, 2 tomato
		  wedges, and 2 egg quarters.

Salad dressing[a]	1½–2 qt	Serve salad with choice of dressings.

[a] Suggested salad dressings: Mayonnaise, Thousand Island, Roquefort, Creamy French, or Ranch.

Variations:
1. **Chicken and bacon salad.**   Delete ham and turkey. Cut 6 lb cooked chicken or turkey into strips or cubes and mix with salad greens. Sprinkle 4 lb chopped, crisply cooked bacon over top of salads, 1 oz per salad.
2. **Seafood chef salad.**   Delete turkey and ham. Substitute 1 oz tuna or salmon, drained and broken into small chunks, and 1 oz shrimp pieces or 2 whole shrimp for each salad.

Chicken salad

YIELD: 50 portions
          6¼ qt
PORTION: ½ cup (4 oz)

Ingredient	Amount	Procedure
Cooked chicken	8 lb	Cut chicken into ½-inch cubes.
Eggs, hard-cooked (p. 306)	12	Peel and dice eggs.
Celery, diced	3 lb	Combine all ingredients. Mix lightly. Chill.
Onion, minced	2 Tbsp	Serve with No. 8 dipper.
Salt	2 Tbsp	
Pepper, white	1 tsp	
Mayonnaise	1 qt	
Lemon juice	4 tsp	

Notes:
1. 24–25 lb chicken AP will yield approximately 8 lb cooked meat.
2. Cubed chicken may be marinated for 2 hours in ⅔ cup French Dressing (Light).

Variations:
1. **Chicken-avocado-orange salad.**   Delete eggs. Gently stir into chicken mixture 1 qt diced orange segments, drained, 12 oz broken or slivered toasted almonds, and 6 oz chopped pimiento. Just before serving, add 6 avocados, diced.
2. **Crunchy chicken salad.**   Add 8 oz sliced water chestnuts or toasted slivered almonds or walnuts.
3. **Curried chicken salad.**   Add 1 Tbsp curry powder to mayonnaise.
4. **Fruited chicken salad.**   Just before serving add 2 lb 8 oz seedless grapes or pineapple chunks, drained, and 8 oz sunflower seeds.
5. **Mandarin chicken salad.**   Delete eggs and pepper. Reduce mayonnaise to 2 cups. Add 2 cups sour cream. Substitute 2 Tbsp lime juice for lemon juice. Gently fold in 1 No. 10 can mandarin oranges and 1 No. 10 can pineapple tidbits, well drained.
6. **Turkey salad.**   Substitute turkey for chicken.

Chicken and pasta salad plate

YIELD: 50 portions
PORTION: 7 oz

Ingredient	Amount	Procedure
Rotini	1 lb 2 oz AP (2 lb 8 oz cooked)	Cook according to directions on p. 402. Drain.
Water, boiling	1 gal	
Salt	1 oz (1½ Tbsp)	
Vinegar, cider	2¾ cups	Combine in mixer bowl.
Lemon juice	⅓ cup	
Prepared mustard	3 Tbsp	
Garlic, minced	3 cloves	
Salt	2 Tbsp	
Oregano, leaf	1 tsp	
Black pepper	2 tsp	
Sugar, granulated	2 tsp	
Salad oil	3½ cups	Add oil very gradually while mixing on medium speed with wire whip attachment.
Cooked chicken, cut in 1-inch pieces	8 lb 8 oz	Add chicken to dressing. Toss to coat well. Add cooked rotini and mix well. Chill overnight.
Broccoli florets	1 lb 4 oz	Steam broccoli until tender-crisp. Add to marinated mixture shortly before serving.
Cherry tomatoes, cut in half	3 lb	Add to marinated mixture shortly before serving.
Zucchini, fresh, cut in julienne strips	2 lb 4 oz	
Carrots, shredded	10 oz	
Green onions, chopped	8 oz	
Leaf lettuce	8 oz	Cover plate with leaf lettuce.
Hard roll	50	Portion 7 oz salad onto lettuce. Place one hard roll on each salad plate shortly before service.

Note:
Salad may be served in a bowl or on a plate with a bed of shredded lettuce.

Cottage cheese salad

		YIELD: 50 portions
		6 qt
		PORTION: ½ cup (4 oz)

Ingredient	Amount	Procedure
Tomatoes, fresh, peeled and diced	3 lb	Prepare vegetables.
Green peppers, chopped	4 oz	
Celery, diced	1 lb	
Cucumber, diced	1 lb	
Radishes, sliced	8 oz	
Cottage cheese, dry curd (see note)	6 lb	Just before serving, add vegetables and mix all ingredients gently.
Salt	2 oz (3 Tbsp)	
Mayonnaise	3 cups	

Note:
If creamed cottage cheese is used, reduce mayonnaise to 1 cup and omit salt.

Crab salad

		YIELD: 50 portions
		6 qt
		PORTION: ½ cup (4 oz)

Ingredient	Amount	Procedure
Eggs, hard-cooked (p. 306)	30	Peel and chop eggs coarsely.
Crabmeat, flaked	5 lb	Add eggs and other ingredients to crabmeat.
Almonds, blanched, slivered (optional)	1 lb	Mix lightly. Chill.
Black olives, sliced	1 lb	Serve with No. 10 dipper.
Lemon juice	⅓ cup	
Mayonnaise	1 qt	

Notes:
    1. Olives may be deleted and 1 lb diced cucumbers added.
    2. If desired, omit mayonnaise and marinate with French Dressing (Light).

Variation:
Lobster salad. Substitute lobster for crab.

Deli plate

	YIELD: 50 portions
	PORTION: 2½ oz salad
	2 oz meat and cheese

Ingredient	Amount	Procedure
Pasta Salad (p. 488) or Potato Salad (p. 493) or Macaroni Salad (p. 491)	9 lb	Prepare salad.
Pastrami, corned beef, or other cold cuts	3 lb	Wafer slice meat.
Lettuce leaves Swiss cheese, sliced	1 lb 8 oz 3 lb	Place lettuce leaf on dinner plate. Place one 1-oz cheese slice on lettuce. Portion 1 oz pastrami on cheese. Place No. 16 dipper pasta, potato, or macaroni salad on plate.
Tomatoes, sliced Dill pickle spears, drained Black olives	6 lb 8 oz (EP) 1 lb 8 oz 6 oz	Arrange on plate: 2 tomato slices 1 dill pickle spear 1 black olive
Rye bread	100 slices	

Suggestions for variation:
Ham rolls or slices, sliced turkey, deviled or hard-cooked egg, green pepper ring, green onion, cucumber slices, onion slices, cherry tomato, marinated mushrooms may be used.

Shrimp salad

YIELD: 50 portions
      6¼ qt
PORTION: ½ cup (4 oz)

Ingredient	Amount	Procedure
Cooked shrimp (see Note 1)	6 lb	Cut shrimp into ½-inch pieces. Place in bowl.
Celery, diced	2 lb	Add vegetables to shrimp.
Cucumber, diced	1 lb	
Lettuce, chopped (optional)	1 head	
Mayonnaise	1 qt	Combine mayonnaise and seasonings.
Lemon juice	2 Tbsp	Add to shrimp mixture. Mix lightly. Chill.
Salt	2 tsp	Serve with No. 10 dipper.
Paprika	1 tsp	
Prepared mustard	2 tsp	

Notes:
   1. 12 lb raw shrimp in shell or 10 lb raw, peeled, and deveined shrimp will yield the 6 lb cooked shrimp needed. Cook according to directions on p. 333.
   2. 1 dozen hard-cooked eggs (p. 306), coarsely chopped, may be added. Reduce shrimp to 5 lb.
   3. Salad may be garnished with tomato wedges or served in a tomato cup.

Shrimp rice salad

YIELD: 50 portions
PORTION: ½ cup (4 oz)

Ingredient	Amount	Procedure
Rice, converted	1 lb	Cook rice according to directions on p. 422. Chill.
Water	1¼ qt	
Salt	1 Tbsp	
Celery	1 lb 8 oz	Cut celery in thin slices crosswise.
Green peppers	1 lb	Slice green peppers in thin strips.
Cooked shrimp, chilled	5 lb	Combine shrimp, rice, and vegetables.
Vinegar, cider	1 cup	Combine and pour over shrimp-rice mixture. Marinate at least 3 hours.
Salad oil	½ cup	
Worcestershire sauce	2 Tbsp	
Sugar, granulated	2 Tbsp	
Salt	1 Tbsp	
Curry powder	2 tsp	
Ginger, ground	¾ tsp	
Pepper, black	½ tsp	
Pineapple chunks, canned or frozen, drained	3 lb	Just before serving, add pineapple. Serve with No. 8 dipper.

Shrimp tortellini salad plate

YIELD: 50 portions
PORTION: 6 oz salad mixture

Ingredient	Amount	Procedure
Spinach tortellini, cheese-stuffed, frozen	4 lb AP (6 lb cooked)	Cook tortellini in boiling water for 3–5 minutes. Drain. Place in bowl.
Italian Dressing (p. 525)	2¼ qt	Pour dressing over pasta and toss gently to coat.
Salad shrimp, cooked, frozen	5 lb	Thaw shrimp under cold running water. Drain well and add to pasta.
Celery, thinly sliced	1 lb 10 oz	Add to pasta mixture. Toss well.
Carrots, cut into ¾-inch-long thin julienne strips	12 oz	Cover. Refrigerate until thoroughly chilled.
Green onions, thinly sliced	10 oz	
Water chestnuts, sliced, drained	1 lb 6 oz	
Leaf lettuce	2 lb 12 oz	Cover plate with leaf lettuce. Portion 6 oz salad onto lettuce.
Black olives	1 lb	Garnish plate with 3 black olives and 1 cherry tomato.
Cherry tomatoes	1 lb	
Bread sticks	100	Serve with 2 breadsticks.

Tuna salad

	YIELD:	50 portions
		6¼ qt
	PORTION:	½ cup (4 oz)

Ingredient	Amount	Procedure
Eggs, hard-cooked (p. 306)	12	Peel and dice eggs.
Tuna, flaked	7 lb	Add vegetables, relish, and eggs to tuna. Mix lightly.
Celery, chopped	1 lb	
Cucumber, diced	1 lb	
Onion, minced	2 oz	
Pickle relish, drained	8 oz	
Mayonnaise	1 qt	Add mayonnaise to tuna mixture. Mix lightly to blend. Chill. Serve with No. 8 dipper.

Variations:
1. **Salmon salad.** Substitute salmon for tuna.
2. **Tuna apple salad.** Substitute tart, diced apples for cucumbers. Omit pickle relish.
3. **Tuna pea salad.** Delete eggs and minced onion. Substitute 5 cups sour cream mixed with ½ cup lemon juice for the mayonnaise. Add 2 lb frozen green peas, thawed, 8 oz green pepper, and 8 oz sliced green onions.

Tuna pasta salad plate

YIELD: 50 portions
PORTION: 3½ oz salad mixture

Ingredient	Amount	Procedure
Shell macaroni	2 lb AP (6 lb cooked)	Cook macaroni according to directions on p. 402.
Water, boiling	2 gal	Drain. Place in bowl.
Salt	2 oz	
Vegetable oil	2 Tbsp	
Italian Dressing (p. 525)	1 qt	Pour dressing over cooked macaroni. Stir to coat evenly. Cover and refrigerate overnight.
Canned tuna	2 lb	Drain tuna. Carefully fold into macaroni.
Green peppers	1 lb 6 oz	Cut peppers into strips approximately 1 inch long. Add to macaroni mixture.
Stuffed green olives, chopped	4 oz	Add chopped olives to macaroni mixture.
Lettuce leaves	1 lb 8 oz	Place 1 lettuce leaf off center on dinner plate. Place 3½ oz (¾ cup) salad on lettuce.
Eggs, hard-cooked (p. 306)	25	Place half of an egg on one side of macaroni salad.
Fresh tomatoes	6 lb	Cut each tomato into 8 wedges.
Hard rolls or crackers	50	Place 2 wedges on other side of salad. Place one hard roll or crackers on plate shortly before serving.

Stuffed tomato salad

YIELD: 50 portions
PORTION: 1 tomato

Ingredient	Amount	Procedure
Tomatoes, medium size	50	Place tomatoes in a wire basket and dip in boiling water. Let stand for 1 minute. Dip in cold water. Remove skins. Chill.
Chicken, crab, shrimp, tuna, or egg salad	10 lb	Turn tomato stem end down. Cut, not quite through, into fourths. Fill with No. 12 dipper of salad.

Note:
50 medium-sized tomatoes will weigh approximately 12 lb.

Variations:
1. **Tomato cabbage salad.**   Combine 1 lb cabbage and 1 lb celery, finely chopped, 1 Tbsp salt, and 1 cup mayonnaise for salad mixture. Fill tomato cup, using a No. 40 dipper.
2. **Tomato cottage cheese salad.**   Substitute 6 lb cottage cheese, seasoned, for salad mixture. Fill tomato cups, using No. 20 dipper.

Fruit salad plate

YIELD: 50 portions
PORTION: 6 oz fruit
4 oz salad or sherbet

Ingredient	Amount	Procedure
Fruit in season (3–4 selections from fruits listed below)	2 lb EP	Prepare fruit. See suggestions below.
Cottage cheese, Chicken Salad (p. 506), or sherbet	12 lb	Prepare salad according to recipe.
Nut bread sandwiches or muffins	50–100	
Lettuce	1 lb 8 oz	Prepare lettuce. Place lettuce leaf on dinner plate. Arrange fruit, salad, and bread on lettuce.

Note:
Choose a combination that offers contrast in shape, color, and flavor from the following lists:

Fruit suggestions:
Apple wedges
Avocado wedges, slices, or halves
Bananas, cut in strips or chunks, rolled in chopped nuts
Cherries, sweet
Grape clusters, red or green
Grapefruit sections
Kiwi fruit
Mangoes
Melon: cantaloupe, honeydew, watermelon; cut in wedges, rings, or balls
Orange slices, half slices, sections
Papayas
Peach halves or slices: cream cheese filling, cranberry sauce, or cottage cheese in halves
Pear halves, filled, or slices
Pineapple chunks, spears, rings
Plums
Strawberries

Salad suggestions:
Cheese strips or slices
Cottage cheese
Chicken salad
Sliced chicken or turkey
Ham roll

Bread suggestions:
Hard roll
Muffin
Finger sandwich: chicken, tuna
Nut bread sandwich
Raisin bread–cream cheese sandwich

Garnishes:
Coconut
Lemon or lime wedge
Pomegranate seeds
Stuffed prune

Relishes

Cranberry relish (raw)

		YIELD: 50 portions
		5 qt
		PORTION: ⅓ cup (3 oz)

Ingredient	Amount	Procedure
Oranges, unpeeled	3 (size 72)	Wash and quarter oranges and apples.
Apples, cored	5 lb	Sort and wash cranberries.
Cranberries, raw	3 lb	Put fruit through chopper or grinder.
Sugar, granulated	2 lb 4 oz	Add sugar to fruit and blend.
		Chill for 24 hours.
		Serve with No. 16 dipper as a relish or salad.

Variation:
Cranberry orange relish.   Delete apples. Increase oranges to 6 and sugar to 3 lb. Add ¼ cup lemon juice.

Buttered apples

	YIELD: 50 portions	
	7 qt	
	PORTION: ½ cup (4 oz)	

Ingredient	Amount	Procedure
Apples, fresh	13 lb EP (16 lb AP)	Wash apples and cut into sections. Remove cores. Arrange in pan.
Margarine or butter, melted	8 oz	Mix remaining ingredients and pour over apples.
Water, hot	2 cups	Cover and simmer until apples are tender, approximately 1 hour.
Sugar, granulated	1 lb 8 oz	
Salt	1½ Tbsp	

Notes:
1. Select apples that will hold their shape when cooked, such as Jonathan, Rome Beauty, or Winesap.
2. Apple sections may be arranged in a counter pan and steamed until tender. Sprinkle margarine and sugar over the top and bake for 15–20 minutes.
3. Hot buttered apples often are served in place of a vegetable.
4. Frozen or canned apples may be used.

Variations:
1. **Apple rings.**   Cut rings of unpared apples, steam until tender. Add sugar and margarine and bake 15 minutes.
2. **Cinnamon apples.**   Cut pared apples into rings. Add cinnamon drops (red-hots) for flavor and color. Proceed as for Buttered Apples but reduce sugar to 12 oz.
3. **Fried apples.**   Melt 1 lb margarine or butter in frying pan. Add sliced apples. Add 8 oz brown sugar, 1 tsp salt, and 1 tsp cinnamon. Cook apples, turning occasionally, until apples are lightly browned and just tender. Frozen apple slices, thawed and drained, may be used.

Cranberry sauce

YIELD: 50 portions
           5 qt
PORTION: ⅓ cup

Ingredient	Amount	Procedure
Cranberries	4 lb AP	Wash cranberries. Discard soft berries.
Sugar, granulated Water	4 lb 1 qt	Combine sugar and water. Bring to a boil. Add cranberries and boil gently until skins burst. Do not overcook. Chill. Serve with No. 12 dipper.

Note:
Make sauce at least 24 hours before using.

Variations:
1. **Pureed cranberry sauce.** Add water to cranberries and cook until skins burst. Puree cranberries and add sugar. Cook until sugar is dissolved.
2. **Royal cranberry sauce.** Make half of cranberry sauce recipe. When cool, add 3 oranges, chopped; 1 lb apples, chopped; 1 lb white grapes, seeded; 1 lb pineapple, diced; and 4 oz coarsely chopped pecans. Serve with No. 24 dipper as a relish. Yield: 1 gal.

Sauerkraut relish

YIELD: 50 portions
PORTION: ⅓ cup (3 oz)

Ingredient	Amount	Procedure
Sauerkraut	1 No. 10 can	Combine all ingredients.
Carrots, shredded	1 lb	Refrigerate for at least 12 hours.
Celery, chopped	12 oz	
Onion, chopped	8 oz	
Green pepper, chopped	1 lb	
Sugar, granulated	1 lb 8 oz	

Note:
Sauerkraut may be chopped before combining with other ingredients.

Pickled beets

YIELD: 50 portions
2 gal
PORTION: 3 oz

Ingredient	Amount	Procedure
Beets, canned, sliced or whole	2 No. 10 cans	Drain beets. Reserve 1 cup juice for next step.
Vinegar, cider	2 qt	Mix vinegar, sugars, spices, and liquid from beets.
Sugar, brown	1 lb	Heat to boiling point. Boil 5 minutes.
Sugar, granulated	8 oz	Pour hot mixture over beets.
Salt	1 tsp	Chill 24 hours before serving.
Pepper, black	½ tsp	
Cinnamon sticks	2	
Cloves, whole	1 tsp	
Allspice, whole	1 tsp	

Notes:
1. If using fresh beets, cook 14 lb (AP) according to directions on p. 634. Peel and slice, then proceed as in the recipe. Substitute 1 cup water for beet juice.
2. Sliced onions, separated into rings, may be added.

SALAD DRESSING RECIPES

Cooked salad dressing

		YIELD: 3 gal
Ingredient	**Amount**	**Procedure**
Sugar, granulated Flour, all-purpose Salt Dry mustard	3 lb 1 lb 8 oz 6 oz 3 oz	Combine dry ingredients in a steam-jacketed kettle or stockpot.
Water, cold	1 qt	Add water to dry ingredients and stir with wire whip until a smooth paste is formed.
Milk, hot Water, hot	1 gal 2 qt	Add hot milk and water, stirring continuously while adding. Cook 20 minutes, or until thickened.
Margarine Vinegar, hot	1 lb 3 qt	Stir in margarine and vinegar.
Egg yolks, beaten (see note)	50 (2 lb)	Add cooked mixture slowly to egg yolks, stirring briskly. Cook 7–10 minutes. Remove from heat and cool.

Note:
25 whole eggs may be substituted for egg yolks, and hot water for hot milk.

Variations:
1. Chantilly dressing.   Combine 1 qt Cooked Salad Dressing and 2 cups cream, whipped.
2. Combination dressing.   Combine 1 qt Cooked Salad Dressing and 1 qt mayonnaise.

Mayonnaise

	YIELD: 1 gal	
Ingredient	**Amount**	**Procedure**
Egg yolks (see Note 1)	8 (5 oz)	Place egg yolks and seasonings in mixer bowl.
Salt	2 oz (3 Tbsp)	Mix thoroughly, using wire whip attachment.
Paprika	2 tsp	
Dry mustard	2 Tbsp	
Vinegar, cider	¼ cup	Add vinegar and blend.
Salad oil	2 qt	Add oil very slowly, beating steadily on high speed until an emulsion is formed. Oil may then be added, ½ cup at a time and later 1 cup at a time, beating well after each addition.
Vinegar, cider	¼ cup	Add vinegar. Beat well.
Salad oil	2 qt	Continue beating and adding oil until all oil has been added and emulsified.

Notes:
1. Eight whole eggs (14 oz) may be used in place of egg yolks.
2. The addition of oil too rapidly or insufficient beating may cause the oil to separate from the other ingredients, resulting in a curdled appearance. Curdled or broken mayonnaise may be reformed by adding it (a small amount at a time) to 2 well-beaten egg yolks or eggs and beating well after each addition. It also may be reformed by adding it to a small portion of uncurdled mayonnaise.

Variations for approximately 2 qt dressing:
1. **Buttermilk dressing.**   To 1 qt mayonnaise, add 1 qt buttermilk, 2 tsp basil, ½ tsp oregano, 1 Tbsp finely chopped fresh parsley, 1 clove garlic, minced, 2 tsp black pepper, 2 oz chopped onion, and 1 tsp tarragon.
2. **Campus dressing.**   To 2 qt mayonnaise, add ⅓ cup chopped parsley, ¼ cup chopped green pepper, and ½ cup finely chopped celery.
3. **Chantilly dressing.**   To 1½ qt mayonnaise, fold in 1½ cups cream, whipped.
4. **Creamy blue cheese dressing.**   To 1 qt mayonnaise, add 2 cups (1 lb) sour cream, ¼ cup lemon juice, 1 Tbsp grated onion, 1 tsp salt, and 8 oz finely crumbled blue cheese.
5. **Dilly dressing.**   To 1½ qt mayonnaise, add 2 cups evaporated milk or buttermilk, 1 Tbsp seasoned salt, 1 tsp garlic powder, and ¼ cup chopped dill weed.
6. **Egg and green pepper dressing.**   To 1¾ qt mayonnaise, add 12 chopped hard-cooked eggs, ¼ cup finely chopped green pepper, 2 Tbsp onion juice, and a few grains cayenne.

7. **Garden dressing.** Combine 3 cups mayonnaise and 1½ qt (3 lb) sour cream. Add 3 oz granulated sugar, 2 tsp salt, and 1 tsp black pepper. Fold in 12 oz thinly sliced green onions, 8 oz thinly sliced radishes, 8 oz chopped cucumbers, and 8 oz minced green pepper. This may be used for a vegetable dip also.

8. **Green peppercorn cream dressing.** To 1 cup mayonnaise, add 1¼ qt (2 lb 8 oz) sour cream, 1 cup Dijon-style mustard, ⅓ cup finely crushed and drained green peppercorns, ¼ cup white wine vinegar, and ⅔ cup chopped parsley (optional).

9. **Honey cream dressing.** Blend together 4 oz cream cheese, 1⅓ cups honey, 1 cup lemon or pineapple juice, and ¼ tsp salt; then fold into 1½ qt mayonnaise.

10. **Honey yogurt dressing.** To 1 cup mayonnaise, add 1½ qt unflavored yogurt, ⅓ cup honey, ¼ cup raspberry vinegar, 2 Tbsp lemon juice, and 1 Tbsp grated fresh orange peel.

11. **Horseradish cream dressing.** To 1 cup mayonnaise, add 1½ qt (3 lb) sour cream, 2 Tbsp lemon juice, 2 tsp curry powder, 5 oz horseradish, 1 tsp salt, and 1 tsp paprika.

12. **Pepper cream dressing.** To 1½ qt mayonnaise, add 1 oz grated Parmesan cheese, 1 clove garlic, minced, 1 Tbsp monosodium glutamate, 2 Tbsp freshly ground black pepper, 1 Tbsp lemon juice, 1½ Tbsp onion juice, 1½ tsp Tabasco sauce, 1 Tbsp cider vinegar, and ¾ cup water.

13. **Roquefort dressing.** To 1½ qt mayonnaise, add 2 cups French dressing, 8 oz crumbled Roquefort cheese, and 2 tsp Worcestershire sauce.

14. **Russian dressing.** To 2 qt mayonnaise, add 2 cups chili sauce, 2 Tbsp Worcestershire sauce, 2 tsp onion juice, and a few grains of cayenne.

15. **Sour cream basil dressing.** To 1 cup mayonnaise, add ¾ cup vinegar, 1½ qt (3 lb) sour cream, 1 oz granulated sugar, 1½ oz salt, 1½ Tbsp celery seed, and 2 Tbsp basil leaves.

16. **Thousand island dressing.** To 1½ qt mayonnaise, add 1½ oz minced onion, 3 oz chopped pimiento, 1 cup chili sauce, 8 chopped hard-cooked eggs, 1 tsp salt, ¼ cup pickle relish, and a few grains of cayenne.

Sour cream dressing

		YIELD: 2 qt
Ingredient	**Amount**	**Procedure**
Eggs, beaten	16 (1 lb 12 oz)	Mix eggs and sour cream.
Sour cream	1 qt	
Sugar, granulated	2 lb	Combine sugar and flour.
Flour, all-purpose	1½ oz	Add water and mix only until smooth.
Water, cold	1 cup	Add to the cream and egg mixture.
Vinegar, cider	2 cups	Add vinegar and cook until thick. Stir as necessary. Chill.

Note:
2 cups cream, whipped, may be added before serving.

Bacon dressing

	YIELD: 2 qt	
Ingredient	**Amount**	**Procedure**
Bacon, sliced, cut into 1-inch pieces	12 oz	Fry bacon until crisp. Remove from fat.
Onions, finely chopped	4 oz	Sauté onions in bacon fat.
Sugar, granulated	8 oz	Add sugar, vinegar, and water to sautéed onions.
Vinegar, cider	¼ cup	Bring to boiling point.
Water	1½ cups	Cool.
Mayonnaise (p. 522)	3 cups	Place Mayonnaise in mixer bowl. Add cooled onion-vinegar mixture slowly, beating on low speed until smooth. Stir in bacon pieces. Serve with tossed green salad.

Chilean dressing

	YIELD: 1½ qt	
Ingredient	**Amount**	**Procedure**
Salad oil	2 cups	Combine all ingredients.
Vinegar, cider	1 cup	Beat on low speed until well blended.
Sugar, granulated	4 oz	Store in covered container.
Salt	2 tsp	Shake or beat well before serving.
Onion, finely chopped	2 oz	
Chili sauce	2 cups	
Catsup	1 cup	

French dressing (light)

		YIELD: 3 qt
Ingredient	**Amount**	**Procedure**
Salt	2 oz (3 Tbsp)	Combine dry ingredients in mixer bowl.
Dry mustard	2 Tbsp	
Paprika	2 Tbsp	
Pepper, black	1 Tbsp	
Vinegar, cider	1 qt	Add vinegar and onion juice to dry ingredients.
Onion juice	4 tsp	
Salad oil	2 qt	Add salad oil slowly. Beat on high speed until thick and blended.
		This is a temporary emulsion that separates rapidly. Beat well or pour into a jar and shake vigorously just before serving.

Note:
An egg white beaten into each quart of dressing just before using will keep it from separating.

Variations:
Prepare by adding the following to 3 qt (1 recipe) French Dressing (Light):
1. **Chiffonade dressing.** Add ⅓ cup chopped fresh parsley, 4 oz chopped onion, 6 oz chopped green pepper, 4 oz chopped red pepper or pimiento, and 16 chopped hard-cooked eggs.
2. **Italian dressing.** Delete paprika. Add 2 tsp oregano, ¼ tsp garlic powder, and 1 Tbsp basil.
3. **Mexican dressing.** Add 3 cups chili sauce, 10 oz chopped green pepper, 2 oz chopped onion, and 1 Tbsp cilantro.
4. **Oil and vinegar.** Delete mustard, paprika, and onion juice.
5. **Roquefort cheese dressing.** Add French Dressing (Light) slowly, while whipping, to 1 lb finely crumbled Roquefort cheese. 1 qt cream may be mixed with cheese before it is added to the dressing.
6. **Sesame seed dressing.** Delete salt, paprika, pepper, and onion juice. Increase mustard to ¼ cup and vinegar to 5½ cups. Add 3½ cups granulated sugar, 1¼ cups soy sauce, and ½ cup toasted sesame seeds.
7. **Tarragon dressing.** Use tarragon vinegar in place of cider vinegar.
8. **Tomato dressing.** Add 1 lb granulated sugar, 1½ qt tomato soup, and ¼ cup celery or poppy seeds. Increase onion juice to 2 Tbsp.

French dressing (thick)

YIELD: 1½ qt

Ingredient	Amount	Procedure
Sugar, granulated	2 lb	Combine sugar and seasonings in mixer bowl, using wire whip attachment.
Paprika	2 Tbsp	
Dry mustard	4 tsp	
Salt	2 Tbsp	
Onion juice	1½ tsp	
Vinegar, cider	1½ cups	Add vinegar. Mix well.
Salad oil	1 qt	Add oil gradually in small amounts. Beat well after each addition.

Note:
If a French Dressing of usual consistency is desired, use only 8 oz of sugar.

Variations:
1. **Celery seed dressing.** Add 2 oz celery seed.
2. **Poppy seed dressing.** Add 1 oz poppy seed.

Honey French dressing

YIELD: 2 qt

Ingredient	Amount	Procedure
Dry mustard	4 tsp	Mix mustard, salt, and celery seed in large mixing bowl.
Salt	1 tsp	
Celery seed or poppy seed	4 tsp	
Honey	2 cups	While mixing, add remaining ingredients in order listed.
Vinegar, cider	1¼ cups	
Lemon juice	¼ cup	
Onion, grated	1 Tbsp	
Salad oil	1 qt	

French dressing (semipermanent)

	YIELD: 1¼ qt	
Ingredient	**Amount**	**Procedure**
Gelatin, unflavored Water, cold	4 tsp ¼ cup	Sprinkle gelatin over cold water. Let stand for 10 minutes.
Water, boiling	½ cup	Add hot water to gelatin. Stir until dissolved. Chill.
Dry mustard Paprika Sugar, granulated Salt Cayenne	4 tsp 4 tsp 3 Tbsp 2 Tbsp Few grains	Combine dry ingredients in mixer bowl.
Salad oil	1 qt	Add oil slowly to dry ingredients while beating on high speed, using wire whip attachment.
Vinegar, cider	1 cup	Add vinegar slowly. Beat on high speed for 5 minutes. Stir in gelatin.

Vinaigrette dressing

YIELD: 2 qt

Ingredient	Amount	Procedure
Vinegar, cider	2 cups	Combine in mixer bowl.
Salt	1½ oz	
Pepper, white	2 tsp	
Cayenne	¼ tsp	
Salad oil	2½ cups	Combine oils. Add very slowly to vinegar mixture, mixing on low speed until oil is blended in.
Olive oil	2¾ cups	
Parsley, fresh, chopped	½ cup	Add to dressing. Mix.
Garlic, minced	5 cloves	Store in refrigerator.
Chives, frozen	½ cup	Stir or shake before serving.
Capers	4 oz	

Variations:
1. **Dijon mustard vinaigrette dressing.** Delete chives, parsley, and garlic. Add 2⅔ cups chopped green onions, ½ cup Dijon mustard, ½ cup granulated sugar, and 1 Tbsp Worcestershire sauce. Red wine vinegar may be substituted for cider vinegar.
2. **Lemon basil dressing.** Combine 2 cups cider vinegar, 1½ cups lemon juice, 6 oz granulated sugar, 1½ oz salt, and 4½ Tbsp dried basil leaves. Gradually add 3 cups salad oil.
3. **Pimiento vinaigrette dressing.** Substitute 4 oz diced pimiento for capers.

Celery seed fruit dressing

YIELD: 2 qt

Ingredient	Amount	Procedure
Sugar, granulated	1 lb 8 oz	Mix dry ingredients in kettle.
Cornstarch	⅓ cup	
Dry mustard	2 Tbsp	
Salt	2 Tbsp	
Paprika	2 Tbsp	
Vinegar, cider	2 cups	Add vinegar to dry ingredients. Cook until thickened and clear.
Onion juice	1 tsp	Add onion juice. Cool to room temperature.
Salad oil	1 qt	Add oil slowly to cooked mixture while beating on high speed.
Celery seed	2 Tbsp	Add celery seed. Serve with any fruit salad combination.

Variation:
Poppy seed dressing.   Add poppy seed in place of celery seed.

Fruit salad dressing

YIELD: 4½ qt

Ingredient	Amount	Procedure
Pineapple juice	1 qt	Combine juices. Heat to boiling point.
Orange juice	3 cups	
Lemon juice	2 cups	
Sugar, granulated	2 lb	Mix sugar and cornstarch.
Cornstarch	5 oz	Add to hot mixture while stirring with a wire whip.
Eggs, beaten	16 (1 lb 12 oz)	Add eggs to hot mixture while stirring. Cook until thickened. Chill.
Cream, whipping	2 cups	Whip cream and fold into dressing just before serving. Serve with fruit salads.

SANDWICHES

Sandwiches have always been good menu choices for the traditional noon and evening meals. They have become popular, however, at breakfast or any meal throughout the day where fast service and flavorful meal is desired. Sandwiches are popular also as hors d'oeuvres or buffet foods. Sandwiches may be closed or open-faced. They may be served hot or cold.

PREPARATION OF INGREDIENTS

Sandwich ingredients include bread, spread, filling, and vegetable accompaniments. Many variations are possible through the selection of ingredients, but the basic procedures for preparing the ingredients are the same.

Breads

A variety of breads and rolls are available that add variety in flavor, texture, size, and shape. Bread should be kept fresh during and after preparation.

Spreads

Bread for sandwiches is first spread with plain or seasoned margarine or butter, mayonnaise, or a Sandwich Spread (p. 538). Covering bread evenly with a spread helps keep the sandwich from becoming soggy. Margarine or butter may be softened by letting it stand at room temperature, or it may be whipped for easy spreading (see p. 538). Allow 1 tsp of spread per slice of bread.

Fillings

Slice meat and cheese into even slices. Tender meats may be sliced thicker than less tender ones. A serving of thinly sliced or wafer-sliced meats usually appears larger than an equal weight of thicker slices. Sliced meats and cheeses dry out quickly. They should be sliced only as needed and kept covered. Mixed fillings should be prepared the day they are served and kept chilled.

Vegetable accompaniments

Prepare greens, tomato and onion slices, and pickles or other vegetable accompaniments. Ingredients should be fresh, crisp, and attractive. See pp. 460–468 for preparing vegetable accompaniments.

PREPARATION OF SANDWICHES
Closed sandwiches

1. Prepare filling and spread.
2. Arrange fresh bread in rows on a baking sheet or a worktable. Four rows of ten slices each is a manageable number.
3. Spread all bread slices to the edges with softened margarine or butter or other spread.
4. Portion filling with dipper or spoon on alternate rows of bread and spread to the edges, or arrange sliced filling to fit the sandwich.
5. If lettuce or other vegetable accompaniment is used, arrange on filling. If sandwiches are to be held for some time, vegetable accompaniments should be omitted.
6. Place plain buttered (or spread) slices of bread on the filled slices.
7. If the sandwiches are to be cut in half or in fourths, stack two or three together and cut with a sharp knife, being careful not to mash bread.
8. To keep sandwiches fresh, place in sandwich bags or plastic wrap. Avoid stacking sandwiches more than three high, because stacking insulates the filling and prevents it from reaching the desired temperature as quickly as it should.
9. Refrigerate until served. If freezing sandwiches for later use, see precautions on p. 535.
10. Handle bread and fillings as little as possible during preparation. Use plastic gloves or tongs when picking up food.

Grilled and toasted sandwiches

1. For a grilled sandwich, place filling between two slices of bread. Fillings may be sliced cheese, meat, or poultry; chopped fillings as in salads; or a combination of fillings as in a Reuben Sandwich (p. 555).
2. Brush the outside with melted margarine or butter. For large quantities, a roller dipped in the melted spread may be used. See Figure 2.46.
3. Brown sandwich on the grill, in a hot oven, or under a broiler.
4. For a toasted sandwich, toast the bread before filling.

Figure 2.46 *Preparing sandwiches for grilling: (a) Place parchment paper in bottom of baking sheet. Apply melted margarine or butter with brush, or with roller as shown here. (b) Place bread slices directly on coated paper. Add filling to all slices in pan. (c) Top with slices of bread. Apply melted margarine or butter with brush or roller.*

Open-faced hot sandwiches

1. Place buttered or unbuttered bread on a serving plate.
2. Cover with hot meat or other filling.
3. Top with gravy, sauce, or other topping.
4. For a hot sandwich that is to be broiled, arrange slices of bread on a baking sheet. Cover with slices of cheese or other topping. Broil just before serving.

Canapés

1. Remove crusts from bread.
2. Cut into desired shapes.
3. Spread with softened margarine or butter.
4. Cover with filling.
5. Decorate with parsley, sliced olives, sliced radishes, pimiento pieces, chopped hard-cooked eggs, or other garnish.

Ribbon sandwiches

1. Remove crusts from two kinds of bread, being careful to have all slices the same size.
2. Spread one or more fillings on slices of bread.
3. Make stacks of five slices of bread, alternating kinds of bread (Figure 2.47).
4. Press together firmly.
5. Arrange stacks in shallow pan; cover with plastic wrap, plastic bag, or waxed paper.
6. Chill for several hours.
7. To serve, cut each slice into thirds, halves, or triangles.

Checkerboard sandwiches

1. Spread slices of white and whole wheat bread with desired filling.
2. Make stacks of ribbon sandwiches by alternating two slices of white and two slices of whole wheat bread. Trim and cut each stack into ½-inch slices.
3. Using butter or smooth spread as a filling, stack three slices together so that white and whole wheat squares alternate to give a checkerboard effect.
4. Chill for several hours.
5. Remove from refrigerator and, with sharp knife, slice into checkerboard slices, ½ inch thick.

Rolled sandwiches

1. Remove crusts from three sides of a loaf of unsliced bread.
2. With crust at left, cut loaf into lengthwise slices ⅛–¼ inch thick.
3. Run rolling pin the length of each slice to make it easier to handle.
4. Spread with softened margarine or butter.

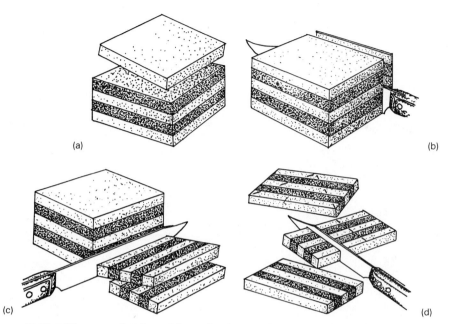

(a)

(b)

(c)

(d)

Figure 2.47 *Ribbon sandwiches: (a) Stack alternately 3 slices white and 2 slices whole wheat bread, filling with one or more spreads. (b) Press each stack of slices firmly together. With a sharp knife, using a sawing motion, slice crusts from all sides of each stack. Arrange stacks in shallow pan. Cover tightly and chill for several hours. (c) Cut in half-inch slices. (d) Cut each slice into thirds, halves, or triangles.*

5. Spread with desired smooth filling.

6. Place olives, watercress, or other foods across the end.

7. Starting at end with garnish, roll tightly, being careful to keep sides straight. Tight rolling makes for easier slicing (Figure 2.48).

8. Wrap rolls individually in waxed paper or aluminum foil, twisting ends securely.

9. Chill several hours or overnight. Rolls may be made ahead of time, then wrapped and frozen. Let thaw about 45 minutes before slicing.

10. Cut chilled rolls into ¼–⅓ inch slices.

FREEZING SANDWICHES

When making sandwiches to be frozen for later use, certain precautions should be taken.

1. Spread bread with margarine or butter instead of mayonnaise or salad dressing.

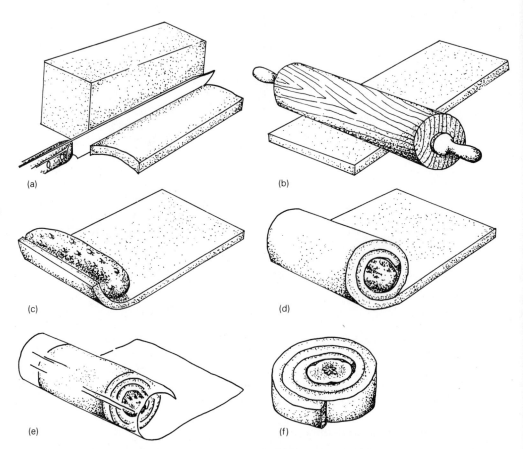

Figure 2.48 *Rolled sandwiches: (a) Place loaf of bread on cutting board. With long, sharp knife (or electric knife) slice off all crusts except bottom one. With crust side of loaf to the left, cut into lengthwise slices, ⅛ to ¼ inch thick. (b) Flatten each slice with rolling pin, starting at narrow end. (Rolling makes the bread easy to handle and less likely to crack.) (c) Spread each slice to the edge with softened margarine or butter. Cover slices with a spread. (d) Starting at the end with the filling, roll up each slice tightly as for a jelly roll, being careful to keep sides in line. Tight rolling makes for easier slicing and neat pinwheels with distinct markings. (e) Wrap rolls individually in waxed paper or plastic wrap, twisting ends securely. Chill thoroughly. (f) Cut chilled rolls into ¼- to ½-inch slices.*

2. Do not use fillings containing mayonnaise, egg white, or some vegetables such as tomatoes and parsley. Chicken, meat, fish, cheese, and peanut butter freeze well.

3. Place large closed sandwiches individually in a sandwich bag or wrap individually in plastic wrap.

4. Pack tea-sized closed sandwiches in layers, separated by waxed paper or

plastic wrap, in freezer boxes; or place in any suitable box and overwrap with moistureproof material.

5. Place open-faced sandwiches on trays, wrap as for closed sandwiches.

6. Wrap ribbon, closed, or other loaf sandwiches uncut.

7. Allow 1 to 2 hours for sandwiches to defrost. Do not remove outer wrapping until sandwiches are partly thawed.

8. If sandwiches are not served immediately after thawing, refrigerate until serving time.

SANDWICH RECIPES

Whipped margarine or butter

YIELD: spread for 50 sandwiches
PORTION: 1 tsp per slice

Ingredient	Amount	Procedure
Margarine or butter	1 lb	Place in mixer bowl. Let stand at room temperature until soft enough to mix.
Milk or boiling water (optional)	½ cup	Add milk or water while whipping. Mix on low speed, gradually increasing to high speed. Whip until fluffy.

Variations:
1. **Honey butter.** Cream 1 lb butter or margarine until light and fluffy. Add 8 oz honey gradually, beating on medium speed until mixture is light. Serve with hot biscuits or other hot bread.
2. **Savory spread.** Add minced cucumber, onion, or pimiento; chopped chives or parsley; horseradish; or prepared mustard to whipped butter or margarine.

Sandwich spread

YIELD: spread for 100 sandwiches
PORTION: 1 tsp per slice

Ingredient	Amount	Procedure
Margarine or butter	8 oz	Whip margarine on high speed until light and fluffy.
Half-and-half	¼ cup	Add cream and mix.
Prepared mustard Mayonnaise Pickle relish	1½ tsp 3 cups ½ cup	Fold in remaining ingredients. Use as a spread for meat or cheese sandwiches.

Cold sandwiches

Cheese salad sandwich

		YIELD: 50 sandwiches
Ingredient	**Amount**	**Procedure**
Cheddar cheese	3 lb 8 oz	Grind or shred cheese.
Salad dressing or cream Salt Cayenne Margarine or butter, softened	2 cups 2 tsp Few grains 4 oz	Combine with cheese.
Bread	100 slices	Assemble filling and bread (p. 532). Portion filling with No. 20 dipper.

Variation:
Pimiento cheese sandwich.   Add 6 oz chopped pimiento.

Egg salad sandwich

YIELD: 50 sandwiches
PORTION: 2 oz filling

Ingredient	Amount	Procedure
Eggs, hard-cooked (p. 306)	36	Peel eggs and chop coarsely.
Mayonnaise or salad dressing	2½ cups	Combine and add to eggs. Mix lightly.
Pickle relish	1 cup	
Salt	2 tsp	
Pepper, white	¼ tsp	
Onion juice	1 tsp	
Pimiento, chopped	4 oz	
Bread	100 slices	Assemble filling, bread, and lettuce (p. 532).
Lettuce, iceburg or leaf	2–3 heads	Portion filling with No. 20 dipper.

Notes:
1. 1 lb chopped celery may be substituted for pickle relish.
2. 2 Tbsp prepared mustard may be added.

Chicken salad sandwich

YIELD: 50 sandwiches
PORTION: 2 oz filling

Ingredient	Amount	Procedure
Cooked chicken	5 lb	Chop chicken coarsely.
Salt	2 tsp	Add remaining ingredients. Mix to blend.
Pepper, white	½ tsp	
Celery, finely chopped	8 oz	
Lemon juice or cider vinegar	¼ cup	
Mayonnaise or salad dressing	2–2½ cups	
Bread	100 slices	Assemble filling, bread, and lettuce (p. 532).
Lettuce, iceberg or leaf	2–3 heads	Portion filling with No. 20 dipper.

Notes:
1. 4 oz chopped, toasted almonds may be added.
2. Alfalfa sprouts may be placed on top of filling for variety.

Ham salad sandwich

YIELD: 50 sandwiches
PORTION: 2 oz filling

Ingredient	Amount	Procedure
Cooked ham	4 lb	Grind ham coarsely.
Eggs, hard-cooked (p. 306)	6	Peel eggs and chop coarsely.
Onion, finely chopped Pickle relish Mayonnaise or salad dressing	4 oz 8 oz 2–2½ cups	Combine all ingredients. Mix lightly.
Bread Lettuce, iceberg or leaf	100 slices 2–3 heads	Assemble filling, bread, and lettuce (p. 532). Portion filling with No. 20 dipper.

Variations:
1. **Ham and cheese sandwich.**   Delete eggs. Reduce ham to 3 lb. Add 1 lb 8 oz cheddar or Swiss cheese, ground.
2. **Meat salad sandwich.**   Substitute ground cooked beef or pork for ham. Add 4 oz finely chopped celery. Check for seasoning and add salt and pepper if needed.

Tuna salad sandwich

YIELD: 50 sandwiches
PORTION: 2 oz filling

Ingredient	Amount	Procedure
Eggs, hard-cooked (p. 306)	7	Peel eggs and chop coarsely.
Tuna, flaked	4 lb	Combine all filling ingredients.
Celery, chopped	4 oz	
Lemon juice	¼ cup	
Onion juice	1 tsp	
Mayonnaise or salad dressing	1½ cups	
Bread	100 slices	Assemble filling, bread, and lettuce (p. 532).
Lettuce, iceberg or leaf	2–3 heads	Portion filling with No. 20 dipper.

Note:
1 cup pickle relish may be substituted for celery.

Variations:
1. **Grilled tuna salad sandwich.** Brush both sides of sandwiches with melted margarine or butter. Grill until golden brown.
2. **Salmon salad sandwich.** Substitute salmon for tuna.

Bacon, lettuce, and tomato sandwich

YIELD: 50 sandwiches

Ingredient	Amount	Procedure
Tomatoes, fresh	7 lb	Wash tomatoes. Peel, if desired, and cut into thin slices.
Lettuce, iceberg or leaf	2–3 heads or 2 lb leaf	Wash lettuce and separate leaves. Drain.
Bacon	150 slices (7 lb)	Cook bacon according to directions on p. 391. Drain.
Bread (white or whole wheat)	100 slices	Spread 50 slices of bread with mayonnaise. Place 3 cooked bacon slices, 2 tomato slices, and a lettuce leaf on each.
Mayonnaise	1 cup	
Whipped Butter or Margarine (p. 538)	8 oz	Top with remaining 50 slices of bread, which have been spread with Whipped Butter or Margarine.

Variations:
1. **Club sandwich.**   Use 150 thin slices white bread toasted. Spread with mayonnaise. Place on first slice 1 lettuce leaf, 2 tomato slices, and 2 strips of bacon. Place second slice of toast on top, spread side down. Spread top with mayonnaise, then add 2 oz thinly sliced turkey or chicken breast and lettuce leaf. Top with third slice of toast, spread side down. Secure with 4 picks. Cut in quarters to serve.
2. **Sliced ham and cheese sandwich.**   Substitute 6 lb 8 oz wafer-sliced ham and 3 lb 2 oz (1 oz slices) cheese for bacon. Herbed Tomato Buns (p. 161) may be substituted for sliced bread.
3. **Turkey club hoagie.**   Reduce bacon to 2 lb. Substitute 7-inch hoagie buns for sliced bread. Prepare turkey breasts to yield 6 lb 8 oz EP (approximately 10 lb AP boneless breast). Each sandwich includes choice of sandwich spread, 2 oz wafer sliced turkey, 1 bacon slice, 1 lettuce leaf, and 2 tomato slices. Garnish plate with dill pickle spears.

Submarine sandwich

YIELD: 50 sandwiches
PORTION: 3 oz meat
                   1 oz cheese

Ingredient	Amount	Procedure
Buns, submarine or hoagie, 4–5 inches	50	Slice buns in half lengthwise. Spread both sides of bun with Sandwich Spread.
Sandwich Spread (p. 538)	1 recipe	
Salami, 1-oz slices	3 lb 2 oz	Cut slices of meat and cheese in half.
Luncheon meat, 1-oz slices	3 lb 2 oz	Arrange 1 oz of each kind of meat and 1 oz cheese on bottom half of each bun.
Ham, pullman, 1-oz slices	3 lb 2 oz	
Cheese, processed, American or Swiss, 1-oz slices	3 lb 2 oz	Alternate meat and cheese and arrange so that full length of each bun is covered.
Tomatoes, fresh, sliced	24	Place 2 slices tomato, ½ oz shredded lettuce, and 2 dill pickle slices on each sandwich.
Dill pickle slices, well drained (optional)	1 qt	Cover with top half of bun.
Shredded head lettuce	1 lb 9 oz	To serve, cut each sandwich in half.

Notes:
1. Other meats such as turkey, corned beef, pastrami, or roast beef may be used (Figure 2.49).
2. Shredded red or green cabbage, alfalfa sprouts, or leaf lettuce may be substituted for shredded head lettuce.
3. Mayonnaise or Italian dressing may be substituted for sandwich spread.

Variation:
Buffet submarine.   Use 12 long, thin buns, approximately 18 inches. Arrange 4 oz each of meats and cheese on each bun. Garnish with 2 tomatoes, sliced, ⅓ cup pickle slices, and 1–2 oz shredded lettuce. Secure with long picks. Portion as served into 4–5-inch sections.

Hot sandwiches

Bierocks

OVEN: 400°F		YIELD: 50 sandwiches
BAKE: 25–30 minutes		

Ingredient	Amount	Procedure
DOUGH		
Yeast, active dry	1¼ oz	Sprinkle yeast over water. Let stand 5 minutes.
Water, warm (110°F)	2 qt	
Sugar, granulated	14 oz	Add sugar, salt, and flour to yeast.
Salt	1 oz	Mix on medium speed, until mixture is
	(1½ Tbsp)	smooth, using dough arm or flat beater.
Flour, all-purpose	2 lb 6 oz	
Eggs	8 (14 oz)	Add eggs and shortening. Continue beating.
Shortening, melted	5 oz	
Flour, all-purpose	5 lb 8 oz	Add flour on low speed to make a soft dough. Knead 5 minutes.
		Cover and let rise until double in bulk.
		When dough has doubled, punch down and divide into 4 or 5 portions.
		Roll dough to ¼-inch thickness.
		Cut into 4 × 6-inch rectangles.
		Place on each piece of dough a No. 8 dipper of filling (recipe follows).
		Fold lengthwise and pinch edges of dough securely to seal.
		Place on baking sheets with sealed edges down.
		Bake at 400°F for 25–30 minutes.
Egg yolk	1	Brush with egg and water mixture.
Water	2 Tbsp	Return to oven for 5 minutes.

FILLING

Ingredient	Amount	Procedure
Ground beef	10 lb AP (7 lb EP)	Brown beef. Drain.
Cabbage, chopped	2 lb 8 oz	Steam cabbage and onion until slightly underdone.
Onion, chopped	3 lb	
Worcestershire sauce	⅓ cup	Add seasonings and vegetables to beef.
Salt	2½ oz	
Pepper, black	1½ tsp	
Savory, ground	1 tsp	
Chili powder	1½ tsp	

Variation:

Bierock pockets.   Scale 3 lb dough onto 18 × 26 × 1-inch greased pans. Cut dough into half lengthwise. Spread 2 lb beef mixture evenly onto each strip of dough. Roll jelly roll fashion and seal tightly. Place seam side down on greased 18 × 26 × 1-inch pan. Bake at 350°F for 30–35 minutes or until done. Cut each roll into 8 portions, 16 per pan.

Hot meat and cheese sandwich

YIELD: 50 portions
PORTION: 2½ oz meat
             1½ oz sauce

Ingredient	Amount	Procedure
Ham, roast beef, or corned beef	8 lb	Wafer-slice meat into 12 × 10 × 2-inch pans. Cover and heat.
Hamburger buns	50	To serve, place open bun on plate. Portion 2½ oz meat on bottom half of bun.
Cheese Sandwich Sauce, American or Cheddar (p. 561) or Swiss (p. 561)	3 qt	Ladle 1½ oz (No. 30 dipper) sauce over meat.

Figure 2.49 *Roast beef submarine sandwich. Photo courtesy of the National Live Stock and Meat Board.*

Grilled sandwiches

GRIDDLE: 350°F		YIELD: 50 portions
		PORTION: 1 sandwich

Ingredient	Amount	Procedure
Bread (white, whole wheat, or rye)	100 slices	See following procedures for preparing sandwiches.
Margarine or butter	1 lb	Grill sandwiches at 350°F on griddle until both sides are delicately brown.

PROCEDURE 1

1. Melt margarine or butter. Pour into 2-inch counter pan.
2. Pick up two slices of bread, one in each hand. Dip one side of one slice in melted margarine or butter. Press dipped slice against second slice.
3. Place buttered side of one slice on 18 × 26-inch baking sheet lined with silicone or waxed paper. Place 24 slices 4 × 6.
4. Top each slice with 2 oz meat and/or cheese.
5. Top meat and/or cheese with buttered bread (from Step 2), buttered side up.
6. Cover layer with silicone or waxed paper.
7. Repeat for a second layer or use another baking sheet. Cover tightly with plastic wrap if the sandwiches are not to be grilled immediately.

PROCEDURE 2

1. Place meat and/or cheese between two slices of bread.
2. Brush sandwiches with melted margarine or butter.
3. Place sandwiches on baking sheet and cover with plastic wrap until grilled.

PROCEDURE 3

See Figure 2.46 for procedure using a roller dipped in melted margarine or butter.

Variations:
1. **Grilled cheese.** Use processed American cheese, two 1-oz slices per sandwich.
2. **Grilled ham and cheese.** Use 1½ oz ham and 1 oz cheese per sandwich. 4 lb 12 oz wafer-sliced ham and 3 lb 2 oz cheese (1-oz slices) will be needed.
3. **Grilled turkey and Swiss on whole wheat.** Use 1½ oz turkey and 1 oz Swiss cheese per sandwich. 4 lb 12 oz wafer-sliced turkey and 3 lb 2 oz cheese (1-oz slices) will be needed.
4. **Hot tuna grill.** Use No. 10 dipper of Tuna Salad Sandwich filling (p. 543) for each sandwich. Other salad sandwich fillings may be used.

Chimichanga

DEEP-FAT FRYER: 350°F		YIELD: 50 portions
		PORTION: 4 oz

Ingredient	Amount	Procedure
Ground beef	10 lb 12 oz	Brown meat in steam-jacketed kettle. Drain.
Onions, chopped	1 lb 10 oz	Add onions and chili peppers to meat.
Green chili peppers, chopped	8 oz	Cook until tender.
Flour, all-purpose	4 oz	Stir flour and seasonings into meat mixture.
Garlic powder	½ tsp	
Cumin, ground	2 tsp	
Chili powder	1 Tbsp	
Salsa (see Note 1)	1 lb 14 oz	Add Salsa, beef base, and water. Cook 15–20 minutes or until very thick.
Beef base	¾ oz	
Water	1 qt	The filling may be prepared the day before and refrigerated.
Flour tortillas, 10-inch	5 lb 8 oz	Separate tortillas and place slightly overlapping in counter pans.
		Cover tightly and heat a few at a time for about 5 minutes or just until soft.
Water, cold	2¼ cups	Mix water and cornstarch.
Cornstarch	2 oz	

To assemble:
1. Brush edges of tortillas with water-cornstarch mixture (Figure 2.50).
2. Place No. 12 dipper or 4 oz meat mixture slightly below center of each tortilla.
3. Fold bottom edge over filling.
4. Fold sides in, then roll into a cylinder. If necessary, brush on more water-cornstarch mixture to help seal edges.
5. Place seam side down on baking sheets until ready to fry. Cover.
6. Fry at 350°F until golden brown and crisp. Internal temperature should be 160°F.
7. Place in counter pans with liners. Do not cover.
8. Serve with topping (recipe follows).

TOPPING

Ingredient	Amount	Procedure
Lettuce, shredded	3 lb 8 oz	Serve each Chimichanga with 1 oz each of
Tomato, chopped	3 lb 8 oz	shredded lettuce, chopped tomato,
Guacamole (p. 87)	3 lb 8 oz	Guacamole, sour cream, and olives; 2 oz
Sour cream	3 lb 8 oz	Salsa. See Note 1.
Black olives, chopped	3 lb 8 oz	
Salsa (p. 569) or Spanish Sauce (p. 570)	3 qt	

Notes:

1. Salsa (p. 569) or commercial salsa may be used.
2. 7 lb shredded cooked beef may be substituted for ground beef. Omit browning the beef and sauté onions and peppers in a little shortening.
3. 3 oz (1½ cups) dehydrated onions, rehydrated in 2½ cups water, may be substituted for fresh onions (p. 50).

Figure 2.50 *Making chimichangas: (a) Portion meat mixture onto flour tortilla. (b) Shape meat mixture into elongated form. Brush tortilla edges with water-cornstarch mixture. (c) Fold bottom edge over filling. (d) Fold in sides of tortilla. (e) Roll into a cylinder shape. (f) Brush water-cornstarch mixture on the top edge to help seal. Place seam side down on baking sheets and cover until ready to fry.*

Oven-baked hamburgers

| OVEN: 400°F | YIELD: 50 portions |
| BAKE: 15–20 minutes | PORTION: 4 oz |

Ingredient	Amount	Procedure
Ground beef	12 lb	Place meat in mixer bowl.
Eggs, beaten Milk	3 (5 oz) 2 cups	Combine eggs and milk and add to meat.
Bread crumbs, soft Onion, chopped Salt Pepper, black	4 oz 4 oz 2 Tbsp 2 tsp	Add crumbs and seasonings. Blend on low speed for approximately 1 minute, using flat beater.
		Portion meat mixture with No. 10 dipper onto lightly greased baking sheets. Flatten into patties. Bake at 400°F for 15–20 minutes.
Hamburger buns	50	Serve patties on warm buns.

Note:
½ oz (¼ cup) dehydrated onions, rehydrated in ½ cup water, may be substituted for fresh onions
(p. 50).

Variations:
1. **Barbecued hamburgers.** Place browned hamburgers in baking pans. Pour Barbecue Sauce
   (p. 568) over patties. Cover with aluminum foil and bake at 325°F until hot, about 10–20 minutes.
2. **Grilled hamburgers and accompaniments.** Cook 4-oz hamburger patties on the grill only
   until they are no longer pink. Place on bun and serve with accompaniments: mayonnaise, mustard, catsup, sliced dill pickles, sliced or chopped onions, sliced tomato, and leaf lettuce.

Fajitas

YIELD: 50 portions
PORTION: 1 fajita, 2 oz meat
2 oz vegetable

Ingredient	Amount	Procedure
Pureed jalapeño peppers, with juice	4 oz	Combine in bowl to make a marinade.
Lemon juice	1½ cups	
Pineapple juice	1½ cups	
Salt	1 Tbsp	
Pepper, black	2 Tbsp	
Meat tenderizer	2 oz	
Water	3 cups	
Beef round	10 lb AP	Cut beef into 1 × 5-inch strips, ¼-inch thick (see Note 1). Pour marinade over meat. Stir to coat meat. Cover and marinate for 24 hours.
		Drain meat in colander. Discard marinade. Stir-fry meat in frying pan with a small amount of oil until cooked.
Onions, sliced, separated in rings	2 lb 8 oz	Add onions and green peppers to meat. Stir-fry until tender-crisp.
Green pepper strips	1 lb 8 oz	Transfer to 12 × 10 × 4-inch pan.
Tomatoes, fresh	2 lb 8 oz	Cut tomatoes into thin wedges. Combine carefully with beef. Gently lift beef and vegetables from juice into 12 × 20 × 2-inch counter pan.
Tortillas, flour, 10-inch	50	Heat tortillas to soften. Keep covered. Do not allow to dry out. Serve 1 tortilla on plate and 4 oz beef and vegetables in center of tortilla. Tortilla may be rolled or folded in half.

Serve with condiments: Guacamole (p. 87), shredded Monterey Jack cheese, shredded lettuce, sour cream, Salsa (p. 569), sliced black olives, sliced jalapeños.

Notes:
1. Meat will slice more easily if it is partially frozen.
2. Fajita meat can be made spicier by substituting additional pureed jalapeños for equal parts of water. More water in proportion to less jalapeños may be used for a less spicy Fajita.
3. Beef strips may be purchased frozen, seasoned or unseasoned.
4. Commercial Fajita marinade mix may be substituted for marinade in the recipe.

Variation:
Chicken fajitas. Delete meat tenderizer. Increase salt to 2 Tbsp. Substitute chicken breasts for beef.

Reuben sandwich

YIELD: 50 sandwiches
PORTION: 3 oz

Ingredient	Amount	Procedure
Cooked corned beef	4 lb 8 oz	Cut corned beef into very thin slices.
Rye bread Mayonnaise or Sandwich Spread (p. 538)	100 slices 2 cups	Spread No. 100 dipper (scant 2 tsp) dressing on bread.

Sauerkraut, well drained
Swiss cheese, 1-oz slices
	1½ qt
	3 lb 2 oz
		Place filling on bread, in order given:
		  1½ oz corned beef
		  2 Tbsp sauerkraut
		  1 oz cheese
		Cover with top slice of bread.

Margarine or butter, melted	1 lb	Brush sandwiches with melted margarine. Preheat grill to 325°F. Grill sandwiches on both sides until delicately browned.

Tacos

YIELD: 50 portions
PORTION: 2 tacos

Ingredient	Amount	Procedure
Ground beef	13 lb AP (9 lb EP)	Brown beef in steam-jacketed or other kettle. Drain off fat.
Onion, chopped	1 lb	Add onions and cook until softened.
Cornstarch	3 Tbsp	Combine cornstarch and seasonings in a bowl.
Chili powder	½ cup	Add to ground beef and onions. Mix well.
Garlic powder	1¾ Tbsp	
Salt	3 Tbsp	
Oregano, leaf	1 Tbsp	
Cumin, ground	2 Tbsp	
Cayenne	1 Tbsp	
Water	1½ qt	Add water to meat mixture. Mix. Simmer 45 minutes, stirring frequently.
Taco shells	100	Place shells in counter pans. Heat in oven until warm and crisp. To serve, fill each taco shell with No. 24 dipper of meat mixture 1½ oz each.

TOPPING

Ingredient	Amount	Procedure
Lettuce, head, chopped	4 lb EP	Cover meat mixture with lettuce, then
Tomatoes, fresh, diced	3 lb EP	tomato, and top with shredded cheese.
Processed cheese, shredded	2 lb	Serve with Salsa (p. 569) to spoon on top.

Notes:
1. Commercial salsa may be substituted for Salsa recipe.
2. Commercial taco seasoning mix may be substituted for spices. Follow manufacturer's directions for amount to use.
3. 2 oz (1 cup) dehydrated onions, rehydrated in 1½ cups water, may be substituted for fresh onions (p. 50).

Variations:
1. **Nacho tostadas.** Place ¾ oz (about 6 large) round unsalted nacho chips on serving plate. Place No. 12 dipper (3 oz) taco meat on top of chips. Ladle 2 oz Nacho Sauce (p. 323) over meat. Place approximately 1½ oz shredded head lettuce and ¾ oz diced fresh tomatoes on top of meat. Serve with condiments: Guacamole (p. 87), sour cream, and Salsa (p. 569).

2. Tostadas. Fry fifty 10-inch flour or corn tortillas in hot oil, 20–30 seconds on each side, until crisp and golden brown. Drain on paper towel. Keep warm. To serve, spread each tortilla with No. 20 dipper Refried Beans (p. 633), then one No. 12 dipper of meat (3 oz). Top with 1½ oz chopped head lettuce, ¾ oz chopped fresh tomatoes, and 1 oz shredded cheese. Serve with condiments: Guacamole (p. 87), sour cream, Salsa (p. 569), chopped green onions, chopped green chilies, and sliced ripe olives.

Western sandwich

| | YIELD: 50 sandwiches | |
| | PORTION: 3 oz | |

Ingredient	Amount	Procedure
Ground beef	10 lb	Brown beef and onion. Drain off fat.
Onion, chopped	1 lb	
Tomato puree	3 cups	Add remaining filling ingredients to meat.
Catsup	3 cups	Simmer 15–20 minutes.
Water	1 cup	
Salt	1 Tbsp	
Paprika	2 tsp	
Dry mustard	2 tsp	
Worcestershire sauce	2 Tbsp	
Chili powder	1 Tbsp	
Hamburger buns	50	Serve with No. 12 dipper of filling on buns.

Notes:
1. If mixture becomes dry, add a small amount of water.
2. 2 oz (1 cup) dehydrated onions, rehydrated in 1½ cups water, may be substituted for fresh onions (p. 50).

Variation:
Pizzaburger. Delete paprika and chili powder. Add 1 Tbsp oregano, 1½ tsp basil, and 8 oz sliced mushrooms. Serve meat on bun and sprinkle with 1 lb 8 oz grated mozzarella cheese, ½ oz per serving.

Hot roast beef sandwich

		YIELD: 50 sandwiches
		PORTION: 3 oz meat
		¼ cup gravy

Ingredient	Amount	Procedure
Beef roast	10 lb EP (15 lb AP)	Roast beef according to directions on p. 346. Slice into 3-oz portions. Place in two 12 × 20 × 2-inch counter pans.
Beef Stock (p. 589)	1½ qt	Heat stock. Pour over meat. Cover with aluminum foil and place in oven to keep warm.
Bread	50 slices	Place 3 oz meat on each slice of bread.
Mashed Potatoes (p. 653) Gravy (p. 566)	12 lb 8 oz 1 gal	Serve No. 12 dipper of Mashed Potato on the plate beside the bread. Cover meat and potato with Gravy, using 2-oz ladle.

Note:
Meat may be covered with additional slice of bread if desired. Omit mashed potatoes. Cover entire sandwich with gravy.

Variations:
1. **Barbecued beef sandwich.** Place thinly sliced beef roast in 2 counter pans and keep warm. Heat 1½ qt Barbecue Sauce (p. 568) and pour 3 cups over each pan of meat. Toss together until sauce is evenly distributed. Serve in warm hamburger buns.
2. **French dip sandwich.** Slice roast beef wafer thin. Place in 12 × 20 × 2-inch counter pan. Pour 1 cup Beef Stock (p. 589) over meat. Cover with aluminum foil and keep warm. To serve, place 3 oz beef on hard roll bun. Serve with side cup of hot seasoned broth for dipping.
3. **Hot roast pork sandwich.** Substitute roast pork for beef.
4. **Hot turkey dip.** Follow directions for French Dip Sandwich, but substitute wafer-sliced turkey for beef and chicken broth for beef broth. Season chicken stock with poultry seasoning.
5. **Hot turkey sandwich.** Substitute roast turkey or turkey roll for beef. Use Chicken Stock (p. 590) in place of Beef Stock.

SAUCES

A sauce serves to complement an entree, vegetable, or dessert. It may be used as a binding agent to hold foods together or as a topping. Sauces add richness, moistness, color, and form to foods and may enhance or offer contrast in flavor or color to foods they accompany.

ENTREE AND VEGETABLE SAUCES

Basic to many sauces is a roux, which is a cooked mixture of fat and flour, usually equal parts by weight. A roux may range from white, in which the fat and flour are cooked only for a short time, to brown, cooked until it is light brown in color and has a nutty aroma. The amount of browning will influence both the flavor and color characteristics of the sauce.

Other starch thickening agents commonly used in sauces are arrowroot, cornstarch, pregelatinized or instant starch, and waxy maize. Waxy maize is preferred for sauces that will be frozen because it will not break and separate as easily as other starches. Egg yolks have a slight thickening power and are used for some sauces. When egg yolks are cooked to too high a temperature, the egg protein will coagulate and cause a curdled effect. When using egg yolks to thicken, care must be exercised to keep the sauce temperature below 158°F and the holding time short.

Most meat and vegetable sauces are modifications of the basic recipes: white sauce, brown sauce, red sauces, and butter sauces.

- White Sauce (p. 560), made with a roux of fat and flour and with milk as the liquid, has many uses in quantity food preparation, as a sauce with vegetables, eggs, and fish and as an ingredient in many casseroles. A White Sauce Mix (p. 562) in which flour, fat, and nonfat dry milk are combined may be made and stored in the refrigerator until needed. Water and seasonings are added when the mixture is to be used. Béchamel Sauce (p. 563) is a white sauce that uses milk and chicken stock as the liquid and, with its variations, usually is served with poultry, seafood, eggs, or vegetables.

- Brown Sauce (p. 565) is made with a well-browned roux and used with meat.

- Red Sauces (pp. 568–571) include tomato as a primary ingredient. These sauces are generally used with meat and pasta.

- Butter Sauces (p. 577) are used with vegetables, fish, meats, and egg dishes.

A broth made with a high-quality commercial stock base can be substituted for the chicken or beef stock called for in sauces, but the salt in the recipe may need to be adjusted if the base is highly seasoned.

Sauces made from concentrated canned soups are time-saving and may be used effectively in many items. Undiluted canned cream soups, such as chicken, mushroom, celery, and cheese, or tomato soup may be used alone or in combination. If the soup is too thick, a small amount of milk or chicken or meat stock may be added. Two soups may be combined for a special flavor effect, or pimiento, green pepper, almonds, curry powder, or other ingredients may be added for variety.

Marinades are used to flavor and tenderize meats and poultry and to flavor raw or cooked vegetables. The less tender cuts of meat should be marinated at least 2 hours; pork, chicken, and the more tender cuts of beef often are basted before and during cooking but do not need to stand in the marinade.

DESSERT SAUCES

Sauces serve as both a garnish and a basic ingredient for many desserts. The choice of sauce should complement the dessert in both color and flavor. Most dessert sauces are added shortly before serving.

ENTREE AND VEGETABLE SAUCE RECIPES

White sauce

		YIELD: 1 gal			
	Ingredients				
Consistency	**Milk**[a]	**Flour**[b]	**Margarine or butter**	**Salt**	**Uses**
Thin	4 qt	6 oz	6 oz	1 oz[c]	Cream soups
Medium	4 qt	8 oz	8 oz	1 oz	Creamed foods, gravy
Thick	4 qt	12 oz	12 oz	1 oz	Soufflés

[a] 1 lb nonfat dry milk and 3¾ qt cool water may be substituted for fluid milk. Combine dry milk and water and whip until smooth. Heat to scalding (185°F). Add, while stirring, roux made of margarine and flour. Cook on low heat, stirring as necessary, until thickened.
[b] All-purpose flour.
[c] 1 oz salt equals 1½ Tbsp.

(continued)

Method 1.   Melt margarine, remove from heat. Add flour and salt. Stir until smooth. Cook 5–10 minutes. Add milk gradually, stirring constantly with wire whip. Cook and stir as necessary until smooth and thick, about 15 minutes.

Method 2.   This method is used for making quantities larger than 4 qt. Make a roux by melting margarine, adding flour, and cooking and stirring until smooth. Add one-fourth of the milk and beat with wire whip until smooth. Gradually add remaining milk while stirring. Cook until smooth and thickened, about 15 minutes.

Method 3.   Combine flour with one-fourth of the milk. Heat remaining milk. Add milk-flour paste, using wire whip. Cook to desired consistency, then add margarine and salt.

Method 4.   This method uses a steamer. Make a paste of flour and margarine. Add cold milk until mixture is the consistency of cream. Heat remaining milk. Add flour and margarine mixture, stirring constantly with wire whip. Place in steamer until flour is cooked; if necessary, stir once during cooking.

Variations to be used with 1 gallon medium white sauce:

1. **A la king sauce.**   Add 12 oz chopped green pepper, 12 oz sliced mushrooms, sautéed, and 1 lb chopped pimiento. Combine with cubed cooked chicken, meats, seafood, vegetables, or eggs.
2. **Bacon sauce.**   Add 1 lb 8 oz cooked chopped bacon. Use bacon fat in making the sauce. Combine with eggs or vegetables in scalloped dishes.
3. **Cheese sauce.**   Add 3 lb sharp cheddar cheese, shredded or ground, 2 Tbsp Worcestershire sauce, and a few grains of cayenne. Serve on fish, egg dishes, soufflés, and vegetables.
4. **Cheese sandwich sauce (American or cheddar).**   Prepare 2 qt (half recipe) Thick White Sauce. Add ¼ cup dry mustard and 1 tsp white pepper with the flour. When sauce has thickened, stir in 2 lb shredded sharp cheese and ½ tsp tabasco sauce. Ladle 1½ oz sauce over meat in sandwich.
5. **Cheese sandwich sauce (Swiss).**   Prepare 2 qt (half recipe) Medium White Sauce. Reduce margarine to 6 oz. After sauce has thickened, add 2 lb shredded Swiss cheese and stir until melted. Serve 1½ oz sauce ladled over meat in sandwich.
6. **Egg sauce.**   Add 20 chopped hard-cooked eggs and 2 Tbsp prepared mustard. Serve over salmon or other fish loaf.
7. **Golden sauce.**   Add 2 cups slightly beaten egg yolks. Serve on fish, chicken, or vegetables.
8. **Mushroom sauce.**   Add 1 lb 8 oz sliced mushrooms and 4 oz minced onion, sautéed in 4 oz margarine or butter. Serve over egg, meat, poultry dishes, or vegetables.
9. **Pimiento sauce.**   Add 1 lb 4 oz finely chopped pimiento and 2 cups finely chopped parsley. Serve with poached fish, croquettes, or egg dishes.
10. **Shrimp sauce.**   Add 4 lb cooked shrimp, 2 Tbsp prepared mustard, and 2 Tbsp Worcestershire sauce. Serve with fish, eggs, or cheese soufflé.
11. **Swiss cheese and mushroom sauce.**   Prepare 2 qt (half recipe) Medium White Sauce. Sauté 8 oz chopped onions, 2 oz chopped green peppers, and 8 oz sliced mushrooms in 6 oz margarine. Stir in 6 oz flour. Cook 10–15 minutes. Add slowly, while stirring, 2 qt milk and heat to 170°F. Add 2 lb 8 oz shredded Swiss cheese and stir until melted.

White sauce mix

	YIELD: 13 lb 8 oz mix	
Ingredient	**Amount**	**Procedure**
Flour, all-purpose	3 lb	Blend flour and milk in 60-qt mixer bowl.
Nonfat dry milk	6 lb	
Shortening	2 lb 4 oz	Using pastry knife or flat beater, blend fats with dry ingredients until mixture is crumbly, scraping sides of bowl occasionally.
Margarine or butter	2 lb 4 oz	
		Store in covered containers in the refrigerator.

TO PREPARE 1 GALLON OF WHITE SAUCE

Water	3¼ qt	Heat water and salt to boiling point.
Salt	1 oz (1½ Tbsp)	
White sauce mix		Add mix for sauce of desired thickness.
Thin	1 lb 12 oz	Stirring with wire whip, continue cooking until thickened.
Medium	2 lb 4 oz	
Thick	2 lb 14 oz	

Béchamel sauce

YIELD: 2 qt
PORTION: 3 Tbsp (1½ oz)

Ingredient	Amount	Procedure
Chicken Stock (p. 590)	1½ qt	Cook stock and seasonings together for 20 minutes. Strain.
Onion slices	4	
Peppercorns, black	2 Tbsp	Save liquid for preparation of sauce. There should be 1 qt liquid.
Carrots, chopped	3 oz	
Bay leaf	1	
Margarine or butter	8 oz	Melt margarine. Add flour and stir until smooth. Cook 5 minutes.
Flour, all-purpose	4 oz	
Seasoned stock (prepared above)	1 qt	Add liquids gradually, stirring constantly with wire whip.
Milk, hot	1 qt	Cook until smooth and thickened.
Salt	½ tsp	Add seasonings.
Pepper, white	½ tsp	Serve with 2-oz ladle (scant) on chicken or meat entrees.
Cayenne	Few grains	

Variations:
1. **Mornay sauce.**   Add gradually to hot Béchamel Sauce 4 oz each of grated Parmesan and Swiss cheese. Let sauce remain over heat until cheese is melted, then remove and gradually beat in 8 oz margarine or butter. Serve with fish or egg entrees.
2. **Velouté sauce.**   Substitute Chicken Stock for milk. Serve on chicken turnovers or other chicken entrees. For fish Velouté, substitute fish stock for milk. Serve on fish.

Fresh mushroom sauce

| | | YIELD: 1 gal |
| | | PORTION: 2½ oz |

Ingredient	Amount	Procedure
Mushrooms, fresh	4 lb	Clean, trim, and slice mushrooms.
Margarine or butter	8 oz	Melt margarine. Sauté onions and mushrooms.
Onions, minced	2 oz	
Flour, all-purpose	4 oz	Add flour and blend. Cook 5 minutes.
Chicken Stock, hot (p. 590)	2 qt	Add stock and milk while stirring with wire whip. Cook until thickened.
Milk or cream	2 cups	
Salt	To taste	Taste for seasoning. Add salt if needed.

Note:
Canned, drained mushrooms may be substituted for fresh mushrooms. Stir into prepared sauce.

Variations:
1. **Mushroom and almond sauce.** Add 1 lb slivered almonds. Serve over rice as an entree.
2. **Mushroom and cheese sauce.** Add 1 lb shredded cheese. Serve over asparagus or broccoli.

Brown sauce

YIELD: 2 qt
PORTION: 3 Tbsp (1½ oz)

Ingredient	Amount	Procedure
Beef Stock (p. 589)	2 qt	Add onions and seasonings to meat stock. If soup base has been used to make stock, taste before adding salt. Simmer about 10 minutes. Strain.
Onion, thinly sliced	4 oz	
Salt	2 tsp	
Pepper, black	¼ tsp	
Shortening	8 oz	Heat shortening and blend with flour. Cook until it becomes uniformly brown in color. Add hot stock while stirring with wire whip. Cook until thickened.
Flour, all-purpose	5 oz	

Variations:

1. **Jelly sauce.**   Add 2 cups currant jelly, beaten until melted, 2 Tbsp tarragon vinegar, and 4 oz sautéed minced onions. Serve with lamb or game.
2. **Mushroom sauce.**   Add 1 lb sliced mushrooms and 2 oz minced onions, sautéed. Serve with steak.
3. **Olive sauce.**   Add 6 oz chopped stuffed olives. Serve with meat or duck.
4. **Piquant sauce.**   Add 2 oz minced onions, 2 oz capers, ½ cup vinegar, 4 oz sugar, ¼ tsp salt, ¼ tsp paprika, and ½ cup chili sauce or chopped sweet pickle. Serve with meats.
5. **Savory mustard sauce.**   Add ½ cup prepared mustard and ½ cup horseradish. Serve with meats.

Pan gravy

YIELD: 1 gal
PORTION: ⅓ cup (2½ oz)

Ingredient	Amount	Procedure
Fat, hot (meat drippings)	8 oz	Add flour to fat and blend.
Flour, all-purpose	8 oz	
Salt	1 Tbsp	Stir in salt and pepper. Cook 5 minutes.
Pepper, black	1 tsp	
Meat or Poultry Stock (pp. 589, 590)	1 gal	Add stock gradually, stirring constantly with wire whip. Cook until smooth and thickened.

Note:
If beef or poultry base is used for stock, delete or reduce salt.

Variations:
1. **Brown gravy.** Use 10 oz flour and brown in the fat.
2. **Cream gravy.** Substitute milk for water or stock.
3. **Giblet gravy.** Use chicken drippings for fat and chicken stock for liquid. Add 1 qt cooked giblets, chopped.
4. **Onion gravy.** Lightly brown 1 lb thinly sliced onions in fat before adding flour.
5. **Vegetable gravy.** Add 1 lb diced carrots, 4 oz chopped celery, and 12 oz chopped onion, cooked in water or meat stock.

Savory cream gravy

	YIELD: 1 gal	
Ingredient	**Amount**	**Procedure**
Chicken Stock (p. 590)	1¾ qt	Combine.
Water	2 cups	
Soy sauce	¾ cup	
Half-and-half	2 cups	
Margarine, melted	8 oz	Sauté vegetables in margarine.
Celery leaves, fresh, coarsely chopped	4 oz	
Green onions, finely chopped	4 oz	
Garlic, minced	2 cloves	
Basil leaves, whole	2 Tbsp	Blend spices and flour into vegetables, while stirring with a wire whip.
Nutmeg, ground	1½ tsp	
Flour, all-purpose	7 oz	Slowly add combined liquids, stirring constantly until mixture thickens.
Sour cream	2½ cups	Blend in sour cream. Do not boil. Keep warm.

Note:
Serve ladled over poultry or meat.

Cooked barbecue sauce

YIELD: 1½ gal

Ingredient	Amount	Procedure
Catsup	1 No. 10 can	Combine all ingredients.
Water	3 qt	Simmer 10 minutes.
Vinegar, cider	2 cups	Baste chicken or meat with sauce during
Salt	2 Tbsp	cooking.
Pepper, black	1 tsp	
Sugar, granulated	4 oz	
Chili powder	1 tsp	
Worcestershire sauce	¼ cup	
Tabasco sauce	1 Tbsp	
Onion, grated	4 oz	

Note:
½ oz (¼ cup) dehydrated onion may be substituted for the fresh onion.

Uncooked barbecue sauce

YIELD: 1 gal

Ingredient	Amount	Procedure
Catsup	1 No. 10 can	Mix all ingredients.
Vinegar, cider	3 cups	Pour over meat or chicken.
Sugar, granulated	12 oz	Follow cooking directions for meat or poultry.
Salt	4 oz	
Onion, grated	4 oz	

Note:
½ oz (¼ cup) dehydrated onion may be substituted for the fresh onion.

Salsa

	YIELD: 1 gal	
Ingredient	**Amount**	**Procedure**
Tomatoes, canned, diced or crushed	5 lb	Drain tomatoes. Reserve juice. Chop tomatoes until pureed. Place chopped tomatoes and reserved juice in kettle.
Green pepper, chopped	12 oz	Add to tomatoes. Simmer about 15 minutes or until of desired consistency.
Onion, chopped	12 oz	
Garlic, minced	2 cloves	
Green chilies, chopped	5 oz	
Jalapeño peppers, diced	2 Tbsp	
Vinegar, cider	1 cup	
Tomato juice	1½ qt	
Salt	1½ tsp	
Sugar, granulated	2 Tbsp	
Tapioca	⅓ cup	
Tabasco sauce	2 Tbsp	
Oregano leaves	½ tsp	
Cayenne	¾ tsp	
Cumin, ground	½ tsp	

Note:
May be served as a condiment with Tacos, Tostadas, Chimichangas, or other Mexican entrees.

Spanish sauce

YIELD: 3 qt
PORTION: 3 Tbsp (2 oz)

Ingredient	Amount	Procedure
Onion, chopped	4 oz	Sauté onion in shortening.
Shortening	4 oz	
Tomatoes, canned, diced	2 qt	Add remaining ingredients.
Celery, diced	1 lb	Simmer until vegetables are tender.
Green pepper, chopped	8 oz	
Pimiento, chopped	6 oz	
Salt	1 Tbsp	
Pepper, black	½ tsp	
Cayenne	Few grains	

Notes:
1. Serve with meat, fish, cheese, or Mexican entrees.
2. ½ oz (¼ cup) dehydrated onions, rehydrated in ½ cup water, may be substituted for fresh onions (p. 50).

Horseradish sauce

YIELD: 5 cups
PORTION: 1½ Tbsp (½ oz)

Ingredient	Amount	Procedure
Horseradish, drained	8 oz	Combine.
Prepared mustard	2 Tbsp	
Salt	½ tsp	
Paprika	¼ tsp	
Cayenne	⅛ tsp	
Vinegar, cider	⅓ cup	
Cream, whipping	2 cups	Whip cream. Fold in horseradish mixture. Chill.

Note:
Serve with ham or roast beef.

Tomato sauce

YIELD: 2 qt
PORTION: 2½ Tbsp (1½ oz)

Ingredient	Amount	Procedure
Tomato juice	2 qt	Combine tomato juice and seasonings.
Onion, finely chopped	4 oz	Simmer 20 minutes.
Sugar, granulated	2 Tbsp	
Salt	1 tsp	
Pepper, black	¼ tsp	
Worcestershire sauce	1 tsp	
Margarine	6 oz	Melt margarine. Add flour and blend.
Flour, all-purpose	4 oz	Add hot tomato juice gradually while stirring with wire whip.
		Cook until thickened.

Note:
½ oz (¼ cup) dehydrated onions, rehydrated in ½ cup water, may be substituted for fresh onions (p. 50).

Cocktail sauce

YIELD: 2 qt
PORTION: 2½ Tbsp (1½ oz)

Ingredient	Amount	Procedure
Chili sauce	1 qt	Mix all ingredients. Chill.
Catsup	2 cups	
Lemon juice	1 cup	
Onion juice	2 Tbsp	
Celery, finely chopped	10 oz	
Worcestershire sauce	5 tsp	
Horseradish	3 oz	
Tabasco sauce	Few drops	

Note:
Serve with clam, crab, lobster, oyster, or shrimp.

Mustard sauce (cold)

YIELD: 1 qt
PORTION: 1 Tbsp

Ingredient	Amount	Procedure
Sugar, granulated	2 Tbsp	Mix dry ingredients.
Salt	½ tsp	
Dry mustard	2 tsp	
Water	2 Tbsp	Add water, vinegar, and eggs to dry ingredients.
Vinegar, cider	¼ cup	
Eggs, beaten	2 (3 oz)	Cook until thick.
Margarine	1 oz	Add margarine. Stir until melted. Cool.
Cream, whipping	2 cups	Whip cream and fold into cooked mixture.

Note:
Serve cold with ham, pork, or beef roast.

Variation:
Hot Chinese mustard.   Combine 8 oz dry mustard, ⅓ cup salad oil, and 1 oz (1½ Tbsp) salt. Add 2 cups boiling water. Stir until smooth. Serve with egg rolls.

Mustard sauce (hot)

YIELD: 2 qt
PORTION: 2 Tbsp (1 oz)

Ingredient	Amount	Procedure
Beef Stock (p. 589)	2 qt	Heat stock to boiling point.
Cornstarch	5 oz	Blend dry ingredients with cold water.
Sugar, granulated	2 Tbsp	Add gradually to hot stock. Cook and stir
Salt	2 tsp	until thickened.
Pepper, white	½ tsp	
Water, cold	½ cup	
Prepared mustard	2 oz	Add remaining ingredients.
Horseradish	4 oz	Stir until blended.
Vinegar, cider	2 Tbsp	
Margarine	1 oz	

Note:
Serve hot with Boiled Beef, fresh or cured ham, or fish.

Sweet-sour sauce

YIELD: 50 portions
            1¼ qt
PORTION: 1½ Tbsp

Ingredient	Amount	Procedure
Sugar, granulated	1 cup	Combine sugar and cornstarch in kettle.
Cornstarch	¼ cup	
Vinegar, cider	2 cups	Add vinegar, water, and soy sauce to dry
Water	2 cups	ingredients and stir until smooth.
Soy sauce	3 Tbsp	
Catsup	⅔ cup	Stir catsup into mixture in kettle. Cook until translucent, stirring constantly. Serve as a condiment with egg rolls or chicken nuggets.

Raisin sauce

YIELD: 1½ qt
PORTION: 2 Tbsp

Ingredient	Amount	Procedure
Seedless raisins	1 lb	Steam raisins or simmer in small amount of water for 3–5 minutes.
Sugar, granulated	4 oz	Mix sugar and water, and heat to boiling point.
Water	2 cups	
Currant jelly	1 lb	Add cooked raisins, currant jelly, and remaining ingredients.
Vinegar, cider	⅓ cup	Simmer 5 minutes or until jelly is dissolved.
Margarine	2 oz	
Worcestershire sauce	1 Tbsp	
Salt	1 tsp	
Pepper, white	¼ tsp	
Cloves, ground	½ tsp	
Mace	⅛ tsp	
Red food coloring (optional)	Few drops	

Note:
Serve with baked ham.

Cucumber sauce

YIELD: 3 cups
PORTION: 1 Tbsp (½ oz)

Ingredient	Amount	Procedure
Cucumbers	1 lb	Peel cucumbers; remove seeds. Grate or chop finely.
Sour cream	1 cup	Combine remaining ingredients and add to cucumber. Chill.
Onion, grated	1 Tbsp	
Vinegar, cider	1 Tbsp	
Lemon juice	1½ Tbsp	
Salt	½ tsp	
Cayenne	Few grains	

Note:
Serve with fish.

Hollandaise sauce

YIELD: 12 portions
PORTION: 1½ Tbsp (¾ oz)

Ingredient	Amount	Procedure
Butter	2 oz	Place butter, lemon juice, and egg yolks over hot (not boiling) water.
Lemon juice	1½ Tbsp	Cook slowly, beating constantly.
Egg yolks	3	
Butter	2 oz	When first portion of butter is melted, add second portion and beat until mixture thickens.
Butter	2 oz	Add third portion of butter and seasonings.
Salt	Few grains	Beat until thickened.
Cayenne	Few grains	Serve immediately.

Notes:
1. Serve with fish or green vegetables such as asparagus or broccoli.
2. If sauce tends to curdle, add hot water, a teaspoon at a time, stirring vigorously.
3. It is recommended that this sauce be made only in small quantity.

Mock hollandaise sauce

YIELD: 2 qt
PORTION: 2½ Tbsp (1½ oz)

Ingredient	Amount	Procedure
Butter or margarine	6 oz	Melt butter. Add flour and stir until smooth.
Flour, all-purpose	3 oz	Cook 3–5 minutes.
Milk	1½ qt	Add milk gradually, stirring constantly with wire whip.
		Cook until smooth and thickened.
Salt	1 tsp	Add seasonings.
Pepper, white	½ tsp	
Cayenne	Few grains	
Egg yolks, unbeaten	12 (8 oz)	Add 1 egg yolk at a time, a little butter, and
Butter, cut in pieces	1 lb	a little lemon juice until all are added.
Lemon juice	½ cup	Beat well.

Tartar sauce

YIELD: 1¾ qt
PORTION: 2 Tbsp (1 oz)

Ingredient	Amount	Procedure
Mayonnaise	1 qt	Mix all ingredients.
Pickle relish	6 oz	
Green pepper, chopped	¼ cup	
Parsley, chopped	¼ cup	
Green olives, chopped	6 oz	
Onion, minced	1 Tbsp	
Pimiento, chopped	2 oz	
Vinegar or lemon juice	½ cup	
Worcestershire sauce	Few drops	
Tabasco sauce	Few drops	

Note:
Serve with fish.

Drawn butter sauce

YIELD: 2 qt
PORTION: 3 Tbsp (1½ oz)

Ingredient	Amount	Procedure
Butter	2 oz	Melt butter. Add flour and blend.
Flour, all-purpose	4 oz	
Water, hot	2 qt	Gradually add hot water, while stirring with wire whip. Cook 5 minutes.
Salt	1 tsp	When ready to serve, add salt and butter. Beat until blended.
Butter, cut into pieces	6 oz	

Note:
Serve with green vegetables, fried or broiled fish, or egg dishes.

Variations:
1. **Almond butter sauce.** Add ¼ cup lemon juice and 6 oz toasted slivered almonds just before serving.
2. **Lemon butter sauce.** Add 1 Tbsp grated lemon peel and ¼ cup lemon juice just before serving. Serve with fish, new potatoes, broccoli, or asparagus.
3. **Maître d'hôtel sauce.** Add ¼ cup lemon juice, ¼ cup chopped parsley, and 8 egg yolks, well beaten.
4. **Parsley butter sauce.** Add 1½ cups minced parsley just before serving. Serve with fish, potatoes, or other vegetables.

Meunière sauce

YIELD: 3 cups

Ingredient	Amount	Procedure
Margarine or butter	1 lb 4 oz	Heat margarine until lightly browned.
Onion, minced	2 oz	Add onion and brown slightly.
Lemon juice	½ cup	Add juice and seasonings.
Worcestershire sauce	1 Tbsp	Serve hot over broccoli, brussels sprouts,
Lemon peel, grated	1 Tbsp	green beans, spinach, or cabbage.
Salt	1 tsp	

Note:
3 oz toasted sliced almonds may be sprinkled over top of vegetable.

Hot bacon sauce

YIELD: 2½ qt

Ingredient	Amount	Procedure
Bacon	1 lb	Dice bacon. Fry until crisp.
Flour, all-purpose	4 oz	Add flour and stir until smooth.
Sugar, granulated	1 lb 4 oz	Mix sugar, salt, vinegar, and water. Boil 1
Salt	¼ cup	minute.
Vinegar, cider	3 cups	Add to fat-flour mixture gradually while
Water	3 cups	stirring.
		Cook until slightly thickened.

Note:
Use to wilt lettuce or spinach; or with hot potato salad or shredded cabbage.

Meat marinade

	YIELD: 2 qt	
Ingredient	**Amount**	**Procedure**
Salad oil	1 qt	Combine ingredients, mixing well.
Worcestershire sauce	¼ cup	Pour over meat. Marinate overnight.
Liquid smoke	¼ cup	
Soy sauce	2 cups	
Vinegar, cider	¼ cup	
Garlic, minced	4 cloves	
Celery salt	¼ cup	
Dry mustard	¼ cup	
Ginger, ground	¼ cup	
Sugar, brown	1 cup	

Note:
Use for pork or beef.

Vegetable marinade

	YIELD: 1½ qt	
Ingredient	**Amount**	**Procedure**
Lemon juice	2½ Tbsp	Combine.
Vinegar, white	⅓ cup	
Salad oil	1 cup	
Worcestershire sauce	1 Tbsp	
Water	⅓ cup	
Onion, finely chopped	3 oz	Add and mix.
Garlic, crushed	2 cloves	
Pimiento, chopped	¼ cup	
Parsley, finely chopped	¼ cup	
Salt	1½ Tbsp	Blend in and mix.
Sugar, granulated	1 Tbsp	Pour over fresh vegetables and marinate.
Pepper, black	⅛ tsp	
Tarragon	1 Tbsp	

Note:
May be used for fresh mushrooms and other fresh vegetables or pasta.

DESSERT SAUCE RECIPES

Butterscotch sauce

YIELD: 1¼ qt
PORTION: 1½ Tbsp (1 oz)

Ingredient	Amount	Procedure
Sugar, brown	1 lb	Combine and cook to soft-ball stage (240°F).
Corn syrup	1⅓ cups	Remove from heat.
Water	⅔ cup	
Margarine or butter	6 oz	Add margarine and marshmallows.
Marshmallows	2 oz	Stir until melted. Cool.
Evaporated milk	1⅓ cups	When cool, add milk.

Caramel sauce

YIELD: 2 qt
PORTION: 2½ Tbsp (1½ oz)

Ingredient	Amount	Procedure
Sugar, brown	1 lb	Mix sugars and flour. Stir in water.
Sugar, granulated	1 lb	Boil until thickened.
Flour, all-purpose	2 oz	
Water	1 qt	
Margarine or butter	8 oz	Stir in margarine and vanilla.
Vanilla	1 Tbsp	

Note:
Serve warm or cold over ice cream or apple desserts.

Chocolate sauce

YIELD: 1½ qt
PORTION: 2 Tbsp (1 oz)

Ingredient	Amount	Procedure
Sugar, granulated	12 oz	Mix dry ingredients.
Cornstarch	2 oz	
Salt	1 tsp	
Cocoa	3 oz	
Water, cold	1 cup	Add cold water gradually to form a smooth paste.
Water, boiling	3½ cups	Add boiling water slowly while stirring. Boil for 5 minutes or until thickened. Remove from heat.
Margarine or butter	6 oz	Add margarine and vanilla. Stir to blend.
Vanilla	1 tsp	

Note:
Serve warm or cold on puddings, cake, cream puffs, or ice cream.

Hot fudge sauce

YIELD: 1½ qt
PORTION: 2 Tbsp (1 oz)

Ingredient	Amount	Procedure
Margarine or butter, soft	8 oz	Combine margarine, sugar, and milk over hot water.
Sugar, powdered	1 lb 8 oz	
Evaporated milk	1 13-oz can	Stir and cook slowly for 30 minutes.
Unsweetened chocolate, chipped or melted	8 oz	Add chocolate and stir until blended.

Notes:
1. Serve hot over ice cream.
2. This sauce may be stored in the refrigerator. Heat over hot water before serving. If too thick or grainy, add evaporated milk before heating.

Custard sauce

YIELD: 1 gal
PORTION: ⅓ cup (2½ oz)

Ingredient	Amount	Procedure
Sugar, granulated Cornstarch Salt	14 oz 2 oz ½ tsp	Mix dry ingredients.
Milk, cold	2 cups	Add cold milk and mix until smooth.
Milk, hot	3 qt	Add cold mixture to hot milk gradually while stirring.
Egg yolks, beaten	10 (6 oz)	Stir in egg yolks gradually. Cook over hot water until thickened, about 5 minutes.
Vanilla	2 Tbsp	Remove from heat and add vanilla. Cool.

Note:
Serve over cake-type puddings.

Fluffy orange sauce

YIELD: 3 qt
PORTION: 3 Tbsp (1½ oz)

Ingredient	Amount	Procedure
Margarine or butter Sugar, powdered	1 lb 5 oz 2 lb 2 oz	Melt margarine. Gradually add sugar. Beat with wire whip until it resembles whipped cream.
Eggs, beaten	10 (1 lb 2 oz)	Add eggs slowly, beating constantly.
Orange juice Orange peel, grated	1¾ cups 1½ Tbsp	Slowly blend in orange juice and peel. Heat 10–15 minutes. Beat again.

Lemon sauce

YIELD: 3 qt
PORTION: 3 Tbsp (2 oz)

Ingredient	Amount	Procedure
Sugar, granulated	2 lb	Mix dry ingredients.
Cornstarch	3 oz	
Salt	½ tsp	
Water, boiling	2 qt	Add boiling water. Cook until clear.
Lemon juice	⅔ cup	Add lemon juice and margarine.
Margarine or butter	1 oz (2 Tbsp)	

Note:
Serve hot with Steamed Pudding (p. 288), Bread Pudding (p. 286), or Rice Pudding (p. 286).

Variations:
1. **Nutmeg sauce.** Omit lemon juice. Add 1 tsp nutmeg. Increase margarine to 4 oz.
2. **Orange sauce.** Substitute orange juice for lemon juice. Add 1 tsp freshly grated orange peel.
3. **Vanilla sauce.** Omit lemon juice and reduce sugar to 1 lb 4 oz. Add 2 Tbsp vanilla.

Brown sugar hard sauce

YIELD: 1 qt
PORTION: 1 Tbsp (½ oz)

Ingredient	Amount	Procedure
Butter	12 oz	Cream butter on medium speed until light.
Sugar, light brown	1 lb 4 oz	Add sugar gradually while creaming.
Vanilla	2 tsp	Add vanilla. Cream until fluffy.
Cream, whipping	¾ cup	Whip cream. Fold into sugar mixture. Chill.

Note:
Serve with Christmas Pudding (p. 288).

Peanut butter sauce

YIELD: 2 qt
PORTION: 2½ Tbsp (1½ oz)

Ingredient	Amount	Procedure
Sugar, granulated	12 oz	Combine sugar, syrup, and water.
Syrup, white	1⅓ cups	Cook to 228°F and turn off heat or remove
Water, hot	¾ cup	from burner.
Margarine or butter	6 oz	Add margarine and marshmallows.
Marshmallows, miniature	3 oz	Stir until melted. Cool.
		Place in mixer bowl.
Evaporated milk	12 oz	Add milk and peanut butter.
Peanut butter	8 oz	Beat until well blended.
		Refrigerate.

Note:
Serve over ice cream.

Brown sugar syrup

YIELD: 2 gal

Ingredient	Amount	Procedure
Sugar, brown	5 lb	Combine all ingredients.
Sugar, granulated	5 lb 8 oz	Stir and heat until sugar is dissolved.
Corn syrup	1 cup	
Water	2½ qt	
Margarine or butter	4 oz	

Notes:
1. Serve warm or cold on pancakes, fritters, or waffles.
2. ½ tsp maple flavoring may be added.

Variation:
Blueberry syrup. Combine 1½ qt water, 12 oz granulated sugar, 1 tsp salt, and ⅓ cup lemon juice. Heat to boiling. Mix 4 oz waxy maize starch and 1½ cups cold water to make a paste. Add slowly to sugar mixture, stirring constantly. Cook until thickened and clear. Fold in 3 lb 8 oz individually quick frozen (IQF) blueberries. Serve warm over pancakes, French toast, or ice cream.

Raspberry sauce

YIELD: 3 qt
PORTION: 3 Tbsp (2 oz)

Ingredient	Amount	Procedure
Red raspberries, frozen	5 lb	Defrost berries. Do not drain.
Sugar, granulated Cornstarch	2 oz 1 oz	Combine sugar and cornstarch and add to berries. Cook until clear.
Currant jelly	1 lb 8 oz	Add jelly. Stir until melted. Cool.

Notes:
   1. Serve over vanilla ice cream or raspberry, lemon, or lime sherbet.
   2. Raspberries may be strained before thickening.

Variations:
1. Fresh strawberry sauce.   Substitute 5 lb fresh strawberries, cleaned and hulled, for raspberries. Mash berries, add 2½ cups water, and strain to remove seeds. Combine 1¼ cups sugar and ⅓ cup cornstarch with juice. Heat to boiling, stirring constantly. Cook until thickened and clear. Chill. Serve over ice cream or other desserts.
2. Peach melba.   Pour 3 Tbsp Raspberry Sauce over a scoop of vanilla ice cream placed in the center of a canned, fresh, or frozen peach half.

Hard sauce

		YIELD: 3⅓ cups
		PORTION: 1 Tbsp (½ oz)

Ingredient	Amount	Procedure
Butter	8 oz	Cream butter on medium speed until soft and fluffy.
Water, boiling	2 Tbsp	Add water and continue to cream until very light.
Sugar, powdered	1 lb 3 oz	Add sugar gradually. Continue creaming.
Lemon juice	½ tsp	Add lemon juice.
		Place in refrigerator to harden.

Note:
Serve with Christmas Pudding (p. 288), Baked Apples (p. 295), or Peach Cobbler (p. 299).

Variations:
1. **Cherry hard sauce.** Add ½ cup chopped maraschino cherries.
2. **Strawberry hard sauce.** Omit lemon juice and water. Add ¾ cup fresh or frozen strawberries, chopped.

SOUPS

Soups may be clear and light or thick and hearty. The type of soup served should complement the other menu items or be hearty enough for the entree. Hot soups should be heated to 180°F and cold soups served chilled.

TYPES OF SOUPS

Stock, the basic ingredient of many soups, is made by simmering meat, poultry, seafood, and/or vegetables in water to extract their flavor. The most frequently used stocks are *brown stock,* made from beef that has been browned before simmering, and *white or light stock,* made from veal and/or chicken.

To prepare stock, cover the meat or poultry with cold water, bring to the boiling point, and simmer for 3 to 4 hours. Strain and cool the broth, and remove the fat. When cold, the fat will congeal on top and may be skimmed off. To clarify the stock after it has been chilled, add egg whites and crushed washed eggshells, boil for 10–15 minutes, then strain (p. 590). Stock is highly perishable. If it is not to be used immediately, it may be reduced in volume by boiling to one-half or one-fourth its volume and frozen for later use.

Bouillon is made from clarified beef broth.

Consommé is made from clarified white or light stock.

Cream soups are made with a thin or medium white sauce combined with either mashed, strained, or finely chopped vegetables or meat, chicken, or fish. Chicken stock may be used to replace part of the milk in the sauce to enhance the flavor. If a stock base is used, it may be added to the margarine-flour roux or may be added to water and used as part of the liquid. Cream soups will curdle if kept at too high a temperature or held for too long a time. For this reason, the milk may be added just before serving and the mixture reheated to serving temperature (180°F).

Bisque is a mixture of chopped shellfish, stock, milk, and seasonings, usually thickened.

Puree is a thick soup made by pressing cooked vegetables or fish through a sieve into their own stock.

Chowder is an unstrained, heavy, thick soup prepared from meat, poultry, seafood, and/or vegetables. Most chowders contain potatoes and milk or cream.

COMMERCIAL SOUP BASES

Because preparation of soups, especially those made from stock, is time-consuming, commercial food or soup bases are often used. The amount of meat concentrate in commercial soup bases varies, so the choice of base should be made carefully to assure a desirable, full-flavored stock. A high-quality base is a concentrate of cooked meat, poultry, seafood, or vegetables, with the concentrated cooking juices and seasonings included. It has a puree-like consistency and may require refrigeration. One pound of soup base produces an average of 5 gallons of ready-to-use-stock. Most granulated soup bases and some paste products are highly salted. When these products are used, the salt listed in the recipe should be deleted or reduced. Soup bases can also be used to prepare sauces, gravies, and stuffings.

SOUP RECIPES
Stock soups

Beef stock

	YIELD: 3 gal	
Ingredient	**Amount**	**Procedure**
Beef shank, lean	15 lb	Pour water over beef shanks in large kettle or
Water, cold	5 gal	steam-jacketed kettle.
Onions, quartered	8 oz	Add vegetables and seasonings.
Celery with leaves, chopped	8 oz	Bring to boiling point. Reduce heat and simmer until meat leaves
Carrots, chopped	8 oz	bone, about 4 hours.
Peppercorns	1 Tbsp	
Bay leaves	2	
Salt	3 oz	
		Remove meat, strain broth, and refrigerate for several hours. Skim congealed fat off top.

Variations:
1. **Beef stock with soup base.**   Add 8 oz concentrated beef base to 2½ gal water. Exact proportion may vary with different manufacturers. If soup base is used for sauces and casseroles, delete or reduce amount of salt specified in recipe.
2. **Brown stock.**   Allow 10 lb beef shank to stand 30 minutes in cold water. Heat slowly to boiling point. Simmer 2 hours. Add vegetables that have been browned with remaining meat. Add seasonings. Simmer 3 hours.

Chicken stock

	YIELD: 3 gal	
Ingredient	**Amount**	**Procedure**
Chicken, uncooked Water, cold	20 lb AP 5 gal	Cut up chicken and place in large kettle or steam-jacketed kettle. Add water.
Onions, quartered Celery, with leaves, chopped Salt Peppercorns Bay leaves Marjoram	8 oz 8 oz 3 oz 1 Tbsp 2 2 tsp	Add vegetables and seasonings. Bring to boiling point. Reduce heat and simmer until chicken is tender.
		Remove chicken and strain broth. Refrigerate. Remove chicken from bones. Cut up for soup or reserve for later use. When broth is cold, fat will congeal on top; skim off.
Egg shells, washed and crushed Egg whites, beaten	3 3	If a clear broth is desired, clarify it by adding egg shells and whites to broth. Bring to boiling point and simmer for 15 minutes. Strain through cheesecloth or fine strainer.

Variations:
1. **Chicken stock with soup base.**   Add 8 oz concentrated chicken base to 2½ gal water. Exact proportion may vary with different manufacturers. If soup base is used for sauces and casseroles, delete or reduce amount of salt specified in recipe.
2. **White stock.**   Substitute knuckle of veal for part of chicken.

Bouillon

YIELD: 3 gal
PORTION: 1 cup (8 oz)

Ingredient	Amount	Procedure
Beef, lean	8 lb	Sear beef. Add bone and water.
Beef bone, cracked	4 lb	Simmer for 3–4 hours. Replace water as
Water, cold	4 gal	necessary.
Carrots, diced	8 oz	Add vegetables and seasonings.
Celery, chopped	8 oz	Cook 1 hour. Strain.
Onions, quartered	8 oz	Chill overnight.
Bay leaf	1	
Peppercorns	1 Tbsp	
Salt	¼ cup	
Egg shells, washed and crushed	3	Remove congealed fat from broth. Add egg shells and whites to clarify the broth.
Egg whites, beaten	3	Bring slowly to boiling point, stirring constantly. Boil 15–20 minutes without stirring. Strain through a fine strainer.

Variations:
1. **Chicken bouillon.**   Substitute 20 lb chicken, cut up, for the beef and bone. Do not sear chicken.
2. **Tomato bouillon.**   To 1½ gal Bouillon, add four 46-oz cans tomato juice, 2 oz chopped onion, 2 oz sugar, 2 oz salt (amount will vary), ½ tsp pepper, and 2 bay leaves.

Beef barley soup

YIELD: 50 portions
       3 gal
PORTION: 1 cup (8 oz)

Ingredient	Amount	Procedure
Beef, cubed	3 lb	Brown beef cubes in kettle. Drain off fat.
Celery, chopped	1 lb 6 oz	Add celery and onions. Sauté until tender.
Onions, chopped	1 lb 6 oz	
Beef Stock (p. 589)	3 gal	Add remaining ingredients. Bring to a boil.
Pepper, black	1 tsp	Lower heat and simmer for 1 hour.
Salt	1 tsp	Taste for seasoning and add salt if needed.
Bay leaf	1	
Carrots, diced	1 lb 6 oz	
Pearl barley	10 oz	

Note:
2¾ oz (1⅓ cups) dehydrated onions may be substituted for fresh onions (p. 50).

Vegetable beef soup

YIELD: 50 portions
3 gal
PORTION: 1 cup (8 oz)

Ingredient	Amount	Procedure
Beef Stock (p. 589)	2 gal	Heat stock in kettle.
Carrots, cubed	8 oz	Add vegetables and seasonings.
Celery, chopped	1 lb	Cover and simmer about an hour. Replace
Onions, chopped	1 lb 8 oz	water as necessary.
Potatoes, cubed	1 lb	Taste for seasoning. Add additional salt if
Salt	1 Tbsp	needed.
Pepper, black	1 tsp	
Tomatoes, diced, canned	1 No. 10 can	
Cooked beef, chopped	2 lb	Add chopped beef. Heat to serving temperature.

Notes:
1. 8 oz raw rice or 4 oz dry noodles may be substituted for the potatoes.
2. Browned beef cubes may be substituted for cooked beef. Brown in kettle before stock is added.
3. 3 oz (1½ cups) dehydrated onions may be substituted for fresh onions (p. 50).

Variations:
1. **Julienne soup.** Cut carrots, celery, and potatoes in long, thin strips.
2. **Vegetable soup.** Delete beef. Increase carrots and celery to 1 lb 8 oz each.

Hearty beef vegetable soup

YIELD: 50 portions
           3 gal
PORTION: 1 cup (8 oz)

Ingredient	Amount	Procedure
Ground beef	8 lb	Brown meat. Drain off fat.
Onions, chopped	1 lb	Add onions to meat and cook until tender.
Margarine Flour, all-purpose	9 oz 9 oz	Melt margarine and stir in flour. Cook for 5 minutes.

Beef Stock (p. 589)
Salt
Pepper, black
	1¼ gal
	1 Tbsp
	½ tsp
		Add stock and seasonings, stirring
		   constantly. Cook until mixture boils and
		   has thickened.
		Add browned meat and onions.

Carrots, fresh, diced Celery, sliced	12 oz 10 oz	Cook vegetables until barely tender. Drain. (Vegetables should be crunchy.)
Mixed vegetables, frozen	4 lb	Cook mixed vegetables until partially done. Add, with other vegetables, to the soup. Stir carefully to blend.
Tomatoes, diced, canned	2 lb 8 oz	Add tomatoes. Heat to serving temperature.

Note:
2 oz (1 cup) dehydrated onions may be substituted for fresh onions (p. 50).

Beef noodle soup

YIELD: 50 portions
3 gal
PORTION: 1 cup (8 oz)

Ingredient	Amount	Procedure
Vegetable oil	½ cup	Heat oil in kettle. Add beef cubes and seasonings and cook until lightly browned. Drain off fat.
Beef, fresh, cubed	2 lb	
Salt	2 tsp	
Pepper, black	½ tsp	
Onions, chopped	8 oz	Add onions and celery, and sauté.
Celery, chopped	12 oz	
Beef Stock (p. 589)	2¾ gal	Add stock. Simmer for one hour.
Noodles	12 oz	Add noodles and simmer until tender, 5–10 minutes. Add salt if needed.

Note:
1 oz (½ cup) dehydrated onions may be substituted for fresh onions (p. 50).

Variations:
1. **Alphabet soup.** Use alphabet noodles.
2. **Beef rice soup.** Substitute 1 lb 8 oz rice for noodles.
3. **Creole soup.** Reduce Beef Stock to 2¼ gal. Add 1 No. 10 can tomatoes, 8 oz shredded green peppers, 1 lb sliced okra, and 4 bay leaves. Substitute rice for noodles.

Chicken noodle soup

		YIELD: 50 portions
		3 gal
		PORTION: 1 cup (8 oz)

Ingredient	Amount	Procedure
Chicken Stock (p. 590)	3 gal	Bring stock to a boil.
Onion, chopped	8 oz	Add onion and celery. Cook until tender.
Celery, chopped	8 oz	
Noodles	1 lb	Add noodles. Cook for about 15 minutes or until noodles are tender.
Margarine, melted	8 oz	Blend margarine and flour.
Flour, all-purpose	4 oz	Add to soup, stirring until slightly thickened.
Salt	1 tsp	Add seasonings.
Pepper, white	½ tsp	
Cooked chicken, diced	1 lb 8 oz	Add chicken and simmer for 5 minutes.

Note:
1 oz (½ cup) dehydrated onions may be substituted for fresh onions (p. 50).

Variation:
Chicken rice soup. Substitute 12 oz rice for the noodles.

Turkey vegetable soup

YIELD:	50 portions
PORTION:	1 cup (8 oz)

Ingredient	Amount	Procedure
Carrots, fresh	1 lb	Cut carrots into thin julienne strips.
Potatoes, red	2 lb	Do not peel potatoes. Dice into ½-inch cubes.
Onions, minced	12 oz	Combine in steam-jacketed kettle.
Celery, chopped	10 oz	Add carrots and potatoes.
Mushrooms, sliced	8 oz	Simmer 20 minutes or until vegetables are
Chicken Stock (p. 590)	2½ gal	tender.
Sage, rubbed	⅛ tsp	Add to soup.
Thyme, ground	¼ tsp	
Pepper, black	¼ tsp	
Cooked turkey, chopped	2 lb	Add turkey and parsley. Heat to 180°F.
Parsley, fresh, chopped	2 oz	

Note:

1½ oz (¾ cup) dehydrated onions may be substituted for fresh onions (p. 50).

Minestrone soup

YIELD: 50 portions
          3 gal
PORTION: 1 cup (8 oz)

Ingredient	Amount	Procedure
Bacon, diced	1 lb	Fry bacon until crisp. Drain.
Onions, chopped Garlic, minced	12 oz 2 cloves	Sauté onion and garlic in a little bacon fat until tender. Place, with bacon, in a large kettle.
Beef Stock (p. 589) Bay leaves Pepper, black	2 gal 2 1 tsp	Add stock and seasonings. Heat to boiling.
Cabbage, chopped Carrots, fresh, diced Potatoes, raw, chopped Celery, chopped Spinach, fresh, chopped Green beans, cut, canned Tomatoes, canned, diced Red beans, canned Spaghetti, long	12 oz 12 oz 12 oz 12 oz 3 oz 12 oz 2 lb 1 lb 12 oz 2 oz	Add vegetables and spaghetti. Simmer 45 minutes.
Flour, all-purpose Water, cold	3 oz 1 cup	Make a smooth paste of the flour and water. Stir into soup. Cook 10 minutes longer.
Parsley, chopped	¼ cup	Add parsley just before serving.

Note:
1½ oz (¾ cup) dehydrated onions may be substituted for fresh onions (p. 50).

Mulligatawny soup

YIELD: 50 portions
3 gal
PORTION: 1 cup (8 oz)

Ingredient	Amount	Procedure
Margarine	6 oz	Melt margarine in steam-jacketed kettle or stockpot.
Onions, finely chopped	12 oz	
Carrots, julienne	12 oz	Add vegetables and apples. Cook 5 minutes.
Celery, thinly sliced	12 oz	
Green peppers, cut in thin strips	1 lb	
Apples, pared and chopped	2 lb	
Flour, all-purpose	12 oz	Stir in flour and seasonings.
Curry powder	1 Tbsp	
Salt	1 Tbsp	
Pepper, black	¼ tsp	
Chicken Stock (p. 590)	2 gal	Slowly add stock, tomatoes, and cloves.
Tomatoes, canned, diced, with juice	1 No. 10 can	
Cloves, whole, tied in a cloth bag for easy removal before serving	8	
Cooked chicken, diced	3 lb	Add chicken. Bring to a boil. Reduce heat and simmer until ingredients are tender, about 30 minutes.
Parsley, chopped	¼ cup	Add parsley. Simmer 5 minutes.

Note:
1½ oz (¾ cup) dehydrated onions may be substituted for fresh onions (p. 50).

Pepper pot soup

YIELD: 50 portions
       3 gal
PORTION: 1 cup (8 oz)

Ingredient	Amount	Procedure
Margarine	12 oz	Sauté vegetables in margarine until lightly browned, about 15 minutes.
Onion, finely chopped	8 oz	
Green peppers, finely chopped	8 oz	
Celery, thinly sliced	6 oz	
Potatoes, diced	3 lb 8 oz	
Flour, all-purpose	5 oz	Add flour to vegetables and stir until well blended.
Beef or Chicken Stock (pp. 589, 590)	2¼ gal	Combine stock and milk. Add to vegetable mixture, while stirring.
Milk, hot	1 qt	If soup base is used for the stock, taste before adding salt.
Salt	1 oz (1½ Tbsp)	
Pimiento, chopped	2 Tbsp	Add pimiento. Keep just below boiling point for 30 minutes, stirring frequently.

Notes:
   1. This soup is good served with Spaetzles (p. 139). Prepare 1 recipe for 50 servings.
   2. 1 oz (½ cup) dehydrated onions may be substituted for fresh onions (p. 50).

Rice soup

YIELD: 50 portions
         3 gal
PORTION: 1 cup (8 oz)

Ingredient	Amount	Procedure
Beef or Chicken Stock (pp. 589, 590)	5 qt	Heat stock in large kettle.
Rice, long-grain Water, boiling Salt	12 oz 3¾ cups 1½ tsp	Cook rice according to directions on p. 422. Add to hot stock.
Milk, hot Onion, finely chopped Salt Pepper, black Parsley, chopped	1 gal 1 Tbsp 1 oz (1½ Tbsp) 1 tsp ¼ cup	Add milk and seasonings to stock and rice. If soup base has been used for stock, taste before adding salt.

Note:
To serve, garnish with parsley.

Tomato rice soup

YIELD: 50 portions
       3 gal
PORTION: 1 cup (8 oz)

Ingredient	Amount	Procedure
Beef or Chicken Stock (pp. 589, 590)	2 gal	Heat stock and puree to boiling point.
Tomato puree	1 gal	
Onion, chopped	2 oz	Add vegetables and rice. Cook until rice is tender.
Green pepper, chopped	4 oz	
Rice, long-grain	8 oz	
Margarine	6 oz	Melt margarine and add flour. Mix until smooth.
Flour, all-purpose	3 oz	Add to soup while stirring. Add salt to taste.

Note:
¼ oz (2 Tbsp) dehydrated onions may be substituted for fresh onions (p. 50).

Variation:
Tomato barley soup.   Add 1 lb barley in place of rice.

French onion soup

YIELD: 50 portions
             3 gal
PORTION: 1 cup (8 oz)

Ingredient	Amount	Procedure
Onions, fresh	8 lb	Cut onions in thin slices.
Margarine or shortening	12 oz	Sauté in margarine in large kettle.
Flour, all-purpose	3 oz	Add flour and pepper. Cook for 10 minutes.
Pepper, black	1 tsp	
Beef Stock (p. 589)	3 gal	Add stock and Worcestershire sauce.
Worcestershire sauce	3 Tbsp	Cook until onions are tender.
Salt	1 tsp (if needed)	
Croutons	12 oz	To serve, ladle soup over croutons or toasted bread.
Parmesan cheese, grated, or Swiss cheese, shredded	2 oz	Sprinkle with cheese.

Navy bean soup

	YIELD:	50 portions
		3 gal
	PORTION:	1 cup (8 oz)

Ingredient	Amount	Procedure
Navy beans, dry	4 lb	Wash beans. Add boiling water. Cover and
Water, boiling	3 gal	let stand 1 hour or longer.
		Simmer beans for about 1 hour.
Ham cubes	3 lb	Add ham and seasonings to beans.
Onion, chopped	12 oz	Cook until beans are tender, 1–1½ hours.
Celery, diced	8 oz	Add water to make volume of 3¼ gal.
Pepper, black	1 Tbsp	Check seasoning. Add salt if needed. Heat to
Water		serving temperature.

Notes:
1. Great Northern beans may be substituted for navy beans.
2. Ham base may be substituted for part of the water.
3. 1½ oz (¾ cup) dehydrated onions may be substituted for fresh onions (p. 50).

Split pea soup

YIELD: 50 portions
          3 gal
PORTION: 1 cup (8 oz)

Ingredient	Amount	Procedure
Split peas	3 lb	Wash peas. Add water and bring to a boil.
Water	2 gal	Boil for 2 minutes, then turn off heat. Cover and let stand for 1 hour.
Ham cubes	2 lb	Add ham, onions, carrots, and potatoes.
Onions, chopped	1 lb	Cook for 1 hour or until peas are soft.
Carrots, fresh, chopped	1 lb 8 oz	
Potatoes, raw, chopped	2 lb	
Margarine	4 oz	Melt margarine and add flour. Stir until smooth. Cook 5 minutes.
Flour, all-purpose	2 oz	Add stock, while stirring, and cook until thickened.
Chicken Stock (p. 590)	2 qt	Add to peas.
Pepper, black	1 tsp	Taste for seasoning. Add pepper and salt if needed.

Notes:
1. If soup becomes too thick, add hot water to bring to desired consistency. If a smoother soup is desired, cook and puree peas before adding ham and vegetables.
2. 1 lb chopped celery may be substituted for 1 lb potatoes.
3. 3 lb sliced Polish sausage may be added to soup before serving. Reduce ham to 1 lb.
4. 2 oz (1 cup) dehydrated onions may be substituted for fresh onion (p. 50).

Variations:
1. **Black bean soup.**   Delete potatoes and carrots. Substitute 6 lb dried black beans for the split peas. Add 3 cloves garlic, minced, ½ tsp cayenne, and 1 tsp cumin. Serve with 1 tsp sour cream on top. Accompany with corn tortillas, cut into thin strips and sautéed briefly in butter, or crusty bread.
2. **Lentil soup.**   Substitute lentils for split peas.

Cream soups

Basic sauce for cream soup

		YIELD: 2½ gal basic sauce
Ingredient	**Amount**	**Procedure**
Margarine or butter Onions, finely chopped	8 oz 2 oz	Melt margarine. Add onions and sauté until tender.
Flour, all-purpose Chicken base Pepper, white	12 oz 3 oz ½ tsp	Add flour, chicken base, and pepper to onions. Stir until blended. Cook for 5 minutes.
Water	2 qt	Add water and stir until mixture thickens.
		Add vegetables and seasonings as suggested below to make a variety of cream soups.
Milk, hot	2 gal	Stir in milk. Heat to 180°F.

Notes:
1. Chicken base may be omitted. Omit the water and use 2½ gal milk. Add 2 oz salt.
2. ¼ oz (2 Tbsp) dehydrated onions, rehydrated in ¼ cup water, may be substituted for fresh onions (p. 50).

Suggestions for cream soups:
To make 3 gallons of soup (50–60 one-cup, 8-oz portions), use 1 recipe Basic Sauce for Cream Soup plus additions suggested below.
1. **Cream of asparagus soup.**   Add 6 lb cooked, chopped, or pureed asparagus.
2. **Cream of broccoli soup.**   Add 6 lb cooked, chopped broccoli.
3. **Cream of cauliflower soup.**   Increase onion to 1 lb 8 oz and water to 1 gal. Reduce milk to 1½ gal. Add 6 lb cauliflower, cut into small florets, and 1 Tbsp Worcestershire sauce. Stir in 1 lb 8 oz processed American cheese, shredded. Stir until melted. Sprinkle with chopped chives.
4. **Cream of celery soup.**   Increase onions to 8 oz. Add 2 lb 8 oz cooked chopped celery and 1 lb cooked diced carrots.
5. **Cream of mushroom soup.**   Increase onion to 8 oz. Add 3 lb mushrooms, sliced or chopped, sautéed with the onion in margarine.
6. **Mushroom barley soup.**   Reduce milk to 3 qt and increase water to 1¾ gal. Increase margarine to 1 lb, onions to 1 lb, and chicken base to 8 oz. Add 3 lb sliced mushrooms, ½ tsp garlic powder, and 1 lb barley after water has been added. Simmer about 30 minutes, then add milk slowly and heat to 180°F. Sprinkle with chopped parsley.

7. **Cream of potato soup.** Increase onions to 12 oz. Add 8 lb cooked diced potatoes and 1 lb cooked chopped celery. Increase chicken base to 5 oz. Potatoes may be mashed or pureed if desired.
8. **Cream of spinach soup.** Increase onion to 8 oz. Add 3 lb chopped spinach, cooked.
9. **Cream of vegetable soup.** Increase onion to 1 lb. Add 1 lb cooked chopped celery, 1 lb 8 oz cooked diced carrots, and 2 lb cooked diced potatoes.

Cream of chicken soup

YIELD: 50 portions
    3 gal
PORTION: 1 cup (8 oz)

Ingredient	Amount	Procedure
Margarine	8 oz	Melt margarine. Sauté celery until tender.
Celery, chopped	1 lb	
Flour, all-purpose	8 oz	Add flour and salt. Stir until blended.
Salt	1 oz (1½ Tbsp)	Cook for 5 minutes.
Chicken Stock (p. 590)	2 gal	Add stock and seasonings. Cook over low
Celery salt	2 tsp	heat until it has the consistency of thin
Pepper, white	½ tsp	white sauce. If chicken base is used for stock, taste before adding celery salt.
Milk	1 gal	Add milk while stirring.
Cooked chicken, chopped	3 lb	Add chicken. Heat to 180°F.

Note:
1 lb cooked rice or noodles may be added. Reduce margarine and flour to 4 oz each.

Variation:
Chicken velvet soup. Substitute 2 qt half-and-half for 2 qt milk. Increase flour to 12 oz.

Cream of tomato soup

YIELD: 50 portions
3 gal
PORTION: 1 cup (8 oz)

Ingredient	Amount	Procedure
Tomato juice	1½ gal	Add onion and bay leaf to tomato juice.
Onion, finely chopped	1 oz	Heat to boiling point.
Bay leaf	½	
Baking soda	1 Tbsp	Add soda to tomato juice.
Margarine	10 oz	Melt margarine. Add flour and seasonings.
Flour, all-purpose	3 oz	Stir until blended.
Salt	2 oz (3 Tbsp)	Cook for 5 minutes.
Pepper, white	1 tsp	
Sugar, granulated	4 oz	
Milk, hot	1½ gal	Add milk while stirring with wire whip.
		Cook until thickened.
		Just before serving, add hot tomato mixture gradually to milk, while stirring.
		Remove bay leaf before serving.

Cheese soup

	YIELD:	50 portions
		3 gal
	PORTION:	1 cup (8 oz)

Ingredient	Amount	Procedure
Margarine	8 oz	Sauté onion in margarine until lightly
Onions, chopped	8 oz	browned.
Flour, all-purpose	4 oz	Add flour and cornstarch. Blend.
Cornstarch	2 oz	Cook for 5 minutes.
Paprika	1 tsp	Add seasonings and blend.
Salt	2 Tbsp	Add milk and stock slowly, while stirring.
Pepper, white	1 tsp	Cook until thickened.
Milk	1 gal	
Chicken Stock (p. 590)	1½ gal	
Carrots, finely diced	1 lb	Cook carrots and celery until tender but
Celery, finely diced	12 oz	slightly crisp.
Cheddar cheese, sharp, shredded	1 lb	Add cheese and blend at low temperature.
Parsley, fresh, chopped	½ cup	Garnish with chopped parsley.

Note:
1 oz (½ cup) dehydrated onions, rehydrated in ¾ cup water, may be substituted for fresh onions (p. 50).

Broccoli and cheese soup

		YIELD: 50 portions
		3 gal
		PORTION: 1 cup (8 oz)

Ingredient	Amount	Procedure
Margarine	10 oz	Melt margarine in steam-jacketed or other large kettle.
Onions, finely chopped	10 oz	Add onions and sauté until tender.
Flour, all-purpose	12 oz	Add flour and seasonings. Stir until blended.
Salt	1 Tbsp	Cook for 5 minutes, stirring often.
Pepper, black	1 tsp	
Chicken base	3 oz	Stir in chicken base, then add water and milk, stirring constantly.
Water	3 qt	Reduce heat and cook until thickened, stirring often.
Milk	1½ gal	
Processed cheese, coarsely shredded	2 lb 8 oz	Add cheese and stir until melted.
Broccoli cuts, frozen	4 lb	Steam broccoli until just tender. Chop, if necessary. Add to cheese mixture and heat to serving temperature.

Note:

1¼ oz (⅔ cup) dehydrated onions, rehydrated in 1 cup water, may be substituted for fresh onions (p. 50).

Chowders

Corn chowder

		YIELD: 50 portions
		3 gal
		PORTION: 1 cup (8 oz)

Ingredient	Amount	Procedure
Potatoes, diced	2 lb	Cook potatoes. Drain.
Margarine, melted Onions, finely chopped Celery, chopped	8 oz 4 oz 6 oz	Sauté onions and celery in margarine until tender.
Flour, all-purpose Pepper, white Chicken base	12 oz 1 tsp 3 oz	Add flour, pepper, and chicken base to onions. Stir until well blended. Cook for 5 minutes.
Water	1½ gal	Add water, stirring constantly. Cook until mixture thickens.
Corn, cream style Chives, frozen	1 No. 10 can 1 cup	Add corn, potatoes, and chives. Heat until hot.
Milk	2½ qt	Stir milk into soup. Heat to 180°F.

Notes:
1. ½ oz (¼ cup) dehydrated onions, rehydrated in ½ cup water, may be substituted for fresh onions (p. 50).
2. 1 lb bacon, diced and cooked until crisp, may be added before serving.

Variations:
1. **Potato chowder.** Omit corn and increase potatoes to 8 lb.
2. **Vegetable chowder.** Substitute 3 lb whole kernel corn for cream style corn. Add 4 oz chopped green pepper and 1 lb cooked diced carrots.

Hearty potato ham chowder

YIELD: 50 portions
         3 gal
PORTION: 1 cup (8 oz)

Ingredient	Amount	Procedure
Margarine	3 oz	Melt margarine in steam-jacketed or other large kettle.
Onion, green, finely chopped	8 oz	
Green pepper, chopped	12 oz	Add onion and green pepper and sauté until tender.
Flour, all-purpose	3 oz	Add flour and seasonings. Stir until blended.
Pepper, white	½ tsp	Cook for 5 minutes, stirring often.
Paprika	1 tsp	
Chicken Stock (p. 590)	3 qt	Add stock and stir until smooth. Cook until mixture begins to thicken.
Ham, coarsely chopped	2 lb 8 oz	Add ham, potatoes, and corn. Heat.
Potatoes, cooked, cubed	5 lb 8 oz	
Corn, whole kernel	3 lb 12 oz	
Milk	2¾ qt	Add milk and mix well. Heat to serving temperature.
Parsley, fresh, chopped	½ cup	Sprinkle parsley over chowder before serving.

Note:
1 oz (½ cup) dehydrated onions, rehydrated in ¾ cup water, may be substituted for fresh onions (p. 50).

New England clam chowder

YIELD: 50 portions
3 gal
PORTION: 1 cup (8 oz)

Ingredient	Amount	Procedure
Potatoes, cubed	6 lb	Cook potatoes until tender. Drain.
Water	1 qt	Reserve potatoes to add in last step.
Salt	1 Tbsp	
Bacon, finely diced	4 oz	Sauté bacon, onion, and celery in steam-
Onion, chopped	8 oz	jacketed or other large kettle for 5 minutes,
Celery, chopped	12 oz	or until lightly browned.
Margarine	8 oz	Add margarine to onion and stir until melted.
Flour, all-purpose	8 oz	Add flour, seasonings, and chicken base. Stir
Pepper, white	1 tsp	until blended.
Chicken base	4 oz	Cook for 5 minutes.
Milk	2 gal	Add milk gradually while stirring. Cook until thickened.
Minced clams, undrained	4 lb	Add clams and potatoes. Heat to serving temperature.

Notes:
1. 1 gal fresh clams may be used. Clean and steam until tender. Drain and chop. Save juice.
2. Garnish with fresh or frozen chives, chopped.
3. 1 oz (½ cup) dehydrated onions, rehydrated in ¾ cup water, may be substituted for fresh onions (p. 50).

Variation:
Fish chowder.   Delete clams. Add 1 tsp thyme, 1 tsp crushed rosemary, 2 tsp Worcestershire sauce, ½ tsp Tabasco sauce, and 3 lb flaked white fish, or 1 lb shrimp and 2 lb minced clams.

Manhattan fish or clam chowder

YIELD: 50 portions
3 gal
PORTION: 1 cup (8 oz)

Ingredient	Amount	Procedure
Bacon, diced	1 lb	Cook bacon until crisp. Drain off excess fat.
Onion, chopped	1 lb 6 oz	Add onion and sauté until tender. Place onion and bacon in large kettle.
Water	3 qt	Add water, vegetables, and spices. Bring to a boil.
Tomatoes, diced, canned	1 No. 10 can	Reduce heat. Simmer 40–45 minutes or until vegetables are tender.
Potatoes, chopped	3 lb	
Carrots, fresh, diced	1 lb 4 oz	
Celery, chopped	1 lb 4 oz	
Catsup	2 cups	
Worcestershire sauce	⅓ cup	
Salt	2 Tbsp	
Pepper, black	1 tsp	
Bay leaves	2	
Thyme, ground	1 tsp	
Fish, boneless, cooked and flaked, or minced clams	3 lb 8 oz	Add fish. Cover and simmer 5–10 minutes.
Parsley, fresh, chopped	¼ cup	Sprinkle parsley over soup before serving.

Note:
2¾ oz (1½ cups) dehydrated onions, rehydrated in 2¼ cups water, may be substituted for fresh onions (p. 50).

Oyster stew

<table>
<tr><td></td><td>YIELD: 50 portions
3 gal
PORTION: 1 cup (8 oz)</td></tr>
</table>

Ingredient	Amount	Procedure
Milk	2½ gal	Scald milk by heating to point just below boiling.
Oysters Butter or margarine	2½ qt 8 oz	Heat undrained oysters and butter only until edges of oysters begin to curl.
Salt Pepper	2 oz (3 Tbsp) ½ tsp	About 10 minutes before serving, add oysters, with the oyster liquor, and seasonings to scalded milk. Serve immediately to avoid curdling.

Chilled soups

Gazpacho (Spanish chilled soup)

YIELD: 50 portions
          1¾ gal
PORTION: ½ cup (4 oz)

Ingredient	Amount	Procedure
Mushrooms, fresh, chopped	4 oz	Sauté mushrooms in olive oil until light brown.
Olive oil	½ cup	
Garlic	3 cloves	Crush garlic in salt.
Salt	2 Tbsp	
Tomatoes, fresh, finely chopped	3 lb	Combine remaining ingredients in a stainless steel or glass container.
Green peppers, finely chopped	1 lb 4 oz	Add mushrooms and garlic.
Celery, finely chopped	12 oz	If too thick, add more tomato juice.
Cucumbers, finely chopped	1 lb	Cover and chill.
Onion, finely chopped	1 lb 8 oz	
Chives, chopped	2 Tbsp	
Parsley, chopped	3 Tbsp	
Pepper, black	1 Tbsp	
Worcestershire sauce	1 Tbsp	
Tarragon wine vinegar	1½ cups	
Tabasco sauce	1 tsp	
Tomato juice	2½ qt	

Vichyssoise (Chilled potato soup)

YIELD: 50 portions
3 gal
PORTION: 1 cup (8 oz)

Ingredient	Amount	Procedure
Chicken Stock (p. 590) Onions, chopped	1 gal 3 lb	Combine stock and onions. Cook until onions are tender. Strain.
Potatoes, diced	6 lb	Steam potatoes until tender. Mash.
Salt Celery salt Garlic salt Pepper, white	1 Tbsp 2 tsp 1 tsp ½ tsp	Add seasonings and chicken stock to potatoes. If soup base is used in stock, salt may need to be reduced.
Cream, half-and-half	1¼ gal	Add cream and mix well. Chill thoroughly.
Parsley, chives, or green onion tops, chopped	⅓ cup	Garnish chilled soup with chopped parsley, chives, or green onion tops.

VEGETABLES

Vegetables have an important place on the menus of most foodservices, and their availability the year around simplifies menu planning for variety and customer appeal. Frozen and canned vegetables are preferred in many foodservices because they require less labor to prepare and have more predictable yields than do the fresh vegetables. However, fresh vegetables should be considered when they are in season, especially those that are not too time-consuming to prepare. Correct preparation and cooking methods are essential to preserving the nutritive value, color, and palatability of fresh vegetables.

The quantity of vegetables to buy depends on the size portion to be served and the method of preparation. One No. 10 can or 5 pounds of frozen vegetables yield 25 3-oz portions of most kinds. For fresh vegetables, the loss in preparation must be considered in determining the amount to purchase. Table 1.2 gives the approximate yield in the preparation of fresh vegetables, and Table 1.1 suggests amounts to buy.

FRESH AND FROZEN VEGETABLES

Fresh or frozen vegetables may be cooked by boiling, steaming, baking, or frying. The method used depends largely on the type of product, the amount to be cooked, and the equipment available.

A small steam-jacketed kettle, if time is controlled carefully, is highly satisfactory for cooking both fresh and frozen vegetables. It should be large enough to prevent crowding and to allow the water to return to the boiling point quickly after vegetables are added. A tilting fry pan may be used successfully also.

Vegetables may be cooked with satisfactory results in a steamer if cooked in small quantities and arranged in thin layers in shallow pans. The time and temperature must be carefully controlled. Quick cooking in a high-pressure or zero-pressure steamer is especially successful. One advantage of steam cooking is that vegetables may be weighed and placed in hot food inset pans as they are prepared, then cooked and served from the same pans, thus minimizing the breakage that results from transferring vegetables.

When steam equipment is not available, top-of-range cooking may be used. Vegetables should be cooked in as small an amount of water as is practicable and as quickly as possible.

Whatever the method used, vegetables should be cooked only until tender. *Do not overcook.* Vegetables should be cooked in as small a quantity at one time as is feasible for the type of service. The needs of most foodservices can be met by the continuous cooking of vegetables in small quantities. Vegetables should be served as soon as possible after cooking for optimum quality and should be handled carefully to prevent breaking or mashing. Appearance is important to customer acceptance of vegetables, as is the seasoning. Individual recipes recommend the amount of salt for 50 portions and suggest seasonings appropriate to that vegetable. If it is necessary to reduce or eliminate salt, many of the herbs and spices suggested may be used in place of salt to make the vegetable more acceptable.

Directions for boiling

1. Prepare vegetables. See pp. 464–469 for directions for preparing fresh vegetables. Frozen vegetables should not be thawed before cooking except for solid-pack frozen vegetables, which should be thawed only long enough to break apart easily.

2. Add prepared vegetables to boiling salted water in steam-jacketed kettle or stockpot. Cook in lots no larger than 10 lb. Use 1 oz (1½ Tbsp) salt to the amount of water specified in Table 2.19, except for corn. Add salt and/or sugar after cooking to prevent toughening and discoloring of corn kernels.

    The amount of water used in cooking all vegetables is important for retention of nutrients. The less water used, the more nutrients retained. Addition of baking soda to the water also causes loss of vitamins. Older root vegetables that need longer cooking require more water than young, tender vegetables. Spinach and other greens need only the water clinging to their leaves from washing.

3. Cover and bring water quickly back to the boiling point. Green vegetables retain their color better if the lid is removed just before boiling begins; strong-flavored vegetables, such as cabbage, cauliflower, and brussels sprouts, should be cooked uncovered to prevent development of unpleasant flavors.

4. Start timing when water returns to the boiling point. Use Table 2.19 as a guide. Stir greens occasionally while boiling.

5. Drain cooked vegetables and place in serving pans. Add 4–8 oz melted margarine or butter to each 50 portions.

6. Adjust seasonings.

Directions for steaming

1. Place prepared vegetables not more than 3–4 inches deep in stainless steel inset pans. Perforated pans provide the best circulation, but if cooking liquid needs to be retained, use solid pans. When cooking winter squash or sweet potatoes, cover with a lid or aluminum foil to prevent water from accumulating in the pan.

TABLE 2.19   TIMETABLE FOR BOILING OR STEAMING VEGETABLES

	Boiling: Approximate cooking time[a] *(minutes)*	*Steaming: Approximate cooking time*[b,c] *(minutes)*		
		5–6 psi[d]	*12–15 psi*[d]	*Pressureless*
Asparagus, fresh, frozen	15–20	7–10	1½	5–8
Beans, black-eyed beans or peas, frozen	30–45	20–30	10–15	20–30
Beans, green or wax, fresh	20	15–25	1	5–6
Beans, green or wax, frozen	10–12	10–15	1	5–7
Beans, lima, frozen	12–14	10–15	1½	6–8
Broccoli, cuts or spears, fresh, frozen	10–15	5–10	1	5–8
Brussels sprouts, fresh, frozen	10–15	5–10	3	6–8
Cabbage, cored, cut	10–20	10–15	1½	7–9
Carrots, fresh	25	18–25	2	10–12
Carrots, frozen	20	9–13	1½	6–8
Cauliflower, fresh, frozen	12	10–15	1	5–8
Celery, fresh	10	4	1	7–8
Corn, whole kernel, frozen	6–8	9–13	½	5–6
Corn on cob, fresh	15–20	10–15	4	10–12
Corn on cob, frozen	15–20	10–15	5–6	8–10
Eggplant, fresh	15–20	10–15	4–6	10–12
Greens, fresh, collard	30–40	10–15	8–10	12–15
Kale, fresh	15–20	10–15	8–10	12–15
Okra, fresh, frozen	10–12	5–8	4–5	10–12
Onions, fresh	15–20	15–20	5	8
Parsnips, fresh	20	15–20	4–6	10–12
Peas, green, fresh, frozen	15–20	6–9	1	5–6
Potatoes, fresh, whole	30–40	20–30	5–6	20–30
For dicing	25–30	20–30	4–6	20–30
For slicing	25–30	20–30	4–6	20–30
For mashing	30–40	20–30	4–6	20–30
Rutabagas, fresh	20	15–20	4–6	10–12
Spinach, fresh	8–10	4–6	1–3	5–8
Spinach, frozen, thawed	8–10	4–6	1–3	8–10
Squash, summer, fresh, frozen	10–15	3–6	2	8–10
Squash, winter, fresh	15–30	15–20	10–12	15–18
Sweet potatoes, fresh	30–40	20–30	5–6	20–30
Turnips, fresh	30–40	25–35	2	8–10
Vegetables, mixed, frozen	12–15	6–9	1	5–6

[a] Figures calculated for boiling 10–12 lb of vegetables in 1–3 qt water. Greens require the addition of no extra water; the water clinging to their leaves is sufficient.
[b] Figures calculated for steaming 5–6 lb vegetables per batch. A steamer filled less than capacity will need the cooking time reduced slightly. An overloaded steamer may require a longer cooking time.
[c] Wherever possible, use 2½-inch-deep perforated steamer pans. For best results, break up frozen vegetables to speed cooking.
[d] Pounds per square inch.

2. Steam, using Table 2.19 as a guide. Begin timing when steamer reaches proper cooking pressure.

3. Add 2–4 oz melted margarine or butter and 2 tsp salt to each 5 lb of drained vegetables.

Directions for stir-frying

1. Select vegetables for color, texture, shape, and flavor.

2. Cut or dice diagonally into small uniform pieces.

3. Heat a small amount of oil in a pan, steam-jacketed kettle, or tilting fry pan.

4. Stir in vegetables, starting with those that take longer to cook (carrots, onions, turnips). Continue to stir for 1 minute until vegetables are coated with oil.

5. Add liquid (water or broth) and seasonings, to vegetables. Cover and steam for 3 minutes or until vegetables are tender but crisp.

6. Add cornstarch mixed with a small amount of cold water (see recipe on p. 669). Cook and stir just until the sauce thickens and vegetables are glazed.

CANNED VEGETABLES

Heating of canned vegetables should be scheduled so they will be served soon after heating. Prepare one to two No. 10 cans at a time, with approximately 25 portions in each can.

Directions for heating

STOCKPOT OR STEAM-JACKETED KETTLE

1. Drain off half the liquid; use for soups, gravies, and sauces.

2. Heat vegetables and remaining liquid in a stockpot or steam-jacketed kettle. Heat only long enough to bring to 160°F.

3. Drain vegetables and place in counter pans. Add 4–8 oz melted margarine or butter.

STEAMER OR OVEN

1. Drain off half the liquid; use for soups, gravies, and sauces.

2. Transfer vegetables and remaining liquid to steamer pans and cover. A 12 × 20 × 2-inch pan will hold contents of 2 No. 10 cans, or 50 portions of most vegetables.

3. Heat in steamer at 5–6 lb pressure for 1 minute, or in a 350°F oven until 160°F is reached.

4. Drain vegetables and add 4–8 oz melted margarine or butter for each lot of vegetables.

DRIED VEGETABLES

To cook dried beans, peas, or lentils:

1. Sort and wash vegetable (5 lb).
2. Heat 1½ gal water to boiling in steam-jacketed kettle.
3. Add vegetable and boil for 2 minutes.
4. Turn off steam and allow to stand for 1 hour.
5. Add salt and cook slowly until vegetables are tender (1–1½ hours).
6. Vegetable may be covered with cold water and soaked overnight, drained, then cooked.

VEGETABLE RECIPES
Seasonings

Herb butter

	YIELD: 1 qt	
Ingredient	**Amount**	**Procedure**
Butter	2 lb	Place butter in mixer bowl. Let stand at room temperature until soft enough to mix.
Lemon juice Seasonings	2 tsp See below	Add lemon juice and seasonings to butter. Mix on low speed, using flat beater, until all ingredients are mixed thoroughly.

For vegetables:

Basil leaves, crushed	1 Tbsp
Marjoram, ground	2 tsp
Savory leaves, crushed	1 Tbsp

For meats:

Marjoram, ground	2 tsp
Dry mustard	4 tsp
Tarragon leaves, crushed	1 Tbsp
Rosemary leaves, crushed	1 Tbsp

Notes:

1. Other spices and herbs may be substituted for those listed in the recipe. See p. 717 for Use of Herbs and Spices in Cooking.
2. White, cider, or wine vinegar may be substituted for part or all of the lemon juice.
3. Unsalted butter may be substituted for salted butter.

Variations:

1. **Curry butter.** Omit seasonings. Add 1 Tbsp curry powder.
2. **Dill butter.** Omit seasonings. Add 1 Tbsp dill weed.
3. **Lemon butter.** Omit seasonings. Increase lemon juice to 1 cup and add 3 Tbsp freshly grated lemon peel.
4. **Onion butter.** Omit seasonings and lemon juice. Blend in 2 oz onion soup mix.
5. **Tarragon butter.** Omit seasonings. Add 4 Tbsp tarragon leaves.

Lemon herb seasoning

YIELD: Approximately 2 cups

Ingredient	Amount	Procedure
Lemons	8	Finely shred lemon peel. Spread on baking pan. Dry in 300°F oven for about 10 minutes. Stir occasionally. Cool.
Basil, dried leaves	5 Tbsp	Crush herbs. Mix with dry lemon peel. Store in airtight container.
Marjoram, dried leaves	5 Tbsp	
Sage, dried leaves	2 Tbsp	
Savory, dried leaves	5 Tbsp	
Parsley, dried leaves	3 Tbsp	
Thyme, dried leaves	5 Tbsp	

Notes:
1. Use Lemon Herb Seasoning sparingly to season soups, stews, meats, fish, poultry, and vegetables.
2. To substitute fresh herbs for dried herbs, use three times more fresh than dried. If using ground herbs, use only one-fourth as much as dried.
3. Variation in flavor may be made by using different combinations of herbs. The following herbs may be substituted for those in the recipe: celery flakes, cilantro, dill weed, oregano, rosemary, or tarragon.

Seasoned salt

YIELD: Approximately 2 cups

Ingredient	Amount	Procedure
Salt	1 lb	Mix all ingredients together thoroughly. Store covered.
Celery salt	2 oz	
Onion powder	2 oz	
Garlic powder	1 oz	
Monosodium glutamate	¼ cup	
Paprika	1 Tbsp	
Chili powder	4 Tbsp	

Note:
Can be used to season meats, salads, or vegetables.

Vegetables

Seasoned fresh asparagus

	YIELD: 50 portions PORTION: 3 oz	
Ingredient	**Amount**	**Procedure**
Asparagus, fresh	18–20 lb AP (10 lb EP)	Break or cut off tough stems. Wash and thoroughly clean remaining portions.
Salt	1 oz (1½ Tbsp)	Arrange spears in pans with tips in one direction, or cut into 1-inch pieces. Sprinkle with salt. Boil or steam (see p. 619).
Margarine or butter, melted	4 oz	Pour margarine over cooked asparagus.

Notes:
1. For frozen asparagus, use 10 lb. See p. 619 for cooking.
2. Seasonings for asparagus: sesame seeds, lemon juice, browned butter, crumb butter.

Variations:
1. **Asparagus with cheese sauce.** Serve 5 or 6 stalks of cooked asparagus with 2 Tbsp Cheese Sauce (p. 561). Make 2 qt sauce.
2. **Asparagus vinaigrette.** Cook asparagus. Marinate in 1½ qt Vinaigrette Dressing (p. 528) or Vegetable Marinade (p. 579).
3. **Creamed asparagus.** Add 1 gal Medium White Sauce (p. 560) to 10 lb asparagus cut in 2-inch lengths and cooked.
4. **Fresh asparagus with hollandaise sauce.** Serve 1 Tbsp Hollandaise Sauce (p. 575) over cooked asparagus spears.

Seasoned fresh green or wax beans

YIELD: 50 portions
PORTION: 3 oz

Ingredient	Amount	Procedure
Green or wax beans, fresh	11–12 lb AP (10 lb EP)	Wash beans. Trim ends. Cut or break beans into 1-inch pieces.
Salt	1 oz (1½ Tbsp)	Boil or steam (see p. 619).
Margarine or butter, melted	4 oz	Pour margarine over cooked beans.

Notes:

1. For frozen beans, use 10 lb. See p. 619 for cooking.
2. For canned beans, use two No. 10 cans. See p. 621 for heating.
3. Seasonings for green beans: basil, dill, marjoram, oregano, savory, tarragon, thyme, onion, chives, mushrooms, bacon.

Variations:

1. **French green beans.** Cook 10 lb frozen French cut green beans. Drain and season with 1 cup mayonnaise, ¾ cup sour cream, 2 Tbsp vinegar, 2 oz chopped onion sautéed in 2 oz margarine or butter, and salt and pepper to taste.
2. **Green beans amandine.** Add 8 oz slivered almonds lightly browned in 8 oz margarine or butter.
3. **Green beans and mushrooms.** Add 2 lb sliced mushrooms that have been sautéed in 8 oz margarine or butter.
4. **Green beans provincial.** Season green beans with 8 oz Onion Butter (p. 623), 2 cloves garlic, minced, 3 Tbsp chopped parsley, and 2 tsp thyme.
5. **Herbed green beans.** Season 10 lb frozen green beans, cooked, or 2 No. 10 cans green beans with 1 lb chopped onions, 8 oz chopped celery, and 1 tsp minced garlic sautéed in 8 oz margarine or butter, 2 tsp basil, and 2 tsp rosemary.
6. **Southern-style green beans.** Cut 1 lb 8 oz bacon into small pieces. Add 6 oz chopped onion and sauté until onion is lightly browned. Add to hot, drained green beans. Good served with ham and corn bread.

Green bean casserole

OVEN: 350°F	YIELD: 50 portions
BAKE: 30 minutes	1 pan 12 × 20 × 2 inches
	PORTION: 4 oz

Ingredient	Amount	Procedure
Green beans, frozen, French cut or cut	7 lb 8 oz	Cook green beans (p. 619). Drain.
Mushrooms, fresh	10 oz	Clean mushrooms and slice.
Margarine or butter, melted	3 oz	Sauté in margarine.
Cream of mushroom soup, undiluted	1 qt	Blend soup, milk, and seasonings.
Milk	1 cup	
Pepper, black	½ tsp	
Onion powder	1 tsp	
Soy sauce	1 Tbsp	
Water chestnuts, sliced, drained	1 lb	Combine soup mixture, mushrooms, and water chestnuts. Add to green beans. Mix lightly. Pour into one 12 × 20 × 2-inch pan.
Swiss cheese, shredded	8 oz	Sprinkle cheese over beans. Bake at 350°F for 25 minutes.
Bread crumbs	4 oz	Combine crumbs and margarine and sprinkle over bean mixture. Bake 5–10 minutes.
Margarine, melted	4 oz	

Notes:
1. Two No. 10 cans cut green beans may be substituted for frozen beans. Drain before using.
2. 8 oz crumbled canned french fried onion rings may be sprinkled over the top during the last 10 minutes of baking.

Spanish green beans

YIELD: 50 portions
PORTION: 3 oz

Ingredient	Amount	Procedure
Bacon, diced	8 oz	Sauté bacon, onion, and green pepper until lightly browned.
Onion, chopped	6 oz	
Green pepper, chopped	4 oz	
Flour, all-purpose	4 oz	Add flour and stir until smooth.
Tomatoes, canned	2 qt	Chop tomatoes and heat. Add salt.
Salt	1 Tbsp	Add gradually to bacon-vegetable mixture. Stir and cook until thickened.
Green beans, drained	2 No. 10 cans	Gently stir tomato sauce into the green beans. Simmer 20–30 minutes or until beans are heated to 160°F.

Note:
8 lb fresh or frozen green beans may be substituted for canned beans. Cook before combining with tomato sauce.

Variations:
1. **Creole green beans.**   Omit bacon. Sauté onion, green pepper, and 8 oz chopped celery in 2 oz margarine. Add 2 oz sugar to tomatoes.
2. **Green beans with dill.**   Delete bacon and onion. Sauté the green pepper in 5 oz margarine. Add 1 tsp pepper and 1 Tbsp dill seeds. Simmer slowly for 10–15 minutes. Tomato may be increased to one No. 10 can.
3. **Hacienda green beans.**   Add 1 oz sugar, 1½ Tbsp chili powder, and ½ tsp garlic powder.

Seasoned lima beans

YIELD: 50 portions
PORTION: 3 oz

Ingredient	Amount	Procedure
Lima beans, baby or fordhook, frozen	10 lb	Boil or steam beans (p. 619).
Salt	1 oz (1½ Tbsp)	
Margarine or butter, melted	4 oz	Pour margarine over beans.

Note:
Seasonings for lima beans: basil, marjoram, oregano, sage, savory, tarragon, thyme, pimiento, mushrooms, onion butter, sour cream.

Variations:
1. **Baked lima beans and peas.**   Thaw 5 lb frozen baby lima beans and 5 lb frozen peas. Combine with 2 Tbsp dried basil, 1 oz (1½ Tbsp) salt, ½ tsp cracked black pepper, and 16 green onions, sliced. Place in baking pan. Sprinkle with 1 cup water and dot with 4–6 oz margarine or butter. Cover and bake at 325°F for 45 minutes. Stir occasionally.
2. **Succotash.**   Use 5 lb lima beans and 5 lb frozen or canned whole kernel corn. Season with 4 oz margarine or butter.

Baked lima beans

OVEN: 350°F
BAKE: 1 hour

YIELD: 50 portions
         2 pans 12 × 20 × 2 inches
PORTION: 5 oz

Ingredient	Amount	Procedure
Lima beans, dry, large	6 lb AP	Wash beans. Add boiling water. Cover. Let stand 1 hour or longer.
Water, boiling	1 gal	Cook beans in the same water until tender, about 1 hour.
Pimiento, chopped	4 oz	Add seasonings.
Bacon fat	8 oz	Scale into two 12 × 20 × 2-inch pans, 8 lb 6 oz per pan.
Salt	1 oz (1½ Tbsp)	
Molasses	1 cup	
Bacon	1 lb 8 oz	Place bacon on top of beans. Bake at 350°F until top is brown, about 1 hour.

Variations:
1. **Baked lima beans and sausage.** Omit bacon and bacon fat. Place 6 lb link sausages on top of beans.
2. **Boiled lima beans and ham.** Omit bacon and seasonings. Add 5 lb diced ham to beans and simmer until tender.

Baked beans

OVEN: 350°F		YIELD: 50 portions
BAKE: 4–5 hours		1 pan 12 × 20 × 4 inches
		PORTION: 5 oz

Ingredient	Amount	Procedure
Beans, navy or Great Northern, dry	5 lb AP	Wash beans. Add boiling water and let stand 1 hour.
Water, boiling	1½ gal	Cook in same water until tender, for about 1 hour. Add more water as necessary.
Salt	4 oz	Add remaining ingredients.
Sugar, brown	6 oz	Pour into one 12 × 20 × 4-inch baking pan.
Dry mustard	1 tsp	Bake uncovered at 350°F for 4–5 hours.
Vinegar	2 Tbsp	Add more water if needed during baking.
Molasses	1 cup	
Catsup (optional)	2½ cups	
Bacon or salt pork, cubed	1 lb	
Onion, chopped	3 oz	

Variations:
1. **Baked pork and beans.** Use two No. 10 cans pork and beans. Fry 1 lb diced bacon until partially cooked. Add 4 oz chopped onion and cook until onions are tender. Pour off fat. Add bacon and onions to pork and beans. Stir in 1 cup catsup, ¼ cup vinegar, 4 oz brown sugar, and 1 Tbsp prepared mustard. Bake at 350°F for 1–2 hours.
2. **Boston baked beans.** Omit catsup.

Ranch style beans

OVEN: 300°F	YIELD: 50 portions
BAKE: 4–5 hours	1 pan 12 × 20 × 4 inches
	PORTION: 5 oz

Ingredient	Amount	Procedure
Beans, red or pinto, dry	5 lb	Wash beans. Add boiling water.
Water, boiling	1½ gal	Cover and let stand for 1 hour or longer.
Salt pork or bacon, 1-inch cubes	2 lb 8 oz	Add salt pork to beans.
		Add cold water to cover. Cook slowly until
Water, cold	To cover	tender, about 1 hour.
Chili peppers	3–4 pods	Soak chili peppers in warm water.
		Remove pulp from pods and add to beans.
Tomatoes, canned	2 qt	Add tomatoes and other seasonings.
Onions, sliced	8 oz	Cook slowly in kettle an additional 4 hours,
Garlic, chopped	2 cloves	or pour into a 12 × 20 × 4-inch baking pan
Salt	1 oz (1½ Tbsp)	and bake at 300°F for 4–5 hours.
Pepper, black	1 Tbsp	
Cayenne	Few grains	

Notes:
1. If chili peppers are not available, 1 oz chili powder may be substituted.
2. Two No. 10 cans red beans may be substituted for dry beans. Reduce baking time to 1–2 hours.

Refried beans

YIELD: 50 portions
PORTION: 4 oz

Ingredient	Amount	Procedure
Beans, pinto, canned	10 lb	Drain beans. Reserve stock. Place beans in mixer bowl and mash thoroughly.
Vegetable oil Onions, chopped	1½ cups 6 oz	Heat oil in frying pan. Add chopped onion. Cook until tender.
Chili powder Garlic powder Salt Tabasco sauce	2 Tbsp 1 tsp 2 tsp Few drops	Add seasonings to onion and mix thoroughly.
Beef Stock (p. 589)	1 qt	Add stock and mix well. Add mashed beans, mixing until well blended. Turn mixture constantly to keep from burning. Small amounts of bean stock may be added if mixture becomes too thick. Cook bean mixture for 45–60 minutes or until dry.

Note:
5 lb dry pinto beans may be substituted for canned beans. Cook according to directions on p. 622.

Seasoned fresh beets

YIELD: 50 portions
PORTION: 3 oz

Ingredient	Amount	Procedure
Beets, fresh	14 lb AP (11 lb EP)	Cut off all but 2 inches of the beet tops. Wash beets and leave whole, with root ends attached. Boil or steam until tender (see p. 619). Drain. Run cold water over beets. Slip off skins and remove root ends. Slice, dice, or cut into shoestring pieces.
Margarine or butter, melted	4 oz	Pour margarine over cooked beets and sprinkle with salt.
Salt	1 oz (1½ Tbsp)	Heat to serving temperature.

Notes:
1. For canned beets, use two No. 10 cans. See p. 621 for heating directions.
2. Seasonings for beets: allspice, bay leaves, caraway seed, cloves, dill, ginger, marjoram, mustard seed, basil, nutmeg, onion, sour cream, vinegar.

Variations:
1. **Beets in sour cream.** Grate fresh cooked beets and season with a mixture of 1½ cups lemon juice, 1½ Tbsp onion juice, 2 tsp salt, and 10 oz sugar. Toss lightly. Serve with a spoonful of sour cream on each portion.
2. **Julienne beets.** Cut 8 lb cooked beets into julienne strips. Season with a mixture of 4 oz margarine or butter, 4 oz sugar, 4 tsp salt, and 1 cup lemon juice.
3. **Pickled beets.** See p. 520.

Harvard beets

YIELD: 50 portions
PORTION: 3 oz

Ingredient	Amount	Procedure
Beets, sliced or diced	2 No. 10 cans	Drain beets. Reserve juice for sauce.
Beet juice Bay leaf Cloves, whole	1½ qt 1 1 tsp	Add bay leaf and cloves to beet juice. Heat to boiling point.
Sugar, granulated Salt Cornstarch	12 oz 1 oz (1½ Tbsp) 6 oz	Combine dry ingredients. Add to beet juice while stirring briskly. Cook until thickened and clear.
Margarine or butter Vinegar, cider	4 oz 2 cups	Add margarine and vinegar. Stir until mixed and margarine is melted. Heat beets. Add sauce.

Note:
For fresh beets, use 10 lb EP (13 lb AP). See p. 634 for cooking procedure.

Variations:
1. **Beets with orange sauce.** Omit bay leaf, cloves, and vinegar. Add 2 cups orange juice and ½ cup lemon juice.
2. **Hot spiced beets.** Drain juice from two No. 10 cans sliced beets and add 1 Tbsp whole cloves, 1½ Tbsp salt, ½ tsp cinnamon, 1 lb brown sugar, 8 oz granulated sugar, and 1 qt cider vinegar. Cook 10 minutes. Pour sauce over beets and heat to serving temperature.

Seasoned broccoli

| | YIELD: 50 portions |
| | PORTION: 3 oz |

Ingredient	Amount	Procedure
Broccoli, fresh	16–20 lb AP (10 lb EP)	Trim off large leaves. Remove tough ends of lower stems. Wash. If stems are thicker than 1 inch, make lengthwise gashes in each stem.
Salt	1 oz (1½ Tbsp)	Boil or steam broccoli spears (p. 619).
Margarine or butter, melted	4 oz	Pour margarine over cooked broccoli.

Notes:
1. For frozen broccoli, use 12 lb spears or 10 lb chopped.
2. Seasonings for broccoli: caraway, dill, or mustard seeds, tarragon, lemon, almond, pimiento, onion butter.

Variations:
1. **Almond buttered broccoli.** Brown slivered almonds in margarine or butter and pour over cooked and drained broccoli.
2. **Broccoli with cheese sauce.** Prepare 2 qt Cheese Sauce (p. 561). Serve 2 Tbsp (1 oz) sauce over each portion of cooked broccoli.
3. **Broccoli with hollandaise sauce or lemon butter.** Serve cooked spears or chopped broccoli with 1 Tbsp Hollandaise Sauce (p. 575) or 1 tsp Lemon Butter (p. 623).

Seasoned brussels sprouts

YIELD: 50 portions
PORTION: 3 oz

Ingredient	Amount	Procedure
Brussels sprouts, fresh	14 lb AP (11 lb EP)	Trim stem end of brussels sprouts. Discard wilted outside leaves. Boil or steam (p. 619) until just tender.
Margarine or butter, melted	4 oz	Pour margarine over brussels sprouts. Sprinkle with salt.
Salt	1 oz (1½ Tbsp)	

Note:
Seasonings for brussels sprouts: dill, celery seed, lemon.

Seasoned whole kernel corn

YIELD: 50 portions
PORTION: 3 oz

Ingredient	Amount	Procedure
Whole kernel corn, frozen	10 lb	Boil or steam corn (p. 619). Do not add salt until after cooking to prevent toughening and discoloring of corn kernels.
Margarine or butter, melted	4 oz	Pour margarine over corn. Stir in salt.
Salt	1 oz (1½ Tbsp)	

Note:
For canned corn, use two No. 10 cans. See p. 621 for heating.

Variations:
1. **Corn in cream.** Add 1¼ qt half-and-half, 6 oz margarine or butter, 1½ Tbsp salt, and 1 Tbsp white pepper to cooked corn. Bring just to boiling point and serve immediately.
2. **Corn O'Brien.** Add 1 lb chopped bacon, 12 oz chopped green pepper, and 12 oz chopped onion that have been cooked together. Just before serving, add 3 oz chopped pimiento, salt, and pepper.
3. **Creamed whole kernel corn.** Combine 2 cups whipping cream, 2 oz granulated sugar, and 1 oz (1½ Tbsp) salt. Bring to a boil. Add 1 cup whipping cream and 1½ oz cornstarch, which have been mixed with a wire whip until smooth. Stir and cook until thick and bubbly. Cook 2 minutes longer. Stir into 10 lb cooked frozen whole kernel corn.

Seasoned cabbage

YIELD: 50 portions
PORTION: 3 oz

Ingredient	Amount	Procedure
Cabbage, fresh	14 lb AP (12 lb EP)	Remove wilted outside leaves. Wash and core. Crisp in cold water, if wilted.
Salt	1 oz (1½ Tbsp)	Cut cabbage into wedges or shred coarsely. Cook until tender (see p. 619). Drain.
Margarine or butter, melted	4 oz	Pour margarine over cabbage.

Note:
Seasonings for cabbage: basil, caraway seed, celery seed, curry powder, dill, nutmeg.

Variations:
1. **Cabbage au gratin.**   Reduce cabbage to 7 lb. Alternate layers of cooked coarsely shredded cabbage, White Sauce, and grated sharp cheese in a 12 × 20 × 2-inch baking pan. Use 2½ qt White Sauce, 1 lb cheddar cheese. Combine 6 oz crumbs and 3 oz melted margarine or butter and sprinkle on top. Bake at 350°F for about 25 minutes.
2. **Cabbage polonaise.**   Arrange cabbage wedges, partially cooked, in baking pans. Cover with 3 qt Medium White Sauce. Sprinkle with buttered bread crumbs. Bake at 350°F for about 25 minutes.
3. **Creamed cabbage.**   Omit margarine or butter. Pour 2 qt Medium White Sauce over shredded, cooked, drained cabbage.
4. **Fried cabbage.**   Melt 6 oz margarine in frying pan. Add 6 lb EP (7 lb AP) shredded cabbage, 12 oz sliced onions, 12 oz diagonally sliced celery. Stir gently while cooking, 6–10 minutes. Just before serving, add 4 lb fresh tomatoes, diced in ½-inch cubes.
5. **Scalloped cabbage.**   Omit margarine or butter. Pour 2 qt Medium White Sauce over chopped, cooked, drained cabbage. Cover with buttered crumbs. Bake at 400°F for 15–20 minutes. Shredded cheese may be added.

Hot cabbage slaw

YIELD: 50 portions
       1¼ gal
PORTION: 3 oz

Ingredient	Amount	Procedure
Cabbage, fresh	7 lb 8 oz AP (6 lb EP)	Remove outside leaves and wash cabbage. Shred.
Sugar, granulated Salt Flour, all-purpose Dry mustard	12 oz 2 tsp 3 oz 1 tsp	Mix dry ingredients in a sauce pan or kettle.
Milk, hot Water, hot	2½ cups 3 cups	Add milk and water while stirring. Cook until thickened.
Eggs, beaten	5 (9 oz)	Add eggs gradually while stirring briskly. Cook for 2–3 minutes.
Vinegar, cider, hot	1½ cups	Add vinegar.
Celery seed	2½ tsp	Pour hot sauce over cabbage just before serving. Add celery seed and mix lightly.

Parsley buttered carrots

YIELD: 50 portions
PORTION: 3 oz

Ingredient	Amount	Procedure
Carrots, fresh	14 lb AP (10 lb EP)	Peel and cut carrots into desired shapes (slices, strips, or quarters).
Salt	1 oz (1½ Tbsp)	Steam or boil until just tender (see p. 619).
Margarine or butter, melted Parsley, chopped	4 oz 1 oz	Pour margarine over carrots. Sprinkle with chopped parsley.

Note:
Seasonings for carrots: allspice, basil, caraway seed, cloves, curry powder, dill, fennel, ginger, mace, marjoram, mint, nutmeg, thyme, parsley.

Variations:
1. **Candied carrots.**   Cut carrots into 1-inch pieces. Cook until tender but not soft. Melt 8 oz margarine or butter. Add 8 oz sugar and 1½ tsp salt. Add to carrots. Bake at 400°F for 15–20 minutes. Turn frequently.
2. **Lyonnaise carrots.**   Arrange cooked carrot strips in baking pan. Add 3 lb chopped onion that has been cooked until tender in 4 oz margarine or butter. Bake at 350°F for 10–15 minutes or until vegetables are lightly browned. Just before serving sprinkle with chopped parsley.
3. **Marinated carrots.**   See p. 480.
4. **Mint-glazed carrots.**   Cut carrots into quarters lengthwise. Cook until almost tender. Drain. Melt 8 oz margarine or butter, 8 oz sugar, 1½ tsp salt, and 1 cup mint jelly. Blend. Add carrots and simmer 5–10 minutes.
5. **Savory carrots.**   Cook carrots in Beef or Chicken Stock. When done, season with 4 oz melted margarine or butter, salt and pepper, and ¼ cup lemon juice. Sprinkle with chopped parsley.
6. **Sweet-sour carrots.**   Add to cooked carrots a sauce made of 1½ qt vinegar, 2 lb 4 oz sugar, 2 Tbsp salt, and 12 oz melted margarine or butter. Bake at 350°F for 15–20 minutes, or simmer until carrots and sauce are thoroughly heated.

Celery and carrots amandine

YIELD: 50 portions
PORTION: 3 oz

Ingredient	Amount	Procedure
Celery	7 lb AP (5 lb EP)	Wash and trim celery. Cut into diagonal slices. Steam (see p. 619).
Salt	2 tsp	
Carrots, fresh	7 lb AP (5 lb EP)	Wash and peel carrots. Cut into strips. Cook (p. 619) until tender but firm. Drain.
Salt	2 tsp	
Margarine or butter	8 oz	Heat margarine in frying pan.
Almonds, blanched, slivered	8 oz	Add almonds and brown lightly.
Lemon juice	⅓ cup	Remove almonds from heat. Add lemon juice. Combine vegetables. Pour almond mixture over vegetables and stir carefully to mix seasoning with vegetables.

Variation:
Creole celery.   Cook 5 lb diced celery until partially done. Add 1 lb chopped onions and 4 oz chopped green pepper that have been sautéed in 6 oz margarine or butter. Add two No. 10 cans tomatoes and 1½ tsp salt. Cook until tender.

Seasoned cauliflower

	YIELD: 50 portions	
	PORTION: 3 oz	

Ingredient	Amount	Procedure
Cauliflower, fresh	16 lb AP (10 lb EP)	Remove outer leaves and stalks. Break into florets. Wash.
Salt	1 oz (1½ Tbsp)	Steam or boil cauliflower (see p. 619).

Note:
Seasonings for cauliflower: caraway seed, celery salt, dill, mace, tarragon, buttered crumbs, cheese.

Variations:
1. **Cauliflower with almond butter.**   Season freshly cooked cauliflower with 12 oz slivered almonds that have been browned in 8 oz margarine or butter.
2. **Cauliflower with cheese sauce.**   Pour 3 qt Cheese Sauce (p. 561) over cooked fresh cauliflower.
3. **Cauliflower with peas.**   Combine 6 lb freshly cooked cauliflower with 4 lb cooked frozen peas. Season with 4 oz melted margarine or butter.
4. **Creamed cauliflower.**   Pour 3 qt White Sauce over cooked cauliflower.
5. **French fried cauliflower.**   See p. 647.

Scalloped corn

OVEN: 350°F	YIELD: 50 portions
BAKE: 35–40 minutes	2 pans 12 × 20 × 2 inches
	PORTION: 4 oz

Ingredient	Amount	Procedure
Corn, cream style Milk Salt Pepper, black	2 No. 10 cans 1 qt 1 Tbsp ½ tsp	Mix corn, milk, and seasonings.
Cracker crumbs Margarine or butter, melted	14 oz 12 oz	Combine crumbs and margarine. Place alternate layers of buttered crumbs and corn mixture in two 12 × 20 × 2-inch baking pans. Bake at 350°F for 35–40 minutes.

Note:
6 oz chopped green pepper and 6 oz chopped pimiento may be added.

Corn pudding

OVEN: 325°F
BAKE: 40–45 minutes

YIELD: 50 portions
2 pans 12 × 20 × 2 inches
PORTION: 5 oz

Ingredient	Amount	Procedure
Corn, whole kernel, frozen	9 lb	Thaw corn.
Egg yolks, beaten	24 (1 lb)	Combine corn and all ingredients except egg whites.
Milk	3 qt	
Margarine or butter, melted	6 oz	
Salt	2 Tbsp	
Pepper, white	1 tsp	
Egg whites	24 (1 lb 10 oz)	Beat egg whites until stiff but not dry. Fold into corn mixture. Pour into two 12 × 20 × 2-inch baking pans. Place in pans of hot water. Bake at 325°F for 40–45 minutes.

Baked eggplant

| OVEN: 375°F | YIELD: 50 portions |
| BAKE: 30 minutes | PORTION: 3 oz |

Ingredient	Amount	Procedure
Eggplant	12 lb AP (10 lb EP)	Pare and cut eggplant into ½-inch slices. Soak in salt water (1 Tbsp salt to 1 qt water) for 30 minutes. Drain.
Eggs, beaten Milk	6 (10 oz) 2 cups	Combine beaten eggs and milk.
Flour, all-purpose Bread crumbs	1 lb 1 lb 8 oz	Dip eggplant slices in flour, then in egg mixture. Roll in crumbs.
Margarine or butter, melted	8 oz	Place on greased baking sheets. Sprinkle with melted margarine. Bake at 375°F for 30 minutes.

Note:
Seasonings for eggplant: basil, garlic, marjoram, onion, oregano, cheese, tomato.

Variations:
1. **Eggplant casserole.** Pare and slice eggplant 1 inch thick. Steam or parboil until fork tender. Place on baking sheets in a single layer. Sprinkle with salt and pepper. Cook 1 lb 8 oz chopped onion and 3 cloves garlic, minced, in 1½ cups vegetable oil and 12 oz margarine. Add to 5 lb peeled chopped fresh tomatoes, 1 cup chopped parsley, ¼ tsp oregano, ½ tsp thyme, 1 tsp basil, and 1 lb bread crumbs. Pile mixture on individual slices of eggplant. Sprinkle grated Swiss cheese (2 lb) over top. Bake at 350°F until eggplant is hot and cheese is melted.
2. **French fried eggplant.** See p. 647.
3. **Sautéed eggplant.** Prepare eggplant as in recipe. Sauté in margarine or butter until tender.

Creole eggplant

OVEN: 350°F
BAKE: 30 minutes

YIELD: 50 portions
         2 pans 12 × 20 × 2 inches
PORTION: 3 oz

Ingredient	Amount	Procedure
Eggplant	10 lb AP (8 lb EP)	Pare eggplant and cut into 1-inch cubes. Cook in boiling salted water for 5 minutes, or
Water, boiling	1½ gal	steam according to directions on p. 619.
Salt	2 Tbsp	
Margarine, melted	1 lb	Cook onion, green pepper, and celery in
Onion, chopped	1 lb 8 oz	margarine until tender.
Green pepper, coarsely chopped	12 oz	
Celery, coarsely chopped	1 lb	
Tomatoes, diced, canned	1 No. 10 can	Combine tomatoes and seasonings with
Salt	2 Tbsp	eggplant and other ingredients.
Pepper, black	2 tsp	Pour into two 12 × 20 × 2-inch baking pans.
Sugar, granulated	2 Tbsp	
Bread crumbs	12 oz	Top with buttered crumbs.
Margarine or butter, melted	8 oz	Bake at 350°F for 30 minutes.

Baked onions

OVEN: 400°F	YIELD: 50 portions
BAKE: 20–30 minutes	PORTION: 1 4-oz onion

Ingredient	Amount	Procedure
Onions, 4 oz, Bermuda or Spanish	50 (15 lb AP)	Peel onions and steam (p. 619) until tender. Place in greased baking pans.
Salt	1 Tbsp	Sprinkle salt and buttered crumbs on onions.
Bread crumbs	8 oz	
Margarine or butter, melted	8 oz	
Beef or Chicken Stock (pp. 589, 590)	1 qt	Pour stock around onions. Bake at 400°F for 20–30 minutes.

Notes:
1. Onions may be cut into thick slices.
2. Seasonings for onions: basil, caraway seed, marjoram, oregano, rosemary, sage, or thyme.

Variations:
1. **Creamed pearl onions.** Cook 12 lb 8 oz small unpeeled white onions (p. 619), then peel. Add 2 qt Medium White Sauce (p. 560) to which 4 oz additional margarine or butter has been added. Garnish with paprika.
2. **Glazed onions.** Mix 1 lb 12 oz brown sugar, 2 cups water, 8 oz margarine or butter, and ½ tsp salt. Pour over cooked onions and bake.
3. **Onion casserole.** Cook 10 lb small pearl onions (p. 619). Combine with 10 oz chopped walnuts, 8 oz pimiento strips, and eight 10½-oz cans cream of mushroom or cream of chicken soup. Cover with 6 oz shredded cheddar or Swiss cheese. Bake at 400°F for approximately 30 minutes.

French fried onion rings

DEEP-FAT FRYER: 350°F	YIELD: 50 portions
FRY: 3–4 minutes	PORTION: 3 oz

Ingredient	Amount	Procedure
Onions, large round	10 lb AP (8 lb EP)	Peel onions and cut crosswise into ¼-inch slices. Separate into rings.
Eggs, beaten Milk	6 (10 oz) 2 cups	Combine eggs and milk.
Flour, all-purpose Baking powder Salt	12 oz 2 tsp 1½ tsp	Combine dry ingredients. Add to egg-milk mixture to make a batter. Dip onion rings in batter and fry in deep fat for 3–4 minutes. Drain.

Variations:
1. **Deep-fat fried bananas.** Cut peeled bananas into 2-inch pieces. Sprinkle with lemon juice and powdered sugar. Let stand 30 minutes. Dip in batter and fry for 1–3 minutes.
2. **French fried cauliflower.** Dip 10 lb cold cooked cauliflower into batter and fry at 370°F for 3–4 minutes.
3. **French fried eggplant.** Peel and cut 13 lb AP eggplant as for French Fried Potatoes (p. 652). Dip in batter and fry at 370°F for 5–7 minutes. Eggplant may be dipped in egg and crumb mixture (p. 41) and fried. Eggplant discolors quickly, so it should be placed in cold water if not breaded immediately.
4. **French fried mushrooms.** Clean small, uniform-sized mushrooms by brushing or rinsing. Do not soak. Dip in batter and fry at 370°F for 4–6 minutes.
5. **French fried zucchini sticks.** Cut unpeeled zucchini lengthwise into strips about ½ inch thick. Dip in batter and fry at 370°F for 4–6 minutes.

Seasoned peas

YIELD: 50 portions
PORTION: 3 oz

Ingredient	Amount	Procedure
Peas, frozen Salt	10 lb 1 oz (1½ Tbsp)	Steam or boil peas (p. 619).
Margarine or butter, melted	4 oz	Pour margarine over cooked peas.

Notes:
1. If using canned peas, heat two No. 10 cans (see p. 621).
2. For fresh peas, use 25 lb AP. Shell and rinse. Steam or boil (p. 619).
3. Seasonings for peas: basil, dill, marjoram, mint, oregano, rosemary, sage, savory, mushrooms, water chestnuts, onions.

Variations:
1. **Creamed peas with new potatoes.**   Combine 7 lb freshly cooked new potatoes and 5 lb cooked frozen peas with 3 qt Medium White Sauce (p. 560).
2. **Green peas and sliced new turnips.**   Combine 5 lb frozen peas, cooked, with 3 lb new turnips, sliced and cooked. Add 4 oz melted margarine or butter and salt to taste.
3. **Green peas with pearl onions.**   Combine 7 lb 8 oz frozen peas, cooked, and 3 lb pearl onions, cooked. Add 4 oz melted margarine or butter or 2 qt Medium White Sauce (p. 560).
4. **Green peas with mushrooms.**   Add 2 lb fresh mushrooms, sliced and sautéed in 8 oz margarine or butter, to 10 lb cooked frozen peas.
5. **Green peas with lemon-mint butter.**   Cream 1 lb butter or margarine, ¼ cup lemon juice, and 1 tsp grated lemon peel. Add ½ cup finely chopped fresh mint. The lemon-mint butter can be made ahead and stored in the refrigerator. When ready to use, melt and pour over hot peas.

Au gratin potatoes

OVEN: 350°F		YIELD: 50 portions
BAKE: 30 minutes		2 pans 12 × 20 × 2 inches
		PORTION: 5 oz

Ingredient	Amount	Procedure
Potatoes Salt	10 lb AP (8 lb EP) 1 Tbsp	Peel and dice potatoes (or dice after cooking). Boil or steam (p. 619) until just tender.
Margarine or butter Flour, all-purpose Salt	12 oz 6 oz 1 Tbsp	Melt margarine. Add flour and salt. Stir until smooth. Cook 2–3 minutes.
Milk	3 qt	Add milk gradually while stirring. Cook until thickened.
Cheddar cheese, shredded	1 lb 8 oz	Add cheese to sauce and stir until cheese is melted. Pour over potatoes. Scale into two 12 × 20 × 2-inch baking pans, 8 lb per pan.
Bread crumbs Margarine or butter, melted	12 oz 8 oz	Combine crumbs and margarine. Sprinkle over top of potatoes, 10 oz per pan. Bake at 350°F for 25–30 minutes.

Notes:
1 lb 10 oz sliced dehydrated potatoes, reconstituted in 5 qt boiling water, and 1½ oz salt may be substituted for fresh potatoes.

Baked potatoes

OVEN: 400°F	YIELD: 50 portions
BAKE: 1–1½ hours	PORTION: 1 potato

Ingredient	Amount	Procedure
Baking potatoes, uniform size	50	Scrub potatoes and remove blemishes. Rub or brush lightly with shortening. Place on baking sheets.
Shortening	4 oz	Bake at 400°F for 1–1½ hours or until tender.

Variations:

1. **Broccoli cheese-topped potato.**   Add 4 lb cooked broccoli cuts to Cheese Sauce (p. 561). Serve over baked potato.
2. **Cheese-topped potato.**   Whip 1 lb softened margarine or butter. Add 2 lb sour cream and mix thoroughly. Fold in 1 lb finely shredded American cheese and 6 oz finely chopped green onions. Serve over baked potato.
3. **Fancy top potato.**   Prepare potatoes and bake (see recipe). Serve with one of the following toppings and one or more of the accompaniments:

    Toppings: Cheese Sauce (p. 561), 3 oz; Chili con Carne (p. 375), 3 oz; Creamed Chicken (p. 442), Ham (p. 390), or Beef (p. 376), 3 oz; Nacho Sauce (p. 323), 3 oz; sour cream, 1 oz.

    Accompaniments: Guacamole (p. 87), chopped broccoli, shredded cheese, sliced mushrooms, chopped green onions, chopped chives, sliced black olives, chopped ham or chicken, chopped lettuce, chopped tomatoes, crumbled cooked bacon, slivered almonds.
4. **Stuffed baked potato.**   Cut hot baked potatoes into halves lengthwise. If potatoes are small, cut a slice from one side. Scoop out contents. Mash, season with 2 Tbsp salt, 1 tsp white pepper, 8 oz melted margarine or butter, and 3–4 cups hot milk. Beat until light and fluffy. Pile lightly into shells, leaving tops rough. Sprinkle with paprika or Parmesan cheese, if desired. Bake at 425°F until potatoes are hot and lightly browned, about 30 minutes.

Cottage fried potatoes

YIELD: 50 portions
PORTION: 4 oz

Ingredient	Amount	Procedure
Potatoes	18 lb AP (15 lb EP)	Peel potatoes. Steam or boil until tender (p. 619).
Fat, hot Salt Pepper, black	As needed 1 oz (1½ Tbsp) 1 tsp	Slice cooked potatoes. Add to hot fat in frying pan. Add salt and pepper. Turn potatoes as needed and fry until browned.

Variations:
1. **American fried potatoes.**   Add raw sliced potatoes to hot fat. Fry until potatoes are brown and tender. Add additional fat as needed.
2. **Hashed brown potatoes.**   Add finely chopped boiled potatoes to hot fat in frying pan. Add salt and pepper. Stir occasionally and fry until browned.
3. **Lyonnaise potatoes.**   Cook 2 lb chopped onion slowly in fat without browning. Add seasoned cut, boiled potatoes and cook until browned.
4. **O'Brien potatoes.**   Cook cubed potatoes in a small amount of fat with chopped onion and pimiento.
5. **Oven-fried potatoes.**   Prepare potatoes as for French Fried Potatoes. Place in greased shallow pans in a thin layer and brush with melted fat, turning to cover all sides. Bake at 450°F for 20–30 minutes, or until browned, turning occasionally. Drain on absorbent paper and sprinkle with salt.

French fried potatoes

DEEP-FAT FRYER: 365°F	YIELD: 50 portions
FRY: 6–8 minutes	PORTION: 3 oz

Ingredient	Amount	Procedure
Potatoes, white	18 lb AP (15 lb EP)	Peel and cut potatoes into uniform strips ¼–⅜ inch thick. Cover with cold water to keep potatoes from darkening.
		Just before frying, drain potatoes or dry with paper towels. Fill fryer basket about one-third full of potatoes. Fry according to Method 1 or 2.

Method 1. Half fill fryer with fat. Preheat to 365°F. Fry potatoes for 6–8 minutes. Drain. Sprinkle with salt. Serve immediately.

Method 2. *Blanching:* Heat fat to 360°F. Place drained potato strips in hot fat, using an 8 to 1 ratio of fat to potatoes, by weight, as a guide for filling fryer basket. Fry 3–5 minutes depending on thickness of potato. (The potatoes should not brown.) Drain. Turn out on sheet pans. Refrigerate for later browning.

Browning: Reheat fat to 375°F. Place about twice as many potato strips in the kettle as for first-stage frying. Fry 2–3 minutes or until golden brown. Drain. Sprinkle with salt if desired. Serve immediately.

Notes:
1. Select a long, mealy potato, such as a russet.
2. To cook frozen French Fried Potatoes, use 12 lb for 50 3-oz portions. Fry at 375°F for 3–5 minutes or until golden brown.

Variations:
1. **Deep-fat browned potatoes.** Partially cook peeled whole or half potatoes. Fry in deep fat at 365°F for 5–7 minutes. Transfer to serving pan. Sprinkle with salt.
2. **Lattice potatoes.** Cut potatoes with lattice slicer. Fry at 365°F for 3–10 minutes. Transfer to serving pan. Sprinkle with salt.
3. **Potato chips.** Cut potatoes into very thin slices. Fry at 365°F for 3–6 minutes. Transfer to serving pan. Sprinkle with salt.
4. **Shoestring potatoes.** Cut potatoes into ⅛-inch strips. Fry at 365°F for 3–6 minutes. Transfer to serving pan. Sprinkle with salt.

Mashed potatoes

YIELD: 50 portions
PORTION: 5 oz

Ingredient	Amount	Procedure
Potatoes	15 lb AP (12 lb EP)	Peel and eye potatoes. Cut into uniform size pieces. Steam or boil (p. 619). When done, drain and place in mixer bowl. Mash, using wire whip attachment, on low speed until there are no lumps. Whip on high speed about 2 minutes.
Milk, hot Margarine or butter Salt	2–2½ qt 8 oz 2 oz (3 Tbsp)	Add hot milk, margarine, and salt. Whip on high speed until light and creamy.

Notes:

1. Potato water may be substituted for part of the milk.
2. 8 oz nonfat dry milk and 2–2½ qt water may be substituted for the liquid milk. Sprinkle dry milk over potatoes before mashing.
3. 2–2½ lb dehydrated potatoes may be substituted for the raw potatoes. Follow processor's instructions for preparation.

Variations:

1. **Duchess potatoes.** Add 18 eggs (2 lb), beaten, to mashed potatoes. Add additional milk if necessary. Pile lightly into baking pans. Bake at 350°F for 20–30 minutes, or until set.
2. **Mashed potato casserole.** Add ½ cup chopped chives, ½ cup crisp, cooked, crumbled bacon, 12 oz cream cheese, 1 tsp white pepper and ¼ tsp garlic powder. Mix until blended. Place in baking pans. Sprinkle lightly with grated Parmesan cheese and paprika. Brush lightly with melted margarine or butter. Bake at 375°F for 30 minutes or until light brown.
3. **Potato croquettes.** Add 18 egg yolks, well beaten. Shape into croquettes and dip in egg-milk mixture and crumbs (p. 41). Chill. Fry in deep fat at 360°F for 5–8 minutes.
4. **Potato rosettes.** Force Duchess Potatoes through a pastry tube, forming rosettes. Bake at 350°F until lightly browned. Use as a garnish for planked steak.

Oven-browned or rissolé potatoes

| OVEN: 450°F | | YIELD: 50 portions |
| BAKE: 1 hour | | PORTION: 1 potato |

Ingredient	Amount	Procedure
Potatoes, baking variety	50	Peel potatoes and partially cook, about 10 minutes.
Margarine, melted Salt	1 lb 1 oz (1½ Tbsp)	Place potatoes on well-greased baking sheets. Pour melted margarine over potatoes. Sprinkle with salt. Bake at 450°F for 1 hour or until tender. Baste every 15 minutes with margarine from pan. Turn potatoes once during baking to ensure uniform browning.

Variations:
1. **Franconia potatoes.** Cook peeled uniform-sized potatoes approximately 15 minutes. Drain and place in pan in which meat is roasting. Bake approximately 40 minutes or until tender and lightly browned, basting with drippings in pan or turning occasionally to brown all sides. Serve with roast.
2. **French baked potatoes.** Select small, uniform potatoes and peel. Roll potatoes in melted margarine or shortening, then in cracker crumbs or crushed cornflakes. Place in shallow pans and bake.
3. **Herbed potato bake.** Peel baking potatoes and cut into ½-inch slices. Place in greased baking pans. Combine 1½ cups melted margarine, 3½ oz dehydrated onion soup mix, and 2 Tbsp rosemary. Sprinkle over potatoes and toss lightly. Bake at 325°F for 1½ hours or until potatoes are tender.

Parsley buttered new potatoes

YIELD: 50 portions
PORTION: 3 oz

Ingredient	Amount	Procedure
New potatoes Salt	15 lb AP (10 lb EP) 1 oz (1½ Tbsp)	Wash and peel potatoes, removing eyes. Cut potatoes into 1½-inch cubes, or leave whole. If whole potatoes, cut as necessary to be of uniform size. Steam or boil (p. 619) until tender.
Butter or margarine, melted	8 oz	Distribute butter uniformly over cooked potatoes.
Fresh parsley, chopped	1 oz	Sprinkle with parsley.

Variations:
1. **Creamed new potatoes.** Add 3 qt Medium White Sauce (p. 560) to cooked potatoes.
2. **Creamed new potatoes and peas.** See p. 648.
3. **New potatoes Parmesan.** Scrub small uniform-sized new potatoes. Remove 1 inch of peeling from around the center of each potato. Steam or boil (p. 619) until just done. Roll potatoes in melted margarine or butter. Place in baking pans. Sprinkle with Parmesan cheese. Bake at 350°F for 20–25 minutes. Canned small whole potatoes may be substituted for fresh potatoes.
4. **Paprika-seasoned new potatoes.** Delete parsley. Sprinkle potatoes with 1 Tbsp paprika. Stir lightly to mix seasoning.
5. **Persillade new potatoes.** Peel and cook uniform, small new potatoes. Pour over them a mixture of lemon juice and melted butter or margarine, then roll in minced parsley.
6. **Potatoes continental.** Peel small potatoes and cook until tender in meat stock, to which 2 or 3 bay leaves have been added. Drain and season with chopped onion browned in margarine. Garnish with minced parsley and paprika.
7. **Potatoes in jackets.** Wash medium-sized potatoes and remove blemishes. Steam or boil until tender. Serve without removing skins.

Potato pancakes

		YIELD: 50 portions
		100 cakes
		PORTION: 2 2-oz cakes

Ingredient	Amount	Procedure
Potatoes	15 lb AP (12 lb EP)	Peel potatoes and onions. Grind. Drain.
Onions	1 lb 8 oz	
Eggs, beaten	8 (14 oz)	Combine and add to potatoes and onion.
Flour, all-purpose	8 oz	
Salt	2 oz (3 Tbsp)	
Baking powder	1 tsp	
Milk	¾ cup	
		Drop potato mixture with No. 20 dipper on hot greased griddle. Fry, turning once, until golden brown on both sides. Serve with applesauce.

Potatoes Romanoff

OVEN: 350°F	YIELD: 60 portions
BAKE: 35–45 minutes	2 pans 12 × 20 × 2 inches
	PORTION: 6 oz

Ingredient	Amount	Procedure
Frozen hashed brown potatoes	16 lb	Thaw potatoes. Steam for 15 minutes.
Sour cream	4 lb 4 oz	Combine in mixer bowl and blend on low speed.
Green onions, sliced	6 oz	
Salt	1½ oz	
Pepper, black	1 Tbsp	
Cheddar cheese, shredded	12 oz	
Paprika	½ tsp	Add cooked potatoes to sour cream mixture. Mix well.
		Scale into two greased 12 × 20 × 2-inch pans, 10 lb per pan.
		Sprinkle lightly with paprika.
		Bake uncovered at 350°F for 35–45 minutes.
		Cut 6 × 5.

Scalloped potatoes

OVEN: 350°F	YIELD: 50 portions
BAKE: 1½–2 hours	2 pans 12 × 20 × 2 inches
	PORTION: 6 oz

Ingredient	Amount	Procedure
Potatoes	15 lb AP (12 lb EP)	Peel and eye potatoes. Slice and place in 2 greased 12 × 20 × 2-inch baking pans, 6 lb per pan.
Salt	2 oz (3 Tbsp)	Sprinkle with salt.
Margarine or butter	8 oz	Melt margarine. Add flour and salt.
Flour, all-purpose	4 oz	Stir until smooth. Cook 5 minutes.
Salt	1 oz (1½ Tbsp)	
Milk	1 gal	Add milk gradually, while stirring with wire whip. Cook until thickened. Pour over potatoes.
Bread crumbs	6 oz	Combine crumbs and margarine.
Margarine or butter, melted	2 oz	Sprinkle over potatoes. Bake at 350°F for 1½–2 hours.

Notes:
1. Potatoes may be partially cooked and hot White Sauce added to shorten baking time.
2. Dehydrated sliced potatoes may be substituted for fresh. Reconstitute according to package directions.

Variations:
1. **Scalloped potatoes with ham.** Add 5 lb cubed ham to White Sauce. Cut salt to 1 Tbsp.
2. **Scalloped potatoes with onions.** Before baking, cover potatoes with onion rings. About 5 minutes before removing from oven, cover potatoes with shredded cheese.

Sour cream potatoes

OVEN: 350°F	YIELD: 50 portions
BAKE: 35–45 minutes	3 pans 12 × 10 × 2 inches
	PORTION: 5 oz

Ingredient	Amount	Procedure
Frozen hashed brown potatoes	10 lb	Thaw potatoes. Steam for 10–15 minutes. Hold for later step.
Margarine Onions, chopped	4 oz 1 lb	Melt margarine in steam-jacketed or other kettle. Add onions and sauté until transparent.
Sour cream Salt (see Note 2) Pepper, black Eggs, beaten slightly Chicken base Water	2 lb 12 oz 1 oz 1 Tbsp 6 (10 oz) 1 Tbsp 2 cups	Add to onions and mix well.
		Add potatoes to onion mixture. Mix lightly. Scale into 3 greased 12 × 10 × 2-inch pans, 5 lb 5 oz per pan.
Cornflake crumbs Margarine	3 oz ⅓ cup	Combine crumbs and margarine in mixer bowl, using flat paddle. Mix until crumbly. Sprinkle 2 oz over each pan of potatoes. Bake at 350°F for 35–45 minutes. To serve, spoon into 50 5-oz portions or cut each pan 4 × 4 for 48 servings.

Notes:
1. Undiluted cream of mushroom, cream of celery, or cream of chicken soup may be substituted for sour cream. Delete salt and chicken base.
2. If a highly salted chicken base is used, delete or reduce salt.
3. 2 oz (1 cup) dehydrated onions, rehydrated in 1½ cups water, may be substituted for fresh onions (p. 50).

Glazed or candied sweet potatoes

OVEN: 400°F		YIELD: 50 portions
BAKE: 20–30 minutes		PORTION: 4 oz

Ingredient	Amount	Procedure
Sweet potatoes or yams	16 lb AP (13 lb EP)	Scrub potatoes. Steam or boil in skins until tender (p. 619). When potatoes are cool enough to handle, peel and cut into halves lengthwise. Arrange in shallow pans.
Sugar, brown Water Margarine or butter Salt	1 lb 12 oz 2 cups 8 oz ½ tsp	Mix sugar, water, margarine, and salt. Heat to boiling point. Pour over potatoes. Bake at 400°F for 20–30 minutes.

Notes:
1. Three No. 10 cans of sweet potatoes may be substituted for fresh sweet potatoes.
2. Seasonings for sweet potatoes: allspice, cardamom, cinnamon, cloves, or nutmeg.

Variations:
1. **Baked sweet potatoes.**   Select small even-sized sweet potatoes or yams. Scrub. Bake at 425°F for 40–45 minutes, or until tender.
2. **Candied sweet potatoes with almonds.**   Proceed as for Glazed Sweet Potatoes. Increase margarine or butter to 12 oz and reduce brown sugar to 1 lb 8 oz. Add 1 cup dark syrup and 2 tsp mace. When partially glazed, sprinkle top with chopped almonds and continue cooking until almonds are toasted.
3. **Glazed sweet potatoes with orange slices.**   Add ¼ cup grated orange peel to syrup. Cut 5 oranges into thin slices; add to sweet potatoes when syrup is added.
4. **Mashed sweet potatoes.**   Cook and mash sweet potatoes or yams (p. 619), following procedure on p. 653. Add 1½ oz salt, ⅓ tsp nutmeg, 1 oz margarine, melted, and 1¼ qt hot milk.
5. **Sweet potatoes and apples.**   Reduce sweet potatoes to 9 lb, cooked, peeled, and sliced. Peel and slice 5 lb tart apples. Place alternate layers of sweet potatoes and apples in baking pans. Pour hot syrup (see recipe for Glazed Sweet Potatoes) over potatoes and apples. Bake at 350°F for 45 minutes.

Sweet potato soufflé

OVEN: 375°F	YIELD: 50 portions
BAKE: 30 minutes	1 pan 12 × 20 × 2 inches
	PORTION: 4 oz

Ingredient	Amount	Procedure
Frozen sweet potatoes	8 lb	Steam potatoes for 25 minutes. Place in mixer bowl and whip on low, medium, and high speeds for 1 minute each, or until smooth.
Margarine, melted Sugar, brown Cinnamon, ground Mace, ground Ginger, ground Cloves, ground Milk Eggs	12 oz 1 lb 8 oz 1 Tbsp 1 Tbsp 1 tsp ¼ tsp 1 cup 9 (1 lb)	Add to sweet potatoes. Mix until thoroughly blended. Begin on low speed and progress to high speed for a total of approximately 5 minutes or until mixture is fluffy.
Miniature marshmallows	6 oz	Fold marshmallows into potato mixture. Scale into greased 12 × 20 × 2-inch pan. Bake at 350°F for 30 minutes or until hot.
Miniature marshmallows	4 oz	Sprinkle marshmallows over sweet potatoes. Return to oven long enough for marshmallows to puff and brown slightly.

Seasoned fresh spinach and other greens

| | | YIELD: 50 portions |
| | | PORTION: 3 oz |

Ingredient	Amount	Procedure
Spinach or other greens, fresh	12 lb AP (10 lb EP)	Sort and trim greens. Remove veins, coarse stems, and roots.
Salt	1 oz (1½ Tbsp)	Wash leaves thoroughly, lifting out of water after each washing. Steam or boil (p. 619).
Margarine or butter, melted	4 oz	Pour margarine over greens.

Notes:
1. Beet greens, chard, collards, kale, mustard greens, or turnip greens may be used. For kale, strip leaves from coarse stems.
2. For frozen spinach, use 10 lb. See p. 619 for cooking.
3. Greens may be garnished with 12 hard-cooked eggs, chopped, and 1 lb 8 oz crisp-cooked bacon, crumbled.
4. Seasonings for spinach: basil, mace, marjoram, nutmeg, oregano, mushrooms, bacon, cheese, hard-cooked eggs, vinegar.

Variations:
1. **Creamed spinach.**   Cook spinach. Drain. Chop coarsely. Add 2 qt White Sauce (p. 560). Season with salt, pepper, and nutmeg.
2. **Wilted spinach or lettuce.**   To 10 lb chopped raw spinach or lettuce, or a combination of the two, add 2 qt Hot Bacon Sauce (p. 578) just before serving.

Spinach soufflé

OVEN: 350°F	YIELD: 48 portions
BAKE: 40 minutes	2 pans 12 × 20 × 2 inches
	PORTION: 4 oz

Ingredient	Amount	Procedure
Margarine or butter	1 lb 4 oz	Melt margarine. Add flour and salt.
Flour, all-purpose	8 oz	Stir until smooth and cook 5 minutes.
Salt	2½ Tbsp	
Milk	1¼ qt	Add milk and sour cream. Blend over low
Sour cream	1¼ qt	heat until smooth, stirring constantly.
		Remove from heat.
Spinach, chopped, frozen	6 lb	Thaw spinach. Drain.
Onion, finely chopped	8 oz	Add spinach, onion, nutmeg, and egg yolks
Nutmeg	1½ Tbsp	to sauce. Mix.
Egg yolks, beaten	18 (12 oz)	
Egg whites	18 (1 lb 5 oz)	Beat egg whites until stiff.
		Fold into spinach mixture.
		Lightly grease two 12 × 20 × 2-inch counter pans on the bottom only. Scale 7 lb 8 oz of the mixture into each pan.
		Set in pans of hot water.
		Bake at 350°F for 40 minutes or until soufflé is set.
		Cut 4 × 6.

Note:
1 oz (½ cup) dehydrated onions, rehydrated in 1½ cups water, may be substituted for fresh onions (p. 50).

Baked acorn squash

OVEN: 350°F		YIELD: 50 portions
BAKE: 30–40 minutes		PORTION: ½ squash

Ingredient	Amount	Procedure
Acorn squash	25	Wash squash and cut in half lengthwise. Scrape out seeds. Place cut side down in shallow pans with a small amount of water. Bake at 350°F for 20–25 minutes, or until just tender. (Squash may be steamed for 20 minutes.)
Margarine or butter, melted	8 oz	Place squash hollow side up. Sprinkle cavities with margarine, salt, and brown sugar.
Salt	1 oz (1½ Tbsp)	
Sugar, brown	12 oz	Bake until sugar is melted, about 10–15 minutes.

Variations:
1. **Acorn squash with sausage.** Place 4-oz sausage patty or 2 link sausages, partially cooked, in each cooked squash half. Continue baking until meat is done.
2. **Stuffed acorn squash.** Half fill cooked squash with No. 12 dipper of the following mixture: 5 qt cooked rice, 4 lb cooked chopped meat, and 4 oz minced onion, sautéed in margarine and moistened with meat stock.

Mashed winter squash

YIELD:	50 portions
PORTION:	3 oz

Ingredient	Amount	Procedure
Winter squash	15 lb AP (10 lb EP)	Pare squash and cut into pieces. Steam or boil until tender (p. 619).
Milk, hot	1½ qt	Mash squash. Add milk and seasonings.
Margarine or butter, melted	8 oz	Whip until light.
		May be garnished with toasted slivered
Salt	2 Tbsp	almonds.
Sugar, brown	8 oz	

Notes:
1. Acorn, butternut, Hubbard, or other winter squash variety may be used.
2. Seasonings for squash: allspice, basil, cinnamon, cloves, fennel, ginger, marjoram, nutmeg, oregano, rosemary, savory.

Variations:
1. **Baked whipped squash.** Mix cooked squash until smooth. Add 12 oz margarine, melted, 1 lb brown sugar, 1 Tbsp ground cinnamon, 1 tsp ground allspice, ½ tsp ground cloves, and 1 oz (1½ Tbsp) salt. Mix thoroughly. Scale into 12 × 20 × 2-inch pan. Bake in 350°F oven for 1 hour or until heated through. Cover with 12 oz miniature marshmallows and heat until marshmallows have browned slightly.
2. **Butternut squash–apple casserole.** Cook 8 lb peeled, cored, and sliced apples, 12 oz margarine or butter, and 12 oz sugar until barely tender. Arrange in baking pans. Cover with mashed butternut squash (use 10 lb). Top with mixture of crushed cornflakes, chopped pecans, melted margarine or butter, and brown sugar. Bake at 350°F for 30–40 minutes.

Seasoned zucchini or summer squash

YIELD: 50 portions
PORTION: 3 oz

Ingredient	Amount	Procedure
Zucchini or other summer squash	11–12 lb AP (10 lb EP)	Wash squash and remove ends. Do not pare. Cut into slices or spears. Steam or simmer until tender (p. 619).
Margarine or butter, melted	4 oz	Pour margarine over squash. Season.
Salt	1 Tbsp	
Pepper, white	1 tsp	

Notes:
1. 1 tsp garlic salt may be substituted for part of salt.
2. ½ cup Parmesan cheese may be sprinkled over zucchini before serving.

Variations:
1. **French fried zucchini.**   See p. 647.
2. **Zucchini casserole.**   Steam or parboil 8 lb sliced zucchini until tender-crisp. Drain. Combine one 46-oz can cream of chicken soup, 3 cups sour cream, 1 cup chopped green onions, and 1 oz shredded carrots. Combine with zucchini. Mix 1 lb 12 oz herb-seasoned bread crumbs and 8 oz melted margarine or butter and spread half in a 12 × 20 × 2-inch counter pan. Pour zucchini mixture over crumbs. Top with remaining crumbs. Bake at 350°F for 30–40 minutes or until heated through. Other vegetables such as broccoli, asparagus, cauliflower, or French cut green beans may be used in this casserole.
3. **Zucchini and summer squash.**   Wash and slice 5 lb zucchini and 5 lb yellow summer squash. Cook until just tender. Season with 8 oz melted margarine or butter, salt and pepper to taste. Add 2 lb cherry tomatoes just before serving.
4. **Zucchini and tomato casserole.**   In 12 × 20 × 2-inch counter pan, layer 7 lb sliced zucchini, 3 lb fresh tomatoes, peeled and chopped, and 1 lb chopped onion. Salt and pepper lightly. Sprinkle 1 lb grated cheddar cheese and 1 lb bacon, cooked and crumbled, over top. Cover with buttered bread crumbs. Bake covered at 400°F for about 1 hour, uncovered for the last 20 minutes.

Baked tomatoes

OVEN: 400°F	YIELD: 50 portions
BAKE: 10–12 minutes	PORTION: ½ tomato

Ingredient	Amount	Procedure
Tomatoes, fresh (5 oz each)	25	Wash tomatoes. Cut in halves.
Salt	1 tsp	Sprinkle each tomato with salt and pepper or
Pepper, black	1 tsp	seasoned salt.
Margarine or butter, melted	6 oz	Combine margarine, bread crumbs, and onion.
Bread crumbs	2 oz	Place 2 tsp mixture on each tomato half.
Onion, finely chopped	6 oz	Bake at 400°F for 10–12 minutes.

Note:
Seasonings for tomatoes: basil, bay leaf, chili powder, garlic, oregano, rosemary, thyme.

Variations:
1. **Mushroom-stuffed tomatoes.** Add 2 lb sautéed mushrooms, sliced or chopped, to crumb mixture.
2. **Broiled tomato slices.** Cut tomatoes in ½-inch slices. Salt, dot with margarine, and broil.
3. **Spinach-stuffed tomatoes.** Wash medium-size fresh tomatoes. Remove core and part of the tomato pulp. Fill center with 2 oz Spinach Soufflé (p. 663). Sprinkle with buttered crumbs and Parmesan cheese. Bake at 350°F for about 1 hour.

Tomato vegetable medley

YIELD: 50 portions
PORTION: 5 oz

Ingredient	Amount	Procedure
Celery, cut in strips	2 lb EP	Steam celery and carrots for 15 minutes
Carrots, cut in 2-inch strips	2 lb EP	(p. 619).
Onions, sliced	2 lb EP	Mix all ingredients and place in two 12 × 20
Green peppers, cut in strips	1 lb EP	× 2-inch pans.
Green beans, cut	1 No. 10 can	Cover with aluminum foil and cook in
Tomatoes, canned	1 No. 10 can	steamer for 30 minutes.
Salt	2 Tbsp	
Tapioca, quick-cooking	6 oz	
Margarine, melted	10 oz	
Pepper, black	¾ tsp	
Sugar, granulated	6 oz	

Note:
Vegetables may be baked at 350°F for 1–1½ hours. Do not precook celery and carrots.

Variations:
1. **Breaded tomatoes.**   Add 1 lb cubed bread, 8 oz margarine, and 6 oz sugar to two No. 10 cans tomatoes. Bake at 350°F for about 30 minutes.
2. **Creole tomatoes.**   Drain two No. 10 cans tomatoes. To the juice add 1 lb celery, 4 oz onion, and 8 oz green pepper, coarsely chopped. Cook for about 15 minutes. Add the tomatoes, 2 Tbsp salt, and ¾ tsp pepper, and place in baking pan. Cover with 2 qt toasted bread cubes and bake at 350°F for about 30 minutes.
3. **Tomatoes and celery.**   Combine two No. 10 cans tomatoes, 8 oz celery, cut into ¾-inch lengths, 1 Tbsp sugar, 1 Tbsp salt, 2 oz margarine. Cover and simmer for 15 minutes or until celery is tender.

Stir-fried vegetables

YIELD: 50 portions
PORTION: 3 oz

Ingredient	Amount	Procedure
Cornstarch Water	⅓ cup 1 cup	Combine cornstarch and water. Set aside for last step.
Assorted vegetables (see Note 2 for suggestions)	7–8 lb AP (6 lb 8 oz EP)	Prepare vegetables. Cut into uniform-size thin slices, strips, or diagonal slices. Pat dry before frying.
Cooking oil Garlic, minced Ginger root, fresh, minced	1 cup 2 cloves ½ tsp	Combine oil, garlic, and ginger root in frying pan. Heat to 350°F.
Water chestnuts, sliced, drained	8 oz	Add water chestnuts and prepared vegetables to heated oil. Stir with long spatulas in a folding motion. Cook until vegetables are tender-crisp.
Chicken Stock (p. 590) Soy sauce	3 cups ½ cup	Combine stock and soy sauce. Mix quickly into vegetables. Reduce heat. Pour cornstarch mixture over vegetables. Cook and stir just until sauce thickens and vegetables are glazed.

Notes:
1. Select vegetables for contrast in color, shape, texture, and flavor. At least three vegetables should be selected. Cut vegetables into small enough pieces to cook quickly. Frozen vegetables should be thawed before stir-frying.
2. Suggested vegetables: cauliflower, broccoli, green beans, snow peas, carrots, celery, onions, zucchini or summer squash, mushrooms, or red, green, or yellow pepper strips.

Vegetable timbale

OVEN:	300°F
BAKE:	2 hours

YIELD: 40 portions
            1 pan 12 × 20 × 2 inches
PORTION: 3 oz

Ingredient	Amount	Procedure
Eggs	16 (1 lb 9 oz)	Beat eggs.
Salt	2 Tbsp	Add salt, margarine, and milk.
Margarine or butter, melted	5 oz	
Milk	1½ qt	
Spinach, chopped, frozen	3 lb	Cook spinach (p. 619). Drain well. Add to egg mixture. Mix until well blended.
		Pour into greased 12 × 20 × 2-inch pan. Set into another pan with 3 cups hot water in it. Bake at 300°F for 2 hours. Test with a silver knife as for custard. Cut 5 × 8. Serve with 1 oz Cheese Sauce (p. 561).

Note:
Spinach, broccoli, brussels sprouts, asparagus, or any combination of these vegetables may be used.

Variation:
Chicken timbale.   Use 32 eggs (3 lb 8 oz), 1 oz salt, 1 lb margarine, melted, 1 tsp white pepper, 12 oz bread crumbs, and 6 lb chopped cooked chicken. Mix melted margarine, bread crumbs, and milk. Cook for 5 minutes. Add beaten eggs, seasonings, and chicken. Bake as for Vegetable Timbale. Cut 6 × 8. Serve with Béchamel Sauce (p. 563).

Part three

MENU DEVELOPMENT

MENU PLANNING

Dining away from home has become an integral part of the American life-style, and statistics indicate that more than one-third of all meals are eaten outside the home. This change in eating style has created a challenge for menu writers to plan menus that are creative, exciting, and nutritious. A careful analysis and understanding of menu types, factors affecting menu planning, and planning procedures is important before the writing of menus can begin.

TYPES OF MENUS

The menu is an outline of food items to be included in each meal, and the variety of choices must be decided before menus are planned. Menus used in foodservices may be classified according to the following groups:

Static or set menus include the same foods every day. Many commercial and some hospital foodservices use the static menu. Most menus of this type offer a wide variety of choices.

Single-use menus are planned for a specific day or event and are not usually repeated in exactly the same form.

Nonselective menus have a single item in each menu category. To assure nutritional adequacy, foods from each of the basic food groups should be included. A general pattern for a nonselective menu is given on p. 685. A nonselective menu may be modified to include a limited selection; for example, a choice of two vegetables may be given, or a soup and salad may be offered as an alternative to an entree and vegetable for those who wish a lighter meal.

Selective menus offer two or more items within each category. Foods from which the individual patron may choose a well-balanced meal should be included. Most commercial and noncommercial foodservices use this type of menu extensively. A suggested pattern for a selective menu, using the same format for lunch and dinner, is given on p. 685.

A *cycle menu* is a carefully planned series of menus that offer different items from day to day for one week, two weeks, or other time period, after which the menus are repeated. The length of the cycle depends on the type of foodservice. A short cycle is appropriate for foodservices having a frequent change of clientele, such as hospitals. Some hospitals can utilize a five-day cycle, but in extended care facilities the cycle usually is three or four weeks or longer. If the cycle is short, the number of days in the cycle should not be divisible by seven. Using a cycle other than seven days assures that the same menu is not served on the same day of the week too frequently. Restaurants may prefer to use monthly or seasonal cycles or may use the same menu throughout the year. Many foodservices recognize seasonal changes by having spring, summer, autumn, and winter cycles.

Cycle menus save time for the planner and are effective tools for food and labor cost control, forecasting, and purchasing. Repetition of the same or nearly the same menu helps standardize preparation procedures and gives the employees an opportunity to become more efficient through repeated use of familiar recipes. Menus can become monotonous and repetitious if not carefully planned, however. Regardless of the length of the cycle, menus should be constantly reviewed and updated. Each day's menus should be analyzed shortly after service, and any production problems or adverse reactions by the clientele should be noted and corrected before the next cycle. The menu planner must allow flexibility for changes resulting from holidays, special occasions, leftover food, and inability to obtain specific food items for production.

FACTORS AFFECTING MENU PLANNING

A well-planned menu is the cornerstone of a successful foodservice and the focal point from which many functions and activities start. The menu must offer a selection of foods that is satisfying to the clientele, but it must be one that can be produced within the constraints and demands of the particular facility. Factors to consider when planning a menu include the following:

Clientele

The menu planner must consider the makeup of the group to be served—age, sex, nutritional needs, food habits, and individual preferences. This is especially important if the foodservice offers a limited choice of food, as in some extended care facilities, child care centers, and retirement complexes. Menus for this type of foodservice are planned to meet the needs of the majority of patrons, with enough flexibility for satisfying all clientele. Planning menus for foodservices with a static population requires strict attention to the complete nutritional needs of the group and also must offer enough variety to minimize monotony.

In foodservices offering a variety of menu items and in those having turnover of clientele, providing nutritionally adequate choices is important. An emphasis for people today is for good nutrition and healthful eating styles. Menu choices offered must reflect this change.

Clientele are increasingly more knowledgeable about new and different foods and desire greater variety and an opportunity to select trendy or contemporary foods. Ethnic, vegetarian, and regional foods have increased in popularity, and menus may need to be expanded to meet these changes.

Planning menus that are acceptable requires the menu planner to be aware of food preferences and periodically evaluate acceptance of foods and food combinations. Plate-waste analysis, customer preference surveys, food usage data, meal census information, and informal interactions with clientele are a few ways to assess menu acceptability.

Type of foodservice

The type of foodservice is not the limiting factor for the menu planner, and differences among various kinds of facilities are becoming less evident. For example, many college foodservices offer menu choices similar to commercial cafeterias and full-service or fast-service restaurants. Hospital menus for general diet patients may be no different from those for any other segment of the foodservice industry. Menu variation among types of foodservices is based on philosophy and limitation differences among particular facilities rather than on foodservice function.

Financial limitations

The budget plays a critical role in planning menus. The costs of food, labor, and supplies for menu items must be considered in relation to projected income and expenses. Commercial foodservices often must price menu items within a predetermined range. Food costs are used in establishing selling price, making the choice of menu items important. Forecasted need and menu mix in relation to cost must be considered. Offering a high-priced item along with a popular lower-cost item will help reduce costs.

Adhering to strict financial standards in menu planning and monitoring unforeseen cost fluctuations are necessary to meet financial goals of both commercial and noncommercial foodservices.

Production capabilities

AVAILABLE EQUIPMENT
The type, size, and amount of food preparation, holding, and transporting equipment available is an important factor in planning menus that can be produced. Special attention should be given to oven capacity, number of grills or fryers, refrigerator and freezer facilities, number and size of steam-jacketed kettles and steamers, and availability and capacity of mixers. Certain combinations of menu items often must be avoided because of lack of production equipment or serving pans and dishes.

NUMBER AND EXPERIENCE OF EMPLOYEES

The man-hours of labor available and the efficiency and skill of employees are important to the successful preparation of any meal.

DISTRIBUTION OF WORK

Menus should be planned that will distribute the work evenly among the different areas of preparation. In determining a day's work load, the menu planner should consider not only one day's menu but also any preparation necessary for meals for the following day. Care should be exercised so menus are not planned in a way that creates an excessive work load for employees one day and underutilizes them the next. To introduce variety in the menu, a limited number of foods requiring time-consuming processes may be included if combined with other food items that require minimum preparation. Some foods require last-minute cooking to assure products of high quality. To avoid confusion and delayed meal service, the menu should be planned so there is a balance between items that may be prepared early and those that must be cooked just prior to serving.

MENU-PLANNING PROCEDURES

There are no absolute rules on how to approach menu planning as long as the menu writer satisfies the needs and demands of the clientele and the policies of the foodservice are met. It is suggested that menu planning be done without interruptions and that the following materials be available:

1. Menu forms as dictated by type and needs of the foodservice.
2. Standardized recipe file.
3. Current trade periodicals and other foodservice publications.
4. Menu suggestions lists, as shown on p. 688.
5. Previous menus if available.
6. Summaries of menu evaluation data.

Key points in menu planning

PLAN FOR VARIETY

1. Include a wide variety of foods from day to day to assure adequate nutrients. Unless you provide a choice, avoid the same form of food on consecutive days—for example, meat loaf on one day and spaghetti and meatballs the next.
2. Avoid repeating the same food on the same day of the week. For this reason, a short cycle where the days are divisible by seven is undesirable.

3. Vary the method of preparation. For example, serve vegetables raw or cooked, buttered, stir-fried, marinated, or with a sauce.

4. Introduce new foods occasionally, and, on a selective menu, pair a new food with a familiar well-liked food.

PLAN FOR EYE APPEAL

1. Try to visualize the appearance of the food on the plate or on the cafeteria counter.

2. Use at least one or two colorful foods on each menu.

3. Use colorful foods in combination with foods having little color.

PLAN FOR CONTRAST IN TEXTURE AND FLAVOR

1. Offer crisp foods with soft foods.

2. Use strong and mild flavored foods together.

3. Balance light and heavy foods; for example, in a nonselective menu use light desserts with hearty entrees.

PLAN FOR CONSUMER ACCEPTANCE

1. Include food combinations most acceptable to the clientele.

2. The completed menu should, if possible, have a predominance of familiar and well-accepted menu items, with the introduction of new and less well-liked foods spaced throughout the menu period.

3. In nonselective menus, it is important that the less popular foods be accompanied by some that are well liked by the majority of the clientele.

4. Periodically assess the food preferences of the consumers.

PLAN FOR FINANCIAL, PRODUCTION, AND SERVICE LIMITATIONS

1. Include food combinations that can be prepared with available personnel and equipment.

2. Select menu items that will keep food costs within the budget allowance.

Steps in menu planning

DETERMINE A TIME PERIOD

Plan menus for at least a week, preferably longer. If a cycle menu is being planned, decide on the length of the cycle.

PROCEED SYSTEMATICALLY

Select menu items systematically, in approximately the following order:

Entrees   Select meat and other entrees for the entire cycle or length of time for which menus are being planned. If planning a week's menus only, choose entrees for a month or longer, then complete the menus as needed. In this way, an entree cycle can be developed that would simplify planning each week's menus.

On a selective menu, offer at least one meat and a meatless entree, along with poultry and fish to complete the number of entrees required.

Be specific about method of preparation when recording the menu; for example, show pork chops as baked, stuffed, barbecued, breaded, or whatever method of preparation is desired.

Soups and sandwiches   Plan soups and sandwiches at the same time as entrees if they are to be offered as a main dish in lieu of meat or other entree. On a selective menu, offer a cream soup and a stock soup. In a cafeteria, a variety of sandwiches may be offered, and these may not change from day to day.

Vegetables   Select vegetables that are compatible with the entrees. Potatoes, rice, or pasta may be included as one choice. On a selective menu, pair a popular vegetable with one that is less well liked.

Salads   If only one salad is to be offered, select one that complements or is a contrast in texture to the other menu items. On a selective menu, include a green salad and fruit, vegetable, and gelatin salads to complete the desired number. Certain salad items may be offered daily such as tossed salad, cottage cheese, or cabbage slaw; or a salad bar may be a standard menu feature. See p. 461 for salad bar suggestions.

Breads   Vary the kinds of breads offered or provide a choice of white or whole grain bread and a hot bread.

Desserts   If no choice is offered, plan a light dessert with a hearty meal and a rich dessert when the rest of the meal is not too heavy. On a selective menu, include a two-crust pie, a soft pie, cake, pudding, and gelatin dessert. Ice cream, yogurt, baked custard, and fruit may be offered daily.

Breakfast items   Certain breakfast foods such as cooked and cold cereal, toast, and fruit juices may be standard. Variety may be introduced through a choice of entrees, hot breads, and fresh fruits.

Beverages   A choice of beverages usually is provided. Coffee, decaffeinated coffee, tea, and milk, including lowfat, usually are offered. Lemonade, fruit punch, and a variety of juices may be included also.

EVALUATE THE COMPLETED MENU

After the menu has been planned, check carefully to see if it has met the established criteria. Evaluate the menu again after the meals have been served. Make notations of satisfactory menus and difficulties encountered in production and service of the meals. If the cycle is to be repeated, desired alterations should be noted.

The responsibility of the menu planner does not end with the writing of the menu. The task is completed only when the food has been prepared and served and the reaction of the consumer noted.

MENU PLANNING FOR DIFFERENT TYPES OF FOODSERVICES

ELEMENTARY AND SECONDARY SCHOOLS

The school lunch program is designed to provide nutritious, reasonably priced lunches to schoolchildren and children in residential child care centers, to contribute to a better understanding of good nutrition, and to foster good food habits. School foodservice has become a basic part of the nutrition and education program of the nation's schools. The School Breakfast Program has further expanded this role.

The nutrition goal for school lunches is to provide approximately one-third of the Recommended Dietary Allowances (RDA) by age and grade categories. In the years since passage of the School Lunch Act, the implementation of its provisions has been changed to permit more choice and greater flexibility in menu patterns and adjustment in portion sizes for various age groups. School lunch patterns for various age/grade groups are given on pp. 682–683.

To qualify for reimbursement, a school is required to use this framework, but other foods may be added to help improve acceptability and to satisfy students' appetites.

An "offer versus serve" provision allows students to choose less than all of the food items within the lunch pattern. Students must be offered all five food items of the school lunch, and the student must choose at least three of these items for the lunch to be reimbursed. Schools are required to implement the "offer versus serve" provision for senior high school students. The implementation of this provision in middle and junior high schools is left to the discretion of local school food authorities, but it is not allowed in elementary schools.

The cycle menu is used to some extent in school foodservices, and many schools are using selective menus in which students may select from two items of comparable nutritional value for part of the menu; for example, a student may have a choice of two vegetables and two or more desserts. Some schools offer multiple menus in which more than one complete menu is offered, such as a soup and sandwich meal that meets federal requirements and a plate lunch. Some junior and senior high schools offer a la carte menus. The trend is for more menu choices for students.

Many foods on the Menu Planning Suggestions listed on p. 688 are suitable for school lunches, keeping in mind the nutritional requirements; cost, labor, and equipment restraints; and food preferences of the age group to be served. Many schools include salad, deli, and potato bars, and most schools introduce ethnic and international foods through special promotions.

An amendment to the National School Lunch Act provides assistance to eligible foodservices for preschool and school-age children in day care centers, settlement houses, recreation centers, and summer day camps. In planning food for children in these centers, the total daily food requirements of children should be considered. The combination of meals and snacks will vary according to the age group, their time of arrival at the center, and their length of stay. It is important that the planner consider the nutritional needs of the children, their food preferences, regional food habits, and equipment, personnel, and other management functions.

Young children need nutritious foods at frequent intervals, but it is important to schedule the service of food to allow sufficient time between meals and supplements. Young children enjoy food they can handle easily. Finger food, snacks, and bite-sized pieces are most popular. Apple wedges, banana slices, berries, dried peaches or pears, fresh peach, pear, or pineapple wedges, grapefruit or orange sections, pitted plums and prunes, raisins, cabbage wedges, carrot and celery sticks, cauliflower florets, tomato wedges, cheese cubes, crackers or rusks with peanut butter or cheese, and small sandwiches are examples of finger foods.

Those responsible for foodservice in child care centers should provide the opportunity for children to learn to eat and enjoy a variety of nutritious foods.

COLLEGES AND UNIVERSITIES

College and university foodservices have every style of foodservice found in the commercial sector of the foodservice industry. Many residence halls are operated on a board contract basis or an a la carte modification of one. Cash cafeterias, snack bars, specialty shops, and retail bakeries are also represented. Banquet and catered functions, both on and off campus, are commonplace.

Planning cafeteria menus for students is similar to that for a commercial cafeteria. Because clientele eat most of their meals in the same location there is a responsibility to provide foods students will select that meet their nutritional requirements.

The selective menu pattern on p. 685 is appropriate for college and university foodservices. Certain salad items, such as tossed salad, cottage cheese, fruit, and gelatin, may be offered each day on a salad bar. Likewise, fruit, yogurt, and ice cream may be served at each meal, with other desserts added for variety. Fast-service lines that serve soups and salads, milk shakes, hamburgers and french fries,

SCHOOL LUNCH PATTERNS FOR VARIOUS AGE/GRADE GROUPS

U.S. Department of Agriculture, National School Lunch Program

USDA recommends, but does not require, that you adjust portions by age/grade group to better meet the food and nutritional needs of children according to their ages. If you adjust portions, Groups I–V are minimum requirements for the age/grade groups specified. If you do not adjust portions, Group IV are the portions to serve all children.

Components		Minimum Quantities		
		Preschool		Grades K–3, Ages 5–8 (Group III)
		Ages 1–2 (Group I)	Ages 3–4 (Group II)	
Meat or meat alternate	A serving of one of the following or a combination to give an equivalent quantity:			
	Lean meat, poultry, or fish (edible portion as served)	1 oz	1½ oz	1½ oz
	Cheese	1 oz	1½ oz	1½ oz
	Large egg(s)	1	1½	1½
	Cooked dry beans or peas	½ cup	¾ cup	¾ cup
	Peanut butter	2 Tbsp	3 Tbsp	3 Tbsp
Vegetable and/or fruit	Two or more servings of vegetable or fruit or both to total	½ cup	½ cup	½ cup
Bread or bread alternate	Servings of bread or bread alternate A serving is: • 1 slice of whole grain or enriched bread • A whole grain or enriched biscuit, roll, muffin, etc. • ½ cup of cooked whole grain or enriched rice, macaroni, noodles, whole grain or enriched pasta products, or other cereal grains such as bulgur or corn grits • A combination of any of the above	5 per week	8 per week	8 per week
Milk	A serving of fluid milk	¾ cup (6 fl oz)	¾ cup (6 fl oz)	½ pt (8 fl oz)

Source: From *Menu Planning Guide for School Food Service,* USDA Food and Nutrition Service, PA 1260, 1980.

Grades 4–12,[a] Ages 9 and Over (Group IV)	Recommended Quantities Grades 7–12,[b] Ages 12 and Over (Group V)	Specific Requirements
		• Must be served in the main dish or the main dish and one other menu item.
		• Textured vegetable protein products, cheese alternate products, and enriched macaroni with fortified protein may be used to meet part of the meat/meat alternate requirement. Fact sheets on each of these alternate foods give detailed instructions for use.
2 oz	3 oz	*Note:* The amount you must serve of a single meat alternate may seem too large for the particular age group you are serving. To
2 oz	3 oz	make the quantity of that meat alternate more reasonable, use
2	3	a smaller amount to meet part of the requirement and
1 cup	1½ cups	supplement with another meat or meat alternate to meet the
4 Tbsp	6 Tbsp	full requirement.
¾ cup	¾ cup	• No more than one-half of the total requirement may be met with full-strength fruit or vegetable juice.
		• Cooked dry beans or peas may be used as a meat alternate or as a vegetable but not as both in the same meal.
8 per week	10 per week	• At least ½ serving of bread or an equivalent quantity of bread alternate for Group I, and 1 serving for Groups II–V must be served daily.
		• Enriched macaroni with fortified protein may be used as a meat alternate or as a bread alternate but not as both in the same meal.
		Note: Food Buying Guide for School Food Service, PA-1257 (1980) provides the information for the minimum weight of a serving.
½ pt (8 fl oz)	½ pt (8 fl oz)	At least one of the following forms of milk must be offered:
		• Unflavored lowfat milk
		• Unflavored skim milk
		• Unflavored buttermilk
		Note: This requirement does not prohibit offering other milks, such as whole milk or flavored milk along with one or more of the above.

[a] Group IV is the one meal pattern which will satisfy all requirements if no portion size adjustments are made.
[b] Group V specified recommended, not required, quantities for students 12 years and older. These students may request smaller portions, but not smaller than those specified in Group IV.

683

submarine sandwiches, or pizza are well liked by students. Special meals depicting regional and international themes, holiday specialties, and ethnic foods are popular in many university settings.

HOSPITALS

Although hospital menus may be more complex, the principles of meal planning for health care facilities are the same as those for other types of foodservices. Foods must be provided for many kinds of diets, ranging from liquid, ground, soft, or regular to bland, low sodium, low carbohydrate, or fat restricted, with a wide range in caloric requirements. In addition, a cafeteria generally is available for hospital personnel and visitors.

When developing a hospital meal pattern, the first step is to plan a regular or normal diet that will supply all food essentials necessary for good nutrition. This pattern then becomes the foundation for most diets required for therapeutic purposes and is the core of all meal planning in a hospital of any type or size. Patients requiring other than a normal diet will receive various modifications of the regular diet to fit their particular needs.

In planning a normal or regular diet, meals should be planned for each day as a unit. Each day's menu then can be checked to be sure that all essential foods have been included. A suggested three-meal-a-day menu pattern for a normal diet is given on p. 685.

The selective menu adds much to the satisfaction of patients and also helps to prevent waste. Choices that appeal to various patients usually can be made available with little extra work, if careful planning is used in pairing items on the menu. The main items on the selective menu are the same as those on the general menu. Some items, such as the choice of meat and vegetables, may be the same as foods prepared for one of the modified diets or for the cafeteria. Other choices may be soup or fruit juice, or fruit or ice cream in place of a prepared dessert. On the dinner menu, choices of light or heavy items may do much to promote patient acceptance. Some hospitals have adopted a selective menu similar to the table d'hôte menu of the commercial field. A varied selection of foods is listed and offered each day. Patients may order any food item on the menu unless it is restricted on their diets.

Hospitals may find it advantageous to use a five-meal plan, also known as the 3–2 plan. Some patients require smaller meals served more often. In this plan, breakfast is served in midmorning and dinner in late afternoon, with snacks and light foods offered between meals.

EXTENDED CARE FACILITIES AND RETIREMENT COMMUNITIES

For people residing in extended health care facilities and retirement communities, food satisfies a basic emotional and physical need.

NONSELECTIVE MENU PATTERN

Breakfast	Lunch	Dinner
Fruit	Soup (optional)	Soup (optional)
Cereal	Entree	Entree
Protein item	Salad and/or vegetable	Two vegetables (one may
Bread, butter or	Bread, butter or	be potato or starchy food)
margarine	margarine	Salad
Beverage	Fruit or other light	Bread, butter or margarine
	dessert	Dessert
	Beverage	Beverage

SELECTIVE MENU PATTERN[a]

Breakfast	Lunch and Dinner
Fruits: 2 or more juices, fresh fruit in season	Soups: 1 cream, 1 broth
Cereals: cooked, choice of cold cereals	Entrees: at least 2 meats, 1 meatless, 1 meat extender, poultry or fish, and a cold plate.
Entrees: eggs, bacon, ham, or sausage, potatoes, breakfast casserole	Sandwiches: 1 hot, 1 or more cold
	Rice or pasta: in addition to or as alternative to potatoes
Breads: toast, white and whole grain; one or more hot breads	Vegetables: 3 or 4, including potatoes in some form
Beverages: coffee, decaffeinated coffee, tea, milk (whole and lowfat)	Salads: 4 to 10, including entree, tossed green, vegetable, gelatin, fruit, cottage cheese, relishes
	Breads: 2 to 3, including white and whole grain, 1 hot bread
	Desserts: 4 to 8, including 2-crust pie, soft pie, cake and/or cookies, pudding, yogurt, ice cream or sherbet, fruit
	Beverages: coffee, decaffeinated coffee, tea, milk (whole and lowfat), fruit juice or fruit flavored drinks.

[a] Menu variety may be increased or decreased to fit the demands of the foodservice.

MENU PATTERN FOR A NORMAL HOSPITAL DIET

Breakfast	Lunch	Dinner
Fruit or juice	Cream soup *or*	Soup (optional)
Cereal with milk	Main dish (made with meat,	Meat, poultry, or fish
Egg	fish, poultry, egg, or cheese)	Potato or alternate
Bread or toast	Vegetable or salad	starchy vegetable
Butter or margarine	Bread with butter or	Green or yellow vegetable
Beverage	margarine	Salad: fruit or vegetable
	Fruit or other simple dessert	Bread with butter or
	Beverage	margarine
		Dessert
		Beverage

Those persons planning meals for older adults should be aware of the problems peculiar to this age group. Their fixed habits and food preferences developed through many years may influence but should not determine entirely the meals planned for them. Healthy adults regardless of age need a well-balanced diet and, in planning the day's food, the basic pattern for the normal diet should be followed. Individual problems of the group members, such as difficulty in chewing, special diet requirements, and limited mobility and activity, must also be considered.

At least three well-planned meals should be served daily, with a hot food at each meal. The menu pattern is similar to that of the regular hospital diet (p. 685), with adjustments in portions and some modification for residents with individual eating problems. The caloric intake or quantity of food eaten usually is smaller because of lessened activity.

The daily food plan should include the following:

1. At least one food of good-quality protein at each meal—fish, poultry, lean meat, eggs, or cheese.

2. Milk offered at mealtime, with at least 2 cups a day for each person.

3. Four or more servings of fruits and vegetables, including a green leafy or yellow vegetable and a citrus fruit, such as grapefruit, orange, or some other high source of vitamin C. Although chewing may be difficult for some, raw vegetables or fruits should be included.

4. Four or more servings from the bread/cereal group, which includes bread, breakfast cereals, pasta, rice, and baked goods made with whole grain or enriched flour.

Additional foods containing fat, sweets, and flavoring add to the acceptance of meals.

If a nonselective menu is used, some modification will add to the residents' acceptance of the food. Choice may be provided by offering certain menu items daily in addition to a set menu or through a choice of two items in each menu category for the dinner meal. Foodservice in this type of long-term facility offers opportunity for use of the eight-week or longer cycle.

COMMERCIAL FOODSERVICES

Menu planning for commercial foodservices varies according to the type and size of operation, its goals, and the expected check average. Menus range from the fast-food concept of limited menu for high volume and speedy service to the elaborate table d'hôte menu of a formal seated-service restaurant.

In planning menus for the commercial foodservice, the basic rules of meal planning should be followed, with special attention given to the specific requirements of the clientele. As in any other foodservice, labor is one of the largest items of expense and one of the most difficult to control. The use of preportioned foods, portion-ready entrees, ready-to-cook foods, and other labor-saving items is of major importance in effecting economies of time and cost.

Some restaurants have a fixed menu with daily specials featured; others have found the use of cycle menus to be valuable in reducing the time spent in planning and as an aid in the equitable distribution of labor and food. In commercial cafeterias, the noon and evening meals may be essentially the same with a wide selection of entrees, sandwiches, and desserts. It is not uncommon to have five or six entrees, eight to ten salads, and eight to ten desserts.

MENU-PLANNING SUGGESTIONS

ENTREES

Meat

BEEF

Roast
  Chuck
  Corned beef
  Pot roast
  Round
  Rolled rib
  Standing rib
  Sauerbraten
  Smoked beef
    brisket

Steak
  Broiled: club
    Filet mignon
    Sirloin
    T-Bone
  Chicken-fried
    steak
  Country-fried
    steak
  Pepper steak
  Spanish steak
  Swiss steak
  Steak teriyaki

Ground beef
  Bacon-wrapped
    beef
  Chuck wagon
    steak
  Salisbury steak
  Meat loaf
  Meatballs
    Swedish
    Spanish
    with Spaghetti

Beef birds
Kabobs
Liver, braised
  Grilled with
    onions
  with Bacon

VEAL

Veal birds
Veal cacciatori

Breaded veal cutlets
Veal New Orleans
Veal Parmesan
Veal piccata
Veal scallopini

LAMB

Roast leg of lamb
Roast lamb
  shoulder
Broiled lamb chops
Lamb stew
Curried lamb with
  rice

PORK

Pork chops
  Breaded
  Baked

Barbecued
Deviled
  with Dressing
Stuffed
Breaded pork cutlets
Pork roast, loin
  Fresh ham
  Shoulder
  with Dressing
Spareribs
  Barbecued
  Sweet-sour
  with Dressing
  with Sauerkraut
Sweet-sour pork
Bacon
Glazed baked ham
Grilled ham slices
Ham balls
Ham loaf

Meat extenders

Beef stew
  with Vegetables
  with Biscuits
Beef pot pie
Beef stroganoff
Hungarian
  goulash

Beef, pork, and
  noodle casserole
Pasta, beef, and
  tomato casserole
Creole spaghetti
Spanish rice
Chop suey

Cheeseburger pie
Beef biscuit roll
Stuffed peppers
Baked hash
Creamed beef
Creamed chipped
  beef

Chipped beef and
  noodles
Chili con carne
Taco salad
  casserole
Pizza
Lasagne

Frankfurters
  Cheese-stuffed
  with Sauerkraut
Meat turnovers
Sweet-sour pork
Pork and noodle
  casserole
Creamed ham on
  spoonbread or
  biscuits

Plantation
  shortcake
Ham à la king
Ham soufflé
Ham timbales
Ham and egg
  scallop
Ham biscuit roll

Ham turnovers
  with cheese
  sauce
Ham and cheese
  quiche
Sausage rolls
Sausage gravy on
  biscuits

Sausage cakes
Baked acorn
  squash with
  sausage
Fried scrapple
See also pasta
  entrees

Poultry

Chicken cutlets
Pan-fried chicken
Chicken Cantonese
Chicken cacciatore
Oven-fried chicken
Chicken Parmesan
Barbecued chicken
Chicken fricassee
Chicken Tahitian
Broiled chicken
Breast of chicken
  with ham slice
Chicken teriyaki
Chicken with
  dumplings

Sweet-sour
  chicken
Chicken turnovers
Creamed chicken
  on Biscuits
  on Chow mein
    noodles
  on Spoonbread
  in Patty shell
  in Toast cups
Chicken à la king
Herb baked
  chicken
Scalloped chicken

Szechwan chicken
Chicken crepes
Hot chicken salad
Chicken loaf
Chicken pie with
  batter crust
Brunswick stew
Chicken soufflé
Chicken and
  noodles
Chicken rice
  casserole
Singapore curry

Chicken chow
  mein
Chicken biscuit
  roll
Chicken fried rice
Spaghetti with
  chicken sauce
Roast turkey with
  dressing
Turkey divan
Turkey and
  dumplings
Turkey tetrazzini
Turkey à la king
See Entree salads

Fish

Baked fish fillets
Lemon baked fish
Breaded fish fillets
Fillet of sole
  amandine

Salmon loaf
Scalloped salmon
Scalloped tuna
Tuna and noodles
Creamed tuna
  with peas

Tuna à la king
Tuna soufflé
Tuna patties
Scalloped oysters
Creole shrimp

Deviled crab
Seafood quiche
Shrimp fried rice
See Entree salads

Eggs and cheese

Egg and sausage
  bake
Creamed eggs

Curried eggs
Eggs à la king
Scotch woodcock

Goldenrod eggs
Scrambled eggs
Omelets

Quiche
Egg cutlets
Egg foo yung

(continued)

*Eggs and cheese
(continued)*
Hot stuffed eggs
Scalloped eggs and
cheese
Welsh rarebit

Cheese balls on
pineapple slice
Cheese croquettes
Cheese soufflé
with Shrimp
sauce

Cheese fondue
Macaroni and
cheese
Cheese and
broccoli strata

Nachos
Spinach lasagne
Spinach cheese
crepes

Pasta

Macaroni and
cheese
with Ham
Pasta, beef,
tomato casserole
Pasta with clam
sauce
with Vegetable
sauce

Garden pasta
Italian sausage
pasta
Pasta primavera
Swiss broccoli
pasta
Lasagne

Spinach lasagne
Noodles Romanoff
Beef on noodles
Chicken and
noodles
Hungarian
goulash

Creole spaghetti
Spaghetti with
meat sauce
with Meatballs
with Chicken
sauce
Vegetarian
spaghetti

Sandwich entrees

COLD
SANDWICHES
Cheese salad
Chicken salad
Egg salad
Ham salad
Tuna salad
Bacon, lettuce,
tomato
Club sandwich
Turkey club
hoagie
Sliced turkey

Baked ham
with cheese
Submarine
Deli plate

HOT
SANDWICHES
Barbecued beef
Hot roast beef
French dip
Hot roast pork
Hot turkey

Grilled sandwiches
Cheese
Ham and cheese
Turkey and
swiss on
whole wheat
Hot tuna grill
Italian sausage
Reuben
Hot meat and
cheese
Bierocks
Chimichangas

Fajitas
Chili dog
Nacho dog
Tacos
Bacon and tomato
on bun
with Cheese
sauce
Chicken cutlet
Hamburgers
Barbecued
with Cheese
Meat loaf
Western

Salad entrees

Chef's salad bowl
Seafood chef salad
Chicken-orange-
avocado salad
Pasta and chicken
salad

Chicken or turkey
salad
Crunchy
Curried
Fruited

Mandarin
and Bacon
Chicken pasta
salad plate

Italian pasta
salad
Taco salad
Crab salad

Shrimp salad
Shrimp-rice salad
Shrimp tortellini
  salad plate

Tuna salad
Tuna pasta salad

Cottage cheese
  salad
Tomato cottage
  cheese salad

Stuffed tomato
  salad
Fruit salad plate

VEGETABLES

Potatoes

WHITE

Au gratin
Baked
  Fancy topped
  Stuffed
  French
  Herbed potato
  Lyonnaise
Browned
Chips
Creamed

Croquettes
Duchess
Fried
French fried
Hashed brown
Lyonnaise
Mashed
New
    Buttered
    Creamed
    Creamed with
      peas

Parmesan
Persillade
Continental
  in Jackets
O'Brien
Potato cakes
Potato pancakes
  with applesauce
Potato salad, hot
  or cold
Rissolé

Rosettes
Shoestring
Scalloped

SWEET

Baked
Candied or glazed
  with Almonds
  with Apples
Mashed
Soufflé

Pasta and rice

Macaroni and
  cheese
Macaroni salad

Spaghetti
  with tomato
  sauce
Buttered noodles

Noodles Romanoff
Herbed fettuccini
Barley casserole
Buttered rice
Curried rice

Fried rice
  with almonds
Green rice
Rice pilaf
Mexican rice

Starchy vegetables

CORN

Buttered
in Cream
on Cob
with Tomato
Corn pudding
O'Brien

Scalloped
Succotash

LIMA BEANS

Buttered
in Cream
with Bacon

with Mushrooms
with Almonds

PARSNIPS

Buttered
Browned
Glazed

SQUASH

Baked acorn
Baked Hubbard
Mashed butternut
Mashed Hubbard
Stuffed acorn

Green vegetables

ASPARAGUS
Buttered or
  creamed
with Cheese or
  hollandaise
  sauce

BEANS, GREEN
Buttered
Casserole
Creole
Herbed
with Almonds or
  mushrooms
with Dill
Southern style

BROCCOLI
Almond buttered
Buttered

with Cheese sauce
with Lemon butter
with Hollandaise
  sauce
with Crumb butter

BRUSSELS SPROUTS
Buttered

CABBAGE
Au gratin
Buttered or
  creamed
Creole
Hot slaw
Polonaise
Scalloped

CELERY
Buttered or
  creamed
Creamed with
  almonds
Creole
with Carrots
  amandine

PEAS
Buttered or in
  cream
with Carrots,
  cauliflower,
  onions, or
  turnips
with Mushrooms,
  almonds, mint,
  lemon

SPINACH
Buttered
Creamed
Wilted
with Egg or bacon
with New beets
Soufflé

SQUASH, ZUCCHINI
Fried
Buttered
Baked
Casserole

STIR-FRIED
Asparagus
Broccoli
Carrots
Green beans
Mushrooms
Onions

Other vegetables

BEETS
Buttered
Harvard
Julienne
in Sour cream
with Orange sauce
Hot spiced
Pickled

CARROTS
Buttered or
  creamed
Candied or glazed
Mint glazed
Lyonnaise
Marinated

Savory
with Celery
with Peas
Parsley buttered
Sweet-sour

CAULIFLOWER
Buttered or
  creamed
French fried
with Almond
  butter
with Cheese sauce
with Peas

EGGPLANT
Creole
Casserole
Baked
Fried or french
  fried

MUSHROOMS
Broiled
Sautéed
French fried

ONIONS
Au gratin
Baked

Buttered or
  creamed
French fried
Stuffed

RUTABAGAS
Buttered
Mashed

SQUASH, SUMMER
Buttered
with Zucchini
Creole

TOMATOES
Baked
Breaded

Broiled tomato
    slices
Creole
Scalloped
Stewed

with Celery
Tomato vegetable
    medley
Stuffed

TURNIPS
Buttered
in Cream
Mashed
with New peas

Fruits served as vegetables

APPLES
Buttered
Fried
Hot baked

BANANAS
Baked
French fried

GRAPEFRUIT
Broiled

PEACHES
Broiled
with Chutney

PINEAPPLE RING
Broiled
Sautéed
Glazed
with Chutney

SALADS AND RELISHES
Vegetable salads

Salad bar
Mixed green
Tossed vegetable
Hawaiian tossed
Brown bean
Garbanzo bean
Triple bean
Cauliflower bean
Oriental bean
Carrifruit

Carrot raisin
Carrot celery
Marinated carrots
Cole slaw
Creamy cole slaw
Green pepper slaw
Cauliflower-
    broccoli
Creamy
    cauliflower

Sliced cucumbers
    and onions
German
    cucumbers
Marinated garden
    salad
Marinated
    asparagus
Marinated green
    beans

Vegetable collage
Oriental
Spinach-cheese
Spinach-
    mushroom
Potato salad
Sour cream potato
    salad
Hot potato salad

Fruit salads

Acini de pepe
Ambrosia fruit
Waldorf
Apple-cabbage

Apple-carrot
Creamy fruit
Grapefruit orange
    with Avocado
    with Apple

Frozen fruit
Banana log
Melon ball
Mixed fruit

Peach half with
    cream cheese
Blushing pear
Pineapple ring

Gelatin salads

Perfection
Tomato aspic
Applesauce
Apple cinnamon
  swirl
Arabian peach

Autumn salad
Bing cherry
Blueberry
Boysenberry mold
Cranberry mold
Cranberry apple

Cucumber soufflé
Frosted cherry
Frosted lime
Jellied Waldorf
Lemon cream

Pineapple cheese
Ribbon gelatin
Sunshine
Swedish green top
Under-the-sea

Protein salads

Cottage cheese
Chicken or turkey

Deviled egg
Shrimp

Tuna

See also salad
  entrees

Pasta and rice salads

Garbanzo and
  pasta

Dilled rice
Macaroni

Italian pasta
Chicken and pasta

Ham and pasta

Sherbet as salad

Cranberry
Lemon

Lime
Mint

Orange
Pineapple

Raspberry

Relishes

Marinated
  mushrooms
Spiced apples
Buttered apples
Cranberry relish
Cranberry sauce
Pickled beets
Sauerkraut relish
Sweet pickles

Dill pickles
Carrot curls or
  sticks
Marinated carrots
Marinated
  mushrooms
Celery sticks
Cauliflower florets

Cherry tomatoes
Green pepper rings
Olives, green, ripe,
  stuffed
Radishes
Spiced pear
Spiced peach
Spiced crabapples
Stuffed celery

Tomato slices or
  wedges
Turnip sticks or
  slices
Watermelon
  pickles
Zucchini sticks or
  slices

SOUPS
Stock soups

Chicken bouillon
Chicken gumbo
Chicken noodle
Chicken rice
Mulligatawny
French onion

Julienne
Tomato barley
Tomato bouillon
Tomato rice
Vegetable
Beef alphabet

Beef barley
Beef noodle
Beef rice
Creole beef
Hearty beef
  vegetable

Pepper pot
Vegetable beef
Minestrone
Manhattan fish
  chowder

Cream soups

Chicken velvet
Cream of chicken
Corn chowder
Fish chowder
Clam chowder

Potato chowder
Vegetable chowder
Spinach
Tomato
Vegetable

Cream of
  Asparagus
  Broccoli
  Celery

Corn
Mushroom
Potato

Entree soups

Chicken with
  spaetzles
Brunswick stew
Beef stew
Chili con carne

Chili spaghetti
Hearty beef
  vegetable
Hearty potato
  ham chowder

Mulligatawny
Split pea
Navy bean
Broccoli cheese
Cheese

Clam or fish
  chowder
Oyster stew
See cream soups

Chilled soups

Gazpacho
Vichyssoise

DESSERTS
Cakes

Angel food
  Chocolate
  Frozen filled
  Yellow
Orange chiffon

Walnut chiffon
Boston cream pie
Dutch apple
Pound cake
Lazy daisy

Marble
Praline
Pineapple upside-
  down

White, with
  variations
Lady Baltimore
Applesauce
Banana

(continued)

Cakes (continued)
Burnt sugar
Carrot
Chocolate

Fudge
German chocolate
Pineapple cashew
Jelly roll

Chocolate roll
Ice cream roll
Pumpkin roll
Gingerbread

Pumpkin cake
Fruit cake
Cupcakes

Cookies

Butter tea
Thimble
Butterscotch drop
Chocolate drop
Butterscotch pecan
Butterscotch
    refrigerator
Chocolate chip

Jumbo chunk
    chocolate
Chocolate tea
Coconut
    macaroons
Crisp ginger
Molasses drop
Oatmeal crispies
Oatmeal drop

Peanut cookies
Peanut butter
    cookies
Sandies
Snickerdoodles
Sugar, rolled
    Drop
    Whole wheat
Brownies

Butterscotch
    squares
Coconut pecan
    bars
Dreamland bars
Date bars
Oatmeal bars
Marshmallow
    squares

Pies

FRUIT

Apple
    Sour cream
    Crumb
Apricot
Berry
Cherry
Gooseberry
Peach
Pineapple

Raisin
Rhubarb
    custard

SOFT PIES

Chiffon
    Apricot
    Lemon
    Chocolate
    Strawberry

Cream
    Banana
    Butterscotch
    Chocolate
    Date
    Pineapple
Custard
    Coconut

Pumpkin
    Praline
Pecan
    Cream cheese
Lemon
Eggnog
Black bottom
Frozen mocha
    almond
Ice cream pie

Frozen desserts

SUNDAES AND
PARFAITS

Hot fudge sundae
Peanut butter
    sundae
Caramel sundae
Strawberry sundae
Chocolate parfait
Strawberry parfait

ICE CREAM

Butter brickle
Chocolate
Chocolate chip
Chocolate almond
Coffee
Lemon custard

Peach
Pecan
Peppermint
Pistachio
Strawberry
Toffee
Vanilla

SHERBET

Cranberry
Lemon
Lime
Orange
Pineapple
Raspberry

Puddings

Cream
  Banana
  Butterscotch
  Chocolate
  Coconut
  Pineapple

Tapioca
Vanilla
Custard, baked
  Caramel
  Rice

Floating island
Bread pudding
Date pudding
Fudge pudding

Lemon cake
  pudding
Christmas
  pudding
  (steamed)
Russian cream

Miscellaneous desserts

Cheese cake
Cream puffs
English toffee

Strawberry
  Bavarian cream
Apple brown betty
Apple crisp

Fruit crisp
Fruit cobbler
Baked apples

Apple dumplings
Strawberry
  shortcake

GARNISHES
Yellow-orange

CHEESE AND EGGS

Cheese balls,
  grated, strips
Cheese rosettes
Egg, hard-cooked
  or sections
Deviled egg halves
Riced egg yolk

FRUIT

Apricot halves,
  sections
Cantaloupe balls
Lemon sections,
  slices
Orange sections,
  slices
Peach slices
Peach halves with
  jelly

Spiced peaches
Tangerines

VEGETABLES

Carrots, rings,
  shredded, strips
Banana peppers

SWEETS

Apricot preserves
Orange
  marmalade

Peanut brittle,
  crushed
Sugar, yellow or
  orange

MISCELLANEOUS

Butter balls
Coconut, tinted
Gelatin cubes
Mayonnaise

Red

FRUIT

Cherries
Cinnamon apples

Cranberries
Plums
Pomegranate seeds

Red raspberries
Maraschino
  cherries

Strawberries
Watermelon
  cubes, balls

(continued)

Red (continued)

VEGETABLES

Beets, pickled,
　julienne
Beet relish
Red cabbage
Peppers, red,
　rings, strips,
　shredded

Pimiento,
　chopped, strips
Radishes, red,
　sliced, roses

SWEETS

Cranberry glacé,
　jelly
Gelatin cubes
Red sugar

Red jelly
　Apple
Cherry Currant
　Loganberry
　Raspberry

MISCELLANEOUS

Paprika
Tinted coconut

Stuffed olives,
　sliced
Tomato, aspic,
　catsup, chili
　sauce, cups,
　sections, slices,
　broiled
Cinnamon drops
　(red-hots)

Green

FRUIT

Avocado
Cherries
Frosted grapes
Green plums
Honeydew melon
Lime wedges

SWEETS

Citron
Green sugar
Gelatin cubes

Mint jelly
Mint pineapple
Mints

VEGETABLES

Broccoli
Capers
Celery
Endive
Green pepper,
　strips, chopped

Green onions
Lettuce cups
Lettuce, shredded
Mint leaves
Olives
Parsley, sprig,
　chopped
Pickles
　Burr gherkins
　Strips, fans,
　　rings

Spinach leaves
Watercress
Zucchini sticks,
　slices

MISCELLANEOUS

Coconut, tinted
Sunflower seeds
Pistachios

White

FRUIT

Apple rings
Apple balls
Grapefruit sections
Pear balls
Pear sections

VEGETABLES

Cauliflower florets
Celery cabbage
Celery curls,
　hearts, strips
Cucumber rings,
　strips, wedges,
　cups
Mashed potato
　rosettes

Onion rings
Onions, pickled
Radishes, white

MISCELLANEOUS

Cream cheese
　frosting
Sliced hard-cooked
　egg white

Shredded coconut
Marshmallows
Almonds
Mints
Whipped cream
Powdered sugar
Popcorn
Parmesan cheese

Brown-tan

BREADS

Crustades
Croutons
Fritters, tiny
Toast, cubes,
   points, strips,
   rings

MISCELLANEOUS

Cinnamon
Dates
French fried
   cauliflower

French fried
   onions
Mushrooms
Nutmeats

Nut-covered
   cheese balls
Potato chips
Rosettes
Toasted coconut

Black

Caviar
Chocolate,
   shredded or
   shaved

Olives, ripe
Prunes

Prunes, spiced
Pickled walnuts

Raisins, currants
Truffles

Part four

SPECIAL MEALS & RECEPTIONS

PLANNING SPECIAL MEALS & RECEPTIONS

Foodservices, for a variety of reasons from income producing to fulfilling educational or social obligations, are often responsible for planning special meals. The types of functions may include coffees, teas, receptions, brunches, buffets, banquets, and catered events on and off the premises. Regardless of the type of service provided, considerable planning is required to ensure a successful foodservice event.

PLANNING RESPONSIBILITIES

Careful advance planning is important to the success of any special function. If the food is to be prepared by regular employees, some preparation should be scheduled in advance. Many foods, especially those for receptions, may be prepared ahead and frozen. The other meals on the day of the special function may need to be simplified to avoid work overloads. Extra service personnel, if needed and if inexperienced, should be provided with detailed instructions.

The major responsibilities of the foodservice staff in charge of a special meal or other function are as follows:

1. Confer with representatives of the group to be served to determine the type of function, time and place, number to be served, service desired, and financial arrangements. Program arrangements and responsibility for table decorations should be discussed also.

2. Plan the menu with the organization's representative. Duplicate copies of the menu plans should be signed and kept by the group's representative and the food director. This procedure confirms the agreement and may prevent a misunderstanding of details and avoid last-minute changes.

3. Determine quantity and estimated cost of food to be served.

4. Place food orders. It is important that orders for special or unusual foods be made early enough to ensure delivery.

5. Check the dish and equipment list and make arrangements for obtaining any additional items needed. A list including the amount and kind of linen, dishes, silverware, glassware, and serving utensils required should be compiled by the manager and arrangements made for assembling these at least one day before they are to be used.

6. Prepare work schedules. A detailed work schedule includes preparation, cooking, serving, and cleanup assignments. If workers are inexperienced, the schedule should indicate time for each task, detailed procedures, and other special instructions. For a seated service luncheon or dinner, assign personnel to the serving counter from which the plates will be filled. Assign and instruct servers for dining room service. See pp. 710–716 for directions for table setting and service.

7. Supervise the preparation and service of food.

8. Supervise the dishwashing and cleanup of preparation and service areas.

9. Prepare, and keep on file, a detailed report including information concerning menu, numbers served, income and expenses, and useful comments for service of similar meals in the future.

RECEPTIONS AND TEAS

Receptions and teas may vary in degree of formality and may accommodate a few or many guests. The menu may be simple or elaborate and should be planned according to the type of event, the time of day, the number to be served, and the money and labor available.

One or two beverages usually are offered, coffee and tea or coffee and punch. The menu may be limited to an attractive dessert with nuts and mints, or it may include several kinds of sandwiches, cookies, or cakes. The following are suggested choices for a reception or tea:

Beverages	Coffee, tea, hot spiced tea or cider, punch, wine.
	See Tables 4.1 and 4.2, pp. 705, 706 for wine purchasing and selection guides.
Breads	Open-face sandwiches spread with a variety of fillings and decorated attractively.
	Rolled, ribbon, checkerboard, or pinwheel sandwiches.
	Nut bread or fruit bread sandwiches with cream cheese filling, cut in square, triangular, round, or oblong shapes.
	Cheese wafers or cheese straws.
	Miniature cream puffs filled with chicken or fish salad.
Dips	Dips with cheese, cream cheese, or sour cream base.
	Served with crisp raw vegetables, fruits, and/or crackers and chips.

TABLE 4.1 WINE SELECTION GUIDE

Wine	Temperature	To accompany
Champagne	Chilled (40°F)	Appetizers or main course
Dessert wines	Cool room temperature (65°F)	Desserts
Cream sherry		
Marsala		
Muscatel		
Port		
Sweet champagne		
Red wine	Slightly cool (60°F)	Hearty entrees
Burgundy		
Claret		
Rosé	Slightly cool (60°F)	Any entree
Sherry, port	Chilled or room temperature (50–65°F)	Appetizers
White wine	Chilled (50°F)	Light entrees
Chablis		
Rhine		
Riesling		
Sauterne		

Cakes, cookies, and tarts	Petits fours or small decorated cupcakes.
	Meringue shells with whipped cream and fruit fillings.
	Small pecan or fruit tarts.
	Small tea cookies that offer a variety of shapes, flavors, and colors.
Nuts and candies	Salted, toasted, or spiced nuts.
	Candied orange or grapefruit peel.
	Mints in pastel colors.

Figure 4.1 suggests a table arrangement for a reception or tea, using two lines of service and set up so that a guest may start by placing a beverage cup on a plate, then selecting food items. The silverware and napkin usually are last. Placing the cup on the plate first assures adequate space for both food and beverage. If only one or two food selections are offered, beverages may be served last. Use the same directions as in Figure 4.1, but start with plates and end with the beverage or beverages.

The table covering, centerpiece, tea service, silverware, and serving dishes should be attractive, and the food should be colorful and interestingly arranged. To prevent a crowded appearance, there should be a limited amount of silverware, china, napkins, and food on the table when the serving begins. A small serving table with extra china and silverware near the tea table is a convenience. Replace-

TABLE 4.2 WINE PURCHASING GUIDE

Size	Volume (ounces)	Servings per container[a]	
		Dinner	Cocktail
375 milliliters	12.7	4	4–6
750 milliliters	25.4	8	8–12
1 liter	33.8	11	12–14
1.5 liters	50.7	16	20–25
3 liters	101.4	32	40–50
4 liters	135.2	43	52–64

[a] Number of servings per container is based on dinner portion size 3–3½ oz, cocktail portion size 2–2½ oz. If larger glasses are used, adjustment in the servings per container will need to be made.

ments of small dishes and appointments are brought on trays from the kitchen. If two beverages are served, they are placed at either end of the table. Cookies, sandwiches, and other foods should be arranged so they do not appear crowded. It is best to use small serving plates and replace them frequently so there is an assortment of food at all times. Arrangements should be made for people to pour the beverages, and employees or hostesses should be assigned to replenish the tea table and to take empty plates from guests.

COFFEES AND BRUNCHES

Coffees and brunches are easy and popular ways to entertain a few or many guests. An ample supply of hot fresh coffee is necessary, and an alternate choice of tea or decaffeinated coffee may be offered. One or more hot breads are served, and the menu may be expanded to include fresh fruit or juice. A fruit tray, with bite-sized pieces of fresh fruit arranged on a silver or other appropriate tray, is an attractive centerpiece and an interesting addition to a coffee hour or brunch.

Brunch, a cross between breakfast and lunch, usually includes a wider variety of food than does a coffee. The menu may be made up of foods normally served at breakfast or may resemble a luncheon menu, depending partly on the hour of service. It may be quite simple, consisting of fruits, hot breads, and coffee, or it may be a more substantial meal that will replace lunch. The food usually is placed on a buffet table for self-service but may be served to guests seated at tables. Brunch often starts with fruit juice or sparkling wines served to guests before they go to the buffet table. The main entree may be one or several that are typical of breakfast, such as eggs in some form, bacon, ham, sausage, or a breakfast casserole, or a luncheon-type entree of chicken, turkey, or fish. An assortment of breads usually is offered. A dessert may be served if the meal is scheduled late in the

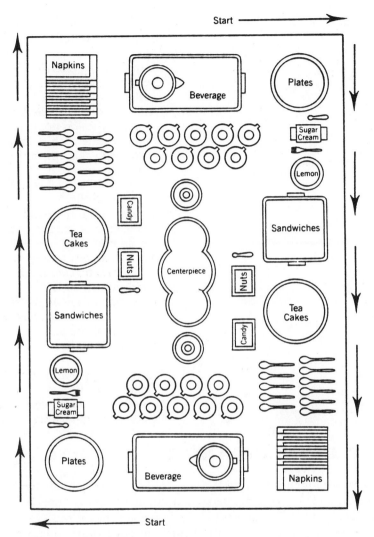

Figure 4.1 *Table arrangement for a reception or tea.*

morning, but it should be light. Suggested foods for coffee hours and brunches are as follows:

Fruits and juices	Orange, pineapple, or tomato juice. Fresh fruit cup or fresh strawberries. Melon wedges, fruit kebobs.
Fruit trays	Fresh pineapple chunks, banana wedges, orange sections, and fresh strawberries.

Fruit trays (*continued*)	Apple slices, honeydew melon wedges, kiwi fruit, and frosted grapes.
	Plums or bing cherries, pear slices, cantaloupe wedges, green grapes, and cheese cubes.
Entrees	Canadian bacon, grilled ham, sausage patties on apple rings.
	Small biscuits with ham slice.
	Scrambled eggs, egg cutlets, egg and sausage casserole.
	Cheese and broccoli strata, quiche, cheese soufflé.
	Chicken and mushroom crepes, chicken a la king in patty shells or on rice.
Breads	Small pecan or orange rolls, scones, kolaches, toasted English muffins with marmalade.
	Coffee cake, Danish pastry.
	Small doughnuts or doughnut holes, cinnamon puffs.
	Small nut bread or fruit bread sandwiches.
Desserts	Fresh pineapple and strawberries, ambrosia, sherbet.
	Strawberry–sour cream crepes.
	Cookies or small cakes.

BUFFET DINNERS AND LUNCHEONS

Buffet dinners and luncheons provide a means of serving relatively large groups of people with a minimum of service personnel. An assortment of hors d'oeuvres and a beverage may be served to guests before they go to the buffet.

A greater variety of food generally is included in a buffet menu than can be offered at table d'hôte meals, although the extent of the variety will depend on preparation time and space on the buffet table, among other factors. The menu may be built around two to three entrees, one or two vegetables, a salad or salad bar, relishes, hot bread, dessert, and beverage. The menu may consist of a more elaborate offering of entrees, such as sliced cold meats, a chicken or fish casserole, and a hot meat, with accompanying vegetables, a variety of salads and relishes, bread, and dessert.

In planning a buffet menu, consideration should be given to contrasts in colors, shapes, and sizes of food and to ease of serving and eating, as well as to pleasing flavor combinations. An assortment of breads adds interest and variety to the buffet table. Desserts usually are "finger foods" such as cookies, small cakes or tarts, or a fresh fruit and cheese tray. If the dessert is to be served to the guests, however, only one is planned, and it might be pie, cake, ice cream, or a baked dessert. Foods appropriate for buffets may be selected from the Menu-Planning Suggestions, pp. 688–698.

Certain precautions should be observed in planning a buffet:

1. Keep the service as simple as possible (i.e., avoid foods that are difficult to serve or soft or runny on the plate). Foods that require extra silverware, such as bread and butter spreaders and salad or cocktail forks, should be avoided.

2. Include a few attractively decorated foods, assorted salads, and an assortment of relishes. Attractive garnishing is important.

3. Plan hot foods that can be prepared ahead and served easily. A hot counter, chafing dishes, or heated trays are essential if hot food is to be served.

4. Plan the arrangement of the table at the same time the menu is planned to be sure of adequate table space and suitable serving dishes.

5. Plan enough food so that the last person in the buffet line will have a choice and will see an attractive display. This objective can be accomplished partly by having the serving dishes or pans not too large and replenished often. The amount of each food to prepare will depend to a great extent on the variety of foods being offered. Unless there is a limited choice, most people will take smaller servings than normal, and some may select only a few items.

The success of a buffet meal depends not only on the quality of food but also on the attractiveness of the buffet table. Interesting colors may be introduced in the table covering, the serving dishes, the food, or the decorations.

Food in a buffet service is arranged in the order in which it usually is served: meats or other entrees, potato or substitute, vegetables, salads, and relishes. Figure 4.2 illustrates a typical buffet arrangement with a single service line. A double line, as shown in Figure 4.3, will speed service but requires more space and duplicate serving dishes. Figure 4.4 illustrates a straight-line buffet arrangement when clientele serve themselves from both sides of the table.

Desserts may be placed on a separate table from which the guests will later serve themselves. If the guests are seated, dishes from the first course usually are removed and the desserts brought to the guests by service personnel.

The type of service depends largely on the equipment available. If ample table space is provided, places may be set with covers, rolls, and water, and provisions may be made for the beverage to be served by employees. If table room for all is not available, each guest may be given an individual tray on which to place silverware, napkin, water glass, and the plate containing the assembled food. Hot beverages and rolls are served.

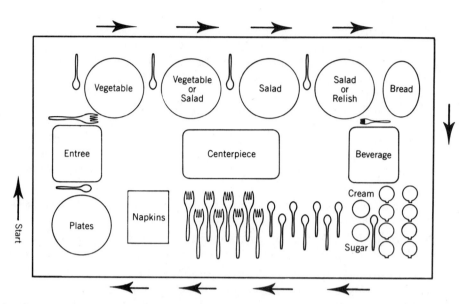

Figure 4.2 *Table arrangement for buffet service, single line. Beverages may be served at tables. Desserts may be served from a dessert table or to guests at the individual tables.*

BANQUET SERVICE

Although table service for banquets in hotels and many other commercial food-services may be elaborate, a simplified service may be the most practical for foodservices in which only an occasional banquet is served. The discussion of table setting and plate service that follows is intended primarily for this type of facility.

Preparation of the dining room

Arrangement of tables and chairs should provide adequate space for serving after the guests are seated. Chairs should be placed so that the front edge of each touches or is just below the tablecloth. If there is to be a head table, it should be placed so that it is easily seen by the guests, with a podium and microphone available for the program. Audiovisual equipment, if needed, should be properly placed and adjusted. Serving stands, conveniently place, facilitate service. These are especially important when the distance to the kitchen is great.

Setting the tables

TABLECLOTH

Tablecloths generally are used for banquets, although place mats make an attractive table setting when the finish of the table top permits, and they are appropriate

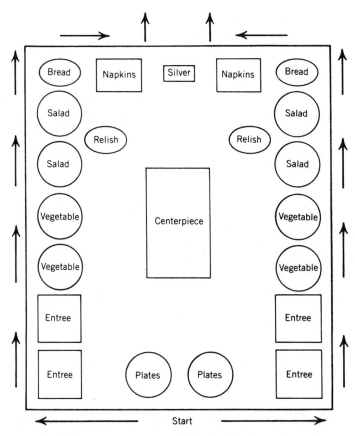

Figure 4.3 *Table arrangement for buffet service, double line. Beverages may be served at tables. Desserts may be served from a dessert table or to guests at the individual tables.*

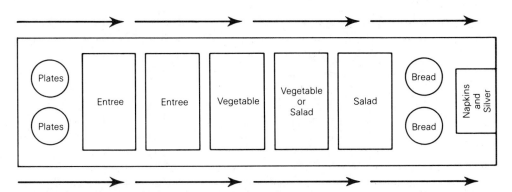

Figure 4.4 *Double straight-line service for a buffet. Guests serve themselves from either side of a single line of food items. Beverages and desserts may be served at a separate table or individually to each guest.*

for informal meals. Place the cloth on the table so that the center lengthwise fold comes exactly in the middle of the table and the four corners are an equal distance from the floor. The cloth should hang 6–12 inches below the table top and should not touch the chair seat.

THE COVER

The setting of plate, silverware, glasses, and napkin to be used by each person is called a cover (see Figure 4.5). Consider 20 inches of table space as the smallest permissible allowance for each cover; 25–30 inches is better. Place all silverware and dishes required for one cover as close together as possible without crowding.

SILVERWARE

Place knives, forks, and spoons about 1 inch from the edge of the table and in the order of their use (see Figure 4.5). Some prefer to place the salad or dessert fork next to the plate as the menu dictates. If the menu requires no knife, omit it from the cover. When cocktail forks are used, they are placed at the extreme right of the cover. If a butter spreader is used, lay it across the upper right-hand side of the bread and butter plate, with the cutting edge toward the center of the plate. It may be placed straight across the top of the plate or with the handle at a convenient angle. Dessert silverware often is not placed on the table when the cover is laid, except when the amount of silver required for the entire meal is small or if it is necessary to simplify the service. If a dessert fork is used, it is sometimes placed in the area above the dinner plate, so the guest will use it for the final course.

NAPKIN

Place the napkin at the left of the fork with the loose corner at the lower right and the open edges next to the edge of the table and the plate. It may be placed between

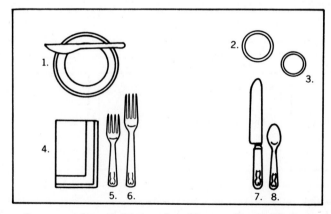

Figure 4.5 *Cover for a served meal: (1) Bread and butter plate, with butter knife. (2) Water glass. (3) Wine glass. (4) Napkin. (5) Salad fork. (6) Dinner fork. (7) Knife. (8) Teaspoon.*

the knife and fork if space is limited, and it may be folded into an accordion shape and placed upright.

GLASSES

Place the water glass at the tip of the knife or slightly to the right. Goblets and footed tumblers often are preferred for luncheon or dinner and should be used for a formal dinner. Wine glasses are placed to the right and slightly below the water glass.

BREAD AND BUTTER PLATE

Place the bread and butter plate at the tip of the fork or slightly to the left.

SALT AND PEPPER

Salt and pepper shakers should be provided for every six covers. They should be placed parallel to the edge of the table and in line with sugar bowls and creamers.

DECORATIONS

Some attractive decorations should be provided for the center of the table. A centerpiece should be low so the view across the table will not be obstructed. Candles should not be used in the daytime unless the lighting is inadequate or the day is dark. When used, they should be the sole source of light. Do not mix candlelight and daylight or candlelight and electric light. Tall candles in low holders should be high enough so that the flame is not on a level with the eyes of the guests. If place cards are used, they are set on the napkin or above the cover.

Seating arrangement

The guest of honor, if a woman, usually is seated at the right of the host; if a man, at the right of the hostess. At banquets and public dinners, a woman is seated at the right of her partner.

Plate service

Food should be served from hot counters, or, if these are not available, the pans containing food should be placed in hot water. Some provision must be made also for keeping plates and cups hot. For serving 50 plates or less, the plan should provide one person to serve each food item. Such an arrangement for serving may be termed a setup. For 60–100 persons, two setups should be provided in order to hasten service. For more than 100 persons, it is well to provide additional setups.

Food is placed on the hot counter in the following order: meat, potato or substitute, vegetables, sauces, and garnish. The supervisor should demonstrate the size of portions to be given and their arrangement on the plate. There should be a checker at the end of the line to remove with a damp cloth any food spots from the plate and to check the plate for completeness, arrangement, and uniformity of servings. The importance of standardized servings can hardly be overemphasized; on this may depend the enjoyment of the guests and the financial success or failure of a meal.

Table service

1. Service personnel should report to the supervisor to receive final instructions at least 15 minutes before the time set for serving the banquet.

2. If the salad is to be on the table when the guests arrive, it should be placed there by the service personnel not more than 15 minutes before serving time. It should be placed at the left of the fork (Figure 4.6). If space does not permit this arrangement, place the salad plate at the tip of the fork and the bread and butter plate, if used, directly above the dinner plate between the water glass and the salad plate. If the salad is to be served as a separate course, it is placed between the knife and the fork, then removed before the main course is served.

3. Place creamer beside the sugar bowl.

4. Place relishes on the table, if desired.

5. For small dinners, the first course may be placed on the table before dinner is announced. For large banquets, however, it is best to wait until the guests are seated. Hot soups or plated appetizers are served after the guests are seated. A first course of beverages and appetizers may be offered as the guests arrive in the reception area.

Figure 4.6 *Placement of food and cover for a served meal: (1) Bread and butter plate. (2) Water glass. (3) Wine glass. (4) Salad plate. (5) Dinner plate. (6) Cup and saucer. The salad is placed at the left of the fork when salad and beverage are both served with the main course. If space does not permit, place salad plate at tip of fork and bread and butter plate, if used, above the dinner plate.*

6. Place butter on the right side of the bread and butter plate. If no bread and butter plate is used and the salad is to be on the table when guests arrive, place the butter on the side of the salad plate. This procedure is often necessary where dishes and table space are limited.

7. Place glasses filled with ice water on the table just before guests are seated.

8. When the guests are seated, service personnel line up in the kitchen for trays containing the first course. It is helpful if two persons work together, one carrying the tray and the other placing the food. Place the cocktail glasses, soup dishes, or canapé plates on the service plates, which are already on the table.

9. Place and remove all dishes from the left with the left hand, except those containing beverages, which are placed and removed from the right with the right hand.

10. Serve the head table first, progressing from there to the right. It is preferable to have the head table the one farthest from the kitchen entrance.

11. When the guests have finished the first course, service personnel remove the dishes. Follow the same order used in serving.

12. For the main course, plates may be brought to the dining room on plate carriers or on large trays holding several plates and set on tray stands. Each worker serves the plates to a specified group of guests.

An alternate method often is used in serving large groups. A tray of filled plates is brought from the kitchen by bus personnel to a particular station in the dining room, from which the plates are served. The dining room service personnel remain at their stations during the serving period.

13. Place the plate 1 inch from the edge of the table with the meat nearest the guest.

14. As soon as a table has been served with dinner plates and salad, specially appointed workers should follow immediately with rolls and coffee.

15. Place the coffee cups at the right of the spoons with the handles toward the right at about the 5 o'clock position. If the coffee is served with the main course, the cup and saucer may be placed on the table with the rest of the cover. If it is served with the dessert only, the cups are not placed on the table until the dessert is served.

16. Serve rolls at least twice. Offer them from the left at a convenient height and distance. Plates or baskets of rolls may be placed on the table to be passed by the guests.

17. Refill water glasses as necessary. If the tables are crowded, it may be necessary to remove the glasses from the table to fill them. Handle the glass near the base.

18. Refill coffee cups as necessary. Do not remove cups from table when filling.

19. At the end of the course, remove all dishes and food belonging to that course. Remove dishes from the left of the guest.

20. If the silverware for the dessert was not placed on the table when the table was set, take it in on a tray and place at the right of the cover.

21. Serve desserts two at a time and in the same order that the plates were served. When pie is served, place it with the point toward the guest.

22. If possible, the table should be cleared except for decorations before the program begins. The handling of dishes should cease before the start of the program.

Appendix

USE OF HERBS AND SPICES IN COOKING

Herb or spice	Use[a]
Allspice (ground or whole)	Pot roast, baked products, fruits, puddings, squash, sweet potatoes
Basil	Roasted meat and poultry, stews, fish, pasta, green salads, salad dressings, vegetables
Bay leaf	Beef, fish, chicken, soups, stews, marinades
Caraway seed	Rye bread, apples, beets, cabbage, cheese spreads
Cardamom	Coffee cakes, Danish pastry, curries, soups
Cayenne (red pepper)	Meats, fish, sauces, Mexican dishes
Celery salt, seeds, flakes	Meat, poultry, eggs, soups, salads. If celery salt is used, reduce amount of salt in recipe.
Chili powder	Chili, Mexican dishes, eggs, meat sauces, dips
Cilantro	Guacamole, chili, dips, salsa
Cinnamon (ground or stick)	Baked products, apples, peaches, beverages, squash
Cloves (ground or whole)	Pork, lamb, marinades, squash, sweet potatoes. Use whole to stud ham, fruit, glazed pork, or onions.
Coriander (ground or whole)	Curries, baked products
Cumin	Chili, curries, stews
Curry powder	Chicken, lamb, pork, fish, eggs, rice
Dill (seed or weed)	Lamb, eggs, salads, vegetables
Fennel seed	Italian and Swedish cookery
Ginger (fresh, ground, candied)	Meats, poultry, oriental dishes, fruits, baked products, carrots, squash, sweet potatoes
Mace	Meats, poultry, fish, baked products
Marjoram	Meats, poultry, fish, soups, stews, tomato dishes, vegetables
Mint leaves	Lamb, veal, iced tea, sauces, carrots, peas
Mustard (ground or seed)	Meat, poultry, eggs, cheese, salad dressings, cheese spreads, sauces
Nutmeg	Meatballs, veal, chicken, seafood, baked products, carrots, spinach, sweet potatoes, eggnog, custards
Oregano	Meat, poultry, seafood, eggs, cheese, soups, stews, pizza, chili, pasta sauces, barbecue sauce, tomatoes
Paprika	Veal, chicken, fish, salad dressings, garnish
Parsley	Meat, poultry, fish, soups, eggs, cheese, cheese spreads, vegetables, garnish
Poppy seed	Cakes, cookies, bread toppings, fruit salad dressing, sprinkled on noodles, sweet roll fillings
Rosemary	Roasted meat and poultry, baked or broiled fish, eggs, soups, stews, vegetables
Saffron	Veal, poultry, rice, soups
Sage (leaf or ground)	Meats, poultry, stuffings, chowders

Herb or spice	Use[a]
Savory	Meats, poultry, fish, eggs, soups, stews, green vegetable salads, rice
Sesame seeds	Bread, rolls, salads, oriental cooking
Tarragon	Poultry, seafood, eggs, tomatoes, green salads, salad dressings
Thyme	Meat, poultry, fish, eggs, soups, stews, vegetables
Turmeric, ground	Ingredient of curry powder, coloring for condiments

[a] Spices and herbs can be creatively combined to enhance the flavor of foods. The art of skillfully adding the right amount of seasonings is basic to successful cookery. Both low-sodium and low-calorie foods can be made more interesting by the addition of spices and herbs. Experimentation, using this chart, may add to patron satisfaction.

GLOSSARY OF MENU AND COOKING TERMS

à la (ah lah), French. In the manner of.

à la carte (ah lah cart), French. On the menu, but not part of a meal, usually prepared as ordered and individually priced.

à la king, French. Served in cream sauce containing green pepper, pimiento, and mushrooms.

à la mode (ah lah mohd), French. When applied to desserts, means with ice cream. *A la mode, boeuf,* a well-larded piece of beef cooked slowly in water with vegetables, similar to braised beef.

al dente (al den' tay), Italian. The point in cooking pasta at which it is still fairly firm to the bite.

allemande (ahl mahnd'), French. A smooth yellow sauce consisting of white sauce with the addition of cream, egg yolk, and lemon juice.

amandine. Served with almonds.

antipasto (ahn tee pahs' toe), Italian. Appetizer; a course consisting of relishes, vegetables, fish, or cold cuts.

aspic. A jellied meat juice or liquid held together with gelatin.

au gratin (oh grah' ton), French. Made with crumbs, scalloped. Often refers to dishes made with cheese sauce.

au jus (oh zhu), French. Meat served in its natural juices or gravy.

bake. To cook in the oven by dry heat.

barbecue. To cook on a grill or spit over hot coals, or in an oven, basting intermittently with a highly seasoned sauce.

bar-le-duc (bahr luh dük'), French. A preserve made of currants and honey. It frequently forms a part of the cheese course.

baron. Double sirloin of beef.

baste. To moisten meat while roasting to add flavor and to prevent drying of the surface. Melted fat, meat drippings, water, or water and fat may be used for basting.

batch cooking. Dividing the estimated amount needed into smaller quantities and cooking as required to meet the demand.

batter. Flour and liquid mixture, usually combined with other ingredients, thin enough to pour or drop from a spoon.

béarnaise (bay ar nayz'), French. Sauce of melted butter, egg yolks, vinegar, onion, and spices.

beat. To mix ingredients with a rotating motion, using spoon, wire whip, or paddle attachment to mixer.

béchamel (bay sha mel'), French. A cream sauce made with equal parts of chicken stock and cream or milk.

beurre (buhr), French. Butter. *Au beurre noire* (oh buhr nwor), with butter sauce browned in a pan. *beurre manie* (buhr mah nee), French. Well-blended mixture of butter and flour used to add thickening to hot soups.

bisque (bisk), French. A thick soup usually made from fish or shellfish. Also a frozen dessert. Sometimes defined as ice cream to which finely chopped nuts are added.

blanch. To dip briefly in boiling water.

blanquette (blang ket'), French. A white stew usually made with veal, lamb, or chicken.

blend. To thoroughly mix two or more ingredients.

bleu (bluh), French. Blue.

boeuf (buff), French. Beef. *Boeuf à la jardinière* (buff a lah zhar de nyoyr), braised beef with vegetables; *boeuf roti* (buff rotee), roast beef.

boil. To cook foods in water or a liquid in which the bubbles are breaking on the surface and steam is given off.

bombe (bahm), French. A frozen dessert made of a combination of two or more frozen mixtures packed in a round or melon-shaped mold.

bordelaise (bor d'layz'), French. Of Bordeaux. *Sauce bordelaise,* a sauce with Bordeaux wine as its foundation, with various seasonings added.

borscht (borsht), Russian. A soup made with beets and served with thick sour cream.

bouillabaisse (boo yah bes'), French. A highly seasoned fish soup made with two or more kinds of fish.

bouillon (boo yon'), French. Clear, white meat stock.

bouquet (boo kay'). Volatile oils that give aroma.

bouquet garni (boo kay' garnee'), French. Herbs and spices tied in a cloth bag, used for flavoring soups, stews, and sauces, then removed after cooking is completed.

bourguignon (bohr ghee n'yang), French. In the Burgundy style, especially a beef stew made with red wine (for which Burgundy is noted), mushrooms, salt pork, and onions.

braise (brays), French. To brown in a small amount of fat, cover, add a small amount of liquid, and cook slowly.

bread. To coat food with an egg-milk mixture and then bread crumbs before frying.

brew. To cook in liquid to extract flavor, as with beverages.

brioche (bree ohsh'), French. A slightly sweetened rich bread used for rolls or babas.

brochette à la (bro shet'), French. Food arranged on a skewer and broiled.

broil. To cook over or under direct heat, as in a broiler or over live coals.

broth. A thin soup or water in which meat or vegetables have been cooked.

brunoise (broo noyz), French. Finely shredded vegetables, such as celery, carrots, leeks, and turnips for soups and sauces.

buffet (boo fay'), French. A table displaying a variety of foods.

cacciatore (ca chi a tor' ee), Italian. Stewed with tomatoes, onion, and garlic.

café au lait (ca fay' oh lay'), French. Coffee with hot milk.

café noir (ca fay' nwar), French. Black coffee, after-dinner coffee.

canapé (can ah pay'), French. An appetizer of meat, fish, egg, or cheese arranged on a bread base.

candy. To preserve or cook with heavy syrup.

caper (kay' per). Small pickled bud from wild caper bush; used in salads and sauces.

caramelize. To heat sugar until a brown color and a characteristic flavor develops.

carte au jour (kart o zhur'), French. Bill of fare or menu for the day.

caviar (cav ee ar'), French. Salted roe of sturgeon or other large fish. May be black or red.

chantilly (shang te' ye), French. Foods containing whipped cream.

charlotte (shar' lot), French. Dessert with gelatin, whipped cream, fruit, or other flavoring, in a mold, garnished with lady fingers.

chiffonade (shee' fahn ahd), French. With minced or shredded vegetables, as in salad dressing.

chill. To refrigerate until thoroughly cold.

chop. To cut food into fairly fine pieces with a knife or other chopping device.

choux paste (shoo paste), French. Cream puff batter.

chowder. A thick soup of fish or vegetables and milk.

chutney (chut-ni). A spicy relish made from several fruits and vegetables.

cilantro. The pungent leaf of the coriander plant, also known as Chinese parsley. Used to season Oriental and Mexican foods.

clarified butter. Butter that has been melted and chilled. The solid is then lifted away from the liquid and discarded. Clarification heightens the smoke point of butter.

clarify. Make clear by skimming or adding egg white and straining.

cloche (klosh), French. Bell, dish cover. *Sous cloche* (soo klosh), under cover.

coat. To cover entire surface with flour, fine crumbs, sauce, batter, or other food as required.

cocktail. An appetizer, either a beverage or a light, highly seasoned food, served before a meal.

coddle. To simmer gently in liquid for a short time.

compote (kom' poht), French. Mixed fruit, either raw or stewed in syrup; a stemmed serving dish.

consommé (kon so may'), French. A clear soup usually made from two or three kinds of meat.

court bouillon (cor boo yon'), French. Seasoned broth in which fish, meat, or vegetables are cooked.

cream. To mix fat and sugar until soft and creamy.

creole (kre' ohl), French. Foods containing meat or vegetables with tomatoes, peppers, onions, and other seasonings.

crepe (krayp), French. Thin, delicate pancake, often rolled and stuffed, served as appetizers, entree or dessert. *Crepe suzette,* a small, very thin and crisp pancake served for tea or as dessert.

crisp. To make foods firm and brittle, as in chilling vegetables or heating cereals or crackers in the oven to remove excessive moisture.

croissant (krwa sang'), French. Crescent; applied to rolls and confectionary of crescent shape.

croquette (crow ket'). Mixture of chopped, cooked meat, poultry, fish, or vegetables bound with thick cream sauce, shaped, breaded, and fried.

croustade (krus tad'). A toasted case or shell of bread.

croutons (kroo tons'). Bread cubes, toasted, for use in garnishing soups and salads.

crudités (croo dee tays'), French. Raw vegetables.

cube. To cut into ½-inch squares.

curry (kur' ee). Highly spiced condiment from India; a stew seasoned with curry.

cut in. To cut a solid fat into flour with knives or mixer until fat particles are of desired size.

cutlet. Thin slice of meat, usually breaded, for frying; also croquette mixture made in a flat shape.

deep fry. To cook in fat deep enough for food to float.

deglaze. To dilute and wash down pan juices by adding liquid.

de la maison (de lah mayzon), French. Specialty of the house.

demitasse (deh mee tahss'), French. Small cup of black coffee served after dinner.

dice. To cut into ¼-inch cubes.

dot. To scatter small bits of butter or margarine over surface of food.

dough. A mixture of flour, liquid, and other ingredients, thick enough to roll or knead.

drawn butter. Melted butter.

dredge. To thoroughly coat a food with flour or other fine substance.

drippings. Fat and liquid residue from frying or roasting meat or poultry.

du jour (doo zhoor'), French. Of the day, such as soup of the day.

dust. To sprinkle lightly with flour.

eau (oh), French. Water.

éclair (ay klair'), French. Finger-shaped cream puff paste filled with whipped cream or custard.

egg and crumb. To dip a food into diluted, slightly beaten egg and dredge with crumbs. This treatment is used to prevent soaking of the food with fat or to form a surface easily browned.

enchilada (en chee lah' dah), Mexican. Tortillas filled and rolled, served with sauce.

en cocotte (ahn ko cot′), French. In individual casserole.

entree (ahn′ tray), French. The main course of a meal or a single dish served before the main course of an elaborate meal.

espagnole (ays pah nyol), French. Brown sauce.

farci (far′ see), French. Stuffed.

fillet (fee lay′), French. Flat slice of lean meat or fish, without bone.

flake. To break into small pieces, usually with a fork.

flan. In France, a filled pastry; in Spain, a custard.

flambé (flam bay′), French. To flame, using alcohol as the burning agent.

florentine. A food containing or placed upon spinach.

fold in. To blend ingredient into a batter by cutting vertically through the mixture, and turning over and over by sliding the implement across the bottom of the mixing bowl with each turn.

frappé (fra pay′), French. Mixture of fruit juices frozen to a mush.

french fry. To cook in deep fat.

fricassee (frik a see′). To cook by browning in a small amount of fat, then stewing or steaming; most often applied to fowl or veal cut into pieces.

frijoles (free hol′ ays), Mexican. Beans cooked with fat and seasonings.

fritter. A deep-fat fried batter containing meat, vegetables, or fruit.

frizzle. To pan fry in a small amount of fat until edges curl.

froid (frwä), French. Cold.

fry. To cook in hot fat. The food may be cooked in a small amount of fat (also called sauté or pan fry), or in a deep layer of fat (also called deep-fat fry).

glacé (glah say′), French. Iced, frozen, or coated with sugar syrup.

glaze. To make a shiny surface. In meat preparation, a jellied broth applied to meat surface; in breads and pastries, a wash of egg or syrup; for doughnuts and cakes, a coating with a sugar preparation.

goulash (goo′ lash), Hungarian. Thick beef or veal stew with vegetables and seasoned with paprika.

grate. To rub food against grater to form small particles.

gratinée (grah teen ay′), French. To brown a food sprinkled with cheese or bread crumbs; or a food covered with a sauce that turns brown under a broiler flame or intense oven heat.

grease. To rub lightly with fat.

grill. To cook by direct heat.

grind. To change a food to small particles by putting through grinder or food chopper.

grits. Coarsely ground corn, served either boiled or boiled and then fried.

gumbo. A rich, thick Creole soup containing okra or filé.

herbs. Aromatic plants used for seasoning and garnishing of foods.

hollandaise (hol′ ahn days), French, of Dutch origin. Sauce of eggs, butter, lemon juice, and seasonings; served hot with fish or vegetables.

hors d'oeuvre (oh durv′), French. Small portions of food served as appetizers.

Italienne (e tal yen′), French. Italian style.

jalapeño. A hot pepper used for seasoning Mexican food.

jardinière (zhar de nyayr′), French. Mixed vegetables in a savory sauce or soup.

jicama. Tuberous root used in salads.

julienne (zhu lee en′), French. Vegetables or other foods cut into fine strips or shreds.

jus (zhoo), French. Juice or gravy.

kebobs. Marinated meat and vegetables cooked on skewers.

kippered. Lightly salted and smoked fish.

knead. To work dough with a pressing motion accompanied by folding and stretching.

kolach (ko′ lahch), Bohemian. Fruit-filled bun.

kosher (ko′ sher). Food handled in accordance with the Jewish religious customs.

kuchen (koo′ ken), German. Cake, not necessarily sweet.

lait (lay), French. Milk.

lard. To insert small strips of fat into or on top of uncooked lean meat or fish to give flavor or prevent dryness.

lebkuchen (lab koo′ ckhen), German. Famous German cake; sweet cake or honey cake.

leek. Seasoning vegetable resembling a large spring onion with wide leaves, always cooked.

limpa. Swedish rye bread.

lox. Yiddish. Smoked salmon.

lyonnaise (lee′ oh nayz), French. Seasoned with onions and parsley, as lyonnaise potatoes.

macédoine (mah say dwan′), French. Mixture or medley of cut vegetables or fruits cut in uniform pieces.

maître d'hôtel (mai tre doh tel′), French. Steward. *maître d'hôtel butter,* a well-seasoned mixture of butter, minced parsley, and lemon juice.

marinade (mah ree nahd′), French. Mixture of oil, acid, and seasonings used to flavor and tenderize meats and vegetables; French dressings often used as marinades.

marinate. To steep a food in a marinade long enough to modify its flavor.

marzipan (mahr′ zi pan). Powdered sugar and almond paste colored and formed into fruit and vegetable shapes.

mask. To coat a food with a thick sauce before it is served. Cold foods may be masked with a mayonnaise mixture or white sauce, which gels after chilling.

melt. To liquify by the application of heat.

meringue (mah rang′). Stiffly beaten egg white and sugar mixture used as a topping for pies or other desserts; or formed into small cakes or cases and browned in the oven.

meunière, à la (meh nyair′), French. Floured, sautéed in butter and served with butter sauce and lemon and sprinkled with chopped parsley; usually refers to fish.

milanaise (me lan ayz′), French. Food cooked in a style developed in Milan, Italy. Implies the use of pasta and cheese with a suitable sauce, often béchamel.

mince. To chop food into very small pieces—not so fine and regular as grinding, yet finer than those produced by chopping.

minestrone (mee ne stroh′ nay), Italian. Thick vegetable soup with beans and pasta.

mirepoix (meer′ pwa), French. Mixture of chopped vegetables used in flavoring soup stock, usually 25% carrots, 50% onions, and 25% celery.

mix. To combine two or more ingredients by stirring.

mocha (moh′ ka). Coffee flavor or combination of coffee and chocolate.

monosodium glutamate (MSG). White crystalline material made from vegetable protein, used to enhance natural flavor of food.

mornay (mohr nay′), French. Sauce of thick cream, eggs, cheese, and seasonings.

mousse (moose), French. Frozen dessert with fruit or other flavors, whipped cream and sugar; also a cold dish of pureed chicken or fish with egg whites, gelatin, and unsweetened whipped cream.

mulligatawny (mul i ga taw′ ni). A highly seasoned thick soup, of Indian origin, flavored with curry powder and other spices.

napoleons. Puff pastry kept together in layers with a custard filling, cut into portion-size rectangles, and iced.

neopolitan (also harlequin and panachée). Molded dessert of two to four kinds of ice cream or ices arranged in layers.

Nesselrode pudding. Frozen dessert with a custard foundation to which chestnut puree, fruit, and cream have been added.

Newburg, à la. Creamed dish with egg yolk added, flavored with sherry; most often applied to lobster, but may be used with other foods.

noisette (nooa zet′), French. Nut-brown color; may imply nut-shaped. A small round piece of lean meat. *Potatoes noisette,* potatoes cut into the shape and size of hazelnuts and browned in fat.

oeuf (oof), French. Egg.

paella (pä ay′ yah), Spanish. Dish with rice, seafood, chicken, and vegetables, usually served in a wide shallow pan in which it is cooked.

pan broil. To cook, uncovered, on hot metal, such as a fry pan, pouring off the fat as it accumulates. Liquid is never added.

pan fry. To cook in a skillet in a small amount of fat.

papillote (pah pe yote′), French. Meat, chicken, or fish cooked in a closed paper container.

parboil. To boil until partially cooked, the cooking being completed by another method.

parch. To cook in dry heat until slightly browned.

pare. To cut off the outside covering, usually with a knife.

parfait (par fay′), French. A mixture containing whipped cream, egg, and syrup that is frozen without stirring. May be ice cream layered with fruit or syrup in parfait glasses.

parmigiana (par mee zhan′ ah), Italian. Parma style, particularly veal, chicken, or eggplant covered with tomato sauce, mozzarella cheese, and Parmesan cheese and browned under the broiler or in the oven.

pasta, Italian. Any of a large family of flour paste products, such as macaroni, spaghetti, and noodles.

paste. Soft, smooth mixture of a dry ingredient and a liquid.

pastrami (pahs tram′ ee), Yiddish. Boneless meat cured with spices and smoked.

pâté (pah tay′), French. Paste, dough; highly seasoned meat paste used as an appetizer.

pâté de foie gras (pah tay d′fwah grah′), French. Paste of fat goose livers.

patty shell. Shell or case of pastry or puff paste used for individual portions of creamed mixtures.

peel. To strip off the outside covering.

persillade (payr se yad′), French. Served with or containing parsley.

petit pois (puh tee pooá), French. A fine grade of very small peas with a delicate flavor.

petits fours (pe teet foor′), French. Small fancy cakes frosted and decorated.

picante. A highly spiced tomato sauce used as a condiment with Mexican foods.

pilaf or pilau (pih lahf or pih low), Turkish. Dish of rice cooked with meat, fish, or poultry, and seasoned with spices.

piquant (pee kahnt′), French. Sharp, highly seasoned.

pizza (peet′ zah), Italian. Flat yeast bread covered with tomato, cheese, and meat, or other toppings.

plank. Hardwood board used for cooking and serving broiled meat or fish. *Planked steak,* a broiled steak served on a plank and garnished with a border of suitable vegetables.

poach. To cook gently in a hot liquid, held just below the boiling point, the original shape of the food being retained.

polenta (poh lent′ ah), Italian. Thick cornmeal mush; cheese is usually added before serving.

polonaise (po lo nays′), French. Dishes prepared with bread crumbs, chopped eggs, browned butter, and chopped parsley.

pomme de terre (pom de tare′), French. Potato; literally, apple of the earth.

pot-au-feu (poh toh fu′), French. Meat and vegetables boiled together in broth.

pot roast. To cook large cuts of meat by braising.

potage (po tazh′), French. Soup, usually of a thick type.

prawn. Large shrimp.

preheat. To heat oven or other cooking equipment to desired temperature before putting in the food.

prosciutto (pro shoot' toh), Italian. Ham, usually thinly sliced and served as an appetizer or as a component in veal dishes.

puff paste. Rich dough, made flaky by repeated folding and rolling.

puree (pu ray'), French. Foods rubbed through a sieve; also a nutritious vegetable soup in which milk or cream is seldom used.

quiche (keesh). Custard, cheese, and seasonings baked in a pie shell and served warm.

ragout (ra goo'), French. A thick, well-seasoned stew containing meat.

ramekin (ram'e kin). Small baking dish for individual portions.

rarebit. Mixture of white sauce, cheese, and seasonings.

ravioli (rav vee oh' lee), Italian. Bite-sized cases of pasta dough filled with finely ground meat, cheese, and spinach; served with a highly seasoned tomato sauce.

reconstitute. To restore concentrated foods to their normal state, usually by adding water, as in fruit juice and milk.

reduce. To boil down, evaporating liquid from a cooked dish.

rehydrate. To cook or soak dehydrated foods or restore water lost during drying.

remoulade (ray moo lad'), French. Pungent sauce made of hard-cooked eggs, mustard, oil, vinegar, and seasonings. Served with cold dishes.

risotto (ri sot' toh), Italian. Rice dish with meat, vegetables, seafood, cheese, or other accompaniments.

rissolé (ree sall'), French. Savory meat mixture encased in rich pastry and fried in deep fat.

roast. To cook uncovered in oven by dry heat, usually meat or poultry.

roe. Eggs of fish.

rosette (roh zet'), French. Thin, rich batter made into fancy shape with special iron and fried in deep fat.

roulade (roo lahd'), French. Rolled thin piece of meat, usually stuffed and roasted or braised.

roux (roo), French. Browned flour and fat used for thickening sauces, stews, and soups.

sabayon (sa by on'), French. Custard sauce with wine added.

salsa. A highly spiced tomato sauce used as a condiment with Mexican foods.

sauerbraten (sour brah' ten), German. Beef marinated in spiced vinegar, pot-roasted, and served with gingersnap gravy.

sauté (soh tay'), French. To cook in a small amount of fat.

scald. To heat a liquid to a point just below boiling; pour boiling water over or dip food briefly into boiling water.

scallion. An onion that has not developed a bulb.

scallop. To bake food, cut into pieces and cover with a liquid or sauce and crumbs. The food and sauce may be mixed together or arranged in alternate layers in a baking dish, with or without crumbs. *Escalloped* is a synonymous term.

scallopine (skol a pee' nee), Italian. Small flat pieces of meat, usually veal, sautéed and served in a sauce.

scone (scahn). Scottish quick bread containing currants.

score. To make shallow lengthwise and crosswise slits on the surface of meat.

sear. To brown the surface of meat quickly at high temperatures.

set. Allow to stand until congealed, as in gelatin and puddings.

shallot. Onion having a stronger but more mellow flavor than the common variety.

shirr. To break eggs into dish, cover with cream and crumbs, and bake.

shortening. Fat suitable for baking or frying.

simmer. To cook in a liquid in which bubbles form slowly and break just below the surface.

skewer. Pin of metal or wood used for fastening meat or poultry while cooking; or long pins used for holding bits of food for broiling or roasting.

skim. To remove surface fat or foam from liquid mixture.

sliver. To cut into long, slender pieces, as in slivered almonds.

smorgasbord (smor gas bohrd'), Swedish. Arrangement of appetizers and other foods on a table in attractive assortment.

sorbet (sor bay'), French. Sherbet made of several kinds of fruits.

soubise (soo' bees), French. White sauce containing onion and sometimes parsley.

soufflé (soo flay'), French. A light fluffy baked dish with beaten egg whites; may be sweet or savory.

soy sauce. Chinese sauce made from fermented soy beans.

spaetzle (spet' zel), Austrian. Fine noodles made by pressing batter through colander into boiling water or broth.

spoon bread. Southern corn bread baked in a casserole and served with a spoon.

springerle (spring' er le), German. A Christmas cookie. The dough is rolled into a sheet and pressed with a springerle mold before baking.

spumoni (spoo moh' nee), Italian. Rich ice cream made in different layers, usually containing fruit and nuts.

steam. To cook in steam with or without pressure. Steam may be applied directly to the food, as in a steamer, or to the vessel, as in a double boiler.

steep. To cover with boiling water and let stand to extract flavors and colors.

stew. To simmer in a small amount of liquid.

stir. To mix food materials with a circular motion.

stir-fry. To cook quickly in oil over high heat, using light tossing and stirring motion to preserve shape of food.

stock. Liquid in which meat, fish, poultry or vegetables have been cooked.

stroganoff (stro' gan off), Russian. Sautéed beef in sauce of sour cream, with mushrooms and onions.

strudel (stroo' dl), German. Pastry of flaky, paper-thin dough filled with fruit.

Tabasco (tah bas'koh), Mexican. Hot red pepper sauce.

table d'hôte (tabl doht'), French. Meal at a fixed price.

tacos (tah′ cos), Mexican. Rolled sandwiches of tortillas filled with meat, onions, lettuce, and hot sauce.

tamale (ta mah′ lee), Mexican. Highly seasoned meat mixture rolled in cornmeal mush, wrapped in corn husks, and steamed.

tart. Small pie or pastry.

tartar sauce. Mayonnaise to which chopped pickles, onions, and other seasonings have been added; usually served with fish.

tender crisp. The point in cooking vegetables at which they are firm and slightly crisp.

terrine (tay reen′), French. Tureen, an earthenware pot resembling a casserole. *Chicken en terrine,* chicken cooked and served in a tureen.

timbale. Thin fried case for holding creamed mixtures; or unsweetened baked custard with meat, poultry, or vegetables.

toast. To apply direct heat until the surface of the food is browned.

torte (tor′te), German. Rich cake made from crumbs, eggs, and nuts; or meringue in the form of a cake.

tortilla (tohr tee′yah), Mexican. A round thin unleavened flour or cornmeal cake baked on a griddle.

toss. To mix ingredients lightly without crushing.

tournedos, Spanish. Small round fillets of beef.

trifle, English. Dessert made with sponge cake soaked in fruit juice and wine and covered with jam, custard, almonds, and whipped cream.

truffle. A dark mushroom-like fungus, found chiefly in France. Used mainly for garnishing and flavor.

truss. To tie or skewer poultry or meat so that it will hold its shape while cooking.

turnover. Food encased in pastry and baked.

tutti frutti. Mixed fruit.

velouté (ve loo tay′), French. A rich white sauce, usually made of chicken or veal broth.

vinaigrette (vee nay groit′), French. French dressing with chopped eggs, capers, and herbs.

whip. To beat rapidly to increase volume by the incorporation of air.

Wiener schnitzel (ve′ner schnit sel), German. Breaded cutlets, frequently served with tomato sauce or lemon.

wonton. Stuffed dumplings cooked in chicken broth.

Yorkshire pudding, English. Accompaniment for roast beef, a popover-like mixture baked in drippings of the roast.

zeste, French. Peel of citrus fruits, such as orange or lemon, which contains aromatic oil.

zwieback (tsvee′ bahk), German. Toasted bread, crisp and slightly sweet.

Index